BH

125

Robert Penn Warren

A Descriptive Bibliography

1922 – 79

ROBERT PENN WARREN

A Descriptive Bibliography
1922–79

James A. Grimshaw, Jr.

Published for the Bibliographical Society
of the University of Virginia
by the University Press of Virginia
Charlottesville

A Linton R. Massey Descriptive Bibliography

THE UNIVERSITY PRESS OF VIRGINIA
Copyright © 1981 by the Rector and Visitors
of the University of Virginia

First published 1981

Frontispiece: bronze head of Robert Penn Warren,
made from life in Venice, Italy, in 1972 by
Joan FitzGerald, sculptor. Height: 13 in. (+ marble
base). Photo by Edmondo Tich.

Library of Congress Cataloging in Publication Data

Grimshaw, James A.
    Robert Penn Warren: a descriptive bibliography, 1922–1979.

    "A Linton R. Massey descriptive bibliography."
    Includes index.
    1. Warren, Robert Penn, 1905–   —Bibliography.
I. Title.
Z8949.73.G75 [PS3545.A748]   016.813'52   81-3003
ISBN 0-8139-0891-4   AACR2

Printed in the United States of America

To
Darlene
and for
Robert Penn Warren

Contents

Foreword

When a writer looks at such a hefty bibliography as this, covering the large part of a lifetime, made with bloodcurdling scrupulousness, his first thought is—at least, mine is—a painful and shocking recognition of forgotten failures, forgotten struggles, forgotten hopes and foolish aspirations, forgotten joy of moments when you thought a word had come right (though the word may be to you now not only dead, but dead-wrong), all the forgotten vanities of youth and the courage bred of old idiocies. The bibliography puts you in your place. Your face looks up, but as in a coffin, a very fine coffin. To regard it inspires humility—rather like a religious conversion, or a psychoanalysis, I suppose, or the doctor's report that the laboratory indicates carcinomatous tissue.

If humility is a virtue, then a whacking bibliography is the medicine ready for the disease of complacency. Not only because every little failed poem or story or novel, which memory had rejected, now stares you in the face, and what you had thought your best work may seem too close for comfort to those failures and fractional successes, but because it is very likely that the bibliography will re-awaken for you the context from which composition had sprung. It reminds you that the most objective of words, big or little, is torn from the once living tissue of experience, now made to live again as memory is stung; so you must not only face the poor cringing little failure, or half-success, but the old experiences from which all your work came, and now you see it newly torn and blood streaked. You are confronted with big chunks of your life process, and you are likely to be panicked into the question: Was this my life?

Certainly I am aware—how could a writer ever be unaware—that there are a multitude of objective considerations in trying to write a piece of fiction, poetry, or play. There is, indeed, a law of the medium—rather, many laws of the medium. By law I do not mean formula or rule, but an understanding much deeper than such, too deep and complex to go into here. But only a pedant or a fool or a fashionmonger would fail to realize that literature of what ever scale is of more worth than a parlor trick. It springs from the incessant need, in the flux of life and history, to try to get to the depth of, and assess, experience.

This, of course, seems far from the obvious function of a bibliography, even if a bibliography may well be, among other things, an essential tool for investigating this question. But I have been speaking, not of the various functions of a bibliography, but of the response of a writer—me—facing his own bibliography. I, at least, have found myself driven a little way back to look for the alleyways, couloirs, blazing events, and secret distortions that lie behind the printed page, and have been absorbed into life.

ROBERT PENN WARREN

Preface

When I began this work in early 1969, I envisioned a bibliography that would serve graduate students, teachers at all levels, research scholars, librarians, booksellers, and collectors. At that time the only bibliography on Robert Penn Warren was Mary Nance Huff's enumerative bibliography. During the past twelve years only one other bibliography has been added to the Warren stockpile, another enumerative compilation by Neil Nakadate. Perhaps, then, this descriptive bibliography will serve a more comprehensive purpose in Warren studies. It is arranged in two parts plus appended matter. The first part, in ten sections, encompasses Warren's writings; the second part, in eight sections, includes material by others about Warren's writing.

Fifty-eight years, from 1922 and Warren's first published poem "Prophecy" to 1979 and a little volume entitled *Two Poems*, are indeed a rich and long career for an artist, especially one whose talents are as versatile as Robert Penn Warren's: every genre is here represented.

The key to the entire volume is the index, which enables users to find what they are looking for by author's name, by title of selection, or by subject for select topics. Additionally, this index offers listings by journal titles to facilitate library work, by publishers and printers to assist other bibliographers and more specialized students, by select subject references for students preparing to write on Warren topics, and by other authors to aid those wanting to make connections among authors on a broader scale.

Since headnotes to each of the sections explain the parameters for their respective catalogs, my comments about arrangement are necessarily brief. Section A enters titles chronologically by edition and by country, American editions followed by English editions. For example, the designation "A7.a1" translates as follows:

A = the section in this bibliography and hence the work in relation to RPW, i.e., a title for which RPW is the sole author.

7 = within that category, it is RPW's seventh publication.

a = roughly, the edition or family relationship, in this example, the first edition.*

1 = the printing within the edition or particular issue.

*Occasionally, there are exceptions. For example, in "A32.b1," "b" indicates a special

Paperback editions are in chronological order among the hardback editions. That arrangement should be of particular help to teachers who are selecting textbooks and who want to ensure that their students are using the same, preferred text.

Section B includes works and products on which Warren collaborated and which constitute an important part of his literary reputation. These titles are perhaps of secondary interest to all but the most ardent collectors and consequently contain descriptions of only first editions, first printings. Subsequent editions are listed in respective notes with size of printings to suggest the acceptance and potential influence of the work.

Sections C-G list individual titles with printing histories. Among poems, for example, each poem is listed in chronological order based on publication rather than composition date. However, users of this bibliography should know that Warren is constantly revising his poems. Consequently, they should take particular care in choosing a version of a poem to cite. For example, "To a Face in the Crowd" (**C32**) has appeared in print under Warren's watchful eye six times. The first version begins, "My brother, brother, whither do you pass," and the second, "Brother, my brother, whither do you pass?" From minor rearrangements to substantive changes, Warren is honing and polishing his poems. The implications of the changes are left to the textual critics; by identifying the appearances of the different versions, I can only hope that this bibliography has helped their labors somewhat. Designations for entries in these and subsequent sections are enumerative: "N45a" reads the first entry (a) for the forty-fifth title in section N.

Section H is a selective listing of anthologies in which Warren's works appear. Editors' selections pinpoint Warren's most popular works and provide a clue about neglected areas. Section I lists unpublished works for which manuscripts are on file and available. Manuscripts of published works are listed in appendix I. The translations listed in Section J supply a measure of Warren's popularity in foreign countries.

The second part, an enumerative bibliography of secondary sources, provides for users' convenience a checklist of criticism about Warren's work. These contents are a standard bill of fare and are not annotated. Readers might refer to the basic abstracts—*AES*, MLA (1970–1975), and Nakadate's reference guide—for annotations or, better yet, might secure copies of the articles for themselves.

---

limited edition of the first edition, with one additional leaf and a slight variation in binding, hence a different member of the same family.

The appendixes give space for the odds and ends that need to be listed but do not fit neatly into other categories: manuscripts, a listing which must remain tentative until Warren's primary deposit at the Beinecke Library finally comes to rest somewhere and is properly cataloged; miscellaneous items that follow every author of note but defy classification; and some of the significant events, awards, and recognitions in Warren's distinguished literary career.

With that said, two comments come to mind. The first is A. T. Hazen's trenchant reminder that "bibliography is the scholar's servant, not his master." The second is Fredson Bowers's statement which to neophyte bibliographers sounds prophetic and to experienced bibliographers is a truism: "Bibliographical work cannot be ground out to schedule and should not be engaged in unless the writer is willing to allow considerably more time than he originally estimated for its production." To the former, I invite users to respond to this book's usefulness with suggestions. To the latter, I simply say, how true, how true.

The enjoyment and reward in doing a project of this scope and magnitude lie in the associations that I have made among these various bibliographical wanderings. This bibliography has offered a rich and divers number of such associations due largely to the far-reaching impact of its subject, Robert Penn Warren. With pleasure and gratitude, then, I acknowledge the assistance, the patient responses, the friendly "tips," and the gentle suggestions of the following individuals, libraries, firms, and bibliophiles.

To these individuals go a special and warm note of thanks: Mrs. Betty Fogler, USAF Academy Library; Brigadier General Jesse C. Gatlin, Jr. (USAF, Retired), former Professor and Head, Department of English and Fine Arts, USAF Academy; Mr. and Mrs. James A. Grimshaw, Sr., Fort Worth; Mr. and Mrs. J. J. Hargett, Fort Worth; Brigadier General William A. Orth, Dean of the Faculty, USAF Academy; Dr. Stephen L. Peterson, Librarian, Beinecke Rare Book and Manuscript Library, Yale; Colonel Jack M. Shuttleworth, Professor and Head, Department of English, USAF Academy; Boyd Professor Lewis P. Simpson, Louisiana State University; and Mr. Robert Penn Warren, who has gone above and beyond the call of even an interested party with his assistance and cooperation.

Professor P. G. Adams, University of Tennessee; Professor Edmund J. Bojarski, General Editor of Thesis Bibliographical Series; Professor Fredson Bowers, University of Virginia; Professor Emeritus Cleanth Brooks, Yale; Professor Matthew J. Bruccoli, University of South Carolina; Mr. Brainard Cheney, Smyrna, TN; Ms. Betsy Colquitt, Fort Worth; Mr. Wayne Dodd, Senior Editor, *Ohio Review*;

Mrs. Jane Davis Doggett, Architectural Graphics Association, Inc.; Professor Maurice Duke, Editor, *Resources for American Literary Studies*; Ms. Susan Dwyer, Editor, *Antaeus*; Mrs. Sarah S. East, Business Manager, *The Southern Review*; Mr. Paul W. Edwards, Austin, TX; Mr. Dean Elkins, Quinnipiac College; Ms. Ann English, Colorado Springs; Professor William Ferris, Director, Center for the Study of Southern Culture, University of Mississippi; Captain James N. Fujita, USAF Academy; Professor Laurence Goldstein, University of Michigan; Professor Erwin Hauer, Yale; Professor C. Hugh Holman, University of North Carolina at Chapel Hill; Major Robert C. Hughes, Washington, D.C.; Professor M. Thomas Inge, Editor, *Resources for American Literary Studies*; Colonel Frederick S. Kiley, Washington, D.C.; Lieutenant Colonel Donald M. Kington (U.S. Army, Retired); Mr. Owen Laster, William Morris Agency; Professor Richard G. Law, Washington State University; Professor James W. Lee, Editor, *Studies in the Novel*; Mr. Stanley W. Lindberg, Editor, *Georgia Review*; Mr. Charles C. Loveridge, *Dialogue*, U.S. Intelligence Agency; Mr. Andrew Lytle, Monteagle, TN; Major William E. McCarron, USAF Academy; Professor Joseph T. McCullen, Texas Tech University; Major and Mrs. Jennings Mace, Colorado Springs; Captain Paul K. Maruyama, USAF Academy; Professor Stephen E. Meats, University of Tampa; Professor James B. Meriwether, University of South Carolina; Professor Harrison T. Meserole, Bibliographer for the Modern Language Association; the late Professor William J. Olive, Louisiana State University; Professor John Clark Pratt, Colorado State University; Mrs. Ilse Rothrock, Kimbell Art Museum, Fort Worth; Mrs. Tsuruko Sadanaga, USAF Academy; Professor John B. Shipley, Editor, *Abstracts of English Studies*; Mr. Robert Shnayerson, Editor, *Quest*; Professor Darwin H. Shrell, Louisiana State University; Professor Donald E. Stanford, Editor, *The Southern Review*; Mr. C. M. Starns, Fort Worth; Mrs. Mary Barbara Tate, Milledgeville, GA; Captain Michael L. Tihomirov, USAF Academy; Professor Joseph F. Tuso, New Mexico State University; Professor Otis B. Wheeler, Louisiana State University; Mrs. Joanne Widner, Wesleyan College, GA; Professor John Hazard Wildman, Louisiana State University; Major George K. Williams, U.S. Military Academy; Mr. Stuart Wright, Winston-Salem, NC; Professor H. Yoshida, Hiroshima University; and those others who, over the years, have passed along to me notes, notices, and references.

Mr. J. R. K. Kantor, University Archivist, University of California at Berkeley; Ms. Martha Campbell, Government Publications, Norlin

Library, University of Colorado; Mr. William J. Marshall, Head of Special Collections, and Ms. Claire McCann, Manuscript Librarian, King Library, University of Kentucky; Mr. Frank W. Robert and Ms. Marice Wolfe, Head of Special Collections, Joint University Libraries, Nashville; Mr. Robert H. Land and Mr. William Matheson, Library of Congress; Mr. D. H. Varley, University of Liverpool Library; Mr. G. J. Guidry, Jr., Ms. Jane P. Kleiner, Mr. Richard Klenk, Mr. Ben Lawson, Mrs. Evangeline Lynch, Mr. T. N. McMullen, Professor Thomas S. Shaw, and Mr. Paul G. Wank, Middleton Library, Louisiana State University; Mrs. J. L. Coleman, Lieutenant Colonel Benjamin C. Glidden, Lieutenant Colonel Claude J. Johns, Jr. (USAF, Retired), Ms. Florence Klemm, and Ms. Mary Ann Robinson, USAF Academy Library; Ms. Christine I. Andrew and Mrs. Elaine Etkin, Sterling Library, Yale; Professor Donald C. Gallup, Ms. Joan Hofmann, and Ms. Anne Whelpley, Beinecke Rare Book and Manuscript Library, Yale; and more than 150 other librarians who responded to my queries regarding materials in their holdings.

Mr. W. Alan Syer, Argus South African Newspapers Ltd.; K. Graff, Bantam Books; Mr. Dale G. Copps, Berkley Publishing Corp.; Blackwell's, Oxford, England; S. Reid-Foster, Collins Publishers; Mr. Charles R. Kahn, Copp Clark Publisher; Mr. Harry Duncan, formerly of the Cummington Press; Mr. Dennis Dalrymple, Dell Publishers; Mr. James Bohan, Dramatists Play Service; Ms. D. C. M. Young, East African *Standard*; Ms. Maria Lyras, Eyre Methuen Ltd.; Ms. Nancy Meiselas, Farrar, Straus & Giroux; Mr. Charles Skilton, Fortune Press; Ms. Karyn M. Berry, Franklin Mint; Mr. Gerard G. Vaughan, Harcourt Brace Jovanovich; Mr. Hugh Van Dusen, Harper & Row, Publishers; Mr. Arthur J. Rosenthal, Harvard University Press; Ms. Jennifer Josephy and Mr. Kenney Withers, Holt, Rinehart and Winston/CBS; Mrs. Barbara E. Amidon, Houghton Mifflin Company; Ms. Barbara Ann Bowden, Literary Guild of America; Ms. Marilyn Hall, London *Observer*; Mr. Charles East, Louisiana State University Press; Ms. Rhona Findley and H. G. Mathews, George J. McLeod; Ms. Muriel Brocklehurst, Manchester *Guardian*; Mr. John Ervin, Jr., Minnesota University Press; V. Andrews, Frederick Muller Ltd.; Mrs. Dorothy Houghton, New English Library; Ms. Marilyn Brauer, Mr. Bruce Kennan, and Mr. R. H. West, Prentice-Hall; Mr. Albert Erskine and Mr. Jim Wilcox, Random House; Mr. D. V. Bradstreet, Random House of Canada; Mrs. David W. Knepper, San Jacinto Museum of History Association; Ms. Ellen C. Wynn, St. Martin's Press; W. P. Neill-Hall and Mr. T. G. Rosenthal, Martin

Secker & Warburg Ltd.; Mrs. Charlotte Campbell, Southern Press; S. Sahay, *The Statesman, Ltd.* (Calcutta); Nicholas Benton and the late Ms. Loraine Winard, Time, Inc.; Ms. Sharon E. Horton, Xerox, University Microfilms.

Mr. Jerry Finder, American Book-Stratford Press; Mr. Charles Willis, Anchor Press Ltd.; V. Flynn, Hunt Barnard Printing Ltd.; M. S. Burden, Cox & Wyman Ltd.; Mr. Jeffrey V. Johnson, Kingsport Press; I. B. Kreidberg, North Central Publishing Company; Mr. Harold Morgan, Quinn & Boden Company; Pat Falzarano, Rae Publishing Company; and N. Gardner, Redwood Burn Ltd.

Mrs. Louis Henry Cohn, House of Books Ltd.; the late Mr. Harold L. Leisure, Plantation Bookshop, Natchez, MS; the late Mr. Linton Massey, President, Bibliographical Society of the University of Virginia, who first showed an interest in this project; Mr. Dick Mohr, International Bookfinders; Mr. Samuel R. Morrill, Edward Morrill & Son; Mr. William Pieper, Bookdealer; Mr. Ralph B. Sipper, Joseph the Provider; Mr. Henry W. Wenning, formerly of C. A. Stonehill; Mr. D. P. Williams, Dalian Books; and Mr. William B. Wisdom, New Orleans.

Mr. William L. Asher, Bibliographer, Library of Congress, provided most of the LC dates of deposit; Dr. Christine Bernstein, London, England, researched for me the British Library date-stamps; and Hiro gave permission to use his photograph of Robert Penn Warren: to all three, a special acknowledgment.

In addition, I wish to thank the Bibliographical Society of the University of Virginia for patient sponsorship, the United States Air Force Academy for granting a year's sabbatical for the completion of this project, and the Robert Penn Warrens for their kindness, patience, and time with this errant bibliographer over the years.

Finally, for their patience with what became a way of life, I want to thank my daughter Courtney and my son James—both of whom grew up with *Robert Penn Warren*—and my wife Darlene, who endured it.

Always a constant concern are the omissions which seem inevitable and which are certainly unintentional. Those who have helped are in no way responsible for the shortcomings of this work. For all their many kindnesses, I am deeply grateful.

JAGJr

Colorado Springs, Colorado

Abbreviations

WORKS

A   *Audubon: A Vision*
AHG   *At Heaven's Gate*
AKM   *All the King's Men*
AKM(p)   *All the King's Men* (play)
ALMM   *American Literature: The Makers and the Making*
ATL   *An Approach to Literature*
BA   *Band of Angels*
BD   *Brother to Dragons*
BD(nv)   *Brother to Dragons: A New Version*
BW   *Blackberry Winter*
CA   *The Circus in the Attic*
Cave   *The Cave*
DP   *Democracy and Poetry*
EP   *Eleven Poems on the Same Theme*
F   *Flood*
FCCE   *Faulkner: A Collection of Critical Essays*
FGW   *Fundamentals of Good Writing*
GMO   *The Gods of Mount Olympus*
HTD   *Homage to Theodore Dreiser*
HTWF   *How Texas Won Her Freedom*
I   *Incarnations*
ITMS   *I'll Take My Stand*
JB   *John Brown: The Making of a Martyr*
JGWP   *John Greenleaf Whittier's Poetry*
LCW   *The Legacy of the Civil War*
MMGG   *Meet Me in the Green Glen*
MR   *Modern Rhetoric*
NR   *Night Rider*
NSH   *A New Southern Harvest*
NT   *Now and Then*
OEP   *Or Else—Poem*
P   *Promises*
PCCE   *Katherine Anne Porter: A Collection of Critical Essays*
PM   *A Plea in Mitigation: Modern Poetry and the End of an Era*
"PPI"   "A Poem of Pure Imagination"

PTCT   A Place to Come To
RA   Remember the Alamo!
RAM   The Rime of the Ancient Mariner
RJ   Randell Jarrell
SCGP   Six Centuries of Great Poetry
SE   Selected Essays
Seg   Segregation: The Inner Conflict in the South
SF   The Scope of Fiction
SH   A Southern Harvest
SP   Selected Poems, 1923–1943
SPDD   Selected Poems by Denis Devlin
SPHM   Selected Poems of Herman Melville
SPNO   Selected Poems: New and Old, 1923–1966
SP75   Selected Poems, 1923–1975
SSM   Short Story Masterpieces
TSP   Thirty-Six Poems
UF   Understanding Fiction
UP   Understanding Poetry
W   Wilderness: A Tale of the Civil War
WET   World Enough and Time
WSN?   Who Speaks for the Negro?
YEO   You, Emperors, and Others

PERIODICALS AND SERIES

Note: These abbreviations correspond to those in the MLA *Annual Bibliography*.

Acc   Accent
AES   Abstracts of English Studies
AL   American Literature
AmOx   American Oxonian
AmPM   American Poetry Magazine
AmPf   American Prefaces
AmRd   Die Amerikanische Rundschau
AN&Q   American Notes and Queries
AQ   American Quarterly
ArlQ   Arlington Quarterly
ArQ   Arizona Quarterly
ASch   American Scholar
AtMo   Atlantic Monthly
BA   Books Abroad
BMCN   Book-of-the-Month Club News
BotOs   Botteghe Oscure

BR*MA*   Baton Rouge *Morning Advocate*
BRMMLA   Bulletin of the Rocky Mountain Modern Language Association
BR*ST*   Baton Rouge *State Times*
BUOP   Bulletin of the University of Osaka Prefecture
BYUS   Brigham Young University Studies
CaSE   Carnegie Series in English
CathW   Catholic World
CE   College English
ChScM   Christian Science Monitor
CL   Comparative Literature
CLAJ   College Language Association Journal
ColQ   Colorado Quarterly
Crit   Critique: Studies in Modern Fiction
DD   Double Dealer
DR   Daily Reveille (LSU)
DVLG   Deutsche Vierteljahrsschrift für Literaturwissenschaft und Geistesgeschichte
EJ   English Journal
ELH   Journal of English Literary History
ELN   English Language Notes
Expl   The Explicator
Fug   The Fugitive
GaR   Georgia Review
HAd   Harvard Advocate
Hor   Horizon
HudR   Hudson Review
JA   Jahrbuch für Amerikastudien
JBR   Journal of Bible and Religion
JEGP   Journal of English and Germanic Philology
JSH   Journal of Southern History
KAL   Kyusha American Literature
KR   Kenyon Review
KyR   The Kentucky Review
LaL   Louisiana Leader
L&P   Literature and Psychology
LitD   Literary Digest
LJ   Library Journal
MAQR   Michigan Alumnus Quarterly Review
McNR   McNeese Review
MCR   Melbourne Critical Review
MFS   Modern Fiction Studies
MissQ   Mississippi Quarterly
MLN   Modern Language Notes
MLQ   Modern Language Quarterly
MP   Modern Philology

NH*Reg*   New Haven *Register*
NNRF   *(Nouvelle) Nouvelle Revue Française*
NO*TP*   New Orleans *Times-Picayune*
NRep   *New Republic*
NY   *New Yorker*
NY*HTBR*   New York *Herald Tribune Book Review*
NYRB   *New York Review of Books*
NY*T*   New York *Times*
NY*TBR*   New York *Times Book Review*
PMLA   *Publications of the Modern Language Association*
PR   *Partisan Review*
PRev   *Paris Review*
PrS   *Prairie Schooner*
PubW   *Publisher's Weekly*
PULC   *Princeton University Library Chronicle*
QJLC   *Quarterly Journal of the Library of Congress*
REL   *Review of English Literature*
RGPFE   *Revue Générale des Publications Françaises et Etrangères*
RGB   *Revue Générale Belge*
RLM   *La Revue des Lettres Modernes*
RLV   *Revue des Langues Vivantes* (Brussels)
SAB   *South Atlantic Bulletin*
SAmL   *Studies in American Literature* (The Hague)
SatEP   *Saturday Evening Post*
SatR   *Saturday Review*
SHR   *Southern Humanities Review*
SLJ   *Southern Literary Journal*
SNNTS   *Studies in the Novel* (North Texas State University)
SoR   *The Southern Review*
SoWS   Southern Writers Series
SR   *Sewanee Review*
SSF   *Studies in Short Fiction*
SWR   *Southwest Review*
SWS   Southwest Writers Series
TCL   *Twentieth-Century Literature*
TCV   Twentieth-Century Views Series
THQ   *Tennessee Historical Quarterly*
TLS   London *Times Literary Supplement*
TQ   *Texas Quarterly*
TSL   *Tennessee Studies in Literature*
TSLL   *Texas Studies in Literature and Language*
TUSAS   Twayne's United States Authors Series
UCQ   *University College Quarterly*
UDQ   *University of Denver Quarterly*

UKCR *University of Kansas City Review*
VMas *Vanderbilt Masquerader*
VQR *Virginia Quarterly Review*
VSH *Vanderbilt Studies in the Humanities*
WHR *Western Humanities Review*
WSCL *Wisconsin Studies in Contemporary Literature*
WWR *Walt Whitman Review*
YDN *Yale Daily News*
YFS *Yale French Studies*
YLM *Yale Literary Magazine*
YR *Yale Review*

DEPOSITORIES AND COLLECTIONS

Note: Many of these abbreviations correspond to those in the *National Union Catalog*.

AAP Auburn Univ., Auburn
AU Univ. of Alabama
BL British Library
CoC Penrose Public Library, Colorado Springs
CoCA United States Air Force Academy, CO
CoCC Colorado College, Colorado Springs
CoD Denver Public Library
CoDU Univ. of Denver
CoFS Colorado State Univ., Fort Collins
CoGrS Colorado State College, Greeley
CoU Univ. of Colorado, Boulder
CSf San Francisco Public Library
Ctb Beinecke Rare Book and Manuscript Library, Yale
CtU Univ. of Connecticut, Storrs
Ctw Robert Penn Warren Deposit, Beinecke Library, Yale
CtY Sterling Library, Yale
CU Univ. of California, Berkeley
DPU Pan American Union Library, Washington, D.C.
FMU Univ. of Miami, Coral Gables, FL
FSU Florida State Univ.
FU Univ. of Florida, Gainesville
ICarbS Southern Illinois Univ., Carbondale
IEN Northwestern Univ., Evanston
IU Univ. of Illinois, Urbana
JAG James A. Grimshaw, Jr., Collection
KU Univ. of Kansas, Lawrence
KyU Univ. of Kentucky, Lexington

L   Louisiana State Library, Baton Rouge
LBR   East Baton Rouge Parish Library
LC   Library of Congress
LPR   Louisiana Polytechnic Institute, Ruston
LU   Middleton Library, Louisiana State Univ., Baton Rouge
MH   Harvard Univ., Cambridge
MiD   Detroit Public Library
MiU   Univ. of Michigan, Ann Arbor
NbU   Univ. of Nebraska, Lincoln
NcD   Duke Univ., Durham
NcU   Univ. of North Carolina, Chapel Hill
NIC   Cornell Univ., Ithaca, NY
NJP   Princeton Univ.
NN   New York Public Library
NNC   Columbia Univ., New York
OCl   Cleveland Public Library
OrCS   Oregon State Univ., Corvallis
PJB   Beaver College, Jenkintown, PA
PPD   Drexel Institute of Tech., Philadelphia
PPL   LaSalle College, Philadelphia
RPB   Brown Univ., Providence
RPW   Robert Penn Warren's Library, Fairfield, CT
ScU   Univ. of South Carolina, Columbia
STW   Stuart T. Wright Collection
TNJ   Vanderbilt University Library, Nashville
TxDaM   Southern Methodist Univ., Dallas
TxFTC   Texas Christian Univ., Fort Worth
TxHR   Rice Univ., Houston
TxLT   Texas Tech Univ., Lubbock
TxU   Univ. of Texas, Austin
ViU   Univ. of Virginia, Charlottesville

MISCELLANEOUS

alt.   alternate, -ing
anon.   anonymous
anth.   anthology, -ized
bds.   boards
beg.   beginning
bf.   boldface
BIP   *Books in Print*
b-w   black and white
ca.   circa
chm.   chairperson

cm.   centimeter
coll.   collation
cont'd   continued
DA   *Dissertation Abstracts*
dw   dust wrapper
hf. tit.   half title
horiz.   horizontal (across)
HT   head title
illus.   illustrated, -or, -ions
ital.   italics
l., ll.   line, -s; leaf, leaves
ltr.   letter
nar.   narrow
obl.   oblong
orn.   ornament
p., pp.   page, -s
q.v.   *quod vide*, which see
r.   recto
ref.   reference
rpt.   reprint
RPW   Robert Penn Warren
RT   running title
st., sts.   stanza, -s
v.   verso
vert.   vertical (down)
w.   with

SYMBOLS

[ ]   interpolated note; inferred, illegible notation
⟨ ⟩   mutilation

Works by
Robert Penn Warren

———————————

A

Books as Sole Author

A1 *John Brown: The Making of a Martyr*

A1.a1 first American edition, first impression (1929)

JOHN BROWN | The Making of | A Martyr | [*quadruple rule*, inverted pyramid (each 0.2 cm. thick: 3.1, 2.3, 1.4, and 0.6 cm.)] | By Robert | Penn Warren | [*quadruple rule*, pyramid (each measures as above in reversed order)] | PAYSON & CLARKE LTD | New York 1929

Colophon, p. [475]: '[logo] | COMPOSITION, PRESSWORK | AND BINDING | *by* THE PLIMPTON PRESS | NORWOOD · MASSACHUSETTS'.

Collation: medium 8° (trimmed: 22.8 × 15.2 cm.); *unsigned* [1–30⁸], 240 leaves + 9 ll. illus.; pp. [i–iv], [1–8] 9–474 [475–476]; numbers centered at foot of type page; plates (9) facing pp. [iii], 10, 104, 364, 381, 399, 410, 434, and 439.

Contents: p. [i]: hf. tit. 'JOHN BROWN'; p. [ii]: blank; p. [iii]: title page; p. [iv]: 'COPYRIGHT 1929 BY | PAYSON & CLARKE LTD | ERRATUM | *Due to a misunderstanding, certain footnotes originally prepared only | for the Author's convenience have been printed in this text. The Author | and the Publishers crave the Reader's indulgence for this unfortunate error.*'; p. [1]: dedication 'To | R. F. W. AND A. R. P. W.'; p. [2]: blank; p. [3]: 'CONTENTS'; p. [4]: blank; p. [5]: 'ILLUSTRATIONS'; p. [6]: blank; p. [7]: hf. tit.; p. [8]: blank; p. 9: text headed '1 | BUT NOT IN A RENTED HOUSE'; p. 25: '2 | THE MERCHANT PRINCE'; p. 87: '3 | A SOUND REASON'; p. 107: '4 | THE TIGHT-ROPE ACT'; p. 125: '5 | JONES GETS SLAPPED'; p. 154: '6 | "A LITTLE COMPANY | BY OURSELVES"'; p. 191: '7 | LETTERS OF MARQUE | FROM GOD'; p. 223: '8 | PASSING THE HAT'; p. 247: '9 | THE BIRTH OF A NATION'; p. 290: '10 | DO YOU BELIEVE QUETELET?'; p. 320: '11 | THE SUMMER IDYL';

A1.a1, B16, A15.a1, A7.a1, A11.a1, A15.b1, A8.a1, A7.k1

p. 352: '12 | THE SWORD OF | FREDERICK & WASHING-
TON'; p. 382: '13 | THE SOUR APPLE TREE'; p. [440]: blank;
p. 441: 'BIBLIOGRAPHICAL NOTE | A Matter of Opinions'; p.
463: 'INDEX'; p. [475]: colophon; p. [476]: blank.

Typography and Paper: text: 32 ll., 15.9 (17.0) × 10.0 cm.; Scotch Roman 11/12-pt. RT: 'JOHN BROWN' on v. except pp. 154, 290, 320, 352,
382, 464ff.; chapter titles on respective r.: 'BUT NOT IN A RENTED
HOUSE'; etc.; 'INDEX' on v. and r., pp. 464–474. Paper: white, laid,
vertical chainlines (1.8 cm.), unwatermarked; sheets bulk 4.0 cm.

Plates: lithographs with titles in type. Facing title page: oval-framed
picture of John Brown (11.0 × 8.2 cm.) '[facsimile signature] John
Brown | (Courtesy of Houghton Mifflin Co.) | (This picture is re-
produced from "John Brown A Biogra-|phy Fifty Years After" by
Oswald Garrison Villard by | courtesy of Mr. Villard.)'; facing
p. 10: (16.5 × 10.2 cm.) 'U.S. MARINES STORMING ENGINE
HOUSE AT HARPER'S FERRY | (From *Frank Leslie's Weekly*, Octo-
ber 29, 1859)'; facing p. 104: square b-w map (11.85 cm.) 'SKETCH
TO SHOW TOWNS NEAR OSSAWATOMIE'; facing p. 364:
(16.45 × 10.2 cm.) 'INTERIOR OF THE ENGINE HOUSE
DURING ATTACK BY MARINES | (From *Frank Leslie's Weekly*,
November 5, 1859)'; facing p. 381: (16.55 × 10.2 cm.) 'GOV. WISE
EXAMINING PRISONERS | (From *Frank Leslie's Weekly*, October
29, 1859)'; facing p. 399: (16.5 × 10.2 cm.) 'MRS. BROWN ES-
CORTED TO HER HUSBAND IN JAIL | (From *Frank Leslie's
Weekly*, December 17, 1859)'; facing p. 410: (12.0 × 10.2 cm.) 'JOHN
BROWN RIDING TO HIS EXECUTION | (From *Frank Leslie's
Weekly*, December 17, 1859)'; facing p. 434: (16.5 × 10.2 cm.) 'JOHN
BROWN ASCENDING SCAFFOLD | (From *Frank Leslie's Weekly*,
December 10, 1859)'; facing p. 439: (16.45 × 10.2 cm.) 'EXECU-
TION OF JOHN BROWN | (From *Frank Leslie's Weekly*, December
17, 1859)'.

Binding: maroon, coarse cloth. Front and back covers: blank. Spine,
gilt-stamped: '[vert.] JOHN BROWN [*quadruple rule*, inverted pyra-
mid] WARREN | [horiz.] PAYSON & | CLARKE LTD'. All edges
trimmed with top stained orange; orange endpapers: map printed both
front and back with legend 'MILITARY MAP | SHOWING THE |
TOPOGRAPHICAL FEATURES OF THE COUNTRY | ADJA-
CENT TO | HARPER'S FERRY, VA. | INCLUDING | Maryland,
Loudoun and Bolivar Heights, and | portions of South and Short
Mountains, | WITH THE POSITIONS OF THE | DEFENSIVE

WORKS, | ALSO THE | Junction of the Potomac and Shenandoah Rivers and their | Passage through the Blue Ridge | Surveyed from August 3ᵈ to Sept. 30ᵗʰ 1863 | UNDER THE DIRECTION OF | CAPT. N. MICHLER, CORPS OF ENGᴿˢ U. S. ARMY | BY | MAJOR JOHN E. WEYSS, PRINCIPAL ASSISTANT | ENGI-NEER DEPARTMENT | ARMY OF THE POTOMAC. | Scale | [Scale in thousand-foot increments] | —— *Union* | Note | [The vertical c]*urves indicate the heights in feet of the several points above the level of the canal at the pontoon bridge.* | *The horizontal curves indicate distances of 20 feet perpendicular height'.*

Dust wrapper: front: '[beige border around edges of cover except spine edge; on reddish brown in black] JOHN-BROWN | THE MAKING OF A MARTYR | BY ROBERT PENN WARREN | [thin black rule] | [woodcut in beige, reddish brown, and black of man with a pistol in his right hand]'. Spine: '[continuation of beige border; on reddish brown in black] JOHN | BROWN | WARREN | [thin black rule] | [cont. of illus.] | [on reddish brown in black] Payson & Clarke Ltd'. Back cover, beige background: '[on outer edge, on beige in black] Robert Penn [two rules—reddish brown and black—make corner frame] | [under Robert] Warren | [in reddish brown] JOHN | BROWN | [toward spine, as if one of a two-column page, in black, about the book] | [two rules—as above—on outer edge make corner frame approximately 5 cm. from bottom] | [on outer edge in reddish brown] PAYSON & | CLARKE LTD | [in black, publisher's device] | [two rules as above on spine edge to make corner frame in lower right]'. Front flap: about the author. Back flap: publisher's advertisement.

Copies: CoCA, CtY, JAG, KyU, LC, LU (rebound), NJP, RPW, STW, TNJ.

Notes: 1. Published 2 Nov. 1929 at $5.00. LC copyright 2 Nov. 1929 (A15518); two copies deposited 7 Nov. 1929. Although the exact number of copies printed is unconfirmed, RPW believes it to be 500 from type.

2. CoCA, JAG, and LU copies have similar ink smudges: p. 66 in top left margin of text between the headline and the first line of text (CoCA and JAG); p. 136 a line the width of the text between the headline and the first line (JAG and LU); pp. 87 and 154 the 'U' in 'SOUND' and 'OURSELVES', respectively, in the chapter head is smeared slightly on the left curve (CoCA, JAG, LU); p. 469 a vertical smudge between the index columns (CoCA and LU).

3. TNJ copy is inscribed on r. of frontispiece, diagonally inner to

upper edges: 'For Dr. and Mrs. Curry | in all affection & esteem, | Red.' KyU copy has a bookplate on the front endpaper from the library of Samuel M. Wilson.

4. Although the original publishing house, Payson & Clarke Ltd., changed hands thrice during the Depression—1930, Brewer & Warren; 1931, Brewer, Warren & Putnam; 1933, Harcourt, Brace & Company—there is no evidence that any of them changed the title page of *JB*.

A1.b1   first American edition, reprint, by offset (1970)

[Title page as in A1.a1 with the following added at foot of page] Republished, 1970 | Scholarly Press, 22929 Industrial Drive East | St. Clair Shores, Michigan 48080

Collation: demy 8° (trimmed: 20.9 × 13.2 cm.); leaf 30₈ canceled.

Contents: added to p. [iv]: 'Library of Congress Catalog Number: 73-145360 | Standard Book Number: 403-01266-X | [at foot of p.] This edition is printed on a high-quality, | acid-free paper that meets specification | requirements for fine book paper referred | to as "300-year" paper'.

Paper: white, wove, unwatermarked; sheets bulk 3.3 cm.

Binding: dark blue bds. Front and back: blank. Spine, in black on very light brown strip: 'JOHN | BROWN | The | Making | of a | Martyr | · | WARREN | Scholarly | Press'. All edges trimmed and unstained; white endpapers (no map).
   Dust wrapper: none found.

Copies: AU, IEN, LC, TxFTC.

Note: published at $19.00, but "publisher has not set a date for availability" of publication information (note, C. Karbowski, Scholarly Press, Inc., 30 Jan. 1975).

A2   *Thirty-Six Poems*

A2.a1   first American edition, first impression (1935)

THIRTY-SIX POEMS | BY | ROBERT PENN WARREN | NEW YORK | THE ALCESTIS PRESS | 551 Fifth Avenue | 1935

Colophon, p. [71]: 'THIS FIRST EDITION OF THIRTY-|SIX POEMS IS STRICTLY LIMITED | TO 165 COPIES, SIGNED

THIRTY-SIX POEMS

BY

ROBERT PENN WARREN

NEW YORK
THE ALCESTIS PRESS
551 Fifth Avenue
1 9 3 5

A2.a1 title page

BY THE | AUTHOR. TWENTY COPIES, NUM-|BERED I-XX ARE PRINTED ON | DUCA DI MODENA, AN ITALIAN | HANDMADE PAPER, FOR PRESEN-|TATION PURPOSES: 135 COPIES, | NUMBERED 1-135 ON STRATH-|MORE PERMANENT ALL-RAG | PAPER, ARE FOR SALE, AND 10 | COPIES, MARKED OUT OF SERIES, | ARE FOR REVIEW. PUBLISHED BY | J. RONALD LANE LATIMER AT | HIS ALCESTIS PRESS IN | NOVEMBER, 1935. | THIS COPY IS NUMBER | [number entered by hand in ink] | [ink signature] Robert Penn Warren | DESIGNED AND PRINTED BY LEW NEY WITH IN-KUNABULA | TYPE SET BY HAND AND THE | TYPE HAS BEEN DISTRIBUTED'.

Collation: royal folio 8° (rough trimmed: 23.7 × 16.2 cm.); *unsigned* [1–4⁸ 5⁶], 38 leaves; pp. [i–ii], [1–5] 6–7 [8] 9–69 [70–74]; numbers are printed in the corner formed by the tail and outer margins.

Contents: pp. [i–ii]: blank; p. [1]: hf. tit. 'THIRTY-SIX POEMS'; p. [2]: blank; p. [3]: title page; p. [4]: 'COPYRIGHT, 1935, BY THE ALCESTIS PRESS | These poems have appeared in | the *Nation*, the *New Republic*, the *Fugitive*, the | *Saturday Review of Literature*, the *Southern* | *Review*, *Poetry: A Magazine of Verse*, the | poetry supplement of the *American Review* (1934), | the *Virginia Quarterly Review*, the *Southwest* | *Review*, and the *American Caravan*'; p. [5]: 'To E. C. B. W.'; pp. 6–7: '*CONTENTS*'; p. [8]: blank; pp. 9–13: 'THE RETURN: AN ELEGY'; p. 14: 'KENTUCKY MOUNTAIN FARM | i. Rebuke of the Rocks'; p. 15: 'ii. At the Hour of the Breaking of the Rocks'; pp. 16–17: 'iii. History among the Rocks'; pp. 17–18: 'iv. The Cardinal'; p. 18: 'v. The Jay'; p. 19: 'vi. Watershed'; p. 20: 'vii. The Return'; pp. 21–24: 'PONDY WOODS'; p. 25: 'EIDOLON'; pp. 26–27: 'LETTER OF A MOTHER'; p. 28: 'GENEALOGY'; pp. 29–33: 'HISTORY'; pp. 34–36: 'RESOLUTION'; pp. 37–40: 'LETTER FROM A COWARD TO A HERO'; p. 41: 'LATE SUBTERFUGE'; p. 42: 'RANSOM'; p. 43: 'AGED MAN SURVEYS THE PAST TIME'; p. 44: 'TOWARD RATIONALITY'; p. 45: 'TO A FRIEND PARTING'; p. 46: 'LETTER TO A FRIEND'; p. 47: 'AUBADE FOR HOPE'; pp. 48–49: 'MAN COMING OF AGE'; p. 50: 'CRŒSUS IN AUTUMN'; p. 51: 'SO FROST ASTOUNDS'; pp. 52–54: 'THE LAST METAPHOR'; pp. 55–56: 'PACIFIC GAZER'; pp. 57–58: 'CALENDAR'; p. 59: 'PROBLEM OF KNOWLEDGE'; p. 60: 'COLD COLLOQUY'; pp. 61–62: 'FOR A SELF-POSSESSED FRIEND'; p. 63: 'FOR A FRIEND WHO THINKS

HIMSELF URBANE'; pp. 64–65: 'THE GARDEN'; p. 66: 'TO ONE AWAKE'; p. 67: 'GARDEN WATERS'; pp. 68–69: 'TO A FACE IN THE CROWD'; p. [70]: blank; p. [71]: colophon; pp. [72–74]: blank.

Typography and Paper: text: 26 ll., 15.4 (16.3) × 10.5 cm.; see type description in colophon, 14-pt. Paper: white, wove, unwatermarked; sheets bulk 0.6 cm.

Binding: off-white paper. Front cover, in black: 'THIRTY-SIX POEMS | ROBERT PENN WARREN'. Spine, vert., in black: 'THIRTY-SIX POEMS ROBERT PENN WARREN'. Back cover: blank. All edges unstained; top edge trimmed, fore and bottom edges rough trimmed.

Dust wrapper: issued in clear wax-paper jacket.

Copies: Ctb (no. 94), Ctw (no. 63), LU (nos. 18 & 116), NJP (no. 124), RPW (no. 64), STW (nos. xix, 27, 50, & 108), TNJ (no. 123, rebound).

Notes: 1. Published 15 Feb. 1936 in 165 copies at $7.50. No LC copyright registration was found (ltr., William L. Asher, Bibliographer, Library of Congress, 5 Nov. 1979).

2. LU (no. 18) collation is 37 leaves with leaf 5_6 canceled; Ctw (no. 63) is signed; and LU (no. 116) contains an inscription in blue ink on p. [i] in the upper left corner in script: 'To | Helen & Marcus [Wilkerson] | with sincere regards | Red Warren | Baton Rouge, | May, 1942 ||'. Both LU copies have been bound around the original covers.

3. No subsequent impressions; however, a Xerox copy (no. 121) is available from University Microfilms, Ann Arbor, MI.

A3 *Night Rider*

A3.a1   first American edition, first impression (1939)

[in gray, on two pp.: p. (ii)] Night [p. (iii)] Rider | BY ROBERT PENN WARREN | [publisher's device] | HOUGHTON MIFFLIN COMPANY · BOSTON | [black letter] The Riverside Press Cambridge | 1939

Collation: demy 8° (untrimmed: 20.5 × 14.0 cm.); *unsigned* [1^4 2^6 3–30^8], 234 leaves; pp. [i–viii], [1] 2–460, except the first page of each chapter is unnumbered; numbers located in the corner formed by the head and outer margins.

Contents: p. [i]: hf. tit. 'NIGHT RIDER'; pp. [ii–iii]: title pages; p. [iv]: 'COPYRIGHT, 1939, BY ROBERT PENN WARREN | ALL RIGHTS RESERVED INCLUDING THE RIGHT TO REPRODUCE | THIS BOOK OR PARTS THEREOF IN ANY FORM | [black letter] The Riverside Press | CAMBRIDGE · MASSACHUSETTS | PRINTED IN THE U.S.A.'; p. [v]: 'TO | DOMENICO BRESCIA | AND | DANIEL JUSTIN DONAHOE | IN GRATITUDE'; p. [vi]: blank; p. [vii]: disclaimer, 'Although this book was suggested by certain events | which took place in Kentucky in the early years of | this century, it is not, in any strict sense, a historical | novel. And more particularly, the characters in this | book are not to be identified with any actual persons, | living or dead, who participated in those events'; p. [viii]: blank; p. [1]: 'Chapter one', consistent pattern throughout to p. [427]: 'Chapter sixteen'; on p. 460 'THE END'.

Typography and Paper: text: 34 ll., 16.5 (17.1) × 10.0 cm.; Baskerville 12/14-pt. In lieu of a RT, on each page, except at the beginning of each chapter, a single rule extends from the page number to the inner margin. Paper: white, wove, unwatermarked; sheets bulk 2.6 cm.

Binding: gray cloth. Front, in maroon: 'Night | Rider'. Spine, in maroon: 'Night | Rider | WARREN | HOUGHTON | MIFFLIN | COMPANY'. Back: blank. All edges unstained; top edge trimmed, fore and bottom edges rough trimmed; white endpapers.

   Dust wrapper: front cover, sky with streaks of orange: '[in black] BY ROBERT PENN WARREN | [in white, shadowed ltrs.] *Night* | *Rider* | [in white on black rectangle, quote of Allen Tate] | [in black] A HOUGHTON MIFFLIN [publisher's device] FELLOWSHIP NOVEL'. Spine: '[horiz., in black] WARREN | [vert., in white, shadowed ltrs.] *Night Rider* | [in horiz., in black] HOUGHTON MIFFLIN | COMPANY'. Back cover: about HM literary fellowships. Front flap: about the book. Back flap: publisher's advertisement.

Copies: CoCC, Ctb, CtY, JAG, KyU (2), LC, LU (2), STW (2), TNJ, TxFTC.

Notes: 1. Published 14 March 1939 in one printing of 5,000 copies bound in separate lots of 3,000 and 2,000 at $2.50. Printed by The Riverside Press. "In October 1947, the plates and dies were ordered sent [to] Quinn & Boden and the copyright certificate was returned to the author, c/o William Morris Agency" (ltrs., Barbara E. Amidon, Permissions Dept., Houghton Mifflin Company, 16 March 1973 and

27 Jan. 1975). LC copyright 14 March 1939 (A127478); deposited 18 March 1939; copyright renewal 19 Oct. 1966 (R395458).

2. An abridged version appeared in *Omnibook Magazine*, Nov. 1948, pp. 69–112.

3. KyU has typescripts of background material on the novel: early warning notes dating back to 1 Jan. 1908; no sources for the material are indicated on the notes.

A3.a2 first American edition, second impression (1948)

[p. (iv)] NIGHT [p. v] RIDER | Robert Penn Warren | [publisher's device] Random House, New York

Collation: demy folio 8° (trimmed: 22.0 × 13.5 cm.); *unsigned* [1–13¹⁶ 14¹² 15¹⁶], 236 leaves; pp. [i–xii], [1] 2–460.

Contents: p. [i]: hf. tit. 'NIGHT RIDER'; p. [ii]: blank; on p. [iii] '*Books by Robert Penn Warren* | [list ends with *The Circus in the Attic*]'; pp. [iv–v]: title pages; p. [vi]: copyright page; p. [vii]: dedication; p. [viii]: blank; p. [ix]: disclaimer; p. [x]: blank; p. [xi]: hf. tit.; p. [xii]: blank; pp. [1]–460: text; on p. 460 'THE END'.

Typography and Paper: reprinted from the original plates. Paper: white, wove, unwatermarked; sheets bulk 2.7 cm.

Binding: cream bds. Front, in black: 'NIGHT | RIDER'. Spine, in black: 'ROBERT | PENN | WARREN | Night | Rider | RANDOM | HOUSE'. Back: blank. All edges trimmed with top edge stained red; white endpapers.

Dust wrapper: none available.

Copies: Albert Erskine.

Note: reprinted 27 Aug. 1948 in 5,000 copies with subsequent printings 18 June 1965 of 1,000 copies and 19 Nov. 1968 of 1,000 copies. Printed at Haddon Bindery, Camden, NJ. According to Random House records, "plates & rights bought from Houghton Mifflin 30 June 1941 for $920.99" (ltr., Jim Wilcox, Random House, Inc., 31 July 1974).

A3.a3 first American edition, third impression (1965)

Binding: reddish brown, calico-texture cloth, not embossed. Front, on black rectangle in gilt: 'NIGHT | RIDER'. Spine, in gilt: 'ROBERT | PENN | WARREN | [title on black] Night | Rider | RANDOM |

HOUSE'. Back: blank. All edges trimmed and unstained.
Dust wrapper: none available.

Copies: CoC, CoCA, JAG, LC.

A3.a4 first American edition, fourth impression (1968)

Contents: p. [i]: blank; on p. [ii] *'Books by Robert Penn Warren* | [list ends
with *Incarnations: Poems 1966–1968]*'; p. [iii]: hf. tit. 'NIGHT RIDER';
pp. [iv–v]: title pages; p. [vi]: 'COPYRIGHT, 1939, COPYRIGHT
RENEWED 1966 BY ROBERT PENN WARREN'.

Binding: navy blue, embossed calico-grain cloth. Front, in light blue:
'NIGHT | RIDER'. Spine: '[in silver] ROBERT | PENN | WARREN
| [in light blue] Night | Rider | [in silver] RANDOM | HOUSE'. Back:
blank. All edges trimmed with top stained red.
  Dust wrapper: front cover, red flames on black background: '[in red]
Robert Penn Warren | [in white overlettering] Night | Rider | [in red]
by the author of the Pulitzer Prize Novel, | "ALL THE KING'S MEN"'.
Spine, continuation of front background: '[in red] ROBERT | PENN |
WARREN | [in white] Night | Rider | RANDOM | HOUSE'. Back
cover, black on white: excerpts of reviews by Lorine Pruette, Mina
Curtiss, Christopher Isherwood, and Hassoldt Davis; across the bot-
tom, *'Night Rider* | *by* | *Robert Penn Warren'*.

Copies: JAG, LC.

A3.b1 second American edition, first impression, paperback
(abridged) (1950)

[orn. rule] | NIGHT RIDER | *by* | Robert Penn Warren | [orn. rule] |
Abridgment and Introduction by | George Mayberry | [within oval—
N · A · L | SIGNET | BOOKS] | A SIGNET BOOK | Published by
THE NEW AMERICAN LIBRARY

Collation: post folio 8° (trimmed: 18.1 × 10.7 cm.); *unsigned* 128 ind.
leaves; pp. [1–5] 6–256; numbers centered at foot of text.

Contents: on p. [1] 'INTRODUCTION TO THE SIGNET EDI-
TION' by George Mayberry, dated April 1950; p. [2]: disclaimer;
p. [3]: title page; p. [4]: copyright page includes 'INTRODUCTION TO THE
SIGNET EDITION COPYRIGHT, 1950, BY | GEORGE MAYBERRY | FIRST
PRINTING, AUGUST, 1950 | [dedication] | This edition of *Night Rider* has
been | abridged with the author's approval.'; on p. [5] text begins with
'CHAPTER ONE'; on p. 256 'THE END'.

Typography and Paper: text: 47 ll., 15.75 (16.0) × 8.9 cm.; Times New Roman 9/10-pt. Paper: white, wove, unwatermarked; sheets bulk 1.1 cm.

Binding: paper. Front cover, top, on orange stripe continuing around to back, in black: on left '804 | [Signet device]'; on right '*A STRONG, PASSIONATE, HUMAN NOVEL* | *By the author of "All the King's Men"*'. Center: '[in yellow] NIGHT RIDER | [in white] ROBERT | PENN | WARREN' over a picture of a man sitting on the edge of a bed, looking at a woman who is standing by a window. Bottom, on orange stripe, in black: 'Abridgment and Introduction by George Mayberry'; on rose stripe continuing around to back, in white: 'A SIGNET BOOK'. Spine, on orange background, in black: '[horiz.] 804 | [vert.] NIGHT RIDER ROBERT PENN WARREN'. Back: about the book and the author. All edges trimmed and stained reddish orange.

Copies: Ctw (2), JAG, KyU, LC, STW.

Notes: 1. Published Aug. 1950; introduction copyrighted 1 Aug. 1950 (A47117).
    2. Omits pp. 78–83 (A3.a1) from chapter 3 and portions of chapters 1off., and paragraphs have been excised throughout as well.

A3.c1   third American edition, first impression, paperback (1956)

NIGHT RIDER | ROBERT PENN WARREN | *Winner of the PULITZER PRIZE for FICTION* | BERKLEY PUBLISHING CORP. | 145 West 57th Street · New York 19, N.Y.

Collation: foolscap folio 8° (trimmed: 16.2 × 10.6 cm.); *unsigned* 192 ind. leaves; pp. [i–ii], [1–4] 5–378 [379–382]; numbers centered at foot of text.

Contents: p. [i]: about the novel and an excerpt from a review from *The Nation*; p. [ii]: blank; p. [1]: title page; p. [2]: copyright page includes dedication; p. [3]: disclaimer; p. [4]: blank; on p. 5 text begins with 'Chapter one'; on p. 378 'THE END'; pp. [379–382]: publisher's advertisement.

Typography and Paper: text: 43 ll., 14.25 (14.5) × 8.7 cm.; Times New Roman 10-pt. unleaded. Paper: white, wove, unwatermarked; sheets bulk 2.05 cm.

Binding: paper. Front cover, illus. in multicolors of fire in background, man on horseback with flaming torch in center, and woman fleeing in foreground: '[in yellow] ROBERT PENN WARREN | [in white] NIGHT RIDER [down outer edge] 50¢ | BERKLEY | [fleur-de-lis] | BOOKS | BG-35 | K [white irregular spot] | by the author of | *ALL THE KINGS* [sic] *MEN* | and *BAND OF ANGELS* | COMPLETE | AND | UNABRIDGED'. Spine, on white, in black: '[vert.] NIGHT RIDER WARREN | [horiz.] 50¢ | BERKLEY | [fleur-de-lis] | BOOKS | BG-35'. Back cover: blue stripe across top, paragraph about the book, and blue-tone illus. of woman in lower right corner. All edges trimmed and stained yellow.

Copies: ScU (but see note 2), STW.

Notes: 1. Published 22 Oct. 1956 in 139,385 copies (BG-35) at 50¢. Printed by W. F. Hall Printing Company. (Ltr., Dale G. Copps, Assistant to the Editor, Berkley Pub. Corp., 3 Feb. 1975.)

2. The ScU library no longer has among its holdings the 1956 copy (BG-35) which had been rebound (ltr., Matthew J. Bruccoli, Univ. of South Carolina, postmarked 10 April 1975).

A3.d1 fourth American edition, first impression, paperback (1965)

NIGHT | RIDER | Robert | Penn | Warren | [publisher's device] | A BERKLEY MEDALLION BOOK | published by | BERKLEY PUBLISHING CORPORATION

Collation: post folio 8° (trimmed: 17.8 × 10.7 cm.); *unsigned* 184 ind. leaves; pp. [1–4] 5–368; numbers centered at foot of text.

Contents: p. [1]: excerpts from reviews by Walter Allen and in *Atlantic Monthly*; p. [2]: blank; p. [3]: title page; p. [4]: copyright page includes dedication, disclaimer, and copyright notice; on p. 5 text begins with 'CHAPTER ONE'; text ends on p. 368.

Typography and Paper: text: 45 ll., 15.6 (16.0) × 8.7 cm.; Times New Roman 10/11-pt. Paper: white, wove, unwatermarked; sheets bulk 2.1 cm.

Binding: paper. Front cover: '[white background, black lettering] BERKLEY | [in blue and black, publisher's device] | MEDALLION | [in black] N1048 | 95¢ | Robert Penn | Warren | A NOVEL BY THE AUTHOR OF | ALL THE KING'S MEN | [in purple] NIGHT | RIDER | [in color, picture of barn burning]'. Spine: '[horiz., in black] N1048 | 95¢ | [vert., in purple] NIGHT RIDER [in black] Robert Penn Warren | [horiz., in purple, publisher's device]'. Back cover: '[in purple, quote by Walter Allen] | [in black, about the book] | [in color, picture of barn burning]'. All edges trimmed and stained red.

Copies: JAG, KyU.

Note: Published as "Berkley Medallion Edition" 26 Feb. 1965 in 66,352 copies (N1048) at 95¢ and 23 May 1967 in 15,506 copies.

A3.d4 fourth American edition, fourth impression, by offset, paperback (1968)

NIGHT RIDER || ROBERT PENN WARREN | [publisher's device]

Collation: post folio 8° (trimmed: 17.7 × 10.7 cm.); *unsigned* 184 ind. leaves; pp. [1–4] 5–368; numbers centered at foot of text.

Contents: p. [1]: about the author; p. [2]: publisher's advertisement; p. [3]: title page; on p. [4] '*This low-priced Bantam Book | has been completely reset in a type face | designed for easy reading, and was printed | from new plates. It contains the complete | text of the original hard-cover edition.* | NOT ONE WORD HAS BEEN OMITTED.' plus dedication, printing history, disclaimer, and copyright notice; on p. 5 text begins with 'CHAPTER ONE'; text ends on p. 368.

> *Note*: does not acknowledge the Berkley "editions" in the printing history.

Typography and Paper: text: 45 ll., 15.6 (16.0) × 8.8 cm.; Times New Roman 10/11-pt. Paper: white, wove, unwatermarked; sheets bulk 2.1 cm.

> *Note*: This Bantam Modern Classic "edition" appears to be from the Berkley impression (**A3.d1**), the statement on p. [4] notwithstanding. Compare, for example, the following similarities between the two impressions: p. 26.31, "Jown" for "John"; p. 195.10, broken font *n* and *d* in "and"; and p. 202.25, broken font *s* in "songs."

Binding: paper. Front cover, in white: '[on purple background, vert. from bottom to top] NY4075 * 95¢ * A BANTAM MODERN CLASSIC | [at top, horiz., trademark] Robert | Penn | Warren || Night | Rider | The powerful | American tragedy | by the Pulitzer | Prize-winning | author of | ALL THE KING'S MEN | [against orange (flame), figure in blue shirt on green horse]'. Spine, on white: '[horiz., in black] 95¢ || NY4075 | [in blue, trademark] | [in black] A BANTAM | MODERN | CLASSIC || [vert.] Night Rider · Robert Penn Warren'. Back cover: quotation by Walter Allen, publisher's device, and 'BY

THE | AUTHOR OF | ALL THE KING'S MEN'. All edges trimmed and unstained.

Copies: Ctw, JAG, RPW.

Note: published March 1968 as a Bantam Modern Classic "edition" (NY4075) in 110,000 copies at 95¢—"the only printing on this title" by Bantam (ltr., K. Graff, Bantam Statistical Dept., Bantam Books, Inc., 30 April 1975). Printed by W. F. Hall, Inc.

A3.d5 fourth American edition, fifth impression, by offset, paperback (1979)

NIGHT | RIDER | Robert Penn Warren | [publisher's device] | VINTAGE BOOKS | A Division of Random House | New York

Collation: post folio 8° (trimmed: 17.7 × 10.6 cm.); *unsigned* 184 ind. leaves; pp. [1–4] 5–368; numbers centered at foot of text.

Contents: p. [1]: hf. tit. 'NIGHT | RIDER'; p. [2]: blank; p. [3]: title page; p. [4]: 'FIRST VINTAGE BOOKS EDITION, April 1979' plus copyright information and LC Cataloging in Publication Data; on p. 5 text begins with 'CHAPTER ONE'; text ends on p. 368.

Typography and Paper: text: 45 ll., 15.5 (15.8) × 8.8 cm.; Times New Roman 10/11-pt. Paper: white, wove, unwatermarked; sheets bulk 1.6 cm.

> *Note*: This Vintage Book appears to have been reproduced by photo-offset from the Berkley impression (**A3.d1**). (See note under typography for **A3.d4**.)

Binding: paper. Front cover, on black background: '[in gilt] $2.95 · IN CANADA $3.75 · V-817 · 394-72817-3 | [in red] Night | Rider | [horseback rider against image of flames] | [gilt and red rules] | [in gilt] ROBERT | PENN | WARREN'. Spine, on black: '[vert., in red] NIGHT RIDER [in gilt with red underline] ROBERT PENN WARREN | [horiz., in gilt, publisher's device] | VINTAGE | V-817'. Back cover, on black: '[in red] FICTION | [in white, about the novel and author]'. All edges trimmed and unstained.

Copies: JAG, RPW, STW.

Note: published April 1979 as a Vintage Book (V-817) in 15,000 copies at $2.95 (ltr., Albert Erskine, Random House, Inc., 27 Nov. 1979). Printed by W. F. Hall.

A3.e1 first English edition, first impression (1940)

ROBERT PENN WARREN | [four rules in decreasing thicknesses] | Night | Rider | EYRE & SPOTTISWOODE | LONDON | [four rules in increasing thicknesses]

Collation: demy folio 8° (trimmed: 21.6 × 13.6 cm.); signed, [1]–28⁸ 29⁴, 228 leaves; pp. [1–8] 9–454 [455–456]. Page numbers are located in the corner formed by the head and outer margins, except on chapter pages, on which numbers are centered at foot of type page.

Contents: p. [1]: hf. tit. 'NIGHT RIDER'; p. [2]: blank; p. [3]: title page; p. [4]: *'First printed in January,* 1940 | *Made and printed in Great Britain for* | *Eyre and Spottiswoode (Publishers), London*'; p. [5]: dedication (sans "in gratitude"); p. [6]: blank; p. [7]: hf. tit.; p. [8]: disclaimer; pp. 9–454: text; on p. 454 'THE END'; pp. [455–456]: blank.

Typography and Paper: text: 37 ll., 15.9 (16.4) × 9.8 cm.; Caslon Old Face 10/12-pt. Paper: white, wove, unwatermarked; sheets bulk 3.4 cm.

Binding: bluish green, calico-texture cloth not embossed. Front and back: blank. Spine, in white: 'NIGHT | RIDER | PENN | WARREN | EYRE & | SPOTTISWOODE'. All edges trimmed and unstained; white endpapers.
  Dust wrapper: none available.

Copies: Ctw, JAG, RPW, ScU.

Note: published in Jan. 1940 with a second impression, so stamped on p. [4], in Feb. 1940. Printed by Lowe and Brydone Ltd., London. The number of copies printed is not available (ltr., Maria Lyras, Publicity Dept., Eyre Methuen Ltd., 6 June 1975). British Library datestamp 3 April 1940.

A3.e3   first English edition, third impression (1955)

NIGHT RIDER || Robert Penn Warren | London | EYRE & SPOTTISWOODE

Collation: crown folio 8° (trimmed: 18.5 × 12.2 cm.); signed [A⁴] B-P¹⁶, 228 leaves; pp. [i–ii], [1–8] 9–454; numbers as in **A3.d1**.

Contents: p. [i]: hf. tit. 'NIGHT RIDER'; p. [ii]: blank; p. [1]: title page; p. [2]: *'First printed January 1940* | *Reprinted February 1940* | *Reprinted March 1955* | *This book is printed in Great Britain for* | *Eyre & Spottiswoode (Publishers) Ltd.,* | *15 Bedford Street, London, W. C. 2,* | *by Lowe & Brydone (Printers) Ltd., London, N. W. 10*'; p. [3]: dedication; p. [4]:

blank; p. [5]: disclaimer; p. [6]: blank; p. [7]: hf. tit.; p. [8]: blank; pp. 9–454: text; on p. 454 'THE END'.

Typography and Paper: text: 37 ll., 14.7 (15.3) × 9.2 cm.; Caslon Old Face 10/12-pt. Paper: white, wove, unwatermarked; sheets bulk 2.6 cm.

Binding: blue bds. Front and back: blank. Spine, in gold: '[thin and thick rules] | NIGHT | RIDER | · | ROBERT | PENN | WARREN | [thick and thin rules] | EYRE & | SPOTTISWOODE'.

Dust wrapper: front cover, against a red and black background of buildings burning and riders coming toward the lower edge: '[in beige] *Robert Penn Warren* | [in black with white outline] | NIGHT | RIDER'. Spine, in beige: '*Robert* | *Penn* | *Warren* | NIGHT | RIDER | [picture from front continues] | *Eyre and* | *Spottiswoode*'. Back cover: on white in blue, publisher's advertisement. Front and back flaps: on white in blue, about the novel.

Copies: Ctw, PPL, STW.

Note: published in March 1955. Printed by Lowe and Brydone Ltd., London. The number of copies printed is not available (ltr., Maria Lyras, Publicity Dept., Eyre Methuen Ltd., 6 June 1975). Not located in British Library (ltr., Dr. Christine Bernstein, 24 Oct. 1979).

A3.f1   second English edition, first impression, paperback (1959)

A FOUR [publisher's device] SQUARE BOOK | NIGHT RIDER | ROBERT PENN WARREN | [publisher's device] | LANDS-BOROUGH PUBLICATIONS LIMITED | 173 NEW BOND STREET, LONDON, W.1

Collation: crown folio 8° (trimmed: 18.4 × 12.1 cm.); signed, [A¹⁶] B–E¹⁶ [F¹⁶] G–L¹⁶, 176 leaves; pp. [1–4] 5–349 [350–352]; page numbers centered at foot of type page.

Contents: p. [1]: about the book; on p. [2] 'PRINTING HISTORY | First published in Great Britain by | Eyre & Spottiswoode (Publishers) Ltd. in 1940 | Second impression February 1940 | Third impression 1955 | Published as a Four Square Book in 1959'; p. [3]: title page; p. [4]: books by RPW and dedication; pp. 5–349: text; on p. 349 'THE END'; pp. [350–352]: publisher's advertisements.

Typography and Paper: text: 44 ll., 15.7 (16.0) × 9.6 cm.; Times New Roman 10-pt. Paper: white, wove, unwatermarked; sheets bulk 2.0 cm.

Binding: paper. Predominantly blue background with black lettering; illus. on front cover continues around to back. Front: '[vert., upper left] FOUR [green device] SQUARE BOOKS | [center] NIGHT RIDER | *"This is a majestic and lyrical and violent novel"* | ——*IRISH TIMES* | ROBERT PENN WARREN | 3/6 | [picture in color]'. Spine: '[vert.] A FOUR SQUARE [green device] BOOK | [in white against picture] NIGHT RIDER ROBERT PENN WARREN | [horiz., in white] 144'. Back cover: [quotation; picture continues]. All edges trimmed and unstained.

Copies: BL, Ctw.

Note: published by Landsborough Publications, Ltd., 1959; printed by Love and Malcomson, Ltd., London, and Redhill, Surrey. Additional information about publication is not available (ltr., Dorothy Houghton, Managing Editor, Paperbacks, New English Library, 29 May 1975). British Library date-stamp 6 July 1959.

A3.g1   third English edition, first impression, by offset (1973)

NIGHT RIDER | [fancy rule] | *Robert Penn Warren* | Secker & Warburg | LONDON

Collation: demy folio 8° (trimmed: 21.5 × 13.6 cm.); *unsigned* [1–13 ^{16} 14 ^{12} 15 ^{16}], 236 leaves; pp. [i–x], [1] 2–460 [461–462], with numbering identical with **A3.a1**.

Contents: pp. [i–ii]: blank; p. [iii]: hf. tit. 'NIGHT RIDER'; on p. [iv] '*Books by Robert Penn Warren* | [list ends with 'MEET ME IN THE GREEN GLEN']'; p. [v]: title page; p. [vi]: 'First published in England 1940 by | Eyre & Spottiswoode Limited | This edition published in England 1973 by | Martin Secker & Warburg Limited | 14 Carlisle Street, London W1V 6NN | Copyright, 1939, Copyright renewed 1966 by | Robert Penn Warren | SBN 436 56313 4 | Printed in Great Britain by | Redwood Press Limited | Trowbridge, Wiltshire'; p. [vii]: dedication (as printed in **A3.a1**); p. [viii]: blank; p. [ix]: disclaimer; p. [x]: blank; pp. [1]–460: text; on p. 460 text ends sans 'THE END'; pp. [461–462]: blank.

Typography and Paper: printed by offset lithography from **A3.a1**. Paper: white Mallex Litho wove, 85 gsm, vol. 15, unwatermarked. Size at printing 88.8 × 112.8 cm. (2 × 32 page sections); sheets bulk 3.0 cm. (Ltr., N. Gardner, General Manager, Printing Div., Redwood Burn Ltd., 24 Feb. 1975.)

Binding: brown bds. Front and back: blank. Spine, in gilt: 'Night | Rider | [orn.] | *Robert* | *Penn Warren* | Secker & | Warburg'. All edges trimmed and unstained; white endpapers.

Dust wrapper, brown background: front and back covers: '[in white] Robert | Penn Warren | [in orange] Night | Rider | [in white] Re-issue | of his famous novel'. Spine: '[in white] Robert | Penn | Warren | [in orange] Night | Rider | [in white] SECKER & | WARBURG'. Front flap, in brown on white: about the book. Back flap, in brown on white: about the author.

Copies: BL, Ctw, JAG, RPW, STW.

Note: published 9 July 1973 at £2.80. Printed by Redwood Press Ltd., Trowbridge, Wiltshire. The publisher prefers not to disclose the number of copies printed (ltr., T. G. Rosenthal, Managing Director, Martin Secker & Warburg Ltd., 6 Feb. 1975). British Library date-stamp 25 July 1973.

A3.h1   fourth English edition, first impression, paperback (1975)

> *Note*: This New English Library (T-19977) edition bears a British Library date-stamp 19 May 1975 (ltr., Dr. Christine Bernstein, 24 Oct. 1979). I have been unable to obtain a copy for examination.

A4   *Eleven Poems on the Same Theme*

A4.a1   first American edition, first impression (1942)

[in black] ROBERT PENN WARREN | [in red] 11 | [in black] ELEVEN POEMS | ON THE SAME THEME | THE POET OF THE MONTH | NEW DIRECTIONS · NORFOLK · CON-NECTICUT

> *Note*: Each figure of the numeral eleven is 5.85 × 1.5 cm. with an 0.8 cm. extension left at the top. The "OE" of "POEMS" is printed over the red of the first "1".

Colophon, p. [31]: '[in script and within a fancy elliptical frame] FEP | Eleven Poems on the Same Theme | by Robert Penn Warren was printed | at The Fine Editions Press, New York, | under the direction of Gustav Davidson. | The types are Bodoni and Futura bold.'

Collation: royal 4° (trimmed: bds. 22.3 × 15.3 cm.; paper 22.3 × 14.9 cm.); *unsigned* [1 ^16], 16 leaves; pp. [1–32]; unnumbered throughout.

Contents: p. [1]: hf. tit. 'ELEVEN POEMS | ON THE SAME THEME'; p. [2]: blank; p. [3]: title page; p. [4]: 'COPYRIGHT, 1942,

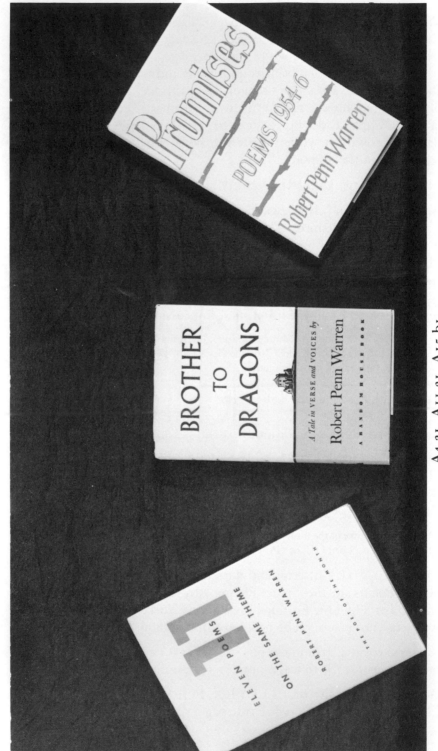

BY NEW DIRECTIONS | Acknowledgment is due to *The Nation*, | *Scribner's*, *The Virginia Quarterly Review*, | *Poetry: A Magazine of Verse*, *The Kenyon* | *Review*, and the Poetry Society of South Caro-|lina for permission to reprint these poems. | *New Directions books are published by James Laughlin*'; p. [5]: 'TO | Cleanth Brooks, Jr. | AND | Albert Russel Erskine, Jr.'; p. [6]: blank; p. [7]: 'MONOLOGUE AT MIDNIGHT'; pp. [8–9]: 'BEARDED OAKS'; pp. [10–11]: 'PICNIC REMEMBERED'; pp. [12–13]: 'CRIME'; pp. [14–15]: 'ORIGINAL SIN: A SHORT STORY'; pp. [16–17]: 'END OF SEASON'; pp. [18–19]: 'REVELATION'; pp. [20–21]: 'PURSUIT'; pp. [22–24]: 'QUESTION AND ANSWER'; pp. [25–27]: 'LOVE'S PARABLE'; pp. [28–30]: 'TERROR'; p. [31]: colophon; p. [32]: 'THE POET OF THE MONTH | 1941'.

Typography and Paper: text: 34 ll., 14.4 (15.35) × 10.4 cm.; Bodoni Monotype 11/12-pt.; titles in Futura Roman bold. Paper: white, wove, unwatermarked; sheets bulk 0.2 cm.

Binding: gray bds.; white paper. Front and back covers: bds. identical with dw; paper, blank. Paper, pamphlet format with stapled leaves. All edges trimmed and unstained; white endpapers (bds. only).

   Dust wrapper: gray paper printed in black and red. Front: '[in red] 11 | [in black] ELEVEN POEMS | ON THE SAME THEME | ROBERT PENN WARREN | THE POET OF THE MONTH'. The figure eleven is printed as on the title page. Back cover: blank. Front flap: brief discussion of *EP*, an evaluation of RPW's poetic talent, and a brief biography. Back flap: list of the poets and their works from which the 1942 series was to have been chosen.

Copies: Ctb, Ctw, CtY (2), JAG (2), KyU, LC (2), LU, RPW, STW (2), TNJ.

Notes: 1. Published 4 April 1942 in bds. at $1.00 and in paper at 35¢. Additional publication information is not available. LC copyright 10 March 1942 (A164482); two copies deposited 25 May 1942; copyright renewed 15 May 1969 (R461636).

   2. JAG copies carry the following advertisement on the back flap: 'A series of poetry pamphlets, issued monthly, | at an annual subscription price of $4. Each | number is printed by a different fine press. | Single copies, 35¢; bound $1.'

A5   *At Heaven's Gate*

A5.a1   first American edition, first impression (1943)

At Heaven's Gate | ROBERT PENN WARREN | NEW YORK | HARCOURT, BRACE AND COMPANY

Collation: demy folio 8° (trimmed: 20.3 × 13.6 cm.); *unsigned* [1–11 ¹⁶ 12 ⁸ 13 ¹⁶], 200 leaves; pp. [i–vi], [1–2] 3–391 [392–394]; numbers centered at foot of type page.

Contents: p. [i]: hf. tit. 'AT HEAVEN'S GATE'; on p. [ii] *'Books by Robert Penn Warren'*; p. [iii]: title page; p. [iv]: 'COPYRIGHT, 1943, BY | HARCOURT, BRACE AND COMPANY, INC. | *All rights reserved, including | the right to reproduce this book | or portions thereof in any form.* | *first edition* | PRINTED IN THE UNITED STATES OF AMERICA'; p. [v]: 'TO | FRANK LAWRENCE OWSLEY | AND | HARRIET OWSLEY'; p. [vi]: blank; p. [1]: hf. tit.; p. [2]: blank; on p. 3 *'One'*; on p. 35 *'Two | Statement of Ashby Wyndham. Sheriff's Office, | The Jail, Mulcaster County'*: headings of chapters 4, 6, 8, 10, 12, 14, 16, 18, 20, and 23 also contain the words *'Statement of Ashby Wyndham'*; on p. 391 'THE END'; pp. [392–394]: blank.

Typography and Paper: text: 42 ll., 16.7 (17.15) × 10.45 cm.; Linotype Baskerville 11-pt. Paper: white, wove, unwatermarked; sheets bulk 2.7 cm.

Binding: issued in both light blue and green cloth. Front and back: blank. Spine, in yellow: 'AT | HEAVEN'S | GATE | ROBERT | PENN | WARREN | Harcourt, Brace | and Company'. All edges trimmed and unstained; white endpapers.

   Dust wrapper: front cover, blue with white ltr. and yellow illus.: 'ROBERT PENN WARREN | [rendering of golden gate] | *at* | HEAVEN'S | *gate* | [up right edge] LIEBERMAN'. Spine, blue with white ltrs. and yellow drawing: *'at* | HEAVEN'S | *gate* | [rendering of golden gate] | ROBERT | PENN | WARREN | Harcourt, Brace | and Company'. Back cover, white with blue ltr. framed in blue double border: a buy-war-bonds advertisement. Front flap, white with blue ltr.: about the book. Back flap, white with blue ltr.: about the author.

Copies: Ctb, Ctw, CtY (2), JAG, KyU, LC, LU, STW (2).

Notes: 1. Published 19 Aug. 1943; first impression (23 April 1943) of 5,000 copies bound in separate lots of 3,500 and 1,500 (17 Aug. 1943) copies at $2.50. Printed by Quinn & Boden Company, Inc., Rahway, NJ. Distributed in Canada by George J. McLeod, Ltd. Out of print March 1950. (Ltr., Gerard G. Vaughan, Trade Dept., Harcourt Brace Jovanovich, Inc., 4 June 1975.) LC copyright 19 Aug. 1943

(A174971); two copies deposited 25 Aug. 1943; copyright renewed 2 Sept. 1970 (R490422).

    2. Excerpt: "Statement of Ashby Wyndham," *SR*, 51 (Spring 1943), 183–236.

A5.a2   first American edition, second impression (1943)

Contents: p. [iv]: '[b·9·43] | This book is complete and unabridged. | It is manufactured under wartime | conditions in conformity with all gov-|ernment regulations controlling the | use of paper and other materials.'

Binding: green cloth.

Copies: LU, TxFTC.

Note: printed 29 Sept. 1943 in 1,500 copies.

A5.a3   first American edition, third impression (1959)

AT HEAVEN'S | GATE | Robert Penn Warren | [publisher's device] | RANDOM HOUSE · NEW YORK

Collation: demy folio 8° (trimmed: 20.3 × 13.6 cm.); *unsigned* [1–10^{16} 11^8 12–13^{16}], 200 leaves; pagination and numbering identical with **A5.a1**.

Contents: p. [i]: hf. tit. 'AT HEAVEN'S GATE'; on p. [ii] 'Books by Robert Penn Warren'; p. [iii]: title page; p. [iv]: 'Copyright, 1943, by Robert Penn Warren | All rights reserved | Library of Congress Catalog Card Number: 59-5736 | Manufactured in the United States of America'; p. [v]: dedication; p. [vi]: blank; p. [1]: hf. tit.; p. [2]: blank; pp. 3–391: text; p. [392]: blank; p. [393]: 'ABOUT THE AUTHOR | [publisher's device] || '; p. [394]: blank.

Typography and Paper: text: 43 ll., 16.8 (17.2) × 10.5 cm.; Linotype Baskerville 11-pt. Paper: white, wove, unwatermarked; sheets bulk 2.8 cm.

Binding: medium brown cloth. Front and back: blank. Spine, in gilt: '[top, on black, publisher's device] | [double gilt border around black rectangle] AT | HEAVEN'S | GATE | [star] | Robert | Penn Warren | [bottom] RANDOM HOUSE'. All edges trimmed and unstained; white endpapers.

    Dust wrapper: front cover, top and bottom edges have a light yellow stripe and a black stripe, both of which continue around the spine and across the back cover. Then, '[on brown in white] *At* | *Heaven's* | *Gate* | [black-yellow-black stripes] | [on brown in white] *A Novel by* | ROBERT PENN | WARREN'. Spine: '[on brown in white] ROBERT | PENN | WARREN | *At* | *Heaven's* | *Gate* | [black-yellow-black stripes] | [in brown on white, publisher's device] | *Random House*'. Back cover, on white in black: publisher's advertisement. Front flap: about the book. Back flap: about the author.

Copies: CoCC, CoCA, CtY, JAG, KyU, LC, LU, STW.

Note: published 28 Jan. 1959 in one printing of 6,000 copies. Plates and stock were purchased from Harcourt Brace. A "second printing" (fourth impression) of 1,000 copies was run 8 Nov. 1968 at $5.95. Both were printed by American Book-Stratford Press, Inc., and both were distributed in Canada by Random House of Canada Limited. (Ltr., Jim Wilcox, Random House, Inc., 31 July 1974.)

A5.b1 second American edition, first impression, paperback (abridged) (1949)

At Heaven's Gate | *by* | *Robert Penn Warren* | Abridgment and Introduction | by George Mayberry | [publisher's device] | A SIGNET BOOK | Published by THE NEW AMERICAN LIBRARY

Collation: post folio 8° (trimmed: 18.1 × 10.7 cm.); *unsigned* 96 ind. leaves; pp. [1–6] 7–191 [192]; numbers centered in tail margin.

Contents: p. [1]: hf. tit. '*AT HEAVEN'S GATE*'; p. [2]: dedication; p. [3]: title page; p. [4]: '[copyright] | First Printing, June, 1949'; pp. [5–6]: introduction; pp. 7–191: text; p. [192]: publisher's advertisement.

Binding: paper. Front cover: '[on purple in black, upper left corner] 725 | [publisher's device] | [across top in white] A frank, rich novel of the new south | [in yellow on illus.] *AT* HEAVEN'S GATE | [on lower right edge of illus., in white] ROBERT | PENN | WARREN | [on purple in white] ABRIDGMENT AND INTRODUCTION BY GEORGE MAYBERRY | [on yellow in black] SIGNET BOOKS | A Special Edition'. Spine: [horiz., on purple in black] 725 | [vert., on yellow in black] AT HEAVEN'S GATE ROBERT PENN WARREN | [purple stripe] | [yellow stripe at bottom]'. Back cover: purple, white, purple, yellow stripes with excerpts from reviews and a biographical sketch on white in black.

Copies: Ctw (2), LC, RPW.

Notes: 1. Published June 1949. Additional publication information is not available. Introduction copyright 1 June 1949 (A37685).

2. Changes: omits part of chapter 4; chapter 3 corresponds with chapter 7. Omits the Ashby Wyndham statements. Gives main plot in fourteen rather than in twenty-seven chapters.

A5.c1   third American edition, first impression, paperback (1962)

AT HEAVEN'S GATE | Robert Penn Warren | A SIGNET BOOK PUBLISHED BY | THE NEW AMERICAN LIBRARY | [publisher's device]

Collation: post folio 8° (trimmed: 18.0 × 10.6 cm.); *unsigned* 192 ind. leaves; pp. [1–4] 5–384; page numbers located in the corner formed by the head and outer margins except for p. 5 where the number is centered at foot of type page.

Contents: p. [1]: about the book and author; p. [2]: publisher's advertisement; p. [3]: title page; p. [4]: dedication and copyright on same page; pp. 5–384: text.

Typography and Paper: text: 46 ll., 15.1 (15.6) × 8.7 cm.; Times New Roman 9/10-pt. Paper: white, wove, unwatermarked; sheets bulk 2.0 cm.

Binding: paper. Front cover: '[on dark brown in yellow] T2298 | SIGNET | [on white oval in black] 75¢ | [on brown in yellow, numerals with curved line underneath on line with 75¢] A famous novel by Pulitzer Prize Winner | [on brown in white] ROBERT PENN WARREN | "There are alternating violence and tenderness, coarse-| ness and poetic beauty, in this rich story." | ——ATLANTIC MONTHLY | [on brown in yellow] AT HEAVEN'S | GATE | A SIGNET BOOK | COMPLETE AND | UNABRIDGED | [lower left half, shaded—man's face; lower right half—man looking at woman sitting on a bed]'. Spine: '[horiz., on black in white] SIGNET [circled] | [on white in black] T | 2298 | [vert., on white in green] AT HEAVEN'S GATE [on white in black] ROBERT PENN WARREN'. Back cover: '[photograph of RPW] | [on white in green] AT HEAVEN'S GATE | [on white in black, about the novel] | [on green in yellow, white, and black, publisher's advertisement]'. All edges trimmed and stained red.

Copies: ICarbS, JAG.

Note: published 1962 at 75¢ with a sixth printing (apparently the publisher's enumeration of printings includes the abridged edition as well, that is, **A5.b1**) in May 1963 (p. [4]). Other publication information is not available from the publisher.

A5.d1   first English edition, first impression (1946)

Robert Penn Warren | [double rule] | AT HEAVEN'S | GATE | EYRE & SPOTTISWOODE | LONDON

Collation: demy folio 8° (trimmed: 21.5 × 13.8 cm.); signed, [1⁸(−1₁)] 2–18⁸, 143 leaves; pp. [i–ii], [1–4] 5–282 [283–284]; page numbers located in the corner formed by the head and outer margins except on p. 5 where the number is centered at foot of type page.

Contents: pp. [i–ii]: blank; p. [1]: hf. tit. '*AT HEAVEN'S GATE*'; on p. [2] '*Also by Robert Penn Warren*'; p. [3]: title page; p. [4]: '[dedication] | *First Published* 1946 | *Printed in Great Britain for* | *Eyre & Spottiswoode (Publishers) Limited* | 14–16 *Bedford Street, London, W.C.* 2'; pp. 5–282: text; on p. 282 'THE END'; pp. [283–284]: blank.

Typography and Paper: text: 53 ll., 16.7 (17.2) × 10.5 cm.; Century expanded 9-pt. Paper: white, wove, unwatermarked; sheets bulk 1.0 cm.

Binding: gray cloth. Front and back: blank. Spine, in gilt: 'At | Heaven's | Gate | [star] | Robert | Penn | Warren | Eyre & | Spottiswoode'. All edges trimmed and unstained; white endpapers.
   Dust wrapper: front cover: '[on black rectangle in white] author of "Night Rider" [on gray and green background in yellow] ROBERT PENN WARREN | [on white in green (torn sheet tied to iron-picket fence)] at | Heaven's | Gate'. Spine: '[on gray in white, outlined] At | Heaven's | Gate | [in yellow, outlined] Penn | Warren | [in white, outlined] E. & S.' Back cover, on white in black: publisher's advertisement (first ad is for "All the King's Horses"). Front flap: about the book. Back flap: blank.

Copies: BL, Ctw, JAG.

Note: published in 1946, but additional publication information is not available. British Library date-stamp 23 Sept. 1946.

A5.e1   second English edition, first impression, by offset (1959)

AT HEAVEN'S | GATE | Robert Penn Warren | LONDON, 1959 | EYRE & SPOTTISWOODE

Collation: demy folio 8° (trimmed: 20.6 × 13.4 cm.); signed, [A]–L¹⁶ M⁸ N¹⁶, 200 leaves; pp. [i–vi], [1–2] 3–391 [392–394]; numbers centered at foot of type page.

Contents: p. [i]: hf. tit. 'AT HEAVEN'S GATE'; on p. [ii] 'Books by Robert Penn Warren'; p. [iii]: title page; p. [iv]: *'Reprinted by Cedric Chivers Ltd., Bath at the request of | the London & Home Counties Branch of the Library | Association. | Printed offset by Billing & Sons Ltd., Guildford and London | 1965'*; p. [v]: dedication; p. [vi]: blank; p. [1]: hf. tit.; p. [2]: blank; pp. 3–391: text; p. [392]: blank; on p. [393] 'ABOUT THE AUTHOR | [Random House publisher's device] || [five paragraphs]'; p. [394]: blank.

Typography and Paper: identical with **A5.a3**. Paper: white, wove, unwatermarked; sheets bulk 2.75 cm.

> *Note*: similarities to **A5.a3**: on p. 391 sans 'THE END' and on p. [393] the same biographical sketch.

Binding: medium green, calico-texture cloth, not embossed. Front and back: unmarked. Spine, in gilt: '[double rule] | [on dark blue] AT | HEAVEN'S | GATE | [1-em rule] | ROBERT PENN | WARREN | [double rule]'. All edges trimmed and stained speckled green; white endpapers.

> *Dust wrapper*: front cover, on pink in black: '[both letters boxed] L [down half line] A | AT HEAVEN'S | GATE | ROBERT PENN WARREN'. Spine: 'AT HEAVEN'S | GATE | ROBERT PENN | WARREN | PORTWAY'. Back cover: 'Reprinted by Cedric Chivers Ltd. of Bath at the request of | the London & Home Counties Branch of the Library Association'. Both flaps: blank.

Copies: KyU.

Note: not found in British Library (ltr., Dr. Christine Bernstein, 24 Oct. 1979), and publication information is not available.

A6 *Selected Poems, 1923–1943*

A6.a1 first American edition, first impression (1944)

[shaded] SELECTED POEMS | 1923–1943 | ROBERT | PENN | WARREN | HARCOURT, BRACE AND COMPANY, NEW YORK

Collation: demy folio 8° (trimmed: 20.05 × 13.5 cm.); *unsigned* [1–7⁸],

56 leaves; pp. [i–vi] vii–viii [ix–x], [1–2] 3–71 [72–74] 75–102; numbers centered at foot of type page.

Contents: p. [i]: hf. tit. 'SELECTED POEMS'; on p. [ii] '*by the same author*'; p. [iii]: title page; p. [iv]: 'COPYRIGHT, 1944, BY | HARCOURT, BRACE AND COMPANY, INC. | COPYRIGHT, 1935, BY | THE ALCESTIS PRESS | COPYRIGHT, 1942, BY | NEW DIRECTIONS | *All rights reserved, including* | *the right to reproduce this book* | *or portions thereof in any form.* | *first edition* | [on banner streaming from the mouth of a diving eagle that is clutching a book in its claws] BOOKS ARE WEAPONS IN THE WAR OF IDEAS | A WARTIME BOOK | *This complete edition is produced in full* | *compliance with the government's regu-|lations for conserving paper and other* | *essential materials.* | PRINTED IN THE UNITED STATES OF AMERICA'; p. [v]: '*To* | *E. C. B. W.*'; p. [vi]: 'These poems have appeared in *The Nation, The New Re-|public, The Saturday Review of Literature, The Fugitive,* | *The Partisan Review, Poetry: A Magazine of Verse*, the | Poetry Supplement of *The American Review* (1934), *The* | *Virginia Quarterly Review, The Kenyon Review, The South-|ern Review, The Southwest Review, Scribner's,* and *The* | *American Caravan*'; pp. vii–viii: 'CONTENTS'; p. [ix]: 'NOTE | [¶] The *Late* poems in this collection have been drawn from among pieces | composed during the last eight or nine years. Most of them, however, are | relatively recent. The *Early* poems belong to the previous decade, some | of them going back into student days. | [right side] R. P. W. | [left side] *Minneapolis,* | *July 26,* 1943.'; p. [x]: blank; p. [1]: 'LATE'; p. [2]: blank; pp. 3–17: 'THE BALLAD OF BILLIE POTTS'; pp. 18–20: 'TERROR'; pp. 21–22: 'PURSUIT'; pp. 23–24: 'ORIGINAL SIN: A SHORT STORY'; pp. 25–26: 'CRIME'; pp. 27–29: 'LETTER FROM A COWARD TO A HERO'; pp. 30–33: 'HISTORY'; pp. 34–36: 'QUESTION AND ANSWER'; pp. 37–38: 'END OF SEASON'; p. 39: 'RANSOM'; p. 40: 'AGED MAN SURVEYS THE PAST TIME'; p. 41: 'TOWARD RATIONALITY'; p. 42: 'TO A FRIEND PARTING'; p. 43: 'LETTER TO A FRIEND'; p. 44: 'AUBADE FOR HOPE'; p. 45: 'EIDOLON'; pp. 46–47: 'REVELATION'; pp. 48–50: 'VARIATION: ODE TO FEAR'; pp. 51–52: 'MEXICO IS A FOREIGN COUNTRY: | FIVE STUDIES IN NATURALISM | I. BUTTERFLIES OVER THE MAP | II. SIESTA TIME IN VILLAGE PLAZA BY RUINED BANDSTAND AND BANANA TREE'; p. 53: 'III. THE WORLD COMES GALLOPING: A TRUE STORY'; pp. 54–55: 'IV. SMALL SOLDIERS WITH DRUM IN LARGE LANDSCAPE'; pp. 56–57: 'V. THE MAN-

GO ON THE MANGO TREE'; p. 58: 'MONOLOGUE AT MID-NIGHT'; pp. 59–60: 'BEARDED OAKS'; pp. 61–62: 'PICNIC RE-MEMBERED'; pp. 63–64: 'RESOLUTION'; pp. 65–67: 'LOVE'S PARABLE'; p. 68: 'LATE SUBTERFUGE'; p. 69: 'MAN COMING OF AGE'; pp. 70–71: 'THE GARDEN'; p. [72]: blank; p. [73]: 'EARLY'; p. [74]: blank; pp. 75–78: 'THE RETURN: AN ELEGY'; pp. 79–80: 'KENTUCKY MOUNTAIN FARM | I. REBUKE OF THE ROCKS | II. AT THE HOUR OF THE BREAKING OF THE ROCKS'; pp. 80–81: 'III. HISTORY AMONG THE ROCKS'; p. 81: 'IV. THE CARDINAL'; pp. 81–82: 'V. THE JAY'; p. 82: 'VI. WATERSHED'; p. 83: 'VII. THE RETURN'; pp. 84–86: 'PONDY WOODS'; pp. 87–88: 'LETTER OF A MOTHER'; p. 89: 'CROESUS IN AUTUMN'; p. 90: 'SO FROST ASTOUNDS'; pp. 91–92: 'THE LAST METAPHOR'; pp. 93–94: 'PACIFIC GAZER'; pp. 95–96: 'CALENDAR'; p. 97: 'PROBLEM OF KNOWLEDGE'; p. 98: 'FOR A SELF-POSSESSED FRIEND'; p. 99: 'FOR A FRIEND WHO THINKS HIMSELF URBANE'; p. 100: 'COLD COLLOQUY'; p. 101: 'GARDEN WATERS'; p. 102: 'TO A FACE IN THE CROWD'.

Typography and Paper: text: 41 ll., 16.8 (17.3) × 10.9 cm.; Bodoni Linotype 10/12-pt. Paper: white, wove, unwatermarked; sheets bulk 0.7 cm.

Binding: grayish green cloth. Front, in dark green: 'SELECTED | POEMS | 1923 1943'. Spine, in dark green: '[vert.] *Robert Penn Warren* SELECTED POEMS *Harcourt Brace | and Company*'. Back: blank. All edges trimmed and unstained; white endpapers.

    Dust wrapper: front cover, on olive green in white: 'SELECTED | POEMS | 1923 1943 | ROBERT | PENN | WARREN'. Spine, on olive green in white: '[vert.] *Robert Penn Warren* SELECTED POEMS *Harcourt Brace | and Company*'. Back cover, on white in olive green: excerpts from reviews. Front flap: about the book. Back flap: blank.

Copies: Ctb, Ctw, CtY, KyU, LC (2), STW (3), TNJ.

Notes: 1. Published 6 April 1944 in 1,500 copies at $2.50. Out of print July 1946. Printed by Quinn & Boden Company, Inc., 14 Feb. 1944. Distributed in Canada by George J. McLeod, Ltd. (Ltr., Gerard G. Vaughan, Trade Dept., Harcourt Brace Jovanovich, Inc., 4 June 1975.) LC copyright 6 April 1944 (A179892); two copies deposited 29 March 1944; copyright renewed 14 May 1971 (R507092).

    2. Variants: in *EP* (**A4.a1**) the poems "Terror" and "Original Sin"

have unequal first and second stanzas; "Question and Answer" has two additional lines in the first stanza, "And the choices / Lost," as ll. 6–7. In *TSP* (**A2.a1**) the poem "Resolution" has an initial twelve-line stanza which is omitted in *SP*.

A6.a2 first American edition, second impression (1947)

Contents: p. [ii]: includes *AKM* in list of works by RPW; p. [iv]: '[b·4·47]' and omits the wartime clause; p. 8: the fourth word in the first line of the last stanza reads "hi" instead of "his".

Binding: black bds. Front and back: blank. Spine, vert. in gilt: '*Robert Penn Warren* SELECTED POEMS *Harcourt, Brace | and Company*'. All edges trimmed and unstained; white endpapers.
  Dust wrapper: none found.

Copies: CoCA, CtY, JAG, LU (2), TxFTC.

Note: reprinted 17 July 1947 in 1,000 copies. Out of print July 1953. Reproduced by Polygraphic Company of America, and bound by Quinn & Boden 11 April 1947.

A6.b1 first English edition, first impression (1952)

SELECTED | POEMS | 1923–1943 | *by* | ROBERT PENN WAR-REN | THE FORTUNE PRESS | 21 Belgrave Road | London, S.W. 1

Collation: crown folio 8° (rough trimmed: 18.7 × 12.6 cm.); *unsigned* [1⁴ 2–7⁸], 52 leaves; pp. [i–iv] v–vi [vii–viii], [1–2] 3–68 [69–70] 71–96; numbers centered at foot of type page.

Contents: p. [i]: title page; on p. [ii] '*by the same author* | [list] | PRINTED IN ENGLAND BY GIBBS AND SONS, ORANGE STREET, CANTERBURY'; p. [iii]: dedication; p. [iv]: previous appearance of poems; pp. v–vi: 'CONTENTS'; p. [vii]: author's note; p. [viii]: blank; p. [1]: 'LATE'; p. [2]: blank; pp. 3–96: text.

Typography and Paper: text: 41 ll., 14.0 (14.5) × 9.3 cm.; 10/12-pt. (I have been unable to identify the type.) Paper: white, laid, vertical chainlines (2.5 cm.), watermarked: '[crown] Gla[tt]onbury'; sheets bulk 0.5 cm.

Binding: black bds. Front and back: blank. Spine, in gilt: '[up] SE-LECTED POEMS——Robert Penn Warren'.
  Dust wrapper: front cover, on rose in white: 'SELECTED | POEMS

| 1923–1943 | ROBERT | PENN | WARREN | THE FORTUNE PRESS'. Spine, on white in rose: '[up] SELECTED POEMS —— Robert Penn Warren'. Back cover, on white in rose: publisher's advertisement. Front flap, on white in rose: about the book. Back flap: blank.

Copies: BL, Ctw, STW.

Note: "No records of any description and no correspondence dating back any earlier than about 1955" exist in the Fortune Press files (ltr., Charles Skilton, London, 6 Feb. 1975). British Library date-stamp 3 May 1952.

A7 *All the King's Men*

A7.a1   first American edition, first impression (1946)

All the King's Men | *By* | ROBERT PENN WARREN | *Mentre che la speranza ha fior del verde.* | La Divina Commedia, Purgatorio, III | *New York* | HARCOURT, BRACE AND COMPANY

Collation: large post 8° (trimmed: 20.3 × 13.7 cm.); *unsigned* [1⁸ 2–15¹⁶ 16⁸], 240 leaves; pp. [i–viii], [1–2] 3–464 [465–472]; numbers centered at foot of type page.

Contents: pp. [i–ii]: blank; p. [iii]: hf. tit. '*ALL THE KING'S MEN*'; on p. [iv] '*Books by Robert Penn Warren*'; p. [v]: title page; p. [vi]: 'COPYRIGHT, 1946, BY | HARCOURT, BRACE AND COMPANY, INC. | *All rights reserved, including the right to reproduce this book* | *or portions thereof in any form* | *first edition* | PRINTED IN THE UNITED STATES OF AMERICA'; p. [vii]: '*TO* | JUSTINE AND DAVID MITCHELL CLAY'; p. [viii]: blank; p. [1]: hf. tit.; p. [2]: blank; on p. 3 '*Chapter One*' with other chapters designated similarly and respectively on pp. 55, 117, 167, 203, 243, 286, 331, 377, and 426; on p. 464 '*THE END*'; pp. [465–472]: blank.

Typography and Paper: text: 43 ll., 16.65 (17.1) × 10.5 cm.; Baskerville Monotype 11-pt. Paper: white, wove, unwatermarked; sheets bulk 2.5 cm.

Binding: dark red (maroon) cloth. Front and back: blank. Spine, in gilt: '[fancy A, T, K, and M] ALL | THE | KING'S | MEN | Robert | Penn | Warren | Harcourt, Brace | and Company'. All edges trimmed and unstained; white endpapers.

   Dust wrapper: front cover, against background of blue-black—red-

All the King's Men

By

ROBERT PENN WARREN

Mentre che la speranza ha fior del verde.
LA DIVINA COMMEDIA, PURGATORIO, III

New York
HARCOURT, BRACE AND COMPANY

A7.a1 title page

dish black-gray (scarf with chess symbols): '[in red] Robert Penn Warren | [in bluish gray] ALL | THE | KING'S | MEN'. Spine: '[in red] ALL | THE | KING'S | MEN | [in white] Robert | Penn | Warren | [in white] HARCOURT BRACE | AND COMPANY'. Back cover, on white in black: 'What SINCLAIR LEWIS Says | About *All the King's Men*'. Front and back flaps: about the novel.

Copies: Ctb, Ctw, CtY (2), JAG, KyU, L (2), LC, LU (2), STW (2), TNJ.

Notes: 1. Published 17 Aug. 1946 in two runs of 7,500 copies each at $3.00. Printed by Quinn & Boden Company, Inc. Subsequent impressions: 25 Aug. 1946, 6,000; 10 Sept. 1946, 12,500; 15 Oct. 1946, 8,727; 29 Jan. 1947, 5,044 (Greystone Press); 22 April 1947, 484 (Greystone Press); 9 May 1947, 3,500; 17 June 1947, 2,500; 27 Oct. 1947, 500 (Greystone Press); 11 Nov. 1947, 500 (Greystone Press); 3 Feb. 1950, 504; 24 April 1951, 497; 7 Aug. 1952, 1,000; 19 Sept. 1956, 1,000; 22 Aug. 1958, 1,000; 12 Feb. 1960, 2,000; 18 Oct. 1962, 2,000; 1 June 1964, 2,000; Dec. 1965, 3,000; Sept. 1967, 4,000; Feb. 1970, 2,000; Sept. 1972, 1,000; Dec. 1974, 1,500. Distributed in Canada by George J. McLeod Ltd. (Ltr., Gerard G. Vaughan, Trade Dept., Harcourt Brace Jovanovich, Inc., 4 June 1975.) LC copyright 19 Aug. 1946 (A5679); two copies deposited 10 Aug. 1946; copyright renewed 22 Aug. 1973 (R557575).

2. Additional copies were bound in inexpensive boards by American Book-Stratford Press, Inc. They bear similar impression designations, '[f·11·46]', but publication data on those copies are unavailable.

3. Excerpts: "Cass Mastern's Wedding Ring," *PR*, 11 (Fall 1944), 375–407 [from chapter 4]; *Omnibook Magazine*, Dec. 1946, pp. 1–50; *The Australian Woman's Weekly Omnibook Magazine*, May 1948, pp. 1–51; and "Mason City," in *Reading for Writing*, ed. Arthur Mizener [from chapter 1].

A7.a4   first American edition, fourth impression (1946)

Contents: p. [vi]: '[d·8·46]'·

Binding: medium red calico-texture cloth, not embossed. Front and back: blank. Spine, in gilt: identical with **A7.a1**.

A7.a6   first American edition, sixth impression (1947)

Contents: p. [vi]: '[f·11·46] | PRINTED IN THE UNITED STATES

OF AMERICA | AMERICAN BOOK-STRATFORD PRESS, INC., NEW YORK'.

Binding: medium blue bds. Front and back: blank. Spine, in light blue: identical with **A7.a1**.

A7.b1   first American edition, reissue (1948)

All the King's Men | *By* | ROBERT PENN WARREN | [publisher's device] || GROSSET & DUNLAP | *Publishers* | NEW YORK

Collation: large post 8° (trimmed: 20.2 × 13.6 cm.); *unsigned* [1–15 ¹⁶], 240 leaves; pp. [i–viii], [1–2] 3–464 [465–472]; numbers centered at foot of type page.

Contents: identical with **A7.a1** except for title page.

Paper: white, wove, unwatermarked; sheets bulk 3.0 cm.

Binding: light reddish bds. Front and back: blank. Spine, in black: '[fancy A, T, K, and M] ALL | THE | KING'S | MEN | Robert | Penn | Warren | GROSSET | & DUNLAP'. All edges trimmed with top edge stained red; white endpapers.

   Dust wrapper: front cover, background identical with **A7.a1**; '[on red rectangle, in white] FIRST TRIPLE-AWARD WINNER | [in black] ·PULITZER PRIZE | ·N.Y. FILM CRITICS' AWARD | ·MOTION PICTURE ACADEMY "OSCAR" | [in bluish gray] ALL | THE | KING'S | MEN | [on red rectangle, in black] "*Magnificently vital reading, a book so charged with | dramatic tension it almost crackles with blue sparks . . .*" | Orville Prescott, NEW YORK TIMES | [in white] ROBERT PENN WARREN'. Spine: '[in red] ALL | THE | KING'S | MEN | [in white] Robert | Penn | Warren | [on red rectangle, bordered in white; ltrs. in white] GROSSET | & DUNLAP'. Back cover: publisher's advertisement. Front flap: about the book. Back flap: advertisement for *Sanctuary*.

Copies: JAG, KyU, STW.

Note: published 1948 at $1.49. Letter from Robert Giroux of Harcourt, Brace and Company to RPW, 30 Dec. 1949, states that the Grosset $1.49 edition had sold 19,200 copies to date (Ctw). Total sales: 39,264 copies. The agreement for this edition ended Feb. 1951 (ltr., Gerard G. Vaughan, Trade/Sales Dept., Harcourt Brace Jovanovich, Inc., 26 Jan. 1976).

A7.c1 first American edition, Modern Library reissue (1953)

ALL | THE KING'S | MEN | *by* ROBERT PENN WARREN | WITH A NEW INTRODUCTION BY THE AUTHOR | *Mentre che la speranza ha fior del verde.* | LA DIVINA COMMEDIA, PUR-GATORIO, III | [publisher's device] || THE MODERN LIBRARY · NEW YORK ||

Collation: post folio 8° (trimmed: 17.7 × 11.8 cm.); *unsigned* [1–15 ¹⁶], 240 leaves; pp. [" 1–4], i–vi, [1–2] 3–464 [465–470]; page numbers centered at foot of type page.

Contents: p. [" 1]: 'THE MODERN LIBRARY | OF THE WORLD'S BEST BOOKS | [rule, thicker in the middle] | ALL THE KING'S MEN | [rule, thicker in the middle] | *The publishers will be pleased to send, upon request, an* | *illustrated folder setting forth the purpose and scope of* | THE MODERN LIBRARY, *and listing each volume* | *in the series. Every reader of books will find titles he* | *has been looking for, handsomely printed, in definitive* | *editions, and at an unusually low price.*'; p. [" 2]: blank; p. [" 3]: title page; p. [" 4]: '[copyright] | *First Modern Library Edition, 1953*'; pp. i–vi: '*Introduction*'; p. [1]: hf. tit. '*ALL THE KING'S MEN*'; p. [2]: blank; pp. 3–464: text; pp. [465–470]: publisher's advertisement.

Typography and Paper: identical with **A7.a1** and reduced to 9/11-pt. Paper: white, wove, unwatermarked; sheets bulk 1.3 cm.

Binding: medium blue calico-texture cloth, not embossed. Front: gilt rectangle; smaller gilt rectangle bordering red field, which bears the following in gilt: 'ALL | THE | KING'S | MEN | · | WARREN'; between rectangles, in lower right corner, in gilt, publisher's device. Spine, in gilt: '[publisher's device] | [gilt border around red field] ALL | THE | KING'S | MEN | · | ROBERT | PENN | WARREN | · | MODERN | LIBRARY'. Back: blank. All edges trimmed with top edge stained red; gray-and-white design on endpapers—an "l," "m," and open-book device, with publisher's device centered on each; verso of front free endpaper and recto of back free endpaper, white.

Dust wrapper: front cover: top and bottom, photograph of crowd of people; on black across middle: '[in blue] ROBERT PENN WARREN | [in white] PULITZER PRIZE NOVEL | [in red] All the King's Men | [in white] INTRODUCTION BY THE AUTHOR | [in blue] A MODERN LIBRARY BOOK | [red rule]'. Spine, continuation from front, on black: '[in white] ROBERT | PENN | WARREN | [in red] All the | King's | Men | [inside red rectangle on black, in blue] 170 | [in white] MODERN | LIBRARY'. Back cover, on white in black and in red: publisher's advertisement. Front flap: about the novel. Back flap: publisher's advertisement. Inner side of cover, horiz.: list of Modern Library editions.

Copies: Ctb, Ctw, CtY, JAG, LC, STW, TNJ.

Notes: 1. Published 1 Sept. 1953 in 7,500 copies at $1.25. Printed by Murry Printing Co. Subsequent impressions: 18 March 1954, 5,000; 28 Dec. 1954, 5,000; 25 May 1955, 5,000; 9 March 1956, 5,000; 18 Oct. 1956, 5,000; 27 Aug. 1957, 5,000; 11 April 1958, 5,000; 6 Feb. 1959, 5,000; 17 April 1959, 7,000; 26 Jan. 1960, 10,000; 7 April 1961, 10,000; 11 Aug. 1964, 8,175; 6 Aug. 1965, 8,125; 14 April 1966, 8,025; 14 Sept. 1967, 8,175 at $1.95; 23 Jan. 1970, 3,000; 20 April 1971, 3,000—for a total of 41,900 copies. Distributed in Canada by Random House of Canada Limited. Licensed from Harcourt Brace (ltr., Jim Wilcox, Random House, Inc., 31 July 1974). Introduction copyright 18 Aug. 1953 (A105925).

2. The 1967 printing (JAG):

Collation: pp. [$^\pi$1–2], [i–iv] v–ix [x], [1–2], 3–464 [465–468]; otherwise identical with **A7.c1**.

Contents: p. [$^\pi$1]: hf. tit. 'ALL THE KING'S MEN'; p. [$^\pi$2]: blank; p. [i]: title page; p. [ii]: copyright; p. [iii]: dedication; p. [iv]: blank; pp. v–[x]: *Introduction*; p. [1]: hf. tit. *'ALL THE KING'S MEN'*; p. [2]: blank; pp. 3–464: text; pp. [465–466]: publisher's advertisement; pp. [467–468]: blank.

Binding: blue cloth. Front, blind stamped: '[publisher's device inside hexagon] | MODERN LIBRARY'. Spine, in gilt: '[horiz., publisher's device] || [vert.] ALL THE KING'S MEN | *Robert Penn Warren* || [horiz.] MODERN | LIBRARY'. Back: blank. All edges trimmed and unstained; gray-and-white endpapers with checkerboard design: 'l [upper half] m [lower half, open book]'; verso of front free endpaper and recto of back free endpaper, white. Publisher's device in center of each page on gray background in white.

Dust wrapper: identical with **A7.c1**.

3. The introduction appeared in *SR*, 61 (Summer 1953), 476–480.

A7.d1   second American edition, Armed Services edition, paperback (1946)

1201 AN ARMED SERVICES EDITION PUBLISHED BY AR-RANGEMENT WITH | HARCOURT, BRACE AND COM-PANY, INC., NEW YORK || ALL THE | KING'S MEN | BY | ROBERT PENN WARREN | *Mentre che la speranza ha fior del verde.* | LA DIVINA COMMEDIA, PURGATORIO, III | [device] | *Edition for the Armed Services, Inc.* | A NON-PROFIT ORGANIZATION ESTAB-LISHED BY | THE COUNCIL ON BOOKS IN WARTIME, NEW YORK

Collation: foolscap folio 8° (trimmed: 16.0 × 10.4 cm.); *unsigned* 256 leaves; pp. [1–2] 3–512; numbers in corner formed by head and outer margins.

Contents: p. [1]: title page; p. [2]: dedication and copyright; pp. 3–512: text.

Typography and Paper: text: 43 ll., 13.7 (14.1) × 8.2 cm.; Baskerville Monotype 9-pt. Paper: white, wove, unwatermarked; sheets bulk 1.6 cm.

Binding: paper. Front cover, top ¾ with white background, bottom ¼ with blue background; picture of hardcover edition predominates white portion: '[on red circle, half on white and half on blue, in white] ARMED | SERVICES | EDITION | [on blue in white, statement about edition] | THIS IS THE COMPLETE BOOK—NOT A DI-GEST'. Spine, vert.: '[on white in black] WARREN——ALL THE KING'S MEN [on blue in white] 1201'. Back cover: five blue 5-point stars across top and bottom on white background; superimposed over outline of light blue national symbol—eagle with olive branch and ar-rows; also, in black, about the book; about the edition. Inside front cover: about Armed Services editions. Inside back cover: list of other Armed Services editions. All edges trimmed and unstained.

Copies: Ctw, LC, STW.

Note: number 1201 on the "JJ" list. Publication information is not available.

A7.e1   third American edition, first impression, paperback (1951)

[p. (ii)] All the | [rule of twenty-four 5-point stars] | [rooster] | Bantam Books | *NEW YORK* [p. (iii)] KING'S | MEN | *BY* | Robert Penn War-ren | [rule of forty 5-point stars] | [epigraph] | [source of epigraph]

Collation: foolscap folio 8° (trimmed: 16.3 × 10.8 cm.); *unsigned* 296 leaves; pp. [i–viii], 1–580 [581–584]; numbers indented 0.65 cm. from the corners formed by the tail and outer margins.

Contents: p. [i]: about the novel; pp. [ii–iii]: title pages; p. [iv]: printing history and copyright; p. [v]: dedication; p. [vi]: blank; p. [vii]: hf. tit. 'ALL THE KING'S MEN'; p. [viii]: blank; pp. 1–580: text; p. [581]: editor's note; p. [582]: about this edition; p. [583]: publisher's advertisement; p. [584]: blank.

Typography and Paper: text: 36 ll., 13.8 (14.1) × 8.8 cm.; Garamond No. 3 Linotype 10/11-pt. Paper: white, wove, unwatermarked; sheets bulk 2.8 cm.

Binding: paper. Front: '[upper left corner in black] A939 [device] | [arched] Every Book Complete. [in blue across top] A BANTAM GIANT. [upper right corner, in red] 35¢ | [on light background in black] *The Fearless Southern Novel* | *that won the* PULITZER PRIZE | [in blue] All the [in red] ROBERT PENN | WARREN | [in blue] KING'S | MEN | [illus.]'. Spine: '[horiz., in black] A939 | [vert. in blue,] ALL THE KING'S MEN [in yellow] ROBERT PENN | WARREN | [horiz., in white, publisher's device] | [in yellow] 35¢'. Back: two scenes with a quotation from a review. All edges trimmed and stained yellow.

Copies: Ctw, JAG, STW.

Note: published 1 Nov. 1951 in runs of 250,000 and 60,000 copies. Printed by W. F. Hall, Inc. (Ltr., K. Graff, Statistical Dept., Bantam Books, Inc., 30 April 1975.)

A7.f1   fourth American edition, first impression, paperback (1955)

All the | King's Men | By | Robert Penn Warren | [epigraph] | [source of epigraph] | [publisher's device] | BANTAM BOOKS · NEW YORK

Collation: post folio 8° (trimmed: 17.8 × 10.7 cm.); *unsigned* 224 leaves; pp. [i–vi], 1–438 [439–442]; numbers in corners formed by the tail and outer margins.

Contents: p. [i]: about the novel; p. [ii]: blank; p. [iii]: title page; p. [iv]: copyright page and printing history; p. [v]: dedication; p. [vi]: about the Bantam edition; pp. 1–438: text; pp. [439–441]: advertisements; p. [442]: publisher's advertisements.

Typography and Paper: text: 48 ll., 15.6 (15.9) × 8.7 cm.; Times New Roman 9/10-pt. Paper: white, wove, unwatermarked; sheets bulk 1.7 cm.

Binding: paper. Front: '[upper left corner, on gold in black] F 1338 | [on gray in white, publisher's device; beneath device, in maroon] A BAN-TAM | FIFTY. [upper center to upper right, on gold in black] ROBERT PENN WARREN | [in red, outlined in black] All the | King's Men. | [black and white sketch of man seated, smoking] | [on gold seal in black] Pulitzer | Prize | Novel | [on red in white, sketch extends into the red] The world-famous American novel of power and corruption, | and the meteoric rise and fall of Willie Stark——politi-cian.' Spine: '[horiz., on black in white] F 1338 || 8 | [vert.] ALL THE KING'S MEN ROBERT PENN WARREN | [on white in red, pub-lisher's device] | [beneath device, in black] BANTAM | BOOKS'. Back, upper left: photograph of RPW; '[top, on white in red] Robert Penn Warren | [on gold in black, excerpts from reviews] | [bottom, black border around white rectangle, publisher's advertisement]'.

Copies: Ctw, JAG, KyU.

Notes: 1. Published April 1955 in 50,000 copies at 50¢. Printed by W. F. Hall, Inc. Subsequent impressions: Oct. 1955, 50,000; March 1957, 35,000; April 1958, 25,000; March 1959, 50,000; Sept. 1959, 35,000; Nov. 1960, 50,000; March 1961, 35,000; Oct. 1961, 35,000; June 1962, 35,000; Dec. 1962, 25,000; April 1963, 25,000; Sept. 1963, 35,000; Feb. 1964, 50,000; Oct. 1964, 50,000; April 1965, 50,000; Dec. 1965, 75,000; May 1966, 75,000; March 1967, 25,000; July 1967, 25,000; Oct. 1967, 100,000; April 1968, 75,000; Sept. 1968, 75,000; July 1969, 35,000; Oct. 1969, 75,000; Feb. 1970, 50,000; Aug. 1970, 75,000; Aug. 1971, 60,000; May 1972, 50,000; July 1972, 35,000; Nov. 1972, 50,000; Aug. 1973, 85,000; April 1974, 50,000; April 1975, 50,000—for a total of 2,060,000 paperback copies in print. Dis-tributed in Canada by Bantam Books of Canada. (Ltr., K. Graff, Sta-tistical Dept., Bantam Books, Inc., 30 April 1975.)

    2. Variants: p. 278.38: "down [to] the hotel"; p. 282.25: "alignment" for "adjustment"; p. 307.38: "of" for "or"; p. 388.41: double colon.

A7.f5   fourth American edition, fifth impression, paperback (1959)

Binding: reprinted as a Bantam Classic in June 1959 in red covers (FC @ 50¢, HC 123 @ 60¢, and SC 167 @ 75¢) and in March 1963 in black covers (same design) (SC 202 @ 75¢ and NC 202 @ 95¢). '*The illustration on the cover was used by the* | *National Broadcasting Company in an advertisement* | *for the Kraft television production of* ALL THE KING'S MEN' (p. [iv]).

Copies: JAG, LU.

A7.f21   fourth American edition, twenty-first impression, paperback (1968)

Binding: reprinted as a Bantam Modern Classic in Jan. 1968 with close-up photograph (red tone) of man's face (NY 4009 @ 95¢ and QY 5249 @ $1.25).

Copies: JAG.

A7.f28   fourth American edition, twenty-eighth impression, paperback (1971)

Binding: reprinted as a Bantam edition in November 1971 in dark blue cover with small depiction (bottom, center) of politician on bunting-draped platform (Q 5249 @ $1.25, T 8003 @ $1.50, Y 6475 @ $1.95, and 12688-1 @ $2.50).

Copies: JAG.

A7.g1   fifth American edition, Time Reading Program edition, paperback (1963)

ALL | THE | KING'S | MEN | *Robert Penn Warren* | WITH A NEW INTRODUCTION | BY THE AUTHOR | [publisher's device] TIME Reading Program Special Edition | TIME INCORPORATED · NEW YORK

Colophon, p. [604]: 'The typeface for the text of this special | edition of *All the King's Men* is Old Style | Number 7, based on an old English face | and adapted for modern use by Linotype | in 1905.

'The type was set by Arrow Composi-|tion, Inc., of Worcester, Massachusetts, | and was printed by The Safran Printing | Company of Detroit, Michigan. The bind-|ing was done by J. W. Clement Co. of | Buffalo, New York. The cover was printed | by Livermore and Knight Co., a division | of Printing Corporation of America, in | Providence, Rhode Island.'

Collation: demy folio 8° (trimmed: 20.4 × 13.1 cm.); *unsigned* 312 leaves; pp. [1–2], [i–vii] viii–ix [x–xi] xii–xvii [xviii], [1–3] 4–71

[72–73] 74–151 [152–153] 154–215 [216–217] 218–261 [262–263] 264–313 [314–315] 316–369 [370–371] 372–427 [428–429] 430–487 [488–489] 490–551 [552–553] 554–602 [603–604]; numbers centered at top of type page.

Contents: pp. [1–2]: blank; p. [i]: hf. tit. 'ALL | THE | KING'S | MEN'; p. [ii]: blank; p. [iii]: title page; p. [iv]: copyright page; p. [v]: dedication; p. [vi]: blank; pp. [vii]–ix: *'Editors' Preface'*; p. [x]: blank; pp. [xi]–xvii: Author's *'Introduction'*; p. [xviii]: blank; p. [1]: epigraph; p. [2]: white on black, *'Chapter One'* with subsequent chapter pages done similarly; pp. [3]–602: text, first letter of each chapter 1.8 cm. high, in bold type; on p. 602 *'The End'*; p. [603]: blank; p. [604]: colophon.

Typography and Paper: text: 36 ll., 16.4 (17.2) × 9.6 cm.; Old Style Number 7 Linotype 12/14-pt. Paper: white, wove, unwatermarked; supplied by the Mead Corporation of Dayton, OH; sheets bulk 3.0 cm.

Binding: paper. Illustration continues from front to back. Front, in various colors, illus. of speaker on platform as seen by audience; flag is background for speaker; two-rail fence in front of speaker: '[in light blue] ALL | THE | KING'S | MEN | [in black] ROBERT PENN WARREN'. Spine, in light blue: 'ROBERT | PENN | WARREN | ALL | THE | KING'S | MEN | TIME INC.' Back, fence rails and more audience; in various colors against black background. All edges trimmed and unstained. Inside covers: light brown.

Copies: Ctw, JAG, KyU, LC, STW, TNJ.

Notes: 1. Published Dec. 1963 for participants in the Time Reading Program. Printing runs were Oct. 1963, 65,000; April 1965, 20,000; Sept. 1967, 14,000; Jan. 1968, 35,000; and May 1969, 21,000. It is now out-of-print (ltr., Nicholas Benton, Public Relations Director, Time-Life Books, 25 March 1975). Introduction copyrighted 2 Dec. 1963 (A673691).

    2. The introduction appeared in *YR*, 53 (Winter 1964), 161–167.

A7.h1   sixth American edition, Ladder edition, paperback (abridged) (1973)

ALL THE KING'S MEN | *by Robert Penn Warren* | A Ladder Edition | at the 3,000-Word Level | *Adapted by* | *Elinor Chamberlain* | Fawcett Publications, Inc. | Greenwich, Connecticut

Collation: post folio 8° (trimmed: 17.8 × 10.5 cm.); *unsigned* 72 leaves; pp. [1–6] 7–23 [24] 25–41 [42] 43–71 [72] 73–87 [88] 89–95 [96] 97–127 [128] 129–139 [140] 141–144; numbers centered at foot of type page.

Contents: p. [1]: about Ladder Series books; p. [2]: blank; p. [3]: title page; p. [4]: copyright; p. [5]: hf. tit. '*ALL THE KING'S MEN*'; p. [6]: blank; pp. 7–139: text in nine chapters; pp. [24, 42, 72, 88, 96, 128, 140]: blank; pp. 141–143: '*Glossary*'; p. 144: publisher's advertisement.

Typography and Paper: text: 45 ll., 15.6 (15.9) × 8.8 cm.; Times New Roman 10-pt. Paper: white, wove, unwatermarked; sheets bulk 1.0 cm.

Binding: paper. Front, dark brown background: '[in gold, outlined] A [toward outer edge] L-137 | 20¢ | [in rectangle] LADDER EDITION | PUBLISHED BY | Fawcett Publications | [in white] This Ladder Edition was adapted to | an English vocabulary of 3,000 words. | [in gold] ALL THE | KING'S MEN | [in red] Robert Penn Warren | [illus., man with back toward viewer, left arm outstretched] | [in gold] The story of the rise and fall of Willie Stark, | a classic study of power and morality in politics.' Spine, on white: '[horiz., in black] L-137 | [vert., in gold] ALL THE KING'S MEN [in red] Robert Penn Warren'. Back: about the book. Front and back inside covers: white. All edges trimmed and stained yellow.

Copies: Ctw, JAG.

Note: published June 1973 at 20¢. Additional publication information is not available.

A7.i1   seventh American edition, Franklin Library edition (1976)

Pulitzer Prize 1947 | ALL THE | KING'S MEN | ROBERT PENN WARREN | Illustrated by Bernard Fuchs | [illus.] | *A Limited Edition* | THE FRANKLIN LIBRARY | Franklin Center, Pennsylvania | 1976

Collation: royal folio 8° (trimmed: 24.0 × 15.3 cm.); *unsigned* [1–41⁸], 324 leaves; pp. [i–xiv], 1–2 [3] 4–38 [39] 40–118 [119] 120–155 [156] 157–200 [201] 202–223 [224] 225–258 [259] 260–346 [347] 348–412 [413] 414–445 [446] 447–504 [505] 506–566 [567] 568–586 [587] 588–628 [629–634]; numbers in outer margins on line with last line of text.

Contents: pp. [i–iii]: blank; p. [iv]: hf. tit. 'ALL THE KING'S MEN';

p. [v]: editors' introduction to the novel; p. [vi]: blank; p. [vii]: '*This limited edition of* | ALL THE KING'S MEN | *is published by* | *The Franklin Library* | *exclusively for subscribers*'; pp. [viii–ix]: illus.; p. [x]: blank; p. [xi]: title page; p. [xii]: copyright; p. [xiii]: dedication; p. [xiv]: epigraph; on p. 1 'CHAPTER ONE' with first letter of text two lines high, display; on p. 628 'THE END'; pp. [629–634]: blank.

Typography and Paper: text: 38 ll., 17.2 (18.1) × 9.7 cm.; Aster 11/13-pt. RT: on v. from outer margin, '*Robert Penn Warren*'; on r. on outer margin, '*All the King's Men*'. Paper: white, wove, watermarked 'Warren's Olde Style' (60 lb.); sheets bulk 4.1 cm.

Illustrations: pp. [viii–ix], [3], [39], [119], [201], [259], [347], [413], [505], [567], and [587].

Binding: dark brown leather. Front and back, in gilt: single-line frame; figures (chess pawns) side by side as frame; single-line frame; thicker, smaller frame; and on gilt rectangle background, chess piece (king). Spine, in gilt: '[three rows of eight figures (pawns) each] | [rib] | ALL | THE KING'S | MEN | · | ROBERT | PENN WARREN | [rib] | [fig. of chess piece (king)] | [rib] | [four rows of eight figures (pawns) each] | [rib] | THE | FRANKLIN LIBRARY | [two rows of eight figures (pawns) each]'. All edges trimmed and gilded; burnt red, silk endpapers. Burnt red ribbon (place marker) sewn in.

Dust wrapper: none.

Copies: JAG, RPW, STW.

Note: publication information is not available.

A7.j1 eighth American edition, Franklin Library signed edition (1977)

[red rule with fleur-de-lis in the center] || [in black] ALL THE | KING'S MEN | ROBERT PENN WARREN | *Illustrated by Jim Sharpe* | [in red] A LIMITED EDITION | [in black] THE FRANKLIN LIBRARY | Franklin Center, Pennsylvania | 1977 | [red rule with inverted fleur-de-lis in the center]

Collation: crown folio 4° (trimmed: 23.4 × 16.0 cm.); *unsigned* [1^8 (+1$_2$) 2–40^8], 321 leaves; pp. [$^\pi$1–2], [i–xvi], [1–4] 5–69 [70–74] 75–151 [152–156] 157–218 [219–222] 223–266 [267–270] 271–320 [321–324] 325–377 [378–382] 383–437 [438–442] 443–498 [499–502] 503–563 [564–568] 569–616 [617–624]; numbers centered at foot of type page.

Contents: pp. [i–ii]: blank; p. [ᵗ 1]: signature in ink: 'Robert Penn Warren'; p. [ᵗ 2]: blank; p. [iii]: ' || *This limited edition of* | ALL THE KING'S MEN | *by Robert Penn Warren* | *has been privately printed,* | *and individually signed* | *by the author* || '; p. [iv]: blank; p. [v]: '[in red] BOOKS BY ROBERT PENN WARREN | [in black—list of books]'; pp. [vi–ix]: '*A special message to subscribers* | *from Robert Penn Warren*'; p. [x]: blank; p. [xi]: title page; p. [xii]: copyright; p. [xiii]: dedication; p. [xiv]: blank; p. [xv]: hf. tit. '[red rule with fleur-de-lis in the center] | ALL THE | KING'S MEN'; p. [xvi]: epigraph; on p. [1] red rule with fleur-de-lis in the center, 'CHAPTER ONE'; pp. [2–3]: illus.; p. [4]: blank; on p. [5] text begins with first letter three lines high, in red; other chapters similarly designated and illus.; pp. [5]–[617]: text; on p. [617] 'THE END'; pp. [618–624]: blank.

Typography and Paper: text: 37 ll., 16.8 (17.7) × 10.1 cm.; Baskerville 11/13-pt. RT: in black, centered above red rule: on v., 'ROBERT PENN WARREN'; on r., 'ALL THE KING'S MEN'. Paper: white, wove, unwatermarked: "a 70-pound '1854 Publishers White' paper was specially made for this book by the Warren Mills" (*Notes from the Editors* pamphlet, pp. 21–22); sheets bulk 4.1 cm.

Illustrations: double-page reproductions of watercolors on pp. [2–3], [72–73], [154–155], [220–221], [268–269], [322–323], [380–381], [440–441], [500–501], and [566–567], i.e., following each chapter page.

Binding: dark green leather. Front and back, in gilt: between triple outer frame with outermost frame orn. and double inner frame, fleur-de-lis orns. at corners, one each centered at top and bottom of frame, and three each equally spaced along sides of frame—all orns. mirrored inside double frame. Four fleur-de-lis orns. centered on cover inside frames. Spine, in gilt: '[triple rule, top orn.] | [fleur-de-lis] | [double rule] | [leather rib] | [double rule] | ALL | THE KING'S | MEN | [double rule] | [leather rib] | [double rule] | ROBERT | PENN | WARREN | [double rule] | [leather rib] | [double rule] | [fleur-de-lis] | [double rule] | [leather rib] | [double rule] | THE | FRANKLIN | LIBRARY | [double rule] | [leather rib] | [double rule | [fleur-de-lis] | [triple rule, bottom orn.]'. All edges trimmed and gilded; dark green silk endpapers. Medium green ribbon (place marker) sewn in.

Dust wrapper: none.

Copies: JAG, STW.

Notes: 1. Published by the Franklin Mint Corporation for $39.00. Additional publication information is not available.

    2. Accompanied by a twenty-two-page pamphlet, *Notes from the Editors*, which contains a background to the novel and to RPW's career as a writer.

A7.k1   first English edition, first impression (abridged) (1948)

ROBERT PENN WARREN | [rule with 5-point star in middle] | *ALL THE* | *KING'S MEN* | LONDON | EYRE & SPOTTISWOODE | [rule with 5-point star in middle]

Collation: crown folio 8° (trimmed: 18.3 × 12.3 cm.); signed, [A]¹⁶ B–P¹⁶ˣQ² Q*¹⁶, 258 leaves; pp. [1–4] 5–514 [515–516]; number on p. 5 in corner formed by tail and outer margins; other numbers in corner formed by head and outer margins.

Contents: p. [1]: hf. tit. '*All the King's Men*'; on p. [2] 'NOVELS BY ROBERT PENN WARREN'; p. [3]: title page; p. [4]: 'THIS BOOK, FIRST PUBLISHED IN 1948, IS MADE AND | PRINTED IN GREAT BRITAIN FOR EYRE & SPOTTISWOODE | (PUBLISHERS) LTD., 14, 15 & 16 BEDFORD STREET, | LONDON, W.C. 2, BY T. & A. CONSTABLE LTD., | HOPETOUN STREET, EDINBURGH'; pp. 5–514: text of ten altered chapters, designated by Roman numerals; pp. [515–516]: blank.

Typography and Paper: text: 36 ll., 15.0 (15.7) × 9.7 cm.; Bembo Monotype 11/12-pt. RT: v. and r., 'ALL THE KING'S MEN'. Paper: white, wove, unwatermarked; sheets bulk 2.8 cm.

Binding: black bds. Front and back: blank. Spine, in gilt: 'ALL | THE | KING'S | MEN | ROBERT PENN | WARREN | EYRE & | SPOTTISWOODE'. All edges trimmed with top edge stained blue; white endpapers.

    Dust wrapper: front cover, on blue background: '[on white oval in blue, outlined] *ALL THE* | *KING'S MEN* | [on blue in white] ROBERT PENN WARREN | Pulitzer Prise Novel 1974'. Spine: '[on white background in blue, outlined] ALL THE | KING'S MEN | [not outlined] ROBERT | PENN | WARREN | [on blue in white] EYRE & | SPOTTISWOODE'. Back cover, on white in blue: excerpts from reviews. Front flap: about the book. Back flap: blank.

Copies: BL, Ctw, JAG, STW.

Notes: 1. Published in 1948 at 12s. 6d. Printed by T. & A. Constable,

Ltd. British Library date-stamp 4 May 1948. Additional publication information is not available.

2. Omits the Cass Mastern story in chapter IV and includes chapter five (**A7.a1**) in IV. Chapters VIII and IX are chapter nine; other variations are evident.

A7.l1   second English edition, first impression (abridged) (1960)

[title, ltrs. shaded] ALL THE | KING'S MEN | [fancy rule] | Robert Penn Warren | 1960 | EYRE & SPOTTISWOODE | LONDON

Collation: demy folio 8° (trimmed: 22.0 × 13.2 cm.); signed, 'A.K.M.—[no.]', [1]⁴ [1*]¹² 2–14⁴ 2–14¹², 224 leaves; pp. [1–6] 7–447 [448]; numbers centered at foot of type page.

Contents: p. [1]: hf. tit. 'ALL THE KING'S MEN'; on p. [2] '*Also by Robert Penn Warren*'; p. [3]: title page; p. [4]: 'First Published in Great Britain 1948 | Second Edition (reset) 1960 | Printed in Great Britain by | Love and Malcomson Ltd., Redhill | Catalogue number 6/5060'; p. [5]: hf. tit.; p. [6]: blank; pp. 7–[448]: text.

Typography and Paper: text: 42 ll., 14.6 (15.2) × 9.6 cm.; Times New Roman 10-pt. Paper: white, wove, unwatermarked; sheets bulk 3.0 cm.

Binding: medium blue, calico-texture cloth, not embossed. Front and back: unmarked. Spine, in gilt: 'All the | King's | Men | [seven dots] | ROBERT | PENN | WARREN | E&S'. All edges trimmed and unstained; white endpapers.

Dust wrapper: Front cover: '[on white in red] Robert Penn Warren | [on red in white irregular ltrs.] ALL THE | KING'S | MEN'. Spine: '[horiz., on white in red] Robert | Penn | Warren | [vert., on red in white irregular ltrs.] ALL THE KING'S MEN | [horiz., on white in red] E & S'. Back cover: excerpts of reviews from *TLS*; Marghanita Laski, *The Observer*; Angus Wilson, *Encounter*; and Marie Scott-James, *Sunday Times*. Front flap: '18s net'. Back flap: publisher's advertisement.

Copies: KyU, MiU, TNJ.

Note: published 1960 at 18s. Printed by Love and Malcomson, Ltd., Redhill. Not located in the British Library (ltr., Dr. Christine Bernstein, 24 Oct. 1979). Additional publication information is not available.

A7.l3 second English edition, third impression, by offset (abridged) (1969)

Binding: dark blue bds. Front and back: blank. Spine, in gilt: 'All the | King's Men | [seven dots] | ROBERT | PENN | WARREN | E & S'. All edges trimmed and unstained; white endpapers.

Dust wrapper: identical with **A7.l1** except: back cover: photograph of RPW, labeled at bottom on white in red 'Robert Penn Warren'. Front flap: '[about the novel] | PRICE NET | 35s=£1.75'. Back flap: 'BOOKS BY | ROBERT PENN WARREN || [list includes *F*]'.

Copies: JAG.

Note: printed by Redwood Press Ltd. Title page omits date.

A7.m1 second English edition, first impression, by offset, paper-back (abridged) (1960)

A FOUR [device] SQUARE BOOK | ALL THE KING'S MEN | ROBERT PENN WARREN | [device] | LANDSBOROUGH PUB-LICATIONS LIMITED | 173 NEW BOND STREET, LONDON, W.1

Collation: post folio 8° (trimmed: 18.3 × 11.8 cm.); signed, [1]–14⁴ [1*]–14*¹², 224 leaves; pp. [1–6] 7–447 [448]; numbers centered at foot of type page.

Contents: p. [1]: quote from review; p. [2]: 'PRINTING HISTORY'; p. [3]: title page; p. [4]: '*By the same author*'; pp. [5–6]: blank; pp. 7–[448]: text.

Typography and Paper: text: 42 ll., 14.7 (15.2) × 9.6 cm.; Times New Roman 10-pt. Paper: white, wove, unwatermarked; sheets bulk 2.15 cm.

Binding: paper. Front: '[upper left corner, vert., in white] FOUR [green device] SQUARE BOOKS [centered on red in yellow] ALL THE | KING'S MEN | [in white] ROBERT PENN WARREN | [on outer edge, in white] 3/6 | [white rule] | [illus.] | [in bottom left corner in black] Pulitzer Prize winning | novel . . . one man's | ruthless fight to control | an American state [*note*: cover by Chantrell]'. Spine, ltrs. in black on blue: '[vert.] A FOUR SQUARE [green device] BOOK All the King's Men ROBERT PENN WARREN | [horiz.] 227'. Back cover, on blue in black: about the novel. All edges trimmed and unstained.

Copies: BL, Ctw (2).

Note: published 1960 by Landsborough Publications, Ltd. Printed by Love & Malcomson, Ltd. The publisher, NEL, prefers not to divulge additional printing information (ltr., Dorothy Houghton, Managing Editor, Paperbacks, New English Library, 29 May 1975). British Library date-stamp 25 April 1960.

A7.n1   third English edition, first impression, by offset (1974)

ALL THE KING'S MEN | [fancy rule] | *Robert Penn Warren* | Secker & Warburg | LONDON

Collation: demy folio 8° (trimmed: 21.5 × 13.5 cm.); *unsigned* [1–15 ^{16}], 240 leaves; pp. [i–vi] vii–xv [xvi], [1–2] 3–463 [464]; numbers centered at foot of type page.

Contents: p. [i]: hf. tit. 'ALL THE KING'S MEN'; on p. [ii] '*Books by Robert Penn Warren*'; p. [iii]: title page; p. [iv]: copyright page; p. [v]: dedication; p. [vi]: blank; pp. vii–xv: '*Introduction to the 1974 English Edition*'; p. [xvi]: blank; p. [1]: hf. tit. '*ALL THE KING'S MEN*'; p. [2]: blank; pp. 3–[464]: text.

Typography and Paper: printed by offset lithography from **A7.a1**. Paper: "Mallex Litho Wove, 85 gsm, vol. 15. Size at printing 88.8 × 112.8 cm. (2 × 32 page sections)" (ltr., N. Gardner, General Manager, Printing Div., Redwood Burn Ltd., 24 Feb. 1975), white, unwatermarked; sheets bulk 3.1 cm.

Binding: blue bds. Front and back: blank. Spine, in gilt: 'All the | King's | Men | [orn.] | Robert | Penn | Warren | Secker & | Warburg'. All edges trimmed and unstained; white endpapers.

   Dust wrapper: front and back covers, on blue background: '[in red] Robert | Penn Warren | [in white] All the | King's | Men | [in red] The complete edition | published for the first time in England | with a new introduction'. Spine, on blue background: '[in red] Robert | Penn | Warren | [in white] All the | King's | Men | SECKER & | WARBURG'. Front flap, on white in blue: about the novel. Back flap: about the author.

Copies: Ctw, JAG, LC, RPW, STW.

Notes: 1. Published 7 Jan. 1974 in one impression at £2.75. Printed by Redwood Press Ltd., Trowbridge, Wiltshire. The publisher prefers not to disclose the number of copies printed (ltr., T. G. Rosenthal, Managing Director, Martin Secker & Warburg, Ltd., 6 Feb. 1975).

Not in the British Library (ltr., Dr. Christine Bernstein, 24 Oct. 1979).

2. A slightly longer version of the introduction appeared in the London *Times*, 5 Jan. 1974, p. 5.

A7.01   fourth English edition, first impression, paperback (1974)

All The King's Men | Robert Penn Warren | NEW ENGLISH LI-BRARY || TIMES MIRROR

Collation: post folio 8° (trimmed: 17.9 × 10.7 cm.); signed, 1–30⁸, 240 leaves; pp. [1–4] 5–13 [14] 15–479 [480]; numbers centered at foot of type page.

Contents: p. [1]: hf. tit. 'ALL THE KING'S MEN'; on p. [2] '*Also by this author and available in the NEL series*'; p. [3]: title page; p. [4]: copyright and dedication; pp. 5–13: '*Introduction to the 1974 English Edition*'; p. [14]: blank; pp. 15–479: text; p. [480]: publisher's advertisement.

Typography and Paper: text: 44 ll., 14.7 (15.1) × 8.7 cm.; Plantin Intertype 9½-pt. Ink: "Fishburn's Solvent based liquid ink—Letterpress rotary novel black AP.2998 (1691/1) 511." Paper: white, wove, unwatermarked; "Norwegian Bulky News, 005/54 gsm. 36″ Reel width" (ltr., V. Flynn, Managing Director, Hunt Barnard Printing Ltd., 18 March 1975); sheets bulk 3.3 cm.

Binding: paper. Front, on white: '[in purple] NEW ENGLISH LI-BRARY [publisher's device] | [in black] ROBERT | PENN WARREN | All the King's Men | [color illus. of man looking and pointing toward viewer, with automobile and street scene behind]'; illus. continues over spine to back cover. Spine: '[horiz., in purple, publisher's device] | [in black] FICTION | [vert., in black] ROBERT PENN WARREN | All the King's Men | [illus. continued from front]'. Back cover, in black: about the novel; lower left corner, worldwide distribution; lower right corner, illus. Inside covers: white. All edges trimmed and unstained.

Copies: BL, JAG, RPW.

Notes: 1. Published 1 Aug. 1974 at 75p. The number of copies printed is not available. Printed by Hunt Barnard Printing Ltd., Aylesbury, Bucks. (ltr., Dorothy Houghton, Senior Editor, New English Library, 19 Feb. 1975). British Library date-stamp 31 July 1974.

2. Also distributed in Cyprus, Gibraltar, Malta, New Zealand, Spain, Trinidad (W.I.), and Australia.

A8   Blackberry Winter

A8.a1   first American edition, first impression (1946)

[in black and blue] ROBERT PENN WARREN | [in blue] Blackberry Winter | A STORY ILLUSTRATED BY | WIGHTMAN WILLIAMS | The Cummington Press/[month] 1946

Colophon, p. [51]: 'THIS COPY IS NUMBER [entered by hand] | of a first edition limited to three-hundred-thirty copies | hand-printed from Poliphilus types set up by hand, those | numbered 1 to 280 being on Arches paper from France, | and those i to l, signed by the author and the illustrator, | on Kelmscott Crown & Sceptre paper from England. | Done at Cummington, Massachusetts. | H. D. & W. W. finx. & fec.'

Collation: crown 8° (rough trimmed: 19.3 × 12.6 cm.); *unsigned* [1−7⁴], 28 leaves; pp. [i–ii], [1–6] 7–49 [50–54]. Numbers are located below the type page, set in 3 ems from the outer margin; p. [35] is unnumbered.

Contents: pp. [i–ii]: blank; p. [1]: hf. tit. 'Blackberry Winter'; p. [2]: blank; p. [3]: title page; p. [4]: 'Copyright 1946 by Robert Penn Warren'; p. [5]: 'TO | DAGMAR & | JOSEPH WARREN BEACH'; p. [6]: blank; pp. 7–49: text, with first letter of first word two lines high and in brown and entire first line in caps.: 'IT WAS GETTING INTO JUNE &'; p. [50]: blank; p. [51]: colophon; pp. [52−54]: blank.

Typography and Paper: text: 28 ll., 12.4 (12.9) × 7.45 cm.; 12/13-pt. (see statement under colophon and n. 3). Paper: white, laid, vertical chainlines (2.6 cm.), watermarked 'ARCHES (FRANCE)' in tail margin; sheets bulk 0.8 cm.

Ilustrations: p. 7 design on top half of page in black and brown; p. 12 design on right half of type page, between ll. 3–21, in black and blue; p. 19 between ll. 4–22 in black and brown; p. 22 on right half of page, between l. 16 and bottom of type page, in black and blue; p. 29 between ll. 10–25, in black and brown; p. [35] between l. 12 and bottom of type page, in black and blue; p. 40 on left half of type page, between ll. 4–21, in black and brown; and p. 45 between top of type page and l. 22, in black and blue.

Binding: black bds. Front: outer edge decorated with brown, blue, and white horizontal argyles (1.95 cm.). Spine, top, in blue on white rectangle: 'Warren | Black-|berry | Winter'. Back: blank. All edges rough trimmed and unstained; white endpapers.

Dust wrapper: issued in clear wax-paper and in plain white paper jackets.

Copies: CoU, Ctw (nos. i and 186), JAG (no. 173), KyU (no. 106), LC (nos. 52 and 53), LU (no. 62), NJP (no. 176), RPW (no. 202), STW (nos. xliv and 183), TNJ (no. 36).

Notes: 1. Published 1 Nov. 1946 in the limited edition of 330 copies at $5.00 unsigned and $10.00 signed. LC copyright 15 Nov. 1946 (A7703); two copies deposited 25 Feb. 1947.

2. Ctw (no. i) is signed by the illustrator only.

Collation: [1–8⁴], 32 leaves; pp. [i–vi] . . . [55–58].

Collation: [$1-8^4$], 32 leaves; pp. [i–vi] . . . [55–58].

Contents: pp. [i–vi]: blank; pp. [55–58]: blank.

Binding: bds. Front: cream backgrounds with inked "tepees" in six double rows plus single row over vertical, spaced marks, which appear to be watercolor. Spine, black leather, vert., in gilt: 'BLACK-BERRY WINTER'. Back: blank.

3. From Harry Duncan's "recollections of its production" (ltr., St. Valentine's Day 1975): "we must have worked on setting the type, cutting the linoleum, hand printing the sheets, and folding and collating during the winter and spring of 1946. John Marchi of Portland, Maine, did the binding, and it usually took him three or four months. There was only one printing, which consisted of less (for we've inveterately been over-sanguine about the number of fair copies we'll finally get) than three hundred and thirty copies, of which fifty were in quarter leather and the remainder in full cloth. . . . we printed as I recall eight pages up, and there were of course additional impressions for each of the sheets with red or blue ink. The type is Monotype Poliphilus 13-point for the body face (it may have been cast on 12-point body and leaded one point); Monotype Poliphilus 10-point is on the title, copyright, dedication, and colophon pages; one line on the title is in 18-point Monotype Centaur. All the type was set up by hand, and since we hadn't enough for all forty-nine pages, Mr. Warren had to read proof piecemeal."

A9 *The Circus in the Attic and Other Stories*

A9.a1 first American edition, first impression (1947)

The Circus in the Attic | and Other Stories | ROBERT PENN WAR-
REN | *New York* | HARCOURT, BRACE AND COMPANY

Collation: demy 8° (trimmed: 20.2 × 13.6 cm.); *unsigned* [1–9¹⁶], 144
leaves; pp. [i–xii], [1–3] 4–276, except chapter pages are unnumbered:
[3], [63], [88], [96], [108], [120], [134], [143], [163], [170], [175], [190],
[199], and [211]; numbers located in the corner formed by the head
and outer margins on the RT line.

Contents: p. [i]: hf. tit. 'THE CIRCUS IN THE ATTIC | AND OTH-
ER STORIES'; on p. [ii]: *'Books by Robert Penn Warren'*; p. [iii]: title
page; p. [iv]: 'COPYRIGHT, 1931, 1935, 1936, 1937, 1941, 1943, |
1945, 1946, 1947, BY | ROBERT PENN WARREN | *All rights re-
served, including* | *the right to reproduce this book* | *or portions thereof in any*
form. | *first edition* | PRINTED IN THE UNITED STATES OF
AMERICA'; p. [v]: *'To* | KATHERINE ANNE PORTER'; p. [vi]:
blank; p. [vii]: *'Contents* | [titles in ital.]'; p. [viii]: blank; p. [ix]: 'For
permission to reprint the stories in this collection the | author wishes
to thank the editors of *The Virginia Quarterly* | *Review, Cosmopolitan, The*
Southern Review, Mademoiselle, | *Cronos,* and the Macaulay Company';
p. [x]: blank; p. [xi]: 'NOTE | The earliest story in this book was writ-
ten in 1930, the | latest in 1946, but the order here is not chronologi-
cal.'; p. [xii]: blank; p. [1]: hf. tit.; p. [2]: blank; on p. [3] 'The Circus in
the Attic'; on p. [63] *'Blackberry Winter* | *To* JOSEPH WARREN *and*
DAGMAR BEACH'; on p. [88] *'When the Light Gets Green'*; on p. [96]
'Christmas Gift'; on p. [108] *'Goodwood Comes Back'*; on p. [120] *'The Pa-
tented Gate and the Mean* | *Hamburger'*; on p. [134] *'A Christian Educa-
tion'*; on p. [143] *'The Love of Elsie Barton:* | *A Chronicle'*; on p. [163]
'Testament of Flood'; on p. [170] *'The Confession of Brother Grimes'*; on p.
[175] *'Her Own People'*; on p. [190] *'The Life and Work of Professor* | *Roy*
Millen'; on p. [199] *'The Unvexed Isles'*; on p. [211] *'Prime Leaf'*.

Typography and Paper: text: 37 ll., 15.55 (16.2) × 9.7 cm.; Linotype
Caledonia 11/12-pt. RT: [centered on all v. except chapter pages] 'THE
CIRCUS IN THE ATTIC'; [centered on all r. except chapter pages,
story titles in full except the following]: 'THE PATENTED GATE',
'THE LOVE OF ELSIE BARTON', 'CONFESSION OF BROTH-
ER GRIMES', and 'LIFE OF PROFESSOR MILLEN'. Paper: white,
wove, unwatermarked; sheets bulk 1.9 cm.

Binding: black cloth. Front and back: blank. Spine, in gilt: 'THE |
CIRCUS | IN THE | ATTIC | *Robert* | *Penn* | *Warren* | *Harcourt Brace* |
and Company'. All edges trimmed and unstained; white endpapers.

Dust wrapper: front cover, in three colors, with diagonal white background cutting from spine to outer edge: '[on red in white] ROBERT | PENN | WARREN | [on black strip in white] *AUTHOR OF THE PULITZER PRIZE NOVEL* | "ALL THE KING'S MEN" | [female and male figures in three colors within a large C, with name 'Arens' along diagonal; on green in white] *The* | CIRCUS | IN THE | ATTIC'. Spine: '[on white in red] ROBERT | PENN | WARREN | [black stripe] | [on white in green] *The* | CIRCUS | IN THE | ATTIC | [on white in black] *Harcourt, Brace | and Company*'. Back cover: photograph of author above publisher's advertisement. Front flap: about the book. Back flap: reviewers' comments about *AKM*.

Copies: Ctb, Ctw, CtY, JAG, KyU, LC, LU (2), STW, TNJ (2).

Notes: 1. Published 22 Jan. 1948 from two impressions of 3,500 (3 Oct. 1947) and 2,500 (3 Feb. 1948) copies at $3.00. Printed by Quinn & Boden Company, Inc. Out of print May 1957. Distributed in Canada by George J. McLeod Ltd. (ltr., Gerard G. Vaughan, Trade Dept., Harcourt Brace Jovanovich, Inc., 4 June 1975). LC copyright not located (ltr., William L. Asher, Bibliographer, Library of Congress, 5 Nov. 1979).

2. Second impression bears imprint '[b·1·48]' on copyright page.

A9.b1 first American edition, first impression, by offset, paperback (1968)

The Circus in the Attic | and Other Stories | ROBERT PENN WARREN | [publisher's device] | HARBRACE PAPERBOUND LIBRARY | HARCOURT, BRACE & WORLD, INC., NEW YORK

Collation: post folio 8° (trimmed: 18.1 × 10.4 cm.); *unsigned* 144 leaves; pp. [i–xii], [1–3] 4–276; numbers located as in **A9.a1**.

Contents: p. [i]: hf. tit. 'THE CIRCUS IN THE ATTIC | AND OTHER STORIES'; p. [ii]: blank; on p. [iii] '*By Robert Penn Warren*'; p. [iv]: blank; p. [v]: title page; p. [vi]: copyright; p. [vii]: dedication; p. [viii]: blank; p. [ix]: '*Contents*'; p. [x]: acknowledgments; on p. [xi] 'NOTE'; p. [xii]: blank; p. [1]: hf. tit.; p. [2]: blank; pp. [3]–276: text.

Typography and Paper: reproduced from **A9.a1** by photo-offset. Paper: white, wove, unwatermarked; sheets bulk 1.8 cm.

Binding: paper. Front cover, on orange: '[in black] HARBRACE PAPERBOUND LIBRARY HPL 34 | $1.25 SLIGHTLY HIGHER IN CANADA | [figure of ringmaster in center, facing spine edge; on spine side of figure, in white] The | Circus | in the | Attic | [in yellow] AND OTHER | STORIES | [on outer edge side of figure, in white] Robert | Penn | Warren | [in yellow] AUTHOR OF THE PULITZER-PRIZE | NOVEL [in black] All The | King's | Men'. Spine, on orange: '[vert., in white] The Circus in the Attic [in yellow] Robert Penn Warren | [horiz., in black] HPL | 34'. Back cover, on white: in black, about the book; in pink, quotes from reviews; publisher's device; series; in black, publisher; 'Cover design by Paul Bacon Studio'. Inside covers: white. All edges trimmed and unstained.

Copies: JAG, KyU, LC.

Note: published 23 Oct. 1968 in 20,000 copies at $1.25. Printed by Colonial Press in Aug. 1968. (Ltr., Gerard G. Vaughan, Trade Dept., Harcourt Brace Jovanovich, Inc., 4 June 1975.)

A9.c1 second American edition, first impression, paperback (1959)

The Circus | In the Attic | and other stories | by | Robert Penn Warren | A DELL BOOK

Collation: foolscap folio 8° (trimmed: 16.3 × 10.6 cm.); *unsigned* 144 leaves; pp. [1–9] 10–286 [287–288], except chapter pages are unnumbered: [9], [69], [94], [103], [116], [128], [143], [153], [173], [180], [185], [200], [209], and [221]; numbers located in corner formed by upper and outer margins.

Contents: p. [1]: three reviewers' comments; p. [2]: blank; p. [3]: title page; p. [4]: copyright data and dedication; p. [5]: 'CONTENTS'; p. [6]: blank; p. [7]: acknowledgments; on p. [8] 'NOTE'; pp. [9]–286: text; pp. [287–288]: publisher's advertisement.

Typography and Paper: text: 39 ll., 13.8 (14.2) × 8.6 cm.; Linotype Baskerville 9½/10½-pt. RT: same arrangement as **A9.a1** except located at inner margins, in ital. instead of caps., and no abbreviated titles. Paper: white, wove, unwatermarked; sheets bulk 1.4 cm.

Binding: paper. Front cover, on black: '[upper left corner, on pink square, in black] DELL | [on black in white] F82 | [upper right corner, in blue] 50¢ | [in center, in yellow] ROBERT | PENN | WARREN | [in white] Author of ALL THE KING'S MEN, and BAND OF ANGELS | [in multicolored stripes, down each letter] THE | CIRCUS | IN THE | ATTIC | [in white] A COLLECTION OF SHORT STORIES'. Spine, on pink triangle: '[vert., in black on pink triangle] F82 [in blue] THE [in green] CIRCUS [in pink] IN [in red] THE [in blue]

ATTIC [in white] ROBERT PENN WARREN | [horiz., in pink] DELL'. Back cover, in pink and in white: about the stories. From each edge, a different colored line. Inside covers: white. All edges trimmed and stained greenish blue.

Copies: JAG, NNC, OrCS, STW(2).

Notes: 1. Published May 1959 at 50¢. Additional publication information is not available (ltr., Dennis Dalrymple, Copyrights Editor, Dell Publishing Co., Inc., 13 May 1975). "Designed and produced by Western Printing & Lithographing Company" (p. [4]).

2. At the bottom of the back cover is a list of RPW's novels which includes *The Man Below*, the original title for *The Cave*.

A9.d1   first English edition, first impression, by offset (1952)

The Circus in the Attic | and Other Stories | ROBERT PENN WARREN | London | EYRE & SPOTTISWOODE

Collation: demy folio 8° (trimmed: 20.0 × 13.5 cm.); signed, [1]⁸ 2–18⁸, 144 leaves; pagination identical with **A9.a1**.

Contents: p. [i]: hf. tit.; on p. [ii] '*Novels by Robert Penn Warren*'; p. [iii]: title page; p. [iv]: '*This book, first published in 1952, is made and | printed in Great Britain for Eyre & Spottiswoode | (Publishers), Ltd., 15 Bedford Street, London, W. C. 2 | by Jarrold and Sons, Limited, Norwich*'; p. [v]: dedication; p. [vi]: blank; p. [vii]: '*Contents*'; p. [viii]: blank; p. [ix]: '*Author's Note*'; p. [x]: blank; p. [xi]: '*Note*'; p. [xii]: blank; p. [1]: hf. tit.; p. [2]: blank; pp. 3–276: text.

Typography and Paper: text: 37 ll., identical with **A9.a1**. Paper: white, wove, unwatermarked; sheets bulk 2.1 cm.

Binding: green bds. Front and back: blanks. Spine, in red: 'THE | CIRCUS | IN THE | ATTIC | *& other* | *stories* | ROBERT | PENN | WARREN | EYRE AND | SPOTTISWOODE'. All edges trimmed and unstained; white endpapers.

Dust wrapper: similar to **A9.a1** but on coarser paper: front cover, on black stripe in white: '*AUTHOR OF THE WORLD FAMOUS NOVELS | "WORLD ENOUGH AND TIME" | & "ALL THE KING'S MEN"*'. Spine, on white: '[in red] ROBERT | PENN | WARREN | [in green script] *The* | [in black] CIRCUS | IN THE | ATTIC | *Eyre & | Spottiswoode*'. Back cover: excerpts from British reviews. Front flap: about the book. Back flap: blank.

Copies: BL, Ctw.

Note: published 1952 at 15s. Printed by Jarrold and Sons, Limited, Norwich. Additional publication information is not available (ltr., Maria Lyras, Publicity Dept., Eyre Methuen Ltd., 6 June 1975). British Library date-stamp 20 March 1952.

A9.d2   first English edition, second impression, by offset (1956)

ROBERT PENN WARREN | *The Circus in the Attic* | *and other stories* | [publisher's device] | *London 1956* | EYRE & SPOTTISWOODE

Contents: p. [i]: 'THE CIRCUS IN THE ATTIC | *and other stories* | [about the collection]'; p. [ii]: '*Also by Robert Penn Warren* | [list ends with *BA*]'; p. [iii]: title page; on p. [iv] '*First published 1952* | *First cheap edition 1956*'.

Dust wrapper: back cover: publisher's advertisement for *WET*.

Copies: AU, JAG.

Note: published June 1956 at 7s. Publisher's device: '[curved down, around top of circle, in black] POPULAR | [in white on black circle] e & s | [curved up, around bottom of circle, in black] FICTION'.

A10   *World Enough and Time*

A10.a1   first American edition, first impression (1950)

[p. (iv), in black] Robert Penn | Warren | [brown hourglass orn.] | [in black] RANDOM HOUSE | NEW YORK | [brown rule] [p. (v), in brown] World Enough | and Time | [in black] A ROMANTIC | NOVEL | [publisher's device]|||

Collation: demy 8° (trimmed 20.85 × 13.8 cm.); *unsigned* [1⁴ 2–17¹⁶], 260 leaves; pp. [i–viii], [1–2] 3-512; numbers, preceded and followed by asterisks, centered at foot of type page.

Contents: p. [i]: hf. tit., in brown, 'WORLD ENOUGH AND TIME'; p. [ii]: blank; on p. [iii] 'BOOKS BY | ROBERT PENN WARREN'; pp. [iv–v]: title page; p. [vi]: '*Copyright, 1950*, | *by* ROBERT PENN WARREN | *Copyright in Canada, 1950*, | *by Robert Penn Warren* | *All rights reserved under Interna-|tional and Pan American Copyright* | *Conventions. Published in New York | by Random House, Inc., and simul-|taneously in Toronto, Canada, by | Random House of Canada, Limited.* | FIRST PRINTING | *Manufactured in the United States of America* | *by H. Wolff, New*

York | *Designed by Marshall Lee*'; p. [vii]: 'To Dixon and Elizabeth Wector'; p. [viii]: blank; p. [1]: hf. tit., in black; p. [2]: '[27 ll. epigraph] | EDMUND SPENSER: *from the Prologue of the Fifth* | *Booke of the Faerie Queene Contayning the* | *Legend of Artegall or of Justice*.'; on p. 3 upper half of page, in black, 'I' with first line extended in caps.; pp. 3–512: text, with respective chapter pages following the same format as chapter I, on pp. 42, 77, 125, 160, 226, 274, 312, 345, 382, 429, and 450.

Typography and Paper: text: 40 ll., 16.7 (17.3) × 10.5 cm.; Linotype Caledonia 11/12-pt. Paper: white, wove, unwatermarked; sheets bulk 3.0 cm.

Binding: brown cloth. Front, stamped in gilt: 'WORLD ENOUGH AND TIME'. Spine, in gilt: '[publisher's device] | [gilt frame, black backgound] World | Enough | and | Time | [brown hour-glass orn.] | [in gilt] Robert | Penn | Warren | RANDOM HOUSE'. Back: blank. All edges trimmed with top edge stained gray; gray endpapers.

Dust wrapper: front cover, on black: '[in orange] World | Enough | and Time | [in green] A ROMANTIC NOVEL | [in yellow] *Robert Penn Warren* | [in green] Author of the Pulitzer Prize Novel | "ALL THE KING'S MEN" | [illus.]'. Spine, on black in yellow: 'World | Enough | and | Time *Robert* | *Penn* | *Warren* | [illus.] | *Random House*'. Back cover, on black: '[in orange] World | Enough | and | Time | [in green] A ROMANTIC NOVEL | [in yellow] *Robert Penn Warren* | [illus.]'. Front flap: '[brief review] | [publisher's advertisement] | *Jacket Design by Jules Gottlieb*'. Back flap: biographical sketch.

Copies: Ctb, CtY, JAG (2), KyU, LC, LU, STW (2), TNJ, TxFTC.

Notes: 1. Published 20 June 1950 in 37,000 copies (printed 27 Feb. 1950) at $3.50. Printed by American Book-Stratford Press, Inc. Subsequent impressions: 23 June 1950, 10,000; 6 April 1968, 1,500; and 20 Feb. 1974, 500. Distributed in Canada by Random House of Canada Limited. (Ltr., Jim Wilcox, Random House, Inc., 31 July 1974.) LC copyright 27 March 1950 (A42423); two copies deposited 3 April 1950; copyright renewed 6 June 1977 (R664522).

2. Excerpts appear in *Omnibook Best-Seller Magazine*, Dec. 1950, pp. 2–58; and "Portrait of La Grand' Bosse," *KR*, 12 (Winter 1950), 41–50.

3. A pamphlet was published in conjunction with *WET*: *Background of a Novel*: World Enough and Time, A Romantic Novel *by Robert Penn Warren* (New York: Random House, n.d.), 7 pp.

4. Supplemental material related to *WET*: J. Winston Coleman, Jr.,

The Beauchamp-Sharp Tragedy: An Episode of Kentucky History During the Middle 1820's (Frankfort, KY: Roberts Printing Company, 1950). (Ctw)

A10.b1 first American edition, special limited edition (booksellers) (1950)

Contents: p. [ii]: 'THIS IS NUMBER [entered by hand] OF A LIMITED EDITION | SPECIALLY MADE FOR PRESENTATION TO | THE BOOKSELLERS OF AMERICA'.

Binding: gray cloth. Front, stamped in gilt: 'WORLD ENOUGH AND TIME | *PRESENTATION EDITION*'. Spine: '[in gilt, publisher's device] | [gilt frame, dark blue background] World | Enough | and | Time | [gray hourglass orn.] | [in gilt] Robert | Penn | Warren | RANDOM HOUSE'. Back: blank. All edges trimmed with top edge stained gray; cream endpapers.

Dust wrapper: issued in clear plastic wrap.

Copies: JAG, RPW, STW.

Note: numbered, but unsigned.

A10.c1 first American edition, special limited edition (Kentucky) (1950)

Collation: *unsigned* [1^4 (+1_2) 2–17^{16}]; pp. [$^{\pi}$1–2], [i–viii], [1–2] 3–512.

Contents: p. [$^{\pi}$1]: 'This special | KENTUCKY EDITION | is limited to one thousand copies, | signed by the author | [ink signature] Robert Penn Warren'; p. [$^{\pi}$2]: blank.

Copies: Ctb, KyU, STW.

Note: KyU copy is inscribed on free endpaper (r.): 'To Herman Lee Donovan [former president, University of Kentucky] | Sincerely | Robert Penn Warren | Lexington | October 18, 1960 || '.

A10.d1 first American edition, book-club edition (1950)

Title Page: identical with **A10.a1**.

Collation: demy 8° (trimmed / rough trimmed: 20.9 × 13.6 cm.); *unsigned* [1–15^{16}], 240 leaves; pp. [i–x], [1–2] 3–465 [466–470]; numbers, unadorned, centered at foot of type page.

Contents: pp. [i–ii]: blank; p. [iii]: hf. tit., in brown, 'WORLD ENOUGH AND TIME'; pp. [iv–v]: title pages; p. [vi]: '*Copyright*,

MCML, | *by* ROBERT PENN WARREN | *Copyright in Canada,* *MCML*.| *by Robert Penn Warren* | *All rights reserved under International* | *and Pan-American Copyright Conventions.* | *Manufactured in the United States of America* | *Based on a design by Marshall Lee*'; p. [vii]: dedication; p. [viii]: blank; p. [ix]: epigraph; p. [x]: blank; p. [1]: hf. tit., in black; p. [2]: blank; on p. 3 in brown, 'I'; pp. 3–465: text; pp. [466–470]: blank.

Typography and Paper: text: 44 ll., 16.9 (17.4) × 10.25 cm.; Caledonia 11-pt. Paper: white, wove, unwatermarked; sheets bulk 3.1 cm.

Binding: in brown cloth, not embossed; otherwise identical with **A10.a1**. Top and bottom edges trimmed, fore edge rough trimmed with top edge stained dark blue; white endpapers.

Copies: Ctw, JAG (2), STW.

Note: a Literary Guild Selection for July 1950, but no publication data are available (ltr., Barbara Ann Bowden, Literary Guild of America, Inc., 29 April 1975).

A10.e1   first American edition, book-club edition, paperback (1951)

[p. (iv), in black] Robert Penn | Warren | [in brown, publisher's device] | [in black] GARDEN CITY BOOKS | GARDEN CITY, N.Y. | [brown rule]; [p. (v), in brown] World Enough | and Time | [in black] A ROMANTIC | NOVEL | [black rule]

Collation: demy 8° (trimmed: 21.0 × 13.6 cm.); *unsigned* 240 leaves; pagination and numbering identical with **A10.d1**.

Contents: on p. [vi] 'GARDEN CITY BOOKS REPRINT EDITION 1951, | by special arrangement with Random House'.

Binding: paper, greenish yellow and white pattern. Front cover, in white on bluish green rectangle: '*World Enough* | *and Time* | ROBERT PENN WARREN'. Spine: '[vert., in white on bluish green rectangle] World Enough and Time *ROBERT PENN WARREN* | [horiz.] GAR-DEN CITY'. Back cover: patterned. All edges trimmed with top edge stained red.

   Wrapper: a publisher's advertising band: front: 'A 3-STAR BEST SELLER | *Only* 75¢'. Spine: title and author. Back: about the book.

Copies: Ctw, KyU, STW, TNJ.

Note: Publication information is not available.

A10.f1   second American edition, first impression, paperback (1952)

World Enough | and Time | A ROMANTIC NOVEL | by Robert Penn Warren | [publisher's device] | A SIGNET BOOK | Published by The New American Library

Collation: crown folio 8° (trimmed: 18.1 × 10.6 cm.); *unsigned* 256 ind. leaves; pp. [1–8] 9–510 [511–512]; numbers centered at foot of type page.

Contents: p. [1]: about the novel and the author; p. [2]: publisher's advertisement; p. [3]: title page; p. [4]: copyright; p. [5]: dedication; p. [6]: blank; p. [7]: hf. tit. 'World Enough | and Time'; p. [8]: epigraph; pp. 9–510: text; pp. [511–512]: publisher's advertisement.

Typography and Paper: text: 44 ll., 15.4 (15.8) × 8.9 cm.; Times New Roman 10-pt. Paper: white, wove, unwatermarked; sheets bulk 2.4 cm.

Binding: paper. Front cover, on light blue: '[upper left corner in black] D975 | [on black in light blue] SIGNET | [on white in black] 50¢ | [on black in light blue] DOUBLE | [on light blue in black] VOLUME | [across remaining top] A Great Novel of Passionate Love and Betrayal | By the Pulitzer Prize Winner——author of *All the King's Men* | [in white across top of illus. of man and woman embracing in room with candle on table] World Enough and Time | Robert Penn Warren | [across bottom on dark blue in white] A SIGNET DOUBLE VOLUME | Complete and Unabridged'. Spine, right half light blue, left half dark blue: '[printed twice, on light blue in black and on dark blue in white; horiz.] D975 | [vert.] WORLD ENOUGH AND TIME Robert Penn Warren | [at lower edge, background colors switch halves; and across on black in white] SIGNET | [on white in black] 50¢ | [on black in white] DOUBLE | [on white in black] VOLUME'. Back cover, across top on dark blue: '[upper left corner, as on spine] SIGNET-50¢-DOUBLE-VOLUME [in white] SIGNET DOUBLE VOLUME EDITIONS | Great Books at a Low Price . . . | [three illus. in color with captions, against white background] | [across bottom on light blue in black] Published by the New American Library'. Inside covers: white. All edges trimmed and stained orange.

Copies: Ctw, JAG, KyU.

Note: published Dec. 1952 at 50¢. Additional publication information is not available.

A10.f2   second American edition, second impression, paperback (1966)

Binding: Signet Book in white cover with small illus. at lower edge: house, red-haired woman, and two men (one dead) (Q2917 @ 95¢). All edges trimmed and stained red.

Copies: JAG (2), KyU.

A10.g1   third American edition, first impression, paperback (1979)

World Enough | and Time || A ROMANTIC NOVEL || Robert Penn | Warren | [publisher's device] | VINTAGE BOOKS | A DIVISION OF RANDOM HOUSE | NEW YORK

Collation: crown folio 8° (trimmed: 17.8 × 10.4 cm.); *unsigned* 240 ind. leaves; pp. [i–viii], [1–2] 3–469 [470–472]; page numbers in corner formed by upper and outer margins.

Contents: pp. [i–ii]: blank; p. [iii]: hf. tit. 'WORLD ENOUGH AND TIME'; p. [iv]: blank; p. [v]: title page; p. [vi]: copyright and LC Cataloging in Publication Data; p. [vii]: dedication; p. [viii]: blank; p. [1]: hf. tit.; p. [2]: epigraph; pp. 3–469: text; pp. [470–472]: blank.

> *Note*: p. [vi] erroneously lists 'Copyright renewed 1978 by Robert Penn Warren'. LC copyright renewal 6 June 1977 (R664522).

Typography and Paper: text: 45 ll., 15.4 (16.0) × 8.8 cm.; Times New Roman 10-pt. Paper: white, wove, unwatermarked; sheets bulk 2.2 cm.

Binding: paper. Front cover, on dark green: '[in white] $2.95 · IN CANADA $3.75 · V-818 · 394-72818-1 | World | Enough | & [illus. in color, hand holding knife] Time | [gold rule] | [red rule] | [in gold] ROBERT | PENN | WARREN'. Spine: '[vert., in white] World Enough & Time · [in gold] Robert Penn | Warren | [horiz., in gold, publisher's device] | VINTAGE | V-818'. Back cover, in white: 'FICTION | [about the novel and author]'. Inside covers: white. All edges trimmed and unstained.

Copies: JAG, RPW, STW.

Note: published April 1979 in 15,000 copies at $2.95. Printed by W. F. Hall. (Ltr., Albert Erskine, Random House, Inc., 27 Nov. 1979.)

A10.h1   first English edition, first impression (1951)

ROBERT PENN WARREN | [fancy rule] | WORLD ENOUGH AND TIME | 1951 | EYRE & SPOTTISWOODE | LONDON

Collation: large crown 8° (trimmed: 20.0 × 13.5 cm.); signed, [A] B–P^{16} Q^{14}, 254 leaves; pp. [1–8] 9–508; numbers inset fourteen characters from outer margin at foot of type page.

Contents: p. [1]: hf. tit. 'WORLD ENOUGH AND TIME'; on p. [2] '*Also by Robert Penn Warren*'; p. [3]: title page; p. [4]: '*This book is printed for | Eyre & Spottiswoode (Publishers) | Ltd., 15 Bedford Street, London, | W.C.2, by Butler & Tanner, | Ltd., Frome and London*'; p. [5]: dedication; p. [6]: blank; p. [7]: epigraph; p. [8]: blank; pp. 9–508: text.

Typography and Paper: text: 38 ll., 16.0 (16.3) × 10.5 cm.; Fournier Monotype 12-pt. Paper: white, wove, unwatermarked; sheets bulk 3.8 cm.

Binding: bluish green cloth. Front and back: blank. Spine, in blue: 'WORLD | ENOUGH | AND | TIME | ROBERT | PENN | WARREN | EYRE & | SPOTTISWOODE'. All edges trimmed and unstained; white endpapers.

Dust wrapper: similar to **A10.a1** with the following exceptions: front cover: omits 'A ROMANTIC NOVEL'. Spine: title in orange, and in yellow, '*Eyre & Spottiswoode*'. Back cover: omits subtitle. Front flap: about the novel and excerpts from reviews. Back flap: same format as front flap.

Copies: BL, Ctw, RPW, STW.

Notes: 1. Published 1951 at 15s. Printed by Butler & Tanner Ltd., Frome and London. Additional publication information is not available (ltr., Maria Lyras, Publicity Dept., Eyre Methuen Ltd., 6 June 1975). British Library date-stamp 20 Aug. 1951.

2. Ctw copy has a slip pasted on front endpaper, in red: 'NOT FOR SALE | Sample Complete Copy | [scratched out] Proof Copy | Manuscript'.

3. JAG copy is uncorrected page proofs in brown wrappers; front cover identical with title page.

A10.i1   second English edition, first impression, by offset (1973)

WORLD ENOUGH | AND TIME | [fancy rule] | *Robert Penn Warren* | Secker & Warburg | LONDON

Collation: demy folio 8° (trimmed: 21.5 × 13.7 cm.); *unsigned* [1–15^{16}

16⁴ 17¹⁶], 260 leaves; pp. [i–viii], [1–2] 3–511 [512]; numbering identical with **A10.a1**.

Contents: pp. [i–ii]: blank; p. [iii]: hf. tit. 'WORLD ENOUGH AND TIME'; on p. [iv] '*Books by Robert Penn Warren*'; p. [v]: title page; p. [vi]: 'First published in England 1951 by | Eyre & Spottiswoode Limited | This edition published in England 1973 by | Martin Secker & Warburg Limited | 14 Carlisle Street, London, W1V 6NN | Copyright, 1950, by Robert Penn Warren | SBN: 436 56314 2 | Printed in Great Britain by | Redwood Press Limited | Trowbridge, Wiltshire'; p. [vii]: dedication; p. [viii]: blank; p. [1]: hf. tit.; p. [2]: epigraph; pp. 3–[512]: text.

Typography and Paper: printed by offset lithography from **A10.a1**. Paper: white Mallex Litho Wove, 85 gsm, vol. 15, unwatermarked. Size at printing 88.8 × 112.8 cm. (2 × 32 page sections). (Ltr., N. Gardner, General Manager, Printing Div., Redwood Burn Ltd., 24 Feb. 1975.) Sheets bulk 3.6 cm.

Binding: red cloth. Front and back: blank. Spine, in gilt: 'World | Enough | and Time | [orn.] | *Robert* | *Penn Warren* | Secker & | Warburg'. All edges trimmed and unstained; white endpapers.

Dust wrapper, red background: front and back covers: '[in white] Robert | Penn Warren | [in yellowish gold] World | Enough | and Time | [in white] Re-issue | of his famous novel'. Spine: '[in white] Robert | Penn | Warren | [in yellowish gold] World | Enough | and | Time | [in white] SECKER & | WARBURG'. Front flap, on white in red: about the book. Back flap: about the author.

Copies: BL, JAG, LC, STW.

Note: published 7 Jan. 1974 at £3.75. Printed by Redwood Press Ltd., Trowbridge, Wiltshire. The publisher prefers not to disclose the number of copies printed (ltr., T. G. Rosenthal, Managing Director, Martin Secker & Warburg Ltd., 6 Feb. 1975). British Library date-stamp 14 Feb. 1974.

A10.j1   second English edition, first impression, by offset, paperback (1978)

WORLD ENOUGH | AND TIME | Robert Penn Warren | NEW ENGLISH LIBRARY/TIMES MIRROR

Collation: crown folio 8° (trimmed: 17.75 × 10.6 cm.); signed, [A]¹⁶

'W.E.T.—' B–H^{16} I^8 K–R^{16}, 264 leaves; pp. [i–viii], [1–3] 4–512 [513–520]; numbers, unadorned, centered at foot of type page.

Contents: p. [i]: hf. tit. 'WORLD ENOUGH AND TIME'; p. [ii]: blank; p. [iii]: title page; p. [iv]: 'First published in England 1951 | by Eyre and Spottiswoode | © 1950 by Robert Penn Warren | First NEL edition December 1978 | . . . '; p. [v]: hf. tit.; p. [vi]: blank; p. [vii]: dedication; p. [viii]: blank; p. [1]: hf. tit.; p. [2]: epigraph; pp. [3]–512: text; pp. [513], [515], [517], and [519]: publisher's advertisement; pp. [514], [516], [518], and [520]: blanks.

Typography and Paper: reprinted by photo-offset and reduced to 14.6 (14.95) × 9.0 cm.; 9/10½-pt. Paper: white, wove, unwatermarked; sheets bulk 3.0 cm.

Binding: paper. Front cover, on white: '[upper left corner in black, up] NEW ENGLISH LIBRARY | [publisher's device] | [centered, in green] WORLD ENOUGH | AND TIME | [illus. in color—man, woman in large hat, another man | slaves] | [in black] ROBERT | PENN | WARREN'. Spine: '[in black, publisher's device] | FICTION | [in green] WORLD | ENOUGH | AND | TIME | [illus. in color, woman in large hat] | [in black] ROBERT | PENN | WARREN | [vert., in black] 35182'. Back cover, on white in green and in black: about the book. Inside covers: white. All edges trimmed and unstained.

Copies: BL, JAG, RPW.

Note: published Dec. 1978 at £1.50 from Barnard's Inn, Holborn, London. Printed by William Collins Sons & Co. Ltd., Glasgow. "Unfortunately it is company policy not to divulge our print runs" (ltr., Dorothy Houghton, Managing Editor—Paperbacks, New English Library, 20 March 1975). British Library date-stamp 29 Nov. 1978.

A11   *Brother to Dragons: A Tale in Verse and Voices*

A11.a1   first American edition, first impression (1953)

BROTHER TO DRAGONS | *A Tale in Verse and Voices* | BY | *ROBERT PENN WARREN* | [publisher's device] *RANDOM HOUSE*

Collation: demy 8° (trimmed: 20.3 × 13.6 cm.); *unsigned* [1–7^{16} 8^{14}], 126 leaves; pp. [1–2], [i–viii] ix–xii [xiii–xiv], [1–4] 5–230 [231–234] [235–236]; numbers within reversed parentheses centered above type page in head margin, except on pp. ix, 5, and 217 where the numbers are unadorned and centered below the type page in the tail margin.

Contents: pp. [1–2]: blank; p. [i]: hf. tit. '*BROTHER TO DRAGONS*'; on p. [ii] '*Books by* ROBERT PENN WARREN'; p. [iii]: title page; p. [iv]: '*First Printing* | *Copyright, 1953, by Robert Penn Warren. All rights reserved under* | *International and Pan-American Copyright Conventions. Published* | *in New York by Random House, Inc., and simultaneously in* | *Toronto, Canada, by Random House of Canada, Limited.* | *Library of Congress Catalog Card Number: 53-5009* | *Designed by George Salter* | *Manufactured in the United States of America*'; p. [v]: '*To* CLEANTH *and* TINKUM BROOKS'; p. [vi]: blank; p. [vii]: '[7-l. epigraph] | HISTORY OF CHRISTIAN COUNTY, by W. H. Perrin | (Chicago and Louisville, 1884) | [1-l. epigraph] | Letter of Wovoka, the Messiah——Arapaho version. | FOURTEENTH ANNUAL REPORT OF THE BUREAU OF | ETHNOLOGY, Part 2 (Washington, 1893) | [7-l. epigraph] | *Lucretius:* DE RERUM NATURA, III | (*translated by* W. H. D. Rouse)'; p. [viii]: blank; pp. ix–xii: 'FOREWORD'; on p. xii below last line of text, a 5.0-cm. rule; p. [xiii]: in ital., author's note about the poem; p. [xiv]: blank; p. [1]: hf. tit.; on p. [2] 'THE SPEAKERS *in the order of appearance*'; p. [4]: blank; pp. 5–216: text; pp. 217–230: notes; on p. [231] '*About the AUTHOR*'; pp. [233–234]: blank; pp. [235–236]: blank.

Typography and Paper: text: 27 ll., 14.8 (15.5) × 9.6 cm.; Linotype Caledonia 11/16-pt.; speakers' names in small caps. throughout. Paper: white, laid, vertical chainlines (2.35 cm.), unwatermarked; sheets bulk 1.8 cm.

Binding: dark blue cloth. Front, in gilt: '*BROTHER TO DRAGONS*'. Spine, in navy blue: '[on red background] ROBERT | PENN | WARREN | [on gilt background] BROTHER | TO | DRAGONS | [on gray background, publisher's device]'. Back: blank. All edges trimmed with top edge stained dark blue. Endpapers: lining paper on front and back identical with paper described above; no free endpapers.

Dust wrapper: front cover, on cream background in black: 'BROTHER | TO | DRAGONS | [in orange, publisher's device] | [black rule] | [on orange in black] *A Tale in* VERSE *and* VOICES *by* | Robert Penn Warren | A RANDOM HOUSE BOOK'. Spine, same background colors: 'Brother | to | Dragons | [orn.] | ROBERT | PENN | WARREN || RANDOM | HOUSE | [publisher's device]'. Back cover, on cream background: '[in black] ROBERT PENN WARREN | [in orange, fancy rule] | [in black, brief biographical sketch]'. Front and back flaps, in orange and in black: about the book.

Copies: Ctb, Ctw, CtY (2), JAG, KyU, LC, LU (2), STW (3), TNJ, TxFTC.

Notes: 1. Published 21 Aug. 1953 in 4,975 copies at $3.50. Printed by Kingsport Press, Kingsport, TN. Subsequent impressions: 14 March 1958, 1,000; 26 Dec. 1963, 1,000; 24 Jan. 1967, 1,000; 2 April 1968, 1,000. (Ltr., Jim Wilcox, Random House, Inc., 31 July 1974.) LC copyright 30 July 1953 (A107785); two copies deposited 24 Aug. 1953.

2. Excerpts appeared in *KR*, 15 (Winter 1953), 1–103; *Poetry*, 82 (June 1953), 125–133; *PR*, 20 (July–Aug. 1953), 393–396; and in *Object and Image in Modern Art and Poetry: An Essay and an Exhibition at the Yale University Art Gallery, 30 April 1954 through 14 June 1954*, p. [xvi].

A11.a6   first American edition, sixth impression (n.d.)

Contents: p. [vi]: '*Sixth Printing*'; pp. [231–232]: about the author.

Binding: dark blue cloth. Front, in red: '*BROTHER TO DRAGONS*'. Spine, in red: 'ROBERT | PENN | WARREN | BROTHER | TO | DRAGONS | [publisher's device]'. Back: blank. All edges trimmed and unstained.

Dust wrapper: back cover bears number: '394-40312-6'.

Copies: Ctw, STW.

A11.b1   second American edition, first impression (1979)

Robert Penn Warren | [orn.] | BROTHER | TO | DRAGONS | [orn.] | *A Tale in Verse and Voices* | A NEW VERSION | [publisher's device] | *Random House* | *New York*

Collation: royal folio 8° (trimmed: 23.5 × 15.6 cm.); *unsigned* [1–5 ^{16}], 80 leaves; pp. [i–x] xi–xiv [xv–xvi], [1–4] 5–141 [142–144]; numbers at foot of type page, inset 5 ems from outer margin on v., from inner margin on r.

Contents: p. [i]: blank; on p. [ii] 'BOOKS BY ROBERT PENN WARREN'; p. [iii]: hf. tit. 'BROTHER TO DRAGONS'; p. [iv]: blank; p. [v]: title page; p. [vi]: copyright and LC Cataloging in Publication Data, '*First Edition*'; p. [vii]: dedication; p. [viii]: blank; p. [ix]: epigraphs; p. [x]: blank; pp. xi–xiv: 'FOREWORD' [revised]; p. [xv]: author's note; p. [xvi]: blank; p. [1]: hf. tit.; on p. [2] 'THE SPEAKERS *in the order of appearance*'; p. [4]: about the spacing between sections; pp. 5–132: text; pp. 133–141: notes; p. [142]: blank; p. [143]: biographical sketch; p. [144]: blank.

Typography and Paper: text: 40 ll., 18.4 (19.2) × 11.4 cm.; Linotype

Janson 11/13-pt. Paper: white, wove, unwatermarked; sheets bulk 1.1 cm.

Binding: black cloth, ¼-embossed calico grain. Front, in copper on cloth: '[orn.] | RPW | [orn.]'. Spine, in copper on black cloth, vert.: 'Robert Penn Warren BROTHER TO DRAGONS [publisher's device] *Random House*'. Back: blank. All edges trimmed and unstained; white endpapers.

Dust wrapper: front cover, on black: '[gray rule] | [in orange] BROTH-ER | TO | DRAGONS | [in green] A TALE IN VERSE | & [extends beneath the line] VOICES | [gray rule] | [in orange] A New Version | [in gray] ROBERT | PENN WARREN'. Spine, on black: '[vert., in orange] BROTHER TO DRAGONS [in gray] ROBERT PENN WARREN | [horiz., in green, publisher's device] | RANDOM | HOUSE'. Back cover, on black: photograph of RPW by Dennis O'Kain; and in white, about the author. Front flap: about the book. Back flap: excerpts from reviews of *BD* (1953); jacket design by Mark Huie.

Copies: CoCA, Ctb, Ctw, JAG, RPW, STW.

Notes: 1. Published Sept. 1979 in 5,000 copies at $8.95. Printed by R. R. Donnelley & Sons, Co. (Ltr., Albert Erskine, Random House, Inc., 27 Nov. 1979.)

2. JAG collection also contains "uncorrected proofs," in red wrappers (20.9 × 13.6 cm.); front cover identical with title page but marked 'UNCORRECTED PROOFS'.

A11.c1   first English edition, first impression, by offset (1954)

BROTHER TO DRAGONS | *A Tale in Verse and Voices* | BY | *ROBERT PENN WARREN* | *EYRE & SPOTTISWOODE*

Collation: demy 8° (trimmed: 20.0 × 13.7 cm.); signed, [A]⁴ B–Q⁸, 124 leaves; pp. [i–viii] ix–xii [xiii–xiv], [1–4] 5–230 [231–234]; numbers identical with **A11.a1**.

Contents: p. [i]: hf. tit. '*BROTHER TO DRAGONS*'; on p. [ii] 'Books by ROBERT PENN WARREN'; p. [iii]: title page; p. [iv]: '[copyright] | *This book is printed in Great Britain for Eyre & Spottiswoode* | *(Publishers) Ltd.*, *15 Bedford Street, London, W.C.2, by Lowe* | *& Brydone (Printers) Limited, London, N.W. 10.*'; p. [v]: dedication; p. [vi]: blank; p. [vii]: epigraphs; p. [viii]: blank; pp. ix–xii: foreword; p. [xiii]: author's note; p. [xiv]: blank; p. [1]: hf. tit.; pp. [2–3]: dramatis personae; p. [4]: blank;

pp. 5–216: text; pp. 217–230: notes; pp. [231–232]: about the author; pp. [233–234]: blank.

Typography and Paper: identical with **A11.a1**; sheets bulk 2.3 cm.

Binding: dark blue cloth. Front and back: blank. Spine, on red in dark blue: 'BROTHER | TO | DRAGONS | · | ROBERT | PENN | WARREN | [on dark blue in red] E & S'. All edges trimmed with top edge stained red; white endpapers.

   Dust wrapper: front cover identical with **A11.a1** except no publisher's device and name. Spine: 'Brother | to | Dragons | ROBERT | PENN | WARREN || EYRE & | SPOTTISWOODE'. Back cover: advertisement for *WET*. Front and back flaps: about the book and a brief biographical sketch about RPW.

Copies: BL, Ctw, JAG, KyU.

Notes: 1. Published 1954. Printed by Lowe & Brydone Ltd. Additional publication information is not available (ltr., Maria Lyras, Publicity Dept., Eyre Methuen Ltd., 6 June 1975). British Library date-stamp 26 April 1954.

   2. The "edition" offered in 1976 by Secker & Warburg was **A11.a6**.

A12   *Band of Angels*

A12.a1   first American edition, first impression (1955)

[p. (iv): sans serif, in black] ROBERT | PENN | WARREN | [publisher's device in burnt orange] [p. (v): sans serif, in burnt orange] BAND | OF | ANGELS | RANDOM HOUSE | NEW YORK

Collation: demy 8° (trimmed: 20.85 × 13.75 cm.); *unsigned* [1–12^{16}], 192 leaves; pp. [i–viii], [1–3] 4–375 [376], except the first page of each chapter is unnumbered: [3], [26], [57], [84], [111], [134], [169], [204], [254], [299], and [330]; numbers centered in the head margins.

Contents: p. [i]: hf. tit. 'BAND OF ANGELS'; p. [ii]: blank; on p. [iii] 'BOOKS BY ROBERT PENN WARREN'; pp. [iv–v]: title page; p. [vi]: 'FIRST PRINTING | *Copyright, 1955, by Robert Penn Warren. All rights reserved under International | and Pan-American Copyright Conventions. Published in New York by Random | House, Inc., and simultaneously in Toronto, Canada, by Random House of | Canada, Limited.* Library of Congress Catalog Card Number: 55-5814 | Manufactured in the United States of America | by H. Wolff, New York'; p. [vii]: '*To Elea-*

nor'; p. [viii]: blank; p. [1]: hf. tit.; p. [2]: epigraph by A. E. Housman; pp. [3]–375: text; p. [376]: about the author.

Typography and Paper: text: 39 ll., 16.3 (17.65) × 10.5 cm.; 40 ll., 16.95 (17.65) × 10.5 cm.; Linotype Caledonia 10/12-pt. Paper: white, wove, unwatermarked; sheets bulk 2.9 cm.

Binding: white embossed calico grain cloth. Front, in gilt: 'R P W'. Spine: '[on black rectangle, in gilt] BAND | OF | ANGELS | [on white rectangle, in gold] ROBERT | PENN | WARREN | [gold orn. similar to orns. on chapter pages] | [in gold, publisher's device] | [in black] RANDOM | HOUSE'. Back: blank. All edges trimmed with top edge stained yellow; brown endpapers.

Dust wrapper: front cover, over chocolate and light brown stripes that extend from the bottom halfway up the cover: '[in white] A NOVEL BY | [in green] Robert | Penn | Warren | [in white] *author of "All the King's Men" and "World Enough and Time"* | [in yellow] BAND OF | ANGELS'. Spine: '[in green] Robert | Penn | Warren | [in yellow] BAND OF | ANGELS | [in green and white, publisher's device] | [in white] *Random House*'. Back cover, on white: photograph of RPW by Sylvia Salmi and same biographical sketch as on p. [376]. Front flap: review of novel. Back flap: review continued and publisher's advertisement.

Copies: Ctb (2), Ctw, CtY (2), JAG (3), KyU, LC, LU, STW, TNJ.

Notes: 1. Published 22 Aug. 1955 in 25,000 copies at $3.95. Printed 20 June 1955 by American Book-Stratford Press, Inc. Subsequent impressions: 27 Sept. 1955, 10,000; 21 Dec. 1955, 3,500; and 7 Nov. 1969, 1,500. (Ltr., Jim Wilcox, Random House, Inc., 31 July 1974.) LC copyright 1 Aug. 1955 (A204686); two copies deposited 12 Oct. 1955.

    2. Excerpt: "Destiny of Hamish Bond," *SR*, 63 (Summer 1955), 349–381.

    3. LU copy is inscribed 'To Herman [*sic*] Deutsch | with regards & gratitude | Red Warren | N.O. | November 9, 1955 || '.

A12.b1   second American edition, book-club edition (1955)

Title Page: identical with **A12.a1**.

Collation: demy 8° (trimmed/rough trimmed: 20.9 × 13.7 cm.); *unsigned* [1–11¹² 12⁴ 13–14¹²], 160 leaves; pp. [i–vi], [1–2] 3–314; numbers centered at foot of type page.

Contents: p. [i]: hf. tit. 'BAND OF ANGELS'; pp. [ii–iii]: title pages; p. [iv]: copyright; p. [v]: dedication; p. [vi]: blank; p. [1]: hf. tit.; p. [2]: blank; pp. 3–313: text; p. 314: about the author.

Typography and Paper: text: 45 ll., 17.25 (17.8) × 10.3 cm.; Linotype Electra 10/11-pt. Paper: white, wove, unwatermarked; sheets bulk 1.8 cm.

Binding: beige calico-texture cloth, not embossed. Front and back: blank. Spine: '[horiz., in black] ROBERT | PENN | WARREN | [vert., on black rectangle, in gilt] BAND OF ANGELS | [horiz., in black] RANDOM | HOUSE'. Top and bottom edges trimmed, fore edge rough trimmed with top edge stained red; white endpapers.

  Dust wrapper: identical with **A12.a1**, but on coarser paper. Front flap, lower right corner bears imprint in brown: 'BOOK CLUB | EDITION'; and back flap does not include publisher's address.

Copies: CoCA, CtY, JAG, STW.

Note: a Literary Guild selection for Sept. 1955. Publication and printing data, however, are not available (ltr., Barbara Ann Bowden, Literary Guild of America, Inc., 29 April 1975).

A12.c1   third American edition, Best-in-Books edition (1956)

[p. (4): in black] *A Complete Novel* | [in red, figures of man with whip and woman in red] | [in black, figures of four men's heads facing inner margin] [p. (5): in black] by ROBERT PENN WARREN | [in red] BAND OF | ANGELS | [in black] NELSON DOUBLEDAY, INC. | *Garden City* | *New York* | [two figures of men in black and two in red facing inner margin]

Collation: demy 8° (trimmed/rough trimmed: 20.9 × 13.8 cm.); *unsigned* [1–2²⁴ 3–5¹² 6⁴ 7²⁴ 8²⁰ 9²⁴ 10²⁰ (end *BA*) 11–12⁸ 13²⁰ 14¹² 15²⁰ 16¹⁶ 17²⁰], 280 leaves; pp. [1–7] 8–27 [28] 29–55 [56] 57–80 [81] 82–105 [106] 107–126 [127] 128–159 [160] 161–191 [192] 193–238 [239] 240–280 [281] 282–309 [310] 311–352 (end *BA*) [π16] [353–355] 356–363 [364] 365–371 [372] 373–385 [386] 387–431 [432] 433–463 [464–467] 468–476 [477] 478–483 [484] 485–501 [502] 503–510 [511–513] 514–516 [517] 518–526 [527] 528–532 [533] 534–540 [541] 542–544; numbers in headline against outer margin of type page.

Contents: p. [1]: table of contents; p. [2]: copyright; p. [3]: 'BAND OF ANGELS'; pp. [4–5]: title pages; p. [6]: editor's note; pp. [7]–352: text; pp. [π16]: 'HAZEL | RIDES AGAIN'; pp. [353]–463: 'THE

FIVE | FATHERS | OF PEPI'; p. [464]: blank; pp. [465]–510: 'ANI-MALS | *And Other People*'; pp. [511]–544: 'John Goffe's | Legacy'.

Typography and Paper: text: 40 ll., 16.8 (17.4) × 10.8 cm.; Linotype Electra 11/12-pt. RT: v. and r., 'BAND OF ANGELS'. Paper: white, wove, unwatermarked; sheets bulk 2.2 cm. (*BA*); 3.5 cm. total.

Binding: ¼ red cloth; beige cloth. Front and back: blank. Spine, in gilt on black background: '[three rules on red] | BAND OF | ANGELS | Robert Penn | Warren | [three rules on red] | [orn.] | . . . | [bottom] Nelson Doubleday, Inc.'

   Dust wrapper: front cover: '[across top on red in white] BEST · IN · BOOKS | [on black background in white] 2 BOOKS COMPLETE | [on beige in red] BAND OF ANGELS | [in black] Robert Penn Warren [toward outer edge, illus. of *BA* in dust wrapper (**A12.a1**)]' . . . .

Copies: Ctw, JAG.

Note: publication data arc not available (ltr., Barbara Ann Bowden, Literary Guild of America, Inc. [for Doubleday & Co.], 29 April 1975).

A12.d1   fourth American edition, first impression, paperback (1956)

|| BAND | OF | ANGELS || Robert Penn Warren | [publisher's device] | A SIGNET BOOK | Published by The New American Library

Collation: crown folio 8° (trimmed: 17.9 × 10.6 cm.); *unsigned* 160 ind. leaves; pp. [1–4] 5–316 [317–320]; numbers centered at foot of type page.

Contents: p. [1]: about the novel; p. [2]: publisher's advertisement; p. [3]: title page; p. [4]: copyright and dedication; p. 5: begins with epigraph; pp. 5–316: text; pp. [317–320]: publisher's advertisement.

Typography and Paper: text: 51 ll., 16.0 (16.3) × 8.8 cm.; Times New Roman 9-pt. Paper: white, wove, unwatermarked; sheets bulk 1.8 cm.

Binding: paper. Front cover, gilt border: '[upper half has pink background with white border; upper left corner, in black] D 1330 | [on black in pink] SIGNET | [on pink in black] 50¢ | [on black in pink] DOUBLE | [on pink in black] VOLUME | [across remaining top] THE GREAT BESTSELLER | About a Kentucky Belle Sold into | Slavery During the Civil War | [in black shadowed in white] Band of Angels | [in white] ROBERT PENN WARREN | Pulitzer Prize-

Winning Author | [figure of woman in front of multiscene illus.] | [bottom quarter again pink bordered by white, in black] A SIGNET BOOK | Complete and Unabridged'. Spine, on gilt in black: '[horiz.] D | 1330 | [vert.] BAND OF ANGELS ROBERT PENN WARREN [horiz.—emblem of Signet Double Volume Books]'. Back cover, gilt and white borders around pink background, in black: about the novel and about the author with RPW's photograph in lower left corner. Inside covers: white. All edges trimmed and stained red.

Copies: JAG, STW.

Note: published Aug. 1956 at 50¢. Additional publication information is not available.

A12.d3   fourth American edition, third impression, paperback (1961)

[outlined, in sans serif] BAND | OF | ANGELS || [with serifs] ROBERT PENN WARREN | [publisher's device] A SIGNET BOOK | Published by The New American Library

Collation: crown folio 8° (trimmed: 17.9 × 10.6 cm.); *unsigned* 176 ind. leaves; pp. [1–5] 6–349 [350–352]; numbers centered at foot of type page.

Contents: p. [1]: about the novel; p. [2]: publisher's advertisement; p. [3]: title page; p. [4]: copyright and dedication; p. [5]: begins with epigraph; pp. [5]–349: text; pp. [350–352]: publisher's advertisement.

Typograph and Paper: text: 46 ll., 15.7 (16.1) × 8.8 cm.; Times New Roman 9/10-pt. Paper: white, wove, unwatermarked; sheets bulk 1.7 cm.

Binding: paper. Front cover, on black: upper left corner, in blue: 'T 1872 | [publisher's device with black 75¢ on white oval inside]'; from inner margin, in white, 'BAND | OF | ANGELS', with orns.; starting in upper right corner: '[in orange shaded in yellow] ROBERT | PENN | WARREN | author of | THE CAVE | [in white] The Pulitzer Prize | winner's great bestseller | about a Kentucky belle | sold into slavery | during the Civil War. | [illus. in color beneath with woman in foreground larger and extending beyond the boundary of the illus.; beneath the illus., in orange shaded in yellow] A SIGNET BOOK · Complete and Unabridged'. Spine, on black: '[horiz., in white] T | 1872 | [vert., in yellow] BAND OF ANGELS [horiz., in white] ROBERT PENN WARREN'. Back cover, on black: upper left corner, illus.; upper right corner, in yellow: '"THE | LUSH SPLEN-

DOR | OF | GONE WITH | THE WIND"'; in white, about the book; in yellow, excerpts from reviews; in white, about the author with photograph toward inner margin on orange rectangle; in yellow: 'Published by the NEW AMERICAN LIBRARY | Cover Printed in U.S.A.' Inside covers: white. All edges trimmed and stained red.

Copies: JAG.

Note: published Feb. 1961 as Signet T1872 at 75¢. Additional publication information is not available.

A12.d5 fourth American edition, fifth impression, by offset, paperback (n.d.)

Contents: on p. [4] '*FIFTH PRINTING*' but no date.

Binding: paper. Front cover, on white: '[in gray] T 2826 | A SIGNET BOOK | [publisher's device] COMPLETE AND UNABRIDGED | [in maroon, shaded in pink] ROBERT | PENN | WARREN | [black rule] | [in pink] BAND OF | ANGELS | [black rule] | [illus. in color as described in **A12.d3**] | [in black] The Pulitzer Prize winner's | great bestseller about a | Kentucky belle sold into | slavery during the Civil War.' Spine, on white: publisher's device, white on black; '[horiz., in black] T | 2826 | [vert., in pink] BAND OF ANGELS [in black] ROBERT PENN WARREN'. Back cover: top half, on white in pink and in black—about the book; bottom half, on red and black—publisher's advertisement. Inside covers: white. All edges trimmed and stained red.

Copies: JAG.

Note: no date indicated and publication information is not available.

A12.d7 fourth American edition, seventh impression, by offset, paperback (n.d.)

Contents: on p. [4] '*SEVENTH PRINTING*' but no date.

Binding: paper. Front cover on greenish yellow: '[in black] ROBERT PENN WARREN | A GREAT PULITZER PRIZE AUTHOR'S FAMED BESTSELLER | ——THE UNFORGETTABLE STORY OF A KENTUCKY BELLE SOLD | INTO SLAVERY DURING THE CIVIL WAR. | BAND OF | ANGELS'; in upper right-hand corner, vert., in gray: '[publisher's device] A SIGNET NOVEL · Y5316 · $1.25'; bottom two-thirds of page, illus.

of woman in large room with others looking at her. Spine, on white in black: '[horiz.; publisher's device] | SIGNET | Y | 5316 | [vert.] Band of Angels Robert Penn Warren 451-Y5316-125'. Back cover, on white in black: excerpts from book reviews and publisher's advertisement. Inside covers: white. All edges trimmed and unstained.

Copies: JAG.

Note: no date indicated and publication information is not available.

A12.d9   fourth American edition, ninth impression, by offset, paper-back (1979)

Contents: on p. [4] '9 10 11 12 13 14 15 16 17'.

Binding: paper. Front cover on reddish yellow in black: 'SIGNET · 451 · E7398 · $1.75 [publisher's device] | A GREAT PULITZER PRIZE-|WINNING AUTHOR'S TORRID NOVEL | OF PLAN-TATION LIFE—— | AND LUST AND LOVE IN | THE OLD SOUTH. | ROBERT PENN | WARREN | THE AUTHOR OF A PLACE TO COME TO | BAND | OF ANGELS | [illus. in color of man in foreground holding a woman, crowd of slaves and antebellum house in background]'. Spine, on reddish yellow in black: '[horiz.; publisher's device] | SIGNET | E | 7398 | [vert.] BAND OF AN-GELS ROBERT PENN WARREN 0-451-07398-3175 | FICTION'. Back cover on white, in black: about the novel. Inside covers: white. All edges trimmed and stained yellow.

Copies: JAG.

A12.e1   first English edition, first impression (1956)

ROBERT PENN WARREN | [fancy rule] | BAND OF ANGELS | 1956 | EYRE & SPOTTISWOODE | LONDON

Collation: large crown 8° (trimmed: 20.0 × 13.7 cm.); signed, [A]⁴ (each sig. preceded by 'B.A.—') A*¹² B–M⁴ B*–M*¹² N² N*⁴, 198 leaves; pp. [1–8] 9–394 [395–396]; numbers centered at foot of type page.

Contents: p. [1]: synopsis; on p. [2] '*Also by Robert Penn Warren*'; p. [3]: title page; p. [4]: '*This book is printed in Great Britain for* | *Eyre & Spot-tiswoode (Publishers)* | *Ltd., 15 Bedford Street, London* | *W. C. 2, by Butler & Tanner,* | *Ltd., Frome and London*'; p. [5]: dedication; p. [6]: blank; p. [7]: hf. tit. 'BAND OF ANGELS'; p. [8]: blank; pp. 9–394: text; pp. [395–396]: blank.

Typography and Paper: text: 37 ll., 15.4 (15.8) × 10.0 cm.; Fournier 10/12-pt. Paper: white, wove, unwatermarked; sheets bulk 2.5 cm.

Binding: blue cloth. Front and back: blank. Spine, in gilt: 'BAND | OF | ANGELS | ROBERT | PENN | WARREN | EYRE & | SPOT-TISWOODE'. All edges trimmed and unstained.

Dust wrapper: front cover: '[illus. of three faces on green] | [on darker green in red] BAND OF | ANGELS | [in yellow] ROBERT PENN | WARREN | [illus. of steamboat]'. Spine, on green: '[in white] BAND | OF | ANGELS | [in yellow] ROBERT | PENN | WARREN | [illus. of flag, rifle, bonds, leaves] | [in yellow] *EYRE & | SPOTTISWOODE*'. Back cover, on white: publisher's advertisement. Front and back flaps: about the book.

Copies: BL, Ctw, IU, JAG, KyU.

Note: published in two impressions in 1956 at 18s. Printed by Butler & Tanner, Ltd. Number of copies printed is not available (ltr., Maria Lyras, Publicity Dept., Eyre Methuen Ltd., 6 June 1975). British Library date-stamp 5 June 1956.

A12.f1   second English edition, first impression, by offset (1973)

BAND OF ANGELS | [fancy rule] | *Robert Penn Warren* | Secker & Warburg | LONDON

Collation: demy folio 8° (trimmed: 21.5 × 13.6 cm.); *unsigned* [1–12 ^{16}], 192 leaves; pp. [i–vi], [1–3] 4–375 [376–378], except the first page of each chapter is unnumbered as listed in **A12.a1**.

Contents: pp. [i–ii]: blank; p. [iii]: hf. tit. 'BAND OF ANGELS'; p. [iv]: '*Books by Robert Penn Warren* | [list ends with *MMGG*]'; p. [v]: title page; p. [vi]: 'First published in England 1956 by | Eyre & Spottiswoode Limited | This edition published in England 1973 by | Martin Secker & Warburg Limited | 14 Carlisle Street, London W1V 6NN | Copyright, 1955, by Robert Penn Warren | SBN: 436 56311 8 | Printed in Great Britain by | Redwood Press Limited | Trowbridge, Wiltshire'; p. [1]: dedication; p. [2]: epigraph; pp. [3]–375: text; p. [376]: about the author; pp. [377–378]: blank.

Typography and Paper: printed by offset lithography from **A12.a1**. Paper: white Mallex Litho wove, 85 gsm, vol. 15, unwatermarked. Size at printing 88.8 × 112.8 cm. (2 × 32 page sections). (Ltr., N. Gardner, General Manager, Printing Div., Redwood Burn Ltd., 24 Feb. 1975.) Sheets bulk 2.3 cm.

Binding: reddish brown cloth. Front and back: blank. Spine, in gilt: 'Band of | Angels | [orn.] | *Robert* | *Penn Warren* | Secker & | Warburg'. All edges trimmed and unstained; white endpapers.

Dust wrapper: front and back covers, green background: '[in orange] Robert | Penn Warren | [in white] Band | of | Angels | [in orange] Re-issue | of his famous novel'. Spine: '[in orange] Robert | Penn | Warren | [in white] Band | of | Angels | SECKER & | WARBURG'. Front flap, in green on white: about the book. Back flap: about the author.

Copies: BL, Ctw, JAG, RPW, STW.

Note: published 9 July 1973 in one impression at £2.50. Printed by Redwood Press Ltd. The publisher prefers not to disclose the number of copies printed (ltr., T. G. Rosenthal, Managing Director, Martin Secker & Warburg Ltd., 6 Feb. 1975). British Library date-stamp 25 July 1973.

A12.g1   third English edition, first impression, paperback (1975)

Band of Angels | ROBERT PENN WARREN | NEW ENGLISH LIBRARY || TIMES MIRROR

Collation: crown folio 8° (trimmed: 17.9 × 10.5 cm.); signed, $[1-2]^8$ $3-20^8[21-22]^8$, 176 leaves; pp. [1–6] 7–352; numbers centered at foot of type page.

Contents: p. [1]: hf. tit. 'BAND OF ANGELS | [about the author]'; p. [2]: publisher's advertisement; p. [3]: title page; p. [4]: '[copyright] | FIRST NEL PAPERBACK EDITION AUGUST 1975 | [condition of sale] | [about NEL books]'; p. [5]: dedication; p. [6]: epigraph; pp. 7–352: text; on p. 352 'THE END'.

Typography and Paper: text: 43 ll., 15.1 (15.5) × 8.6 cm.; Times New Roman 10-pt. Paper: white, wove, unwatermarked; sheets bulk 2.4 cm.

Binding: paper. Front cover, on white: '[in grayish green] NEW EN-GLISH LIBRARY [publisher's device] | [in black] ROBERT | PENN WARREN | Band of Angels | By the author of | All the King's Men | [illus. in color with woman in foreground holding parasol, of slaves and others before a house with large tree behind it]'. Spine, on white: '[horiz.; publisher's device] | FICTION | [vert.] ROBERT PENN WARREN | Band of Angels | [horiz., illus. continues from front] | 019225'. Back cover on off-white, in black: about the book with illus.

continuing from front, at bottom. Inside covers: white. All edges trimmed and unstained.

Note: RPW copy has two 14⁸ gatherings (pp. 209–224) bound in.

Copies: Ctw, RPW.

Note: published Aug. 1975 at 6op. Additional publication information is not available (ltr., Dorothy Houghton, Managing Editor—Paperbacks, New English Library, 20 March 1975). Not located in British Library (ltr., Dr. Christine Bernstein, 24 Oct. 1979).

A13 *Segregation: The Inner Conflict in the South*

A13.a1 first American edition, first impression (1956)

[p. (iv): publisher's device] RANDOM HOUSE | NEW YORK | [black vert. stripe from top to bottom on inner margin] [p. (v)] SEGREGATION | THE INNER CONFLICT IN THE SOUTH | ROBERT PENN WARREN

Collation: demy 8° (trimmed: 20.25 × 13.5 cm.); *unsigned* [1–5⁸], 40 leaves; pp. [i–x], [1–2] 3–66 [67–70]. On r. numbers appear in the corner formed by the tail and inner margins; on v., in the corner formed by the tail and outer margins.

Contents: p. [i]: hf. tit. 'SEGREGATION'; p. [ii]: blank; on p. [iii] 'BOOKS BY ROBERT PENN WARREN'; pp. [iv–v]: title pages; p. [vi]: 'FIRST PRINTING | *Copyright, 1956, by Robert Penn Warren* | *All rights reserved* | *under International and Pan-American Copyright Conventions.* | *Published in New York by Random House, Inc., and* | *simultaneously in Toronto, Canada, by Random House of Canada, Limited.* | *Library of Congress Catalog Card Number: 56-11268* | *Manufactured in the United States of America* | *by H. Wolff, New York* | DESIGN: *Marshall Lee*'; p. [vii]: '*to Jack and Eunice*'; p. [viii]: blank; p. [ix]: author's note; p. [x]: blank; p. [1]: hf. tit.; p. [2]: blank; on p. 3 black vert. stripe from top to bottom on inner margin, conjugate leaf to pp. [iii–iv], text with orn. between spaced sections; p. [67]: blank; p. [68]: publisher's device and about the author; pp. [69–70]: blank.

Typography and Paper: text: 32 ll., 15.8 (16.5) × 9.4 cm.; 33 ll., 16.0 (16.8) × 9.4 cm.; Linotype Caledonia 12/14-pt. Paper: white, wove, unwatermarked; sheets bulk 0.8 cm.

Binding: black cloth with upper one-third in antiqued paper. Front:

'[on paper in light brown] SEGREGATION | [on cloth, lower right corner, in gray, publisher's device]'. Spine, vert.: '[on paper in light brown] SEGREGATION [on cloth in white] ROBERT PENN WARREN [on cloth in gray] RANDOM HOUSE'. Back: blank. All edges trimmed with top edge stained gray; gray endpapers.

Dust wrapper: front cover, on black, ltrs. in white: 'Segregation | THE INNER CONFLICT IN THE SOUTH | [brown rule] | BY ROBERT PENN WARREN | AUTHOR OF "ALL THE KING'S MEN" AND "BAND OF ANGELS" | [publisher's device, in brown] A Random House Book'. Spine, on black, ltrs. in white: '[vert.] SEG-REGATION [brown rule continued from front cover] ROBERT PENN WARREN [horiz., in brown, publisher's device] | RANDOM | HOUSE'. Back cover, on white: '[photograph of RPW] | *Sylvia Salmi* | [biographical sketch] | (*continued on back flap*)'. Front flap: about the book. Back flap: about the author cont'd.

Copies: CtY (2), JAG, KyU, LC, LU, STW, TNJ, TxFTC.

Notes: 1. Published 31 Aug. 1956 in two impressions of 4,500 (25 July 1956) and 1,000 (27 Aug. 1956) at $1.95. Printed by American Book-Stratford Press, Inc. Subsequent impressions: 21 Sept. 1956, 2,500; 22 Oct. 1956, 2,500; 26 Dec. 1956, 2,000; 5 June 1959, 1,000; 30 Dec. 1960, 1,000; 29 Jan. 1963, 1,200; 24 July 1964, 1,500; 13 Nov. 1968, 1,500. (Ltr., Jim Wilcox, Random House, Inc., 31 July 1974.) LC copyright 15 Aug. 1956 (A253644); two copies deposited 2 Oct. 1956.

2. Excerpt: "Divided South Searches Its Soul," *Life*, 9 July 1956, pp. 98–99, 101–102, 105–106, 108, 111–112, and 114.

3. KyU has background material—newspaper clippings, pamphlets, handouts, and news reports—on the segregation issue.

A13.b1 second American edition, first impression, paperback (1957)

[first word in sans serif] SEGREGATION | THE INNER CON-FLICT IN THE SOUTH | ROBERT PENN WARREN | [publisher's device] | PUBLISHED BY RANDOM HOUSE | *New York*

Collation: post folio 8° (trimmed: 18.3 × 11.1 cm.); *unsigned* [1–16⁴], 64 leaves; pp. [i–viii], [1–2] 3–115 [116–120]. Page numbers are located in the corner formed by the tail and outer margins.

Contents: p. [i]: excerpts from reviews; p. [ii]: blank; p. [iii]: title page; p. [iv]: copyright; p. [v]: dedication; p. [vi]: blank; p. [vii]: author's note; p. [viii]: blank; p. [1]: hf. tit. 'SEGREGATION'; p. [2]: blank;

pp. 3–115: text; p. [116]: blank; pp. [117–118]: about the note and publisher's device; p. [119]: publisher's advertisement; p. [120]: blank.

Typography and Paper: text: 23 ll., 12.1 (13.7) × 8.0 cm.; Linotype Caledonia 12/15-pt. RT: v., 'SEGREGATION'; r., '*The inner conflict in the South*'. Paper: white, wove, unwatermarked; sheets bulk 1.4 cm.

Binding: paper, white background. Front: '[upper right corner, in black] 95¢ | [in purple] Segregation | [in black] THE INNER CONFLICT IN THE SOUTH | Robert Penn Warren | Author of ALL THE KING'S MEN and BAND OF ANGELS | [framed in purple rectangle, in black, quotation from *J. C. Furnas*] | [framed in second purple rectangle, in black, quotation from *Dallas Times-Herald*] | [in black] A MODERN LIBRARY PAPERBACK'. Spine: '[vert., in purple] Segregation [in black] Robert Penn Warren | [horiz., in black, publisher's device] | P30'. Back cover: '[in white on purple, publisher's device] [in black toward the spine] Modern Library | [in purple] PAPERBACKS | [in black, list of selections] | [in purple, publisher's address]'. Inside covers: white. All edges trimmed and unstained.

Copies: AAP, FMU, JAG, MiU, NcU.

Note: published in 1957 at 95¢. Manufactured by H. Wolff, New York. Distributed in Canada by Random House of Canada Limited. Additional publication information is not available.

A13.b2   second American edition, by offset, paperback (n.d.)

SEGREGATION | THE INNER CONFLICT IN THE SOUTH | ROBERT PENN WARREN | [publisher's device] | VINTAGE BOOKS | A DIVISION OF RANDOM HOUSE | *New York*

Collation: in 64 leaves, pagination identical with **A13.b1**.

Contents: p. [i]: 'SEGREGATION | BY ROBERT PENN WARREN'; p. [117]: publisher's device omitted in heading; pp. [119–120]: publisher's advertisement.

Paper: sheets bulk 0.9 cm.

Binding: paper, white background. Front cover: '[irregular letters in bluish green] SEGREGATION | [in brown] THE INNER CONFLICT | IN THE SOUTH | [in bluish green, between three figures of people on spine side and one figure on outer edge side] ROBERT PENN | WARREN | [in brown] AUTHOR OF | ALL THE KING'S

| MEN | AND | BAND OF | ANGELS | [in white against black, lower left corner—publisher's device] A VINTAGE BOOK | V-145 $1.45'. Spine: '[irregular letters, vert., on white in bluish green] SEGREGATION [on black in white] ROBERT PENN WARREN | [horiz., publisher's device] | VINTAGE | V-145]. Back cover: '[irregular letters on white in bluish green] SEGREGATION | ROBERT PENN | WARREN | [in black and white, men's faces in illus.] | on black in white, excerpts from reviews] | A VINTAGE BOOK COVER DESIGN BY PETER MAX'. Inside covers: white. All edges trimmed and unstained.

Copies: Ctw, JAG, STW (3).

Note: no date indicated and publication information is not available.

A13.c1 first English edition, first impression (1957)

[p. (2)] EYRE & SPOTTISWOODE | LONDON 1957 | [black vert. stripe from top to bottom on inner margin] [p. (3)] SEGREGATION | THE INNER CONFLICT IN THE SOUTH | ROBERT PENN WARREN

Collation: crown folio 8° (trimmed: 18.4 × 12.3 cm.); signed, [A]–F^8, 48 leaves; pp. [i–iv], [1–10] 11–86 [87] 88 [89–92]; numbers located in corner formed by tail and outer margins.

Contents: pp. [i–ii]: blank; p. [iii]: hf. tit. 'SEGREGATION'; p. [iv]: blank; on p. [1] 'BOOKS BY ROBERT PENN WARREN'; pp. [2–3]: title pages; p. [4]: copyright and '*This book, first published in 1957, is printed in Great | Britain for Eyre & Spottiswoode (Publishers) Ltd.,* | 15 *Bedford Street, London, W. C. 2., by C. Tinling & | Co. Ltd., Liverpool, London and Prescot*'; p. [5]: dedication; p. [6]: blank; p. [7]: author's note; p. [8]: blank; p. [9]: hf. tit.; p. [10]: blank; pp. 11–86: text; p. [87]: blank; p. 88: about the author; pp. [89–92]: blank.

Typography and Paper: text: 29 ll., 14.2 (14.8) × 8.8 cm.; Linotype Caledonia 12/14-pt. Paper: white, wove, unwatermarked; sheets bulk 0.8 cm.

Binding: black cloth with ¼ white cloth. Front and back: blank. Spine, on white in black: '[vert.] SEGREGATION PENN WARREN | [horiz., fancy ltrs. in oval] E & S'. All edges trimmed and unstained; white endpapers.

Dust wrapper: front cover, on white in black: 'SEGREGATION | [on black in white] ROBERT | PENN WARREN | author of ALL

THE KING'S MEN and BAND OF ANGELS'. Spine: '[vert., on white in black] SEGREGATION [on black in white] PENN WARREN | [horiz., fancy ltrs. in oval] E & S'. Back cover on white in black: about the book. Front flap: refers reader to back of jacket. Back flap: other works by RPW and excerpts from reviews.

Copies: BL, Ctw, JAG, STW.

Note: published 10 Jan. 1957 at 9s.6d. Printed by C. Tinling & Co. Ltd. Additional publication information is not available (ltr., Maria Lyras, Publicity Dept., Eyre Methuen Ltd., 6 June 1975). British Library date-stamp 3 Jan. 1957.

A14 *To a Little Girl, One Year Old, in a Ruined Fortress*

A14.a1 private limited edition (1956)

[p. (2)] *a poem in five parts by* ROBERT PENN WARREN [p. (3)] TO A LITTLE GIRL, ONE YEAR OLD, IN A RUINED FORTRESS

Colophon, p. [36]: '*This book was designed, illustrated, and printed | by Jane Doggett in the Department of Graphic Arts, | School of Design, Yale University.*'

Collation: ob imperial 12° (trimmed: 17.9 × 18.8 cm.); *unsigned* [1–3⁶], 18 leaves; pp. [1–36]; unnumbered.

Contents: p. [1]: blank; pp. [2–3]: title pages; p. [4]: '*Copyright 1956, by Robert Penn Warren. | Printed in the School of Design, Yale University. | These poems appeared in "The Partisan Review" Spring 1955.*'; p. [5]: illus.; p. [6]: blank; p. [7]: '*for Rosanna*'; p. [8]: blank; pp. [9–33]: text; pp. [14], [17], [26], [29], and [34–35]: blank; p. [36]: colophon.

Typography and Paper: text: 25 ll., 13.4 (14.1) × 11.6 cm.; Monotype Bell 9-pt. Paper: white, wove, unwatermarked; sheets bulk 0.25 cm.

Illustrations: appear to be woodcuts, bluish green and white, on pp. [13], [18], [25], [30], and [33].

Binding: paper bds. Front cover, against bluish green and white woodcut in white: 'TO A LITTLE GIRL, ONE YEAR OLD, IN A RUINED FORTRESS'. Spine and back cover: woodcut cont'd. All edges trimmed and unstained; white endpapers.

   Dust wrapper: none.

Copies: Ctw, JAG, RPW, STW.

Notes: 1. Approximately 175 copies were printed (ltr., Jane Davis Doggett, 20 May 1976).

2. In the poem "The Child Next Door," last line, the word "*ciao*" is printed "*ciaou*."

A15   *Promises: Poems, 1954–1956*

A15.a1   first American edition, first impression (1957)

Robert Penn Warren | Promises | *Poems 1954–1956* | Random House, New York

Collation: super royal 8° (trimmed: 2.7 × 16.9 cm.); *unsigned* [1–6⁸], 48 leaves; pp. [i–x], [1–2] 3–13 [14–16] 17–84 [85–86]; ital. numerals off-center, left, at foot of type page.

Contents: p. [i]: hf. tit. 'Promises | *Poems 1954–1956*'; p. [ii]: blank; on p. [iii] 'Books by Robert Penn Warren'; p. [iv]: blank; p. [v]: title page; p. [vi]: ' © Copyright, 1955, 1957, by Robert Penn Warren | All rights reserved under International and Pan-American Copyright Conventions. | Published in New York by Random House, Inc., and simultaneously in Toronto, Can-|ada, by Random House of Canada, Limited. Manufactured in the United States of | America. | These poems have appeared in *The Partisan Review, The Kenyon Review, The Yale | Review*, and *Encounter*. "Boy's Will, Joyful Labor without Pay, and Harvest Home | (1918)" first appeared in *Botteghe Oscure*. | Library of Congress Catalog Card Number: 57–7894 | First Printing'; p. [vii]: '*To Rosanna and Gabriel*'; pp. [viii–ix]: 'Contents'; p. [x]: blank; pp. [1]–13: 'To a Little Girl, One Year Old, | in a Ruined Fortress | To Rosanna'; p. [2]: blank; p. 3: 'I Sirocco'; p. 4: "II Gull's Cry'; p. 5: 'III The Child Next Door'; pp. 6–10: 'IV The Flower'; pp. 11–13: 'V Colder Fire'; p. [14]: blank; pp. [15]–84: 'Promises | To Gabriel'; p. [16]: blank; pp. 17–18: 'I What Was the Promise That Smiled | from the Maples at Evening?'; pp. 19–23: 'II Court-martial'; pp. 24–25: 'III Gold Glade'; pp. 26–31: 'IV Dark Woods'; pp. 26–27: '*1 Tonight the Woods Are Darkened*'; pp. 28–29: '*2 The Dogwood*'; pp. 30–31: '*3 The Hazel Leaf*'; pp. 32–33: 'V Country Burying (1919)'; pp. 34–36: 'VI School Lesson Based on Word of Tragic Death | of Entire Gillum Family'; pp. 37–38: 'VII Summer Storm (Circa 1916), and God's Grace'; pp. 39–41: 'VIII Founding Fathers, Nineteenth-Century Style, | Southeast U.S.A.'; pp. 42–43: 'IX Foreign Shore, Old

Woman, Slaughter of Octopus'; pp. 44–47: 'X Dark Night Of';
pp. 48–53: 'XI Infant Boy at Midcentury'; pp. 48–49: '*1 When the
Century Dragged*'; pp. 50–51: '*2 Modification of Landscape*'; pp. 52–53: '*3
Brightness of Distance*'; pp. 54–55; 'XII Lullaby: Smile in Sleep'; pp.
56–61: 'XIII Man in Moonlight'; pp. 56–57 '*1 Moonlight Observed from
Ruined Fortress*'; pp. 58–59: '*2 Walk by Moonlight in Small Town*'; pp.
60–61: '*3 Lullaby: Moonlight Lingers*'; pp. 62–63: 'XIV Mad Young
Aristocrat on Beach'; pp. 64–66: 'XV Dragon Country: To Jacob
Boehme'; pp. 67–75: "XVI Ballad of a Sweet Dream of Peace'; pp.
67–68: '*1 And Don't Forget Your Corset Cover, Either*'; pp. 69–70: '*2 Keepsakes*'; p. 71: '*3 Go It, Granny——Go It, Hog!*'; p. 72: '*4 Friends of the
Family, or Bowling a Sticky Cricket*'; p. 73: '*5 You Never Knew Her Either,
Though You | Thought You Did, Inside Out*'; p. 74: '*6 I Guess You Ought to
Know Who You Are*'; p. 75: '*7 Rumor Unverified Stop Can You Confirm
Stop*'; p. 76: 'XVII Boy's Will, Joyful Labor without Pay, | and Har-
vest Home (1918)'; pp. 76–81: '*1 Morning*'; p. 77: '*2 Work*'; pp. 78–79:
'*3 The Snake*'; pp. 80–81: '*4 Hands Are Paid*'; pp. 82–83: 'XVIII Lullaby: A Motion like Sleep'; p. 84: 'XIX The Necessity for Belief'; p.
[85]: blank; p. [86]: 'About the Author'.

Typography and Paper: text: 36 ll., 17.5 (18.6) × 12.5 cm.; Monotype
Bodoni 10/12-pt. Paper: white, wove, unwatermarked; sheets bulk 0.8
cm.

Binding: black cloth. Front, in silver: '*Poems 1954–1956*'. Spine, vert.:
'[in blue] Robert Penn Warren [in silver] Promises [in blue] Random
House'. Back: blank. All edges trimmed with top edge stained dark
blue; white endpapers.
   Dust wrapper: front cover, on black: '[in white] Robert Penn Warren
| [in light blue] Promises | *Poems 1954–1956* | [in white] A Random
House Book'. Spine, vert. on black: '[in white] Robert Penn Warren
[in light blue] Promises [in white] Random House'. Back cover, on
white in black: photograph and brief biographical sketch. Front flap:
about the book. Back flap: publisher's advertisement.

Copies: Ctb, CtY, JAG, KyU, LBR, LC, MH, NbU, STW (2), TNJ
(2), TxFTC, ViU.

Notes: 1. Published 15 Aug. 1957 at $3.00. The publisher has been un-
able to locate the records of *P* (ltr., Jim Wilcox, Random House, Inc.,
31 July 1974). LC copyright 2 Aug. 1957 (A305231); two copies deposited 10 Oct. 1957.
   2. KyU copy is inscribed: 'To | Lawrence Thompson | warm re-

gards | Red Warren | Fairfield | September 3, 1957'. Thompson was Director of Libraries at the University of Kentucky. STW copy: 'To Amory ⟨name illegible⟩ | My best love | Red | NYC | August 8, 1957' with top edge unstained (ltr., Stuart Wright, 8 May 1980).

A15.b1 first English edition, first impression (1959)

ROBERT PENN WARREN | [outlined] PROMISES | Poems 1954–1956 | 1959 | EYRE & SPOTTISWOODE · LONDON

Collation: demy folio 8° (trimmed: 21.7 × 13.6 cm.); signed, [A]–D⁸ E⁴ F⁸, 44 leaves; pp. [i–viii], [1–2] 3–14 [15–16] 17–78 [79–80]; numbers, in square brackets, located on v. in corner formed by tail and outer margins and on r. in corner formed by tail and inner margins.

Contents: p. [i]: 'PROMISES | *Poems 1954–1956*'; on p. [ii] 'By the same author'; p. [iii]: title page; p. [iv]: ' © 1955, 1957, BY ROBERT PENN WARREN | THIS EDITION FIRST PUBLISHED IN GREAT BRITAIN 1959 | BY EYRE & SPOTTISWOODE (PUB-LISHERS) LTD | PRINTED BY THE SHENVAL PRESS LTD | LONDON, HERTFORD AND HARLOW | CATALOGUE NO 6/2377'; p. [v]: dedication; p. [vi]: acknowledgments; pp. [vii–viii]: 'Contents'; p. [1]: '*To a Little Girl,* | *One Year Old,* | *in a Ruined Fortress* | TO ROSANNA'; p. [2]: blank; pp. 3–14: poems; p. [15]: '*Promises* | TO GABRIEL'; p. [16]: blank; pp. 17–78: poems; pp. [79–80]: blank.

Typography and Paper: text: 34 ll., 16.1 (16.7) × 9.4 cm.; Simoncini Garamond 12/14-pt. Paper: white, laid, vertical chainlines (2.7 cm.), unwatermarked; sheets bulk 0.7 cm.

Binding: medium blue cloth. Front and back: blank. Spine, vert. in silver: '*Promises* [diamond-shaped orn.] POEMS 1954–6 [same orn.] *Robert Penn Warren* [same orn.] E&S'. All edges trimmed and unstained; white endpapers.

Dust wrapper: front cover, on grayish blue in red, shaded: '*Promises* | [irregular rule] | *POEMS 1954–6* | [irregular rule] | [solid ltrs.] *Robert Penn Warren*'. Spine, in red, vert.: '*Promises* [diamond-shaped orn.] POEMS 1954–6 [same orn.] *Robert Penn Warren* [same orn.] E&S'. Back cover, in red: excerpts from reviews of *BD*. Front flap, in red: about the book. Back flap: '*Also by Robert Penn Warren*'.

Note: A 4.4-cm. band which fits over the dust wrapper and is of the same paper notes in red that 'Robert Penn Warren's PROMISES has been awarded | THE PULITZER PRIZE | NATIONAL BOOK AWARD | EDNA ST. VINCENT MILLAY MEMORIAL AWARD'.

Copies: BL, Ctw, JAG, RPW, STW (2), TNJ.

Note: published 1959 at 18s. Printed by the Shenval Press Ltd. Additional publication information is not available (ltr., Maria Lyras, Publicity Dept., Eyre Methuen Ltd., 6 June 1975). British Library date-stamp 14 April 1959.

A16 *Selected Essays*

A16.a1 first American edition, first impression (1958)

Robert Penn Warren | Selected Essays | [publisher's device] Random House *New York*

Collation: crown 8° (trimmed 19.0 × 11.3 cm.); *unsigned* [1–10^{16}], 160 leaves; pp. [i–xi] xii–xiii [xiv], [1–3] 4–305 [306]. On v. numbers are in the corner formed by head and inner margins; on r., in the corner formed by head and outer margins; pp. [59], [80], [170], and [184] are unnumbered.

Contents: p. [i]: hf. tit. 'Selected Essays'; on p. [ii] 'BOOKS BY | *Robert Penn Warren*'; p. [iii]: title page; p. [iv]: '*First Printing* | © COPYRIGHT, 1941, 1943, 1944, 1946, 1947, | 1958 BY ROBERT PENN WARREN | COPYRIGHT, 1951, BY RANDOM HOUSE, INC. | COPYRIGHT, 1947, BY THE UNIVERSITY OF MICHI-|GAN | COPYRIGHT, 1935, BY THE BOOKMAN PUBLISHING | CO., INC. | ALL RIGHTS RESERVED UNDER INTERNATIONAL | AND PAN-AMERICAN COPYRIGHT CONVENTIONS. | PUBLISHED IN NEW YORK BY RANDOM HOUSE, | INC., AND IN TORONTO, CANADA, BY RANDOM | HOUSE OF CANADA, UNLIMITED. | LIBRARY OF CONGRESS CATA-LOG CARD NUMBER: | 58-7674 | MANUFACTURED IN THE UNITED STATES OF AMERICA | By Kingsport Press, Inc., Kingsport, Tennessee'; p. [v]: 'ACKNOWLEDGMENTS'; p. [vi]: blank; p. [vii]: 'To Milton and Zaro Starr'; p. [viii]: blank; p. [ix]: '*Contents* | [in Roman type, date of each essay's composition provided in parentheses after each title]'; p. [x]: blank; pp. [xi–xiii]: '*Preface*'; p. [xiv]: blank; p. [1]: hf. tit.; p. [2]: blank; p. [3]: 'Pure and Impure Poetry'; p. 31: beg. bottom half of p., '"The Great Mirage": | CONRAD and *Nostromo*'; p. [59]: 'WILLIAM FAULKNER'; p. [80]: 'ERNEST HEMINGWAY'; p. 118: beg. bottom half of p., 'The Themes | of ROBERT FROST'; p. 136: beg. bottom half of p., 'Irony with a Center: | KATHERINE ANNE | PORTER'; p. 156: beg. bottom two-thirds of p., 'Love and Separateness | in EUDORA WELTY'; p. [170]: 'A Note on the Hamlet | of THOMAS WOLFE'; p. [184]: 'MELVILLE the Poet'; p. 198: beg. bottom half of p., 'A Poem of Pure | Imagination: | an Experiment in Reading'; p. [306]: '[publisher's device] ABOUT THE AUTHOR'.

Typography and Paper: text: 42 ll., 15.5 (16.0) × 8.1 cm.; Primer 11-pt. RT: on p. xii and all v. beg. with p. 4, except pp. [80], [170], and [184], *'Selected Essays'*; on r., except p. [59], essay titles in full except '"THE GREAT MIRAGE"'; 'IRONY WITH A CENTER'; 'LOVE AND SEPARATENESS'; 'A NOTE ON . . . THOMAS WOLFE'; and 'A POEM OF PURE IMAGINATION'. Paper: white, wove, unwatermarked; sheets bulk 2.5 cm.

Binding: navy blue cloth. Front, stamped in gilt: 'RPW'. Spine: '[stamped in silver] Selected | Essays | [stamped in gilt] *Robert | Penn | Warren* | [in gilt, publisher's device] | RANDOM | HOUSE'. Back: blank. All edges trimmed with top edge stained dark blue; white endpapers.

Dust wrapper: front cover: '[on sky blue in white block ltrs.] ROB-ERT | PENN | WARREN | [on white in black] SELECTED | [on white in blue] ESSAYS | [on yellow in black—complete list in double column of essays]'. Spine: '[on blue in white] ROBERT | PENN | WARREN | [on white in black] SELECTED | ESSAYS | [on yellow in black, publisher's device] | RANDOM | HOUSE'. Back cover, on white in black: publisher's advertisement which lists other Random House books by RPW. Front flap: '$4.00 | SELECTED | ESSAYS | by ROBERT | PENN | WARREN | [brief review] | Jacket design by Glanzman-Parker | [publisher's advertisement | 6/58'. Back flap: bio-graphical sketch.

Copies: Ctb, CtY, JAG, KyU, LC, LU, STW (2), TNJ, TxFTC.

Notes: 1. Published 25 June 1958 in an impression of 4,000 copies at $4.00. Printed by Vail-Ballou Press. Subsequent impressions: 1 June 1962, 1,500; 27 April 1967, 100. (Ltr., Jim Wilcox, Random House, Inc., 31 July 1974.) LC copyright 16 June 1958 (A346966); two copies deposited 21 July 1958.

A16.b1   first American edition, first impression, by offset, paperback (1966)

[within rectangle frame of square dots] SELECTED | ESSAYS | by | Robert Penn Warren | [publisher's device] | VINTAGE BOOKS | A Division of Random House | New York | [rule of square dots]

Collation: post folio 8° (trimmed: 18.3 × 10.8 cm.); *unsigned* 160 ind. leaves; pp. [i–xi] xii–xiii [xiv], [1–3] 4–58 [59] 60–79 [80] 81–169 [170] 171–183 [184] 185–305 [306]; numbered identical with **A16.a1**.

Contents: p. [i]: hf. tit. 'Selected Essays'; p. [ii]: blank; p. [iii]: title page; p. [iv]: copyright and 'FIRST VINTAGE EDITION, September, 1966'; p. [v]: acknowledgments; p. [vi]: blank; p. [vii]: dedication; p. [viii]: blank; p. [ix]: contents; p. [x]: blank; pp. [xi]–xiii: preface; p. [xiv]: blank; p. [1]: hf. tit.; p. [2]: blank; pp. [3]–305: essays; p. [306]: about the author.

Typography and Paper: reproduced photographically from **A16.a1**. Paper: white, wove, unwatermarked; sheets bulk 2.0 cm.

Binding: paper. Front cover, similar to **A16.a1** but with the addition at top, in white: 'A Vintage Book [publisher's device] V-347 $1.95'. Spine: '[vert., on purple in white] ROBERT PENN WARREN [on white in purple] SELECTED [on gold in black] ESSAYS | [horiz., on white, publisher's device; in black] Vintage | V-347'. Back cover, on white: '[in purple] SELECTED ESSAYS | [in gold] by Robert Penn Warren | [in black, excerpts from reviews with sources in purple] | [in gold] Also available in a hardcover edition from Random House | A Vintage Book'. Inside covers: white. All edges trimmed and unstained.

Copies: JAG, STW, TNJ.

Note: published 3 Oct. 1966 in 6,000 copies at $1.95. Printed by Colonial Press. Subsequent impression: 1 June 19767, 3,000. Distributed in Canada by Random House of Canada Limited. (Ltr., Jim Wilcox, Random House, Inc., 31 July 1974.)

A16.c1   first English edition, first impression, by offset (1964)

Selected Essays by | Robert Penn Warren | EYRE & SPOTTISWOODE · LONDON

Collation: demy folio 8° (trimmed: 20.3 × 12.4 cm.); *unsigned*, [1–10^{16}], 160 leaves; pagination and numbering identical with **A16.a1**.

Contents: on p. [iv] 'FIRST PUBLISHED IN GREAT BRITAIN 1964' and the catalogue no. 5/2516/1.

Typography and Paper: identical with **A16.a1**. Paper: white, wove, unwatermarked; sheets bulk 2.5 cm.

Binding: purple cloth. Front and back: blank. Spine, stamped in gilt:

'Selected | Essays || ROBERT | PENN | WARREN | E & S'. All edges trimmed and unstained; white endpapers.

Dust wrapper: front, on white: '[in purple, orn. script] R P | [in black] Selected | Essays | [purple rule] | [in black] | ROBERT | PENN WARREN | [in purple, orn. script] W'. Spine: '[in black] Selected | Essays | ROBERT | PENN | WARREN | [purple rule continued from front] | [in purple] E & S'. Back cover, in purple and in black: publisher's advertisement. Front flap: about the book. Back flap: 'PRINTED IN GREAT BRITAIN'.

Copies: BL, IEN, RPW, STW.

Note: published 23 Jan. 1964 at 30s. Additional publication information is not available (ltr., Maria Lyras, Publicity Dept., Eyre Methuen Ltd., 6 June 1975). British Library date-stamp 12 Feb. 1964.

A17 *Remember the Alamo!*

A17.a1 first American edition, first impression (1958)

[ltrs. in black] REMEMBER | THE ALAMO! | Robert Penn Warren | Illustrated by William Moyers | [in black, brown, white, illus. of Alamo, front view | RANDOM HOUSE · NEW YORK

Collation: medium folio 8° (trimmed: 21.0 × 14.2 cm.); *unsigned* [1–6¹⁶], 96 leaves; pp. [i–viii], [1–2] 3–92 [93] 94–131 [132–133] 134–148 [149] 150–151 [152–153] 154–171 [172–173] 174–177 [178] 179–182 [183–184]; numbers centered at foot of type page.

Contents: p. [i]: hf. tit. 'REMEMBER THE ALAMO!' | [Landmark Books device]'; p. [ii]: blank; p. [iii]: title page; on p. [iv] copyright, LC no. 58-6178, and 'FIRST PRINTING'; p. [v]: '*To Gabriel*'; p. [vi]: blank; p. [vii]: contents with chapter numerals in Arabic; p. [viii]: blank; p. [1]: hf. tit. 'REMEMBER THE ALAMO!'; p. [2]: blank; on p. 3 '1 | How the Alamo | Got Its Name'; on p. 10 '2 | Why the Spaniards | Were Afraid'; on p. 16 '3 | First Blood at the Alamo'; on p. 30 '4 | Stephen Austin Was an | Honest Man'; on p. 39 '5 | A Young Fellow Who Didn't | Mind Trouble'; on p. 48 '6 | Sam Houston Gets a Razor'; on p. 61 '7 | Jim Bowie: The Deadliest | Man Alive'; on p. 71 '8 | Trouble Means Texas'; on p. 82 '9 | "We Will Rather Die in | These Ditches . . . "'; on p. 90 '10 | The Long Rifle Comes In'; on p. 98 '11 | The Gates Are Closed: Victory or Death'; on p. 118 '12 | A Sword Point and a Line in the Dust'; on p. 135 '13 | Last Blood'; on p. 161 '14 |

Remember the Alamo!'; on p. 179 'Index'; pp. [183–184]: publisher's advertisement for Landmark Books.

Typography and Paper: text: 24 ll., 14.95 (15.8) × 9.7 cm.; Linotype Caledonia 12/14-pt. RT: on v., 'REMEMBER THE ALAMO!'; on r., full chapter titles in ital. except on chapter pages and pages with illus. in top half of page. Paper: white, wove, unwatermarked; sheets bulk 1.8 cm.

Illustrations: all twenty-five on white background in black; captions in ital. beneath illus.: pp. 8–9, 18, 21, 24, 32, 41, 52, 59, 64, [69], [75], 84, 87, [93], 102, 109, 113, 128–129, [132–133], 141, [149], [152–153], 165, 169, and [172–173].

Binding: green cloth. Front, in blue: '[front view of Alamo] | [encircled by red wreath and blue flowers] REMEMBER | THE ALAMO!'. Spine: '[red stem, blue flower] | [blue rule] | [horiz., in blue] WARREN | [in red border, blue ltrs., vert.] Remember the Alamo! | [blue rule] | [inverted flowers] | [horiz., in blue] Landmark Books [device] | Random House'. Back: blank. All edges trimmed with top edge stained yellow; endpapers have pictorial argyles in blue on beige.

Dust wrapper: front cover, in upper right corner on orange: '[in black, publisher's device] 79 | [fancy] *Landmark* | BOOKS [in white] REMEMBER | THE ALAMO! | [in black] by Robert Penn Warren | ILLUSTRATED BY WILLIAM MOYERS | [picture of fighting soldiers in front of Alamo]'. Spine, in white: REMEMBER | THE | ALAMO! | WARREN | [publisher's device] | RANDOM | HOUSE'. Back cover: publisher's advertisement. Front flap: about the book. Back flap: about the author and illustrator. Reverse side: list of Landmark Books.

Copies: Ctb, Ctw, KyU, LC (rebound), STW, TxFTC.

Notes: 1. Published 28 Aug. 1958 at $1.80. Number of impressions for "first seven editions on unavailable records." Printed by Colonial Press. Subsequent impressions: 20 Jan. 1964, 5,500; 2 June 1965, 7,500; 15 Feb. 1966(?), 8,000; 28 Oct. 1966, 15,000; 14 March 1968, 12,500; 1 May 1970, 4,000. (Ltr., Jim Wilcox, Random House, Inc., 31 July 1974.) Distributed in Canada by Random House of Canada Limited. LC copyright 20 Aug. 1958 (A353799); two copies deposited 15 Sept. 1958.

2. Portions of this book were excerpted in *Holiday*, Feb. 1958, pp. 52–55, 106, 108–110, and 112–113.

A17.a3 first American edition, third impression (1959)

Contents: p. [iii]: title page, and beneath illustrator's name: 'A LAND-MARK BOOK | [illus.]'; on p. [iv] 'THIRD PRINTING'.

Binding: endpapers: a series of colored illus. on white with free end leaf, v. and r., having on top half a U.S. map with Landmark Book device superimposed over it.

Copies: Ctw, RPW.

A17.b1 first American edition, library edition (1958)

[p. (ii), in gold] REMEMBER | [illus. of men charging—outlined in black on white with touches of gold on hat, horn, belt, sleeve, and saber] [p. (iii), in gold] THE ALAMO! | [in black] Robert Penn Warren | Illustrated by William Moyers | RANDOM HOUSE · NEW YORK | [other figures of men in the distance; in gold, publisher's device including the words] *Landmark* [fancy] | BOOKS

Collation: demy 8° (trimmed: 20.85 × 13.7 cm.); *unsigned* [1–8^{12}], 96 leaves; pagination and numbering identical with **A17.a1**.

Contents: p. [i]: hf. tit. 'REMEMBER THE ALAMO!'; pp. [ii–iii]: title pages; p. [iv]: copyright; p. [v]: dedication; p. [vi]: blank; p. [vii]: contents with chapters designated in Arabic numerals, in gold; p. [viii]: blank; p. [1]: hf. tit.; p. [2]: blank; pp. 3–[178]: text; p. 179: index; pp. [183–184]: blank.

Typography and Paper: identical with **A17.a1**. Paper: white, wove unwatermarked; sheets bulk 1.6 cm.

Illustrations: identical with **A17.a1** except printed in gold and black.

Binding: paper covered bds., "library binding." Front cover, in upper right corner on red in black: '[publisher's device] 79 | [fancy] *Landmark* | BOOKS'; '[on olive green, in white] REMEMBER | THE ALAMO! | [in black] by Robert Penn Warren | ILLUSTRATED BY WILLIAM MOYERS | [white rule] | [illus. of fighting soldiers in front of the Alamo]'. Spine, on white: '[horiz., in black] WARREN | [red, white, and blue emblem of eagle] | [red five-point star outlined in black] | [vert., in red] REMEMBER THE ALAMO! | [horiz.—red, white, and blue publisher's device] | [in black] RANDOM | HOUSE'. Back cover: blank. All edges trimmed and unstained; gray endpapers.
 Dust wrapper: none.

Copies: JAG, STW, TNJ.

Note: published Oct. 1958 at $1.95. Printed by E. M. Hale & Company, Eau Claire, WI. Additional publication information is not available (ltr., unsigned, E. M. Hale and Company, n.d., postmarked 10 Feb. 1975).

A18   *How Texas Won Her Freedom*

A18.a1   first American edition, first impression (1959)

[ltrs. in black] ROBERT PENN WARREN | [in burnt orange, woodcut of eagle] | HOW TEXAS WON | HER FREEDOM | *The Story of Sam Houston | & the Battle of San Jacinto* | 1959 San Jacinto Museum of History · San Jacinto Monument, Texas

Colophon, p. [23]: '[burnt orange orn.] | The eagle on the title page was | cut in wood for this book by | FRITZ KREDEL'.

Collation: medium 8° (trimmed: 22.9 × 15.2 cm.); *unsigned* [1 ¹⁸], 18 leaves; pp. [i–x], 1–22 [23–26]; numbers centered at bottom of type page.

Contents: pp. [i–v]: blank; on p. [vi] 'BOOKS BY | *Robert Penn Warren*'; p. [vii]: hf. tit. 'HOW TEXAS WON HER FREEDOM'; p. [viii]: blank; p. [ix]: title page; p. [x]: 'LIBRARY OF CONGRESS CATALOG CARD NUMBER 59-12348 | *Reprinted by special permission of* HOLIDAY | *Copyright* © *1958 by the Curtis Publishing Co.* | *Manufactured in the United States of America* | *by the Kingsport Press, Inc., Kingsport, Tennessee*'; pp. 1–22: text with first line of text in large and small caps.; p. [23]: colophon; pp. [24–26]: blank.

Typography and Paper: text: 30 ll., 15.6 (16.5) × 10.0 cm.; Linotype Janson 10/12-pt. Paper: white, wove, watermarked 'CURTIS RAG'; sheets bulk 0.3 cm.

Binding: green paper-covered bds. and green cloth spine: Front, on green in brown: eagle as on title page. Spine, vert., in gilt: 'ROBERT PENN WARREN'. Back: blank. All edges trimmed and unstained; white lining paper, no free endpaper.
   Dust wrapper: none located.

Copies: CU, KyU, LC, MH, NN, STW, TxU.

Notes: 1. Published 1959 in 512 cloth and 2,147 paper copies. Second printing, 1961 in 68 cloth and 4,884 paper copies. Both printings by Kingsport Press, Inc. Subsequent printings by May Printing & Lithographing, Inc., include: 1965, 4,936 paper; 1966, 4,969 paper; 1969, 5,075 paper at $1.00. (Ltr., Mrs. David W. Knepper, Director, San Jacinto Museum of History Association, 24 Feb. 1975.) LC copyright could not be located (ltr., William L. Asher, Bibliographer, Library of Congress, 5 Nov. 1979).

2. Appeared originally in *Holiday*, March 1958, pp. 72–73, 160, 162–167.

A18.a5 first American edition, fifth impression, by offset, paperback (1969)

Collation: 16 leaves.

Paper: white, laid, vertical chainlines (2.1 cm.), watermarked 'Hilmory Text'; sheets bulk 0.3 cm.

Binding: paper, stapled. Front, in two-tone green: 'ROBERT PENN WARREN | How Texas Won Her Freedom | [outlined] SAM HOUSTON | & THE BATTLE OF | SAN JACINTO | [illus. of horseback rider]'. Back: blank. All edges trimmed and unstained.

Copies: JAG.

A19 *The Cave*

A19.a1 first American edition, first impression (1959)

[brown irregular "circle" as background on upper half of p.; in black] THE CAVE | *Robert Penn Warren* | [publisher's device] | *Random House · New York*

Collation: large post 8° (trimmed: 20.8 × 14.0 cm.); *unsigned* [1–13^{16}], 208 leaves; pp. [i–viii], [1–2] 3–403 [404–408]; numbers square-bracketed and centered at foot of type page.

Contents: p. [i]: hf. tit. 'THE CAVE'; on p. [ii]: '*Books by Robert Penn Warren*'; p. [iii]: title page; p. [iv]: 'FIRST PRINTING | © *Copyright, 1959, by Robert Penn Warren* | *All rights reserved under International and Pan-American Copyright* | *Conventions. Published in New York by Random House, Inc., and* | *simultaneously in Toronto, Canada, by Random House of Canada, Limited.* | *Library of Congress Catalog Card Number: 59-5719* | *Manufactured in the United States of America* | *by H. Wolff, New York* | *De-*

sign: Marshall Lee'; p. [v]: '*To Denis and Caren Devlin*'; p. [vi]: blank;
p. [vii]: '[7 ll. epigraph] | Plato, *The Republic*, Book VII'; p. [viii]: blank;
p. [1]: hf. tit.; p. [2]: blank; pp. 3–403: text, with chapters designated
in Roman numerals within black, irregular "circle" on upper half of
page: pp. 3, 36, 81, 135, 179, 207, 226, 243, 277, 310, 325, 352, and
373; p. [404]: blank; p. [405]: about the author; pp. [406–408]: blank.

Typography and Paper: text: 34 ll., 15.3 (16.3) × 10.1 cm.; 35 ll., 15.95
(17.0) × 10.1 cm.; Linotype Caledonia 10/13-pt. Paper: white, wove,
unwatermarked; sheets bulk 3.2 cm.

Note: size of type page varies: pp. 217, 292, 329, and 376 have 32 ll., 14.45 (15.45)
× 10.1 cm.; and p. 38 has 33 ll., 14.95 (15.95) × 10.1 cm.

Binding: brown cloth. Front, on brown background inside black irreg-
ular circle in white ltrs.: '*R P W*'. Spine, on black: '[in white] THE |
CAVE | [in gilt] *Robert* | *Penn* | *Warren* | [publisher's device] | *Random
House*'. Back: blank. All edges trimmed with top edge stained yellow;
gray endpapers.

Dust wrapper: front cover, on streaked gray background: '[in yellow]
ROBERT PENN | WARREN | [in white] THE | CAVE | A NOVEL
| [in yellow] A RANDOM HOUSE BOOK [publisher's device]'.
Spine, on same background: '[in white] THE | CAVE | [in yellow]
ROBERT | PENN | WARREN | [in white, publisher's device] | RAN-
DOM HOUSE'. Back cover, on white: photograph of RPW by Sylvia
Salmi and a short biographical sketch. Front flap: about the book.
Back flap: bio. sketch continued from back cover.

Copies: Ctb, CtY (2), JAG (2), KyU, LC, LU (2), STW, TNJ.

Notes: 1. Published 24 Aug. 1959 in 25,000 copies at $4.95. Printed by
American Book-Stratford Press, Inc. Subsequent impressions: 26
Aug. 1959, 12,500; 26 Oct. 1959, 7,500; 14 Dec. 1959, 5,000; 15 Aug.
1969, 500. (Ltr., Jim Wilcox, Random House, Inc., 31 July 1974.) LC
copyright 17 July 1959 (A404751); two copies deposited 4 Sept. 1959.

2. Excerpts: "Love and Death in Johntown, Tennessee," *PR*, 26
(Summer 1959), 392–419; "Natural History of Ikey Sumpter, Formerly of Johntown, Tennessee," *SR*, 67 (Summer 1959), 347–400;
and "Black Is Not the Color of My True Love's Hair," *Esquire*, Sept.
1959, p. 112.

A19.b1 second American edition, book-club edition (abridged)
(1960)

[in triple rectangular frame] The Cave | ROBERT PENN WARREN | [publisher's device] AN ABRIDGEMENT

Collation: large post 8° (trimmed: 20.8 × 13.7 cm.); *unsigned* [1–14¹⁶], 224 leaves; pp. [1–6] 7–120 [121–122] 123–228 [229–230] 231–326 [327–328] 329–448; numbers in corner formed by outer and tail margins.

Contents: p. [1]: 'BOOKS [publisher's device] ABRIDGED'; p. [2]: blank; p. [3]: inside triple frame with publisher's device interrupting top of frame, 'The Cave | ROBERT PENN WARREN | [diamond shaped orn.] | The Armada | GARRETT MATTINGLY | [diamond shaped orn.] | Fuel For The Flame | ALEC WAUGH | [diamond shaped orn.] | Celia Garth | GWEN BRISTOW | [outside frame] BOOKS ABRIDGED, INC. *New York*'; p. [4]: copyright; p. [5]: title page for *Cave*; p. [6]: about the author and individual copyright; pp. 7–120: text.

> *Note*: omits chapters VII, VIII, X, XI, and portions of others; and combines XII and XIII.

Typography and Paper: text: 37 ll., 17.0 (18.1) × 9.7 cm.; Times New Roman 10/13-pt. RT, on outer margins: on v., 'Robert Penn Warren'; on r., 'The Cave'. Paper: white, wove, unwatermarked; sheets bulk 3.2 cm.

Binding: bluish green cloth with black cloth spine. Front and back: blank. Spine, in bluish green: '[fifteen rules] [inside triple frame, top; double, side] THE CAVE | [asterisk orn.] | THE ARMADA | [orn.] | FUEL FOR | THE FLAME | [orn.] | CELIA GARTH | [publisher's device] | BOOKS ABRIDGED, INC. | [thirty rules]'. All edges trimmed with top stained green; white endpapers.

Dust wrapper: all sides on cream background with orange and black patterns. Front cover, inside black double frame: '[in black] The Cave | ROBERT PENN WARREN | [in orange, asterisk orn.] | The Armada | GARRETT MATTINGLY | [orn.] | Fuel for the Flame | ALEC WAUGH | [orn.] | Celia Garth | GWEN BRISTOW | [in orange and black, publisher's device] | [in black] Books Abridged, Inc.' Spine, with words in black: '[black double rule] | THE CAVE | [orange asterisk orn.] | THE ARMADA | [orn.] | FUEL FOR | THE FLAME | [orn.] | CELIA GARTH | [in orange and black, publisher's device] | BOOKS ABRIDGED, INC.' Back cover, in black double frame, in black: about the authors. Front and back flaps: about each selection.

Copies: JAG, STW.

Note: from the dw: '*BOOKS ABRIDGED volumes are issued every second* | *month and are available only by subscription at $2.19 per* | *volume, plus 24¢* | *for postage and shipping. . . .*' Additional publication information is not available.

A19.c1 third American edition, first impression, paperback (1960)

[inside an irregular "circle"] THE | CAVE | *ROBERT PENN WARREN* | [publisher's device] | A SIGNET BOOK | Published by THE NEW AMERICAN LIBRARY

Collation: post folio 8° (trimmed: 17.9 × 10.6 cm.); *unsigned* 192 ind. leaves; pp. [1–6] 7–382 [383–384]; numbers centered at foot of type page.

Contents: p. [1]: about the novel; p. [2]: publisher's advertisement; p. [3]: title page; p. [4]: copyright; p. [5]: dedication; p. [6]: epigraph; pp. 7–382: text; pp. [383–384]: publisher's advertisements.

Typography and Paper: text: 42 ll., 16.0 (16.4) × 8.8 cm.; Times New Roman 10/11-pt. Paper: white, wove, unwatermarked; sheets bulk 1.8 cm.

Binding: paper. Front cover, on white: '[in black] T1866 | [arched slightly] SIGNET | [on black ellipse in white] 75¢ | [on white, between black ellipse and black elliptical line, in black] BOOKS | [illus. in color along left half; lettering along right half] The | Cave | A BRUTALLY POWERFUL NOVEL BY | [in red] Robert | Penn Warren | [in black] PULITZER PRIZE WINNER | [in red, excerpt from a review by Arthur Mizener] | [in black] A SIGNET BOOK Complete and Unabridged'. Spine, on white: '[horiz., in black] T | 1866 | [vert.] THE CAVE [in red] Robert Penn Warren'. Back cover, on white: '[in red] Death | Carnival | [in black, about the book and two excerpts from reviews] | [in red] Published by the New American Library | [in black] Cover Printed in U.S.A.' Inside covers: white. All edges trimmed and stained red.

Copies: JAG, KyU, STW.

Note: published Oct. 1960 at 75¢ by The New American Library. Additional publication information is not available.

A19.d1 first English edition, first impression (1959)

THE CAVE | ROBERT PENN WARREN | 1959 | EYRE & SPOT-
TISWOODE | LONDON

Collation: demy folio 8° (trimmed: 20.0 × 13.1 cm.); signed, [A]–Y⁸
Z⁴ AA⁸, 188 leaves; pp. [1–8] 9–376; numbers centered at foot of
type page.

Contents: p. [1]: 'THE CAVE | [story outline]'; on p. [2] '*Books by Robert
Penn Warren*'; p. [3]: title page; p. [4]: ' © 1959 ROBERT PENN
WARREN | FIRST PUBLISHED IN GREAT BRITAIN 1959 | BY
EYRE & SPOTTISWOODE (PUBLISHERS) LTD | 22 HENRI-
ETTA ST, LONDON, WC 2 | PRINTED BY THE SHENVAL
PRESS | LONDON, HERTFORD AND HARLOW | CATA-
LOGUE NUMBER 6/4208'; p. [5]: dedication; p. [6]: blank; p. [7]:
epigraph; p. [8]: blank; pp. 9–376: text.

Typography and Paper: text: 38 ll., 15.9 (16.3) × 9.7 cm.; Linotype Janson 12-pt. Paper: white, wove, unwatermarked; sheets bulk 2.5 cm.

Binding: blue cloth. Front and back: blank. Spine, in gilt: 'The | Cave |
[eight dots] | ROBERT | PENN | WARREN | E & S'. All edges
trimmed and unstained; white endpapers.

Dust wrapper: front cover, illus. on golden beige background: '[in ir-
regular letters, in black] THE | CAVE | [in black and white, face and
hand] | [on black irregular octagon in white] ROBERT | PENN |
WARREN | [irregular designs in red, white, black, and black speckles
along outer edge]'. Spine, on golden beige: '[irregular letters in black]
THE | CAVE | [regular letters, in black] ROBERT | PENN | WAR-
REN | [in red] EYRE & | SPOTTISWOODE'. Back cover, on white:
picture of RPW along outer margin; quotes and excerpts along inner margin. Front flap: about the story. Back flap: publisher's advertisement.

Copies: BL, JAG, RPW, ScU, STW.

Note: published 1959 at 18s. Printed by Shenval Press. Additional
publication information is not available (ltr., Maria Lyras, Publicity
Dept., Eyre Methuen Ltd., 6 June 1975). British Library date-stamp
18 Nov. 1959.

A19.e1   second English edition, first impression, paperback (1961)

The | Cave | ROBERT PENN WARREN | [publisher's device] | THE
NEW ENGLISH LIBRARY LTD BARNARD'S INN LON-
DON EC 1

Collation: post folio 8° (trimmed: 18.0 × 10.9 cm.); signed, A–M¹⁶, 176 leaves; pp. [1–4] 5–351 [352]; numbers centered at foot of type page.

Contents: p. [1]: about the novel; p. [2]: publisher's advertisement; p. [3]: title page; p. [4]: 'First published in England by Eyre & Spottiswoode | (Publishers) Ltd. in 1959 | First Four Square edition 1961 | © 1959 Robert Penn Warren | [dedication] | [epigraph] | [publishing statement]'; pp. 5–351: text; on p. 351: 'Conditions of Sale'; p. [352]: publisher's advertisement.

Typography and Paper: text: 42 ll., 14.1 (14.7) × 8.7 cm.; Times New Roman 10-pt. Paper: white, wove, unwatermarked; sheets bulk 1.9 cm.

Binding: paper. Front cover, on yellow: '[upper left corner, in black] FOUR | [four red squares form a square] | [in black] SQUARE | 3'6'; '[in black, bottom of top word touching top of bottom word] THE | CAVE | [in red] ROBERT | PENN | WARREN | [illus. of man unconscious at mouth of hole] | [in black] his dying father, | the girl who carried his child, | the whole state, | watched . . . | and waited . . .'. Spine, on green: '[vert., in black] FOUR [publisher's device] SQUARE THE CAVE ROBERT PENN WARREN | [horiz.] 385'. Back cover, on yellow, in red and in blue: about the novel. Inside covers: white. All edges trimmed and unstained.

Copies: BL, RPW.

Note: published 1961 at 3s. 6d. by the New English Library. Printed by Love and Malcomson Ltd., London and Redhill, Surrey. Additional publication information is not available (ltr., Dorothy Houghton, Senior Editor—Paperbacks, New English Library, 19 Feb. 1975). British Library date-stamp 14 March 1962.

A20 *The Gods of Mount Olympus*

A20.a1 first American edition, first impression (1959)

[on light blue background, in black] By ROBERT PENN WARREN | [in white] THE GODS | OF MOUNT | OLYMPUS | [in black] Illustrated by WILLIAM MOYERS | [in white] LEGACY | [publisher's device—phoenix] | BOOKS | [in black] RANDOM HOUSE · NEW YORK

Collation: demy 8° (trimmed: 21.2 × 14.3 cm.); *unsigned* [1–4⁸], 32 leaves; pp. [i–viii], 1–2 [3] 4–6 [7] 8–16 [17] 18–24 [25] 26–28 [29] 30

[31] 32–46 [47] 48–50 [51] 52 [53–56]; light blue numbers at foot of page in extreme outer margins.

Note: pagination includes endpapers which are part of gatherings 1 and 4, respectively.

Contents: p. [i]: lining paper; pp. [ii–iii]: endpapers with illus.; p. [iv]: blank; p. [v]: title page; p. [vi]: 'To Rosanna | FIRST PRINTING | [copyright]'; on p. [vii] 'THE PRINCIPAL GODS | AND GODDESSES OF | ANCIENT GREEK | MYTHOLOGY'; p. [viii]: illus.; pp. 1–52: text with all chapter headings on light blue strips in black and the initial ltr. of each chapter light blue and enlarged: 'THE DARK BEGINNINGS'; p. 5: 'THE BIRTH OF ZEUS'; p. 9: 'ZEUS REIGNS SUPREME'; p. 11: 'POSEIDON'; p. 13: 'HADES'; p. 16: 'PERSEPHONE AND | DEMETER'; p. 20: 'THE WIVES OF ZEUS'; p. 22: 'THE FAVORITE CHILD | OF ZEUS'; p. 24: 'PHOEBUS APOLLO'; p. 30: 'ARTEMIS AND THE MOON'; p. 33: 'APHRODITE'; p. 35: 'HEPHAESTUS'; p. 37: 'HERMES AND ARES'; p. 39: 'DIONYSUS, | THE STRANGE GOD'; p. 42: 'HOW MAN WAS | CREATED'; p. 44: 'PROMETHEUS | AND PANDORA'; p. 49: 'THE FLOOD AND THE ARK'; p. [53]: '[in black] *Legacy Books* [in blue, publisher's device]; pp. [54–55]: illus., same as on pp. [ii–iii]; p. [56]: glued to bd.

Typography and Paper: text: 26 ll., 16.4 (18.3) × 10.05 cm.; Linotype Electra 12/14-pt. Paper: Gorham offset 44 × 66, 70 lb. Basis 490 m.; white, wove, unwatermarked. Ink: Seaboard Litho. (Ltr., Pat Falzarano, Production Dept., Rae Publishing Co., Inc., 20 Feb. 1975.) Sheets bulk 0.6 cm.

Illustrations: All illus. in light blue, gray, and black; no captions: pp. [ii–iii], [viii], [3], [7], 12, 14–15, [17], 21, [25], 28, [31], 36, 41, [47], [51], and [54–55].

Binding: blue cloth. Front: '[in red] LEGACY | [in gold on red—publisher's device] | [in red] BOOKS'. Spine: '[vert., in red] WARREN [gilt on red] THE GODS OF | MOUNT OLYMPUS [horiz., in red] RANDOM | HOUSE | [in gold] LEGACY | [publisher's device] | BOOKS'. Back: blank. All edges trimmed with top edge stained red; illus. endpapers.

Dust wrapper: front cover, gold background: '[in corner formed by upper and outer edges, on blue scroll which is outlined in black, in black ltrs.] LEGACY | [phoenix] | BOOKS | Y-1 | [in black on line with bottom of scroll] *The* GODS *of* | MOUNT | OLYMPUS | [in blue] BY

ROBERT PENN WARREN | [illus. in color of four of the gods]'. Spine, yellow on blue background: '[vert.] The Gods of Mount Olympus · WARREN | [horiz.] LEGACY | [phoenix] | BOOKS | Y-1 | RANDOM | HOUSE'. Back cover: white background, in black and in red, about Legacy Books. Front flap: about the book. Back flap: about the author and the illustrator.

Copies: KyU, LC, RPW, STW.

Note: published 28 Sept. 1959 at $1.50. No records of the first run are available. Printed by Rae Publishing, Cedar Grove, NJ. Subsequent impressions: 20 March 1970, 2,000. Distributed in Canada by Random House of Canada Limited. (Ltr., Jim Wilcox, Random House, Inc., 31 July 1974.) LC copyright 15 Sept. 1959 (A409016); two copies deposited 2 Oct. 1959.

A20.b1   first American edition, library edition (1965)

Contents: p. [i] and p. [56]: blue, blank.

Binding: paper-covered bds., "library binding." Front cover, in upper right corner on light blue, publisher's device, and: '[in black] LEGACY | [publisher's device] | BOOKS | Y-1 [on gold, in black] *The* GODS *of* | MOUNT | OLYMPUS | [in dark blue] BY ROBERT PENN WARREN | [illus.]'. Spine, on dark blue, in yellow: '[vert.] The Gods of Mount Olympus · WARREN | [horiz.] LEGACY | [device] | BOOKS | Y-1 | RANDOM | HOUSE '. Back cover, lower right corner in oval frame, on dark blue, in yellow: '[elephant standing on opened book and facing inner margin] GIBRALTAR | LIBRARY | BINDING'. Lining paper: black.

Copies: JAG, TNJ.

Note: published 23 Dec. 1965 in 3,750 copies; 30 April 1970, 2,000 copies.

A20.c1   first English edition, first impression, by offset (1962)

[on light blue, in black] by ROBERT PENN WARREN | [in white] THE GODS | OF MOUNT | OLYMPUS | [in black] Illustrated by WILLIAM MOYERS | [on white publisher's device] LEGACY | LIBRARY | FREDERICK MULLER LIMITED | LONDON

Collation: demy 8° (trimmed: 21.0 × 14.0 cm.); *unsigned* [1–4^8], 32 leaves; pagination and numbering identical with **A20.a1**.

Contents: p. [vi]: 'FIRST PUBLISHED IN GREAT BRITAIN IN 1962 BY | FREDERICK MULLER LIMITED | THIS BOOK HAS BEEN PRINTED IN GREAT BRITAIN BY | OFFSET LITHO AT TAYLOR GARNETT EVANS & CO. LTD, | WATFORD, HERTS, AND BOUND BY THEM | [publisher's (FM) device] | COPYRIGHT © 1959 BY RANDOM HOUSE, INC. | TO ROSANNA'.

Typography and Paper: reproduced by offset from **A20.a1**. Paper: white, wove, unwatermarked; sheets bulk 0.5 cm.

Binding: maroon cloth. Front and black: blank. Spine, in gold, vert.: 'The Gods of Mount Olympus *Robert Penn Warren* MULLER'. All edges trimmed and unstained; illus. endpapers.

Dust wrapper: front cover: '[in blue on yellow] *The* GODS | *of* MOUNT | OLYMPUS | [in black] Robert Penn Warren | [colored illus. of four-horse chariot with figures against clouds and mountains] | [upper right edge, in black on white] LEGACY LIBRARY | 3 [publisher's device]'. Spine, in black on red, vert.: 'The Gods of Mount Olympus Robert Penn Warren MULLER'. Back cover: about the Legacy Library. Front flap: about Greek worship. Back flap: blank.

Copies: BL, RPW, STW.

Notes: 1. Published 20 Aug. 1962 at 9s.6d. net in 5,000 copies and in 1965 in 5,000 copies. Both printed by Taylor Garnett Evans, Watford, Herts. A 1971 impression in 3,000 copies was printed by Anchor Press, Tiptree, Essex. (Ltr., V. Andrews, Frederick Muller Ltd., 12 Feb. 1975.) British Library date-stamp 16 July 1962.

2. RPW copy is marked 'Sample Complete Copy | Proof Copy | Manuscript'.

A21 *All the King's Men: A Play*

A21.a1 first American edition, first impression (1960)

ALL | THE | KING'S | MEN | *A Play by* | ROBERT PENN | WARREN | [publisher's device] | RANDOM HOUSE · NEW YORK

Collation: medium folio 8° (trimmed: 22.5 × 13.5 cm.); *unsigned* [1–9⁸], 72 leaves; pp. [i–x], 1–7 [8–10] 11–48 [49–50] 51–102 [103–104] 105–134; numbers in corner formed by tail and outer margins.

Contents: p. [i]: hf. tit. 'ALL THE KING'S MEN'; p. [ii]: blank; p. [iii]: title page; on p. [iv] 'FIRST PRINTING | [copyright information] | CAUTION: [warning about production] | *All inquiries should be ad-dressed* | *to the author's agent, William Morris Agency, 1740 Broadway, New York 19,* | *New York.* | *The amateur acting rights of* ALL THE KING'S MEN *are controlled exclusively by* | *the Dramatists' Play Service, 14 East 38th Street, New York, N.Y., without* | *whose permission in writing no amateur perfor-mance of it may be made.* | Library of Congress Catalog Card Number: 60-8377 | Manufactured in the United States of America'; p. [v]: 'To Francis Fergusson | and the memory of Marion Crowne Fergusson'; p. [vi]: blank; p. [vii]: 'ALL THE KING'S MEN *was presented by Michel Bouché, Arnold* | *M. Brockman and Iris Michaels at the East 74th Street The-atre,* | *New York City, on October 16, 1959, with the following cast:* | *(In order of appearance)* | [cast] | [director, producer, et al.]'; p. [viii]: 'The action takes place in a state of the deep South. | There are a prologue and three acts.'; on p. [ix] 'A NOTE ON PRODUCTION'; p. [x]: blank; pp. 1–7: prologue; p. [8]: blank; on p. [9] 'ACT ONE'; p. [10]: blank; pp. 11–48: act one; on p. [49] 'ACT TWO'; p. [50]: blank; pp. 51–102: act two; on p. [103] 'ACT THREE'; p. [104]: blank; pp. 105–134: act three.

Typography and Paper: text: 35 ll., 14.9 (16.35) × 9.2 cm.; Linotype Granjon 10/13-pt. RT: except on p. 1 and unnumbered pages, 'ALL THE KING'S MEN'. Paper: white, wove, unwatermarked; sheets bulk 1.3 cm.

Binding: purplish red cloth, embossed linen grain. Front, upper half in gilt: publisher's device in square. Spine: '[horiz., in gilt] ROBERT | PENN | WARREN | [vert., on black in gilt with gilt border] ALL THE KING'S MEN | [horiz., in gilt] RANDOM | HOUSE'. Back: blank. All edges trimmed with top edge stained dark blue; white endpapers.

  Dust wrapper: front cover: '[on cream in black] ALL | THE | KING'S | MEN | [publisher's device in antique gold] | [black rule | [on antique gold, in black] BY | Robert Penn Warren | A RANDOM HOUSE PLAY'. Spine, in black: '[on cream] ALL | THE | KING'S | MEN | ROBERT | PENN | WARREN || [on antique gold] Random | House | [publisher's device]'. Back cover, in black on cream: '*Books by Robert Penn Warren* | *available from Random House*'. Front flap: excerpts from reviews. Back flap: about the author.

Copies: CoCA (3), Ctw, CtY, KyU, LC, LU (rebound), STW, TNJ (2).

Notes: 1. Published 25 April 1960 in 4,000 copies at $2.95. Printed by

American Book-Stratford Press, Inc. Subsequent impressions: 24 Oct. 1969, 1,000; 5 Oct. 1971, 1,000; 8 Jan. 1973, 750. Distributed in Canada by Random House of Canada Limited. (Ltr., Jim Wilcox, Random House, Inc., 31 July 1974.) LC copyright 29 March 1960 (D4049); two copies deposited 23 June 1960.

    2. This play appeared complete in *SR*, 68 (Spring 1960), 177–239.

    3. TNJ copy is inscribed on the free endpaper: 'To | Bill & Alice | with best love | Red || Fairfield, Connecticut | May 1, 1960 || '.

A21.a2   first American edition, second impression (1969)

Contents: on p. [iv] 'SECOND PRINTING'.

Binding: medium red, calico-texture cloth, not embossed. Front: publisher's device blind stamped. Spine, in gilt: '[horiz.] ROBERT | PENN | WARREN | [vert., in gilt frame] ALL THE KING'S MEN | [horiz.] RANDOM | HOUSE'. Back: blank. All edges trimmed with top edge stained dark blue; white endpapers.

Copies: JAG.

Note: sold for $4.50.

A21.a3   first American edition, third impression (1971)

Binding: light red cloth, embossed calico grain. Front and back: blank. Spine: identical with **A21.a2**. All edges trimmed with top edge stained dark blue; white endpapers.

Copies: JAG, RPW.

Note: sold for $5.50.

A21.b1   second American edition, script edition, paperback (1960)

[down left side, seven bold rules, 9.25 cm.] ALL THE | KING'S MEN | A PLAY | BY ROBERT PENN WARREN | [five-point solid star] | [horiz., seven bold rules, 9.25 cm.] | [five-point solid star] | DRAMATISTS | PLAY SERVICE | INC. [down right side, seven bold rules, 3.3 cm.]

Collation: pott folio 4° (trimmed: 19.6 × 13.2 cm.); *unsigned* 34 leaves; pp. [1–2] 3–5 [6] 7–66 [67–68]; numbers centered at foot of text in tail margin.

Contents: p. [1]: title page; p. [2]: copyright and caution; p. 3: Off-

Broadway cast; p. 4: list of characters; p. 5: note on production; p. [6]: blank; on p. 7 'ALL THE KING'S MEN | PROLOGUE'; pp. 11–28: act one; pp. 29–51: act two; pp. 52–65: act three; on p. 66 'PROPERTY PLOT'; pp. [67–68]: publisher's advertisements.

Typography and Paper: text: 40 ll., 15.5 (16.0) × 9.2 cm.; Intertype Weiss Roman with italic and swash capitals 10/11-pt. Paper: white, wove, unwatermarked; sheets bulk 0.3 cm.

Binding: paper, stapled. Front cover, on gray in black: '[left side, vert., eight bold rules, 12.9 cm.] ALL THE | KING'S MEN | A PLAY | BY ROBERT PENN WARREN | [five point, solid star] | [horiz., eight bold rules, 13.2 cm.] | [five-point solid star] | DRAMATISTS | PLAY SERVICE | INC. [vert., seven bold rules, 4.6 cm.]'. Spine: 'ALL THE KING'S MEN——WARREN'. Back cover: publisher's advertisement. Inside front and back covers: publisher's advertisements. All edges trimmed and unstained.

Copies: Ctw, JAG, RPW, STW, ViU.

Note: published 24 Ot. 1960 in 1,000 copies. Subsequent impressions: 6 Aug. 1962, 1,000; 1 March 1965, 1,000; 26 July 1967, 1,000; 15 Jan. 1970, 2,000. (Ltr., James Bohan, Play Leasing Dept., Dramatists Play Service, Inc., 13 Feb. 1975.)

A22   *You, Emperors, and Others: Poems, 1957–1960*

A22.a1   first American edition, first impression (1960)

YOU, EMPERORS, AND OTHERS | Poems 1957–1960 | [orn.] ROBERT PENN WARREN | RANDOM HOUSE NEW YORK

Collation: super royal 8° (trimmed: 22.7 × 17.2 cm.); *unsigned* [1–3^{16}], 48 leaves; pp. [i–xii], [1–2] 3–79 [80] 81 [82–84]; on v., numbers are located in the corner formed by the tail and outer margins; on r., in corner formed by the tail and inner margins.

Contents: p. [i]: hf. tit. '*YOU, EMPERORS, AND OTHERS: Poems 1957–1960*'; p. [ii]: blank; on p. [iii] 'BOOKS BY ROBERT PENN WARREN'; p. [iv]: blank; p. [v]: title page; p. [vi]: 'First Printing | [copyright statements] | Library of Congress Catalog Card Number: 60-12123 | Manufactured in the United States of America | These poems have appeared in the *Partisan Review, Yale Review,* | *American Scholar, Saturday Review, Kenyon Review, Virginia Quarterly Review,* |

Prairie Schooner, Sewanee Review, Delta, and [*sic*] *Botteghe Oscure*.'; p. [vii]:
'*To Max and Carol Shulman*'; p. [viii]: blank; on p. [ix] '*Contents*'; p. [xii]:
blank; p. [1]: hf. tit.; p. [2]: blank; pp. 3–4: '*Garland for You* | 1
CLEARLY ABOUT YOU'; pp. 5–6: '2 LULLABY: EXERCISE IN
HUMAN CHARITY AND SELF-KNOWLEDGE'; pp. 7–8: '3
MAN IN THE STREET'; pp. 9–10: '4 SWITZERLAND'; pp.
11–12: '5 A REAL QUESTION CALLING FOR SOLUTION';
pp. 13–16: '6 THE LETTER ABOUT MONEY, LOVE, OR
OTHER COMFORT, IF ANY'; pp. 17–18: '7 ARROGANT LAW';
p. 19: '8 THE SELF THAT STARES'; pp. 20–22: '*Two Pieces after
Suetonius* | 1 APOLOGY FOR DOMITIAN'; pp. 22–23: '2 TI-
BERIUS ON CAPRI'; pp. 24–25: '*Mortmain* | 1 AFTER NIGHT
FLIGHT SON REACHES BEDSIDE OF ALREADY | UNCON-
SCIOUS FATHER, WHOSE RIGHT HAND LIFTS | IN A
SPASMODIC GESTURE, AS THOUGH TRYING | TO MAKE
CONTACT: 1955'; pp. 26–27: '2 A DEAD LANGUAGE: CIRCA
1885'; pp. 28–29: '3 FOX-FIRE: 1956'; pp. 30–31: '4 IN THE TUR-
PITUDE OF TIME: N.D.'; pp. 32–33: '5 A VISION: CIRCA
1880'; pp. 34–36: '*Fatal Interview: Penthesilea and Achilles*'; p. 37: '*Some
Quiet, Plain Poems* | 1 ORNITHOLOGY IN A WORLD OF FLUX';
p. 38: '2 HOLLY AND HICKORY'; p. 39: '3 THE WELL HOUSE';
pp. 40–41: '4 IN MOONLIGHT, SOMEWHERE, THEY ARE
SINGING'; pp. 42–43: '5 IN ITALIAN THEY CALL THE BIRD
CIVETTA'; pp. 44–45: '6 DEBATE: QUESTION, QUARRY,
DREAM'; p. 46: '*Ballad: Between the Boxcars (1923)* | 1 I CAN'T
EVEN REMEMBER THE NAME'; pp. 47–48: '2 HE WAS FOR-
MIDABLE'; pp. 49–50: '3 HE HAS FLED'; p. 51: '*Two Studies in
Idealism: Short Survey of American, and Human, History* | *For Allan Nevins*
| 1 BEAR TRACK PLANTATION: SHORTLY AFTER SHI-
LOH'; pp. 52–53: '2 HARVARD '61: BATTLE FATIGUE'; pp.
54–55: '*Nocturne: Traveling Salesman in Hotel Bedroom*'; pp. 56–57: '*So
You Agree with What I Say? Well, What Did I Say?*'; pp. 58–59: '*Prog-
nosis: A Short Story,* | *the End of Which You Will Know Soon Enough* | 1
AND OH——'; p. 60: '2 WHAT THE SAND SAID'; p. 61: '3
WHAT THE JOREE SAID, THE JOREE BEING ONLY A
BIRD'; pp. 62–63: '*Autumnal Equinox on Mediterranean Beach*'; pp.
64–65: '*Nursery Rhymes* | 1 KNOCKETY-KNOCKETY-KNOCK';
pp. 66–67: '2 NEWS OF UNEXPECTED DEMISE | OF LITTLE
BOY BLUE'; pp. 68–69: '3 MOTHER MAKES THE BISCUITS';
p. 70: '4 THE BRAMBLE BUSH'; p. 71: '*Short Thoughts for Long
Nights* | 1 NIGHTMARE OF MOUSE'; p. 72: '2 NIGHTMARE OF

MAN'; p. 73: '3 COLLOQUY WITH COCKROACH'; p. 74: '4 LITTLE BOY ON VOYAGE'; p. 75: '5 OBSESSION'; p. 76: '6 JOY'; p. 77: '7 CRICKET, ON KITCHEN FLOOR, ENTERS HISTORY'; p. 78: '8 LITTLE BOY AND GENERAL PRINCIPLE'; p. 79: '9 GRASSHOPPER TRIES TO BREAK SOLIPSISM'; p. [80]: blank; on p. 81 *'About the Author'*; pp. [82–84]: blank.

Typography and Paper: text: lines vary, (16.75) × 12.6 cm.; Bodoni Monotype 10/14-pt. Paper: white, wove, unwatermarked; sheets bulk 0.8 cm.

Binding: black cloth. Front cover, in silver, fancy: 'RWP [W larger than R and P]'. Spine, vert., in silver: *'ROBERT PENN WARREN YOU, EMPERORS, AND OTHERS* RANDOM HOUSE'. Back: blank. All edges trimmed with top edge stained blue-black; white endpapers.

Dust wrapper: front cover, on blue: '[in white] *YOU, EMPERORS,* | *AND OTHERS* | *Poems 1957–1960* | [black orn.] [in white] *Robert Penn Warren'*. Spine, in white on black: '[vert.] *YOU, EMPERORS, AND OTHERS* | [horiz.] RANDOM | HOUSE | [vert.] *Robert Penn Warren'*. Back, on white, in blue and in black: brief biographical sketch. Front flap: about RPW's poetry. Back flap: publisher's advertisement.

Copies: Ctb, CtY, JAG, KyU, LC, LU (2), STW (2), TxFTC.

Notes: 1. Published 31 Aug. 1960 in 4,000 copies at $3.50. Printed by Quinn & Boden Co. "This is the only printing. No record as to plate location" (ltr., Jim Wilcox, Random House, Inc., 31 July 1974). Distributed in Canada by Random House of Canada Limited. LC copyright 16 Aug. 1960 (A470451); two copies deposited 7 Nov. 1960.

2. On p. [vi] the word "and" in the acknowledgments is inadvertently italicized.

A23 *The Legacy of the Civil War: Meditations on the Centennial*

A23.a1 first American edition, first impression (1961)

THE LEGACY OF | THE CIVIL WAR | *Meditations on the Centennial* | BY | ROBERT PENN WARREN | [publisher's device] | *Random House* · *New York*

Collation: large post 8° (trimmed: 20.25 × 12.7 cm.); *unsigned* [1–8⁸], 64 leaves; pp. [i–x], [1–2] 3–109 [110–118]; numbers centered at foot of type page.

Contents: pp. [i–iv]: blank; p. [iii]: hf. tit. 'THE LEGACY OF | THE CIVIL WAR'; on p. [iv]]BOOKS BY ROBERT PENN WARREN'; p.

[v]: title page; p. [vi]: 'First Printing | [copyright statements] | Library of Congress Catalog Card Number: 61-7261 | Manufactured in the United States of America | by Quinn & Boden Company, Inc., Rahway, N.J.'; p. [vii]: 'To *Sidney Hook*'; p. [viii]: blank; p. [1]: hf. tit.; p. [2]: blank; pp. 3–109: text, with the initial words in the first sentence of each section printed in small caps. and three five-point stars separating each section; p. [110]: blank; on pp. [111–112] 'ABOUT THE AUTHOR'; pp. [113–118]: blank.

Typography and Paper: text: 20 ll., 14.25 (16.15) × 8.7 cm.; Linotype Granjon 12/21-pt., "25 × 42 picas overall. The display type used was 30-pt. Ultra Bodoni with Monotype 10-pt. #301 stars." RT: v., 'THE LEGACY OF'; r., 'THE CIVIL WAR'. Paper: "44 × 66 Perkins and Squire Standard wove sheet," white, unwatermarked. Ink: "General Printing Ink Book black" (ltr., Harold Morgan, Quinn & Boden Company, Inc., 21 Feb. 1975). Sheets bulk 1.2 cm.

Binding: gray bds. with white cloth spine. Front: blind-stamped rectangular frame with orn. in each corner enclosing an oval frame with 'R P W' in the center. Spine, vert., in red: '*Robert Penn Warren* THE LEGACY OF THE CIVIL WAR *Random House*'. Back: blank. All edges trimmed with top edge stained red; white lining paper and no free endpapers.

Note: 1₁ and 8₈ are used as lining papers.

Dust wrapper: front cover: '[on light brown, in white] THE LEGACY | OF THE | CIVIL WAR | [red rule] | [in black] Meditations on the Centennial | [black rule] | [darker brown background of rectangular frame with black and red inner frames and a light brown orn. in each corner; within a red oval outlined in white with white ltrs. in script] *Robert Penn Warren*'. Spine, vert., on white: '[in white] *Robert Penn Warren* [in red] THE LEGACY OF THE CIVIL WAR [in black] *Random House*'. Back cover, on white, in black and in red: publisher's advertisement. Front flap: '$2.75 | [review] | [publisher's imprint] | *Jacket design by Guy Fleming* | 2/61'. Back flap: biographical sketch.

Copies: CtY, JAG, KyU, LC, LU, STW, TNJ, TxFTC.

Notes: 1. Published 27 Feb. 1961 in 10,000 copies at $2.75. Printed by Quinn & Boden Company, Inc. (Ltr., Jim Wilcox, Random House, Inc., 31 July 1974.) Distributed in Canada by Random House of Canada Limited. LC copyright 4 April 1961 (A513763); two copies deposited 31 July 1961.

2. In a letter, 19 May 1961, Albert Erskine, Random House, mentions that RPW signed 1,000 copies; however, those copies were not issued in a special edition. (Ctw)

3. An adaptation from *LCW* appeared as "A Mark Deep on a Nation's Soul," *Life*, 17 March 1961, pp. 82–89.

A23.b1 first American edition, first impression, by offset, paperback (1964)

THE LEGACY | OF | THE CIVIL WAR | *Meditations on the Centennial* | [orn.] | ROBERT PENN WARREN | [publisher's device] | VINTAGE BOOKS | *A Division of* RANDOM HOUSE: *New York*

Collation: post folio 8° (trimmed: 18.4 × 10.85 cm.); *unsigned* 64 ind. leaves; pp. [i–vi], [1–2] 3–109 [110–122]; numbering identical with **A23.a1**.

Contents: p. [i]: hf. tit. 'THE LEGACY | OF | THE CIVIL WAR'; p. [ii]: blank; p. [iii]: title page; p. [iv]: 'FIRST VINTAGE EDITION, September, 1964 | [copyright data]'; p. [v]: dedication; p. [vi]: blank; p. [1]: hf. tit.; p. [2]: blank; pp. 3–109: text; p. [110]: blank; p. [111]: biographical sketch; pp. [112–122]: publisher's advertisements.

Typography and Paper: identical wtih **A23.a1**. Paper: white, wove, unwatermarked; sheets bulk 0.9 cm.

Binding: paper. Front cover, identical with **A23.a1** except across lower edge: '[in red on light brown] A Vintage Book [in black, publisher's device] [in red] V-265 $1.25'. Spine, on beige: after title: '[horiz., in black, publisher's device] | [vert., in red] Vintage | [horiz., in black] V-265'. Back cover, in red and in black: publisher's advertisement. Inside covers: white. All edges trimmed and unstained.

Copies: JAG, KyU.

Note: published Sept. 1964 at $1.25. Distributed in Canada by Random House of Canada Limited. Additional publication information is not available (ltr., Jim Wilcox, Random House, Inc., 31 July 1974).

A24 *Wilderness: A Tale of the Civil War*

A24.a1 first American edition, first impression (1961)

[condensed type] Wilderness | [orn. rule] | Tale of the Civil War | by

Robert Penn Warren | Random House · New York | [publisher's device]

Collation: demy 8° (trimmed: 21.2 × rough trimmed: 14.3 cm.); *unsigned* [1–10¹⁶], 160 leaves; pp. [i–viii], [1–2] 3–310 [311–312]; numbers centered beneath 1.6 cm. rule at foot of type page.

Contents: p. [i]: hf. tit. 'WILDERNESS'; on p. [ii] 'BOOKS BY ROBERT PENN WARREN'; p. [iii]: title page; p. [iv]: 'FIRST PRINTING | [copyright statement] | *Library of Congress Catalog Card Number: 61-6248* | *Manufactured in the United States of America by H. Wolff, New York*'; p. [v]: 'TO Hugh AND Ethelyn Cox'; p. [vi]: blank; p. [vii]: '[epigraph] | *King Henry V*, WILLIAM SHAKESPEARE | [epigraph] | *Pensées*, 397–398, PASCAL'; p. [viii]: blank; p. [1]: hf. tit.; p. [2]: blank; pp. 3–310: text, with chapter headings consisting of three-dimensional shaded Arabic numerals underscored by an orn. rule on pp. 3, 18, 25, 39, 55, 82, 95, 132, 162, 196, 227, 246, 269, 282, and 291; p. [311]: about the author; p. [312]: blank.

Typography and Paper: text: 30 ll., 14.5 (15.7) × 9.0 cm.; Linotype Caledonia 11/14-pt. Paper: white, wove, unwatermarked; sheets bulk 2.5 cm.

Binding: orange cloth, embossed calico grain. Front, in white shaded ltrs.: 'R P W'. Spine: '[in black, publisher's device] | [on black oblong in white] Wilderness | [orn. rule] | [in orange] Robert | Penn | Warren | [orange on orange] Random | House'. Back: blank. Fore edge rough trimmed, top and bottom edges trimmed with top edge stained black; cream endpapers.

Dust wrapper: front cover, on motley gray: '[in black] WILDER-| NESS | [in white] *A Tale of the Civil War* | [dark blue illus. begins at outer edge and continues to spine] | [in red] ROBERT PENN | WARREN | [in black, publisher's device] [in white] A RANDOM HOUSE NOVEL'. Spine, on motley gray: '[in black] Wilder-|ness | [dark blue illus.] | [in red] ROBERT | PENN | WARREN | [in black, publisher's device] | [in white] RANDOM | HOUSE'. Back cover, on white: photograph of RPW by Peter Fink. Front flap: about the story. Back flap: about the author.

Copies: Ctb, CtY, JAG, KyU, LC, LU, STW, TNJ, TxFTC.

Note: published 15 Nov. 1961 in 28,350 copies at $4.95. Printed by American Book-Stratford Press, Inc. Subsequent impressions: 21 Nov. 1969, 1,000. (Ltr., Jim Wilcox, Random House, Inc., 31 July

1974.) Distributed in Canada by Random House of Canada Limited. LC copyright 20 Oct. 1961 (A552567); two copies deposited 29 March 1962.

A24.b1   first American edition, book-club edition (1961)

Title Page: The title, orn. rule, and publisher's device are in blue.

Collation: demy folio 8° (trimmed: 21.0 × rough trimmed: 13.9 cm.).

Contents: p. [ii]: blank; p. [iv]: omits LC Catalog Card Number and manufacturer's name; pp. 3ff.: numbers and rules designating chapters in blue; p. [311]: shorter biographical sketch (17 ll.).

Paper: white, wove, unwatermarked; sheets bulk 2.3 cm.

Binding: bds., gray with quarter orange. Front, in dark blue shaded ltrs.: 'R P W'. Spine, in dark blue on orange: '[publisher's device] | Wilderness | [orn. rule] | Robert | Penn | Warren | Random | House'. Back: blank. Fore edge rough trimmed, top and bottom edges trimmed with top edge stained dark blue; white endpapers.
  Dust wrapper: front flap: 'BOOK CLUB | EDITION' with title and author's name in black rather than in red.

Copies: Ctw, JAG (2), STW.

Note: A Literary Guild selection, Dec. 1961. "Robert Penn Warren Tells About *Wilderness*," *Wings: The Literary Guild Review*, Dec. 1961, pp. [3]–4.

A24.c1   second American edition, first impression, paperback (1962)

[shaded] WILDERNESS | *A Tale of the Civil War* | *by* | ROBERT PENN WARREN | [publisher's device] | A SIGNET BOOK | Published by THE NEW AMERICAN LIBRARY

Collation: post folio 8° (trimmed: 17.9 × 10.5 cm.); *unsigned* 96 ind. leaves; pp. [1–6] 7–190 [191–192]; numbers centered beneath type page on pp. 7, 28, 152; others in corner formed by outer and head margins.

Contents: p. [1]: excerpts from reviews; p. [2]: publisher's advertisement; p. [3]: title page; p. [4]: dedication and copyright; p. [5]: epigraphs; p. [6]: blank; pp. 7–190: text, with chapters designated by shaded Arabic numerals above two rules, one thicker than the other; pp. [191–192]: publisher's advertisements.

Typography and Paper: text: 44 ll., 15.3 (15.8) × 8.7 cm.; Times New Roman 10-pt. RT: v., '*Robert Penn Warren*'; r., 'WILDERNESS'. Paper: white, wove, unwatermarked; sheets bulk 1.0 cm.

Binding: paper. Front cover, against a yellowish gold background: '[in black, curved] SIGNET | [on white] 60¢ | BOOKS | [half oval frame] P2231 | [within white rectangle with thin black frame] THE POWER-FUL NEW NOVEL BY | PULITZER PRIZE WINNER | [in purple] ROBERT PENN | WARREN | [in black, fancy rule] | WILDER-NESS | A Tale of the Civil War | [beneath white rectangle, against background of illus., quotation from NEW YORK TIMES] | [illus. of encamped troops] | [next to spine edge, beginning toward lower edge, in yellow] A SIGNET BOOK · Complete and Unabridged'. Spine, white background: '[horiz., on black in white ltrs., encircled] SIG-NET | [on white in black] P | 2231 | [vert., in blue] WILDERNESS [in black] · ROBERT PENN WARREN'. Back cover, upper two-thirds on white: about the novel, excerpts from reviews, about the author; lower one-third on dark brown: publisher's advertisement. Inside covers: white. All edges trimmed and stained red.

Copies: Ctw, JAG (2), KyU, STW.

Note: published Dec. 1962 at 60¢. Additional publication information is not available.

A24.d1   first English edition, first impression (1962)

Robert Penn Warren | [outlined] WILDERNESS | London | EYRE & SPOTTISWOODE | 22 Henrietta Street · WC₂

Collation: demy folio 8° (trimmed: 19.95 × 13.2 cm.); signed, [A]⁸ B–Q⁸, 128 leaves; pp. [1–8] 9–255 [256]; numbers centered at foot of type page.

Contents: p. [1]: synopsis; on p. [2] '*by the same author*'; p. [3]: title page; p. [4]: ' © 1961 Robert Penn Warren | This edition published 1962 | Printed in Great Britain | by Cox & Wyman Limited | London, Fakenham and Reading | Catalogue Number 6/4269/2'; p. [5]: dedication; p. [6]: blank; p. [7]: epigraphs; p. [8]: blank; pp. 9–[256]: text.

Typography and Paper: text: 33 ll., 14.8 (15.4) × 9.6 cm.; Monotype Baskerville 11/13-pt. Paper: white, wove, unwatermarked; sheets bulk 1.9 cm.

Binding: blue cloth. Front and back: blank. Spine, vert.: '[in silver]

Robert Penn Warren [in gilt] Wilderness [in silver] eyre & spottis-woode'. All edges trimmed and unstained; white endpapers.

Dust wrapper: front cover, against patterned background: '[on green and gold patches in white] Wilder | ness | [lower left on purple in white] Robert | Penn | Warren | [lower right, in black and white, silhouette of human form]'. Spine: '[horiz., on green in white] Robert | Penn | Warren | [vert., on purple in white] Wilderness | [horiz., on purple in white] E & S'. Back cover: other books by RPW. Front flap: about the book; jacket design by Pamela Stokes. Back flap: 'PRINTED IN GREAT BRITAIN'.

Copies: BL, Ctw (3), JAG, KyU, STW.

Note: published 1962 at 18s. Printed by Cox & Wyman Limited. Additional publication information is not available (ltr., Maria Lyras, Publicity Dept., Eyre Methuen Ltd., 6 June 1975). British Library date-stamp 29 May 1962.

A25   *Flood: A Romance of Our Time*

A25.a1   first American edition, first impression (1964)

|| [Thorne shaded ltrs.] FLOOD || *A Romance of Our Time* | [orn. rule] | ROBERT | PENN WARREN || [publisher's device] | *Random House New York*

Collation: demy 8° (trimmed: 21.15 × rough trimmed: 14.35 cm.); *unsigned* [1–14^{16}], 224 leaves; pp. [i–viii], [1–3] 4–440; in parentheses, numbers inset from outer margin at top of type page on line with RT, except book and chapter pages, which are unnumbered throughout: pp. [14], [22], [32], [42], [58], [78], [97], [112], [129–131], [142], [152], [164], [172], [178], [191–193], [207], [221], [234], [252], [264], [275], [291], [299–301], [320], [340], [350], [368], [379], [389], [400–403], [415], and [428].

Contents: p. [i]: hf. tit. '[script] Flood | [orn. rule]'; on p. [ii] '*Books by* ROBERT PENN WARREN'; p. [iii]: title page; p. [iv]: 'FIRST PRINTING | [copyright statements] | *Library of Congress Catalog Card Number: 64-10357* | *Manufactured in the United States of America* | *by H. Wolff, New York* | *Design by Tere Loprete*'; p. [v]: 'TO | *Albert and Marisa Erskine*'; p. [vi]: blank; p. [vii]: '[epigraph in ital.] *Amos* IX:15'; p. [viii]: blank; p. [1]: '[script] Book | [Thorne shaded ltrs.] ONE | [orn. rule]'; p. [2]: blank; pp. [3]–440: text, with each chapter designated: ' || *Chapter* || [Arabic numeral] || '.

Typography and Paper: text: 43 ll., 16.1 (16.75) × 9.7 cm.; Linotype Primer 11-pt. RT: v., '*Robert Penn Warren*'; r., 'FLOOD'. Paper: white, wove, unwatermarked; sheets bulk 3.3 cm.

Binding: blue-green cloth. Front, stamped in blue-green, 4 ll. of two orns. each (orns. represent water). Spine: '[in blue-green, 2 ll. of two "water" orns. each] | [in gilt] FLOOD | [in yellowish green, 1 l. of two "water" orns.] | [in gilt] Robert Penn | *WARREN* | [in blue-green, 3 ll. of two "water" orns. each] | [in gilt, publisher's device] | *Random House*'. Back: blank. Fore edge rough trimmed, top and bottom edges trimmed with top edge stained yellowish green; yellow endpapers.

Dust wrapper: front cover, within brown, thin-lined frame, with background of bluish green and light green undulating lines separated by dark green undulating lines: '[in white] Robert | Penn | Warren | [in orange] FLOOD | [in white] *A Romance of Our Time* | [in orange] A Random House Novel'. Spine, within brown, thin-lined frame: '[vert., on bluish green in orange] FLOOD | [horiz., on light green square in white] Robert | Penn | Warren | [on bluish green in brown, publisher's device] | [on bluish green in white] Random House'. Back cover, on white in light green and in bluish green: publisher's advertisement. Front flap: about the novel; jacket design by Lawrence Ratzkin. Back flap: continuation from front flap.

Copies: Ctb, CtY, JAG, KyU, LC, LU, STW, TNJ, TxFTC.

Notes: 1. Published May 1964 in 35,000 copies at $5.95. Printed by American Book-Stratford Press, Inc. Subsequent impressions: 15 Oct. 1968, 1,000. (Ltr., Jim Wilcox, Random House, Inc., 31 July 1974.) Distributed in Canada by Random House of Canada Limited. LC copyright 18 March 1964 (A707704); two copies deposited 10 Aug. 1964.

2. On p. 439.2: "fact" should read "face" (ltr., Stuart Wright, 8 May 1980).

3. Excerpts: "Fiddlersburg Preacher," *Esquire*, July 1963, pp. 55–56; "Have You Seen Sukie?" *VQR*, 39 (Autumn 1963), 574–586; "How to Make a Movie in Fiddlersburg, Tennessee," *North American Review*, March 1964, pp. 42–49, 82–83; "Moths Against the Screen," *Saturday Evening Post*, 4 April 1964, pp. 42–43, 46–50, and 52–55; "It's a Long Way from Central Park to Fiddlersburg," *KR*, 26 (Winter 1964), 129–143.

A25.b1   first American edition, book-club edition (1964)

Title Page: lettering identical wtih **A25.a1**, but in orangish red; rules, orn., publisher's device in black.

Collation: (trimmed: 20.9 × rough trimmed: 13.9 cm.).

Contents: p. [i]: script in red, orn. in black; p. [ii]: blank; p. [iv]: omits LC number and manufacturer's name; p. [1]: script in red, orn. in black.

Binding: brownish-gray quarter, light green cloth. Front, medium green on light green: orns. Spine, bluish green orns. on brownish gray; ltrs. in gilt, identical with **A25.a1**. Back cover: blank. Same trim with top edge stained orange; white endpapers.

    Dust wrapper: front cover, no frame; medium blue and very light green undulating lines separated by bluish green undulating lines; publisher's name is deleted and title is in lighter orange. Spine, no frame; title is lighter orange; author's name vert., in white: 'Robert | Penn Warren'; publisher's device in white. Back cover, on white in blue: '*Great Writers on Reading*'. Front flap: lower right corner, 'BOOK CLUB | EDITION'. Back flap: omits publisher's address.

Copies: JAG, STW, TNJ.

Note: A Literary Guild selection, May 1964. Essay by RPW for *Wings: The Literary Guild Review*, May 1964: about the novel, pp. [i] [1–3]; essay, pp. 4–5; about the author, p. 6.

A25.c1   second American edition, first impression, paperback (1965)

[Thorne shaded ltrs.] FLOOD | *A Romance of Our Time* | Robert Penn Warren | [publisher's device] | A SIGNET BOOK | Published by | THE NEW AMERICAN LIBRARY

Collation: post folio 8° (trimmed: 18.0 × 10.5 cm.); *unsigned* 184 leaves; pp. [1–8] 9–368; numbers are centered below type page in tail margin.

Contents: p. [1]: about the novel; p. [2]: publisher's advertisement; p. [3]: title page; p. [4]: dedication and copyright; p. [5]: epigraph; p. [6]: blank; p. [7]: hf. tit. '[Thorne shaded ltrs.] FLOOD'; p. [8]: blank; pp. 9–368: text.

Typography and Paper: text: 47 ll., 15.8 (16.0) × 8.9 cm.; Times New Roman 10-pt. Paper: white, wove, unwatermarked; sheets bulk 2.1 cm.

Binding: paper: '[on white in black] A SIGNET BOOK COMPLETE AND UNABRIDGED | [in olive green and brown, publisher's device] | [in black] Q2611 | The Magnificent new novel by one of America's | great writers——the Pulitzer Prize-winning author | [in red rectangular frame with blunted corners, on black, in olive green] Robert Penn Warren | [in black rectangular frame with rounded corners, on blue above illus., in black open ltrs.] FLOOD | [quotations from two reviews]'. Spine: '[horiz., on red oval, which is on black square, in white] SIGNET | [on white in black] Q | 2611 | [vert., blue open ltrs.] FLOOD [in black] Robert Penn Warren'. Back cover: about the novel, quotations from reviews, about the author (including small photograph). Inside covers: white. All edges trimmed and stained red.

Copies: Ctw, JAG, KyU, STW.

Note: published April 1965 at 95¢. Additional publication information is not available.

A25.d1   first English edition, first impression (1964)

ROBERT PENN WARREN | *Flood* | A NOVEL | *Collins* | ST JAMES'S PLACE, LONDON | 1964

Collation: demy folio 8° (trimmed: 21.0 × 13.4 cm.); signed, [A]–2E⁸, 224 leaves; pp. [1–10] 11–134 [135–136] 137–195 [196–198] 199–302 [303–306] 307–405 [406–408] 409–446 [447–448]; numbers centered at foot of type page.

> *Note*: Signatures toward outer margins; 'F' appears near inner margin on signature page.

Contents: p. [1]: hf. tit. '*Flood*'; on p. [2]: 'BOOKS BY ROBERT PENN WARREN'; p. [3]: title page; p. [4]: ' © 1963, 1964, *by Robert Penn Warren* | *Printed in Great Britain* | *Collins Clear-Type Press* | *London and Glasgow*'; p. [5]: dedication; p. [6]: blank; p. [7]: epigraph; p. [8]: blank; p. [9]: '*Book One*'; p. [10]: blank; pp. 11–446: text, with chapters designated by bold Arabic numerals, centered above single rule; pp. [447–448]: blank.

Typography and Paper: text: 39 ll., 17.1 (17.5) × 10.05 cm.; Mergenthaler Linotype Caslon Old Face 11/13-pt. Paper: white, wove, unwatermarked; sheets bulk 2.7 cm.

Binding: olive green cloth. Front and back: blank. Spine, in gilt: '*Flood* | [double rule] | *ROBERT* | *PENN* | *WARREN* | *COLLINS*'. All edges trimmed and unstained; white endpapers.

Dust wrapper: cover, dark blue-green. Front: '[in yellow] *Flood* | [black rule] | [in black] ROBERT | PENN | WARREN | AUTHOR OF | [in light blue] ALL THE | KING'S MEN | [in black] A NOVEL'. Spine: '[in yellow] Flood | [black rule] | [in black] Robert | Penn | Warren | A NOVEL | COLLINS'. Back cover: blank. Front flap: about the novel. Back flap: about the author.

Copies: BL, JAG, STW.

Note: published Oct. 1964 in 8,000 copies at 25s. Printed June 1964 by Collins Clear-Type Press. Out of print April 1972. (Ltr., S. Reid-Foster, Collins Publishers, 12 Feb. 1975.) British Library date-stamp 21 Oct. 1964.

A26 *Who Speaks for the Negro?*

A26.a1 first American edition, first impression (1965)

WHO SPEAKS | *FOR THE NEGRO?* || *Robert Penn Warren* | [publisher's device] | *Random House New York*

Collation: demy 8° (trimmed: 21.3 × rough trimmed: 14.4 cm.); *unsigned* [1–13^{16} 14^{12} 15^{16}], 236 leaves; pp. [$^{\pi}$1–2], [i–xii], [1–3] 4–454 [455–458]; numbers in ital.; in v., preceded by a double colon and inset from inner margin at top of type page; on r., followed by double colon and inset from inner margin at top of type page. Chapter pages are unnumbered.

Contents: pp. [$^{\pi}$1–2]: blank; p. [i]: hf. tit. '*Who Speaks for the Negro?*'; on p. [ii] 'BOOKS BY ROBERT PENN WARREN'; p. [iii]: title page; p. [iv]: 'FIRST PRINTING | [copyright information] | *Library of Congress Catalog Card Number: 65-16759* | *The author and publisher wish to thank the following for permission* | *to use material quoted:* [acknowledgments] | MANUFACTURED IN THE UNITED STATES OF AMERICA BY | THE HADDON CRAFTSMEN, SCRANTON, PA. | *Design by Tere Loprete*'; p. [v]: '*With thanks to all those who speak here*'; p. [vi]: blank; p. [vii]: '[epigraph] | A character in *Under Western Eyes,* | by JOSEPH CONRAD'; p. [viii]: blank; p. [ix]: '*Foreword* | [message] | *Robert Penn Warren* | February, 1965'; p. [x]: blank; p. [xi]: contents; p. [xii]: blank; p. [1]: hf. tit.; p. [2]: blank; p. [3]: '1 [orn.] *The Cleft Stick* | : 1 : [other sections numbered similarly] | [text]'; on p. [44] '2 [orn.] *A Mississippi Journal*'; on p. [132] '3 [orn.] *The Big Brass*'; on p. [268] '4 [orn.] *Leadership from* | *the Periphery*'; on p. [355] '5 [orn.] *The Young*'; on

p. [405] '6 [orn.] *Conversation Piece*'; on p. [445] '[orn.] *Index*'; pp. [455–458]: blank.

Typography and Paper: text: 39 ll., 16.3 (16.9) × 9.15 cm.; Monotype Times Roman 10/12-pt. RT: v., '*Who Speaks for the Negro?*'; r., respective chapter titles in ital. Paper: 45 × 68 in., International Paper's I. P. opaque text, 50 lb., 450 pp./in. (telecon, Meredith White, Halliday Lithograph, 26 Feb. 1975); white, wove, unwatermarked; sheets bulk 3.1 cm.

Binding: maroon cloth. Front, in gilt: '[4 four-point star orns., arranged in diamond shape] | *R·P·W*'. Spine, in black: '[same star orn. arrangement] | [in gilt] *Who* || *Speaks* || *for the* || *Negro?* | [in black, one star orn.] | [in gilt] Robert | Penn | Warren | [publisher's device] | *Random House*'. Back: blank. Fore edge rough trimmed, top and bottom edges trimmed with top edge stained red; white endpapers.

Dust wrapper: front cover, within white frame on black: '[in white with gray question mark: 'WHO | SPEAKS | FOR THE | NEGRO? | [in red] ROBERT | PENN | WARREN | [in gray] A RANDOM HOUSE BOOK'. Spine, within white frame: '[vert., on black in red] ROBERT PENN WARREN | [in white with gray question mark] WHO SPEAKS | FOR THE NEGRO? | [horiz., in white, publisher's device] | RANDOM | HOUSE'. Back cover, in red and black on white: publisher's advertisement. Front flap: about the book; jacket design by Muriel Nasser. Back flap: continued from front flap.

Copies: Ctb, CtY, JAG, KyU, LC, LU, STW, TNJ.

Notes: 1. Published 27 May 1965 in 10,000 copies at $5.95. Printed by Halliday Lithograph. Subsequent impressions: 17 Aug. 1965, 1,500; 1 April 1966, 1,200; 24 March 1967, 1,500; 1 May 1968, 1,550; 13 Nov. 1968, 1,550; 17 Nov. 1969, 1,550; 21 Dec. 1972, 800. (Ltr., Jim Wilcox, Random House, Inc., 31 July 1974.) Distributed in Canada by Random House of Canada Limited. LC copyright 4 May 1965 (A789281); two copies deposited 20 Sept. 1965.

2. Variant: p. 5, "5:."—i.e., a missing dot.

3. Excerpts: *Look*, 23 March 1965, pp. 23–31; *Reporter*, 25 March 1965, pp. 42–46 and 48; *Commentary*, 39 (April 1965), 38–48; [in Polish] "Ellison: Pisarz murzyński o sytuaeji murzyńow," *Ameryka*, May 1967, pp. 59–64; [in Russian] "Ellison: Kto govorit ot imeni negrov," *Amerika*, May 1976, pp. 59–64; "Who Speaks for the Negro?: A Talk with Ralph Ellison," *Dialogue*, 2, no. 4 (1969), 79–89; [in Spanish] "¿Quien habla por el negro?: Por Robert Penn Warren y Ralph Elli-

son," *Facetas*, 2 (1969), 95–106; [in French] "Qui plaide pour le noir? Entretien avec Ralph Ellison," *Dialogue*, 1, no. 3 (1970), 100–111; [in French] "'Moi, je suis content d'être un noir!' un entretien avec Ralph Ellison," *Mensuel: Journal de Genève*, no. 30 (July 1970), pp. 2–3.

4. Related material, with marginalia (Ctw): James Baldwin, Nathan Glazer, Sidney Hook, and Gunnar Myrdal, "Liberalism and the Negro: A Round-Table Discussion," *Commentary*, 37 (March 1964), 25–42; Charles B. Turner, Jr., "The Black Man's Burden: The White Liberal," *Dissent: A Major Document from Russia*, 10 (Summer 1963), 215–219; Staughton Lynd and Roberta Yancy, "The Unfamiliar Campus: 1. Southern Negro Students: the College and the Movement," *Dissent: A Major Document from Russia*, 11 (Winter 1964), 39–45. KyU: A listing of taped interviews conducted by RPW indicates 81 tapes for *WSN?* (list received 12/23/64); 34 interviews by RPW are with civil rights leaders—some on tape, some transcripts, some both (ltr., Susan Emily Allen, Oral History Program, KyU, 3 Oct. 1979).

A26.b1   first American edition, first impression, by offset, paperback (1966)

WHO SPEAKS | *FOR THE NEGRO?* || *Robert Penn Warren* | [publisher's device] | *VINTAGE BOOKS* | *A Division of Random House* | *New York*

Collation: post folio 8° (trimmed: 18.4 × 10.9 cm.); *unsigned* 240 ind. leaves; pp. [i–xiv], [1–3] 4–43 [44] 45–131 [132] 133–267 [268] 269–354 [355] 356–404 [405] 406–444 [445] 446–454 [455–466]; numbering identical with **A26.a1**.

Contents: p. [i]: hf. tit.; p. [ii]: blank; p. [iii]: title page; p. [iv]: copyright and acknowledgments; p. [v]: dedication; p. [vi]: blank; p. [vii]: epigraph; p. [viii]: blank; p. [ix]: preface to the Vintage edition; p. [x]: blank; p. [xi]: foreword; p. [xii]: blank; p. [xiii]: contents; p. [xiv]: blank; p. [1]: hf. tit.; p. [2]: blank; pp. [3]–444: text; pp. [445–454]: index; p. [455]: about the author; p. [456]: blank; pp. [457–466]: blank.

Typography and Paper: identical with **A26.a1**. Paper: white, wove, unwatermarked; sheets bulk 2.3 cm.

Binding: paper. Similar to **A26.a1** with the following differences: front cover, between title and author's name, in gray, quotation from C. Vann Woodward; beneath author's name, in gray: 'A VINTAGE BOOK [publisher's device] V-323 [price]'. Spine: '[vert., in red]

ROBERT PENN WARREN [in white] WHO SPEAKS FOR THE NEGRO? [question mark in gray] | [horiz., in gray, publisher's device] | [in red] VINTAGE | [in white] V-323'. Back cover, on white: excerpts from reviews. Inside covers: white. All edges trimmed and unstained.

Copies: JAG, LC, STW.

Note: published 21 Feb. 1966 in 7,850 copies. Printed by Colonial Press. Subsequent impressions: 29 June 1966, 3,000; 14 Nov. 1966, 5,000; 15 Dec. 1967, 3,500; 19 Dec. 1968, 5,000; 22 Jan. 1970, 5,000. (Ltr., Jim Wilcox, Random House, Inc., 31 July 1974.) "Preface to the Vintage Edition" copyrighted 21 Feb. 1966 (A853085).

A27 *A Plea in Mitigation: Modern Poetry and the End of an Era*

A27.a1 first American edition, first impression (1966)

A Plea in Mitigation | Modern Poetry and the End of An Era | ROBERT PENN WARREN | EUGENIA DOROTHY BLOUNT LAMAR LECTURE | Delivered at Wesleyan College | February 1966 | WESLEYAN COLLEGE | MACON, GEORGIA | iii

Collation: royal 4° (trimmed: 21.5 × 13.8 cm.); *unsigned* [1¹⁴], 14 leaves; pp. [i–ii] iii–vi, 1–20 [21–22]; numbers centered at the bottom of the type page.

Contents: p. [i]: blank; p. [ii]: photograph; p. iii: title page; p. iv: 'Copyright 1966 | ROBERT PENN WARREN | Printed by | SOUTHERN PRESS, INC., MACON, GEORGIA'; on p. v 'FOREWORD'; on p. vi 'Leah A. Strong | Professor of United States | Language and Literature | Wesleyan College | Macon, Georgia'; pp. 1–20: text; pp. [21–22]: blank.

Typography and Paper: text: 37 ll., 15.7 (16.7) × 10.05 cm.; Monotype Century 10/12-pt. Paper: white, wove, watermarked 'WARREN'S OLDE STYLE'; sheets bulk 0.2 cm.

Plates: p. [ii]: 15.3 × 10.3 cm.; photograph of RPW seated, autographing a book for a student, with caption: '*Robert Penn Warren at Wesleyan College*'.

Binding: paper, stapled. Front cover: '[on red in white] *A Plea in Mitigation* | MODERN | POETRY | *and the* | END OF | AN ERA | [bottom ¼, on white in red] *Robert Penn Warren*'. Back cover, top ¾ red, bottom ¼ white. Pamphlet format. All edges trimmed and unstained.

Copies: Ctb, Ctw (3), JAG, L, LC, RPB, RPW, STW (2).

Notes: 1. Published 14 Feb. 1966 in 400–500 copies for the Lamar Lecture program at Wesleyan College (ltr., Charlotte Campbell, Southern Press, Inc., 25 April 1975). LC copyright 15 Sept. 1966 (A871575); two copies deposited 2 Nov. 1966.

   2. Variation: p. 3.2 belongs properly as 3.4; on p. 5.2, "abstration" for "abstraction."

A28   *Selected Poems: New and Old, 1923–1966*

A28.a1   first American edition, first impression (1966)

Selected Poems: | NEW AND OLD, 1923–1966 | ROBERT PENN WARREN | RANDOM HOUSE NEW YORK [publisher's device]

Collation: royal 8° (trimmed: 23.8 × rough trimmed: 16.0 cm.); *unsigned* [1–10¹⁶], 160 leaves; pp. [ᵖ 1–2], [i–viii] ix–xv [xvi], [1–2] 3–91 [92–94] 95–143 [144–146] 147–219 [220–222] 223–300 [301–302]; numbers off-center at foot of type page: on v., inset from outer margin; on r., from inner margin.

Contents: p. [ᵖ 1]: blank; on p. [ᵖ 2] '*Books by Robert Penn Warren*'; p. [i]: hf. tit. 'SELECTED POEMS | *New and Old 1923–1966*'; p. [ii]: blank; p. [iii]: title page; p. [iv]: '*First Printing* | [copyright statements] | *Library of Congress Catalog Card Number: 66-21460* | *Manufactured in the United States of America by Kingsport Press, Inc., Kings-|port, Tennessee* | *Design by Betty Anderson* | ACKNOWLEDGMENT | *The poems in this volume that have not previously been published in book form | appeared first in the following periodicals (the page numbers in parentheses | refer to pages in this book and indicate which poems appeared in each):* | Encounter *(pp. 19–39, 58–66)*, The New Leader *(pp. 67–68)*, The New | Yorker *(pp. 3, 6–7, 9–12, 40–49, 52–57)*, The New York Review of Books | *(pp. 8, 50–51, 81, 84–85, 90–91)*, Partisan Review *(p. 5)*, The Sewanee | Review *(pp. 13–18)*, The Saturday Review *(pp. 82–83, 86–89)*, The Yale | Review *(pp. 68–80)*'; p. [v]: '*To* ELEANOR, ROSANNA, *and* GABRIEL'; p. [vi]: blank; p. [vii]: 'PREFATORY NOTE | [9 ll. text] | *Stratton, Vermont,* | *March 6, 1966*'; p. [viii]: blank; pp. ix–xv: contents; p. [xvi]: blank; p. [1]: 'TALE OF TIME | *New Poems 1960–1966*'; p. [2]: '*This symbol is used to indicate a space between sections | of a poem whenever such spaces are lost in pagination*'; p. 3: 'NOTES ON A LIFE TO BE LIVED | I Stargazing'; p. 4: 'II Small White House'; p. 5: 'III Blow, West Wind'; pp. 6–7: 'IV Composition in Gold and

Red-Gold'; p. 8: 'V Little Boy and Lost Shoe'; pp. 9–10: 'VI Patriotic Tour and Postulate of Joy'; pp. 11–12: 'VII Dragon-Tree'; pp. 13–14: 'VIII Vision Under the October Mountain: A Love Poem'; p. 15: 'IX Chain Saw at Dawn in Vermont in Time of Drouth | 1'; pp. 16–17: '2'; p. 18: 'X Ways of Day'; pp. 19–20: 'TALE OF TIME | I What Happened'; pp. 21–22: 'II The Mad Druggist'; p. 23: 'III Answer Yes or No'; pp. 24–32: 'IV The Interim', in eight parts; p. 33: 'V What Were You Thinking, Dear Mother?'; pp. 34–39: 'VI Insomnia', in four parts; pp. 40–41: 'HOMAGE TO EMERSON, | ON NIGHT FLIGHT TO NEW YORK | TO PETER AND EBIE BLUME | I His Smile'; p. 42: 'II The Wait'; p. 43: 'III The Spider'; pp. 44–45: 'IV One Drunk Allegory'; p. 46: 'V Multiplication Table'; p. 47: 'VI Wind'; pp. 48–49: 'VII Does the Wild Rose?'; pp. 50–51: 'Shoes in Rain Jungle'; pp. 52–53: 'Fall Comes in Back-Country Vermont | TO WILLIAM MEREDITH | (1 One Voter Out of Sixteen)'; pp. 53–55: '(2 The Bear and the Last Person to Remember)'; pp. 55–56: '(3 The Human Fabric)'; pp. 56–57: '(4 Afterwards)'; pp. 58–59: 'THE DAY DR. KNOX DID IT | TO WILLIAM AND ROSE STYRON | I Place and Time'; p. 60: 'II The Event'; pp. 61–62: 'III A Confederate Veteran Tries to Explain the Event'; p. 63: 'IV The Place Where the Boy Pointed'; pp. 64–66: 'V And All That Came Thereafter'; pp. 67–68: 'HOLY WRIT | TO VANN AND GLENN WOODWARD | I Elijah on Mount Carmel'; pp. 69–80: 'II Saul at Gilboa | (Samuel Speaks)', in eight parts; p. 81: 'DELIGHT | I Into Broad Daylight'; p. 82: 'II Love: Two Vignettes | 1 Mediterranean Beach, Day after Storm'; p. 83: '2 Deciduous Spring'; pp. 84–85: 'III Something Is Going to Happen'; p. 86: 'IV Dream of a Dream the Small Boy Had'; pp. 87–88: 'V Two Poems About Suddenly and a Rose | 1 Dawn'; p. 89: '2 Intuition'; p. 90: 'VI Not to Be Trusted'; p. 91: 'VII Finisterre'; p. [92]: blank; p. [93]: 'From YOU, EMPERORS, | AND OTHERS | Poems 1957–1960'; p. [94]: blank; p. 95: 'GARLAND FOR YOU | I Clearly About You'; pp. 96–99: 'II The Letter About Money, Love, or Other Comfort, If Any'; pp. 100–101: 'III Man in the Street'; pp. 102–103: 'IV Switzerland'; pp. 104–105: 'V A Real Question Calling for Solution'; p. 106: 'VI Arrogant Law'; pp. 107–108: 'TWO PIECES AFTER SUETONIUS | I Apology for Domitian'; pp. 109–110: 'II Tiberius on Capri', in two parts; pp. 111–112: 'MORTMAIN | I After Night Flight Son Reaches Bedside of Already Unconscious | Father, Whose Right Hand Lifts in a Spasmodic Gesture, as | Though Trying to Make Contact: 1955'; p. 133: 'II A Dead Language: Circa 1885'; pp. 114–115: 'III

Fox-Fire: 1956'; p. 116; 'IV In the Turpitude of Time: N.D.'; pp. 117–118: 'V A Vision: Circa 1880'; p. 119: 'SOME QUIET, PLAIN POEMS | I Ornithology in a World of Flux'; p. 120: 'II Holly and Hickory'; p. 121: 'III The Well House'; p. 122: 'IV In Moonlight, Somewhere, They Are Singing'; p. 123: 'V In Italian They Call the Bird *Civetta*'; pp. 124–125: 'VI Debate: Question, Quarry, Dream'; p. 126: 'BALLAD BETWEEN THE BOXCARS (1923) | I I Can't Even Remember the Name'; pp. 127–128: 'II He Was Formidable'; p. 129: 'TWO STUDIES IN IDEALISM: SHORT SUR-|VEY OF AMRICAN, AND HUMAN, HISTORY | FOR ALLAN NEV-INS | I Bear Track Plantation: Shortly After Shiloh'; pp. 130–131: 'II Harvard '61: Battle Fatigue'; pp. 132–133: 'Autumnal Equinox on Mediterranean Beach'; pp. 134–135: 'NURSERY RHYMES | I Knockety-Knockety-Knock'; pp. 136–137: 'II News of Unexpected Demise of Little Boy Blue'; pp. 138–139: 'III Mother Makes the Biscuits'; p. 140: 'SHORT THOUGHTS FOR LONG NIGHTS | I Nightmare of Mouse'; p. 141: 'II Colloquy with Cockroach'; p. 142: 'III Cricket, on Kitchen Floor, Enters History'; p. 143: 'IV Grasshop-per Tries to Break Solipsism'; p. [144]: blank; p. [145]: '*From* PROM-ISES | *Poems 1954–1956*'; p. [146]: blank; p. 147: 'TO A LITTLE GIRL, ONE YEAR OLD, | IN A RUINED FORTRESS | TO ROSANNA | I Sirocco'; p. 148: 'II Gull's Cry'; p. 149: 'III The Child Next Door'; pp. 150–154: 'IV The Flower'; pp. 155–157: 'V Colder Fire'; pp. 158–159: 'PROMISES | TO GABRIEL | I What Was the Promise That Smiled from the Maples | at Evening?'; pp. 160–164: 'II Court-Martial'; pp. 165–166: 'III Gold Glade'; pp. 167–168: 'IV Dark Woods | 1 Tonight the Woods Are Darkened'; pp. 169–170: '2 The Dogwood'; pp. 171–172: '3 The Hazel Leaf'; pp. 173–174: 'V Coun-try Burying (1919)'; pp. 175–177: 'VI School Lesson Based on Word of Tragic Death | of Entire Gillum Family'; pp. 178–179: 'VII Sum-mer Storm (Circa 1916), and God's Grace'; pp. 180–182: 'VIII Founding Fathers, Nineteenth-Century Style, | Southeast U.S.A.'; pp. 183–184: 'IX Foreign Shore, Old Woman, Slaughter of Octopus'; pp. 185–188: 'X Dark Night of the Soul'; p. 189: 'XI Infant Boy at Midcentury | 1 When the Century Dragged'; p. 190: '2 Modification of Landscape'; p. 191: '3 Brightness of Distance'; pp. 192–193: 'XII Lul-laby: Smile in Sleep'; pp. 194–195: 'XIII Man in Moonlight | 1 Moon-light Observed from Ruined Fortress'; pp. 196–197: '2 Walk by Moonlight in Small Town'; pp. 198–199: '3 Lullaby: Moonlight Lin-gers'; pp. 200–201: 'XIV Mad Young Aristocrat on Beach'; pp. 202–203: 'XV Dragon Country: To Jacob Boehme'; pp. 204–205:

'XVI Ballad of a Sweet Dream of Peace | 1 And Don't Forget Your Corset Cover, Either'; pp. 206–207: '2 Keepsakes'; p. 208: '3 Go It, Granny——Go It, Hog!'; p. 209: '4 Friends of the Family, or Bowling a Sticky Cricket'; p. 210: '5 You Never Knew Her Either, Though You Thought You Did'; p. 211: '6 I Guess You Ought to Know Who You Are'; p. 212: '7 Rumor Unverified Stop Can You Confirm Stop'; p. 213: 'XVII Boy's Will, Joyful Labor Without Pay, | and Harvest Home (1918) | 1 Morning'; p. 214: '2 Work'; p. 215: '3 The Snake'; pp. 216–217: '4 Hands Are Paid'; pp. 218–219: 'XVIII Lullaby: A Motion Like Sleep'; p. [220]: blank; p. [221]: '*From* SELECTED POEMS | *1923–1943*'; p. [222]: blank; pp. 223–239: 'THE BALLAD OF BILLIE POTTS'; pp. 240–242: 'Terror'; pp. 243–244: 'Pursuit'; pp. 245–246: 'Original Sin: A Short Story'; pp. 247–248: 'Crime'; pp. 249–251: 'Letter from a Coward to a Hero'; pp. 252–255: 'History'; pp. 256–257: 'End of Season'; p. 258: 'Ransom'; p. 259: 'To a Friend Parting'; p. 260: 'Eidolon'; pp. 261–262: 'Revelation'; p. 263: 'MEXICO IS A FOREIGN COUNTRY: | FOUR STUDIES IN NATURALISM | I Butterflies over the Map'; pp. 264–265: 'II The World Comes Galloping: A True Story'; pp. 266–268: 'III Small Soldiers with Drum in Large Landscape'; pp. 269–270: 'IV The Mango on the Mango Tree'; pp. 271–272: 'Monologue at Midnight'; pp. 273–274: 'Bearded Oaks'; pp. 275–276: 'Picnic Remembered'; pp. 277–280: 'Love's Parable'; p. 281: 'Late Subterfuge'; pp. 282–283: 'Man Coming of Age'; pp. 284–285: 'The Garden'; pp. 286–289: 'The Return: An Elegy'; p. 290: 'KENTUCKY MOUNTAIN FARM | I Rebuke of the Rocks'; p. 291: 'II At the Hour of the Breaking of the Rocks'; p. 292: 'III History Among the Rocks'; p. 293: 'IV The Return'; pp. 294–296: 'Pondy Woods'; pp. 297–298: 'Letter of a Mother'; pp. 299–300: 'To a Face in a Crowd'; p. [301]: blank; p. [302]: about the author.

Typography and Paper: text: 32 ll., 16.1 (17.4) × 12.6 cm.; Linotype Times 11/13-pt. Paper: white, laid, vertical chainlines (2.0 cm.), unwatermarked; sheets bulk 2.0 cm.

Binding: red cloth. Front, in gilt, facsimile signature: 'Robert Penn Warren'. Spine, in gilt: '[vert.] *Robert Penn Warren · Selected Poems · New and Old · 1923–1966* | [horiz., publisher's device] | RANDOM | HOUSE'. Back: blank. Top edge trimmed, fore and bottom edges rough trimmed with top edge stained blue-black; white endpapers.

Dust wrapper: front cover, gold rule; ltrs. black on beige: 'ROBERT | PENN | WARREN | [gold rule] | [red rule, thick] | SELECTED

POEMS | [red rule, thick] | [gold rule] | NEW & OLD | 1923–1966 | [in gold] A RANDOM HOUSE BOOK [publisher's device] | [gold rule]'. Spine, vert., black on gold: 'ROBERT PENN WARREN | SELECTED POEMS [in red, publisher's device] RANDOM | HOUSE'. Back cover, black and red on beige, gold frame: publisher's advertisement. Front flap: about the book. Back flap: biographical sketch and publisher's advertisement.

Copies: CtY, JAG, KyU, LC, LU, STW, TNJ.

Notes: 1. Published 7 Oct. 1966 in 5,300 copies at $7.95. Printed by American Book-Stratford Press, Inc. Subsequent impressions: 24 March 1967, 2,500; 15 Sept. 1967, 2,250; 26 Jan. 1972, 1,000; and on order as of 31 July 1974, 1,000. (Ltr., Jim Wilcox, Random House, Inc., 31 July 1974.) Distributed in Canada by Random House of Canada Limited. LC copyright 19 Sept. 1966 (A897975); "Tale of Time" (AI10265); two copies deposited 16 March 1967.

2. Variations from *YEO* (**A22.a1**): in the sequence "Garland for You," two poems—"Lullaby: Exercise in Human Charity and Self-Knowledge" and "The Self That Stares"—have been omitted. Epigraphs for "V A Real Question Calling for Solution" and "VI Arrogant Law" have been omitted. In the sequence "Nursery Rhymes," "4 The Bramble Bush" is omitted. The sequence "Short Thoughts for Long Nights" omits "2 Nightmare of Man," "4 Little Boy on Voyage," "5 Obsession," "6 Joy," and "8 Little Boy and General Principle."

3. Variations from *P* (**A15.a1**): the stanzas differ and the last line is omitted in "IV The Flower." In "III Gold Glade," the last stanza is omitted. Three stanzas are omitted in "VI School Lesson Based on Word of Tragic Death of Entire Gillum Family." In "VII Summer Storm (Circa 1916), and God's Grace," the last stanza is omitted. In "X Dark Night of Soul," the stanza beginning "The cows drift up the land" (p. 187) has been shortened by two lines and the last twenty lines have been rearranged and shortened by one line. One stanza is omitted from "XV Dragon Country." The words "Inside Out" are left off the end of the title, "5 You Never Knew Her Either."

4. Variations from *SP* (**A6.a1**): In "The Ballad of Billie Potts," the refrain "In the land between the rivers" is sometimes omitted in the second and subsequent stanzas. On p. 229, two ten-line stanzas are shortened from *SP*, pp. 8–9; p. 231, four lines omitted; p. 232, two lines omitted; p. 233, two lines omitted; p. 234, six lines omitted; p. 235, one five-line stanza omitted; p. 236, four lines omitted;

p. 237, two lines omitted and stanzas divided differently; and p. 238, six lines omitted. In "History," the next-to-last stanza (p. 255) is altered and increased one line. In the poem sequence "Mexico Is a Foreign Country," one poem—"II Siesta Time . . ."—is omitted; "III Small Soldiers . . ." is shortened by two stanzas. In "The Return: An Elegy," the first stanza on p. 289 omits one line. The poem sequence "Kentucky Mountain Farm" is shortened by three poems—"IV The Cardinal," "V The Jay," and "VI Watershed."

5. TNJ copy is inscribed on the free endpaper: 'To | Bill & Alice | love, as always | Red | Magagnosc | November 13, 1966 || '.

A28.b1   first American edition, special limited edition (1966)

[in reddish orange] *Selected Poems:* | NEW AND OLD, 1923–1966 | [in black] ROBERT PENN WARREN | RANDOM HOUSE NEW YORK [publisher's device]

Collation: [1 ¹⁶ (+1₁) 2–10¹⁶], 161 leaves; pp. [1–4], otherwise identical with **A28.a1**.

Contents: p. [1]: extended ltrs.: '[in black] OF THE FIRST EDITION OF [above and below line, in red] SELECTED POEMS | *New and Old 1923–1966* | [in black] TWO HUNDRED AND FIFTY COPIES HAVE BEEN | PRINTED ON SPECIAL PAPER AND SPECIALLY BOUND. | [¶] EACH COPY IS SIGNED BY THE AUTHOR AND | NUMBERED. *No.* [entered in ink by hand on line provided] | [signature in ink]'. pp. [2–3]: blank; p. [4]: 'Books by Robert Penn Warren | [list]'.

Typography and Paper: identical with **A28.a1**. Paper: white, laid, vertical chainlines (2.4 cm.); watermarked 'WARREN'S | OLDE STYLE'; sheets bulk 2.1 cm.

Binding: off-white embossed calico grain cloth with alternating wide and narrow impressions horiz. (2.3 cm. between wide, 2.3 cm. between narrow), front and back. Spine, in gilt: '[vert.] *Robert Penn Warren · Selected Poems · New and Old · 1923–1966* | [horiz., publisher's device] | RANDOM | HOUSE'. Top edge trimmed and stained blue-black, fore and bottom edges rough trimmed; dark red, textured endpapers.

Dust wrapper: front and back covers, black on light brown: alternating wide and narrow rules, each 2.3 cm. apart. Spine, in black: '[vert.] *Robert Penn Warren · Selected Poems · New and Old · 1923–1966* | [horiz., publisher's device] | RANDOM | HOUSE'. Front and back flaps: blank.

Copies: JAG (no. 57), RPW (no. 50), STW (marked "OUT OF SE-RIES"), TNJ (no. 176).

Note: published 7 Oct. 1966 in 250 boxed copies for $12.50.

A29   *Incarnations: Poems, 1966–1968*

A29.a1   first American edition, first impression (1968)

[p. (iv)] *Robert Penn Warren* [p. (v)] *INCARNATIONS* | *POEMS 1966–1968* | *RANDOM HOUSE NEW YORK* [publisher's device]

Collation: royal 8° (trimmed: 23.75 × rough trimmed: 15.9 cm.); *unsigned* [1–5 ^{8}], 40 leaves; pp. [i–xii], [1–2] 3–28 [29–30] 31–54 [55–56] 57–59 [60] 61–64 [65–68]; numbers in ital.; on v., in corner formed by tail and outer margins; on r., in corner formed by tail and inner margins.

Contents: p. [1]: blank; on p. [ii] 'BOOKS BY Robert Penn Warren'; p. [iii]: hf. tit. 'INCARNATIONS | *POEMS* | *1966–1968*'; pp. [iv–v]: title pages; p. [vi]: 'FIRST PRINTING | [copyright statements] | *Some of the poems in this collection have appeared in* Encounter, Northwest | Review, Harper's, The Reporter, Saturday Review, The New York Review of Books, | The University of Denver Quarterly, Yale Review, and The New Yorker. | *Library of Congress Catalog Card Number: 68-28529* | *Manufactured in the United States of America* | *Design by Betty Anderson*'; p. [vii]: 'TO John Palmer'; p. [viii]: blank; p. [ix]: '[epigraph] | —NEHEMIAH 5.5 | [epigraph] | —A FOLK BALLAD'; p. [x]: blank; pp. [xi–xii]: contents; p. [1]: 'I · ISLAND OF SUMMER'; p. [2]: statement about spacing; p. 3: 'ISLAND OF SUMMER | 1 | WHAT DAY IS'; p. 4: '2 | WHERE THE SLOW FIG'S PURPLE SLOTH'; pp. 5–6: '3 | NATURAL HISTORY'; p. 7: '4 | RIDDLE IN THE GARDEN'; pp. 8–9: '5 | PAUL VALÉRY STOOD ON THE CLIFF AND | CONFRONTED THE FURIOUS ENERGIES OF NATURE'; p. 10: '6 | TREASURE HUNT'; p. 11: '7 | MOONRISE'; pp. 12–16: '8 | MYTH ON MEDITERRANEAN BEACH: | APHRODITE AS LOGOS'; p. 17: '9 | MISTRAL AT NIGHT'; p. 18: '10 | THE IVY'; p. 19: '11 | WHERE PURPLES NOW THE FIG'; p. 20: '12 | THE RED MULLET'; p. 21: '13 | A PLACE WHERE NOTHING IS'; pp. 22–23: '14 | MASTS AT

DAWN'; pp. 24–28: '15 | THE LEAF', in four parts; p. [29]: 'II · IN-TERNAL INJURIES'; p. [30]: blank; pp. 31–32: 'PENOLOGICAL STUDY: SOUTHERN EXPOSURE | *To Brainard and Frances Cheney* 1 | KEEP THAT MORPHINE MOVING, CAP'; p. 33: '2 | TO-MORROW MORNING'; pp. 34–35: '3 | WET HAIR: IF NOW HIS MOTHER SHOULD COME'; p. 36: '4 | NIGHT: THE MO-TEL DOWN THE ROAD FROM THE PEN'; pp. 37–38: '5 | WHERE THEY COME TO WAIT FOR THE BODY: A GHOST STORY'; pp. 39–41: '6 | NIGHT IS PERSONAL'; p. 42: '7 | DAWN'; pp. 43–44: 'INTERNAL INJURIES | 1 | THE EVENT'; p. 45: '2 | THE SCREAM'; pp. 46–47: '3 | HER HAT'; p. 48: '4 | THE ONLY TROUBLE'; pp. 49–50: '5 | THE JET MUST BE HUNTING FOR SOMETHING'; p. 51: '6 | BE SOMETHING ELSE'; p. 52: '7 | THE WORLD IS A PARABLE'; pp. 53–54: '8 | DRIVER, DRIVER'; p. [55]: 'III · ENCLAVES'; p. [56]: blank; pp. 57–58: 'THE TRUE NATURE OF TIME | 1 | THE FARING'; p. 59: '2 | THE ENCLAVE'; p. [60]: blank; p. 61: 'IN THE MOUN-TAINS | *To Baudouin and Annie de Moustier* 1 | SKIERS'; pp. 62–64: '2 | FOG', in three parts; pp. [65–66]: blank; p. [67]: about the author; p. [68]: blank.

Typography and Paper: text: 32 ll., 15.4 (20.7) × 12.1 cm.; Monotype Scotch Roman 11/13-pt. Paper: white, laid, vertical chainlines (2.1 cm.), unwatermarked; sheets bulk 0.5 cm.

Binding: white cloth and mustard paper-covered bds. Front, gilt on mustard, facsimile signature: 'Robert Penn Warren'. Spine, in gilt on white: '[vert.] *ROBERT PENN WARREN* / *INCARNATIONS: POEMS 1966–1968* / *RANDOM HOUSE* | [horiz., publisher's device]'. Back: blank. Fore edge rough trimmed, top and bottom edges trimmed with top edge stained light blue; black endpapers.

Dust wrapper: front cover, superimposed on black background with random blue-black ltrs.: '[in yellow] *Robert Penn Warren* | [in white] INCARNATIONS | [in yellow] *Poems 1966–1968*'. Spine, vert., on black: '[in yellow] *Robert Penn Warren* [in white] *Incarnations:* [in yellow] *POEMS 1966–1968* [publisher's device] *Random House*'. Back cover: left side, photograph of RPW with credit: 'JOEL KATZ / YALE ALUMNI MAGAZINE'; right side on yellow: biographical sketch. Front flap: about the book; jacket design by Betty Anderson. Back flap: publisher's advertisement.

Copies: Ctb, CtY, JAG, LC, LU, STW, TNJ, TxFTC.

Note: published 16 Oct. 1968 in 5,000 copies at $4.00. Printed by Kingsport Press. Subsequent impression: 19 March 1969, 2,500. (Ltr., Jim Wilcox, Random House, Inc., 31 July 1974.) Distributed in Canada by Random House of Canada Limited. LC copyright 7 Oct. 1968 (A70253); two copies deposited 28 April 1969.

A29.b1 first American edition, special limited edition (1968)

Title Page: identical with **A29.a1**.

Collation: [1^8 (+1,) 2–5^8], 41 leaves; pp. [$^\pi$1–2], otherwise identical with **A29.a1**.

Contents: p. [$^\pi$1]: '*Of the first edition of* | *INCARNATIONS: Poems 1966–1968* | *two hundred and fifty copies* | *have been printed on special* | *paper and specially bound.* | *Each copy is signed by the author* | *and numbered* | [entered by hand in ink] | [signature in ink]'. p. [$^\pi$2]: blank.

Typography and Paper: identical with **A29.a1**. Paper: white, laid, vertical chainlines (2.5 cm.), unwatermarked; sheets bulk 0.6 cm.

Binding: medium blue embossed calico grain cloth. Front, upper edge, blind-stamped, interlocking ltrs.: 'RPW'. Spine, in gilt: '[vert.] *ROBERT PENN WARREN* / *INCARNATIONS: POEMS 1966–1968* / *RANDOM HOUSE* | [horiz., publisher's device]'. Back: blank. Fore edge rough trimmed, top and bottom edges trimmed with top edge stained yellowish green; yellow endpapers.
    Dust wrapper: identical with **A29.a1** except on nonglossy paper.

Copies: JAG (no. 126), KyU (no. 218), RPW (no. 5), STW (no. 112).

Note: published 16 Oct. 1968 in 250 boxed copies at $10.00.

A29.c1 first English edition, first impression, by offset (1970)

[p. (iv)] *Robert Penn Warren* [p. (v)] *INCARNATIONS* | *POEMS 1966–1968* | *LONDON · W. H. ALLEN · 1970*

Contents: identical with **A29.a1**, but with the following differences: p. [vi]: '© *Robert Penn Warren, 1967, 1968* | *First British edition, 1970* | *Printed in Great Britain by William Lewis & Co. Ltd.,* | *Cardiff, for the publishers W. H. Allen & Co. Ltd.,* | *Essex Street, London, W.C. 2.* | *Bound in Tiptree by William Brendon & Son Ltd.* | *Some of the poems* [. . . same as **A29.a1**] | *491 00244 0*'; p. [67]: blank.

Typography and Paper: identical with **A29.a1**. Paper: white, laid, horiz. chainlines (2.8 cm.), unwatermarked; sheets bulk 0.6 cm.

Binding: yellowish white cloth. Front and back: blank. Spine, vert., in gilt: '*INCARNATIONS: POEMS 1966–1968 Robert Penn Warren* W. H. ALLEN'. All edges trimmed and unstained; goldish brown endpapers.

Dust wrapper: front cover, in olive green border, on black rectangle with rounded corners: '[in white] *ROBERT | PENN WARREN | IN-CARNATIONS | Poems 1966·1968 |* [olive green design]'. Spine, on olive green in black: '[vert.] *Robert Penn Warren INCARNATIONS Poems 1966·1968 |* [horiz.] W. H. | ALLEN'. Back cover, in olive green and black on white: publisher's advertisement. Front flap: about RPW's work. Back flap: blank.

Copies: BL, JAG, RPW, STW.

Note: published 1970 at £1.25. Printed by William Lewis & Co. Ltd. Additional publication information is not available. British Library date-stamp 23 March 1970.

A30   *Audubon: A Vision*

A30.a1   first American edition, first impression (1969)

Robert Penn Warren | [orn. extending to first ltr.] Audubon | a vision | Random House New York [publisher's device]

Collation: royal 8° (rough trimmed: 23.8 × 15.8 cm.); *unsigned* [1–3 ^{8}], 24 leaves; pp. [i–xii], [1–2] 3–32 [33–36]; numbers in ital.; on v., in corner formed by the tail and outer margins; on r., in corner formed by tail and inner margins.

Contents: p. [i]: blank; on p. [ii] 'Books by Robert Penn Warren'; p. [iii]: hf. tit. 'Audubon | *a vision*'; p. [iv]: blank; p. [v]: title page; p. [vi]: 'FIRST PRINTING | [copyright statements] | *Library of Congress Catalog Card Number: 70-89694 | Manufactured in the United States of America | by Kingsport Press, Inc., Kingsport, Tennessee | Design by Betty Anderson | ACKNOWLEDGMENT | Parts of* AUDUBON: | A Vision *have previously been | published in the following periodicals:* Harper's Magazine (*Part* II) | The New Yorker (*Parts* IA; IVA, C, E; VA, B; VI; VIIB) | The Yale Review (*Parts* IB; IVB, D; VC)'; p. [vii]: 'To Allen and Helen Tate'; p.[viii]: blank; p.[ix]: '[epigraph] | ——PSALMS: 56,8 | [epigraph] | ——*Carlos Drummond de Andrade*: | "Travelling in the Family" | Translated by *Elizabeth Bishop*'; p. [x]: blank; p. [xi]: contents; p. [xii]: blank; p. [1]: hf. tit.; p. [2]: prefatory note and a note about the spacing; p. 3: 'I Was Not the Lost Dauphin | [A]'; p. 4: '[B]'; p. 5: 'II The Dream He Never Knew the End Of | [A]'; p. 6: '[B]'; p. 7: '[C]'; pp. 8–9: '[D]'; p. 10: '[E]'; p. 11: '[F]'; p. 12: '[G]'; p. 13: '[H]'; p. 14: '[I]'; p. 15: '[J]'; p. 16: '[K]'; p. 17: '[L]'; p. 18: '[M]'; p. 19: 'III We Are Only Ourselves'; p. 20: 'IV The Sign Whereby He Knew | [A]'; p. 21: '[B]'; p. 22: '[C]'; p. 23: '[D]'; p. 24: '[E]'; pp. 25–27: 'V The Sound of That Wind | [A]'; p. 28: '[B]'; p. 29: '[C]'; p. 30: 'VI Love and Knowledge'; p. 31: 'VII Tell Me a Story | [A]'; p. 32: '[B]'; pp. [33–34]: blank; p. [35]: about the author; p. [36]: blank.

Typography and Paper: text: 33 ll., 15.95 (19.2) × 12.0 cm.; Monotype Scotch Roman 11/14-pt. Paper: white, laid, vert. chainlines (3.05 cm.), unwatermarked; sheets bulk 0.3 cm.

Binding: light blue cloth and white paper-covered bds. Front, in gilt on white, facsimile signature: 'Robert Penn Warren'. Spine, in gilt on light blue: '[vert.] ROBERT PENN WARREN || AUDUBON: A VISION || RANDOM HOUSE | [horiz., publisher's device]'. Back: black. Top edge trimmed, fore and bottom edges rough trimmed; all edges unstained; light blue endpapers.

Dust wrapper: front cover, against a dark blue background and landscape setting, a light blue heron's head with a fish in its beak; '[at top, in white] ROBERT PENN WARREN | [at bottom, in white with blue colon] *Audubon*: | [in blue] A VISION'. Spine, vert.: '[in white with blue colon] *Audubon*: [in blue] A VISION ROBERT PENN WARREN [publisher's device] RANDOM HOUSE'. Back cover, in black on light blue: publisher's advertisement. Front flap: about the book and the jacket illus.; jacket design by Betty Anderson. Back flap: photograph of RPW by Harold Strauss and biographical sketch.

Copies: CoCA, Ctb, CtY, JAG, KyU, LC, LU, STW, TxFTC.

Note: published 20 Nov. 1969 in 6,300 copies at $4.00. Printed by Kingsport Press. Subsequent impressions: 1 April 1970, 1,500. (Ltr., Jim Wilcox, Random House, Inc., 31 July 1974.) Distributed in Canada by Random House of Canada Limited. LC copyright 3 Nov. 1969 (A162308); two copies deposited 22 June 1970.

A30.b1   first American edition, special limited edition (1969)

Title Page: identical with **A30.a1**.

Collation: [1⁸ (+1₂) 2–3⁸], 25 leaves; pp. [π1–2], otherwise as in **A30.a1**.

Contents: p. [π1]: blank; p. [π2]: 'Books by Robert Penn Warren | [list]'; p. [i]: '*Of the first edition of* | AUDUBON: *A Vision* | three hundred copies have been printed | on *special paper and specially bound.* | *Each copy is signed by the author* | *and numbered*. [no. entered by hand in ink] || [signature in ink]'. p. [ii]: blank.

Typography and Paper: identical with **A30.a1**. Paper: yellowish white, laid, vert. chainlines (2.4 cm.), watermarked '[arched] WARREN'S | [horiz.] OLDE STYLE'; sheets bulk 0.4 cm.

Binding: dark blue, embossed calico grain cloth. Front, upper right corner, impressed: 'R P | [orn.] | W'. Spine, in gilt: '[vert.] ROBERT PENN WARREN || AUDUBON: A VISION || RANDOM HOUSE | [horiz., publisher's device]'. Back: blank. All edges trimmed with top edge stained blue; grayish blue endpapers.

   Dust wrapper: identical with **A30.a1** in design, but on nonglossy paper, laid, vert. chainlines (2.4 cm.).

Copies: JAG (no. 62), STW (no. 30).

Note: published 20 Nov. 1969 in 300 boxed copies at $10.00.

A30.c1   first American Edition, pirated Taiwan edition, by offset (n.d.)

Robert Penn Warren | Audubon | *a vision*

Collation: medium folio 8° (trimmed: 20.8 × 14.4 cm.); *unsigned* [1–3⁸], 24 leaves; pp. [i–xii], [1–4] 5–32 [33–36]; numbering identical with **A30.a1**.

Contents: p. [vi]: 'FIRST PRINTING | *Copyright © 1969 by Robert Penn Warren* | [in Chinese]'.

Paper: white, wove, unwatermarked; sheets bulk 0.3 cm.

Binding: dark red embossed calico grain cloth. Front and back: blank. Spine, vert., in silver: 'ROBERT PENN WARREN || AUDUBON: A VISION'. All edges trimmed and unstained; white endpapers.

   Dust wrapper: identical with **A30.a1** except publisher's name has been omitted.

Copies: JAG, STW, TNJ.

A31   *Homage to Theodore Dreiser, August 27, 1871–December 28, 1945, on the Centennial of His Birth*

A31.a1   first American edition, first impression (1971)

HOMAGE TO | Theodore | Dreiser | *August 27, 1871——December 28, 1945* | *ON THE CENTENNIAL OF HIS BIRTH* | [two small, crosslike orns.] ROBERT | PENN | WARREN | [publisher's device] | RANDOM HOUSE | *New York*

Collation: demy 8° (rough trimmed: 21.15 × 14.3 cm.); *unsigned* [1–6¹⁶], 96 leaves; pp. [i–xiv], [1] 2–143 [144] 145–171 [172] 173 [174–178]; numerals, preceded and followed by two stacked, crosslike orns., at foot of type page and indented 7 ems from the outer margin.

Contents: pp. [i–iii]: blank; on p. [iv] 'BOOKS BY ROBERT PENN WARREN'; p. [v]: hf. tit. 'HOMAGE TO THEODORE DREISER'; p. [vi]: a 14.4 × 11.4 cm., b-w reproduction of Theodore Dreiser without caption; p. [vii]: title page; p. [viii]: '[copyright statements] | *ISBN: 0-394-41027-0* | *Library of Congress Catalog Card Number: 73-156965* | *Excerpts from* An American Tragedy *are reprinted by permission of The World Publishing Company.* | [additional copyright information] | *First Edition*'; p. [ix]: acknowledgments; p. [x]: blank; p. [xi]: '*TO* | *VANN AND GLENN WOODWARD*'; p. [xii]: blank; p. [xiii]: '[epigraph] | W. B. YEATS | [epigraph] | JOHN KEATS'; p. [xiv]: blank; p. [1]: hf. tit.; p. 2: '[reproduction of sheet music] | From "On the Banks of the Wabash, Far Away"; | words by Theodore Dreiser and Paul Dresser, music by Paul Dresser'; pp. 3–4: 'PORTRAIT I. PSYCHOLOGICAL PROFILE'; pp. 5–7: 'II. VITAL STATISTICS'; p. 8: 'III. MORAL ASSESSMENT'; pp. 9–143: text, with spacing between sections and the first ltr. of the first word in each section in bf., enlarged; p. [144]: blank; pp. 145–168: notes, identified by page no.; pp. 169–170: biographical summary; p. 171: bibliographical note; p. [172]: blank; p. 173: about the author; pp. [174–178]: blank.

Typography and Paper: text: 31 ll., 15.05 (16.75) × 9.65 cm.; Monotype Aster 11/13-pt. Paper: white, laid, vert. chainlines (2.4 cm.), unwatermarked; sheets bulk 1.5 cm.

Binding: purple cloth and light brown paper-covered bds. Front, on light brown in gilt, facsimile signature: 'Robert Penn Warren'. Spine, in gilt on purple: '[vert.] Homage to Theodore Dreiser [two pair of stacked crosslike orns.] ROBERT PENN WARREN | [horiz., publisher's device] | RANDOM | HOUSE'. Back: blank. Fore and bottom edges rough trimmed, top edge trimmed and stained purple; black endpapers.

Dust wrapper: front cover, olive green frame, purple frame with four white dots, on black: '[in white] HOMAGE | TO | THEODORE | DREISER | [orn. extending from fancy "R"] | [in olive green] *On the Centennial of His Birth* | [in white] ROBERT | PENN | WARREN'. Spine: '[vert., on olive green in white] 'ROBERT PENN WARREN | [in black] HOMAGE

TO THEODORE DREISER | [horiz., publisher's device] | RANDOM | HOUSE'. Back cover: across top, photograph of RPW by Michael V. Carlisle; below, purple and black on beige, biographical sketch. Front flap: about the book. Back flap: publisher's advertisement; jacket design by Muriel Nasser.

Copies: CtY, JAG, KyU, STW, TNJ, TxFTC.

Notes: 1. Published 27 Aug. 1971 in 5,000 copies at $5.95. Printed by the Haddon Craftsmen. (Ltr., Jim Wilcox, Random House, Inc., 31 July 1974.) Distributed in Canada by Random House of Canada Limited. LC copyright 27 July 1971 (A291164); two copies deposited 10 Dec. 1971.

2. Portions of the text appeared in *SoR*, NS 7 (Spring 1971), 345–410; as "Theodore Dreiser: *An American Tragedy*," in *Der amerikanische Roman im 19. und 20. Jahrhundert*, ed. Edgar Lohner (Berlin: Erich Schmidt, 1974), pp. 152–161, with slight modifications to pp. 112–129 of *HTD*.

A32 *Meet Me in the Green Glen*

A32.a1 first American edition, first impression (1971)

[ltrs. in black] Meet Me | in the | Green Glen | [four gray barren-tree orns.] | ROBERT | PENN WARREN | RANDOM HOUSE [publisher's device] NEW YORK

Collation: demy 8° (trimmed: 21.2 × rough trimmed: 14.3 cm.); *unsigned* [1–12 ^{16}], 192 leaves; pp. [i–viii], [1–2] 3–376; numbers in parentheses, centered at foot of type page, except on book pages: pp. [1], [95–96], [260–262], and [334–336].

Contents: p. [i]: hf. tit. 'MEET ME | IN THE | GREEN GLEN'; on p. [ii] '[barren-tree orn.] BOOKS BY | ROBERT PENN WARREN'; p. [iii]: title page; p. [iv]: '[copyright statements] | *ISBN*: 0-394-46141-X Tr. | LIBRARY OF CONGRESS CATALOG CARD NUMBER: 70-102303 | PRINTED AND BOUND BY HADDON CRAFTS-MEN, | SCRANTON, PENNSYLVANIA | 2 4 6 8 9 7 5 3 | FIRST EDITION'; p. [v]: 'TO ARNOLD | AND BESS STEIN'; p. [vi]: blank; p. [vii]: '[epigraph] | ——John Clare | [epigraph] | ——Andrew Marvell'; p. [viii]: blank; p. [1]: 'BOOK | [four small black barren-tree orns.] I [four small black barren-tree orns.]'; p. [2]: blank; pp. 3–376: text; on p. 3 'CHAPTER ONE' with twelve barren-tree orns. preceding the first word of the first line and with the first ltr. of the first word enlarged and bf. Other chapters are designated similarly: pp. 20, 45, 66, 97, 127, 151, 196, 225, 263, and 301.

Typography and Paper: text: 34 ll., 15.4 (17.0) × 9.8 cm.; Linotype Caledonia 11/13-pt. RT: v., 'ROBERT PENN WARREN'; r., 'MEET ME IN THE GREEN GLEN'. Paper: white, wove, unwatermarked; sheets bulk 2.7 cm.

Binding: white cloth. Front, bottom, in gray: three barren-tree orns. Spine, in gilt: '[vert.] || Meet Me in the | Green Glen || [horiz.] ROBERT | PENN | WARREN || [publisher's device] | RANDOM HOUSE | NEW YORK'. Back: blank. Fore and bottom edges rough trimmed, top edge trimmed and stained lavender; white with scattered short blue hair lines on endpapers.

Dust wrapper: front cover, on purple: '[in white] Robert | Penn | Warren | [in light purple, two lines in one] A | NOVEL [in orange] Meet | Me in the | Green | Glen [in black, three barren-tree orns.]'. Spine: '[vert., in white] Robert Penn Warren | [in orange] Meet Me in the Green Glen | [horiz., in light purple, publisher's device] | [in white] Random | House'. Back cover: across top, photograph of RPW by Michael V. Carlisle; below, in purple and black on white, biographical sketch. Front flap: about the book. Back flap: publisher's advertisement; jacket design by Muriel Nasser.

Copies: CoCA, Ctb, CtY, JAG, KyU, LC, LU, STW, TNJ (2), TxFTC.

Notes: 1. Published 4 Oct. 1971 in 25,300 copies at $7.95. Printed by Haddon Craftsmen. (Ltr., Jim Wilcox, Random House, Inc., 31 July 1974.) Subsequent impressions: 11 Nov. 1971, 5,300; 16 Dec. 1971, 3,000. Distributed in Canada by Random House of Canada Limited. LC copyright 31 Aug. 1971 (A354681); two copies deposited 30 March 1972.

2. Excerpts: "from *Meet Me in the Green Glen*," *PR*, 38, no. 2 (1971), 143–166; in *Works in Progress, No. 4*, ed. Martha Saxton (New York: Literary Guild of America, Inc., 1971), pp. 11–23.

3. Working titles for *MMGG* were "Escape," "Flight," "Love in a Valley," and "But Not the Nightingale."

4. A *Saturday Review of Literature* Book Club selection identical with **A32.a1** was published in 1972.

A32.b1 first American edition, special limited edition (1971)

Title Page: identical with **A32.a1**.

Collation: [1^{16} (+1₁) 2–12^{16}], 193 leaves; pp. [$^{\pi}$1–2], otherwise as in **A32.a1**.

Contents: p. [$^\pi$1]: '*Of the first edition of* | Meet Me in the | Green Glen | three hundred copies have | been printed *on special paper* | *and specially bound. Each copy* | *is signed by the author and* | *numbered.* | [no. entered by hand in ink] || [signature in ink]'; p. [$^\pi$2]: blank.

Typography and Paper: identical with **A32.a1**. Paper: white, laid, vert. chainlines (2.1 cm.), unwatermarked; sheets bulk 2.8 cm.

Binding: beige and ¼ medium brown, embossed calico grain cloth. Front, in gilt, facsimile signature: 'Robert Penn Warren'. Spine, in gilt: '[vert.] || Meet Me in the | Green Glen || [horiz.] ROBERT | PENN | WARREN || [publisher's device] | RANDOM HOUSE | NEW YORK'. Back: blank. Fore and bottom edges rough trimmed, top edge trimmed and stained dark brown; beige endpapers.
    Dust wrapper: clear plastic.

Copies: JAG (no. 268), STW (no. 237).

Note: published 4 Oct. 1971 in 300 boxed copies at $17.50.

A32.c1   first English edition, first impression, by offset (1972)

Meet Me | in the | Green Glen | ROBERT | PENN WARREN | Secker & Warburg | London

Collation: demy folio 8° (trimmed: 21.5 × 13.6 cm.); *unsigned* [1–12 ^{16}], 192 leaves; pagination and numbering identical with **A32.a1**.

Contents: p. [iv]: 'First published in England 1972 by | Martin Secker & Warburg Limited | 14 Carlisle Street, London W1V 6NN | Copyright © 1971 by Robert Penn Warren | 436 56310 X | Printed offset litho and bound in Great Britain by | Cox & Wyman Limited, | London, Fakenham and Reading'.

Typography and Paper: identical with **A32.a1**. Paper: white, wove, unwatermarked, 88.8 × 112.8 Concord Offset Cartridge (ltr., M. S. Burden, Works Manager, Cox & Wyman, 28 Feb. 1975); sheets bulk 2.9 cm.

Binding: medium greenish brown cloth. Front and back: blank. Spine, in gilt: 'Meet Me | in the | Green | Glen | [orn.] | *Robert* | *Penn Warren* | Secker & | Warburg'. All edges trimmed and unstained; white endpapers.
    Dust wrapper: front and back covers, on cream: '[in brown, fancy "R" and "a"] Robert | Penn Warren | [in green with fancy "e" in "th*e*" and "n" in "Gle*n*"] Meet me | in the | Green | Glen'. Spine, in brown:

'[same fancy ltrs.] Meet | me | in the | Green | Glen | SECKER & | WARBURG'. Front flap: about the novel. Back flap: about the author.

Copies: BL, Ctw, JAG (2).

Note: published 10 April 1972 at £2.25. Printed by Cox & Wyman Limited. The publisher prefers not to disclose the number of copies printed (ltr., T. G. Rosenthal, Managing Director, Martin Secker & Warburg Ltd., 6 Feb. 1975). British Library date-stamp 18 April 1972.

A32.d1   second English edition, first impression, paperback (1974)

Meet Me In | The Green Glen | Robert Penn Warren | NEW EN-GLISH LIBRARY || TIMES MIRROR

Collation: post folio 8° (trimmed: 17.8 × 10.6 cm.); signed, $[1]-18^8$, 144 leaves; pp. [1–6] 7–75 [76–78] 79–199 [200–202] 203–255 [256–258] 259–288; numbers centered at foot of type page.

Contents: p. [1]: hf. tit. 'MEET ME IN | THE GREEN GLEN'; p. [2]: blank; p. [3]: title page; p. [4]: dedication and copyright; p. [5]: 'BOOK I'; p. [6]: blank; pp. 7–288: text.

Typography and Paper: text: 45 ll., 15.1 (15.5) × 8.7 cm.; Times-Inter-type 9/10-pt. Paper: Norwegian Bulky News, 005/54 gsm, 36-in. reel width; white, wove, unwatermarked. Ink: Fishburn's solvent-based liquid; Letterpress rotary novel black AP.2998 (1691/1)511 (ltr., V. Flynn, Managing Director, Hunt Barnard Printing Ltd., 18 March 1975); sheets bulk 1.8 cm.

Binding: paper. Front cover, against illus. (reddish brown tones) of a woman: '[in purple] NEW ENGLISH LIBRARY [publisher's device, on purple oval in black] | [in white with fancy ltrs.] *Robert | Penn | War-ren | Meet me | in the | Green Glen*'. Spine: '[horiz., publisher's device, on purple oval in black] | [in white] FICTION | [vert.] *Meet me in the Green Glen | Robert Penn Warren* | [horiz.] 016161'. Back cover, in purple: about the novel. Inside covers: white. All edges trimmed and unstained.

Copies: BL, JAG.

Note: published 7 March 1974 at 50p. The publisher prefers not to disclose the number of copies printed (ltr., Dorothy Houghton, Manag-ing Editor—Paperbacks, New English Library, 20 March 1975). Printed by Hunt Barnard Printing Ltd. Distributed in Cyprus,

Gibraltar, Malta, New Zealand, Spain, Trinidad (W.I.), and Australia. British Library date-stamp 25 Feb. 1974.

A33 *Or Else—Poem/Poems, 1968–1974*

A33.a1 first American edition, first impression (1974)

[p. (iv): orn.] Robert Penn Warren [p. (v)] OR ELSE— | Poem/Poems 1968–1974 | RANDOM HOUSE NEW YORK [publisher's device]

Collation: royal folio 8° (rough trimmed: 23.8 × 15.9 cm.); *unsigned* [1–4¹⁶], 64 leaves; pp. [1–2], [i–ix] x–xi [xii] xiii [xiv] xv [xvi], [1–2] 3–102 [103–110]; numbers in ital.; on v., in corner formed by tail and inner margins; on r., in corner formed by tail and outer margins.

Contents: pp. [1–2]: blank; p. [i]: blank; on p. [ii] 'BOOKS BY ROBERT PENN WARREN'; p. [iii]: hf. tit. 'OR ELSE— | Poem/ Poems 1968–1974'; pp. [iv–v]: title pages; p. [vi]: '[copyright] | FIRST EDITION'; p. [vii]: 'TO CESARE AND RYSIA LOM-BROSO'; p. [viii]: blank; pp. [ix]–xi: contents; p. [xii]: blank; p. xiii: author's note about this book; p. [xiv]: blank; p. xv: '[epigraph] | *Psalms, 78 : 15*'; p. [xvi]: blank; p. [1]: hf. tit.; p. [2]: about spacing between sections; p. 3: 'I [orn.] | THE NATURE OF A MIRROR'; p. 4: 'INTERJECTION #1: | THE NEED FOR RE-EVALUA-TION'; pp. 5–6: 'II [orn.] | NATURAL HISTORY'; pp. 7–9: 'III [orn.] | TIME AS HYPNOSIS | *For I. A. Richards*'; p. 10: 'IV [orn.] | BLOW, WEST WIND'; pp. 11–12: 'INTERJECTION #2: | CAVEAT | *For John Crowe Ransom*'; pp. 13–22: 'V [orn.] | I AM DREAMING OF A WHITE CHRISTMAS: | THE NATURAL HISTORY OF A VISION | *For Andrew Vincent Corry*'; pp. 23–24: 'INTERJECTION #3: | I KNOW A PLACE WHERE ALL IS REAL | *For Austin Warren*'; pp. 25–29: 'VI [orn.] | BALLAD OF MISTER DUTCHER | AND THE LAST LYNCHING IN GUP-TON'; pp. 30–33: 'VII [orn.] | CHAIN SAW AT DAWN IN VER-MONT | IN TIME OF DROUTH'; p. 34: 'VIII [orn.] | SMALL WHITE HOUSE'; pp. 35–36: 'INTERJECTION #4: | BAD YEAR, BAD WAR: | A NEW YEAR'S CARD, 1969 | [epigraph]'; pp. 37–39: 'IX [orn.] | FOREVER O'CLOCK'; pp. 40–48: 'X [orn.] | RATTLESNAKE COUNTRY | *For James Dickey*'; pp. 49–50: 'XI [orn.] | HOMAGE TO THEODORE DREISER | On the Centen-nial of his Birth | (August 27, 1871) | [epigraph] | 1. PSYCHOLOGI-CAL PROFILE'; pp. 51–53: '2. VITAL STATISTICS'; pp. 54: 'MORAL ASSESSMENT'; pp. 55–57: 'XII [orn.] | FLAUBERT IN

EGYPT | *For Dorothea Tanning*'; p. 58: 'INTERJECTION #5: | SOL-IPSISM AND THEOLOGY'; pp. 59–60: 'XIII [orn.] | THE TRUE NATURE OF TIME | 1. THE FARING'; p. 61: '2. THE ENCLAVE'; pp. 62–63: 'XIV [orn.] | VISION UNDER THE OCTOBER | MOUNTAIN: A LOVE POEM'; pp. 64–65: 'XV [orn.] | STARGAZING'; p. 66: 'INTERJECTION #6: | WHAT YOU SOMETIMES FEEL ON | YOUR FACE AT NIGHT'; pp. 67–73: 'XVI [orn.] | NEWS PHOTO | [description of photo]'; p. 74: 'XVII [orn.] | LITTLE BOY AND LOST SHOE'; pp. 75–77: 'XVIII [orn.] | COMPOSITION IN GOLD AND RED-GOLD'; pp. 78–79: 'INTERJECTION #7: | REMARKS OF SOUL TO BODY | (On the Occasion of a Birthday Party) | *For Sergio and Alberta Perosa*'; pp. 80–81: 'XIX [orn.] | THERE'S A GRANDFATHER'S CLOCK | IN THE HALL'; pp. 82–89: 'XX [orn.] | READING LATE AT NIGHT, | THERMOMETER FALLING'; pp. 90–92: 'XXI [orn.] | FOLLY ON ROYAL STREET | BEFORE THE RAW FACE OF GOD'; p. 93: 'INTERJECTION #8: | OR, SOMETIMES, NIGHT | *For Paul Horgan*'; pp. 94–97: 'XXII [orn.] | SUNSET WALK IN THAW-TIME IN VERMONT'; pp. 98–100: 'XXIII [orn.] | BIRTH OF LOVE'; pp. 101–102: 'XXIV [orn.] | A PROBLEM IN SPATIAL COMPOSITION'; p. 103: about the author; pp. [104–110]: blank.

Typography and Paper: text: 33 ll., 15.8 (16.3) × 11.75 cm.; Fairfield 11/14-pt. Paper: white, laid, vert. chainlines (2.1 cm.); unwatermarked; sheets bulk 0.9 cm.

Binding: black cloth. Front, in gilt: '[orn.] ROBERT PENN WARREN'. Spine, vert., in gilt: 'Robert Penn Warren [orn.] OR ELSE—Poem/Poems 1968–1974 [orn.] Random House [publisher's device]'. Back: blank. Fore and bottom edges rough trimmed, top edge trimmed and stained orange; black endpapers.

 Dust wrapper: front cover, on black: '[in white] ROBERT | PENN | WARREN | [in gold, enlarged "O"] OR ELSE | Poem/Poems 1968 · 1974'. Spine, vert., on black: '[in white] ROBERT PENN WARREN [in gold] OR ELSE Poem/Poems 1968 · 1974 [in white, publisher's device] Random | House'. Back cover, in white on black: about the author. Front flap: about RPW's poetry. Back flap: books by RPW.

Copies: CoCA, Ctb, CtY, JAG, LC, STW, TxFTC.

Note: published 7 Oct. 1974 in 6,500 copies at $6.95. Printed by Book Press, Brattleboro, VT. (Ltr., Jim Wilcox, Random House, Inc., 17

Dec. 1976.) LC copyright 10 Sept. 1974 (A594092); two copies deposited 18 Dec. 1974.

A33.b1   first American edition, special limited edition (1974)

Title Page: identical with **A33.a1**.

Collation: [1¹⁶ (+1₂) 2–4¹⁶], 65 leaves; pp. [ᵗ1–4], otherwise as in **A33.a1**.

Contents: pp. [ᵗ1–2]: blank; p. [ᵗ3]: 'Of the first edition of | OR ELSE—POEM/POEMS—1968–1974 | three hundred copies have been specially printed and bound. | These books are signed by the author, | and numbered 1 to 300. | No. [entered by hand in ink] | [signature in ink]'; p. [ᵗ4]: blank.

Typography and Paper: identical with **A33.a1**. Paper: pp. [ᵗ3–4]: cream (color does not match other paper); laid, vert. chainlines (2.1 cm.), unwatermarked; sheets bulk 0.9 cm.

Binding: black embossed calico grain cloth. Markings identical with **A33.a1**.
   Dust wrapper: none.

Copies: JAG (marked "OUT OF SERIES"), RPW (no. 9), STW (no. 262).

Note: published 7 Oct. 1974 in 300 boxed copies at $17.50. Advance proof copies preceded publication (letter, Stuart Wright, 8 May 1980). By 11 Feb. 1975 this edition was out of stock.

A34   *Democracy and Poetry*

A34.a1   first American edition, first impression (1975)

Democracy and Poetry || Robert Penn Warren | Harvard University Press | Cambridge, Massachusetts | and | London, England | 1975

Collation: demy folio 8° (trimmed: 20.9 × 14.0 cm.); *unsigned* [1–7⁸ 8⁴], 60 leaves; pp. [i–x] xi–xvi, [1–2] 3–37 [38–40] 41–94 [95–96] 97–102 [103–104]; numbers centered in tail margin.

Contents: p. [i]: '*Democracy and Poetry* || *The 1974 Jefferson Lecture in the Humanities*'; p. [ii]: '[epigraph] | ——St.-John Perse'; p. [iii]: title page; p. [iv]: copyright; p. [v]: ' || To | Andrew Nelson Lytle | and the memory of | Edna Barker Lytle'; p. [vi]: blank; p. [vii]: acknowledgments;

p. [viii]: blank; p. [ix]: contents; p. [x]: blank; pp. xi–xvi: foreword; p. [1]: '*America and the Diminished Self* || '; p. [2]: blank; pp. 3–37: text; p. [38]: blank; p. [39]: '*Poetry and Selfhood* ||'; p. [40]: blank; pp. 41–94: text; p. [95]: '*Notes* ||'; p. [96]: blank; pp. 97–101: notes; p. 102: credits; pp. [103–104]: blank.

Typography and Paper: text: 29 ll., 15.0 (17.6) × 9.6 cm.; Palatino 12/15-pt. RT: v., '*Robert Penn Warren* || '; r., '*Democracy and Poetry* ||'. Paper: white, wove, unwatermarked; sheets bulk 0.85 cm.

Binding: medium blue cloth. Front and back: blank. Spine, vert., in silver: 'WARREN DEMOCRACY AND POETRY HARVARD'. All edges trimmed and unstained; red endpapers.

   Dust wrapper: front cover, on purple: '[in white] DEMOCRACY | & | POETRY | [in red] ROBERT | PENN | WARREN'. Spine, vert., on purple: '[in red] WARREN [in white] DEMOCRACY AND PO-ETRY [in red] HARVARD'. Back cover, in white on purple: about the author and photograph by Michael V. Carlisle. Front flap: about the book. Back flap: continued from front flap.

Copies: CoCA, Ctb, JAG, KyU, LC, LU, STW, TNJ.

Notes: 1. Published July 1975 in 4,500 copies at $5.95. (letter, Arthur J. Rosenthal, Harvard University Press, 14 Dec. 1976.) LC copyright 21 May 1975 (A639692); two copies deposited 27 May 1975. Advance proof copies preceded publication (letter, Stuart Wright, 8 May 1980).

   2. Excerpts: "Democracy and Poetry," *SoR*, NS 11 (Winter 1975), 1–28 [pp. 41–94]; "Bearers of Bad Tidings: Writers and the American Dream," *NYRB*, 20 March 1975, pp. 12–19 [pp. 4–37].

A34.b1   first American edition, second impression, paperback (1976)

Title Page: identical with **A34.a1** except omits date.

Contents: on p. [iv] 'Second Printing 1976'.

Binding: issued in cloth and paper. Identical with dw. of **A34.a1** except back cover has excerpts from reviews in lieu of photograph and biographical sketch. All edges trimmed and unstained; the red end-papers—two leaves front and two leaves back—are bound into this impression.

Copies: JAG, STW.

Note: published April 1976 in 4,000 copies at $2.25. Printed by Vail-Ballou Press.

A35 *Selected Poems, 1923–1975*

A35.a1 first American edition, first impression (1976)

[ltrs. in black: p. (iv)] Random House [publisher's device] New York [p. (v)] *Robert Penn Warren* | [two gray orns.] SELECTED | POEMS [four gray orns.] | [three gray orns.] 1923–1975

Collation: royal folio 8° (trimmed: 23.4 × 15.5 cm.); *unsigned* [1–11 ¹⁶], 176 leaves; pp. [ᵗ1–2], [i–viii] ix–xvii [xviii], [1–2] 3–17 [18–20] 21–81 [82–84] 85–100 [101–102] 103–138 [139–140] 141–188 [189–190] 191–216 [217–218] 219–268 [269–270] 271–325 [326–332]; numbers off-center at foot of type page: on v., inset from outer margin; on r., inset from inner margin.

Contents: pp. [ᵗ1–2]: blank; p. [i]: blank; on p. [ii] '*Books by Robert Penn Warren*'; p. [iii]: hf. tit., ltrs. in black '[two gray orns.] SELECTED | POEMS [four gray orns.] | [three gray orns.] 1923–1975'; pp. [iv–v]: title pages; on p. [vi] copyright, acknowledgments, and '9 8 7 6 5 4 3 2 | First Trade Edition'; p. [vii]: '*To* | Eleanor | Rosanna | Gabriel'; p. [viii]: blank; pp. ix–xvii: contents; p. [xviii]: blank; p. [1]: '[three gray orns.] CAN I SEE | [two gray orns.] ARCTURUS | FROM WHERE | [three gray orns.] I STAND? | *Poems 1975* [five gray orns.] | *Is* was *but a word for wisdom, its price?* | "RATTLESNAKE COUNTRY"'; p. [2]: about the spacing between sections; pp. 3–4: 'A WAY TO LOVE GOD'; pp. 4–5: 'EVENING HAWK'; pp. 5–6: 'LOSS, OF PERHAPS LOVE, | IN OUR WORLD OF CONTINGENCY'; pp. 6–8: 'ANSWER TO PRAYER | A Short Story That Could Be Longer'; p. 8: 'PARADOX'; p. 9: 'MIDNIGHT OUTCRY'; pp. 10–11: 'TRYING TO TELL YOU SOMETHING | *To Tinkum Brooks*'; pp. 11–12: 'BROTHERHOOD OF PAIN'; pp. 12–13: 'SEASON OPENS ON WILD BOAR IN CHIANTI | *To Guerino and Ginevra Roberti*'; pp. 13–17: 'OLD NIGGER ON ONE MULE CART ENCOUNTERED | LATE AT NIGHT WHEN DRIVING HOME | FROM PARTY IN THE BACK COUNTRY'; p. [18]: blank; p. [19]: '[seven gray orns.] *from* | [three gray orns.] OR ELSE— | *Poem/Poems 1968–1974* | *To Cesare and Rysia Lombroso* | [epigraph]'; p. [20]: blank; pp. 21–81: includes all poems from *OEP* except "News Photo"; p. [82]: blank; p. [83]: '[one gray orn.] AUDUBON | *A Vision* [five gray orns.] | *To Allen and Helen Tate* | [epigraphs]'; p. [84]: on Jean Jacques Audubon; pp. 85–100: complete; p. [101]: '[nine gray orns.] *from* | INCARNATIONS | *Poems 1966–1968* [four gray orns.] | *To John*

Palmer | [epigraphs]'; p. [102]: blank; pp. 103–138: includes all poems from *I* except four—"Moonrise," "Mistral at Night," "The Faring," and "The Enclave"; p. [139]: '[eight gray orns.] *from* | TALE OF TIME | *Poems 1960–1966* [three gray orns.]'; p. [140]: blank; pp. 141–188: omits 10 poems—"Stargazing," "Small White House," "Blow, West Wind," "Composition in Gold and Red-Gold," "Little Boy and Lost Shoe," "Dragon-Tree," "Vision Under the October Mountain: A Love Poem," "Chain Saw at Dawn in Vermont in Time of Drouth," "Dream of a Dream the Small Boy Had," and "Finisterre"; p. [189]: '[nine gray orns.] *from* | YOU, EMPERORS, | [two gray orns.] AND OTHERS | *Poems 1957–1960* [four gray orns.] | *To Max and Carol Shulman*'; p. [190]: blank; pp. 191–216: omits among the poems included in *SPNO*, nine poems—"In Italian They Call the Bird *Civetta*," "Autumnal Equinox on Mediterranean Beach," the three poems in the sequence "Nursery Rhymes," and the four poems in the sequence "Short Thoughts for Long Nights"; p. [217]: '[six gray orns.] *from* | [one gray orn.] PROMISES | *Poems 1954–1956* [one gray orn.]'; p. [218]: blank; pp. 219–268: same selections as those which appear in *SPNO* (**A28.a1**); p. [269]: '[ten gray orns.] *from* | SELECTED POEMS | *1923–1943* [seven gray orns.]'; p. [270]: blank; pp. 271–325: includes same selections as those which appear in *SPNO*, except two—"Man Coming of Age" and "Letter of a Mother"; p. [326]: blank; p. [327]: about the author; pp. [328–332]: blank.

Typography and Paper: text: 40 ll., 18.4 (19.15) × 11.4 cm.; Linotype Janson 11/13-pt. Paper: white, wove, unwatermarked; sheets bulk 2.6 cm.

Binding: black cloth and cream-colored, paper-covered bds. Front, on cream in gilt: '*R P W* | [two orns.]'. Spine, in gilt: '[horiz.] *Robert* | *Penn* | *Warren* | [orn.] | [vert.] SELECTED | POEMS | [orn.] | [horiz.] 1923– | 1975 | [publisher's device] | Random House'. Back: blank. All edges trimmed and unstained; black endpapers.

Dust wrapper: front cover, on cream: '[gold orn.; gold rule] | [in black] ROBERT PENN | WARREN || SELECTED | POEMS | 1923–1975 | [gold rule; gold orn.]'. Spine, on cream: '[gold orn., horiz.] | [vert., in black] ROBERT PENN | WARREN / SELECTED POEMS | 1923–1975 | [gold orn.] | [in black, publisher's device] | RANDOM | HOUSE'. Back cover: photograph of RPW by Rhoda Nathans and biographical sketch. Front flap: about the book. Back flap: books by RPW.

Copies: CoCA, Ctb, Ctw, JAG, KyU, RPW, STW, TNJ.

Notes: 1. Published Jan. 1977 in 6,000 copies at $15.00. Printed by R. R. Donnelley & Sons Co. Distributed in Canada by Random House of Canada Limited. (Ltr., Albert Erskine, Random House, Inc., 27 Nov. 1979.) LC copyright 15 Dec. 1976 (A827363); two copies deposited 11 Feb. 1977.

2. A Book-of-the-Month Club edition is identical to the first trade edition. Also, excerpted in *Four Star Condensations* (Bombay, India: Vakils, Feffer, and Simons, Private Ltd., n.d.), pp. viii, 1–51; USIA distribution. (Ctb)

A35.b1   first American edition, first impression, paperback (1976)

Title Pages: identical with **A35.a1**.

Binding: paper. Identical with **A35.a1** dw. except number in lower right corner, back cover: '394-73264-2'.

Copies: JAG, STW.

Note: published Jan. 1977 in 4,000 copies at $6.95.

A35.c1   first American edition, special limited edition (1976)

Title Pages: identical with **A35.a1**.

Collation: [1 ^{16} (+1 $_2$) 2–11 ^{16}], 177 leaves; pp. [$^\pi$1–4], otherwise identical with **A35.a1**.

Contents: pp. [$^\pi$1–2]: blank; p. [$^\pi$3]: 'Of the first trade edition of | SELECTED POEMS: 1923–1975 | two hundred and fifty copies | have been specially printed and bound. | These books are signed by the author, | and numbered 1 to 250. | No. [no. entered by hand in ink on the blank provided | [signature in ink]'; p. [$^\pi$4]: blank.

Typography and Paper: both identical with **A35.a1**.

Binding: black cloth. Front and back: blank. Spine, in gilt: '[horiz.] *Robert* | *Penn* | *Warren* | [orn.] | [vert.] SELECTED | POEMS | [orn.] | [horiz.] 1923–|1975 | [publisher's device] | Random House'. All edges trimmed with top edge stained harvest gold; black endpapers.

  Dust wrapper: none.

Copies: JAG (marked "out of series"), KyU (no. 183), RPW (nos. 9, 18, 19, 21), STW (no. 52).

Note: published Jan. 1977 in 250 boxed copies at $25.00.

A35.d1   second American edition, Franklin Library edition (1977)

[ltrs. in black] *The First Edition Society* | Selected Poems | 1923–1975 | *Robert Penn Warren* | [illus. in brownish red] | *Illustrated by Leo and Diane Dillon* | THE FRANKLIN LIBRARY | Franklin Center, Pennsylvania | 1976

Collation: crown folio 4° (trimmed: 23.4 × 16.2 cm.); *unsigned* [1–20^8], 160 leaves; pp. [i–xiv] xv–xxi [xxii], [1–2] 3–16 [17–18] 19–72 [73–74] 75–89 [90–92] 93–124 [125–126] 127–168 [169–170] 171–180 [181] 182–193 [194–196] 197–242 [243–244] 245–272 [273] 274–294 [295–298]; numbers, in brownish red, centered at foot of type page.

Contents: pp. [i–ii]: blank; p. [iii]: '[brownish red rule] | [in black] *This limited first edition of* | SELECTED POEMS 1923–1975 | *by Robert Penn Warren* | *has been privately printed* | *exclusively for Members of* | *The First Edition Society* | [brownish red rule]'; p. [iv]: blank; on p. [v] in brownish red '*Other Books by Robert Penn Warren*' with titles in black; p. [vi]: blank; p. [vii]: hf. tit. '[in black] Selected Poems | 1923–1975 | [brownish red illus.]'; pp. [viii–ix]: 'a special message to the members of the First Edition Society from the author'; p. [x]: blank; p. [xi]: title page; p. [xii]: copyright and acknowledgment; p. [xiii]: dedication; p. [xiv]: blank; pp. xv–xxi: contents; p. [xxii]: blank; pp. [1]–294: text, identical with **A35.a1** but with titles of sections of poems in brownish red; pp. [295–298]: blank.

Typography and Paper: text: 42 ll., 17.6 (18.35) × 12.6 cm.; Linotype Baskerville 10/12-pt. RT: only on contents pages, in brownish red, 'CONTENTS'. Paper: white, laid, vert. chainlines (2.4 cm.), watermarked 'THE | FIRST EDITION | SOCIETY'; sheets bulk 2.4 cm.

Illustrations: brownish red woodcuts on pp. [vii], [xi], [1], [17], [73], [91], 107, [125], [169], [181], [195], 204, [243], and [273].

Binding: brownish red leather. Front and back, in gilt: double frame with five rows of orns.: 3-2-3-2-3. Spine, in gilt: '[framed orn.] | [leather rib] || SELECTED | POEMS | 1923–1975 || [rib] || ROBERT | PENN | WARREN || [rib] | [framed orn.] || FIRST | EDITION || [rib] | [framed orn.] || THE | FRANKLIN | LIBRARY ||'. All edges trimmed and gilded; endpapers in burnished orange silk.

Dust wrapper: none.

Copies: RPW, STW.

Note: published by the Franklin Mint Corporation for $39.00. Additional publication information is not available.

A35.e1   first English edition, reissue (1976)

[ltrs. in black: p. (iv)] Secker & Warburg London [p. (v)] *Robert Penn Warren* | [two gray orns.] SELECTED | POEMS [four gray orns.] | [three gray orns.] 1923–1975

Contents: p. [vi]: 'This selection first published in England 1976 | by Martin Secker & Warburg Limited | 14 Carlisle Street, London W1V 6NN'.

Typography and Paper: identical with **A35.a1**: "In fact our edition is identical to that of Random House since we imported bound books from them" (ltr., Laura Morris, Foreign Rights, Martin Secker & Warburg Ltd., 15 May 1975).

Binding: identical wtih **A35.a1** except at bottom of spine, in gilt: 'Secker & | Warburg'.

   Dust wrapper: front and back, on purple: '[in white] Robert | Penn Warren | [in aqua] Selected | Poems | 1923–1975'. Spine, on purple: '[in white] Robert | Penn | Warren | [in aqua] Selected | Poems | 1923–1975 | [in white] SECKER & | WARBURG'. Front flap: about RPW's poetry. Back flap: about the poet and publisher's advertisement.

Copies: BL, JAG, RPW, STW.

Note: published Jan. 1977 at £7.95. Printed in U.S.'A. British Library date-stamp 1 Feb. 1977.

A36   *A Place to Come To*

A36.a1   first American edition, first impression (1977)

[p. (iv): publisher's device] || RANDOM HOUSE | NEW YORK [p. (v)] A Place | to Come To || [two orns.] || A NOVEL BY | Robert Penn | Warren ||

Collation: medium folio 8° (trimmed: 20.8 × 14.1 cm.); *unsigned* [1–13^{16}], 208 leaves; pp. [i–x], [1–2] 3–120 [121–122] 123–314 [315–316] 317–401 [402–406]; numbers beneath 1.25-cm. rule, centered at foot of type page.

Contents: p. [i]: blank; on p. [ii] 'BOOKS BY ROBERT PENN WAR-REN'; p. [iii]: hf. tit. 'A Place | to Come To'; pp. [iv–v]: title pages; p. [vi]: '[copyright] | 24689753 | First Edition'; p. [vii]: 'TO | *my sister Mary* | AND | *my brother Thomas*'; p. [viii]: blank; p. [ix]: '[epigraph] | GERARD MANLEY HOPKINS: | "Carrion Comfort"'; p. [x]: blank; p. [1]: 'Book One'; p. [2]: blank; pp. 3–120: chapters I–IV; p. [121]: 'Book Two'; p. [122]: blank; pp. 123–314: chapters V–XIII; p. [315]: 'Book Three'; p. [316]: blank; pp. 317–401: chapters XIV–XVII; p. [402]: blank; pp. [403–404]: about the author; pp. [405–406]: blank.

Typography and Paper: text: 37 ll., 16.8 (17.8) × 10.1 cm.; Times New Roman 11/13-pt. Paper: white, wove, unwatermarked; sheets bulk 2.95 cm.

Binding: black cloth and orangish gold bds. Front, in copper: ' || [orn.] R W P [orn.] ||'. Spine, on black in copper: ' || [two orns.] | [framed, vert.] A Place to Come To || Robert Penn Warren | [two orns.] || [horiz., publisher's device] | RANDOM | HOUSE'. Back: blank. All edges trimmed and unstained; beige endpapers.

   Dust wrapper: front, on black: '[in yellow] A | PLACE | TO | COME | TO | [white rule] | [in white] A NOVEL | [in orange] ROBERT | PENN | WARREN'. Spine, on black: '[in yellow] A | PLACE | TO | COME | TO | [in orange] ROBERT | PENN | WARREN | [in yellow, publisher's device] | [in white] RANDOM | HOUSE'. Back: photograph of RPW by Nancy Crampton. Front flap: about the novel. Back flap: about the author.

Copies: CoCA, Ctw, JAG, KyU, LU, RPW, STW, TNJ.

Notes: 1. Published March 1977 in 50,000 copies at $10.00. Printed by Haddon Craftsmen. "I am fairly certain . . . that we went to press for another 5,000 copies at some point" (ltr., Albert Erskine, Random House, Inc., 27 Nov. 1979). Distributed in Canada by Random House of Canada Limited. LC copyright 9 Feb. 1977 (A845518) and supplementary registration 3 Feb. 1978 (TX6-334); two copies deposited 19 April 1977.

   2. Excerpts: "Chicago," *GaR*, 30 (Winter 1976), 799–823; "Life and Death with Agnes," *Ohio Review*, 18 (Winter 1977), 49–74; "Rozelle," *Family Circle*, Feb. 1977, pp. 22, 150, 152, and 161.

   3. RPW's after-the-fact changes to the first impression (provided Nov. 1978): p. 33.7: "People said that Mrs. Hardcastle was saving Rozelle" to "People said that Rozelle's stuck-up aunt was saving her"; p. 82.8: "learning will" to "learning, will"; p. 171.36: "*réproduction*" to

"*reproduction*"; p. 216.20: "*foedelité*" to "*féodalité*"; p. 232.3: "*Mantova*" to "*Mantovano*"; p. 283.1: "pickly" to "pickley"; p. 283.21: "Pappa" to "Poppa"; p. 312.34: "Air Lines" to "Airlines"; p. 318.1: "of Gallic wit" to "in Gallic wit"; p. 321.11: "He looked" to "I looked"; p. 324.19 and .23: "di Siena" to "da Siena"; p. 340.24–25: "Académie Française" to "Légion d'Honneur"; p. 351.2: "ministero" to "Ministero" and "Istruzioni" to "Istruzione"; p. 351.3: "suo" to "Suo"; p. 356.33: "my hotel of whose hot and cold running water I had great need" to "my hotel and the hot and cold running water of which I had great need"; p. 357.15: delete ital. in "*Trinità dei Monti*"; and p. 361.26: "fettucine" to "fettuccine."

A36.b1   first American edition, special limited edition (1977)

Title Pages: identical with **A36.a1**.

Collation: [1^{16} (+1$_1$) 2–13^{16}], 209 leaves; pp. [$^\pi$1–2], otherwise identical with **A36.a1**.

Contents: p. [$^\pi$1]: '*Of the first edition of* | A PLACE TO COME TO | *three hundred and fifty copies* | *have been specially printed and bound.* | *These books are signed by the author,* | *and numbered 1 to 350.* | *Number* [no. entered by hand in ink on the blank provided] | [signature in ink]'; p. [$^\pi$2]: blank.

Typography and Paper: identical with **A36.a1**.

Binding: black cloth. Front, in copper: '|| [orn.] *R W P* [orn.] ||'. Spine, in copper: as on **A36.a1**. Back: blank. All edges trimmed with top edge stained reddish orange; beige endpapers.
   Dust wrapper: none.

Copies: JAG (no. 29), Donald A. Keal (no. 317), STW (no. 183), TNJ (no. 106).

Note: published April 1977 in 350 boxed copies at $25.00.

A36.c1   second American edition, book-club edition (1977)

[p. (iv): publisher's device] || RANDOM HOUSE | NEW YORK [p. (v)] A Place | to Come To || [two orns.] || A NOVEL BY | Robert Penn | Warren ||

Collation: demy folio 8° (trimmed: 20.8 × 13.8 cm.); *unsigned* [1–8^{12} 9–16^{10}], 176 leaves; pp. [i–viii], [1] 2–11 [12] 13–36 [37] 38–65 [66] 67–101 [102–103] 104–117 [118] 119–134 [135] 136–159 [160] 161–

181 [182] 183–190 [191] 192–212 [213] 214–223 [224] 225–245 [246] 247–268 [269] 270–283 [284] 285–303 [304] 305–319 [320] 321–341 [342–343] 344; numbers indented from outer margins at top of page.

Contents: p. [i]: blank; on p. [ii] 'BOOKS BY ROBERT PENN WARREN'; p. [iii]: hf. tit. 'A Place | to Come To'; pp. [iv–v]: title pages; p. [vi]: copyright page; p. [vii]: dedication; p. [viii]: epigraph; pp. [1]–101: Book One; p. [102]: blank; pp. [103]–268: Book Two; pp. [269]–341: Book Three; p. [342]: blank; pp. [343]–344: about the author.

Typography and Paper: text: 41 ll., 17.1 (17.8) × 10.8 cm.; Fairfield 10/12-pt. Paper: white, wove, unwatermarked; a coarser paper than in **A36.a1**; sheets bulk 2.3 cm.

Binding: black bds. Front, in gilt: ' || [orn.] R W P [orn.] ||'. Spine, in gilt: ' || [two orns.] | [framed, vert.] A Place to Come To || Robert Penn Warren | [two orns.] || [publisher's device] | [horiz.] RANDOM | HOUSE'. Back: blank. Fore and bottom edges rough trimmed, top edge trimmed, all edges unstained; white endpapers.

Dust wrapper: identical with **A36.a1** and front flap includes: 'Book Club | Edition'.

Copies: JAG, STW.

Notes: 1. Published as the April 1977 Literary Guild selection; *Literary Guild*, April 1977, pp. [i]–1; RPW–Norman O'Connor interview enclosed on flier.

2. Reflects one change from the author's suggestions: p. 26.31: "People said that her aunt was saving Rozelle" (cf. **A36.a1**, n.3).

A36.d1 third American edition, first impression, paperback (1978)

A Place | to Come To | *Robert Penn Warren* | A DELL BOOK

Collation: post folio 8° (trimmed: 17.8 × 10.7 cm.); *unsigned* [1⁸ 2– 13¹⁶], 200 leaves; pp. [1–9] 10–395 [396–400], except chapter and book pages are unnumbered: pp. [21], [49], [82], [123–125], [142], [161], [189], [214], [224], [249], [261], [285], [311–313], [330], [353], and [371]; numbers in corner formed by upper and outer margins.

Contents: p. [1]: about the novel; on p. [2] 'BOOKS BY ROBERT PENN WARREN'; p. [3]: title page; p. [4]: dedication and copyright; p. [5]: epigraph; p. [6]: blank; pp. [7]–395: text; pp. [396–400]: publisher's advertisements.

Typography and Paper: text: 43 ll., 14.9 (15.6) × 8.3 cm.; Times New

Roman 10-pt. RT: v., '*Robert Penn Warren*'; r., 'A PLACE TO COME TO'. Paper: white, wove, unwatermarked; sheets bulk 1.8 cm.

Binding: paper. Front cover against illus. of rural cabin, university building, and people: '[up left-hand side, in black] DELL · 15999 · 2.25 | [in white] A Triumphant Saga of an American Life | By the Author of ALL THE KING'S MEN | "Memorable! . . . One of the best books | of this or any year!—The Pittsburgh Press | [in gold] ROBERT | PENN | WARREN | [in beige] A | PLACE | TO | [in greenish beige] COME | TO [with the title going toward or coming out of face of clock which is superimposed on the center of the illus.]'. Spine, on white: '[horiz., in black] DELL || FIC || 2.25 | [vert., in yellowish green] A PLACE | TO COME TO || [in dark blue] ROBERT | PENN WARREN | [in black] 0-440-15999-7'. Back cover: about the book. Front inside cover: series of rules. Back inside cover: white. All edges trimmed and unstained.

Copies: JAG, STW.

Notes: 1. Published April 1978 at $2.25.

2. Printed from **A36.a1**, e.g., p. 37.38: "People said that Mrs. Hardcastle was saving Rozelle"; does not contain other changes suggested by the author.

A36.e1 first English edition, first impression, by offset (1977)

A Place | to Come To | A NOVEL BY | Robert Penn | Warren | SECKER & WARBURG | LONDON

Collation: medium folio 8° (trimmed: 21.4 × 13.4 cm.); *unsigned* [1–13¹⁶], 208 leaves; pp. [i–viii], [1–2] 3–[408]; numbering identical with **A36.a1**.

Contents: p. [i]: hf. tit. 'A Place | to Come To'; on p. [ii] 'BOOKS BY ROBERT PENN WARREN'; p. [iii]: title page; p. [iv]: 'First published in England 1977 by | Martin Secker & Warburg Limited | 14 Carlisle Street, London W1V 6NN | [copyright]'; p. [v]: dedication; p. [vi]: blank; p. [vii]: epigraph; p. [viii]: blank; otherwise as in **A36.a1**.

Typography and Paper: identical wtih **A36.a1**. Paper: white, wove, unwatermarked; sheets bulk 3.0 cm.

Binding: medium brown cloth. Front and back: blank. Spine, in gilt: 'A Place | to Come To | [five orns.] | *Robert | Penn Warren* | Secker & | Warburg'. All edges trimmed and unstained; white endpapers.

Dust wrapper: front and back, on brown: '[in white] Robert | Penn Warren | [in yellow] A Place | to Come | to | [in white] Author of | ALL THE KING'S MEN'. Spine: '[in white] Robert | Penn | Warren | [in yellow] A Place | to Come | to | [in white] SECKER & | WARBURG'. Front flap, brown on white: about the novel. Back flap: about the author.

Copies: BL, JAG, RPW, STW.

Note: published Feb. 1977 at £4.50. Printed by Cox & Wyman Limited. Additional information is not available (ltr., W. P. Neill-Hall, Martin Secker & Warburg Ltd., 14 Sept. 1976). British Library datestamp 24 March 1977.

A36.f1 second English edition, first impression, paperback (1978)

A Place To Come To | ROBERT PENN WARREN | NEW ENGLISH LIBRARY || TIMES MIRROR

Collation: post folio 8° (trimmed: 17.9 × 10.6 cm.); signed, [1]^8 2–22^8, 176 leaves; pp. [1–4] 5–351 [352]; numbers centered at foot of type page.

Contents: p. [1]: hf. tit. '*A PLACE TO COME TO*'; on p. [2] '*Also by this author and available from New English Library*'; p. [3]: title page; p. [4]: dedication, epigraph, copyright; pp. 5–351: text; p. [352]: publisher's advertisement.

Typography and Paper: text: 44 ll., 15.4 (15.8) × 8.6 cm.; Times New Roman 10-pt. Paper: white, wove, unwatermarked; sheets bulk 2.6 cm.

Binding: paper. Front cover, on white: '[up left side, top, in black] NEW ENGLISH LIBRARY [publisher's device] | [in maroon] A PLACE TO COME TO | [illus., five people and separate scene with automobile (on outer margin)] | ROBERT | PENN | WARREN | [in black] ———— ————*Soon to be a major film* | *starring Robert Redford* ————————'. Spine, on white: '[horiz., in black, publisher's device] | FICTION | [in maroon] A | PLACE | TO | COME TO | [illus., figure of a man] | ROBERT | PENN | WARREN | [vert., in black] 34658'. Back cover, maroon and black on white: about the novel. Inside covers: white. All edges trimmed and unstained.

Copies: BL, JAG, RPW, STW.

Note: published Feb. 1978 at £1.25. The publisher prefers not to disclose the number of copies printed. British Library date-stamp 29 Nov. 1978.

A37 *Now and Then: Poems, 1976–1978*

A37.a1 first American edition, first impression (1978)

NOW | AND | THEN | [orn.] *Poems* | [orn.] *1976–|1978* | [orn.] | Robert | Penn Warren | *Random House* [publisher's device] *New York*

Collation: royal folio 8° (trimmed: 23.4 × 15.5 cm.); *unsigned* [1–3 ^{16}], 48 leaves; pp. [^{π}1–2], [i–x] xi–xii, [1–2] 3–26 [27–28] 29–75 [76–82]; numbers at foot of type page indented 2 ems from outer margin on v., from inner margin on r.

Contents: p. [^{π}1–2]: blank; p. [i]: blank; on p. [ii] 'BOOKS BY ROBERT PENN WARREN'; p. [iii]: hf. tit. 'NOW AND THEN | *Poems 1976–1978*'; p. [iv]: blank; p. [v]: title page; p. [vi]: copyright, acknowledgments, LC Cataloging in Publication Data, 'FIRST EDITION'; p. [vii]: '*To Andrew Vincent Corry*'; p. [viii]: blank; p. [ix]: '[epigraph] | ISAIAH 42:11'; p. [x]: blank; pp. xi–xii: contents; p. [1]: '[orn.] I | NOSTALGIC'; p. [2]: about spacing between sections; pp. 3–7: '*American Portrait: Old Style*'; pp. 8–10: '*Amazing Grace in the Back Country*'; pp. 11–12: '*Boy Wandering in Simms' Valley*'; p. 13: '*Old Flame*'; p. 14: '*Evening Hour*'; pp. 15–16: '*Orphanage Boy*'; pp. 17–21: '*Red-Tail Hawk and Pyre of Youth* | TO HAROLD BLOOM'; p. 22: '*Mountain Plateau* | TO JAMES WRIGHT'; pp. 23–24: '*Star-Fall*'; pp. 25–26: '*Youth Stares at Minoan Sunset*'; p. [27]: '[orn.] II | SPECULATIVE'; p. [28]: blank; p. 29: '*Dream*'; pp. 30–31: '*Dream of a Dream*'; p. 32: '*First Dawn Light*'; pp. 33–34: '*Ah, Anima!*'; pp. 35–36: '*Unless*'; pp. 37–38: '*Not Quite Like a Top*'; pp. 39–40: '*Waiting*'; pp. 41–42: '*The Mission*'; pp. 43–44: '*Code Book Lost*'; pp. 45–46: '*When the Tooth Cracks—Zing!*'; pp. 47–48: '*Sister Water*'; pp. 49–50: '*Memory Forgotten*'; p. 51: '*Waking to Tap of Hammer*'; p. 52: '*Love Recognized*'; p. 53: '*The Smile*'; p. 54: '*How to Tell a Love Story*'; pp. 55–56: '*Little Black Heart of the Telephone*'; pp. 57–58: '*Last Laugh*'; pp. 59–60: '*Heat Lightning*'; pp. 61–62: '*Inevitable Frontier*'; pp. 63–65: '*Heart of the Backlog*'; pp. 66–68: '*Identity and Argument for Prayer*'; p. 69: '*Diver*'; pp. 70–71: '*Rather Like a Dream*'; p. 72: '*Departure*'; p. 73: '*Heat Wave Breaks*'; pp. 74–75: '*Heart of Autumn*'; p. [76]: blank; p. [77]: about the author; pp. [78–82]: blank.

Typography and Paper: text: 36 ll., 16.3 (17.0) × 12.0 cm.; Palatino

10/13-pt. Paper: white, wove, unwatermarked; sheets bulk 0.7 cm.

Binding: ⅔ beige, ⅓ black cloth. Front, in black on beige: '[orn.] RPW'. Spine, vert., in gilt on black: 'Robert Penn Warren [orn.] NOW AND THEN *Poems 1976–1978* [publisher's device] *Random House*'. Back: blank. All edges trimmed and unstained; cream end-papers.

    Dust wrapper: front cover, on medium brown: '[red rule] | [in white outlined in black] NOW | [cream orn.] AND [cream orn.] | THEN | [red rule] | [in black] POEMS 1976–1978 | [red rule] | ROBERT | PENN | WARREN | [red rule]'. Spine, vert., on medium brown: '[in black] ROBERT PENN WARREN [in white] NOW AND THEN [in black] POEMS 1976–1978 [in cream, publisher's device] RAN-DOM HOUSE'. Back cover, on medium brown: photograph of RPW by Nancy Crampton and biographical sketch. Front flap: about RPW as poet. Back flap: books by RPW and jacket design by Robert Gretczko.

Copies: CoCA, Ctb, Ctw, JAG, KyU, LC, RPW, STW (2), TNJ.

Note: published Sept. 1978 in 5,000 copies at $8.95. Printed by the Haddon Craftsmen. (Ltr., Albert Erskine, Random House, Inc., 27 Nov. 1979.) LC copyright 21 March 1979 (TX262-271); two copies deposited 21 March 1979.

A37.b1   first American edition, first impression, paperback (1978)

Title Page: identical with **A37.a1**.

Binding: paper. Cover is identical with **A37.a1** dw. except on back cover, at bottom: '$4.95 394-73515-3'. Inside covers: white. All edges trimmed and unstained.

Copies: JAG, RPW, STW.

Note: published Sept. 1978 in 7,500 copies at $4.95 (ltr., Albert Erskine, Random House, Inc., 27 Nov. 1979).

A37.c1   first American edition, special limited edition (1978)

Title Page: identical with **A37.a1**.

Collation: [1^{16} (+1$_1$) 2–3^{16}], 49 leaves; pp. [$^\pi$1–4], otherwise identical with **A37.a1**.

Contents: p. [$^\pi$1]: 'Of the first edition of | NOW AND THEN | *Poems*

1976–1978 | two hundred copies | have been specially printed and bound. | These books are signed by the author, | and numbered 1 to 200. | No. [entered by hand in ink] | [signature in ink]'; p. [ᵂ2]: blank.

Typography and Paper: identical with A37.a1. Paper: white, wove, unwatermarked; sheets bulk 0.7 cm.

Binding: olive green cloth. Front, in copper: '[upper right corner, floral four-leaf orn.] RPW'. Spine, vert., in copper: 'Robert Penn Warren [orn.] NOW AND THEN *Poems 1976–1978* [publisher's device] *Random House*'. Back: blank. All edges trimmed and unstained; light olive green endpapers.

   Dust wrapper: none.

Copies: Albert Erskine (no. 8), RPW (no. 4), STW (no. 85).

Note: published Sept. 1978 in 200 boxed copies at $27.50.

A38 *Two Poems*

A38.a1 first American edition, special limited edition (1979)

[ltrs. in black] TWO POEMS | *by* ROBERT PENN WARREN | [red fancy rule] | Palaemon Press Limited

Collation: royal folio 12° (trimmed: 16.4 × 13.8 cm.); *unsigned* [1⁶ (+1₇)], 7 leaves; pp. [1–14]; unnumbered.

Contents: p. [1]: title page; p. [2]: 'Copyright © 1979 by Robert Penn Warren | An earlier version of *A Few Axioms for a Young Man* appeared in | THE GEORGIA REVIEW; *Lord Jesus, I Wonder* | is here published for the first time.'; pp. [3–5]: title in red, 'Lord Jesus, I Wonder'; pp. [6–11]: title in red 'A Few Axioms For A Young Man'; p. [12]: blank; p. [13]: 'This first edition of | TWO POEMS by Robert Penn Warren | is limited to 230 copies | signed by the author. 200 copies, num-|bered 1–200, are for sale; 30 copies, | numbered *i–xxx*, are for distribu-|tion by the poet and publisher. | This is copy | [no. entered by hand in ink] | [signature in ink]'; p. [14]: blank.

Typography and Paper: text: 20 ll., 9.9 (9.9) × 10.3 cm.; Linotype Garamond no. 3, 11/14-pt. Paper: white, wove, unwatermarked; sheets bulk 0.15 cm.

Binding: marble-papered bds. Front, on white rectangle (3.1 × 6.7 cm.) framed in green, in red: 'TWO POEMS | *by* ROBERT PENN

WARREN'. Back: blank. All edges trimmed and unstained; white endpapers.

Note: free endpapers are gathered and are of the same paper as the lining paper.

Copies: JAG (no. xii), STW (nos. i and 1).

Note: published Dec. 1979 in 230 copies. Printed by Heritage Printers, Inc., Charlotte, NC (ltr., Stuart Wright, Palaemon Press Ltd., 9 Nov. 1979).

B

Works as Coauthor, Editor, and Panelist

B1 *The Fugitive: A Journal of Poetry* (1923–1925)

Contains: II, no. 7 (June–July 1923), 90–91: "Crusade"; II, no. 8
(Aug.–Sept. 1923), 106: "After Teacups"; II, no. 9 (Oct. 1923), 142:
"Midnight"; III, no. 1 (Feb. 1924): RPW is listed as one of The Fugi-
tives on the masthead; III, no. 2 (April 1924), 54–55: "Three Poems:
I. ['Beyond this bitter shore there is no going'] II. ['So many are the
things that she has learned'] III. ['I knew not down what windy nights
I fled']"; III, no. 3 (June 1924), 69–70: "Death Mask of a Young Man:
I. The Mouse II. The Moon" and "Nocturne"; III, no. 4 (Aug. 1924),
117–118: "Sonnets of Two Summers: I. Sonnet of a Rainy Summer
II. Sonnet of August Drouth" and "Praises for Mrs. Dodd"; III, nos.
5/6 (Dec. 1924), 154–155: "Alf Burt, Tenant Farmer" and "Admonition to Those Who Mourn"; IV, no. 1 (March 1925), 15–16 and
29–30: "Iron Beach," "The Mirror," and a review of *Sunrise Trumpets*
by Joseph Auslander; IV, no. 2 (June 1925), 33–37: "Easter Morning:
Crosby Junction," "Mr. Dodd's Son," "To a Face in the Crowd," and
"The Wrestling Match"; IV, no. 3 (Sept. 1925), 89–92: "Images on
the Tomb: I. Dawn: The Gorgon's Head II. Day: Lazarus III. Evening: The Motors IV. Night: But a Sultry Wind"; IV, no. 4 (Dec.
1925): nothing by RPW.

Binding: paper, stapled. IV, no. 1 (March 1925): front cover, on black
in red: 'THE | FUGITIVE | [on left] SINGLE COPIES | TWENTY-
FIVE CENTS [on right] MARCH | 1925 || PUBLISHED QUAR-
TERLY IN NASHVILLE, TENNESSEE ||'; inside front, on black
in red: '[masthead] THE FUGITIVE || VOL. IV. MARCH, 1925
NO. 1. | THE FUGITIVES—— | [names] EDITORS SERVING FOR 1925—— |
John Crowe Ransom Robert Penn Warren || [address] || [contents]'.

Copies: Ctw.

Note: reprints: New York: Johnson Reprint Corporation, 1966; Glou-
cester, MA: Peter Smith, 1967.

B2 *I'll Take My Stand*

B2.a1   first American edition, first impression (1930)

[ornamental rule] | I'LL TAKE MY STAND | *The South and the Agrarian Tradition* | By *TWELVE SOUTHERNERS* || [device] || HARPER & BROTHERS PUBLISHERS | 19 · *New York and London* · 30 ||

Collation: demy folio 8° (trimmed: 19.3 × 13.4 cm.); *unsigned* [1^{10} (+1₁) 2–19^{10}], 191 leaves; pp. [i–vi] vii–xx [xxi–xxii], 1–359 [360]; numbers in parentheses centered at foot of type page.

Contains: pp. 246–264: "The Briar Patch."

Typography and Paper: text: 30 ll., 14.8 (15.9) × 9.7 cm.; Granjon 12/14-pt. Paper: white, wove, unwatermarked; sheets bulk 3.8 cm.

Binding: bluish green cloth. Front, on gilt strip: 'I'LL TAKE MY STAND | BY TWELVE SOUTHERNERS'. Spine, on gilt: '[in black] I'LL TAKE | MY STAND | [in gilt] BY TWELVE | SOUTHERNERS || HARPER'S'. Back: blank. All edges trimmed with top edge stained red; white endpapers.

   Dust wrapper: on gray in blue: front: 'I'LL TAKE | MY STAND | [wavy rule] | *The South and the Agrarian Tradition* | [wavy rule] | By TWELVE SOUTHERNERS | [lists names of contributors] | [wavy rule] | HARPER & BROTHERS PUBLISHERS ESTABLISHED 1817 | [wavy rule]'. Spine: 'I'LL | TAKE MY | STAND | *by* | *Twelve* | *Southerners* | [two wavy rules] | *The South* | *and the* | *Agrarian* | *Tradition* | [orn.] | [wavy rule] | HARPERS | [wavy rule]'. Back: publisher's advertisement. Front flap: about the book. Back flap: *Harper's Magazine* advertisement.

Copies: Ctb, LC, OCl.

Notes: 1. LC copyright 12 Nov. 1930 (A31038); two copies deposited 12 Nov. 1930; copyright renewed 29 Jan. 1958 (R207715) by Donald Davidson as author.

   2. Reprinted, by offset: New York: Peter Smith, 1951; New York: Harper & Brothers, 1962, as a Harper Torchbook (TB 1072) with an introduction by Louis D. Rubin, Jr., and biographical essays by Virginia Rock; and Baton Rouge, LA: Louisiana State University Press, 1977, with a new introduction by Rubin.

B3   *Southwest Review* (1934–1935)

(Dallas: SMU and LSU), 20 (1934–1935): contributing editor, no. 1; associate editor, nos. 2–4.

B4 *New Republic* (1934)

As editor: "Seven Southern Poets," *New Republic*, 26 Dec. 1934, pp. 184–186; contains "For a Friend Parting," p. 186.

B5 *The Southern Review* (1935–1942)

Charles W. Pipkin, Cleanth Brooks, Jr., and RPW, eds. *The Southern Review*, 1–7 (July 1935–Spring 1942). As managing editor, vols. 1–6; tri-editor, 7, no. 1; co-editor, 7, nos. 2–4; "Editorial," 7 (Autumn 1941), iv, vi, viii, x, and xii; and "Editorial Announcement," 7 (Spring 1942), iv.

B6 *American Review* (1936)

Cleanth Brooks, Jr., and RPW. "Dixie Looks at Mrs. Gerould," *American Review*, 6 (March 1936), 585–595.

B7 *An Approach to Literature*

B7.a1 first American edition, first impression (1936)

[three borders: black, brownish red, black; ltrs. in black] An | Approach | To Literature | *A Collection of Prose and Verse with Analyses and Discussion* | By | CLEANTH BROOKS, JR. JOHN THIBAUT PURSER ROBERT PENN WARREN | *Department of English, Louisiana State University* | BATON [in brownish red, LSU Press seal] ROUGE | 1936

Collation: demy folio 4° (trimmed: 27.3 × 19.9 cm.); *unsigned* [1–18^{16} 19^{12} (+19$_{13}$)], 301 leaves; pp. [i–iv] v–x, 1–7 [8] [$^\pi$2] 9–111 [112] [$^\pi$2] 113–211 [212] [$^\pi$2] 213–308 [$^\pi$2] 309–417 [418] [$^\pi$2] 419–511 [512] [$^\pi$2] 513–572 [$^\pi$2] 573–578; numbers at top, outer margins except for chapter pages, on which they are centered at foot of type page.

Contents: does not contain any creative writing by RPW.

Typography and Paper: text: 54 ll., double column: 23.1 (23.9) × 16.9 cm.; Granjon 10/12-pt. RT: v., 'AN APPROACH TO LITERATURE'; r., titles of selections except in poetry section which lists 'POETRY: SECTION I' (through VII). Paper: white, wove, unwatermarked; sheets bulk 3.0 cm.

Binding: copies examined have been rebound.

Copies: Ctb, LC, OCI.

Notes: 1. Published Sept. 1936 with a second printing Sept. 1938: "we have been unable to find anything in our files concerning that particular book. . . . I know that at least some of our files were damaged or destroyed when water got into the basement of this building in the late 1950's, and that may be the explanation" (ltr., Charles East, Director of the LSU Press, 3 March 1975). LC copyright 24 Sept. 1936 (A100441); two copies deposited 6 Nov. 1936; copyright renewed 18 Nov. 1963 (R326080).

2. The forerunner of this textbook was a mimeographed pamphlet used by LSU sophomore students: cover: 'SOPHOMORE | [triple rule] | POETRY MANUAL | [triple rule] | [LSU seal] | Louisiana State University | 1936'. "The text pages measure 27.5 × 21.2 cm. (the wrappers protrude about 0.5 cm.) and the foliation is: 4 leaves unnumbered, leaves 2–123. The leaves are held together by staples" (ltr., Donald Gallup, Beinecke Rare Book and Manuscript Library, 28 May 1975). *Copy*: Ctb.

3. Subsequent editions: *revised edition*: New York: F. S. Crofts & Co., Publishers, 1939, pp. xii+636, and issued in a shorter edition which omits pp. 25–212 (Ctw, JAG, LC); LC copyright 5 Sept. 1939 (A133335), two copies deposited 25 Sept. 1939, and copyright renewed 8 Sept. 1966 (R392919). *Third edition*: New York: Appleton-Century-Crofts, Inc., 1952, pp. xvi+820, and issued in an alternate third edition (CoCA, Ctw [2], JAG, KyU, LC, TxFTC); LC copyright 18 March 1952 (A64903) with two copies deposited 21 March 1952; copies printed: Sept. 1951 (10,000), June 1952 (7,500), Dec. 1952 (12,500), Jan. 1954 (12,000), Sept. 1954 (10,000), Jan. 1955 (12,335), Sept. 1955 (15,750), Sept. 1956 (16,650), March 1958 (5,000), Sept. 1958 (9,325), Jan. 1959 (10,000), July 1959 (10,000), Sept. 1959 (10,000), Sept. 1960 (10,600), March 1961 (10,700), Jan. 1962 (10,000), and Jan. 1963 (12,000)—for a total of 184,360 copies, outselling the combined totals of the first and second editions (107,580 copies) (ltr., Marilyn Brauer, Humanities Editor, Prentice-Hall, Inc., 18 Jan. 1977). *Fourth edition*: New York: Appleton-Century-Crofts, Educational Division, Meredith Corporation, 1964, pp. xviii+926, and issued in an alternate fourth edition; RPW's essay "Why Do We Read Fiction?", pp. 553–559 and 866–872, respectively (CoCA, Ctw, JAG, LC); LC copyright 1 April 1964 (A682506), two copies deposited 3 April 1964, and for the alt. ed. 4 April 1967 (A902203),

two copies deposited 7 April 1967; copies printed: Oct. 1963 (7,500), April 1964 (23,500), June 1964 (24,500), Oct. 1964 (25,000), April 1965 (25,000), Aug. 1965 (35,000), Oct. 1965 (25,000), March 1966 (28,500), May 1968 (10,500), and Feb. 1970 (5,000)—for a total of 209,500 copies; 76,500 copies of the alt. ed. were printed (ltr., Brauer, 18 Jan. 1977). A Philippine edition (paper) was also printed of the fourth edition. *Fifth edition*: Englewood Cliffs, NJ: Prentice-Hall, Inc., 1975, pp. xxvi+902 (CoCA, Ctw, JAG, LC); LC copyright 4 March 1975 (A625557), two copies deposited 20 March 1975; initial printing of 20,000 copies. This edition is accompanied by a pamphlet, *Notes on An Approach to Literature: Fifth Edition, 1975*, pp. 32, with a photograph of the title page of "Sophomore Poetry Manual" (see note 2 above) (JAG); *Notes* was compiled and edited from a taped interview with Brooks and Warren by P–H (ltr., Bruce Kennan, Marketing Manager, College Div., Prentice-Hall, Inc., 5 April 1976); LC copyright 2 Jan. 1975 (A608008), deposited 7 Feb. 1975.

B8 *American Review* (1937)

With Cleanth Brooks. "II. The Reading of Modern Poetry," *American Review*, 8 (Feb. 1937), 435–449; also in *Purpose* [London], 11 (March 1938).

Note: one of three papers in a modern poetry symposium presented at the Modern Language Association meeting in Richmond, VA, Dec. 1936.

B9 *A Southern Harvest: Short Stories by Southern Writers*

B9.a1 first American edition, first impression (1937)

A | SOUTHERN | HARVEST || SHORT STORIES BY SOUTH-ERN WRITERS | EDITED BY ROBERT PENN WARREN | [rule with publisher's device in middle] | HOUGHTON MIFFLIN COM-PANY——BOSTON | [black letter] The Riverside Press Cambridge | 1937

Collation: demy folio 8° (trimmed: 20.5 × 14.0 cm.); *unsigned* [1–23⁸ 24⁴], 188 leaves; pp. [i–vi] vii [viii–x] xi–xv [xvi], 1–19 [20] 21–30 [31] 32–55 [56] 57–71 [72] 73–78 [79] 80–94 [95] 96–113 [114] 115–150 [151] 152–193 [194] 195–210 [211] 212–225 [226] 227–237 [238] 239–267 [268] 269–280 [281] 282–300 [301] 302–314 [315]

316–330 [331] 332–340 [341] 342–351 [352] 353–359 [360]; numbers centered at foot of type page.

Contains: pp. xi–[xvi]: introduction by RPW.

Typography and Paper: text: 37 ll., 15.3 (16.5) × 10.0 cm.; Linotype Century Expanded 11/12-pt. RT: v., story's title; r., author's name. Paper: white, wove, unwatermarked; sheets bulk 3.1 cm.

Binding: blue bds. Front and back: blank. Spine, in silver: '[double rule] | A | SOUTHERN | HARVEST | [double rule] | ROBERT | PENN | WARREN | [nineteen rules] | HOUGHTON | MIFFLIN | COMPANY'. All edges trimmed and unstained; white endpapers.

Dust wrapper: front, on pinkish red background: '[in dark blue] Representative fiction from the distinguished | writers of the New South. | [multicolored illus. of pickers in cotton field; illus. is bordered in white, then a thin red frame with leaf-vine orn. on each side] | [in dark blue] A SOUTHERN | HARVEST | EDITED BY | ROBERT PENN WARREN'. Spine, in dark blue: 'A | SOUTHERN | HARVEST | [orn.] | WARREN | HOUGHTON | MIFFLIN CO'. Back, on white in dark blue: list of new fiction from HM. Front flap: about the book. Back flap: about *The Best Short Stories 1937*, edited by Edward J. O'Brien.

Copies: CoFS, Ctw, CtY, JAG, KyU, LC, LU.

Notes: 1. Published 5 Nov. 1937 in one printing (10 Sept. 1937) of 2,500 copies by The Riverside Press. Issued simultaneously in Canada by Thomas Allen. (Ltr., Barbara E. Amidon, Permissions Dept., Houghton Mifflin Co., 27 Jan. 1975.) LC copyright 5 Nov. 1937 (A110963), two copies deposited 11 Nov. 1937, and copyright renewed 7 April 1965 (R358869).

2. Reprinted, by offset: Dunwoody, GA: Norman S. Berg, Publisher, 1972, with both trade and library bindings. (CoFS, Ctw, CtY, JAG, KyU, LC, LU.)

B10 *Understanding Poetry*

B10.a1 first American edition, first impression (1938)

UNDERSTANDING POETRY | AN ANTHOLOGY FOR COLLEGE STUDENTS | BY | CLEANTH BROOKS, JR. | AND | ROBERT PENN WARREN | THE LOUISIANA STATE UNI-

VERSITY | [publisher's device] | NEW YORK | HENRY HOLT AND COMPANY

Collation: crown folio 8° (trimmed: 18.7 × 12.7 cm.); *unsigned* [1–22 ¹⁶], 352 leaves; pp. [i–iii] iv–xxiv, 1–25 [26] 27–115 [116] 117–293 [294] 295–381 [382] 383–627 [628] 629–680; numbers at top, outer margins except on chapter pages where they are centered at the foot of the type page.

Typography and Paper: text: 38 ll., 14.8 (15.35) × 9.2 cm.; Granjon 10/11-pt. RT: on v. and r. inner margins, title of poem. Paper: white, wove, unwatermarked; sheets bulk 3.3 cm.

Binding: navy blue cloth. Front: pressed frame around edges. Spine, in gilt: '[pressed frame] *Understanding* | *Poetry* | [design] | BROOKS | AND | WARREN | HOLT'. Back: blank. All edges cut and unstained; white endpapers.
  Dust wrapper: none found.

  Note: To the best of Brooks's recollection, *UP* was issued in brown wrappers (Nov. 1979).

Copies: Ctw (4), JAG, LC, OIC, TxFTC.

Notes: 1. Published 1938 at $1.50. About *UP*'s publication: "First edition of UNDERSTANDING POETRY, published in 1938, printer Montauk (now out of business). No record at all until 2-1949, 10,000; 2-1950, 2,500; 4-1950, 1,500" (ltr., Kenney Withers, Publisher/Humanities, Holt, Rinehart, Winston, Inc., 3 Feb. 1975). LC copyright 6 June 1938 (A118321), two copies deposited 18 June 1938, copyright renewed 10 June 1965 (R363131).
  2. Subsequent editions: *revised edition*: New York: Henry Holt and Company, 1950, pp. lvi+728 (Ctw, JAG, TxFTC); LC copyright 27 July 1950 (A46501), two copies deposited 21 Aug. 1950, copyright renewed 5 Sept. 1978 (RE5-944); published in cloth July 1950 in 5,000 copies, Aug. 1950 (5,000), March 1951 (7,000), Sept. 1953 (5,000), Jan. 1954 (5,000), Sept. 1955 (6,000), Oct. 1955 (10,000), May 1956 (3,000), Sept. 1957 (4,000), June 1958 (3,000), Sept. 1958 (2,000), July 1959 (3,500), and Jan. 1960 (3,500)—for a total of 73,000 copies (ltr., Kenney Withers, Holt, Rinehart and Winston, Inc., 3 Feb. 1975). A *Teacher's Manual to Accompany UP* (rev. ed.) was printed in 2,500 copies, Feb. 1951; and according to Withers, "this was the only printing of the only manual to accompany the Brooks and Warren poetry texts." *Shorter revised edition*: pp. lvi+520 (Ctw, JAG); LC copyright

31 July 1950 (A6500), two copies deposited 21 Aug. 1950, copyright renewed 5 Sept. 1978 (RE5-943); published in paper July 1950 in 5,000 copies, Sept. 1953 (2,500), Feb. 1954 (3,500), Sept. 1955 (2,500), Oct. 1955 (2,500), March 1956 (2,200), Aug. 1957 (2,000), Jan. 1958 (2,500), Nov. 1958 (2,000)—for a total of 24,700 copies (ltr., Withers, 3 Feb. 1975). *Third edition*: New York: Holt, Rinehart and Winston, 1960, pp. xxiv+584 (CoCA, Ctw, JAG, LC, TxFTC [2]); LC copyright 26 April 1960 (A453837), two copies deposited 22 June 1960; published in cloth with dw. April 1960 in 10,000 copies, Oct. 1960 (10,000), May 1961 (15,000), Nov. 1961 (15,000), March 1963 (15,000), Dec. 1963 (10,000), Aug. 1964 (13,000), May 1965 (12,000), June 1966 (8,000), Feb. 1967 (15,000), May 1968 (15,000), April 1970 (13,000), Feb. 1975 (2,000)—for a total of 153,000 copies (ltr., Withers, 3 Feb. 1975). A set of two tapes with transcript accompanied *UP* (3d ed.), *Conversations on the Craft of Poetry* (**B27**). *Fourth edition*: New York: Holt, Rinehart and Winston, 1976, pp. xxii+602 (CoCA, Ctw, JAG [2]); LC copyright 2 Jan. 1976 (A734441), two copies deposited 21 April 1976; published 2 Jan. 1976 in 10,000 copies, followed by a second printing of 20,000 copies, both runs in paper (ltr., Kenney Withers, Publisher, Humanities, Holt, Rinehart and Winston, Inc., 8 Dec. 1976); contains "Birth of Love," pp. 460–461.

B11 *American Prefaces* (1942)

With Cleanth Brooks. "'The Killers,'" *American Prefaces*, 7 (Spring 1942), 195–209.

Notes: 1. Excerpt of a portion of *UF*, 1st edition, pp. 316–324; and second edition, pp. 303–312.

2. Reprinted by Kraus Reprint Corporation (New York, 1967).

B12 *Kenyon Review* (1942–1963)

Advisory editor, *Kenyon Review*, 4, no. 3 (Autumn 1942) through 25, no. 1 (Winter 1963); guest editor, "The Henry James Number," 5 (Autumn 1943), 481–617.

B13 *Aspects of a World at War* (1943)

Conrad Albrizio, Peter A. Carmichael, James B. Trant, RPW, and Ralph W. Steetle, panelists, "Industrialization: The Old South Fades," in *Aspects of a World at War: Radio Forums of the Louisiana State University*, ed. Robert Bechtold Heilman ([Baton Rouge]: Published for the

General Extension Division of the Louisiana State University, 1943), pp. 119–132.

Note: Transcripts of biweekly forums from Nov. 1941 to May 1942, WJBO, Baton Rouge; WSMB, New Orleans; KWKH, Shreveport; and KMLB, Monroe.

B14 *Understanding Fiction*

B14.a1   first American edition, first impression (1943)

Understanding | Fiction | [wavy rule] | *By* CLEANTH BROOKS, Jr. | LOUISIANA STATE UNIVERSITY | *and* ROBERT PENN WARREN | UNIVERSITY OF MINNESOTA | 1943 | F. S. CROFTS *& Company* | NEW YORK

Collation: medium folio 8° (trimmed: 22.0 × 14.1 cm.); *unsigned* [1–20¹⁶], 320 leaves; pp. [i–vi] vii–xix [xx] xxi–xxiii [xxiv] xxv [xxvi–xxx], 1–568 [569] 570–600 [601] 602–608 [609–610]; numbers located in corner formed by head and outer margins except section pages which have numbers centered in tail margin.

Typography and Paper: text: 37 ll., 16.7 (17.4) × 10.5 cm.; Granjon 11/13-pt. RT: v., section title in all caps.; r., titles of stories in all caps. Paper: white (smooth), wove, unwatermarked; sheets bulk 2.5 cm.

Binding: cream bds. Front: '[medium brown wavy rule] | [in dark blue] Understanding | Fiction | [medium brown wavy rule] | [in dark blue] *By* CLEANTH BROOKS, Jr. | *and* ROBERT PENN WARREN | [two medium brown wavy rules]'. Spine, medium brown rules, dark blue ltrs.: '[wavy rule] | Under-|standing | Fiction | [wavy rule] | BROOKS | *and* | WARREN | [wavy rule] | CROFTS | [wavy rule]'. Back: blank. All edges trimmed and unstained; white endpapers.
    Dust wrapper: none found.

Copies: Ctb, Ctw, CtY, JAG, KyU, LC, TxFTC.

Notes: 1. Published Jan. 1943 at $1.75. Subsequent printings: Sept. 1944, Feb. 1945, Jan. 1946, Oct. 1946, April 1947, Jan. 1948, . . . , but not all publication information was transferred from Appleton-Century-Crofts to Prentice-Hall (ltr., Marilyn Brauer, Editor-Humanities, Prentice-Hall, Inc., 11 Feb. 1975). LC copyright 19 Jan. 1943 (A170463), two copies deposited 22 Jan. 1943, copyright renewed 15 June 1970 (R486122).
    2. Portions of *UF* have been printed elsewhere: "'The Killers,'"

AmPf, 7 (Spring 1942), 195–209; "Character Is Action," *Writer*, 63 (June 1950), 181; and in a shorter version, *The Scope of Fiction* (**B26**).

3. Subsequent editions: *second edition*: New York: Appleton-Century-Crofts, Inc., 1959, pp. xxiv+688; contains RPW's translation of "The Killing of the Dragon" by Dino Buzzati, pp. 482–493 (Ctb), "Blackberry Winter," pp. 621–638, and "'Blackberry Winter': A Recollection," pp. 638–643; (CoCA, Ctw, JAG, LC, TxU); LC copyright 18 Nov. 1959 (A417953), two copies received 1 Dec. 1959; published in cloth April 1959 (5,000), Jan. 1960 (5,000), April 1960 (5,000), April 1961 (7,500), Feb. 1962 (5,000), April 1963 (6,500), May 1964 (6,000), Aug. 1964 (6,000), Aug. 1965 (6,000), March 1966 (6,000), Oct. 1966 (6,000), March 1967 (5,000), Jan. 1968 (10,181), Aug. 1968 (10,150)—for a total of 89,331 copies, outselling the first edition of 71,263 copies (ltr., Brauer, 11 Feb. 1975). *Third edition*: Englewood Cliffs, NJ: Prentice-Hall, Inc., 1979, pp. xviii+526; contains RPW's "BW," pp. 362–377 and "'BW': A Recollection," pp. 377–382; (CoCA, JAG, LC, RPW); LC copyright 30 April 1979 (TX234-701) and two copies deposited that date; "publication 5 March 1979 and creation in 1978" (ltr., William L. Asher, Bibliographer, Library of Congress, 5 Nov. 1979).

B15 *U.S. Library of Congress Quarterly Journal of Current Acquisitions* (1944–1945)

Editor, 2 (July 1944–June 1945).

Note: now *QJLC*.

B16 *The Rime of the Ancient Mariner* (1946)

[p. (ii)] ILLUSTRATED BY ALEXANDER CALDER | [illus.] | WITH AN ESSAY BY ROBERT PENN WARREN [p. (iii)] THE RIME OF | THE ANCIENT MARINER | BY SAMUEL TAYLOR COLERIDGE | REYNAL & HITCHCOCK, NEW YORK CITY

Collation: imperial folio 8° (trimmed: 25.3 × 18.6 cm.); *unsigned* [1–10⁸], 80 leaves; pp. [i–viii], [1–2] 3–58 [59–60] 61–117 [118] 119–148 [149–152]; numbers centered in tail margin.

Contains: pp. [59]–117: "A Poem of Pure Imagination: An Experiment in Reading."

Typography and Paper: text: 36 ll., 19.2 (20.4) × 12.6 cm.; Linotype Janson 12/15-pt. (essay). Paper: white, wove, unwatermarked; sheets bulk 0.8 cm.

Illustrations: pp. [i], [ii], [v], 3, 5, 7–9, 11–12, 15, 16, 19–21, 23, 25, 31, 34, 36, 39, 41, 43, 46, 48, 51, 53, 55, and 57.

Binding: red cloth. Front and back: blank. Spine, vert., in black: 'THE RIME OF THE ANCIENT MARINER REYNAL & HITCH-COCK'. All edges trimmed and unstained; white endpapers.

  Dust wrapper: black background. Front: '[in white] THE RIME OF | [in red] THE ANCIENT MARINER | [in white] BY SAMUEL TAYLOR COLERIDGE | [in yellow, irregular circle representing the sun] | [along outer edge, in white, erect figure with albatross hanging around his neck by rope] | [in white] ILLUSTRATED BY | [in red] ALEXANDER CALDER | [in white] WITH AN ESSAY BY | [in red] ROBERT PENN WARREN'. Spine: '[vert., in white] THE RIME OF [in red] THE ANCIENT MARINER [horiz., in white] REYNAL & | HITCHCOCK'. Back: blank. Front flap: about the poem. Back flap: about the essayist and the illustrator.

Copies: Ctb, JAG, LC, LU.

Notes: 1. Published 1946 at $3.75. Additional publication information is not available. Issued in Canada by McClelland & Stewart Ltd., Toronto. LC copyright 2 Dec. 1946 (A91111); two copies deposited 14 Dec. 1946; copyright renewed 11 March 1974 (R572685). Reprinted: Cleveland: Micro Photo, 1962 (NIC).

  2. Excerpted in *KR*, 8 (Summer 1946), 391–427: parts III, IV, and V of the seven-part essay; rpt., *SE*, pp. 198–305 (**A16.a1**). Part of this essay was delivered as a Bergen Foundation Lecture, Yale University, 1945.

  3. Ctb copy is inscribed: 'To | Red Lewis | with warm regards | Red Warren | December 1946'.

B17 *Modern Rhetoric*

B17.a1 first American edition, first impression (1949)

Modern | Rhetoric | [framed] WITH | READINGS | Cleanth Brooks YALE UNIVERSITY | Robert Penn Warren UNIVERSITY OF MINNESOTA | [bold rule] | HARCOURT, BRACE AND COMPANY, NEW YORK

Collation: medium folio 8° (trimmed: 21.3 × 14.3 cm.); *unsigned* [1–30¹⁶], 480 leaves; pp. [i–v] vi–xii [xiii] xiv–xvii [xviii–xx], [1] 2–9 [10–11] 12–30 [31] 32–39 [40] 41–140 [141] 142–217 [218] 219–261 [262] 263–315 [316] 317–334 [335] 336–364 [365] 366–370 [371]

372–402 [403] 404–441 [442] 443–488 [489] 490–532 [$^\pi$2: green divider] [533–535] 536 [537] 538–546 [547] 548–578 [579] 580–623 [624] 625–676 [677] 678–736 [737] 738–772 [773] 774–807 [808] 809–845 [846] 847–876 [877] 878–888 [889–891] 892–896 [897] 898–901 [902] 903–928, [xxi] xxii–xxvii [xxviii–xxix] xxx–xxxii; numbers located in the corner formed by the head and outer margins.

Typography and Paper: text: 39 ll., 16.6 (17.1) × 10.5 cm.; Caledonia 10/12-pt. RT: v., chapter title or designation; r., subheadings. Paper: white, wove, unwatermarked; sheets bulk 3.6 cm.

Binding: light green cloth. Front: '[in black] Modern | Rhetoric | [on blue rectangle, in green] *WITH* | *READINGS* | [in black] Cleanth Brooks | Robert Penn Warren'. Spine, in black: 'Modern | Rhetoric | BROOKS [with blue rectangle on end after "Brooks" and extending toward "Rhetoric"] | & WARREN | HARCOURT, BRACE | AND COMPANY'. Back: blank. All edges trimmed and unstained; white endpapers.

Dust wrapper: none found.

Copies: CoCA, Ctw, CtY, JAG, Ashland Community College (KY).

Notes: 1. Published 28 April 1949 in 9,294 copies with symbol "A" designating first impression. Printed by Quinn & Boden Company, Inc. Subsequent impressions: July 1949 (B), 10,000; Aug. 1949 (B), 10,600; March 1950 (C), 15,450; Oct. 1951 (D), 6,440 and 2,200; Jan. 1953 (E), 2,000; April 1954 (F), 3,040; Aug. 1954 (G), 2,540; Oct. 1955 (H), 4,180; Aug. 1956 (I), 2,000; and May 1958 (J), 1,500—for a total of 69,244 copies (ltr., Gerard G. Vaughan, Trade Dept., Harcourt Brace Jovanovich, Inc., 4 June 1975). LC copyright 28 April 1949 (A32504); two copies deposited 3 May 1949; copyright renewed 11 May 1976 (R632807).

2. *Fundamentals of Good Writing* (**B19**) is a shorter version of *MR*.

3. Subsequent editions: *second edition*: New York: Harcourt, Brace and Company, [1958], pp. xviii+870 (CoCA, Ctw, CtY, JAG, LC, TxFTC); LC copyright 2 Jan. 1958 (A318206), two copies received 9 Jan. 1958; published 28 Jan. 1958 with a Dec. 1957 (A) printing of 7,000 copies, May 1958 (B; 15,000), Aug. 1958 (B; 10,000), Sept. 1958 (C; 7,000), Feb. 1959 (C; 8,700), July 1959 (D; 22,900), Sept. 1960 (E; 9,000), Dec. 1960 (E; 1,000), Aug. 1961 (F; 5,600), July 1962 (F; 1,000), Sept. 1961 (G; 7,000), July 1962 (H; 7,000), Aug. 1963 (I; 7,000), June 1964 (J; 7,600), Oct. 1964 (J; 2,700), March 1965 (K; 9,500), Nov. 1965 (L; 5,300), Aug. 1966 (L; 3,000), Aug. 1967 (L;

2,200), July 1967 (M; 2,900), Sept. 1968 (N; 4,000), Oct. 1969 (N; 3,000)—for a total of 148,400 copies (ltr., Vaughan, 4 June 1975). *Shorter edition*: New York: Harcourt, Brace & World, Inc., [1961], pp. viii+376 (CoCA, Ctw, JAG, LC); LC copyright 21 April 1961 (A501538); published April 1961 (A) in 10,200 copies, July 1961 (B; 20,100), Sept. 1961 (C; 10,100), Sept. 1962 (D; 10,000), Feb. 1963 (E; 20,200), Oct. 1963 (F; 10,200), June 1964 (G; 15,000), Aug. 1964 (H; 25,300), Feb. 1965 (I; 10,000), April 1965 (J; 40,200), June 1966 (K; 15,000), Aug. 1967 (K; 4,900), Sept. 1967 (K; 5,100), March 1968 (L; 5,000), Aug. 1968 (L; 10,700), Dec. 1968 (M; 5,000), Aug. 1969 (M; 10,000), Jan. 1971 (N; 5,000), Oct. 1971 (O; 4,000)—for a total of 236,000 copies (ltr., Vaughan, 4 June 1975). *Third edition*: New York: Harcourt, Brace & World, [1970], pp. [2], xx+882+xxiv (CoCA, CtY, JAG, LC); LC copyright 1 April 1970 (A157424), two copies deposited 5 June 1970; published 11 May 1970 (A) in 14,700 copies, Sept. 1970 (A; 14,200), Feb. 1971 (A; 400), Oct. 1970 (B; 9,800), July 1971 (C; 10,000), Oct. 1974 (C; 2,000) (ltr., Vaughan, 4 June 1975). *Shorter third edition*: New York: Harcourt Brace Jovanovich, Inc., [1972], pp. viii+440 (CoCA, JAG, LC); LC copyright 3 Jan. 1972 (A293039), two copies deposited 5 Jan. 1972; published 31 Jan. 1972 (A) in 15,900 copies, Sept. 1972 (B; 25,600), July 1973 (C; 10,200), and Oct. 1974 (D; 10,300) (ltr., Vaughan, 4 June 1975). *Fourth edition*: New York: Harcourt Brace Jovanovich, Inc., [1979], pp. xiv+402 (CoCA, JAG, RPW); in paper only.

4. *Instructor's Manual* (3d ed.) copyrighted 21 Aug. 1970 (A186445); *Instructor's Manual* (shorter 3d ed.), with Marinus Swets, copyrighted 24 March 1972 (A346027).

B18   *Inventario* (1949–1964)

Redazione americana: Harry Levin, Robert Lowell, Allen Tate, RPW. *Inventario*, 2, no. 1 (1949)—15 (1960); comitato internazionale di redazione: Salvatore Quasimodo, Jorge Guillen, Harry Levin, Jean-Jacques Mayoux, RPW. *Inventario*, 15 (1960)–19 (1964). (Ltr., Kathryn McCrodden, General Reference Service, General Library, University of California, Berkeley, 17 Feb. 1977.)

B19   *Fundamentals of Good Writing*

B19.a1   first American edition, first impression (1950)

Fundamentals | of | Good Writing | *A HANDBOOK OF MODERN*

RHETORIC | Cleanth Brooks | Robert Penn Warren | [script 'hb' in a rectangle frame] Harcourt, Brace and Company · New York

Collation: medium folio 8° (trimmed: 21.2 × 14.3 cm.); *unsigned* [1–17¹⁶], 272 leaves; pp. [i–ix] x–xiv [xv–xvi], [1] 2–9 [10–11] 12–28 [29] 30–37 [38] 39–124 [125] 126–194 [195] 196–236 [237] 238–289 [290] 291–303 [304] 305–328 [329] 330–334 [335] 336–360 [361] 362–389 [390] 391–424 [425] 426–460 [461] 462–471 [472–475] 476–480 [481] 482–485 [486] 487–516 [517–519] 520–523 [524–528]; numbers at top, outer margin.

Typography and Paper: text: 38 ll., 16.7 (17.05) × 10.5 cm.; Caledonia 11/13-pt. RT: v., chapter title; r., section title. Paper: white, wove, unwatermarked; sheets bulk 2.8 cm.

Binding: beige bds. Front and back: blank. Spine, vert., in green: 'Cleanth Brooks and | Robert Penn Warren Fundamentals of | GOOD WRITING | HARCOURT, BRACE | AND COMPANY'. All edges trimmed and unstained; white endpapers.

   Dust wrapper: front cover, red background: '[in white] fundamentals of | [in white box, in black] GOOD | WRITING | [on red in white] a handbook of modern rhetoric | [in black box in white] CLEANTH BROOKS | ROBERT PENN WARREN'. Spine: '[on red in white] CLEANTH | BROOKS | ROBERT | PENN | WARREN | fundamentals | of | [in white box, in black] GOOD | WRITING | [on red in white] HARCOURT, BRACE | AND COMPANY'. Back cover: publisher's advertisement. Front flap: about the book. Back flap: publisher's advertisement.

Copies: Ctb, Ctw, JAG, Regis College Library (Denver), TNJ.

Notes: 1. Published 15 June 1950 at $4.75. Printed by Quinn & Boden Company, Inc. Subsequent impressions: 11 April 1950, two lots of 3,340 and 2,000; 24 July 1950, 1,340; 14 Aug. 1950, 3,000 and 1,000; 13 Nov. 1950, 2,000; 25 Nov. 1952, 2,000 and 1,000; 4 March 1955, 1,026; 15 Jan. 1957, 1,500; 28 Aug. 1959, 2,000 and 1,000; 6 Jan. 1961, 1,000; 1 July 1962, 2,000; Aug. 1965, 2,000; Sept. 1968, 1,000; Dec. 1970, 1,000; Dec. 1971, 1,000; Dec. 1974, 1,000—for a total of 30,206 copies. Distributed simultaneously in Canada by George J. McLeod Ltd. (Ltr., Gerard G. Vaughan, Trade Dept., Harcourt Brace Jovanovich, Inc., 4 June 1975.) LC copyright 15 June 1950 (A45053); two copies deposited 16 June 1950; copyright renewed 22 Sept. 1977 (R672321).

2. Error on p. [iv] lists "*Selected Poems: 1923–1934*" instead of *1923–1943*.

3. Subsequent editions: *first English edition*: London: Dennis Dobson, 1952, pp. xvi+528 (Ctb). *Second English edition*: London: Dennis Dobson, 1956, pp. xvi+528 (FSU). *Note*: both English editions appear to be identical with **B19.a1**, and both repeat the error noted on p. [iv].

B20 "This Very Spot" (1952)

With David M. Clay. "The Conway Cabal." Script no. 1 of a dramatic television series, "This Very Spot." LC copyright 15 Dec. 1952 (D-1321); two copies deposited 26 Jan. 1953.

B21 *An Anthology of Stories from the Southern Review* (1953)

[five-line rule] | *An Anthology of* | STORIES | *from the* | SOUTHERN REVIEW | *Edited by* | CLEANTH BROOKS | *and* | ROBERT PENN WARREN | LOUISIANA STATE UNIVERSITY PRESS | *Baton Rouge* | [five-line rule]

Collation: medium folio 8° (trimmed: 22.8 × 15.0 cm.); *unsigned* [1–14^{16} 15^2], 226 leaves; pp. [i–xi] xii–xvi, [1] 2–15 [16] 17–27 [28] 29–45 [46] 47–57 [58] 59–63 [64] 65–75 [76] 77–92 [93] 94–100 [101] 102–109 [110] 111–118 [119] 120–133 [134] 135–143 [144] 145–192 [193] 194–235 [236] 237–248 [249] 250–261 [262] 263–274 [275] 276–309 [310] 311–328 [329] 330–345 [346] 347–352 [353] 354–386 [387] 388–412 [413] 414–431 [432] 433–435 [436]; numbers located in the corner formed by the head and outer margins.

Contains: pp. [xi]–xvi: introduction; pp. 93–100: "When the Light Gets Green."

Typography and Paper: text: 38 ll., 17.3 (17.9) × 10.5 cm.; Bruce Old Style Monotype 11/13-pt. RT: v., 'STORIES FROM THE SOUTHERN REVIEW'; r., title of story. Paper: white, laid, vert. chainlines (3.0 cm.), unwatermarked; sheets bulk 2.8 cm.

Binding: medium green cloth. Front and back: blank. Spine, in gilt: '[on black rectangle, four rules] | STORIES | *from the* | SOUTHERN | REVIEW | [four rules] | [on green] BROOKS | and | WARREN | LOUISIANA'. All edges trimmed and unstained; white endpapers.

Dust wrapper: front: green background with one large and, beneath it, five small stripes: '[in black] STORIES | *from the* | SOUTHERN |

REVIEW | [five rules] | [on large white stripe] *Edited by* CLEANTH BROOKS *and* ROBERT PENN WARREN | [in white] LOUI-SIANA STATE UNIVERSITY PRESS'. Spine, stripes continued from front: 'STORIES | *from the* | SOUTHERN REVIEW | BROOKS | and | WARREN | [on large white stripe] LOUISIANA | [publisher's device]'.

Copies: Ctw (3), CtY, JAG, KyU, LC, TxFTC.

Note: published 23 Nov. 1953 in 2,923 copies, of which 2,460 were bound in 1953 and 463 bound in April 1965. Printed by Colonial Press, Inc. (ltr., Charles East, Director, LSU Press, 3 March 1975). The 1965 binding has the top edge stained yellow and was issued in wax-paper dw. LC copyright 23 Nov. 1953 (A117529); two copies deposited 14 Dec. 1953.

B22 *Short Story Masterpieces* (1954)

[p. (2)] Short Story | *EDITED BY* | *AND* | A FIRST EDITION [p. (3)] Masterpieces | ROBERT PENN WARREN | ALBERT ERSKINE | DELL BOOKS NEW YORK

Collation: foolscap folio 8° (trimmed: 16.1 × 10.6 cm.); *unsigned* [272] ind. leaves; pp. [1–15] 16–114 [115] 116–123 [124] 125–161 [162] 163–238 [239] 240–288 [289] 290–335 [336] 337–362 [363] 364–367 [368] 369–383 [384] 385–397 [398] 399–439 [440] 441–483 [484] 485–524 [525] 526–542 [543–544]; numbers located in corner formed by the head and outer margins.

Contains: pp. [9–11]: editors' note.

Typography and Paper: text: 39 ll., 13.6 (14.1) × 8.6 cm.; Linotype Baskerville 10-pt. RT: v., title of story; r., author's name. Paper: white, wove, unwatermarked; sheets bulk 2.6 cm.

Binding: paper. Front: '[upper left corner in black] FIRST | EDITION | F16 and [upper right corner] 50¢ | [centered, on white in black] SHORT | STORY | MASTERPIECES | [circles in different colors] | [on black in gray] Edited by ROBERT PENN WARREN | and ALBERT ERSKINE | [in blue, names of selected authors]'. Spine: '[horiz.] F16 | [vert., on white in black] Editors | ROBERT PENN WARREN | ALBERT ERSKINE | [circles in different colors continued] | [vert., on black in red] SHORT STORY | MASTERPIECES | FIRST | EDITION'. Back: about the collection. Inside covers: white. All edges trimmed and stained light blue.

Copies: Ctw, JAG, KU, LC, MiD, PJB, PPD.

Notes: 1. Published 22 April 1954 in 357,933 copies at 50¢. Printed by Western Publishing Company, Inc. Subsequent impressions: 11 Sept. 1958 (101,000), May 1959 (100,500), Oct. 1960 (103,000), March 1962 (49,727), Sept. 1962 (76,738), June 1963 (106,000), Nov. 1968 (100,000), Sept. 1969 (100,713), May 1970 (99,490), March 1972 (51,656), Aug. 1972 (101,611), 11 Sept. 1973 (100,000), May 1974 (50,219), Feb. 1975 (100,000)—for a total of 1,598,587 copies (ltr., Dennis Dalrymple, Copyrights Editor, Dell Publishing Company, Inc., 13 May 1975). LC copyright 17 May 1954 (A141615); two copies deposited 14 June 1954.

2. Subsequent issues: Laurel Edition LX 102 (1958) at 75¢ and 7864 (1962) at 75¢ in same cover; Laurel Editions 7864 at 75¢ and 95¢ in red covers.

B23   *Six Centuries of Great Poetry* (1955)

SIX | CENTURIES | OF GREAT | POETRY | Edited by | ROBERT PENN WARREN | and | ALBERT ERSKINE | A DELL FIRST EDITION

Collation: foolscap folio 8° (trimmed: 16.25 × 10.8 cm.); *unsigned* [272] ind. leaves; pp. [1–8] 9–12 [13] 14–16 [17] 18–44 [45] 46–48 [49] 50–70 [71] 72–75 [76] 77 [78] 79 [80–81] 82–97 [98] 99–110 [111] 112–117 [118] 119–157 [158] 159–164 [165–166] 167–179 [180] 181–185 [186] 187–188 [189] 190–193 [194] 195–205 [206] 207–222 [223] 224–241 [242] 243–274 [275] 276–303 [304] 305–308 [309] 310–346 [347] 348–372 [373] 374–433 [434] 435–438 [439] 440–448 [449–450] 451–452 [453] 454–495 [496] 497–508 [509] 510–521 [522] 523–524 [525] 526–544; numbers located in the corner formed by the head and outer margins.

Contains: pp. [8]–12: introduction.

Typography and Paper: text: 39 ll., 13.7 (14.1) × 8.75 cm.; Caledonia 10-pt. RT: on v. and r., names of poets. Paper: white, wove, unwatermarked; sheets bulk 2.5 cm.

Binding: paper. Front: '[upper left corner on gold in black] FIRST | EDITION | FE 69 | [upper right corner on black in white triangle] 50¢ | [up, under 'FIRST EDITION' on black in white] Edited by | Robert Penn Warren | & Albert Erskine | [horiz., on black in purple] SIX | CENTURIES | OF | GREAT | POETRY | [colored sunburst on

white; ltr. in black across half of sunburst] from Chaucer to Yeats'.
Spine: '[vert., on gold triangle in black] FE 69 [in purple] SIX CEN-
TURIES | OF GREAT POETRY | [horiz., on gold in black] FIRST |
EDITION'. Back, on black in white and purple: about the book. All
edges trimmed and stained gold.

Copies: Ctb, Ctw, CU, FU, JAG, KyU, LC.

Notes: 1. Published 27 Sept. 1955 in 200,000 copies at 50¢. Printed by
Western Publishing Company, Inc. Subsequent impressions: Dec.
1957 (25,000), 3 Feb. 1959 (51,000), Oct. 1960 (25,250), Sept. 1961
(25,952), Aug. 1962 (24,259), April 1963 (25,694), July 1964 (26,702),
May 1965 (25,203), Feb. 1966 (24,328), Jan. 1970 (15,000), March
1971 (15,591), Aug. 1971 (14,596), Aug. 1973 (15,798), Jan. 1975
(15,000)—for a total of 529,373 copies (ltr., Dennis Dalrymple, Copyrights Editor, Dell Publishing Company, Inc., 13 May 1975). LC
copyright 27 Sept. 1955 (A213168); two copies deposited 5 Dec. 1955.
   2. Subsequent issues: Laurel Edition LC 109 (1958), LX 110 (1959),
and 7972 (1962).

B24   *A New Southern Harvest* (1957)

A NEW | SOUTHERN | HARVEST | An Anthology | Edited by |
ROBERT PENN WARREN | and ALBERT ERSKINE | [pub-
lisher's device] BANTAM BOOKS | NEW YORK

Collation: post folio 8° (trimmed: 17.8 × 10.5 cm.); *unsigned* [152] ind.
leaves; pp. [i–vi] vii–ix [x], 1–294; numbers on first page of each
story are centered at foot of type page; others are in the corner formed
by the head and outer margins.

Contains: pp. vii–ix: introduction; pp. 67–86: "Blackberry Winter."

Typography and Paper: text: 47 ll., 13.6 (16.1) × 8.7 cm.; Times New
Roman 9½-pt. RT: v., 'A NEW SOUTHERN HARVEST'; r., author's name in small caps. and title of story in ital. Paper: white,
wove, unwatermarked; sheets bulk 1.5 cm.

Binding: paper. Front cover: '[upper left corner in black] F1556 [on
green in black with red outline] A brilliant gathering | of the new
South's | finest writing selected by | ROBERT PENN WARREN |
and ALBERT ERSKINE | A NEW | SOUTHERN | HARVEST |
[in black with white outline] including short stories by | [five names] |
[green illus.] | [in black, publisher's device] A BANTAM BOOK ·
50¢'. Spine: '[horiz., on black in white] F1556 || 6 | [vert.] A NEW

SOUTHERN HARVEST selected by Robert Penn Warren and Albert Erskine | [on white in red, publisher's device]'. Back: authors' names and publisher's advertisement.

Copies: Ctb, Ctw, CU, JAG, KyU, LC, LU, MH, NcD.

Note: published Jan. 1957 at 50¢. LC copyright 7 Jan. 1957 (A269835); two copies deposited 25 Jan. 1957.

B25 *University of Minnesota Pamphlets on American Writers* (1959–)

As editor with William Van O'Connor, Allen Tate, Leonard Unger; advisers: Willard Thorp, Karl Shapiro, and Philip Rahv.

B26 *The Scope of Fiction*

B26.a1 first American edition, first impression (1960)

[solid black rectangle] CLEANTH BROOKS | [solid black rectangle] ROBERT PENN WARREN | *The SCOPE* | *of FICTION* | [publisher's device] | New York: APPLETON-CENTURY-CROFTS, Inc.

Collation: royal folio 8° (trimmed: 23.4 × 15.5 cm.); *unsigned* [1–11 ^{16}], 176 leaves; pp. [i] ii–iii [iv] v [vi] vii–xvi, 1–336; numbers centered at foot of type page on story title pages and in the corner formed by the head and outer margins elsewhere.

Typography and Paper: text: 44 ll., 18.5 (19.2) × 11.3 cm.; Linotype Janson 10/12-pt. RT: v., title of section in small caps.; r., title of story in ital. Paper: white, wove, unwatermarked; sheets bulk 1.6 cm.

Binding: smooth papered bds. Front: '[on green stripe in gray] THE | [on blue stripe in white] SCOPE | [on green stripe in gray] OF | [on blue stripe in white] FICTION | [on dark green in light green] Cleanth Brooks | Robert Penn Warren | [green stripe]'. Spine, vert.: [on dark green in light green] Brooks & Warren [in white] THE SCOPE OF FICTION [in gray] *Appleton-Century-Crofts*'. Back: dark green. All edges trimmed and unstained; white endpapers.
    Dust wrapper: none found.

Copies: CoCA, Ctw (2), CtY, JAG, LC, TNJ, TxFTC.

Notes: 1. Published May 1960. Printed in March 1960 (5,000), May 1960 (5,350), April 1961 (4,270), Aug. 1961 (5,000), Jan. 1962 (5,000), Aug. 1962 (7,500), April 1963 (2,755), March 1964 (7,500), April 1965 (3,500), Aug. 1965 (5,000), March 1966 (5,127), June 1966 (7,700),

March 1967 (5,000), Jan. 1968 (7,500), May 1968 (7,500), April 1969 (7,500), 1974 (2,675), 1976 (2,100)—for a total of 95,977 copies (ltr., Barbara Tagliani, Prentice-Hall, Inc., 26 Jan. 1977). LC copyright 3 May 1960 (A443676); two copies deposited 9 May 1960.

2. Reissued by Prentice-Hall: *title page*: 'Prentice-Hall, Inc., Englewood Cliffs, New Jersey'; *spine*: '[in white] Prentice | Hall'; issued in bluish green and in olive green cloth.

B27 *Conversations on the Craft of Poetry* (1961)

Conversations | ON THE CRAFT OF Poetry | CLEANTH BROOKS and ROBERT PENN WARREN | with | ROBERT FROST | JOHN CROWE RANSOM | ROBERT LOWELL | THEODORE ROETHKE | A transcript of the tape recording made to accompany | UNDERSTANDING POETRY, | Third Edition || HOLT, RINEHART AND WINSTON · New York

Note: 250 sets of two tapes each were manufactured Dec. 1961, after which Dec. 1966 (36 sets), July 1967 (30 sets), July 1968 (30 sets), and Jan. 1969 (30 sets). The transcript of the tapes was printed in 5,000 copies Nov. 1961. Issued in London in 1962. Both the transcript and the tapes are out of print. (Ltr., Kenney Withers, Publisher/Humanities, Holt, Rinehart and Winston, Inc., 3 Feb. 1975.) LC copyright 18 Aug. 1961 (A536624); two copies deposited 12 Dec. 1961. (Ctw, LC)

B28 *Poetry Pilot* (1962)

As editor. *Poetry Pilot*, Nov. 1962, pp. 1–20. (KyU)

B29 *Selected Poems by Denis Devlin* (1963)

SELECTED POEMS BY DENIS DEVLIN | With a Preface by Allen Tate and | Robert Penn Warren | Holt, Rinehart and Winston · *New York / Chicago / San Francisco*

Collation: demy folio 8° (trimmed: 19.7 × 13.6 cm.); *unsigned* [1–2 ^{16} 3 ^{8} 4 ^{16}], 56 leaves; pp. [1–4] 5–6 [7–8] 9–106 [107–112]; numbers centered at foot of each page.

Contains: pp. 9–14: preface.

Typography and Paper: text: 34 ll., 15.6 (16.3) × 10.1 cm.; Electra 10/13-pt. Paper: white, wove, unwatermarked; sheets bulk 0.8 cm.

Binding: bluish green cloth around spine and whitish patterned paper bds. front and back; pattern has white background with alternating gray and green tear drops in columns. Spine, vert., in green: '*SE-LECTED POEMS BY DENIS DEVLIN* [in white] · Holt · Rinehart · Winston'. All edges trimmed and unstained; green endpapers.

Dust wrapper: front, on white: '[in olive green] Selected | [in bluish green] POEMS | [dark green wide rule] | [in bluish green] Denis Devlin | [in olive green] With a preface by ALLEN TATE | and ROBERT PENN WARREN'. Spine, vert., on white: '[in olive green] Selected [in bluish green] POEMS [dark green thick rule] [in bluish green] Devlin [in olive green] Holt | Rinehart | Winston'. Back: what the critics said about DD. Front flap: about DD's poetry. Back flap: about the poet.

Copies: Ctb, Ctw, KU, LU, RPW.

Note: published 14 Jan. 1963 in 2,500 copies at $3.95. Printed by Vail-Ballou Press, Inc. (Ltr., Jennifer Josephy, Editor, Holt, Rinehart and Winston, Inc., 12 Feb. 1975.) LC copyright 14 Jan. 1963 (A613005); two copies deposited 21 Feb. 1963.

B30   *Faulkner: A Collection of Critical Essays* (1966)

FAULKNER | A COLLECTION OF CRITICAL ESSAYS | Edited by | *Robert Penn Warren* | Prentice-Hall, Inc. [publisher's device with 'A SPECTRUM BOOK' beneath it] *Englewood Cliffs, N.J.*

Collation: demy folio 8° (trimmed: 20.2 × 13.8 cm.); *unsigned* [1–10^{16}], 160 leaves; pp. [i–viii], 1–299 [300–301] 302–311 [312]; numbers located in the corner formed by the head and outer margins except on chapter pages, on which they are centered beneath the text in the tail margin.

Contains: pp. 1–22: "Introduction: Faulkner: Past and Future"; pp. 251–271: "Faulkner: The South, the Negro, and Time."

Typography and Paper: text: 45 ll., 17.2 (17.8) × 11.2 cm.; Linotype Baskerville 10/11-pt. RT: v., contributor's name; r., title of essay. Paper: white, wove, unwatermarked; sheets bulk 2.2 cm.

Binding: black cloth. Front and back: blank. Spine, vert., in gilt: 'FAULKNER *Edited by* Robert Penn Warren Prentice-Hall'. All edges trimmed and unstained; white endpapers.

Dust wrapper: front, on black in pink: 'TWENTIETH CENTURY

VIEWS | FAULKNER | *A Collection of Critical Essays* | *Edited by* ROBERT PENN WARREN | [cover design, *The Sound and the Fury*, by Stanley Wyatt]'. Spine, vert., in pink: 'TWENTIETH | CENTURY VIEWS FAULKNER *Edited by* | ROBERT PENN WARREN | ⟨ ⟩'. Back cover: about the book.

Copies: Ctb, CtY, JAG, LC.

Note: issued in paper and also issued in London (1967). LC copyright 23 Nov. 1966 (A881018); two copies deposited 10 Jan. 1967.

B31 *Randall Jarrell, 1914–1965* (1967)

Randall Jarrell || 1914–1965 | EDITED BY | Robert Lowell, Peter Taylor, | & Robert Penn Warren | [publisher's device] | *Farrar, Straus & Giroux* | NEW YORK

Collation: demy folio 8° (trimmed: 20.3 × 13.9 cm.); *unsigned* [1–5^{16} 6^{16} (+6$_{3,9}$) (+6$_{1,7}$) 7^{16} (+7$_{1,7}$) 8–10^{16}], 169 leaves; pp. [i–vi] vii–xii, [1–2] 3–301 [302–304] 305–307 [308]; bracketed numbers located at the corner formed by the lower and inner margins; plates (8) between pp. 164–165 and 192–193.

Contains: no contribution by RPW.

Typography and Paper: text: 29 ll., 14.2 (16.05) × 9.65 cm.; Granjon 12/14-pt. RT: v., '*Randall Jarrell*, 1914–1965 [device]'; r., contributor's name. Paper: white, laid, vert. chainlines (2.1 cm.), unwatermarked; sheets bulk 2.4 cm.

Plates: between pp. 164–165, seventeen photographs; between pp. 192–193, woodcut.

Binding: brown cloth, embossed linen grain. Front, impressed: '*Randall Jarrell* || 1914–1965'. Spine, in gilt: '*Randall Jarrell* || 1914–|1965 || LOWELL, | TAYLOR, | & | WARREN || [publisher's device] | *Farrar,* | *Straus &* | *Giroux*'. Back: blank. All edges trimmed and stained yellow; bright yellow endpapers.

Dust wrapper: front, on black: '[in white] *Randall Jarrell* | [in yellowish gold] 1914–1965 | [in white] *Edited by* ROBERT LOWELL, PETER TAYLOR, | & ROBERT PENN WARREN | [photograph of RJ by Philippe Halsman]'. Spine: '[vert., in white] *Randall Jarrell* / 1914–1965 | [in yellowish gold] *Edited by* ROBERT LOWELL, PETER TAYLOR, & ROBERT PENN WARREN | [horiz., white rule; in yellowish gold, publisher's device] | [in white] *Farrar*, | *Straus & | Giroux*]'. Back: list of contributors. Front flap: about RJ. Back flap: continuation from front flap; jacket design by Guy Fleming.

Copies: CoCA, Ctb, CtY, KyU, LC, TNJ, TxFTC.

Note: cloth edition published 29 Aug. 1967 in 6,500 copies at $6.50. Printed by H. Wolff Book Manufacturing Company, Inc., which is now part of American Book-Stratford Press, Inc. Paperback edition published 15 April 1968 in 3,000 copies. (Ltr., Nancy Meiselas, Farrar, Straus & Giroux, Inc., 24 April 1975.) LC copyright 28 Aug. 1967 (A935541); one copy each deposited 7 Sept. 1967 and 11 Sept. 1967.

B32 *American Scholar* (1968)

Panelist with William Styron, Robert Coles, and Theodore Solo-taroff. "Symposium: Violence in Literature."
  a. *American Scholar*, 37 (Summer 1968), 482–496.
  b. In *The Writer's World*, ed. Elizabeth Janeway (New York: McGraw-Hill, 1969).

Note: transcript of a panel discussion for the New School for Social Research and The Authors Guild, Inc., "The Writer's World in an Age of Violence," New York, Spring 1968.

B33 *Southern Literary Journal* (1969)

Panelist with Ralph Ellison, William Styron, and C. Vann Woodward. "The Uses of History in Fiction," *Southern Literary Journal*, 1 (Spring 1969), 57–90.

Note: transcript of a panel discussion during the Southern Historical Association meeting, Fall 1968.

B34 *Selected Poems of Herman Melville* (1970)

[orn.] | SELECTED POEMS | *of* HERMAN MELVILLE | *A Reader's Edition* | [orn.] | *Edited with an Introduction* | *by* ROBERT PENN WARREN | [publisher's device] | RANDOM HOUSE NEW YORK

Collation: medium folio 8° (trimmed: 21.1 × untrimmed: 14.3 cm.); *unsigned* [1–15 ¹⁶], 240 leaves; pp. [ᵗ1–2], [i–vii] viii–xiv, [1–2] 3–88 [89–90] 91–199 [200–202] 203–273 [274–276] 277–324 [325–326] 327–340 [341–342] 343–451 [452] 453–455 [456] 457–458 [459–464]; numbers located in the corner formed by the head and outer margins with vertical line between the number and RT; beneath the text in the tail margin with vertical line on either side on chapter pages.

Contains: pp. 3–88: introduction and notes.

Typography and Paper: text: introduction: 36 ll., 16.6 (17.3) × 9.6 cm., 11/13-pt.; notes: 42 ll., 16.6 (17.3) × 9.6 cm.; 10/11-pt.; Caledonia. RT: v., 'SELECTED POEMS OF HERMAN MELVILLE'; r., 'Introduction'; in the body itself, v., title of section; r., title of poem. Paper: white, wove, unwatermarked; sheets bulk 2.7 cm.

Binding: beige cloth. Front, in gilt: open "M" which with horizontal line doubles for an "H"; one orn. on each of the four sides. Spine, on dark brown in gilt: '[orn.] | SELECTED | POEMS | *of* HERMAN | MELVILLE | [orn.] | *Edited by* | ROBERT | PENN | WARREN | [orn.] | [publisher's device] | RANDOM | HOUSE'. Back: blank. Fore edge rough trimmed, top and bottom edges trimmed, all edges unstained; medium brown endpapers.

Dust wrapper: front cover, on beige: vert., fore edge in orange, illus. of man's face; '[in black] SELECTED | POEMS | OF | HERMAN | MELVILLE | [in orange] A Reader's Edition | [in medium brown] Edited, with an Introduction by | Robert Penn Warren'. Spine, vert., on beige: '[in black] SELECTED POEMS OF | HERMAN MEL-VILLE | [in orange] Edited by Robert Penn Warren | [horiz., in medium brown—publisher's device] | RANDOM | HOUSE'. Back cover: same as front, but with illus. on back edge and in lower right corner, '394–40398–3'. Front flap: about the book. Back flap: about the author.

Copies: CoCA, Ctb, CtY, JAG, LC, TxFTC.

Notes: 1. Published 24 Nov. 1970 in 4,000 copies at $8.95. Printed by H. Wolff Book Manufacturing Co., Inc. Issued simultaneously in Canada by Random House of Canada Limited. (Ltr., Jim Wilcox, Random House, Inc., 17 Dec. 1976.) LC copyright 4 Dec. 1970 (A247164); two copies deposited 30 March 1971.

2. The introduction appears slightly modified as "Melville's Poems," *SoR*, NS 3 (Autumn 1967), 799–855.

B35 *John Greenleaf Whittier's Poetry* (1971)

John | Greenleaf | Whittier's | Poetry | *An Appraisal* | *and a Selection* | *by Robert Penn Warren* | UNIVERSITY OF MINNESOTA PRESS, | Minneapolis

Collation: demy folio 8° (trimmed: 21.5 × 12.4 cm.); *unsigned* [1–7 ¹⁶], 112 leaves; pp. [i–xii], [1–2] 3–62 [63–64] 65–208 [209–212]; numbers centered beneath the text in the tail margin.

Contains: pp. 3–63: "John Greenleaf Whittier: Poetry as Experience."

Typography and Paper: text: 36 ll., 16.6 (17.5) × 8.8 cm.; Bodoni Book 10/11-pt. for the poetry, 8/9-pt. introduction to poems and selected reading, 10/13-pt. for the text. Paper: 20½ × 35 basis 60, Ibsen Eggshell, white, wove, unwatermarked. Ink: Letterpress black. Sheets bulk 1.5 cm. (Ltr., I. B. Kreidberg, President, North Central Publishing Company, 18 Feb. 1975.)

Binding: white bds. with ¼ black cloth. Front, on white in blue: illus. of Whittier. Spine, on black in gilt: '[horiz.] Robert | Penn | Warren | [vert.] John Greenleaf Whittier's Poetry | [horiz.] Minnesota'. Back: blank. All edges trimmed and unstained; white endpapers.

  Dust wrapper: front cover: illus. in blue, reduced to lower right corner; '[on white in blue] ROBERT | PENN WARREN | [in black] John Greenleaf | Whittier's Poetry | An | Appraisal | and a | Selection'. Spine, on black in white: '[horiz.] Robert | Penn | Warren | [vert.] John Greenleaf Whittier's Poetry | [horiz.] Minnesota'. Back cover: photograph of RPW by Michael V. Carlisle. Front and back flaps: about the book.

Copies: CoCA, Ctb, CtY, JAG, LC, TxFTC.

Notes: 1. Published 2 June 1971 in 3,000 hard copies at $8.95 and in 3,500 paperbacks at $2.95. Printed by North Central Publishing Co. Distributed in Great Britain, India, and Pakistan by Oxford University Press, London; and in Canada by Copp Clark Publishing Co. Ltd., Toronto. (Ltr., John Ervin, Jr., Director, University of Minnesota Press, 5 Feb. 1975.) LC copyright 2 June 1971 (A248695); two copies deposited 22 June 1971.

  2. The introduction appears in a slightly different form as "Whittier," *SR*, 79 (Winter 1971), 86–135.

B36 *American Literature: The Makers and the Making* (1973)

American | Literature | *The Makers and* | *the Making* | VOLUME I [II] | *Cleanth Brooks R. W. B. Lewis Robert Penn Warren* | St. Martin's Press New York

Collation: post folio 4° (trimmed: 23.3 × 18.5 cm.); *unsigned* I [1–39 ¹⁶] and II [1–57 ¹⁶], 624, 912 leaves, respectively; I: pp. [i–x] xi–xxx [xxxi–xxxii], 1–107 [108] 109–323 [324] 325–1195 [1196], xxxiii–xliv [xlv–lii]; II: pp. [i–iii] iv–xxxiii [xxxiv], 1197–1471 [1472] 1473–1685 [1686] 1687–1725 [1726] 1727–1777 [1778] 1779–1801 [1802] 1803–2041 [2042] 2043–2745 [2746] 2747–2857 [2858] 2859–2915 [2916] 2917–2970, xxxv–l; numbers appear in the corner formed by the head and outer margins, except on heading pages on which they appear in the corner formed by the tail and outer margins.

Typography and Paper: text: introductory material 42 ll., 19.2 (19.75) × 12.5 cm., 12/13-pt.; excerpts 53 ll., double column, 18.7 (19.3) × 15.2 cm., 10-pt.; Electra Linotype. RT: v., major division title; r., author's name. Paper: white, wove, unwatermarked; Sparlite Regular Finish. Ink: Manufacturer's Printing Ink. Sheets bulk: I, 4.0 cm.; II, 5.1 cm. (Ltr., Harold Morgan, Quinn & Boden Company, Inc., 4 March 1975.)

Binding: paper. Front covers: I: blue and yellowish green with illus. of tree-lined pond; II: pinkish orange with photograph of "Railroad Bridge at Harper's Ferry, VA" (p. [iv]); at tops, in white: 'American Literature | The Makers and the Making Volume I [II] | Cleanth Brooks | R. W. B. Lewis | Robert Penn Warren'. Spine: '[horiz.] I [II] | Brooks | Lewis | Warren | [vert.] American Literature The Makers and the Making | [horiz.] St. Martin's'. Back cover: continuation of photograph. All edges trimmed and unstained.

Copies: CoCA, JAG, RPW.

Notes: 1. Volume I published May 1973 at $7.95; II, June 1973 at $8.95. The publisher prefers not to release the schedule of printings and the quantities printed (ltr., Ellen C. Wynn, Deputy Director, College Dept., St. Martin's Press, Inc., 10 Feb. 1975). Printed and bound at Quinn and Boden Company, Inc. LC copyright, vol. I, 16 March 1973 (A518721) and, vol. II, 1 June 1973 (A519970); two copies of each deposited 11 Jan. 1974.

2. Also issued in the following sets: *hardcover, 2 vols.*: brown cloth; both published July 1973 at $12.95 and $14.95, respectively (CoCA, JAG). *Paper, 4 vols.*: parts A–C published May 1974, D June 1974; A, pp. 1+324; B, pp. 1+872; C, pp. 1+606; D, pp. 1+1168 (CoCA, Ctb, JAG). *Bds., 1 vol.*: shorter edition, published June 1974 at $11.95; pp. xxxii+1796 (CoCA, JAG, RPW).

3. According to Cleanth Brooks (13 April 1978), each of the editors wrote specific introductions and then circulated the drafts to the other two. See Appendix (manuscripts) for possible RPW contributions.

Audubon: A Vision appears in II and D, pp. 2924–2931, and in the shorter edition, pp. 1743–1750.

B37   *Katherine Anne Porter: A Collection of Critical Essays* (1979)

KATHERINE ANNE | PORTER | A COLLECTION OF CRITICAL ESSAYS | *Edited by* | Robert Penn Warren | Prentice-Hall, Inc. [publisher's device with 'A SPECTRUM BOOK' beneath it] *Englewood Cliffs, N.J.*

Collation: demy folio 8° (trimmed: 20.0 × 14.0 cm.); *unsigned* [1–6¹⁶ 7⁸], 104 leaves; pp. [i–viii] ix–xii, 1–195 [196]; numbers in italics in corner formed by head and outer margins except on chapter pages on which they are centered beneath the text in the tail margin.

Contains: pp. 1–19: introduction; pp. 93–108: "Irony with a Center."

Typography and Paper: text: 41 ll., 16.8 (17.3) × 11.0 cm.; Linotype Baskerville 10/12-pt. RT, in ital.: v., contributor's name; r., title of essay. Paper: white, wove, unwatermarked; sheets bulk 1.2 cm.

Binding: black cloth. Front: blank. Spine, vert., in gilt: 'KATHERINE ANNE PORTER *Edited by* Robert Penn Warren Prentice-Hall'. Back, in gilt, lower right corner: '0-13-514679-8'. All edges trimmed and unstained; white endpapers.

   Dust wrapper: front cover, on black in lavender: 'TWENTIETH CENTURY VIEWS | KATHERINE ANNE | PORTER | *A Collection of Critical Essays* | *Edited by* ROBERT PENN WARREN | [illus. by Stanley Wyatt of *A Day's Work*]'. Spine: '[vert.] TWENTIETH | CENTURY VIEWS KATHERINE ANNE PORTER *Edited by* | ROBERT PENN WARREN PRENTICE | HALL | [horiz.] S-TC-120'. Back cover: about TCV. Front flap: about the collection of essays. Back flap: about the author.

Copies: CoCA, Ctw, JAG, LC, RPW, STW.

Note: published 23 Jan. 1979 in cloth and paper ($3.95). LC copyright 1 May 1979 (TX239-886); two copies deposited 1 May 1979.

C

Poems

Note: The symbol * indicates the end of a poem sequence, and + indicates the end of a subsequence (sequence within a sequence) of poems. Untitled poems are listed by first lines. Arrangement is chronological by publication date.

C1 "Prophecy." *The Mess Kit: (Food for Thought)*. [Ed.] Edgar Dow Gilman. Camp Knox, KY: Military Training Camps Association (U.S. Army), 1922. P. 41.

C2 "Vision." *American Poetry Magazine*, 5 (Dec. 1922), 23.

C3 "Crusade." *Fugitive*, 2 (June–July 1923), 90–91.

C4 "After Teacups." *Fugitive*, 2 (Aug.–Sept. 1923), 106.
Note: published under the name "Penn Warren."

C5 "Midnight." *Fugitive*, 2 (Oct. 1923), 142.
Note: published under the name "Penn Warren."

C6 "The Fierce Horsemen." *Driftwood Flames*. Nashville: The Poetry Guild, 1923. P. 10.

C7 "Wild Oats." *Driftwood Flames*. Nashville: The Poetry Guild, 1923. P. 17.

C8 "Iron Beach."
  a. *Driftwood Flames*. Nashville: The Poetry Guild, 1923. P. 30.
  b. *Fugitive*, 3 (April 1924), 54.
  Note: as "I" in a group entitled "Three Poems."
  c. *Fugitive*, 4 (March 1925), 15.

C9 "To Certain Old Masters." *Driftwood Flames*. Nashville: The Poetry Guild, 1923. Pp. 36–37.

C10 "The Golden Hills of Hell." *Driftwood Flames*. Nashville: The Poetry Guild, 1923. P. 41.
                    "Three Poems" sequence
  Note: see **C8b**.

C11 "So many are the things that she has learned." *Fugitive*, 3 (April 1924), 54.
  Note: title on MS: "Mrs. Dodd's Daughter."

C12 "I knew not down what windy nights I fled." *Fugitive*, 3 (April 1924), 55.
  Note: title on MS: "Apocalypse."

  *

  "Death Mask of a Young Man" sequence
C13 "I. The Mouse." *Fugitive*, 3 (June 1924), 69.
C14 "II. The Moon." *Fugitive*, 3 (June 1924), 69.

  *

C15 "Nocturne." *Fugitive*, 3 (June 1924), 70.
C16 "Adieu Sentimentale."
  a. *Voices: A Journal of Verse*, 3 (July–Aug. 1924), 112.
  b. *Voices: A Journal of Poetry*, 146 (Sept.–Dec. 1951), 10.
C17 "The Romance Macabre." *Voices: A Journal of Verse*, 3 (July–Aug. 1924), 112.
  "Sonnets of Two Summers" sequence
C18 "I. Sonnet of a Rainy Summer." *Fugitive*, 3 (Aug. 1924), 117.
C19 "II. Sonnet of August Drouth." *Fugitive*, 3 (Aug. 1924), 117.

  *

C20 "Praises for Mrs. Dodd." *Fugitive*, 3 (Aug. 1924), 118.
  Note: title on MS: "Praises for Mrs. Dodd Deceased."
  "Portraits of Three Ladies" sequence
C21 "I. He passed her only once in a crowded street." *Double Dealer*, 6 (Aug.–Sept. 1924), 191.
C22 "II. Since I can neither move you nor the fate." *Double Dealer*, 6 (Aug.–Sept. 1924), 191.
C23 "III. Strangely her heart yet clutched a strange twilight." *Double Dealer*, 6 (Aug.–Sept. 1924), 192.

  *

C24 "Admonition to the Dead." *Double Dealer*, 7 (Oct. 1924), 2.
C25 "Autumn Twilight Piece." *Double Dealer*, 7 (Oct. 1924), 2.
C26 "Apologia for Grief." *The Measure*, no. 44 (Oct. 1924), p. 12.
C27 "Alf Burt, Tenant Farmer." *Fugitive*, 3 (Dec. 1924), 154.
C28 "Admonition to Those Who Mourn." *Fugitive*, 3 (Dec. 1924), 155.
C29 "The Mirror." *Fugitive*, 4 (March 1925), 16.
C30 "Easter Morning: Crosby Junction." *Fugitive*, 4 (June 1925), 33–34.
C31 "Mr. Dodd's Son." *Fugitive*, 4 (June 1925), 35.
C32 "To a Face in the Crowd."
  a. *Fugitive*, 4 (June 1925), 36.

b. *TSP*, pp. 68–69.

c. *SP*, p. 102.

d. *New English Review*, 12 (May 1946), 392.

e. *SPNO*, pp. 299–300.

f. *SP75*, pp. 324–325.

C33 "The Wrestling Match." *Fugitive*, 4 (June 1925), 37.

"Images on the Tomb" sequence

C34 "I. Dawn: The Gorgon's Head." *Fugitive*, 4 (Sept. 1925), 89.

C35 "II. Day: Lazarus." *Fugitive*, 4 (Sept. 1925), 90.

C36 "III. Evening: The Motors." *Fugitive*, 4 (Sept. 1925), 91.

C37 "IV. Night: But a Sultry Wind."

a. *Fugitive*, 4 (Sept. 1925), 92.

b. "Firing Line Section." Nashville *Tennessean*, 27 Sept. 1925, p. 7.

*

C38 "August Revival: Crosby Junction." *SR*, 33 (Oct. 1925), 439.

C39 "To One Awake."

a. *Occident* (University of California, Berkeley), 86 (March 1926), 13.

b. *NRep*, 30 May 1928, p. 47.

c. *TSP*, p. 66.

C40 "Pro Sua Vita." *NRep*, 11 May 1927, p. 333.

C41 "Croesus in Autumn."

a. *NRep*, 2 Nov. 1927, p. 290.

b. *Literary Digest*, 19 Nov. 1927, p. 34.

c. *TSP*, p. 50.

d. *SP*, p. 89.

"Kentucky Mountain Farm" sequence

C42 "i. Rebuke of the Rocks."

a. *Nation*, 11 Jan. 1928, p. 47.

b. *Literary Digest*, 28 Jan. 1928, p. 32.

c. *Vanderbilt Masquerader*, 10 (Dec. 1933), 16.

d. *TSP*, p. 14.

e. *SP*, p. 79.

f. *SPNO*, p. 290.

g. *SP75*, p. 319.

C43 "ii. At the Hour of the Breaking of the Rocks."

a. *American Caravan*. Ed. Van Wyck Brooks et al. New York: The Macaulay Company, 1927. P. 803.

b. *Vanderbilt Masquerader*, 10 (Dec. 1933), 16.

c. *TSP*, p. 15.

d. *SP*, pp. 79–80.

e. *SPNO*, p. 291.

f. *SP75*, pp. 319–320.

C44 "iii. History among the Rocks."

a. *NRep*, 5 Dec. 1928, p. 63.

b. *Vanderbilt Masquerader*, 10 (Dec. 1933), 16.

c. *TSP*, pp. 16–17.

d. *SP*, pp. 80–81.

e. *SPNO*, p. 292.

f. *SP75*, pp. 320–321.

C45 "iv. The Cardinal."

a. In the "Southern Number." Ed. Allen Tate. *Poetry*, 40 (May 1932), 60.

b. *TSP*, pp. 17–18.

c. *SP*, p. 81.

C46 "The Owl." In the "Southern Number." Ed. Allen Tate. *Poetry*, 40 (May 1932), 59–60.

C47 "v. The Jay."

a. As "Blue Cuirassier." *SatR* (*of Literature*), 11 July 1931, p. 953.

b. *TSP*, p. 18.

c. *SP*, pp. 81–82.

C48 "vi. Watershed."

a. In the "Southern Number." Ed. Allen Tate. *Poetry*, 40 (May 1932), 61.

b. *TSP*, p. 19.

c. *SP*, p. 82.

C49 "vii. The Return."

a. *NRep*, 15 Jan. 1930, p. 215.

b. *TSP*, p. 20.

c. *SP*, p. 83.

d. As "IV." *SPNO*, p. 293.

e. *SP75*, pp. 321–322.

*

C50 "Letter of a Mother."

a. *NRep*, 11 Jan. 1928, p. 212.

b. *Vanderbilt Masquerader*, 10 (Dec. 1933), 16–17.

c. *TSP*, pp. 26–27.

d. *SP*, pp. 87–88.

e. *SPNO*, pp. 297–298.

C51 "Garden Waters."

a. *NRep*, 7 March 1928, p. 99.

b. *TSP*, p. 67.

c. *SP*, p. 101.

C52 "Grandfather Gabriel."

a. *Second American Caravan*. Ed. Alfred Kreymborg et al. New York: The Macaulay Company, 1928. P. 120.

b. As "Genealogy." *TSP*, p. 28.

C53 "Pondy Woods."

a. *Second American Caravan*. Ed. Alfred Kreymborg et al. New York: The Macaulay Company, 1928. P. 121–122.

b. *TSP*, pp. 21–24.

c. *SP*, pp. 84–86.

d. *SPNO*, pp. 294–296.

e. *SP75*, pp. 322–324.

C54 "For a Self-Possessed Friend."

a. *NRep*, 27 Nov. 1929, p. 14.

b. *TSP*, pp. 61–62.

c. *SP*, p. 98.

d. *New English Review Magazine*, NS 2 (Jan. 1949), 54.

C55 "Tryst on Vinegar Hill." *This Quarter*, 2 (Jan.–March 1930), 503–504.

C56 "Empire." *This Quarter*, 3 (July–Sept. 1930), 168–169.

C57 "The Last Metaphor."

a. *NRep*, 9 Dec. 1931, p. 105.

b. *TSP*, pp. 52–53.

c. *SP*, pp. 91–92.

C58 "The Limited." *Poetry*, 41 (Jan. 1933), 200.

C59 "Problem of Knowledge."

a. *SWR*, 18 (Summer 1933), 417.

b. *TSP*, p. 59.

c. *SP*, p. 97.

C60 "Letter to a Friend."

a. *American Review*, 3 (May 1934), 236.

b. *TSP*, p. 46.

c. *SP*, p. 43.

C61 "Aubade for Hope."

a. *American Review*, 3 (May 1934), 236–237.

b. *TSP*, p. 47.

c. *SP*, p. 44.

C62 "Eidolon."

a. *American Review*, 3 (May 1934), 237–238.

b. *TSP*, p. 25.

c. *SP*, p. 45.

d. *SPNO*, p. 260.

e. *SP75*, pp. 299–300.

"Two Poems on Truth" sequence

C63 "Aged Man Surveys the Past Time."

a. *American Review*, 3 (May 1934), 238–239.

b. *TSP*, p. 43.

c. *SP*, p. 40.

C64 "Toward Rationality."

a. *American Review*, 3 (May 1934), 239.

b. *TSP*, p. 44.

c. *SP*, p. 41.

*

C65 "So Frost Astounds."

a. *Poetry*, 44 (July 1934), 196.

b. *TSP*, p. 51.

c. *SP*, p. 90.

C66 "The Return: An Elegy."

a. *Poetry*, 45 (Nov. 1934), 85–89.

b. *TSP*, pp. 9–13.

c. *SP*, pp. 75–78.

d. *SPNO*, pp. 286–289.

e. *SP75*, pp. 315–318.

C67 "For a Friend Parting."

a. *NRep*, 26 Dec. 1934, p. 186.

b. As "To a Friend Parting." *TSP*, p. 45.

c. *SP*, p. 42.

d. *SPNO*, p. 259.

e. Revised and read at Allen Tate's 75th birthday celebration as "Old Soldier." *Vanderbilt Alumnus*, Spring 1975, p. 29. Changes listed in note below.

f. *SP75*, p. 299.

Note: In a letter to me 4 Sept. 1976, RPW wrote: "I notice in my copy, now at hand, some scribbled revisions, which must represent the version read: Stanza I, line 2: '*though* scarred'; II.1: 'Yes you who by grove / and shore have walked'; II.3: 'though *like* chaff'; II.5: 'his wings the *full* light'; II.6: 'What can be foresaid?'; III.3: 'The horny clasp of hands / that your hand now seal.'; and III.4: 'ere this *have* kept powder'."

C68 "Letter from a Coward to a Hero."

a. *SoR*, 1 (July 1935), 92–94.

b. *TSP*, pp. 37–40.

c. *SP*, pp. 27–29.

d. *SPNO*, pp. 249–251.

e. *SP75*, pp. 291–293.

C69 "Ransom."

  a. *SoR*, 1 (July 1935), 95.

  b. *TSP*, p. 42.

  c. *SP*, p. 39.

  d. *SPNO*, p. 258.

  e. *SP75*, p. 268.

"Two Poems on Time" sequence

C70 "Resolution."

  a. *VQR*, 11 (July 1935), 352–353.

  b. *TSP*, pp. 34–36.

  c. *SP*, pp. 63–64.

C71 "History."

  a. *VQR*, 11 (July 1935), 353–356.

  b. *TSP*, pp. 29–33.

  c. *SP*, pp. 30–33.

  d. *SPNO*, pp. 252–255.

  e. *SP75*, pp. 294–296.

*

"October Poems" sequence

C72 "The Garden."

  a. *Poetry*, 47 (Oct. 1935), 9–10.

  b. *TSP*, pp. 64–65.

  c. *SP*, pp. 70–71.

  d. *SPNO*, pp. 284–285.

  e. *SP75*, pp. 314–315.

  Note: reprinted in conjunction with the announcement of RPW's winning the Helen Haire Levinson Prize for Poetry in 1936, *Poetry*, 49 (Nov. 1936), 106–107, 112.

C73 "Man Coming of Age."

  a. *Poetry*, 47 (Oct. 1935), 10–11.

  b. *TSP*, pp. 48–49.

  c. *SP*, p. 69.

  d. *SPNO*, pp. 282–283.

*

C74 "Late Subterfuge."

  a. *TSP*, p. 41.

  b. *SP*, p. 68.

    c. *SPNO*, p. 281.

    d. *SP75*, pp. 313–314.

C75 "Pacific Gazer."

    a. *TSP*, pp. 55–56.

    b. *SP*, pp. 93–94.

C76 "Calendar."

    a. *TSP*, pp. 57–58.

    b. *SP*, pp. 95–96.

C77 "Cold Colloquy."

    a. *TSP*, p. 60.

    b. *SP*, p. 100.

C78 "For a Friend Who Thinks Himself Urbane."

    a. *TSP*, p. 63.

    b. *SP*, p. 99.

C79 "Picnic Remembered."

    a. *Scribner's Magazine*, 99 (March 1936), 185.

    b. *EP*, pp. [4–5].

    c. *SP*, pp. 61–62.

    d. *New English Review*, 16 (May 1948), 433–434.

    e. *SPNO*, pp. 275–276.

    f. *SP75*, pp. 309–311.

C80 "Monologue at Midnight."

    a. *VQR*, 12 (July 1936), 395.

    b. *EP*, p. [1].

    c. *SP*, p. 58.

    d. *SPNO*, pp. 271–272.

    e. *SP75*, pp. 307–308.

C81 "Athenian Death." *Nation*, 31 Oct. 1936, p. 523.

C82 "Bearded Oaks."

    a. *Poetry*, 51 (Oct. 1937), 10–11.

    b. *EP*, pp. [2–3].

    c. *SP*, pp. 59–60.

    d. *SPNO*, pp. 273–274.

    e. *SP75*, pp. 308–309.

C83 "Love's Parable."

    Note: copyright 27 March 1940 (B451097); renewed 26 July 1967 (R415291).

    a. *KR*, 2 (Spring 1940), 186–188.

    b. *EP*, pp. [19–21].

    c. *SP*, pp. 65–67.

d. *SPNO*, pp. 277–280.

e. *SP75*, pp. 311–313.

C84 "Crime."

Note: copyright 22 May 1940 (B455689); renewed 26 July 1967 (R415290).

a. *Nation*, 25 May 1940, p. 655.

b. *Living Age*, Jan. 1941, pp. 487–488.

c. *EP*, pp. [6–7].

d. *SP*, pp. 25–26.

e. *SPNO*, pp. 247–248.

f. *SP75*, pp. 290–291.

C85 "Terror."

Note: copyright 5 Feb. 1941 (B486414); renewed 10 May 1968 (R435854).

a. *Poetry*, 57 (Feb. 1941), 285–288.

b. *EP*, pp. [22–24].

c. *SP*, pp. 18–20.

d. *SPNO*, pp. 240–242.

e. *SP75*, pp. 284–286.

C86 "Question and Answer."

a. *Poetry*, 57 (Feb. 1941), 288–291.

b. *EP*, pp. [16–18].

c. *SP*, pp. 34–36.

C87 "Goodbye." *AmPf*, 6 (Winter 1941), 113–114.

C88 "Pursuit."

Note: copyright 5 Dec. 1941 (B524196); renewed 12 May 1969 (R461335).

a. *VQR*, 18 (Jan. 1942), 57–59.

b. *EP*, pp. [14–15].

c. *SP*, pp. 21–22.

d. *Perspectives USA*, no. 13 (Autumn 1955), pp. 23–25.

e. *SPNO*, pp. 243–244.

f. *SP75*, pp. 286–288.

C89 "Revelation."

Note: copyright 9 Jan. 1942 (B527428); renewed 12 May 1969 (R461334).

a. *Poetry*, 59 (Jan. 1942), 202–203.

b. *EP*, pp. [12–13].

c. Rpt. in *Angry Penguins* (Australia), Sept. 1943 [unverified].

d. *SP*, pp. 46–47.

e. *SPNO*, pp. 261–262.

f. *SP75*, pp. 300–301.

C90 "End of Season."

Note: copyright 5 March 1942 (B534078); renewed 12 May 1969 (R461333).

a. *Nation*, 7 March 1942, p. 286.

b. *EP*, pp. [10–11].

c. *SP*, pp. 37–38.

d. *Perspectives USA*, no. 13 (Autumn 1955), pp. 25–26.

e. *SPNO*, pp. 256–257.

f. *SP75*, pp. 297–298.

C91 "Original Sin: A Short Story."

Note: copyright 10 April 1942 (B538867); renewed 12 May 1969 (R461332).

a. *KR*, 4 (Spring 1942), 179–180.

b. *EP*, pp. [8–9].

c. *SP*, pp. 23–24.

d. *SPNO*, pp. 245–246.

e. *SP75*, pp. 288–289.

Note: rpt. in *Poetry in the Age of Anxiety* by Cleanth Brooks. Fifth McGregor Room Seminar in Contemporary Prose and Poetry. Program. Charlottesville: University of Virginia School of English, 31 Oct. 1947, pp. 4–7.

"Mexico Is a Foreign Country: Four [Five] Studies in
Naturalism" sequence

Note: copyright 8 June 1943 (B588979); renewed 2 Oct. 1970 (R491912).

C92 "I. Butterflies Over the Map."

a. *Poetry*, 62 (June 1943), 121–122.

b. *SP*, p. 51.

c. *SPNO*, p. 263.

d. *SP75*, p. 302.

C93 "II. Siesta Time in Village Plaza by Ruined Bandstand and Banana Tree." *SP*, pp. 51–52.

C94 "III. The World Comes Galloping: A True Story."

a. As II. *Poetry*, 62 (June 1943), 122–123.

b. *SP*, p. 53.

c. As II. *SPNO*, pp. 264–265.

d. *SP75*, p. 303.

C95 "IV. Small Soldiers with Drum in Large Landscape."

a. As III. *Poetry*, 62 (June 1943), 123–126.
b. *SP*, pp. 54–55.
c. As III. *SPNO*, pp. 266–268.
d. *SP75*, pp. 304–305.
C96 "V. The Mango on the Mango Tree."
a. As IV. *Poetry*, 62 (June 1943), 126–127.
b. *SP*, pp. 56–57.
c. *Perspectives USA*, no. 13 (Autumn 1955), pp. 22–23.
d. As IV. *SPNO*, pp. 269–270.
e. *SP75*, pp. 305–307.

*

C97 "Variation: Ode to Fear." *SP*, pp. 48–50.
C98 "The Ballad of Billie Potts."
a. *PR*, 11 (Winter 1944), 56–70.
b. *SP*, pp. 3–17.
c. *SPNO*, pp. 223–239.
d. *SP75*, pp. 271–284.
C99 "The Lie." *Poetry*, 82 (June 1953), 125–132.
Note: excerpt from *BD*.
C100 "The Death of Isham." *PR*, 20 (July–Aug. 1953), 393–396.
Note: excerpt from *BD*.
"To a Little Girl, One Year Old, in Ruined Fortress" sequence
Note: published separately, **A14**.
C101 "I. Sirocco."
a. *PR*, 23 (Spring 1955), 171.
b. *P*, p. 3.
c. *SPNO*, p. 147.
d. *SP75*, p. 219.
C102 "II. Gull's Cry."
a. *PR*, 23 (Spring 1955), 172.
b. *P*, p. 4.
c. *SPNO*, p. 148.
d. *SP75*, p. 220.
C103 "III. The Child Next Door."
a. *PR*, 23 (Spring 1955), 172–173.
b. *P*, p. 5.
c. *SPNO*, p. 149.
d. *SP75*, pp. 220–221.
C104 "IV. The Flower."
a. *PR*, 23 (Spring 1955), 173–176.

  b. *P*, pp. 6–10.
  c. *SPNO*, pp. 150–154.
  d. *SP75*, pp. 221–224.
C105 "V. Colder Fire."
  a. *PR*, 23 (Spring 1955), 177–178.
  b. *P*, pp. 11–13.
  c. *SPNO*, pp. 155–157.
  d. *SP75*, pp. 225–226.

*

"Promises" sequence

C106 "Courtmartial."
  a. As I. *YR*, 46 (Spring 1957), 321–325.
  b. As II. *P*, pp. 19–23.
  c. As II. *SPNO*, pp. 160–164.
  d. As II. *SP75*, pp. 228–232.
C107 "School Lesson Based on Word of Tragic Death of Entire Gillum Family."
  a. As II. *YR*, 46 (Spring 1957), 325–328.
  b. As VI. *P*, pp. 34–36.
  c. As VI. *SPNO*, pp. 175–177.
  d. As VI. *SP75*, pp. 239–240.

"Man in Moonlight" subsequence

C108 "Walk by Moonlight in Small Town."
  a. As III. *YR*, 46 (Spring 1957), 328–330.
  b. As XIII.2. *P*, pp. 58–59.
  c. As XIII.2. *SPNO*, pp. 196–197.
  d. As XIII.2. *SP75*, pp. 253–255.
C109 "Moonlight Observed from Ruined Fortress."
  a. As IV. *YR*, 46 (Spring 1957), 330–331.
  b. As XIII.1. *P*, pp. 56–57.
  c. As XIII.1. *SPNO*, pp. 194–195.
  d. As XIII.1. *SP75*, pp. 252–253.
C110 "Lullaby in Moonlight."
  a. As V. *YR*, 46 (Spring 1957), 331–332.
  b. As XIII.3. "Lullaby: Moonlight Lingers." *P*, pp. 60–61.
  c. As **b** above. *SPNO*, pp. 198–199.
  d. As **b** above. *SP75*, pp. 255–256.

+

C111 "Mad Young Aristocrat on Beach."
  a. As VI. *YR*, 46 (Spring 1957), 333–334.

b. As XIV. *P*, pp. 62–63.

c. As XIV. *SPNO*, pp. 200–201.

d. As XIV. *SP75*, pp. 257–258.

C112 "Foreign Shore, Old Woman, Slaughter of Octopus."

  a. As VII. *YR*, 46 (Spring 1957), 334–336.

  b. As IX. *P*, pp. 42–43.

  c. As IX. *SPNO*, pp. 183–184.

  d. As IX. *SP75*, pp. 243–244.

C113 "Dragon Country: To Jacob Boehme."

  a. As VIII. *YR*, 46 (Spring 1957), 336–338.

  b. As XV. *P*, pp. 64–66.

  c. As XV. *SPNO*, pp. 202–203.

  d. As XV. *SP75*, pp. 258–260.

C114 "Lullaby: A Motion Like Sleep."

  a. As IX. *YR*, 46 (Spring 1957), 339–340.

  b. As XVIII. *P*, pp. 82–83.

  c. As XVIII. *SPNO*, pp. 218–219.

  d. As XVIII. *SP75*, p. 268.

C115 "Necessity for Belief."

  a. As X. *YR*, 46 (Spring 1957), 340.

  b. As XIX. *P*, p. 84.

*

"Boy's Will, Joyful Labor Without Pay, and Harvest Home
(1918)" subsequence

C116 "Morning."

  a. As (a). *BotOs*, 19 (1957), 203–204.

  b. As XVII.1. *P*, p. 76.

  c. As XVII.1. *SPNO*, p. 213.

  d. As XVII.1. *SP75*, p. 265.

C117 "Work."

  a. As (b). *BotOs*, 19 (1957), 204.

  b. As XVII.2. *P*, p. 76.

  c. As XVII.2. *SPNO*, p. 214.

  d. As XVII.2. *SP75*, p. 265.

C118 "The Snake."

  a. As (c). *BotOs*, 19 (1957), 204–205.

  b. As XVII.3. *P*, pp. 78–79.

  c. As XVII.3. *SPNO*, p. 215.

  d. As XVII.3. *SP75*, pp. 265–266.

C119 "Hands Are Paid."

  a. As (d). *BotOs*, 19 (1957), 205–206.

b. As XVII.4. *P*, pp. 80–81.

c. As XVII.4. *SPNO*, pp. 216–217.

d. As XVII.4. *SP75*, pp. 266–267.

+

C120 "What Was the Promise That Smiled from the Maples at Evening?"

    a. As I. *Encounter*, 8 (May 1957), 3–4.

    b. As I. *P*, pp. 17–18.

    c. As I. *SPNO*, pp. 158–159.

    d. As I. *SP75*, pp. 227–228.

C121 "Gold Glade."

    a. As II. *Encounter*, 8 (May 1957), 4.

    b. As III. *P*, pp. 24–25.

    c. As III. *SPNO*, pp. 165–166.

    d. As III. *SP75*, pp. 232–233.

C122 "Dark Night Of."

    a. As III. *Encounter*, 8 (May 1957), 5–7.

    b. As X. *P*, pp. 44–47.

    c. As X, "Dark Night of the Soul." *SPNO*, pp. 185–188.

    d. As X. *SP75*, pp. 245–248.

C123 "Country Burying: 1919."

    a. As IV. *Encounter*, 8 (May 1957), 7–8.

    b. As V, "Country Burying (1919)." *P*, pp. 32–33.

    c. As **b** above. *SPNO*, pp. 173–174.

    d. As **b** above. *SP75*, pp. 237–238.

C124 "Summer Storm (Circa 1916) and God's Grace."

    a. As V. *Encounter*, 8 (May 1957), 8.

    b. As VII. *P*, pp. 37–38.

    c. As VII. *SPNO*, pp. 178–179.

    d. As VII. *SP75*, pp. 240–241.

"Dark Woods" subsequence

C125 "Tonight the Woods Are Darkened."

    a. As VI (a). *Encounter*, 8 (May 1957), 9.

    b. As IV.1. *P*, pp. 26–27.

    c. As IV.1. *SPNO*, pp. 167–168.

    d. As IV.1. *SP75*, pp. 233–234.

C126 "The Dogwood."

    a. As VI (b). *Encounter*, 8 (May 1957), 9–10.

    b. As IV.2. *P*, pp. 28–29.

    c. As IV.2. *SPNO*, pp. 169–170.

    d. As IV.2. *SP75*, p. 235.

C127 "The Hazel Leaf."
 a. As VI (c). *Encounter*, 8 (May 1957), 10–11.
 b. As IV.3. *P*, pp. 30–31.
 c. As IV.3. *SPNO*, pp. 171–172.
 d. As IV.3. *SP75*, p. 236.
+

C128 "Founding Fathers, 19th Century Style, South-East USA."
 a. As VII. *Encounter*, 8 (May 1957), 11–12.
 b. As VIII. *P*, pp. 39–41.
 c. As VIII. *SPNO*, pp. 180–182.
 d. As VIII. *SP75*, pp. 241–243.
"Infant Boy at Midcentury" subsequence

C129 "When the Century Dragged."
 a. As VIII (a). *Encounter*, 8 (May 1957), 12.
 b. As XI.1. *P*, pp. 48–49.
 c. As XI.1. *SPNO*, p. 189.
 d. As XI.1. *SP75*, pp. 248–249.

C130 "Modification of Landscape."
 a. As VIII (b). *Encounter*, 8 (May 1957), 12–13.
 b. As XI.2. *P*, pp. 50–51.
 c. As XI.2. *SPNO*, p. 190.
 d. As XI.2. *SP75*, pp. 249–250.

C131 "Brightness of Distance."
 a. As VIII (c). *Encounter*, 8 (May 1957), 13.
 b. As XI.3. *P*, pp. 52–53.
 c. As XI.3. *SPNO*, p. 191.
 d. As XI.3. *SP75*, p. 250.
+

C132 "Lullaby."
 a. As IX. *Encounter*, 8 (May 1957), 13–14.
 b. As XII, "Lullaby: Smile in Sleep." *P*, pp. 54–55.
 c. As **b** above. *SPNO*, pp. 192–193.
 d. As **b** above. *SP75*, pp. 251–252.

*

"Ballad of a Sweet Dream of Peace" subsequence
Note: presented at the Loeb Drama Center Experimental Theatre, Harvard University, 27–29 April 1961. **E9**.
C133 "And Don't Forget Your Corset Cover, Either."
 a. As (a). *KR*, 19 (Winter 1957), 31–32.
 b. As XVI.1. *P*, pp. 67–68.

   c. As XVI.1. *SPNO*, pp. 204–205.
   d. As XVI.1. *SP75*, pp. 260–261.
C134 "Keepsakes."
   a. As (b). *KR*, 19 (Winter 1957), 32–33.
   b. As XVI.2. *P*, pp. 69–70.
   c. As XVI.2. *SPNO*, pp. 206–207.
   d. As XVI.2. *SP75*, pp. 261–262.
C135 "Go It, Granny——Go It, Hog!"
   a. As (c). *KR*, 19 (Winter 1957), 33–34.
   b. As XVI.3. *P*, p. 71.
   c. As XVI.3. *SPNO*, p. 208.
   d. As XVI.3. *SP75*, p. 262.
C136 "Friends of the Family, or Bowling a Sticky Cricket."
   a. As (d). *KR*, 19 (Winter 1957), 34.
   b. As XVI.4. *P*, p. 72.
   c. As XVI.4. *SPNO*, p. 209.
   d. As XVI.4. *SP75*, pp. 262–263.
C137 "You Never Knew Her Either Though You Thought You Did, Inside Out."
   a. As (e). *KR*, 19 (Winter 1957), 34–35.
   b. As XVI.5. *P*, p. 73.
   c. As XVI.5, with "Inside Out" omitted. *SPNO*, p. 210.
   d. As **c** above. *SP75*, p. 263.
C138 "I Guess You Ought to Know Who You Are."
   a. As (f). *KR*, 19 (Winter 1957), 35.
   b. As XVI.6. *P*, p. 74.
   c. As XVI.6. *SPNO*, p. 211.
   d. As XVI.6. *SP75*, p. 264.
C139 "Rumor Unverified Stop Can You Confirm Stop."
   a. As (g). *KR*, 19 (Winter 1957), 36.
   b. As XVI.7. *P*, p. 75.
   c. As XVI.7. *SPNO*, p. 212.
   d. As XVI.7. *SP75*, p. 264.

+

"Prognosis: A Short Story, the End of Which You Will Know
Soon Enough" sequence
C140 "1. And Oh——."
   a. *SR*, 66 (Spring 1958), 252–254.
   b. *YEO*, pp. 58–59.
C141 "2. What the Sand Said."
   a. *SR*, 66 (Spring 1958), 254–255.

b. *YEO*, p. 60.

C142 "3. What the Joree Said, the Joree Being Only a Bird."

    a. *SR*, 66 (Spring 1958), 255.

    b. *YEO*, p. 61.

*

"Two Pieces after Suetonius" sequence

C143 "Apology for Domitian."

    a. As I. *PR*, 25 (Spring 1958), 223–224.

    b. As 1. *YEO*, pp. 20–21.

    c. As I. *SPNO*, pp. 107–108.

    d. As I. *SP75*, pp. 199–200.

C144 "Tiberius on Capri."

    a. As II. *PR*, 25 (Spring 1958), 224–225.

    b. As 2. *YEO*, pp. 22–23.

    c. As II. *SPNO*, pp. 109–110.

    d. As II. *SP75*, pp. 200–201.

*

C145 "Garland for You: Poem."

    a. *YR*, 47 (Summer 1958), 494–495.

    b. As 1, "Clearly About You." *YEO*, pp. 3–4.

    c. As I, "Clearly About You." *SPNO*, p. 95.

    d. As **c** above. *SP75*, pp. 191–192.

    Note: from the sequence "Garland for You."

"[Three] Nursery Rhymes" sequence

C146 "Knockety-Knockety-Knock."

    a. As I. *YR*, 47 (Summer 1958), 495–496.

    b. *YEO*, pp. 64–65.

    c. *SPNO*, pp. 134–135.

C147 "Little Boy Blue."

    a. As II. *YR*, 47 (Summer 1958), 496–497.

    b. As 2, "News of Unexpected Demise of Little Boy Blue." *YEO*, pp. 66–67.

    c. As II, titled as **b** above. *SPNO*, pp. 136–137.

C148 "Mother Makes the Biscuits."

    a. As III. *YR*, 47 (Summer 1958), 497–498.

    b. As 3. *YEO*, pp. 68–69.

    c. As III. *SPNO*, pp. 138–139.

*

C149 "Debate: Question, Quarry, Dream."

    a. *YR*, 47 (Summer 1958), 498–499.

    b. As 6. *YEO*, pp. 44–45.

c. As VI. *SPNO*, pp. 124–125.
d. As V. *SP75*, p. 211.
C150 "Penthesilea and Achilles: Fatal Interview."
  a. *KR*, 20 (Autumn 1958), 599–601.
  b. As "Fatal Interview: Penthesilea and Achilles." *YEO*, pp. 34–36.
C151 "Switzerland."
  a. *KR*, 20 (Autumn 1958), 602–603.
  b. As 4. *YEO*, pp. 9–10.
  c. As IV. *SPNO*, pp. 102–103.
  d. As IV. *SP75*, pp. 196–197.
      "Some Quiet, Plain Poems" sequence
C152 "1. Ornithology in a World of Flux."
  a. *SatR*, 22 Nov. 1958, p. 37.
  b. *YEO*, p. 37.
  c. As I. *SPNO*, p. 120.
  d. *SP75*, p. 208.
C153 "2. Holly and Hickory."
  a. *SatR*, 22 Nov. 1958, p. 37.
  b. *YEO*, p. 38.
  c. As II. *SPNO*, p. 120.
  d. *SP75*, pp. 208–209.
C154 "3. The Well-House."
  a. *SatR*, 22 Nov. 1958, p. 37.
  b. *YEO*, p. 39.
  c. As III. *SPNO*, p. 121.
  d. *SP75*, p. 209.
C155 "4. In Moonlight, Somewhere, They Are Singing."
  a. *SatR*, 22 Nov. 1958, p. 37.
  b. *YEO*, pp. 40–41.
  c. As IV. *SPNO*, p. 122.
  d. *SP75*, p. 210.
      *

"Short Thoughts for Long Nights" sequence
C156 "Nightmare of Mouse."
  a. As I. *BotOs*, 23 (1959), 199.
  b. As 1. *YEO*, p. 71.
  c. As I. *SPNO*, p. 140.
C157 "Nightmare of Man."
  a. As II. *BotOs*, 23 (1959), 199.
  b. As 2. *YEO*, p. 72.
C158. "Human Nature." As III. *BotOs*, 23 (1959), 199.

C159 "Colloquy with Cockroach."
  a. As IV. *BotOs*, 23 (1959), 200.
  b. As 3. *YEO*, p. 73.
  c. As II. *SPNO*, p. 141.
C160 "Little Boy on Voyage."
  a. As V. *BotOs*, 23 (1959), 200.
  b. As 4. *YEO*, p. 74.
C161 "Obsession."
  a. As VI. *BotOs*, 23 (1959), 200.
  b. As 5. *YEO*, p. 75.
C162 "A Long Spoon." As VII. *BotOs*, 23 (1959), 200.
C163 "Joy."
  a. As VIII. *BotOs*, 23 (1959), 200.
  b. As 6. *YEO*, p. 76.
C164 "Theology." As IX. *BotOs*, 23 (1959), 201.
C165 "Cricket, on Kitchen Floor, Enters History."
  a. As X. *BotOs*, 23 (1959), 201.
  b. As 7. *YEO*, p. 77.
  c. As III. *SPNO*, p. 142.
C166 "Little Boy and General Principle."
  a. As XI. *BotOs*, 23 (1959), 201.
  b. As 8. *YEO*, p. 78.
C167 "Grasshopper Tries to Break Solipsism."
  a. As XII. *BotOs*, 23 (1959), 201.
  b. As 9. *YEO*, p. 79.
  c. As IV. *SPNO*, p. 143.

*

C168 "Nursery Rhyme: Why Are Your Eyes as Big as Saucers?"
BotOs, 23 (1959), 201–202.
C169 "Equinox on Mediterranean Beach."
  a. *BotOs*, 23 (1959), 203–204.
  b. As "Autumnal Equinox on Mediterranean Beach." *YEO*, pp. 62–
63.
  c. As **b** above. *SPNO*, pp. 132–133.
        "Garland for You" sequence
C170 "A Real Question Calling for Solution."
  a. As 1. *VQR*, 35 (Spring 1959), 248–249.
  b. As 5. *YEO*, pp. 11–12.
  c. As V. *SPNO*, pp. 104–105.
C171 "Lullaby: Exercise in Human Charity and Self-Knowledge."
  a. As 2. *VQR*, 35 (Spring 1959), 249–251.

b. As 2. *YEO*, pp. 5–6.

C172 "The Letter About Money, Love, or Other Comfort, If Any."
 a. As 3. *VQR*, 35 (Spring 1959), 251–255.
 b. As 6. *YEO*, pp. 13–16.
 c. As II. *SPNO*, pp. 96–99.
 d. As II. *SP75*, pp. 192–195.

C173 "The Self That Stares."
 a. As 4. *VQR*, 35 (Spring 1959), 255–257.
 b. As 8. *YEO*, p. 19.

*

C174 "Nocturne: Traveling Salesman in Hotel Bedroom."
 a. *ASch*, 28 (Summer 1959), 306–307.
 b. *YEO*, pp. 54–55.

C175 "Nursery Rhyme."
 a. *PrS*, 33 (Fall 1959), 244.
 b. As 4, "The Bramble Bush." *YEO*, p. 70.

C176 "In Italian They Call the Bird *Civetta*."
 a. *PrS*, 33 (Fall 1959), 244–245.
 b. As 5. *YEO*, pp. 42–43.
 c. As V. *SPNO*, p. 123.

"Ballad: Between the Box Cars (1923)" sequence

C177 "I Can't Even Remember the Name."
 a. As I, untitled. *PR*, 27 (Winter 1960), 69.
 b. *YEO*, p. 46.
 c. *SPNO*, p. 126.
 d. *SP75*, p. 212.

C178 "He Was Formidable."
 a. As II, untitled. *PR*, 27 (Winter 1960), 70–71.
 b. *YEO*, pp. 47–48.
 c. *SPNO*, pp. 127–128.
 d. *SP75*, pp. 213–214.

C179 "He Has Fled."
 a. As III, untitled. *PR*, 27 (Winter 1960), 72.
 b. *YEO*, pp. 49–50.

*

"Mortmain" sequence

C180 "1. After Night Flight Son Reaches Bedside of Already Unconscious Father, Whose Right Hand Lifts in a Spasmodic Gesture, as Though Trying to Make Contact: 1955."
 a. *YR*, 49 (Spring 1960), 393–394.
 b. *YEO*, pp. 24–25.

c. As I. *SPNO*, pp. 111–112.

d. *SP75*, pp. 202–203.

C181 "2. A Dead Language: Circa 1885."

  a. *YR*, 49 (Spring 1960), 394–395.

  b. *YEO*, pp. 26–27.

  c. As II. *SPNO*, p. 113.

  d. *SP75*, pp. 203–204.

C182 "3. Fox-fire."

  a. *YR*, 49 (Spring 1960), 395–396.

  b. As "Fox-fire: 1956." *YEO*, pp. 28–29.

  c. As III, titled as **b** above. *SPNO*, pp. 114–115.

  d. *SP75*, pp. 264–265.

C183 "4. In the Turpitude of Time."

  a. *YR*, 49 (Spring 1960), 396–397.

  b. As "In the Turpitude of Time: N. D." *YEO*, pp. 30–31.

  c. As V. *SPNO*, pp. 117–118.

  d. *SP75*, pp. 205–206.

C184 "5. A Vision: Circa 1880."

  a. *YR*, 49 (Spring 1960), 397–398.

  b. *YEO*, pp. 32–33.

  c. As V. *SPNO*, pp. 117–118.

  d. *SP75*, pp. 206–207.

*

C185 "Do You Agree with What I Say? Well, What Did I Say?"

  a. *Delta* (LSU), 14 (1960), 1.

  b. *YEO*, pp. 56–57.

"Two Studies in Idealism: A Short Survey of American, and
Human, History" sequence

C186 "1. Bear Track Plantation: Shortly after Shiloh."

  a. *KR*, 22 (Summer 1960), 337–338.

  b. *YEO*, p. 51.

  c. As I. *SPNO*, p. 129.

  d. *SP75*, p. 215.

C187 "2. Harvard '61: Battle Fatigue."

  a. *KR*, 22 (Summer 1960), 338–339.

  b. *YEO*, pp. 52–53.

  c. As II. *SPNO*, pp. 130–131.

  d. *SP75*, p. 216.

*

"Garland for You" sequence

C188 "Man in the Street."

   a. As 3. *YEO*, pp. 7–8.
   b. As VII. *SPNO*, pp. 100–101.
   c. As III. *SP75*, pp. 195–196.
C189 "Arrogant Law."
   a. As 7. *YEO*, pp. 17–18.
   b. As VI. *SPNO*, p. 106.
   c. As V. *SP75*, p. 198.

                                       *

C190 "Elijah on Mt. Carmel."
   a. *New Leader*, 26 Sept. 1960, p. 10.
   b. As I. *SPNO*, pp. 67–68.
   c. *SP75*, pp. 174–175.
   Note: from "Holy Writ" sequence.
                     Lyrics from "Delight" sequence
C191 "Into Broad Daylight."
   a. *NYRB*, 1, no. 1, "Special Issue," 1963, p. 18.
   b. As I. *SPNO*, p. 81.
   c. *SP75*, p. 183.
   Note: sequenced as "Delight."
C192 "It Is Not To Be Trusted."
   a. *NYRB*, 1, no. 1, "Special Issue," 1963, p. 18.
   b. As VI, "Not to Be Trusted." *SPNO*, p. 90.
   c. *SP75*, p. 188.
C193 "Something Is Going to Happen."
   a. *NYRB*, 1, no. 1, "Special Issue," 1963, p. 18.
   b. As III. *SPNO*, pp. 84–85.
   c. *SP75*, pp. 185–186.
C194 "Finisterre."
   a. *NYRB*, 1, no. 1, "Special Issue," 1963, p. 18.
   b. As VII. *SPNO*, p. 91.

                                       *

          "Fall Comes in Back-Country Vermont" sequence
C195 "(1. One Voter Out of Sixteen)."
   a. *NY*, 23 Oct. 1965, p. 56.
   b. *SPNO*, p. 52.
   c. *SP75*, pp. 162–163.
C196 "(2. The Bear and the Last Person to Remember)."
   a. *NY*, 23 Oct. 1965, p. 56.
   b. *SPNO*, pp. 53–54.
   c. *SP75*, pp. 163–165.

C197 "(3. The Human Fabric)."
  a. *NY*, 23 Oct. 1965, pp. 56–57.
  b. *SPNO*, p. 55.
  c. *SP75*, p. 165.
C198 "(4. Afterwards)."
  a. *NY*, 23 Oct. 1965, p. 57.
  b. *SPNO*, pp. 56–57.
  c. *SP75*, p. 166.

*

C199 "Shoes in Rain Jungle."
  a. *NYRB*, 11 Nov. 1965, p. 10.
  b. *SPNO*, pp. 50–51.
  c. *SP75*, pp. 159–160.
C200 "Patriotic Tour and Postulate of Joy."
  a. *NY*, 22 Jan. 1966, p. 28.
  b. As VI. *SPNO*, pp. 9–10.
  c. *SP75*, pp. 160–161.
  Note: from "Notes on a Life to Be Lived" sequence.
              "Notes on a Life to Be Lived" sequence
C201 "Stargazing."
  a. *NY*, 12 Feb. 1966, p. 30.
  b. As I. *SPNO*, p. 3.
  c. As XV. *OEP*, pp. 64–65.
  d. As XV. *SP75*, pp. 60–61.
C202 "Composition in Gold and Red-Gold."
  a. *NY*, 12 Feb. 1966, p. 30.
  b. As IV. *SPNO*, pp. 6–7.
  c. As XVIII. *OEP*, pp. 75–77.
  d. As XVII. *SP75*, pp. 62–64.
C203 "Dragon Tree."
  a. *NY*, 12 Feb. 1966, p. 30.
  b. As VII. *SPNO*, pp. 11–12.

*

C204 "Little Boy and Lost Shoe."
  a. *NYRB*, 17 Feb. 1966, p. 23.
  b. As V. *SPNO*, p. 8.
  c. As XVII. *OEP*, p. 74.
  d. As XVI. *SP75*, p. 62.
                    "Tale of Time" sequence
C205 "I. What Happened."

a. *Encounter*, 26 (March 1966), 16.
b. *SPNO*, pp. 19–20.
c. *SP75*, pp. 141–142.
C206 "II. The Mad Druggist."
a. *Encounter*, 26 (March 1966), 17.
b. *SPNO*, pp. 21–22.
c. *SP75*, pp. 142–143.
C207 "III. Answer Yes or No."
a. *Encounter*, 26 (March 1966), 17.
b. *SPNO*, p. 23.
c. *SP75*, p. 144.
                    "IV. The Interim" subsequence
C208 "1. Between the clod and the midnight."
a. As (a). *Encounter*, 26 (March 1966), 18.
b. *SPNO*, pp. 24–25.
c. *SP75*, pp. 144–145.
C209 "2. Tell me what love is, for."
a. As (b). *Encounter*, 26 (March 1966), 18.
b. *SPNO*, p. 26.
c. *SP75*, p. 145.
C210 "3. Propped in a chair, lying down she."
a. As (c). *Encounter*, 26 (March 1966), 18–19.
b. *SPNO*, p. 27.
c. *SP75*, pp. 145–146.
C211 "4. I am myself, and."
a. As (d). *Encounter*, 26 (March 1966), 19.
b. *SPNO*, p. 28.
c. *SP75*, p. 146.
C212 "5. We stand in the street of Squigg-town."
a. As (e). *Encounter*, 26 (March 1966), 19.
b. *SPNO*, p. 29.
c. *SP75*, p. 147.
C213 "6. There is only one solution. If."
a. As (f). *Encounter*, 26 (March 1966), 20.
b. *SPNO*, p. 30.
c. *SP75*, p. 147.
C214 "7. Planes pass in the night. I turn."
a. As (g). *Encounter*, 26 (March 1966), 20.
b. *SPNO*, p. 31.
c. *SP75*, pp. 147–148.
C215 "8. But the solution: You."

a. As (h). *Encounter*, 26 (March 1966), 20.

b. *SPNO*, p. 31.

c. *SP75*, p. 148.

+

C216 "V. What Were You Thinking, Dear Mother?"

a. *Encounter*, 26 (March 1966), 20–21.

b. *SPNO*, p. 33.

c. *SP75*, pp. 148–149.

"VI. Insomnia" subsequence

C217 "1. If to that place. Place of grass."

a. As (a). *Encounter*, 26 (March 1966), 21.

b. *SPNO*, pp. 34–35.

c. *SP75*, pp. 149–150.

C218 "2. What would we talk about? The dead."

a. As (b). *Encounter*, 26 (March 1966), 21–22.

b. *SPNO*, p. 36.

c. *SP75*, pp. 150–151.

C219 "3. Or does the soul have many faces, and would I."

a. As (c). *Encounter*, 26 (March 1966), 22.

b. *SPNO*, pp. 37–38.

c. *SP75*, p. 151.

C220 "4. Come."

a. As (d). *Encounter*, 26 (March 1966), 23.

b. *SPNO*, p. 39.

c. *SP75*, p. 152.

*

"Notes on a Life to Be Lived" sequence

C221 "Blow, West Wind."

a. *PR*, 33 (Spring 1966), 220.

b. As III. *SPNO*, p. 5.

c. As IV. *OEP*, p. 10.

d. As IV. *SP75*, pp. 24–25.

C222 "Vision Under the October Mountain: A Love Poem."

a. *SR*, 74 (Summer 1966), 589–590.

b. As VIII. *SPNO*, pp. 13–14.

c. As XIV. *OEP*, pp. 62–64.

d. As XIV. *SP75*, pp. 59–60.

C223 "Chain Saw at Dawn in Vermont, in Time of Drouth."

a. *SR*, 74 (Summer 1966), 590–592.

b. As IX. *SPNO*, pp. 15–17.

c. As VII. *OEP*, pp. 30–33.

d. As VII. *SP75*, pp. 39–41.
C224 "Ways of Day."
  a. *SR*, 74 (Summer 1966), 592.
  b. As X. *SPNO*, p. 18.
  c. *SP75*, pp. 161–162.

*

C225 "Saul."
  a. *YR*, 55 (Summer 1966), 481–487.
  b. As II, "Saul at Gilboa." *SPNO*, pp. 69–80.
  c. *SP75*, pp. 175–182.
  Note: from "Holy Writ" sequence
"Homage to Emerson, on Night Flight to New York" sequence
C226 "I. His Smile."
  a. *NY*, 16 July 1966, p. 30.
  b. *SPNO*, pp. 40–41.
  c. *SP75*, pp. 153–154.
C227 "II. The Wart."
  a. *SPNO*, p. 42.
  b. *SP75*, p. 154.
C228 "III. The Spider."
  a. As II. *NY*, 16 July 1966, p. 30.
  b. *SPNO*, p. 43.
  c. *SP75*, pp. 154–155.
C229 "IV. One Drunk Allegory."
  a. As III. *NY*, 16 July 1966, p. 30.
  b. *SPNO*, pp. 44–45.
  c. *SP75*, 155–156.
C230 "V. Multiplication Table."
  a. As IV. *NY*, 16 July 1966, pp. 30–31.
  b. *SPNO*, p. 46.
  c. *SP75*, pp. 156–157.
C231 "VI. Wind."
  a. As V. *NY*, 16 July 1966, p. 31.
  b. *SPNO*, p. 47.
  c. *SP75*, p. 157.
C232 "VII. Does the Wild Rose?"
  a. As VI. *NY*, 16 July 1966, p. 31.
  b. *SPNO*, pp. 48–49.
  c. *SP75*, p. 158.

*

"Delight" sequence; "Love: Two Vignettes" subsequence

C233 "1. Mediterranean Beach, Day after Storm."
　　a. *SatR*, 13 Aug. 1966, p. 21.
　　b. As II.1. *SPNO*, p. 82.
　　c. *SP75*, p. 184.
C234 "2. Deciduous Spring."
　　a. *SatR*, 13 Aug. 1966, p. 21.
　　b. As II.2. *SPNO*, p. 83.
　　c. *SP75*, pp. 184–185.

+

C235 "Dream of a Dream the Small Boy Had."
　　a. *SatR*, 13 Aug. 1966, p. 21.
　　b. As IV. *SPNO*, p. 86.
　"Two Poems about Suddenly and a Rose" subsequence
C236 "1. Dawn."
　　a. *SatR*, 13 Aug. 1966, p. 21.
　　b. As V.1. *SPNO*, pp. 87–88.
　　c. *SP75*, pp. 186–187.
C237 "2. Intuition."
　　a. *SatR*, 13 Aug. 1966, p. 21.
　　b. As V.2. *SPNO*, p. 89.
　　c. *SP75*, p. 187.

*

"The Day Mr. Knox Did It" sequence

C238 "I. Place and Time."
　　a. As 1. *Encounter*, 27 (Sept. 1966), 22.
　　b. *SPNO*, pp. 58–59.
　　c. *SP75*, pp. 167–168.
C239 "II. The Event."
　　a. As 2. *Encounter*, 27 (Sept. 1966), 22.
　　b. *SPNO*, p. 60.
　　c. *SP75*, pp. 168–169.
C240 "III. A Confederate Veteran Tries to Explain the Event."
　　a. As 3. *Encounter*, 27 (Sept. 1966), 23.
　　b. *SPNO*, pp. 61–62.
　　c. *SP75*, pp. 169–170.
C241 "IV. The Place Where the Boy Pointed."
　　a. As 4. *Encounter*, 27 (Sept. 1966), 23.
　　b. *SPNO*, p. 63.
　　c. *SP75*, p. 171.
C242 "V. And All That Came Thereafter."
　　a. As 5. *Encounter*, 27 (Sept. 1966), 24.

b. *SPNO*, pp. 64–66.

c. *SP75*, pp. 171–173.

*

C243 "II. Small White House."
  a. *SPNO*, p. 4.
  b. As VIII. *OEP*, p. 34.
  c. *SatR*, 19 Oct. 1974, p. 30.
  d. As VIII. *SP75*, p. 41.
  Note: from "Notes on a Life to Be Lived" sequence

C244 "Myth on Mediterranean Beach."
  a. *SatR*, 25 Feb. 1967, p. 38.
  b. As "Myth on Mediterranean Beach: Aphrodite as Logos." *I*, pp. 12–16.
  c. *SP75*, pp. 109–112.

C245 "Fairy Story." *NY*, 18 March 1967, p. 123.

C246 "Mistral at Night on Summer Island: For Allan Swallow."
  a. *UDQ*, 2 (Spring 1967), 32.
  b. As "Mistral at Night." *Encounter*, 30 (Jan. 1968), 13.
  c. As 9, titled as **b** above. *I*, p. 17.
  Note: from "Island of Summer" sequence.

C247 "Where the Slow Fig."
  a. *NY*, 10 June 1967, p. 145.
  b. *I*, p. 4.
  c. As "Where the Slow Fig's Purple Sloth." *SP75*, p. 104.
        "Whiteness of Fog on Wintry Mountains" sequence
  Note: As "2. Fog" in the sequence "In the Mountains" in *I*.

C248 "(a) White, white, luminous but."
  a. *Reporter*, 21 Sept. 1967, p. 49.
  b. As [A]. *I*, p. 62.
  c. As "Fog" [1]. *SP75*, p. 137.

C249 "(b) Heart—Oh, contextless—how."
  a. *Reporter*, 21 Sept. 1967, p. 49.
  b. As [B]. *I*, p. 63.
  c. As "Fog" [2]. *SP75*, pp. 137–138.

C250 "(c) At fog-height, unseen."
  a. *Reporter*, 21 Sept. 1967, p. 49.
  b. As [C]. *I*, p. 64.
  c. As "Fog" [3]. *SP75*, p. 138.

*

"Ile de Port Cros: What Happened" sequence
Note: As "Island of Summer" sequence in *I*.

C251 "1. What Day Is."
  a. *Encounter*, 29 (Oct. 1967), 3.
  b. *I*, p. 3.
  c. *SP75*, p. 103.
C252 "2. Natural History."
  a. *Encounter*, 29 (Oct. 1967), 3.
  b. As 3. *I*, pp. 5–6.
  c. As "Natural History I." *SP75*, pp. 105–106.
C253 "3. The Poet Paul Valéry Walked Here and Confronted the Fierce Energies of the World."
  a. *Encounter*, 29 (Oct. 1967), 4.
  b. As "5. Paul Valéry Stood on the Cliff and Confronted the Furious Energies of Nature." *I*, pp. 8–9.
  c. As **b** above. *SP75*, pp. 107–108.
C254 "4. Moonrise."
  a. *Encounter*, 29 (Oct. 1967), 4.
  b. As 7. *I*, p. 11.
  Note: rpt. in "A Poet Probes the Fragility of Relevance," Washington *Post*, 6 Dec. 1970, p. C-3.
C255 "5. A Place Where Nothing Is."
  a. *Encounter*, 29 (Oct. 1967), 4.
  b. As 13. *I*, p. 21.
  c. As 11. *SP75*, pp. 114–115.
C256 "6. Masts at Dawn."
  a. *Encounter*, 29 (Oct. 1967), 5.
  b. As 14. *I*, pp. 22–23.
  c. *QJLC*, 27 (April 1970), [137]–138.
  d. As 12. *SP75*, pp. 115–116.

*

  "Thoughts in Ruined Garden on Summer Isle" sequence
  Note: as "Island of Summer" sequence in *I*.
C257 "1. Riddle in the Garden."
  a. *Encounter*, 30 (Jan. 1968), 13.
  b. As 4. *I*, p. 7.
  c. *SP75*, pp. 106–107.
  Note: rpt. in "A Poet Probes the Fragility of Relevance," Washington *Post*, 6 Dec. 1970, p. C-3.
  "2. Mistral at Night" appears earlier in **C246**.
C258 "3. Where Purples Now the Fig."
  a. *Encounter*, 30 (Jan. 1968), 13.
  b. As 11. *I*, p. 19.

    c. As 9. *SP75*, p. 113.

C259 "4. The Ivy."

    a. *Encounter*, 30 (Jan. 1968), 13.

    b. As 10. *I*, p. 18.

    c. As 8. *SP75*, p. 112.

C260 "5. The Red Mullet."

    a. *Encounter*, 30 (Jan. 1968), 14.

    b. As 12. *I*, p. 20.

    c. As 10. *SP75*, pp. 113–114.

"6. The Leaf" subsequence

C261 "(a) Here the fig lets down the leaf, the leaf."

    a. *Encounter*, 30 (Jan. 1968), 14.

    b. As 15[A]. *I*, p. 24.

    c. As 13[A]. *SP75*, p. 116.

C262 "(b) We have undergone ourselves, therefore."

    a. *Encounter*, 30 (Jan. 1968), 14–15.

    b. As 15[B]. *I*, pp. 25–26.

    c. As 13[B]. *SP75*, p. 117.

C263 "(c) The world is fruitful. In this heat."

    a. *Encounter*, 30 (Jan. 1968), 15.

    b. As 15[C]. *I*, p. 27.

    c. As 13[C]. *SP75*, pp. 117–118.

C264 "(d) The voice blesses me for the only."

    a. *Encounter*, 30 (Jan. 1968), 15.

    b. As 15[D]. *I*, p. 28.

    c. As 13[D]. *SP75*, p. 118.

*

"Internal Injuries" sequence

C265 "1 *Nigger*: as if it were not."

    a. *Harper's*, June 1968, p. 56.

    b. As "1. The Event." *I*, pp. 43–44.

    c. *SP75*, pp. 127–128.

C266 "2 The scream comes as regular."

    a. *Harper's*, June 1968, p. 56.

    b. As "2. The Scream." *I*, p. 45.

    c. *SP75*, pp. 128–129.

C267 "3 They are tearing down Penn Station."

    a. *Harper's*, June 1968, p. 56.

    b. As "3. Her Hat." *I*, pp. 46–47.

    c. *SP75*, pp. 129–130.

C268 "4 The only trouble was, you got up."

a. *Harper's*, June 1968, p. 57.
b. As "4. The Only Trouble." *I*, p. 48.
c. *SP75*, pp. 130–131.
C269 "5 One cop holds the spik delicately between thumb and forefinger."
a. *Harper's*, June 1968, p. 57.
b. As "5. The Jet Must Be Hunting for Something." *I*, pp. 49–50.
c. *SP75*, pp. 131–132.
C270 "6 Be something else be something."
a. *Harper's*, June 1968, p. 57.
b. As "6. Be Something Else." *I*, p. 51.
c. *SP75*, pp. 132–133.
C271 "7 I must hurry, I must go somewhere."
a. *Harper's*, June 1968, p. 58.
b. As "7. The World Is a Parable." *I*, p. 52.
c. *SP75*, pp. 133–134.
C272 "8 Driver, driver, hurry now——"
a. *Harper's*, June 1968, p. 58.
b. As "8. Driver Driver." *I*, pp. 53–54.
c. *SP75*, pp. 134–135.

*

"Penological Study: Southern Exposure" sequence
C273 "1. Keep That Morphine Moving, Cap."
a. *NYRB*, 12 Sept. 1968, p. 32.
b. *I*, pp. 31–32.
c. As II.1. *SP75*, pp. 119–120.
C274 "2. Night Waiting in the Cheap Motel."
a. *NYRB*, 12 Sept. 1968, p. 32.
b. As "4. Night: The Motel Down the Road from the Pen." *I*, p. 36.
c. As II.4. *SP75*, pp. 122–123.
C276 "3. Where They Come to Wait for the Body."
a. *NYRB*, 12 Sept. 1968, p. 33.
b. As "5. [added to title] A Ghost Story." *I*, pp. 37–38.
c. As II.5. *SP75*, pp. 123–124.
C276 "4. Night Is Personal."
a. *NYRB*, 12 Sept. 1968, p. 33.
b. As "6." *I*, pp. 39–41.
c. As II.6. *SP75*, pp. 125–126.
C277 "5. Dawn."
a. *NYRB*, 12 Sept. 1968, p. 33.

b. As "7." *I*, p. 42.

c. As II.7. *SP75*, pp. 126–127.

*

"A Faring" sequence

Note: from "Enclaves" sequence in *I* with heading "The True Nature of Time."

C278 "(a) Once over the water, to you borne brightly."

a. *YR*, 58 (Autumn 1968), 74–75.

b. As "1. The Faring." *I*, pp. 57–58.

c. As XIII.1. *OEP*, pp. 59–60.

d. As XIII.1. *SP75*, pp. 57–58.

C279 "(b) Out of the silence, the saying, into."

a. *YR*, 58 (Autumn 1968), 75.

b. As "2. The Enclave." *I*, p. 59.

c. As XIII.2. *OEP*, p. 61.

d. As XIII.2. *SP75*, pp. 58–59.

*

C280 "6. Treasure Hunt."

a. *I*, p. 10.

b. *SP75*, pp. 108–109.

Note: from "Island of Summer" sequence.

"Penological Study: Southern Exposure" sequence

C281 "2. Tomorrow Morning."

a. *I*, p. 33.

b. As II.2. *SP75*, pp. 120–121.

C282 "3. Wet Hair: If Now His Mother Should Come."

a. *I*, pp. 34–35.

b. As II.3. *SP75*, pp. 121–122.

*

C283 "1. Skiers."

a. *I*, p. 61.

b. *SP75*, p. 136.

Note: from "In the Mountains" sequence. Rpt. in "A Poet Probes the Fragility of Relevance," Washington *Post*, 6 Dec. 1970, p. C-3.

C284 "Bad Year, Bad War: New Year's Card."

a. *NYRB*, 13 March 1969, p. 27.

b. *Sense and Sensibility in Twentieth-Century Writing: A Gathering in Memory of William Van O'Connor*. Ed. Brom Weber. Crosscurrents / Modern Critiques. Carbondale: Southern Illinois University Press, 1970. Pp. 153–154.

c. As "Interjection #4: . . . 1969." *OEP*, pp. 35–36.

d. *SP75*, pp. 42–43.

"II. The Dream He Never Knew the End Of" sequence

C285 "[A] Shank-end of day, spit of snow, the call."

a. As 1. *Harper's*, Aug. 1969, p. 73.

b. *A*, p. 5.

c. *SP75*, pp. 86–87.

C286 "[B] What should he recognize? The Nameless face."

a. As 2. *Harper's*, Aug. 1969, p. 73.

b. *A*, p. 6.

c. *SP75*, p. 87.

C287 "[C] The face, in the air, hangs. Large."

a. As 3. *Harper's*, Aug. 1969, p. 74.

b. *A*, p. 7.

c. *SP75*, p. 87.

C288 "[D] The Indian."

a. As 4. *Harper's*, Aug. 1969, p. 74.

b. *A*, pp. 8–9.

c. *SP75*, p. 88.

C289 "[E] The sons come in from the night, two, and are."

a. As 5. *Harper's*, Aug. 1969, p. 74.

b. *A*, p. 10.

c. *SP75*, p. 89.

C290 "[F] With no sound, she rises. She holds it in her hand."

a. As 6. *Harper's*, Aug. 1969, p. 74.

b. *A*, p. 11.

c. *SP75*, pp. 89–90.

C291 "[G] But no scream now, and under his hand."

a. As 7. *Harper's*, Aug. 1969, p. 74.

b. *A*, p. 12.

c. *SP75*, p. 90.

C292 "[H] The door bursts open, and the travelers enter."

a. As 8. *Harper's*, Aug. 1969, p. 75.

b. *A*, p. 13.

c. *SP75*, p. 90.

C293 "[I] Trussed up with thongs, all night they lie on the floor there."

a. As 9. *Harper's*, Aug. 1969, p. 75.

b. *A*, p. 14.

c. *SP75*, pp. 90–91.

C294 "[J] They stand there under the long, low bough of the great oak."

    a. As 10. *Harper's*, Aug. 1969, p. 75.

    b. *A*, p. 15.

    c. *SP75*, pp. 91–92.

C295 "[K] The affair was not tidy: bough low, no drop, with the clients."

    a. As 11. *Harper's*, Aug. 1969, p. 75.

    b. *A*, p. 16.

    c. *SP75*, p. 92.

C296 "[L] There are tears in his eyes."

    a. As 12. *Harper's*, Aug. 1969, p. 75.

    b. *A*, p. 17.

    c. *SP75*, p. 92.

C297 "[M] And so stood alone, for the travelers."

    a. As 13. *Harper's*, Aug. 1969, p. 75.

    b. *A*, p. 18.

    c. *SP75*, pp. 92–93.

*

"Audubon: A Vision and a Question for You" sequence

C298 "I Was not the lost dauphin, though handsome was only."

    a. *NY*, 20 Sept. 1969, p. 42.

    b. As I [A]. *A*, p. 3.

    c. *SP75*, p. 85.

    Note: from "Was Not the Lost Dauphin" sequence in *A*.

"The Sign Whereby He Knew" subsequence

C299 "II (a) His life, at the end, seemed—even the anguish—simple."

    a. *NY*, 20 Sept. 1969, p. 42.

    b. As IV [A]. *A*, p. 20.

    c. *SP75*, p. 94.

C300 "II (b) Keep store, dandle babies, and at night nuzzle."

    a. *NY*, 20 Sept. 1969, p. 42.

    b. As IV [C]. *A*, p. 22.

    c. *SP75*, p. 95.

C301 "II (c) The world declares itself. That voice."

    a. *NY*, 20 Sept. 1969, p. 42.

    b. As IV [E]. *A*, p. 24.

    c. *SP75*, pp. 95–96.

+

"The Sound of That Wind" subsequence

C302 "III (a) He walked in the world. Knew the lust of the eye."
   a. *NY*, 20 Sept. 1969, pp. 42–43.
   b. As V [A]. *A*, pp. 25–27.
   c. *SP75*, pp. 96–98.
C303 "III (b) So died in his bed, and."
   a. *NY*, 20 Sept. 1969, p. 43.
   b. As V [B]. *A*, p. 28.
   c. *SP75*, p. 98.

+

C304 "IV Their footless dance."
   a. *NY*, 20 Sept. 1969, p. 43.
   b. As "VI. Love and Knowledge." *A*, p. 30.
   c. *SP75*, p. 99.
C305 "V Tell me a story."
   a. *NY*, 20 Sept. 1969, p. 43.
   b. As VII [B]. *A*, p. 32.
   c. *SP75*, p. 100.
   Note: from "Tell Me a Story" sequence in *A*.

*

"Lyrics from Audubon: A Vision" sequence

C306 "October: and the bear."
   a. *YR*, 59 (Autumn 1969), 1.
   b. As I [B]. *A*, p. 4.
   c. *SP75*, pp. 85–86.
   Note: from "Was Not the Lost Dauphin" sequence
      "The Sign Whereby He Knew" subsequence
C307 "In this season the waters shrink."
   a. *YR*, 59 (Autumn 1969), 1.
   b. As IV [B]. *A*, p. 21.
   c. *SP75*, p. 94.
C308 "Listen! Stand very still and."
   a. *YR*, 59 (Autumn 1969), 2.
   b. As IV [D]. *A*, p. 23.
   c. *SP75*, p. 95.

+

C309 "For everything there is a season."
   a. *YR*, 59 (Autumn 1969), 2.
   b. As V [C]. *A*, p. 29.
   c. *SP75*, pp. 98–99.

*

C310 "What You Sometimes Feel on Your Face at Night."

Note: copyright 14 Dec. 1970 (BB38761).
a. *Lit: The Yale Literary Magazine*, Nov. 1970, p. [35].
b. As "Interjection #6." *OEP*, p. 66.
c. *SP75*, p. 61.

C311 "Long ago, in Kentucky, I, a boy, stood." *A*, p. 31.
Note: from "Tell Me a Story" sequence.

C312 "Folly on Royal Street Before the Raw Face of God."
a. *NYRB*, 7 Jan. 1971, p. 33.
b. As XXI. *OEP*, pp. 90–92.
c. As XX. *SP75*, pp. 73–75.

"Homage to Theodore Dreiser: On the Centennial of His
Birth: Portrait" sequence

C313 "I. Psychological Profile."
a. *NYRB*, 12 Aug. 1971, p. 23.
b. *HTD*, pp. 3–4.
c. As XI.1. *OEP*, pp. 49–50.
d. *SP75*, pp. 51–52.

C314 "II. Vital Statistics."
a. As (a) and (b). *NYRB*, 12 Aug. 1971, p. 23.
b. *HTD*, pp. 5–7.
c. As XI.2 [A] and [B]. *OEP*, pp. 51–53.
d. As XI.2. *SP75*, pp. 52–54.

C315 "III. Moral Assessment."
a. *NYRB*, 12 Aug. 1971, p. 23.
b. *HTD*, p. 8.
c. As XI.3. *OEP*, p. 54.
d. *SP75*, p. 54.

*

C316 "Address of Soul to Body (On the Occasion of a Birthday
Party)."
a. *NY*, 11 Sept. 1971, p. 46.
b. As "Interjection #7: Remarks . . . ." *OEP*, pp. 78–79.
c. *SP75*, pp. 64–65.

C317 "Solipsism and Theology."
a. *NY*, 29 Jan. 1972, p. 44.
b. As "Interjection #5." *OEP*, p. 58.
c. *SP75*, p. 57.

C318 "Natural History."
a. *NY*, 1 April 1972, p. 38.
b. As II. *OEP*, pp. 5–6.
c. *SP75*, p. 22.

C319 "Time as Hypnosis."
  a. In *I. A. Richards: Essays in His Honor*. Ed. Reuben Brower, Helen Vendler, and John Hollander. New York: Oxford University Press, 1973. Pp. 3–4.
  b. As III. *OEP*, pp. 7–9.
  c. *SP75*, pp. 23–24.
C320 "The Nature of a Mirror."
  a. *Salmagundi* (Skidmore College, Saratoga, NY), nos. 22–23 (Spring–Summer 1973), pp. 24–25.
  b. As I. *OEP*, p. 3.
  c. *SP75*, p. 21.
C321 "Caveat."
  a. *Sou'wester* (University of Southern Illinois), NS 2 (Fall 1973), 62–63.
  b. As "Interjection #2." *OEP*, pp. 11–12.
  c. *SP75*, pp. 25–26.
C322 "The Natural History of a Vision."
  a. *Atlantic Monthly*, Dec. 1973, pp. 84–90.
  b. As "V. I Am Dreaming of a White Christmas: The Natural History of a Vision [1]–[12]." *OEP*, pp. 13–22.
  c. *SP75*, pp. 26–34.
  Note: reportedly reprinted in *Intellectual Digest*.
C323 "Rattlesnake Country."
  a. *Esquire*, Dec. 1973, pp. 206–209.
  b. As X.1–5. *OEP*, pp. 40–48.
  c. *SP75*, pp. 45–50.
C324 "Ballad of Mr. Dutcher and the Last Lynching in Gupton."
  a. *NYRB*, 24 Jan. 1974, p. 35.
  b. As VI. *OEP*, pp. 25–29.
  c. *SP75*, pp. 35–39.
  Note: title on MS is "Ballad of Mr. Crutcher and the Last Lynching in Guthrie."
C325 "Flaubert in Egypt."
  a. *NYRB*, 8 Aug. 1974, p. 25.
  b. As XII. *OEP*, pp. 55–57.
  c. *SP75*, pp. 55–56.
C326 "Reading Late at Night, Thermometer Falling."
  a. *NY*, 11 March 1974, pp. 34–35.
  b. As XX.[1]–[8]. *OEP*, pp. 82–89.
  c. As XIX. *SP75*, pp. 67–72.
C327 "News Photo."

a. *Atlantic Monthly*, June 1974, pp. 72–75.

b. As XVI.[1]–[5]. *OEP*, pp. 67–73.

Note: title on MS is "News Photo of Man Coming Down Steps of Court House after Acquittal."

C328 "Forever O'Clock."

a. As I. *YR*, 63 (Summer 1974), 545–547.

b. As IX.[1]–[3]. *OEP*, pp. 37–39.

c. *SP75*, pp. 43–45.

C329 "There's a Grandfather's Clock in the Hall."

a. As II. *YR*, 63 (Summer 1974), 548–549.

b. As XIX. *OEP*, pp. 80–81.

c. As XVIII. *SP75*, pp. 65–66.

C330 "Sunset Walk in Thaw-Time in Vermont."

a. *SoR*, NS 10 (Summer 1974), 590–592.

b. As XXII.1–4. *OEP*, pp. 94–97.

c. As XXI. *SP75*, pp. 76–78.

C331 "Birth of Love."

a. *NY*, 22 July 1974, p. 36.

b. As XXIII. *OEP*, pp. 98–100.

c. As XXII. *SP75*, pp. 78–80.

C332 "The Need for Re-evaluation."

a. As "Interjection #1." *OEP*, p. 4.

b. *SP75*, p. 21.

C333 "I Know a Place Where All Is Real."

a. As "Interjection #3." *OEP*, pp. 23–24.

b. In *Teacher & Critic: Essays by and about Austin Warren*. Ed. Myron Simon and Harvey Gross. Los Angeles: Plantin Press, 1976. P. 98.

c. *SP75*, pp. 34–35.

C334 "Or, Sometimes, Night."

a. As "Interjection #8." *OEP*, p. 93.

b. *SP75*, p. 75.

C335 "Answer to Prayer: A Short Story That Could Be Longer."

a. *VQR*, 51 (Spring 1975), 240–242.

b. *TLS*, 28 March 1975, p. 337.

c. *SP75*, pp. 6–8.

C336 "A Problem in Spatial Composition."

a. *Harper's*, April 1975, p. 24.

b. As XXIV.[1]–[3]. *OEP*, pp. 101–102.

c. As XXIII. *SP75*, pp. 80–81.

C337 "One Way to Love God."

a. *YR*, 65 (Autumn 1975), 71–72.

b. *TLS*, 20 Feb. 1976, p. 199.

c. As "A Way to Love God." *SP75*, pp. 3–4.

C338 "Loss, of Perhaps Love, in Our World of Contingency."

a. *NY*, 8 Sept. 1975, p. 34.

b. *SP75*, pp. 5–6.

C339 "Paradox."

a. *NYRB*, 16 Oct. 1975, p. 35.

b. *SP75*, p. 8.

"Two Night Poems" sequence

C340 "I. Evening Hawk."

a. *Atlantic Monthly*, Nov. 1975, p. 54.

b. *SP75*, pp. 4–5.

C341 "II. Midnight Outcry."

a. *Atlantic Monthly*, Nov. 1975, p. 55.

b. *SP75*, p. 9.

*

C342 "Old Nigger on One-Mule Cart Encountered Late at Night When Driving Home from Party in the Back Country."

a. *NY*, 8 Dec. 1975, pp. 46–47.

b. *SP75*, pp. 13–17.

C343 "Hunting Season Opens on Wild Boar in Chianti."

a. *TLS*, 26 Dec. 1975, p. 1530.

b. *SR*, 84 (Spring 1976), 300–301.

c. As "Season Opens . . . ." *SP75*, pp. 12–13.

"Can I See Arcturus from Where I Stand?"

Note: title of section of new poems in *SP75*.

C344 "Trying To Tell You Something."

a. *NY*, 5 Jan. 1976, p. 26.

b. *SP75*, pp. 10–11.

C345 "Brotherhood in Pain."

a. *American Review*. Not located.

b. *SP75*, pp. 11–12.

C346 "American Portrait: Old Style."

a. *NY*, 23 Aug. 1976, pp. 26–27.

b. *NT*, pp. 3–7.

C347 "Youth Stares at Minoan Sunset."

a. *NYRB*, 30 Sept. 1976, p. 15.

b. *NT*, pp. 25–26.

C348 "Sister Water."

a. *NYRB*, 14 Oct. 1976, p. 24.

b. *NT*, pp. 47–48.

C349 "Bicentennial." *Esquire*, Dec. 1976, pp. 132–135, 200–201.

C350 "Waiting."

  a. *Atlantic Monthly*, Dec. 1976, p. 47.

  b. *NT*, pp. 39–40.

C351 "Dream of a Dream."

  Note: copyright 10 Nov. 1976 (A819091).

  a. Boston: G. K. Hall, 1976. Printed separately as a Christmas card.

  b. *SoR*, NS 13 (Winter 1977), 147–148.

  c. *NT*, pp. 30–31.

C352 "Mountain Plateau."

  a. *Ironwood 10*, 5, no. 2 (1977), 73. The "James Wright Special Issue."

  b. *NT*, p. 22.

C353 "A Few Axioms for a Young Man."

  a. *GaR*, 31 (Winter 1977), 785–787.

  b. *Two Poems*, pp. [6–11]. **A38**.

C354 "The Mission."

  a. *Ohio Review*, 18 (Winter 1977), 30–31.

  b. *NT*, pp. 41–42.

  Note: The "RPW Issue."

C355 "Departure."

  a. *Ohio Review*, 18 (Winter 1977), 31.

  b. *NT*, p. 72.

C356 "Amazing Grace in the Back Country."

  a. *Ohio Review*, 18 (Winter 1977), 32–34.

  b. *NT*, pp. 8–10.

C357 "Love at First Sight."

  a. *Ohio Review*, 18 (Winter 1977), 34.

  b. As "Love Recognized." *NT*, p. 52.

C358 "When the Tooth Cracks——Zing!"

  a. *Ohio Review*, 18 (Winter 1977), 35–36.

  b. *NT*, pp. 45–46.

C359 "Orphanage Boy (Octosyllables)."

  a. *NYRB*, 3 March 1977, p. 12.

  b. As "Orphanage Boy." *NT*, pp. 15–16.

C360 "First Dawn Light."

  a. *NY*, 4 April 1977, p. 38.

  b. *NT*, p. 32.

C361 "Little Black Heart of the Telephone."

a. *NY*, 23 May 1977, p. 34.
b. *NT*, pp. 55–56.
C362 "Red-Tail Hawk and Pyre of Youth."
a. *NY*, 18 July 1977, pp. 32–33.
b. *NT*, pp. 17–21.
Note: a Harvard Phi Beta Kappa poem.
"Three Poems in Time" sequence
C363 "I. Heart of Autumn."
a. *Atlantic Monthly*, Oct. 1977, p. 84.
b. *NT*, pp. 74–75.
C364 "II. Dream."
a. *Atlantic Monthly*, Oct. 1977. p. 85.
b. *NT*, p. 29.
C365 "III. Ah, Anima!"
a. *Atlantic Monthly*, Oct. 1977, p. 86.
b. *NT*, pp. 33–34.

*

C366 "Code Book Lost."
a. *SatR*, 29 Oct. 1977, p. 38.
b. *NT*, pp. 43–44.
C367 "Boy Wandering in Simms' Valley."
a. *SatR*, 29 Oct. 1977, p. 39.
b. *NT*, pp. 11–12.
C368 "Old Flame."
a. Winston-Salem, NC: Palaemon Press Limited, 1978. Palaemon Broadside No. Four; issued in 100 numbered and 26 lettered copies. *Copies*: JAG (no. E), RPW (nos. A and B).
b. *NT*, p. 13.
C369 "Somewhere."
a. *TLS*, 20 Jan. 1978, p. 64.
b. *SoR*, NS 14 (Spring 1978), 305–306.
C370 "Heart of the Backlog."
a. *NY*, 30 Jan. 1978, p. 34.
b. *NT*, pp. 63–65.
C371 "Not Quite Like a Top."
a. *NYRB*, 23 Feb. 1978, p. 36.
b. *NT*, pp. 37–38.
C372 "Waking to Tap of Hammer."
a. *YR*, 67 (Spring 1978), 418.
b. *NT*, p. 51.

C373 "Star Fall."
  a. *YR*, 67 (Spring 1978), 419.
  b. *NT*, pp. 23–24.
C374 "Inevitable Frontier."
  a. *NY*, 13 March 1978, p. 36.
  b. *NT*, pp. 61–62.
C375 "Diver."
  a. *SoR*, NS 14 (Spring 1978), 303.
  b. *NT*, p. 69.
C376 "Rather Like a Dream."
  a. *SoR*, NS 14 (Spring 1978), 304–305.
  b. *NT*, pp. 70–71.
C377 "An Argument for Prayer."
  a. *SoR*, NS 14 (Spring 1978), 306–309.
  b. As "Identity and Argument for Prayer." *NT*, pp. 66–68.
C378 "Heat Lightning."
  a. *TLS*, 5 May 1978, p. 491.
  b. *NT*, pp. 59–60.
C379 "Praise." *Atlantic Monthly*, June 1978, p. 45.
C380 "Last Laugh."
  a. *NY*, 12 June 1978, p. 34.
  b. *NT*, pp. 57–58.
C381 "Boyhood in Tobacco Country." *Antaeus*, 30/31 (Summer–Autumn 1978), 241.
C382 "Function of Blizzard." *Antaeus*, 30/31 (Summer–Autumn 1978), 242.
C383 "Evening Hour."
  a. *GaR*, 32 (Summer 1978), 282.
  b. *NT*, p. 14.
            "Love Poems about a Smile" sequence
C384 "How To Tell a Story."
  a. *Quest/78*, July–Aug. 1978, p. 80.
  b. As "How To Tell a Love Story." *NT*, p. 54.
C385 "The Smile."
  a. *Quest/78*, July–Aug. 1978, p. 80.
  b. *NT*, p. 53.
            *
C386 "Heat Wave Breaks." *NT*, p. 73.
C387 "Memory Forgotten." *NT*, pp. 49–50.
C388 "Unless." *NT*, pp. 35–36.
C389 "The Cross (A Theological Study)." *NY*, 2 Oct. 1978, p. 36.

C390 "Better than Counting Sheep." *NYRB*, 9 Nov. 1978, p. 27.

C391 "Why?" Winston-Salem, N.C.: Palaemon Press Limited, 14 Nov. 1978. Broadsheet. For Aaron Copland on the occasion of his 78th birthday; 50 sets numbered with Arabic numerals and 28 sets numbered with Roman numerals. *Copies*: JAG (no. v).

C392 "Truth-Seeker, Half-Naked, at Night, Running Down Beach South of San Francisco." *Atlantic Monthly*, Dec. 1978, pp. 64–65.

C393 "No Bird Does Call." *American Poetry Review*, 8 (Jan.–Feb. 1979), 3.

C394 "Tires on Wet Asphalt at Night." *American Poetry Review*, 8 (Jan.–Feb. 1979), 4.

C395 "Swimming in the Pacific." *American Poetry Review*, 8 (Jan.–Feb. 1979), 5.

C396 "Part of a Short Story." *GaR*, 33 (Spring 1979), 86–88.

C397 "Weather Report." *New England Review*, 1 (Spring 1979), 262.

C398 "Snowshoeing Back to Camp in Gloaming." *New England Review*, 1 (Spring 1979), 263–264.

C399 "Timeless, Twinned." *New England Review*, 1 (Spring 1979), 265.

"Antinomy: Time and Identity" sequence

C400 "1. Alone, alone, I lie. The canoe floats in blackness." *YR*, 68 (Summer 1979), 540.

C401 "2. Do I hear stars speak in a whisper as gentle as breath." *YR*, 68 (Summer 1979), 540.

C402 "3. A dog, in the silence, is barking a county away." *YR*, 69 (Summer 1979), 540.

C403 "4. As consciousness outward seeps, the dark seeps on." *YR*, 68 (Summer 1979), 540.

C404 "5. It is not long till day" *YR*, 68 (Summer 1979), 540–541.

C405 "6. Dawn will burst . . . ." *YR*, 68 (Summer 1979), 541.

C406 "7. One crow, alone, ..." *YR*, 68 (Summer 1979), 541.

*

C407 "Truth." *YR*, 68 (Summer 1979), 541–542.

C408 "What Is the Voice That Speaks?" *YR*, 68 (Summer 1979), 542–543.

C409 "Lessons of History." *American Poetry Review*, 8 (July–Aug. 1979), 5.

C410 "The Only Poem." *American Poetry Review*, 8 (July–Aug. 1979), 5.

C411 "Night Walking." *American Poetry Review*, 8 (July–Aug. 1979), 48.

C412 "Trips to California." *NYRB*, 19 July 1979, p. 24.

C413 "Vision." Washington *Post Book World*, 12 Aug. 1979, p. 1.
Note: not to be confused with **C2**.

C414 "Dreaming in Daylight." *Salmagundi*, no. 46 (Fall 1979), pp. 4–5.

C415 "Prairie Harvest." *Salmagundi*, no. 46 (Fall 1979), p. 6.

C416 "Globe of Gneiss." *Salmagundi*, no. 46 (Fall 1979), pp. 6–7.

C417 "When Life Begins." *Salmagundi*, no. 46 (Fall, 1979), pp. 8–9.

C418 "Grackles, Goodbye!" *Salmagundi*, no. 46 (Fall 1979), p. 9.

C419 "Filling Night with the Name." *Salmagundi*, no. 46 (Fall 1979), p. 10.

C420 "On Into the Night." *Salmagundi*, no. 46 (Fall 1979), pp. 11–12.

C421 "Preternaturally Early Snowfall in Mating Season." *NY*, 10 Sept. 1979, p. 46.

C422 "Acquaintance with Time in Autumn." *NY*, 10 Sept. 1979, pp. 46–47.

C423 "August Moon." *NY*, 10 Sept. 1979, p. 47.

C424 "Speleology." *NY*, 10 Sept. 1979, p. 47.

C425 "October Picnic Long Ago." *Atlantic Monthly*, Oct. 1979, p. 79.

C426 "Aging Man at Noon in Timeless Noon of Summer." *SoR*, NS 15 (Autumn 1979), 996.

C427 "Language Problem." *SoR*, NS 15 (Autumn 1979), 997.

"Synonyms" sequence

C428 "(1) Where eons back earth slipped and cracked." *Poetry*, 135 (Nov. 1979), 76.

C429 "(2) After last thrust knows the hour past song." *Poetry*, 135 (Nov. 1979), 76.

C430 "(3) Lean back, one hand on saddle-horn if you must." *Poetry*, 135 (Nov. 1979), 77.

C431 "(4) Have you—scarcely more than a boy—been." *Poetry*, 135 (Nov. 1979), 77.

C432 "(5) Riding in riot and roil of Aegean blue and gold light." *Poetry*, 135 (Nov. 1979), 78.

C433 "(6) In the narrow, decrepit old street where day-gleam." *Poetry*, 135 (Nov. 1979), 78–80.

C434 "(7) There are many things in the world and I have seen some." *Poetry*, 135 (Nov. 1979), 80.

*

C435 "The Moonlight's Dream." *Poetry*, 135 (Nov. 1979), 81–82.

C436 "Aspen Leaf in Windless World." *Poetry*, 135 (Nov. 1979), 83–84.

C437 "Lord Jesus, I Wonder." *Two Poems*, pp. [3–5]. **A38**.

C438 "Auto-da-Fé." *NY*, 31 Dec. 1979, p. 28.

C439 "Eagle Descending." *Vanderbilt Poetry Review*, 4, nos. 1–2 (1979), 29.

D

Short Fiction

Note: Although most of RPW's short fiction relates in some way to his longer fiction, his later "short stories" are excerpts—advance releases—of his novels. Consequently, only those pieces written as short fiction are listed in this section. Excerpts are identified in the notes under the appropriate entries in section **A**.

D1 "Prime Leaf."
  a. *American Caravan IV*. Ed. Alfred Kreymborg, Lewis Mumford, and Paul Rosenfeld. New York: Macaulay Company, 1931. Pp. 3–61.
  b. *CA*, pp. 211–276.
D2 "Unvexed Isles."
  a. *The Magazine*, 2 (July–Aug. 1934), 1–10; rpt., New York: Kraus Reprint Corporation, 1967.
  b. *CA*, pp. 199–210.
  c. *Perspectives USA*, no. 13 (Autumn 1955), pp. 27–37.
D3 "Testament of Flood."
  a. *The Magazine*, 2 (March–April 1935), 230–234.
  b. *CA*, pp. 163–169.
D4 "Her Own People."
  Note: copyright 15 March 1935 (B255230); renewed 20 Nov. 1962 (R305056).
  a. *VQR*, 11 (April 1935), 289–304.
  b. *Horizon*, 14 (Oct. 1946), 240–252.
  c. *CA*, pp. 175–189.
D5 "When the Light Gets Green."
  Note: copyright 7 April 1936 (B297383); renewed 27 June 1963 (R317677).
  a. *SoR*, 1 (Spring 1936), 799–806.
  b. *CA*, pp. 88–95.
  Note: honorable mention, Edward J. O'Brien Short Story Collection for 1937.

D6 "Christmas Gift."

Note: copyright 15 Dec. 1936 (B320802); renewed 3 March 1964 (R333639).

  a. *VQR*, 13 (Winter 1937), 73–85.

  b. *CA*, pp. 96–107.

  c. *The Dude*, 2 (Jan. 1958), 61–66.

    Note: in the O. Henry Memorial Award Collection for 1937.

D7 "How Willie Proudfit Came Home."

  SoR, 4 (Autumn 1938), 299–321.

    Note: in the Edward J. O'Brien Best Short Story Collection for 1939.

D8 "Goodwood Comes Back."

Note: copyright 27 Dec. 1940 (B482965); renewed 5 July 1968 (R438844).

  a. *SoR*, 6 (Winter 1941), 526–536.

  b. *CA*, pp. 108–119.

D9 "The Life and Work of Professor Roy Millen."

Note: copyright 29 Jan. 1943 (B576788); renewed 28 Aug. 1970 (R490408).

  a. *Mademoiselle*, Feb. 1943, pp. 88, 145–149.

  b. *CA*, pp. 190–198.

D10 "A Christian Education."

Note: copyright 29 Dec. 1944 (B658651); renewed 24 Jan. 1972 (R521908).

  a. *Mademoiselle*, Jan. 1945, pp. 96–97, 155–157.

  b. *New English Review*, 12 (May 1946), 434–439.

  c. *CA*, pp. 134–142.

D11 "The Love of Elsie Barton: A Chronicle."

Note: copyright 29 Jan. 1946 (B7770); renewed 22 Aug. 1973 (R557576).

  a. *Mademoiselle*, Feb. 1946, pp. 161, 282–290.

  b. *CA*, pp. 143–162.

D12 "The Confession of Brother Grimes."

  a. *New English Review*, 12 (June 1946), 561–563.

  b. *Cronos*, 1 (Fall 1947), 29–30.

  c. *CA*, pp. 170–174.

D13 "Blackberry Winter."

  a. Cummington, MA: Cummington Press, 1946. **A8**.

  b. *CA*, pp. 63–87.

D14 "The Patented Gate and the Mean Hamburger."

Note: copyright 31 Dec. 1946 (B58400); renewed 26 July 1974 (R582271).

a. *Mademoiselle*, Jan. 1947, pp. 188–189, 242–243, 245–246.

b. *New English Review*, 13 (Aug. 1946), 148–157.

c. *CA*, pp. 120–133.

D15 "The Circus in the Attic."

Note: copyright 29 Aug. 1947 (B95273); renewed 23 Sept. 1974 (R585909).

a. *Cosmopolitan*, Sept. 1947, pp. 67–70, 73–74, 76, 78, 80, 83–84, 86, 88.

b. *CA*, pp. 3–62.

D16 "Invitation to a Dance."

Today's Woman, Feb. 1949, pp. 45, 88.

E

Drama and Cinema

E1 "Proud Flesh."
a. An unpublished play, 1939. First presented 28 April–4 May
1947, University Theater, University of Minnesota, directed by
Frank Whiting.
b. Program (Ctb) of 1947 presentation mentions a radio adaptation
by Ruth Swanson and Betty Girling for KUOM, 3 May 1947,
6:30–7:30 P.M., with original cast.
Notes: 1. Excerpt, "From *Proud Flesh*." *Modern American Poetry*.
Ed. B. Rajan. *Focus* Five. London: Dennis Dobson, 1950. Pp.
163–167.
2. Kuehl, John, ed. *Creative Writing and Rewriting: Contemporary
American Novelists at Work*. New York: Appleton-Century-Crofts,
1967. Pp. 234–263. Includes verse drama into novel, a comparison
of "Proud Flesh" and *AKM*: III.iii—chapter 9, III.iv—chapter 10,
and I.ii—chapter 6.

E2 *All the King's Men.*
Screen play by Robert Rossen. Columbia Pictures Corporation,
1949. Copyright 5 Jan. 1950. Cast: *Willie*, Broderick Crawford; *Jack
Burden*, John Ireland; *Anne*, Joanne Dru; *Sadie*, Mercedes Mc-
Cambridge; *Adam*, Shepperd Strudwick; *Tiny*, Ralph Dumke; *Tom
Stark*, John Derek; *Sugar Boy*, Walter Burke; *Lucy*, Anne Seymour;
Judge Irwin, Raymond Greenleaf; *Mrs. Burden*, Katherine Warren.
Rereleased by Screen Gems, 1954.
Reviews: "*AKM*: The Prize Novel about a Demagog Makes Year's
Most Exciting Movie." *Life*, 28 Nov. 1949, pp. 111–112, 114,
116–117, 121.
Time, 5 Dec. 1949, pp. 102, 105–106.
Look, 20 Dec. 1949, pp. 114–116.
NY *Tribune*, 28 Dec. 1949, p. 19.
Notes: 1. Rossen received the Look Achievement Award for the
best screen writing of 1949. RPW was consulted as technical ad-

viser about the film and script. The film won an Academy Award for best picture.

2. Casty, Alan. "The Films of Robert Rossen." *Film Quarterly*, 20 (Winter 1966–67), 3–12. RPW ltr., p. 9, praises the movie since the novel provided only the raw material.

3. Rossen, Stephen, ed. *Three Screenplays: "All the King's Men," "The Hustler," "Lilith" by Robert Rossen.* Anchor Octavo Original, AO 34. New York: Doubleday, 1972.

4. A *Teaching Manual* is available with the rental film in the *Literature & Film* program from Audio Brandon Films.

E3 "The Wedding Ring."
An unpublished play, copyright 24 July 1951; revised and copyrighted 27 Dec. 1955; version "D" dated 1 June 1959 and titled "Listen to the Mockingbird: A Drama of the American Civil War" (Ctw).

E4 "This Very Spot."
A dramatic television series (not produced) written with David M. Clay; copyright 15 Dec. 1952. *See* **B20.**

E5 "Willie Stark: His Rise and Fall: A Play in Three Acts."
a. An unpublished play, copyright 17 Oct. 1955.
b. Premiered at the Margo Jones Theater, Dallas, TX, 25 Nov.–14 Dec. 1958.

E6 "Brother to Dragons."
a. An unpublished play when copyrighted 10 April 1957.
b. Presentations: 1955, British Broadcasting Company, a dramatic reading adapted from the poem; 11–12 March 1960, School of Speech, Northwestern University, directed by Charlotte I. Lee; 1964, American Place Theater, directed by Wynn Handman; 21 Nov.–21 Dec. 1968, Trinity Square Repertory Company, Providence, RI, directed by Adrian Hall; 1973, second revision, new Trinity Square Theater, directed by Adrian Hall; 1974, Wilbur Theater, Boston, directed by Adrian Hall.
c. Adapted for television by Adrian Hall and Ken Campbell for BFA Educational Media (56 min.); aired 19 Feb. 1975 on PBS. RPW has a cameo role as the writer's father.
Review: Edwin Wilson, "The Crime of Jefferson's Nephews," *Wall-Street Journal*, 19 Feb. 1975, p. 18.
d. "*BD*: A Play in Two Acts." *GaR*, 30 (Spring 1976), 65–138.

E7 *Band of Angels.*
Screenplay by John Twist. Warner Brothers Pictures, 1957. Copy-

right 3 Aug. 1957. Cast: *Amantha Starr*, Yvonne DeCarlo; *Hamish Bond*, Clark Gable.

E8 *All the King's Men* (play).

a. *SR*, 68 (Spring 1960), 177–239.

b. New York: Random House, 1960. **A21.a1.**

c. New York: Dramatists Play Service, 1960. **A21.b1.**

d. Directed in an unpublished form by Erwin Piscator, 1947. (Ctw).

e. Produced off-Broadway, East 74th St. Theatre, New York, 16 Oct. 1959. Directed by Mark Schoenberg. Cast: *Willie*, Clifton James; *Jack Burden*, John Ragin; *Anne*, Joan Harvey; *Sadie*, Marion Reardon; *Adam*, Richard Kneeland; *Tiny*, Roger C. Carmel; *Tom*, Donald Quine; *Sugar Boy*, Will Corry; *Lucy*, Mary Van Fleet; *Judge Irwin*, Alex Reed.

Notices: Emory Lewis, "The Theatre: A Distinguished Week On and Off Broadway," *Cue*, 31 Oct. 1959, p. 8; Frank Aston, "'King's Men' Packs Wallop," NY *World Telegraph and Sun*, Feature Magazine Section, 17 Oct. 1959, p. 5.

f. Other selected presentations include: 1947 University Theatre world premiere, University of Minnesota; 1–8 Feb. 1952, University of Oregon, directed by Horace W. Robinson; 22 Sept.–1 Oct. 1960, Circle Players at Nashville, TN, directed by Barbara Izard; 22 Feb.–2 March 1963, Department of Theater, University of Connecticut, Harriet S. Jorgensen Theater, directed by John W. Hallauer; 5–29 Oct. 1967, Actors Theater of Louisville, KY, directed by Richard Block.

g. Polish productions: *Ludzie Królestwa*, 26 Jan. 1962, directed by Jerzy Kaliszewski in Katowice; *Wielki Szefv (Willie Stark)*, 8 Feb. 1962, translated by Kazlmierz Piotrowski and Bronislaw Zieliński, directed by Marian Meller in Warsaw.

Note: Ctw has a mimeographed radio script of *AKM* (not by RPW, but author not specified), n.d.

E9 "Ballad of a Sweet Dream of Peace."

a. Presented at the Loeb Drama Center Experimental Theatre, 27–29 April 1961.

b. As "Ballad of a Sweet Dream of Peace: A Charade for Easter," with music by Alexei Haieff, *GaR*, 29 (Spring 1975), 5–36.

E10 "A Place to Come To."

Screenplay by Julian Barry and marked "First Draft / 13 June 1977" with the following note: "This is the original draft by Barry

with which Barry, Robert Redford, and I worked with the director
. . . . His [Barry's] new draft refused & another writer called in on
1 Nov. 1977. . . . 26 Nov. 1978." (Ctw).

F

Articles and Mimeographed Separates

F1 "The Briar Patch." *I'll Take My Stand: The South and the Agrarian Tradition*. By Twelve Southerners. New York: Harper & Brothers Publishers, 1930. Pp. 246–264. **B2**.

F2 "Paul Rosenfeld." *Jewish Journal*, 9 Sept. 1931, pp. 6, 24.

F3 "A Note on Three Southern Poets." *Poetry*, 40 (May 1932), 103–113. On Fletcher, Davidson, and Ransom.

F4 "T. S. Stribling: A Paragraph in the History of Critical Realism." *American Review*, 2 (Feb. 1934), 463–486.

F5 "John Crowe Ransom: A Study in Irony." *VQR*, 11 (Jan. 1935), 93–112.

F6 "A Note on the Hamlet of Thomas Wolfe."
a. *American Review*, 5 (May 1935), 191–208.
b. *SE*, pp. 170–183.

F7 "Some Don'ts for Literary Regionalists." *American Review*, 8 (December 1936), 142–150.

F8 "Homage to T. S. Eliot." *Harvard Advocate*, 125 (Dec. 1938), 46.

F9 "The Present State of Poetry: III. In the United States." *KR*, 1 (Autumn 1939), 384–398.

F10 "The Situation in American Writing, Part II." *PR*, 6 (Fall 1939), 112–113.

F11 "Statement Concerning Wallace Stevens' *Harmonium*." *Harvard Advocate*, 127 (Dec. 1940), 32.

F12 "Katherine Anne Porter (Irony with a Center)."
Note: copyright 13 Dec. 1941 (B524627); renewed 17 Dec. 1968 (R451205).
a. *KR*, 4 (Winter 1942), 29–42.
b. As "Irony with a Center: Katherine Anne Porter." *SE*, pp. 136–156.

F13 "Pure and Impure Poetry."
Note: copyright 16 March 1943 (B579095); renewed 6 April 1970 (R484768). Delivered as "Pure Poetry and the Structure of Poems"

for the Mesures Lecture at Princeton University, spring 1942.

   a. *KR*, 5 (Spring 1943), 228–254.

   b. *SE*, pp. 3–31.

F14 "The Love and Separateness in Miss Welty."

   Note: copyright 15 March 1944 (B623893); renewed 5 April 1971 (R504499).

   a. *KR*, 6 (Spring 1944), 246–259.

   b. As "Love and Separateness in Eudora Welty." *SE*, pp. 156–169.

F15 "The War and the National Muniments." *U.S. Library of Congress Quarterly Journal of Current Acquisitions*, 2 (Nov. 1944), 64–75.

F16 "Melville the Poet."

   a. *KR*, 8 (Spring 1946), 208–223.

   b. *SE*, pp. 184–198.

F17 "A Poem of Pure Imagination: An Experiment in Reading."

   Note: delivered in part as a Bergen Foundation Lecture, Yale University, 1945.

   a. *The Rime of the Ancient Mariner*. Samuel Taylor Coleridge. Illus. Alexander Calder. New York: Reynal & Hitchcock, 1946. Pp. 59–148. *See* **B16**.

   b. *KR*, 9 (Summer 1946), 391–427. Parts III, IV, and V of the seven-part essay.

   c. *SE*, pp. 198–305.

F18 "William Faulkner."

   a. As "Cowley's Faulkner." *NRep*, 12 Aug. 1946, pp. 176–180; 26 Aug. 1946, pp. 234–237.

   b. *SE*, pp. 59–79.

F19 "Hemingway."

   a. *KR*, 9 (Winter 1947), 1–28.

   b. *Horizon*, 15 (April 1947), 156–179.

   c. *Die amerikanische Rundschau*, 3 (Dec. 1947), 89–104.

   d. As "Introduction" to *A Farewell to Arms*. Ernest Hemingway. Modern Standard Authors Edition. New York: Charles Scribner's Sons, 1949. Pp. vii–xxxvii.

   e. As "Ernest Hemingway." *SE*, pp. 80–118.

F20 "Paul Rosenfeld: Prompter of Fiction."

   a. *Commonweal*, 15 Aug. 1947, pp. 424–426.

   b. Rpt. in Jerome Mellquist and Lucie Wiese, eds. *Paul Rosenfeld: Voyager in the Arts*. New York: Creative Age Press, 1948. Pp. 93–97.

F21 "The Themes of Robert Frost."

Note: presented as a Hopwood Lecture in 1947.

a. *Michigan Alumnus Quarterly Review*, 54 (Dec. 1947), 1–11.

b. *SE*, pp. 118–136.

F22 "Introduction." *A Long Fourth and Other Stories*. Peter Taylor. New York: Harcourt, Brace and Company, 1948.

Note: copyright 4 March 1948 (A16501); renewed 9 June 1975 (R607033).

F23 An epistolary essay regarding the dismissal of W. T. Couch, Director of the University of Chicago Press, 20 Nov. 1950. Mimeographed. (Ctw).

F24 "William Faulkner and His South." Mimeographed. Charlottesville, VA: n.p., 13 March 1951.

Note: delivered as the first Peters Rushton seminar in contemporary prose and poetry and the sixteenth in the series sponsored by the Schools of English, University of Virginia.

F25 "*Nostromo.*"

Note: copyright 26 Sept. 1951 (A60209).

a. *SR*, 59 (Summer 1951), 363–391.

b. As "Introduction" to *Nostromo*. Joseph Conrad. Modern Library No. 275. New York: Random House, 1951.

c. As "The Great Mirage: Conrad and *Nostromo*." *SE*, pp. 31–58.

F26 "Introduction." *Katherine Anne Porter: A Critical Bibliography*. Comp. Edward Schwartz. New York: New York Public Library, 1953. Pp. 5–10.

F27 "A Note to *All the King's Men*."

a. *SR*, 61 (Summer 1953), 476–480.

b. As "Introduction" to *AKM*. Modern Library No. 170. New York: Random House, 1953.

F28 "The Way It Was Written" (*BD*). *NYTBR*, 23 Aug. 1953, pp. 6, 25.

F29 "Knowledge and the Image of Man." *SR*, 62 (Spring 1955), 182–192.

Note: an address at the Conference on the Unity of Knowledge at the bicentennial celebration of Columbia University, 1954. RPW was on the panel that discussed "Man's Right to Knowledge," 30 Oct. 1954.

F30 "A Lesson Read in American Books." *NYTBR*, 11 Dec. 1955, pp. 1, 33.

Note: a response from Sloan Wilson and six others in "Letters to the Editor," *NYTBR*, 15 Jan. 1956, p. 32.

F31 "Divided South Searches Its Soul." *Life*, 9 July 1956, pp. 98–99, 101–102, 105–106, 108, 111–112, 114. Excerpt from *Seg*.

F32 "Remember the Alamo!" *Holiday*, Feb. 1958, pp. 52–55, 106, 108–110, 112–113. **A17.a1**.

F33 "How Texas Won Her Freedom." *Holiday*, March 1958, pp. 72–73, 160, 162–167. **A18.a1**.

F34 "Formula for a Poem." *SatR*, 22 March 1958, p. 23.
    Note: excerpt from RPW's acceptance speech for the National Book Award for *P*.

F35 "Writer at Work: How a Story Was Born and How, Bit by Bit, It Grew."
    a. *NYTBR*, 1 March 1959, pp. 4–5, 36.
    b. As "'Blackberry Winter': A Recollection." *UF* (2d ed.), pp. 638–643. **B14**.

F36 "Storia di Jack e Willie." Introduction to *Tutti gli uomini del re*. Trans. Gerardo Guerrieri. *Sipario*, Dec. 1960, p. 52.

F37 Introductory notes to John Webster's *White Devil*, program for Harvard production, Loeb Theatre, 1961.

F38 "Statement on Censorship." *Proceedings of the American Academy of Arts and Letters and the National Institute of Arts and Letters*. Second series, no. 11 (1961), pp. 177–180.

F39 "Letters and Comment: On Civil Disobedience and the Algerian War." *YR*, 50 (Spring 1961), 474–480. Two essay-letters to Nicola Chiaromonte.

F40 "A Mark Deep on a Nation's Soul." *Life*, 17 March 1961, pp. 82–89. Excerpt from *LCW*.

F41 "Note" to accompany "Mortmain" poem sequence in Paul Engle and Joseph Langland, eds. *Poet's Choice*. Chicago: Dial Press, 1962.

F42 "Foreword." *Faith and the Contemporary Arts*. Ed. Finley Eversole. New York: Abingdon Press, 1962.

F43 "Why Do We Read Fiction?"
    a. *SatEP*, 20 Oct. 1962, pp. 82–84.
    b. In five parts: *Time and Tide—John O'London's*, 3 Jan. 1963, p. 27; "——2. Readers Who Play a Double Game," 10 Jan. 1963, p. 27; "——3. Awesome Confrontations," 17 Jan. 1963, p. 27; "——4. The Inner Logic of Fiction," 24 Jan. 1963, p. 28; "——5. The Inner Logic of Motivation," 31 Jan. 1963, p. 27.
    c. *American Journal*, 3 (June 1963), 80–89.
    d. *Writer's Yearbook '67*, pp. 70–73, 146–148.
    e. *ATL* (4th ed.), pp. 553–559. **B7**.

F44 *"An American Tragedy."*
  a. *YR*, 52 (Autumn 1962), 1–15.
  b. As "Introduction" to *An American Tragedy*. Theodore Dreiser. Cleveland: World Publishing Co., 1962.

F45 "Elizabeth Madox Roberts: Life Is from Within."
  a. *SatR*, 2 March 1963, pp. 20–21, 38.
  b. As "Introduction" to *The Time of Man*. Elizabeth Madox Roberts. New York: Viking Press, 1963. Pp. vii–xix.

F46 "John Crowe Ransom: Some Random Remarks."
  a. *Shenandoah*, 14 (Spring 1963), 19–21.
  b. As "A Tribute in New York" (upon JCR's appearance at the Guggenheim Museum Auditorium, 19 Dec. 1963). *John Crowe Ransom: A Tribute from the Community of Letters*. Eds. D. David Long and Michael R. Burr. *The Kenyon Collegian*, a supplement to vol. 90, no. 7, Gambier, OH, 1964. P. 20.

F47 "The Veins of Irony." *University: A Princeton Magazine*, nos. 17–18 (Summer–Fall 1963), pp. 10–12.

F48 "Mightier Than the Sword." *Yale Political*, 3 (Autumn 1963), 17 and 30.

F49 "The World of Daniel Boone." *Holiday*, Dec. 1963, pp. 162, 164, 166–167, 169–174, 176–177.

F50 "William Carlos Williams, 1883–1963." *Proceedings of the American Academy of Arts and Letters and the National Institute of Arts and Letters*. Second series, no. 14 (1964), pp. 383–386.

F51 *"All the King's Men*: The Matrix of Experience."
  a. *YR*, 53 (Winter 1964), 161–167.
  b. As "Introduction" to *All the King's Men*. Time Reading Program Special Edition. New York: Time Incorporated, 1963. Pp. [xi]–xvii.

F52 "Tribute to Flannery O'Connor." *Esprit* (University of Scranton, PA), 8 (Winter 1964), 49.

F53 "Negro Now." *Look*, 23 March 1965, pp. 23–31. Excerpt from *WSN?*.

F54 "Robert Penn Warren and Ralph Ellison: A Dialogue." *Reporter*, 25 March 1965, pp. 42–46, 48. Excerpt from *WSN?*.

F55 "Learning to Write." *Descant* (TCU), 9 (Spring 1965), 2–11.
  Note: lecture given for the Creative Writing Day Convocation at Texas Christian University, Fort Worth, TX, May 1965.

F56 "Two for SNCC." *Commentary*, 39 (April 1965), 38–48. Excerpt from *WSN?*.
  Note: discussed as "Inside Snick." *Time*, 30 April 1965, pp. 73–74.

F57 "Faulkner: The South, the Negro, and Time."
Note: delivered at the Southern Literary Festival, University of Mississippi, 23 April 1965.
a. *SoR*, NS 1 (Summer 1965), 501–529.
b. *FCCE*, pp. 251–271.

F58 "Uncorrupted Consciousness: The Stories of Katherine Anne Porter." *YR*, 55 (Winter 1966), 280–290. An essay-review of KAP's *Collected Stories*.

F59 *A Plea in Mitigation: Modern Poetry and the End of an Era*. Macon, GA: Wesleyan College, 1966. *See* **A27**.
Note: the Eugenia Dorothy Blount Lamar Lecture at Wesleyan College, Feb. 1966.

F60 "Tribute at Chapel Hill." *The Alumni News*, 54 (Spring 1966), 23. Tribute to Randall Jarrell, University of North Carolina, Greensboro.

F61 "Introduction: Faulkner: Past and Future." *Faulkner: A Collection of Critical Essays*. Ed. RPW. TCV. Englewood Cliffs, NJ: Prentice-Hall, 1966. Pp. 1–22.

F62 "Malcolm X: Mission and Meaning." *YR*, 56 (Winter 1967), 161–171. An essay-review of *The Autobiography of Malcolm X*.

F63 "Melville's Poems."
a. *SoR*, NS 3 (Autumn 1967), 799–855.
b. As "Introduction" to *SPHM*, pp. 3–88. **B34**.

F64 "William Styron." *Book-of-the-Month Club News*, Oct. 1967, pp. 6–7, 14.

F65 "Notes on the Poetry of John Crowe Ransom at His Eightieth Birthday." *KR*, 30 (June 1968), 319–349.

F66 "Five Tributes." *Shenandoah*, 20 (Spring 1969), 36–39. One of five tributes to Eudora Welty.

F67 Prefatory note to Cass Mastern episode in Whit Burnett, ed. *This Is My Best in the Third Quarter of the Century*. Garden City, NY: Doubleday, 1970. P. 389.

F68 "Lambert Davis: The Book Editor." *A Statesman of the Republic of Books*. Chapel Hill: University of North Carolina Press, 1970. Pp. 7–9.

F69 National Medal of Literature Acceptance Speech.
a. As "A Poet Probes the Fragility of Relevance." Washington *Post*, 6 Dec. 1970, p. C-3.
b. As "Who Is Relevant?" *Yale Alumni Magazine*, Feb. 1971, pp. 8–11.
c. As "Relevance Without Meaning." *Intercollegiate Review* (Bryn Mawr), 7 (Spring 1971), 149–152.

d. As "Are Writers Relevant?" *Dialogue*, 4, no. 3 (1971), 89–94.

e. As "Hawthorne *Was* Relevant." *Nathaniel Hawthorne Journal*, 2 (1972), 85–89.

F70 "Cooper." *Atlantic Brief Lives*. Ed. Louis Kronenberger and Emily M. Beck. Boston: Little, Brown, 1971.

F71 "Whittier."

　a. *SR*, 79 (Winter 1971), 86–135.

　b. As "Introduction" to *JGWP*, pp. 3–62. **B35**.

F72 "Andrew Lytle's *The Long Night*: A Rediscovery." *SoR*, NS 7 (Winter 1971), 130–139.

F73 "Literature and Crisis." *PTA Magazine*, 65 (Jan. 1971), 35–37.

F74 "Poetry in a Time of Crack-Up."

　a. *NYRB*, 7 Jan. 1971, pp. 32–33.

　b. *Intellectual Digest*, March–April 1971, pp. 19–24.

F75 "Homage to Theodore Dreiser on the Centenary of His Birth." *SoR*, NS 7 (Spring 1971), 345–410. Excerpt from *HTD*.

F76 "Walker Evans." *Walker Evans: 14 Photographs*. New York: Ives-Sillman, 1972. n.p. Portfolio.

F77 "Mark Twain." *SoR*, NS 8 (Summer 1972), 459–492.

F78 "A Dearth of Heroes."

　a. *American Heritage: The Magazine of History*, 23 (Oct. 1972), 4–7, 95–99.

　b. As "Introduction" to *The Hero in America: A Chronicle of Hero Worship*. Dixon Wector. Rpt.; New York: Charles Scribner's Sons, 1972. Pp. xxiii–xxvii.

F79 "Hawthorne Revisited." *SR*, 81 (Winter 1973), 75–111.

F80 "Theodore Dreiser: *An American Tragedy*." *Der amerikanische Roman im 19. und 20. Jahrhundert*. Ed. Edgar Lohner. Berlin: Erich Schmidt, 1974. Pp. 152–161. Excerpt from *HTD*, pp. 112–129.

F81 "The World of Huey Long."

　a. London *Times*, 5 Jan. 1974, p. 5.

　b. As "Introduction" to *AKM*. London: Secker & Warburg, 1974. Pp. vii–xv.

F82 "John Crowe Ransom, 1888–1974."

　a. *Proceedings of the American Academy of Arts and Letters and the National Institute of Arts and Letters*. Second series, no. 25 (1975), p. 84.

　b. *SoR*, NS 11 (Spring 1975), 243–244.

F83 "Democracy and Poetry."

　a. *SoR*, NS 11 (Winter 1975), 1–28. From *DP*, pp. 41–94.

　b. As "Bearers of Bad Tidings: Writers and the American Dream." *NYRB*, 20 March 1975, pp. 12–19. From *DP*, pp. 4–37.

F84 "In Search of the American Dream."
    a. "How Can History Relate to Future Challenges?" Denver *Post*, 23 Jan. 1975, p. 56.
    b. "'Inalienable Rights': What Are They?" Denver *Post*, 30 Jan. 1975, p. 62.
    Note: the 17th and 18th articles in a series offered through the University of California extension program.

F85 "Tribute to Hugh B. Cox." *The Perfect Advocate: A Memoir of the Late Hugh B. Cox, Esquire*. Oxford: Librarian of Christ Church, 1976. Pp. 58–59.

F86 "A Special Message to Subscribers from RPW." *AKM*. Franklin Center, PA: Franklin Library, 1977. n.p. *See* **A7.j1**.

F87 "The Use of the Past." *A Time to Hear and Answer: Essays for the Bicentennial Season*. Ed. Taylor Littleton. Franklin Lectures in Sciences and Humanities, 4th series. University: University of Alabama Press for Auburn University, 1977. Pp. 3–35.

F88 "Two Peters: Memory and Opinion." *Shenandoah*, 28 (Winter 1977), 8–10. Tribute to Peter Taylor.

F89 "Foreword." *Head o' W-Hollow*. Jesse Stuart. Rpt.; Lexington: University of Kentucky Press, 1979. Pp. ix–x.

F90 "A Reminiscence." *Nashville: The Faces of Two Centuries, 1780–1980*. Ed. John Egerton. Nashville: Nashville Magazine, PlusMedia, 1979. Pp. 203–220.

F91 "Introduction." *The Sound and the Fury*. William Faulkner. Franklin Center, PA: Franklin Library, 1979. Pp. ix–xv.

G

Reviews

G1 Rev. of *Chills and Fever*, by John Crowe Ransom. *Voices*, 4 (Nov. 1924), 24–25.

G2 Rev. of *The Flaming Terrapin*, by Ray Campbell. *Voices*, 4 (Jan. 1925), 89–90.

G3 "Sunrise Trumpets." Rev. of *Sunrise Trumpets*, by Joseph Auslander. *The Fugitive*, 4 (March 1925), 29–30.

G4 "Firing Line Section." Rev. of *The Grand Inquisitor*, by Donald Douglas. Nashville *Tennessean*, 12 April 1925, p. 8.

G5 Rev. of *The Great Gatsby*, by F. Scott Fitzgerald. Nashville *Tennessean*, 24 May 1925, n.p.

G6 Rev. of *A Wind Blowing Over*, by Clara Platt Meadowcraft. Nashville *Tennessean*, 26 July 1925, n.p.

G7 "Firing Line Section." Rev. of *Thus Far*, by J. C. Snaith. Nashville *Tennessean*, 9 Aug. 1925, p. 6.

G8 "Firing Line Section." Rev. of *Voices of the Stones*, by A.E. (George William Russell). Nashville *Tennessean*, 3 Jan. 1926, p. 6.

G9 "The Romantic Strain." Rev. of *Rustic Elegies*, by Edith Sitwell. *NRep*, 23 Nov. 1927, pp. 23–24.

G10 "Sacheverell Sitwell's Poems." Rev. of *Cyder Feast and Other Poems*, by Sacheverell Sitwell. *NRep*, 29 Feb. 1928, p. 76.

G11 "The Bright Doom." Rev. of *The Bright Doom*, by John Hall Wheelock. *NRep*, 4 April 1928, p. 227.

G12 "Guinea-Fowl." Rev. of *Guinea-Fowl and Other Poultry*, by Leonard Bacon. *NRep*, 2 May 1928, pp. 330–331.

G13 "Hawthorne, Anderson, and Frost." Rev. of *Nathaniel Hawthorne*, by Herbert Gorman; *Robert Frost*, by Gorham Munson; and *The Phenomenon of Sherwood Anderson*, by N. Bryllion Fagin. *NRep*, 16 May 1928, pp. 399–401.

   Note: see "Correspondence: Munson, Warren, and Tate," *NRep*, 27 June 1928, p. 149, for Munson's rather vehement rebuttal.

G14 "The Gentle Buccaneer." Rev. of *Count Luckner, the Sea Devil*, by Lowell Thomas. *NRep*, 5 Sept. 1928, p. 81.

G15 "Merrill Moore's Sonnets." Rev. of *The Noise That Time Makes*, by Merrill Moore. *NRep*, 29 Jan. 1930, p. 280.

G16 "A French View of Jefferson." Rev. of *Thomas Jefferson: The Apostle of Americanism*, by Gilbert Chinard. *NRep*, 2 April 1930, pp. 196–197.

G17 "The Gamecock." Rev. of *High Stakes and Hair Trigger: The Life of Jefferson Davis*, by Robert W. Winston; and *Jefferson Davis: Political Soldier*, by Elizabeth Cutting. *NRep*, 25 March 1931, pp. 158–159.

G18 "The Second American Revolution." Rev. of *The Critical Year*, by Howard K. Beale; and *The Age of Hate*, by George Fort Milton. *VQR*, 7 (April 1931), 282–288.

G19 "Lavender and Old Ladies." Rev. of *Many Thousands Gone*, by John Peale Bishop. *NRep*, 5 Aug. 1931, p. 321.

G20 "Not Local Color." Rev. of *A Buried Treasure*, by Elizabeth Madox Roberts; *Penhally*, by Caroline Gordon; *God in the Straw Pen*, by John Fort; *A Calendar of Sin*, by Evelyn Scott; *John Henry*, by Roark Bradford; and *These Thirteen*, by William Faulkner. *VQR*, 8 (Jan. 1932), 153–160.

G21 "Two Poets." Rev. of *The Signature of Pain*, by Alan Porter; and *Jane Matthew and Other Poems*, by Eda Lou Walton. *NRep*, 24 Feb. 1932, pp. 51–52.

G22 "Georgian Laureate." Rev. of *The Poems of Lascelles Abercrombie*. *Poetry*, 40 (April 1932), 47–50.

G23 "James Stephens Again." Rev. of *Strict Joy and Other Poems*, by James Stephens. *Poetry*, 40 (July 1932), 229–232.

G24 "Sight Unseen." Rev. of *Ships and Lovers*, by Thomas Caldesot Chubb. *Poetry*, 42 (Aug. 1933), 292–294.

G25 "Old Words." Rev. of *High Perils*, by Cole Young Rice. *Poetry*, 42 (Sept. 1933), 342–345.

G26 "Blind Poet: Sidney Lanier." Rev. of *Sidney Lanier: A Biography and Critical Study*, by Aubrey Harrison Starke. *American Review*, 2 (Nov. 1933), 27–45.

Note: for the debate which ensued from this review, see **M3** and **M4**.

G27 "Georgian Middle Life." Rev. of *Halfway House*, by Edmund Blunden. *Poetry*, 43 (Feb. 1934), 287–288.

G28 "Working Toward Freedom." Rev. of *Now With His Love*, by John Peale Bishop. *Poetry*, 43 (March 1934), 342–346.

G29 "Twelve [*sic*] Poets." Rev. of *Poems, 1924–1933*, by Archibald MacLeish; *A Green Bough*, by William Faulkner; *Now With His Love*, by John Peale Bishop; *A Tale of Troy*, by John Masefield; *The Fleeting* *and Other Poems*, by Walter De La Mare; *Collected Poems*, by E. A. Robinson; *Talifer*, by Robinson Jeffers; *Poems*, by W. H. Auden; *The Orators*, by W. H. Auden; *Poems*, by Stephen Spender; and *Spring Encounter*, by John Pudney. *American Review*, in "Poetry Supplement," ed. Allen Tate, 3 (May 1934), 212–228.

G30 "Americanism." Rev. of *The Yoke of Thunder* and *Ballads of Square-toed Americans*, by Robert P. Tristram Coffin. *Poetry*, 44 (Sept. 1934), 334–337.

G31 "The Fiction of Caroline Gordon." Rev. of *Aleck Maury, Sportsman*, by Caroline Gordon. *SWR*, 20 (Winter 1935), 5–10.

G32 "The Middle Flight." Rev. of *Atlantides*, by Haniel Long. *Poetry*, 45 (Jan. 1935), 226–228.

G33 "Set in a Silver Sea." Rev. of *Collected Poems*, by V[ictoria] Sackville-West. *Poetry*, 46 (Sept. 1935), 346–349.

G34 "Straws in The Wind." Rev. of *Trial Balances*, edited by Ann Winslow. *Poetry*, 48 (June 1936), 172–175.

G35 "Some Recent Novels." Rev. of *Golden Apples*, by Marjorie Kinnan Rawlings; *Red Sky in the Morning*, by Robert P. Tristram Coffin; *Brothers Three*, by John M. Oskison; *Honey in the Horn*, by H. L. Davis; *Free Forester*, by Horatio Colony; *The Wind Blew West*, by Edwin Lanham; *This Body the Earth*, by Paul Green; *A Sign for Cain*, by Grace Lumpkin; *Pier 17*, by Walter Havighurst; *From the Kingdom of Necessity*, by Isidor Schneider; and *South*, by Frederick Wight. *SoR*, 1 (Winter 1936), 624–649.

G36 "Jeffers on the Age." Rev. of *Solstice and Other Poems*, by Robinson Jeffers. *Poetry*, 49 (Nov. 1936), 112.

G37 "Arnold vs. the 19th Century." Rev. of *Matthew Arnold*, by Lionel Trilling. *KR*, 1 (Spring 1939), 217–226.

G38 "The Snopes World." Rev. of *The Hamlet*, by William Faulkner. *KR*, 3 (Spring 1941), 253–257.

G39 "Poor White." Rev. of *Fire in the Summer*, by Robert Ramsey. *Nation*, 28 Feb. 1942, pp. 261–262.

G40 "Homage to Oliver Allston." Rev. of *Opinions of Oliver Allston*, by Van Wyck Brooks. *KR*, 4 (Spring 1942), 259–263.

G41 "Principle and Poet." Rev. of *Out of the Jewel*, by Rolfe Humphries. *Nation*, 11 April 1942, pp. 438–439.

G42 "The Lady of Lourdes." Rev. of *The Song of Bernadette*, by Franz Werfel. *Nation*, 30 May 1942, pp. 635–636.

G43 "Poems by Kenneth Patchen." Rev. of *The Dark Kingdom*. *Nation*, 4 July 1942, p. 17.

G44 "Poets and Scholars." Rev. of *Princeton Verse Between Two Wars:*

An Anthology, edited by Allen Tate. *Nation*, 15 Aug. 1942, p. 137.

G45 "Asides and Diversions." Rev. of *Note Books of Night*, by Edmund Wilson. *Nation*, 5 Dec. 1942, p. 625.

G46 "Button, Button." Rev. of *The Company She Keeps*, by Mary McCarthy. *PR*, 9 (Dec. 1942), 537–540.

G47 "The Poetry of Mark Van Doren." Rev. of *Our Lady of Peace and Other War Poems*. *Nation*, 6 Feb. 1943, pp. 209–211.

G47.1 "Prof. Warren Reviews Two Books on War Time England." Rev. of *I Saw Two Englands*, by H. V. Morton, and *Flight to England*, by I. A. R. Wylie. Chicago *Sunday Tribune Books*, 21 March 1943, p. 11.

G47.2 "Satire on Small Time Politicians." Rev. of *Colonel Effingham's Raid*, by Berry Fleming. Chicago *Sunday Tribune Books*, 28 March 1943, p. 15.

G47.3 "This Is Britain: a Realistic Look in Midst of War." Rev. of *The English People: Impressions and Observations*, by D. W. Brogan. Chicago *Sunday Tribune Books*, 4 April 1943, p. 14.

G47.4 "Another Book Dealing with Immigrants." Rev. of *The Shadows of the Trees*, by Jacques Ducharme. Chicago *Sunday Tribune Books*, 25 April 1943, p. 16.

G48 "Our Literary Harvest." Rev. of *The Shock of Recognition*, by Edmund Wilson. *NYTBR*, 13 June 1943, pp. 5 and 18.

G49 "Rev. of *1 × 1*, by E. E. Cummings. *Accent*, 4 (Summer 1944), 251–253.

G50 "A Sheaf of Novels." Rev. of *Time Must Have a Stop*, by Aldous Huxley; *Freedom Road*, by Howard Fast; *Presidential Agent*, by Upton Sinclair; *The Firing Squad*, by F. C. Weiskopf; *Escape the Thunder*, by Lonnie Coleman; *No Bright Banners*, by Michael DeCapite; *Simone*, by Lion Feuchtwanger; *The History of Rome Hanks*, by J. S. Pennell; *A Walk in the Sun*, by Harry Brown; *Lieutenant Bertram*, by Bedo Uhse; *Lie Down in Darkness*, by H. R. Hays; and *Guerrilla*, by Lord Dunsany. *ASch*, 14 (Winter 1945), 115–122.

G51 "From the Underground." Rev. of *In Sicily*, by Elio Vittorini. *Nation*, 3 Dec. 1949, pp. 547–548.

G52 Rev. of *A Woman of Means*, by Peter Taylor. *NYTBR*, 11 June 1950, p. 8.

G53 "The Redemption of Temple Drake." Rev. of *Requiem for a Nun*, by William Faulkner. *NYTBR*, 30 Sept. 1951, pp. 1 and 31.

G54 "Man with No Commitments." Rev. of *The Adventures of Augie March*, by Saul Bellow. *NRep*, 2 Nov. 1953, pp. 22–23.

G55 "A First Novel." Rev. of *The Innocent*, by Madison Jones. *SR*, 65 (Spring 1957), 347–352.

G56 "Edmund Wilson's Civil War." Rev. of *Patriotic Gore*. *Commentary*, 34 (Aug. 1962), 151–158.

G57 "Race." Rev. of *Why We Can't Wait*, by Martin Luther King; *The New Equality*, by Nat Hentoff; *White and Black: Test of a Nation*, by Samuel Lubell; *Crisis in Black and White*, by Charles E. Silberman; and *To Be Equal*, by Whitney Young. *NYRB*, 8 Oct. 1964, pp. 7–9.

G58 "Who Shall Overcome?" Rev. of *Fire-Bell in the Night*, by Oscar Handlin; and *My People Is the Enemy*, by William Stringfellow. *NYRB*, 22 Oct. 1964, pp. 8 and 10.

G59 "Unity of Experience." Rev. of *Shadow and Act*, by Ralph Ellison. *Commentary*, 39 (May 1965), 91–96.
  Note: Rpt. in *Ralph Ellison: A Collection of Critical Essays*. TCV. Englewood Cliffs, NJ: Prentice-Hall, 1974. Pp. 21–26.

G60 "Death of a Salesman—Southern Style." Rev. of *Old Powder Man*, by Joan Williams. *Life*, 20 May 1966, pp. 10 and 18.

G61 "The Negro Movement in Upheaval." Rev. of *Freedom When?*, by James Farmer. *NYRB*, 18 Aug. 1966, pp. 22–25.

G62 Rev. of *The Zodiac*, by James Dickey. *NYTBR*, 14 Nov. 1976, p. 8.

H

Contributions to Anthologies

Note: This section attempts selectivity, not necessarily completeness, to suggest a paradox about the acceptance of RPW's works: how few selections have been anthologized by so many editors.

H1 *Driftwood Flames*. Nashville: Poetry Guild, 1923.
    Includes: "The Fierce Horsemen," p. 10; "Wild Oats," p. 17; "Iron Beach," p. 30; "To Certain Old Masters," pp. 36–37; and "The Golden Hills of Hell," p. 41.

H2 Brooks, Van Wyck, Alfred Kreymborg, Lewis Mumford, and Paul Rosenfeld, eds. *The American Caravan: A Yearbook of American Literature*. New York: Macaulay Company, 1927.
    Includes: "Kentucky Mountain Farm: At the Hour of the Breaking of the Rocks," p. 803.

H3 Strong, L. A. G., ed. *Best Poems of 1926*. New York: Dodd, Mead & Co., 1927.
    Includes: "Evening: The Motors."

H4 *Fugitives: An Anthology of Verse*. New York: Harcourt, Brace & Company, 1928.
    Includes: "Letter of a Mother"; "Kentucky Mountain Farm: I. Rebuke of the Rocks" and "II. At the Hour of the Breaking of the Rocks"; "To a Face in the Crowd"; "Images on the Tomb: I. Dawn: The Gorgon's Head," "II. Day: Lazarus," "III. Evening: The Motors," and "IV. Night: But a Sultry Wind"; "The Wrestling Match"; "Admonition to the Dead"; "Croesus in Autumn"; and "Pro Sua Vita," pp. 135–150.

H5 Kreymborg, Alfred, Lewis Mumford, and Paul Rosenfeld, eds. *The Second American Caravan: A Yearbook of American Literature*. New York: Macaulay Company, 1928.
    Includes: "Grandfather Gabriel" and "Pondy Woods," pp. 120–122.

H6 Kreymborg, Alfred, ed. *Lyric America (1630–1930)*. New York: Coward-McCann, [1930?].
    Includes: "Croesus in Autumn," "Grandfather Gabriel," and "The Wrestling Match," pp. 560, 564–567.

H7 Kreymborg, Alfred, Lewis Mumford, and Paul Rosenfeld, eds. *American Caravan IV*. New York: Macaulay Company, 1931.

  Includes: "Prime Leaf," pp. 3–61; "Tryst on Vinegar Hill," pp. 392–393.

H8 *The Modern Muse*. New York: Oxford University Press, 1934.

  Includes: "Pro Sua Vita."

H9 Agar, Herbert, and Allen Tate, eds. *Who Owns America? A New Declaration of Independence*. Boston: Houghton Mifflin Company, 1936.

  Includes: "Literature as a Symptom," pp. 264–279.

H10 Parks, Edd Winfield, ed. *Southern Poets: Representative Selections*. American Writers Series. New York: American Book Company, 1936. Rpt.; New York: Phaeton Press, 1970.

  Includes: "Kentucky Mountain Farm: I. Rebuke of the Rocks," "II. At the Hour of the Breaking of the Rocks," and "III. History Among the Rocks," pp. 308–310.

H11 Untermeyer, Louis, ed. *Modern American Poetry: A Critical Anthology*. 5th ed., rev. New York: Harcourt, Brace and Company, 1936.

  Includes: "Aubade for Hope," "Kentucky Mountain Farm: III. History Among the Rocks," "Letter from a Coward to a Hero," "Letter of a Mother," "Letter to a Friend," "The Owl," "Pondy Woods," and "Pro Sua Vita."

H12 Young, Stark, ed. *Southern Treasury of Life and Literature*. New York: Charles Scribner's Sons, 1937.

  Includes: "History Among the Rocks" and "When the Light Gets Green," pp. 626–632.

H13 Zabel, Morton Dauwen, ed. *Literary Opinion in America: Essays Illustrating the Status, Methods and Problems of Criticism in the U.S. Since the War*. New York: Harper & Brothers, 1937.

  Includes: "The Hamlet of Thomas Wolfe" and "T. S. Stribling: A Paragraph in the History of Critical Realism," pp. 359–389.

H14 *Great American Short Stories: O. Henry Memorial Prize Winning Stories, 1937*. New York: Doubleday & Company, 1938.

  Includes: "Christmas Gift."

H15 O'Brien, Edward J., ed. *Best Short Stories 1938*. Boston: Houghton Mifflin Company, 1939.

  Includes: "Christmas Gift."

H16 Beatty, Richmond Croom, and William Perry Fidler, eds. *Contemporary Southern Prose*. Boston: D. C. Heath, 1940.

  Includes: "How Willie Proudfit Came Home," pp. 446–469.

H17 O'Brien, Edward J., ed. *Best Short Stories 1939*. Boston: Houghton Mifflin Company, 1940.

Includes: "How Willie Proudfit Came Home."

H18   Kreymborg, Alfred, ed. *An Anthology of American Poetry*. New York: Tudor Publishing Company, 1941.

Includes: "Croesus in Autumn," "Grandfather Gabriel," and "The Wrestling Match."

H19   Tate, Allen, and John Peale Bishop, eds. *American Harvest: Twenty Years of Creative Writing in the U.S.* New York: L. B. Fischer, 1942.

Includes: "When the Light Gets Green."

H20   Untermeyer, Louis, ed. *Modern American Poetry: A Critical Anthology*. 6th ed., rev. New York: Harcourt, Brace and Company, 1942.

Includes: "Aubade for Hope," "The Ballad of Billie Potts," "Bearded Oaks," "Kentucky Mountain Farm: History Among the Rocks," "Letter of a Mother," "Letter to a Friend," "The Owl," "Pondy Woods," and "Pro Sua Vita."

H21   Swallow, Alan, ed. *American Writing, 1942: The Anthology and Yearbook of the American Noncommercial Magazine*. New York: J. A. Decker Press, 1943.

Includes: "Goodwood Comes Back."

H22   Aiken, Conrad, ed. *Comprehensive Anthology of American Poetry*. Modern Library. New York: Random House, 1944.

Includes: "Bearded Oaks" and "Revelation."

H23   Aiken, Conrad, ed. *Twentieth-Century American Poetry*. Modern Library. New York: Random House, 1944.

Includes: "End of Season," "Pursuit," and "Revelation."

H24   Beatty, Richmond Croom, ed. *A Vanderbilt Miscellany*. Nashville: Vanderbilt University Press, 1944.

Includes: "When the Light Gets Green," pp. 31–38; "Terror," "Pursuit," "Original Sin: A Short Story," and "The Ballad of Billie Potts," pp. 331–355.

H35   Benét, William Rose, and Conrad Aiken, eds. *An Anthology of Famous English and American Poetry*. Modern Library. New York: Random House, 1944.

Includes: "Bearded Oaks and "Revelation."

H26   Caukin, Helen Ferguson, and Alan Swallow, eds. *American Writing, 1944: The Anthology and Yearbook of the American Noncommercial Magazine*. Boston: Bruce Humphries, 1945.

Includes: "Small Soldiers with Drum in Large Landscape," pp. 200–202.

H27   Williams, Oscar, ed. *The War Poets: An Anthology of the War Po-*

etry of the 20th Century. New York: John Day Company, 1945.
Includes: "Terror."

H28 Cooper, Charles W., and John Holmes, eds. *Preface to Poetry*. New York: Harcourt, Brace and Company, 1946.
Includes: "Monologue at Midnight" and "The Wrestling Match."

H29 Foley, Martha, ed. *Best American Short Stories, 1945*. Boston: Houghton Mifflin Company, 1946.
Includes: "Cass Mastern's Wedding Ring."

H30 Williams, Oscar, ed. *A Little Treasury of Modern Poetry: English and American*. New York: Charles Scribner's Sons, 1946.
Includes: "Bearded Oaks," pp. 104–105; "Original Sin: A Short Story," p. 465.

H31 Foerster, Norman, ed. *American Poetry and Prose*. 3d ed. Boston: Houghton Mifflin Company, 1947.
Includes: "The Ballad of Billie Potts," pp. 1519–1526.

H32 Selden, Elizabeth, comp. *The Book of Friendship: An International Anthology*. Boston: Houghton Mifflin Company, 1947.
Includes: "102 To a Friend Parting," p. 192; "213 For a Friend Who Thinks Himself Urbane," pp. 325–326.

H33 Wolpers, Theodore, trans. *American Short Stories*. Vol. 8: *The Twentieth-Century Mid-Century Stories*. Annotated by Heinz Pähler. Herstellung: Ferdinand Schöningh Paderborn, [1947?].
Includes: "Blackberry Winter," pp. 24–50.

H34 Locke, Louis G., William M. Gibson, and George W. Arms, eds. *Readings for Liberal Education*. New York: Rinehart & Company, 1948.
Includes: "On Faulkner's *A Rose for Emily*," pp. 187–191.

H35 O'Connor, William Van, ed. *Forms of Modern Fiction: Essays Collected in Honor of Joseph Warren Beach*. Minneapolis: University of Minnesota Press, 1948.
Includes: "William Faulkner," pp. 125–143.

H36 Schorer, Mark, Josephine Miles, and Gordon McKenzie, eds. *Criticism: The Foundations of Modern Literary Judgment*. New York: Harcourt, Brace & Company, 1948.
Includes: "Pure and Impure Poetry," pp. 366–378.

H37 Williams, Oscar, ed. *A Little Treasury of American Poetry*. New York: Charles Scribner's Sons, 1948.
Includes: "Original Sin: A Short Story," pp. 830–831; "Pursuit," pp. 833–835; and "Revelation," pp. 832–833.

H38 Davis, Joe Lee, John T. Frederick, and Frank Luther Mott, eds. *American Literature: An Anthology and Critical Survey*. New

York: Charles Scribner's Sons, 1949.

Includes: "The Patented Gate and the Mean Hamburger," II, 905–913.

H39 Mayberry, George, ed. *A Little Treasury of American Prose: The Major Writers from Colonial Times to the Present Day*. New York: Charles Scribner's Sons, 1949.

Includes: as work in progress, "Lois," pp. 886–893, from *AKM*.

H40 Rodman, Selden, comp. *100 Modern Poems*. New York: Pellegrini & Cudahy, 1949.

Includes: "Bearded Oaks."

H41 Stallman, Robert Wooster, ed. *Critiques and Essays in Criticism, 1920–1948*. New York: Ronald Press, 1949.

Includes: "Pure and Impure Poetry," pp. 85–104.

H42 Gordon, Caroline, and Allen Tate, eds. *House of Fiction: An Anthology of the Short Story, with Commentary*. New York: Charles Scribner's Sons, 1950.

Includes: "When the Light Gets Green."

H43 Matthiessen, F. O., ed. *The Oxford Book of American Verse*. New York: Oxford University Press, 1950.

Includes: "The Ballad of Billie Potts."

H44 Rajan, B., ed. *Modern American Poetry*. *Focus* Five. London: Dennis Dobson, 1950.

Includes: "From 'Proud Flesh,'" pp. 163–167.

H45 Friar, Kimon, and John Malcolm Brinnin, eds. *Modern Poetry: British and American*. New York: Appleton-Century-Crofts, 1951.

Includes: "Revelation," pp. 289–290; "Pursuit," pp. 290–291; and "Terror," pp. 292–293.

H46 Hoffman, Frederick J., and Olga W. Vickery, eds. *William Faulkner: Two Decades of Criticism*. East Lansing: Michigan State College Press, 1951.

Includes: "William Faulkner," pp. 82–101.

H47 Ransom, John Crowe, ed. *Kenyon Critics: Studies in Modern Literature*. Cleveland, OH: World Publishing Company, 1951.

Includes: "Pure and Impure Poetry," pp. 17–42.

Note: rev. by Louis L. Martz, *SatR*, 9 June 1951, p. 15.

H48 Zabel, Morton Dauwen, ed. *Literary Opinion in America*. Rev. ed. New York: Harper & Brothers, 1951.

Includes: "Hemingway" and "William Faulkner," pp. 444–477.

H49 Aldridge, John Watson, ed. *Critiques and Essays on Modern Fiction, 1920–1951: Representing the Achievement of Modern American and British Critics*. New York: Ronald Press Company, 1952.

Includes: "Ernest Hemingway," pp. 447–473.

H50 West, Ray B., Jr., ed. *Essays in Modern Literary Criticism*. New York: Rinehart & Company, 1952.
Includes: "Pure and Impure Poetry," pp. 246–266.

H51 Palgrave, F. T., ed. Rev. by Oscar Williams. *The Golden Treasury of the Best Songs and Lyrical Poems*. New York: New American Library, 1953.
Includes: "Original Sin: A Short Story," pp. 457–458.

H52 Unger, Leonard, and William Van O'Connor, eds. *Poems for Study: A Critical and Historical Introduction*. New York: Holt, Rinehart & Winston, 1953.
Includes: "Pursuit."

H53 Walser, Richard, ed. *The Enigma of Thomas Wolfe: Biographical and Critical Selections*. Cambridge, MA: Harvard University Press, 1953.
Includes: "The Hamlet of Thomas Wolfe," pp. 120–132.

H54 Lovett, Robert Morss, et al., eds. *The Writer and His Craft: Being the Hopwood Lectures, 1932–1952*. Ann Arbor: University of Michigan Press, 1954.
Includes: "The Themes of Robert Frost," pp. 218–233.

H55 Stallman, Robert Wooster, and R. E. Watters, eds. *The Creative Reader: An Anthology of Fiction, Drama, and Poetry*. New York: Ronald Press, 1954.
Includes: "An Interpretation of T. S. Eliot's 'The Love Song of J. Alfred Prufrock,'" pp. 878–885.

H56 Summers, Hollis S., ed. *Kentucky Story: A Collection of Short Stories*. Lexington: University of Kentucky Press, 1954.
Includes: "Blackberry Winter."

H57 Engle, Paul, and Warren Carrier, eds. *Reading Modern Poetry*. Key Editions. Glenview, IL: Scott, Foresman, 1955.
Includes: "Bearded Oaks," "Original Sin: A Short Story," and "Pursuit."

H58 Gettman, Royal Alfred, and Bruce Harkness, eds. *Book of Stories*. New York: Holt, Rinehart & Winston, 1955.
Includes: "Blackberry Winter."

H59 Thurston, Jarvis A., ed. *Reading Modern Short Stories*. Chicago: Scott, Foresman, 1955.
Includes: "Blackberry Winter."

H60 Williams, Oscar, ed. *New Pocket Anthology of American Verse from Colonial Days to the Present*. PL-35. New York: Pocket Library, 1955.
Includes: "Revelation," pp. 519–520; "Pursuit," pp. 520–521;

"Terror," pp. 521–523; and "To a Little Girl . . . ," pp. 524–531.

H61 Auden, W. H., ed. *The Criterion Book of Modern American Verse.* New York: Criterion Books, 1956.

Includes: "Original Sin: A Short Story" and "Pursuit."

H62 Elliott, George P., ed. *Fifteen Modern American Poets.* Rinehart Edition no. 79. New York: Holt, Rinehart & Winston, 1956.

Includes: "Eidolon," p. 265; "Revelation," pp. 265–266; "Pursuit," pp. 267–268; "Original Sin: A Short Story," pp. 268–270; "Variation: Ode to Fear," pp. 270–272; "Mexico Is A Foreign Country: III. The World Comes Galloping: A True Story," pp. 273–274; "IV. Small Soldiers with Drum in Large Landscape," pp. 274–276; "To a Little Girl . . . ," pp. 276–283; and "Bearded Oaks," pp. 283–284.

H63 Hall, James B., and Joseph Thomas Langland, eds. *Short Story.* New York: Macmillan, 1956.

Includes: "Blackberry Winter."

H64 Wagenheim, Harold H., et al., eds. *Our Reading Heritage.* New York: Henry Holt, 1956.

Includes: "Bearded Oaks," p. 144.

H65 Foerster, Norman, ed. *American Poetry and Prose.* 4th ed. Boston: Houghton Mifflin, 1957.

Includes: "The Reading of Modern Poetry," pp. 1612–1617.

H66 Locke, Louis G., William H. Gibson, and George W. Arms, eds. *Readings for Liberal Education.* 3d ed. New York: Rinehart, 1957.

Includes: "Toward Liberal Education" (originally "A Lesson Read in American Books"), pp. 410–413; and "On Faulkner's *A Rose for Emily*," pp. 443–446.

H67 Moore, Robert T., ed. *Best Poems of 1955.* Borestone Mountain Poetry Awards of 1956: A Compilation of Original Poetry Published in Magazines of the English-Speaking World in 1955. Eighth Annual Issue. Stanford, CA: Stanford University Press, 1957.

Includes: "To A Little Girl . . . ," pp. 97–98.

H68 Rahv, Philip, ed. *Literature in America: An Anthology of Literary Criticism.* New York: Meridian Books, 1957.

Includes: "William Faulkner," pp. 415–430.

H69 Cecil, David, and Allen Tate, eds. *Modern Verse in English, 1900–1950.* New York: Macmillan, 1958.

Includes: "Bearded Oaks," "Kentucky Mountain Farm: History Among the Rocks," "The Cardinal," "Original Sin: A Short Story," and "Colder Fire."

H70 *The Guinness Book of Poetry, 1956–1957.* London: Putnam, 1958.
Includes: "Promises," pp. 112–113.

H71 Mizener, Arthur, ed. *Reading for Writing.* New York: Henry Holt, 1958.
Includes: "Mason City," pp. 266–268, from *AKM.*

H72 West, Ray B., Jr., ed. *American Short Stories.* New York: Thomas Y. Crowell, 1959.
Includes: "Blackberry Winter."

H73 Abels, Cyrilly, and Margarita G. Smith, eds. *Forty Best Stories from* Mademoiselle. New York: Harper & Row, 1960.
Includes: "The Patented Gate and the Mean Hamburger."

H74 Buckler, William Earl, and Arnold B. Sklare, eds. *Stories from Six Authors.* New York: McGraw-Hill, 1960.
Includes: "The Life and Work of Professor Roy Millen," "The Circus in the Attic," and "Blackberry Winter," pp. 66–152.

H75 *Great Reading from* Life*: A Treasury of the Best Stories and Articles Chosen by the Editors.* New York: Harper, 1960.
Includes: "A Divided South Searches Its Soul," pp. 259–273.

H76 Hoffman, Frederick J., and Olga W. Vickery, eds. *William Faulkner: Three Decades of Criticism.* [East Lansing]: Michigan State University Press, 1960.
Includes: "William Faulkner," pp. 109–124.

H77 *Poetry for Pleasure: The Hallmark Book of Poetry.* New York: Doubleday, 1960.
Includes: "The Flower."

H78 Shapiro, Karl, ed. *American Poetry.* New York: Thomas Y. Crowell, 1960.
Includes: "Bearded Oaks," p. 211; "Crime," pp. 211–212; and "Original Sin: A Short Story," pp. 210–211.

H79 Stallman, Robert Wooster, ed. *The Art of Joseph Conrad: A Critical Symposium.* East Lansing: Michigan State University Press, 1960.
Includes: "On *Nostromo*," pp. 209–227.

H80 Summerfield, Jack D., and Lorlyn Thatcher, eds. *The Creative Mind and Method.* Austin: University of Texas Press, 1960.
Includes: "On Writing," pp. 59–63.

H81 Beal, Richard S., and Jacob Korg, eds. *The Complete Reader.* Englewood Cliffs, NJ: Prentice-Hall, 1961.
Includes: "Original Sin: A Short Story," pp. 609–610.

H82 Beaver, Harold, ed. *American Critical Essays: Twentieth Century.*

The World's Classics. London: Oxford University Press, 1961.
Includes: "William Faulkner," pp. 211–233.

H83 Drew, Elizabeth A., and George Connor, eds. *Discovering Modern Poetry*. New York: Holt, Rinehart & Winston, 1961.
Includes: "Pure and Impure Poetry," pp. 391–414.

H84 Gold, Herbert, and David L. Stevenson, eds. *Stories of Modern America*. New York: St. Martin's Press, 1961.
Includes: "The Unvexed Isles."

H85 Harned, Joseph, and Neil Goodwin, eds. *Art and the Craftsman: The Best of the Yale Literary Magazine, 1836–1961*. Carbondale: Southern Illinois University Press, 1961.
Includes: "Courses in Writing," pp. 278–279.
Note: original source unavailable for comparison.

H86 Mack, Maynard, Leonard Dean, and William Frost, eds. *Modern Poetry*. 2d ed. Englewood Cliffs, NJ: Prentice-Hall, 1961.
Includes: "Bearded Oaks," pp. 335–336.

H87 Chase, Richard, ed. *Melville: A Collection of Critical Essays*. TCV. Englewood Cliffs, NJ: Prentice-Hall, 1962.
Includes: "Melville the Poet," pp. 144–155.

H88 Engle, Paul, and Joseph Langland, eds. *Poet's Choice*. Chicago: Dial Press, 1962.
Includes: "Mortmain" sequence which is accompanied by a note on the poem sequence by RPW.

H89 Mizener, Arthur, ed. *Modern Short Stories: The Uses of Imagination*. New York: W. W. Norton, 1962.
Includes: "When the Light Gets Green" and an instructor's manual by Mizener.

H90 Phillips, William, and Philip Rahv, eds. *The Partisan Review Anthology*. New York: Holt, Rinehart & Winston, 1962.
Includes: "To a Little Girl . . . ," pp. 379–380.

H91 Weeks, Robert P., ed. *Hemingway: A Collection of Critical Essays*. TCV. Englewood Cliffs, NJ: Prentice-Hall, 1962.
Includes: "The Discovery of Evil: An Analysis of 'The Killers,'" pp. 114–117.

H92 Brinnin, John Malcolm, and Bill Read, eds. *The Modern Poets: An American-British Anthology*. New York: McGraw-Hill, 1963.
Includes: "Bearded Oaks" and "Pursuit," pp. 384–387.

H93 Litz, A. Walton, ed. *Modern American Fiction: Essays in Criticism*. A Galaxy Book. New York: Oxford University Press, 1963.
Includes: "William Faulkner," pp. 150–165.

H94 Bloom, Edward A., Charles H. Philbrick, and Elmer M. Blistein, eds. *The Variety of Poetry: An Anthology*. New York: Odyssey Press, 1964.

Includes: "Autumnal Equinox on Mediterranean Beach" and "Bearded Oaks."

H95 Brown, Francis, ed. *Opinions and Perspectives*. Boston: Houghton Mifflin, 1964.

Includes: "How a Story Was Born and How, Bit by Bit, It Grew," pp. 307–313.

H96 Driver, Tom F., and Robert Pack, eds. *Poems of Doubt and Belief: An Anthology of Modern Religious Poetry*. New York: Macmillan, 1964.

Includes: "The Dogwood" and "Summer Storm (Circa 1916) and God's Grace."

H97 Hardy, John Edward, ed. *The Modern Talent: An Anthology of Short Stories*. New York: Holt, Rinehart & Winston, 1964.

Includes: "When the Light Gets Green," pp. 167–173.

H98 *John Crowe Ransom: Gentleman, Teacher, Poet, Editor, Founder of the* Kenyon Review: *A Tribute*. Gambier, OH: Kenyon College Press, 1964.

Includes: "Tribute to John Crowe Ransom."

H99 Tambimuttu, ed. *Festschrift for Marianne Moore's Seventy-Seventh Birthday*. New York: Tambimuttu & Mass, 1964.

Includes: "Jingle: In Tribute to a Great Poem by Marianne Moore," p. 103.

H100 Utley, Francis Lee, Lynn Z. Bloom, and Arthur F. Kinney, eds. *Bear, Man, and God: Seven Approaches to William Faulkner's "The Bear."* New York: Random House, 1964.

Includes: "Tradition, Moral Confusion, the Negro: Themes in Faulkner's Work" (excerpt from "William Faulkner"), pp. 166–169.

H101 Pratt, William, ed. *The Fugitive Poets: Modern Southern Poetry in Perspective*. New York: E. P. Dutton, 1965.

Includes: "To a Face in a Crowd," pp. 117–118; "Aubade for Hope," p. 118; "Crime," pp. 119–120; "Original Sin: A Short Story," pp. 120–121; "Pursuit," pp. 122–124; "The Ballad of Billie Potts," pp. 124–140; "Bearded Oaks," pp. 141–142; and "To a Little Girl . . . ," pp. 142–151.

H102 Perrine, Laurence, and James M. Reid, eds. *100 American Poems of the Twentieth Century*. New York: Harcourt, Brace & World, 1966.

Includes: "Dragon Country: To Jacob Boehme," pp. 200–204.

H103 *The Alternative Society*. Bombay [India]: Vakils, Feffer and Simons Private Ltd., [1967?].

Includes: "Notes on a Life to Be Lived," "Tale of Time," "The Day Dr. Knox Did It," "Delight," and "Some Quiet, Plain Poems," IX, 1–51.

H104 Hogins, J. Burl, and Robert E. Yarber, eds. *Reading, Writing and Rhetoric*. Chicago: Science Research Associates, 1967.

Includes: "Why Do We Read Fiction?" pp. 468–476.

H105 Levin, Gerald, ed. *The Short Story: An Inductive Approach*. New York: Harcourt, Brace & World, 1967.

Includes: "Why Do We Read Fiction?" pp. 459–468.

H106 Engle, Paul, and Warren Carrier, eds. *Reading Modern Poetry: A Critical Anthology*. Rev. ed. Glenview, IL: Scott, Foresman, 1968.

Includes: "Bearded Oaks," pp. 79–80; "Original Sin: A Short Story," pp. 82–84; and "Pursuit," pp. 84–86.

H107 Jacobus, Lee A., ed. *Issues and Response*. New York: Harcourt, Brace & World, 1968.

Includes: "Malcolm X: Mission and Meaning," pp. 30–39.

H108 Jaffe, Adrian H., and Virgil Scott, eds. *Studies in the Short Story*. 3d ed. New York: Holt, Rinehart & Winston, 1968.

Includes: "The Patented Gate and the Mean Hamburger," pp. 586–596.

H109 Steward, Joyce S., and Eva M. Burkett, eds. *Introductory Readings in Literary Criticism*. Menlo Park, CA: Addison-Wesley, 1968.

Includes: "Why Do We Read Fiction?" pp. 148–159.

H110 Stillinger, Jack, ed. *Keats's Odes*. TCI. Englewood Cliffs, NJ: Prentice-Hall, 1968.

Includes: "The 'Ode to a Nightingale,'" pp. 44–47.

H111 Timko, Michael, and Clinton F. Oliver, eds. *Thirty-Eight Short Stories: An Introductory Anthology*. New York: Alfred A. Knopf, 1968.

Includes: "Blackberry Winter," pp. 238–260.

H112 Witt-Diamant, Ruth, and Rikutaro Fukuda, eds. *53 American Poets of Today*. Tokyo: Kenkyusha, 1968.

Includes: "History Among the Rocks," pp. 6–7; "When the Century Dragged," pp. 7–9.

H113 Young, Thomas Daniel, ed. *John Crowe Ransom: Critical Essays and a Bibliography*. Baton Rouge: Louisiana State University Press, 1968.

Includes: "John Crowe Ransom: A Study in Irony," pp. 24–40.

H114 Young, Thomas Daniel, Floyd C. Watkins, and Richmond

Croom Beatty, eds. *The Literature of the South*. Rev. ed. Glenview, IL: Scott, Foresman, 1968.

Includes: "Terror," "Pursuit," "Original Sin: A Short Story," "The Ballad of Billie Potts," "Blackberry Winter," and "The Patented Gate and the Mean Hamburger," pp. 1043–1083.

H115   Coyle, William, ed. *The Young Man in American Literature*. New York: Odyssey Press, 1969.

Includes: "Blackberry Winter."

H116   Kohler, Charlotte, ed. *Poems from the Virginia Quarterly Review, 1925–1967*. Charlottesville: University Press of Virginia, 1969.

Includes: "Two Poems on Time: I. Resolution," "II. History"; "Monologue at Midnight"; "Pursuit"; "Garland for You: 1. A Real Question Calling for Solution," "2. Lullaby: Exercise in Human Charity and Self-Knowledge," "3. The Letter About Money, Love, or Other Comfort, If Any," and "4. The Self That Stares," pp. 200–216.

H117   Meserole, Harrison T., Walter Sutton, and Brom Weber, eds. *American Literature: Tradition and Innovation*. Lexington, MA: D. C. Heath, 1969.

Includes: "Blackberry Winter," pp. 3297–3315.

H118   Plimpton, George, and Peter Ardery, eds. *The American Literary Anthology, 2: The Second Annual Collection of the Best from the Literary Magazines*. New York: Random House, 1969.

Includes: "Malcolm X: Mission and Meaning," pp. 409–419.

H119   Burnett, Whit, ed. *This Is My Best in the Third Quarter of the Century*. Garden City, NY: Doubleday, 1970.

Includes: "Cass Mastern" with a brief introduction by RPW, pp. 389–413.

H120   Hughes, Douglas A., ed. *The Way It Is: Readings in Contemporary American Prose*. New York: Holt, Rinehart & Winston, 1970.

Includes: "Malcolm X: Mission and Meaning," pp. 116–123.

H121   Kitzhaber, Albert P., et al., eds. *The Oregon Curriculum: A Sequential Program in English Literature V*. New York: Holt, Rinehart & Winston, 1970.

Includes: "Bearded Oaks," pp. 656–657.

H122   Weber, Brom, ed. *Sense and Sensibility in Twentieth-Century Writing: A Gathering in Memory of William Van O'Connor*. Carbondale: Southern Illinois University Press, 1970.

Includes: "Bad Year, Bad War: New Year's Card," pp. 153–154.

H123   Archer, Jerome W., and Joseph Schwartz, eds. *A Reader for Writers: A Critical Anthology of Prose Readings*. 3d ed. New York: McGraw-Hill, 1971.

Includes: "Malcolm X: Mission and Meaning," pp. 513–521.

H124 Brennecke, John H., and Robert G. Amick, eds. *Significance: The Struggle We Share*. Beverly Hills, CA: Glencoe Press, 1971.
Includes: "Malcolm X," pp. 97–106.

H125 Goldstone, Herbert, Irving Cummings, and Thomas Churchill, eds. *Points of Departure: A Collection of Short Fiction*. Englewood Cliffs, NJ: Prentice-Hall, 1971.
Includes: excerpt from *AKM*, p. 403.

H126 Lydenberg, John, ed. *Dreiser: A Collection of Critical Essays*. TCV. Englewood Cliffs, NJ: Prentice-Hall, 1971.
Includes: "*An American Tragedy*," pp. 129–140.

H127 Lytle, Andrew, ed. *Craft and Vision: The Best Fiction from the Sewanee Review*. New York: Delacorte Press, 1971.
Includes: "Statement of Ashby Wyndham" (excerpt from *AHG*), pp. 366–414.

H128 Madden, David, ed. *Rediscoveries*. New York: Crown Publishers, 1971.
Includes: "Andrew Lytle's *The Long Night*," pp. 17–28.

H129 Salzman, Jack, comp. *The Merrill Studies in* An American Tragedy. Columbus, OH: Charles E. Merrill, 1971.
Includes: "*An American Tragedy*," pp. 99–111.

H130 Foley, Martha, ed. *The Best American Short Stories in 1972 & The Yearbook of the American Short Story*. Boston: Houghton Mifflin; New York: Ballantine, 1972.
Includes: excerpt from *MMGG*, pp. 324–346.

H131 Harrison, Gilbert A. *The Critic as Artist: Essays on Books, 1920–1970*. New York: Liveright, 1972.
Includes: "The Portable Faulkner," pp. 358–377.

H132 Kytle, Ray, and Annette Peterson Kytle, eds. *The Complex Vision: A Collection of Short Stories*. New York: Harcourt Brace Jovanovich, 1972.
Includes: "The Patented Gate and the Mean Hamburger," pp. 193–204.

H133 Rodman, Selden, ed. *100 American Poems*. 2d ed. Mentor, MQ-1123. New York: New American Library, 1972.
Includes: "Love and Knowledge," p. 179, from *A*.

H134 Bradley, Sculley, Richmond Croom Beatty, and E. Hudson Long, eds. *The American Tradition in Literature*. 4th ed. New York: W. W. Norton, 1973.
Includes: "Blackberry Winter."

H135 Clark, C. E. Frazer, ed. *The Nathaniel Hawthorne Journal, 1972*.

Washington, D.C.: NCR Microcard Editions, 1973.

Includes: "Hawthorne *Was* Relevant," pp. 85–89.

H136 Ellmann, Richard, and Robert O'Clair, eds. *The Norton Anthology of Modern Poetry*. New York: W. W. Norton, 1973.

Includes: "History," pp. 684–686; "Revelation," pp. 686–687; "Bearded Oaks," pp. 687–688; "Mexico Is A Foreign Country: Four Studies in Naturalism: IV. The Mango on the Mango Tree"; "VIII. Founding Fathers . . ."; "Notes on a Life to Be Lived: II. Small White House"; "III. Blow, West Wind"; "X. Ways of Day"; "Penological Study: Southern Exposure: 3. Wet Hair . . . ," pp. 688–693.

H137 Schmitter, Dean Morgan, ed. *William Faulkner: A Collection of Criticism*. Contemporary Studies in Literature. New York: McGraw-Hill, 1973.

Includes: "Faulkner: Past and Future," pp. 58–76.

H138 Benson, Jackson J., ed. *The Short Stories of Ernest Hemingway*. Durham, NC: Duke University Press, 1974.

Includes: "Hemingway."

H139 Lohner, Edgar, ed. *Der amerikanische Roman im 19. und 20. Jahrhundert*. Berlin: Erich Schmidt Verlag, 1974.

Includes: "Theodore Dreiser: *An American Tragedy*," pp. 152–161 (in English).

H140 Miller, James E., Jr., Robert Hayden, and Robert O'Neal, eds. *The Lyric Potential*. Glenview, IL: Scott, Foresman, 1974.

Includes: "The Skiers," p. 110.

H141 Ciardi, John, and Miller Williams, eds. *How Does a Poem Mean?* 2d ed. Boston: Houghton Mifflin, 1975.

Includes: "Original Sin: A Short Story," pp. 53–54.

H142 Foley, Martha, ed. *Two Hundred Years of Great American Short Stories*. Boston: Houghton Mifflin, 1975.

Includes: "Cass Mastern's Wedding Ring" from *AKM*.

H143 Higgs, Robert J., and Ambrose N. Manning, eds. *Voices from the Hills: Selected Readings of Southern Appalachia*. New York: Frederick Unger, 1975.

Includes: "Some Don'ts for Literary Regionalists," pp. 357–364.

H144 Litz, A. Walton, ed. *Major American Short Stories*. New York: Oxford University Press, 1975.

Includes: "Blackberry Winter," pp. 603–621.

H145 Stern, Milton R., and Seymour L. Gross, eds. *American Literature Survey*. Vol. 4: *The Twentieth Century*. Rev. ed. Viking Portable Library. New York: Viking Press, 1975.

Includes: "The Last Metaphor," pp. 662–663; "Bearded Oaks," pp. 663–664; and "Revelation," pp. 664–665.

H146 Sergeant, Howard, et al., eds. *Best Poems of 1975.* Borestone Mountain Poetry Awards 1976. Palo Alto, CA: Pacific Books, 1976.

Includes: "Answer to Prayer," pp. 96–97; "One Way to Love God," pp. 98–99; "Evening Hawk," p. 100; and "Midnight Outcry," p. 101.

H147 Cogan, Lee, ed. *Kreuzer and Cogan: Literature for Composition.* 2d ed. New York: Holt, Rinehart & Winston, 1976.

Includes: "Gull's Cry" and "Lullaby: Moonlight Lingers," pp. 283–285.

H148 Zwick, Edward, ed. *Literature and Liberalism: An Anthology of Sixty Years of* The New Republic. Washington, D.C.: New Republic Book Company, 1976.

Includes: "For A Friend Parting," p. 107.

H149 Britton, Norman A., ed. *A Writing Apprenticeship.* New York: Holt, Rinehart & Winston, 1977.

Includes: "Martin Luther King," p. 8.

H150 Rosenberger, Francis Coleman, ed. *Washington and the Poet.* Charlottesville: University Press of Virginia, 1977.

Includes: "Patriotic Tour and Postulate of Joy," p. 13.

H151 Samway, Patrick, and Benjamin Forkner, eds. *Short Stories of the Modern South.* New York: Bantam Books, 1978.

Includes: "Blackberry Winter," pp. 363–384.

H152 Field, Edward, ed. *A Geography of Poets: An Anthology of the New Poetry.* New York: Bantam Books, 1979.

Includes: "Homage to Theodore Dreiser," pp. 423–425.

H153 Rubin, Louis D., Jr. *The Literary South.* New York: John Wiley, 1979.

Includes: "Bearded Oaks," "Summer Storm (Circa 1916) and God's Grace," "Founding Fathers, Nineteenth-Century Style, Southeast U.S.A.," "The Sound of That Wind" (from *A*), and "Evening Hawk," pp. 544–551.

I

Unpublished Works

Note: This section is divided into five subsections: Fiction, Poetry, Drama, Nonfiction, and Speeches and Tributes. The dates provided without square brackets are dates found on the manuscripts; dates in square brackets are conjectures based on external evidence. The entries in this section are not repeated in Appendix I, which lists manuscripts of RPW's published items. The following abbreviations describe the manuscript holdings: OH = original holograph; CH = carbon holograph; OTS = original typescript; CTS = carbon typescript; O/CTS = mixed MS; MTS = multilith typescript.

FICTION

I1　"Goodbye, Jake" (story), n.d. Ctw: OTS, 16 pp.; OTS, 14pp.

I2　"The Apple Tree" (novel), 1930–1932. Ctw: OTS, chapter 8 wanting.

I3　"God's Own Time" (novel), 1932–1933. Ctw: OTS, and 4pp. summary of uncompleted section. KyU: CTS, 128pp.

I4　Untitled (novel), 1933–1934. KyU: CTS, "This untitled & unpublished novel, my second, was written about 1933–34——in Tennessee——R. P. Warren / 1st revised draft," 223pp.

I5　"Waldo, The Good Wolf" (children's story), July 1960. KyU: CTS.

I6　"So Clear, O Victory"; also "Call Me Early" (novel), 1966. Ctw: OH, notes; OH; OTS; CTS (2), frags. KyU: CH, 47pp.; CTS, 63pp.

POETRY

I7　"As, delicate within the stone" (poem), n.d. Ctw: OTS.

I8　"The Bird and Stone" (seq.), n.d. "I. You work injustice to the little streets" and "II. Colder than figments on the wall of sleep." Ctw: OTS.

I9 "Blumlein in April" (poem), n.d. Ctw: OTS (3).

I10 "Body and Soul" (poem), n.d. Ctw: OH.

I11 "Chaste Quaker" (poem), n.d. Ctw: OTS.

I12 "The Concert" (poem), n.d. Ctw: OTS.

I13 "Conquest" (poem), n.d. Ctw: OTS (2).

I14 "The Day Before Christmas" (poem), n.d. Ctw: OTS.

I15 "Devotional Piece: On Seeing Italian with .12 Gauge Stalking Small and Apparently Unobservant Sparrow" (poem), n.d. Ctw: CTS.

I16 "The Door" (poem), n.d. Ctw: OH, OTS.

I17 "Dream scarps and cirques where the tongued glaciers drool" (poem), n.d. Ctw: OTS.

I18 "Far off in Mississippi now" (poem), n.d. Ctw: OTS.

I19 "Farewell of Faustus to Helen" (poem), n.d. Ctw: OTS.

I20 "Greenwood Song" (poem), n.d. Ctw: OTS (2); CTS.

I21 "How cunningly—a spy at night" (poem), n.d. Ctw: OTS.

I22 "I half recall a queen who turned on the stair" (poem), n.d. Ctw: OTS.

I23 "In his great head the gold leaves are falling" (poem), n.d. Ctw: OTS (2).

I24 "In late afternoon, he stops in the road's red dust" (poem), n.d. Ctw: OTS.

I25 "Let summer sum up summer in the blood" (poem), n.d. Ctw: OTS, 2pp., 1 version.

I26 "Let the world's great streaming blackness" (poem), n.d. Ctw: CTS (2).

I27 "Love's Voice" (poem), n.d. Ctw: OTS (2); CTS.

I28 "Notation" (poem), n.d. Ctw: OTS; CTS (2).

I29 "Oxford City Wall" (poem), n.d. Ctw: OTS (2).

I30 "Park Scene" (poem), n.d. Ctw: OTS.

I31 "Riddle of the Dust" (poem), n.d. Ctw: OTS (2).

I32 "San Francisco Night Windows" (poem), n.d. Ctw: OTS.

I33 "September Twilight Piece" (poem), n.d. Ctw: OTS.

I34 "Several Days: I. Thursday" (poem), n.d. Ctw: OH.

I35 "Social Notes" (seq.), n.d. "1. Human Nature," "2. A Long Spoon Advised," and "3. Almanac de Gotha." Ctw: OH; CH; OTS; CTS.

I36 "Spring Off the Gulf" (poem), n.d. Ctw: OH; OTS; CTS.

I37 "Stand back and let them go" (poem), n.d. Ctw: OTS, 3 versions.

I38 "This last grey city holds the travailing sun" (poem), n.d. Ctw: OTS.

I39 "To One Not Quite a Clown" (poem), n.d. Ctw: OTS.

I40 "Two Sonnets of Eternity" (seq.), n.d. "I. The Hours" and "II. My passion is never less than you are wise." Ctw: OTS.

I41 "Watch a Clock Closely" (poem), n.d. Ctw: CTS.

I42 "Where heavy scent of oakleaf under sun" (poem), n.d. Ctw: OTS.

I43 "Why do I love, but the meaningless things I remember?" (poem), n.d. Ctw: OH; OTS; CTS (3).

I44 "Young Men in April Dusk" (poem), n.d. Ctw: OTS.

I45 "Pondy Woods and Other Poems" (collection), 1929. Includes: "Tryst on Vinegar Hill," "Kentucky Mountain Farm: I. Rebuke of the Rocks," "II. At the Hour of the Breaking of the Rocks," "IV. The Owl," "IV. The Moon," "V. The Return," "August Revival: Crosby Junction," "Alf Burt: Tenant Farmer," "Genealogy," "Pro Sua Vita," "To a Face in the Crowd," "The Wrestling Match," "Night Windows for Two," "To One Awake," "Images on the Tomb: I. Dawn: The Gorgon's Head," "II. Day: Lazarus," "III. Evening: The Motors," "IV. Night: But a Sultry Wind," "The Mirror," "Iron Beach," "August Drouth," "September Twilight Piece," "Croesus in Autumn," "Garden Waters," "Easter Morning: Crosby Junction," "The Last Metaphor," "Death Mask of a Young Man: I. The Mouse," "II. The Moon," and "Admonition to the Dead." Ctw: CTS (2).

Note: Payson & Clarke Ltd accepted the manuscript but went bankrupt in the Crash of '29.

I46 "Kentucky Mountain Farm and Other Poems" (collection), 1930. Includes same poems as **I45** with following exceptions: only the first two poems in "Kentucky Mountain Farm" sequence are included, and "Letter of a Mother" is added. Ctw: OTS.

I47 "Cold Colloquy" (collection), 1933. Includes: "Kentucky Mountain Farm: I. Rebuke of the Rocks," "II. At the Hour of the Breaking of the Rocks," "III. History Among the Rocks," "IV. The Owl," "V. The Cardinal," "VI. The Jay," "VII. Watershed," "VIII. The Return," "Pondy Woods," "Croesus in Autumn," "Genealogy," "Pro Sua Vita," "Letter of a Mother," "So Frost Astounds," "The Wrestling Match," "To a Face in the Crowd," "Garden Waters," "The Garden: On Prospect of a Fine Day in Early Autumn," "The Last Metaphor," "To a Friend

Parting," "Letter to a Friend," "Aged Man Surveys the Past Time," "Toward Rationality," "Late Subterfuge," "Ransom," "History," "Resolution," "Calendar," "Pacific Gazer," "Man Coming of Age," "Aubade for Hope," "Problem of Knowledge," "The Limited," "Cold Colloquy," "Eidolon," "For a Friend Who Thinks Himself Urbane," "Images on the Tomb: [same four-poem seq. as in I45]," "To One Awake," and "Death Mask of a Young Man" seq. Ctw: CTS.

I48 "Problem of Knowledge" (collection), [1938–39]. Includes same poems as I47 with the following exceptions: deletes "Pro Sua Vita," "The Wrestling Match," and "The Limited"; adds "Bearded Oaks," "Monologue at Midnight," "Love's Voice," "Picnic Remembered," "Love's Parable," "Question and Answer," "Letter from a Coward to a Hero," "The Return: An Elegy," and "Athenian Death." Ctw: OTS.

I49 "Hold on to Yourself Now" (poem), 1957–60. Ctw: OH.

I50 "Dr. McClinken" [or, McClendon] (poem), 12 Feb. 1965 and 1 March 1965. KyU: CTS, in "Tale of Time" seq.

I51 "Birthday Poem—April 24, 1971" (poem), 1971. Ctw: OTS.

I52 "Rosanna" (poem), Aug. 1976. Ctw: OTS.

I53 "Egyptian Mystery in Connecticut" (poem), 27 Feb.–2 March [1978]. Ctw: OH; OTS (2); CTS (6).

DRAMA

I54 "Proud Flesh" (three-act play), 1939. Ctw: OH and OTS, worksheets; OTS and CTS, early version labeled "This was the first fragment written on *Proud Flesh*, which later became *All the King's Men*. This is the opening of the chorus of Highway Patrolmen / RPW"; OTS, with revisions; OTS (4); CTS (3); and some fragments.

I55 "Don't Bury Me at All: An Original Story for the Screen" (screenplay) with Max Shulman, [1950]. Ctw: OTS; CTS; MTS (8).

Note: ltr., 12 July 1950, from P. M. Pasinetti to RPW about this script.

I56 "The Wedding Ring" (three-act play), 1951. Ctw: OH and OTS worksheets with revisions; two reel-to-reel tapes marked "Early Version——Ready for Robert Rossen"; MTS (6), early version from three-ring binder; MTS (6) marked "old version"; MTS with inserts and revisions; MTS (2), one marked "Eric

Bentley"; OTS and CTS, revisions of various acts labeled "Version B"; CTS worksheets labeled "Version A"; CTS with revisions; CTS marked "1955"; CTS (3), one marked on folder "Intermediate revisions, Act III, 1957"; MTS (2) marked "Version C"; O/CTS labeled "Master Draft"; and an envelope labeled "Notes and rejects, June 1959." KyU: MTS. See also **I59**.

I57 "This Very Spot" (television screenplay) with David M. Clay, 1952. Ctw: OTS. **B20**.

I58 "Willie Stark: His Rise and Fall: A Play in Three Acts," 1955. Ctw: OTS (2), labeled "Old Version"; OTS (2), one marked "This is director's copy for production at Margot Jones Theater, Dallas——November 1958," the other with "Copyright 1 July 1955" on the coversheet; CTS (2), one marked "Lucy"; and CTS in envelope from L. Fitzall (?) postmarked Berkeley, CA, 6 June 1955. KyU: CTS.

I59 "Listen to the Mockingbird: A Drama of the American Civil War" (three-act play), 1959. Formerly "The Wedding Ring," **I56**. Ctw: CTS(4) marked "Version D (revised 1 June 1959)."

NONFICTION

I60 Prospectus for book on modern poetry, with Allen Tate. n.d. Ctw: CTS.

I61 "Garrick and the Plays of Shakespeare" (class paper), 1927. Yale University graduate class. KyU: CTS.

I62 "A Study of John Marston's Satires" (thesis, B.Litt., Oxford), [1933]. KyU: CTS.

I63 Article on Italy and the collapse of Fascism, July 1940. Ctw: OTS with revisions.

I64 "Syracuse" (article), [1948]. About the ancient Greek city. Ctw: CTS.

SPEECHES AND TRIBUTES

I65 "Luigi Berti: a recollection" (obituary), n.d. KyU: OH; CTS.

I66 "Denis Devlin: a recollection" (obituary), n.d. KyU: OH; CTS.

I67 Nomination of Max Ernst to honorary membership in the Academy of Arts and Letters, n.d. Ctw: CTS.

I68 Nomination of Katherine Anne Porter for election into the Academy of Arts and Letters, n.d. Ctw: CTS.

I69 "Conference on Literature and Reading in the South and Southwest" (speech, RPW presiding), 10–11 April 1935. Southern Writers Conference at LSU. Ctw: MTS.

Note: transcript by B. A. Botkin.

I70 "Tradition in Literature" (speech), 1938. MLA. KyU: CTS.

I71 "Poetry and Patriotism" (speech), 1942. Louisiana Poetry Society. KyU: CTS.

I72 A series of radio lectures, 1943–45. For Minneapolis and for Palmer Radio at Connecticut College. KyU: CTS.

I73 "A Tribute to Ezra Pound" (radio), 5 Dec. 1955. WYBC, Yale Broadcasting Co. Ctw: CTS.

I74 "Eberhart" (tribute), [1957]. American Poetry Society Annual Dinner. Ctw: OH.

I75 "Who Do You Work For?" (panel), 10 Aug. 1957. 50th Anniversary Meeting of the MacDowell Colony, Peterborough, NH. Ctw: OTS, pp. 1–4; CTS, pp. 5–22.

Note: with Ben Shahn, Virgil Thomson, and Russell Lynes (moderator).

I76 National Book Award for Poetry acceptance speech, 1958. Ctw: OTS. KyU: OH.

I77 Introduction of T. S. Eliot (speech), 23 Nov. [1961]. Ctw: OTS. KyU: OH; CTS.

I78 On Robert Frost (tribute), 1962. KyU: OH; CTS.

I79 Lecture to Response Symposium of World Affairs, April 1963. Princeton University. KyU: OH; copy of the program.

I80 "A Note on Roethke" (tribute), [1963]. University of Washington, Seattle. Ctw: OTS.

I81 "On Alberto Moravia" (introductory speech), April 1964. Metropolitan Museum of Art, New York. KyU: OH; CTS.

I82 "Viewpoint" (radio), 5–6 June 1965. Over the Mutual Broadcasting Network, WOR (NYC). Ctw: tape reel.

I83 "T. S. Eliot" (obituary), [1965]. For TV channel 13, NYC. Ctw: CTS. KyU: CTS.

I84 "Trends and Fiction" (speech), 10 May 1966. 50th Anniversary of the Pulitzer Prize. Ctw: OH; OTS; CTS (2), one marked "Final." KyU: CTS.

I85 Address given at the University of California at La Jolla, Oct. 1967. KyU: CH.

I86 "Pound" (tribute), [1972]. Yale. Ctw: OH; CTS.

I87 "Katherine Anne Porter" (tribute), 18 Oct. 1976. YMHA, New York City. Ctw: OH; CTS.

188 "William Faulkner: A Life on Paper" (documentary), [1978]. Mississippi Authority for Educational Television. Ctw: OTS, 4 pp.

Note: a 90-minute documentary film which includes 53 interviews, one of which is with RPW.

189 On the program for The Citadel Conference on Literature on the Southern Literary Imagination (speech), 6–7 April 1979. Ctw: OTS.

Note: with William Styron, Louise Cowan, Cleanth Brooks, and Louis D. Rubin, Jr.

J

Translations

J1 Argentina
a. "Terror." Trans. A. Biou Casares and J. L. Borges. *Sur: Revista mensual publicada bajo la dirección de Victoria Ocampo*, 14 (March–April 1944), [120]–127.
Note: in English, pp. [120], 122, 124, and 126;. in Spanish, pp. [121], 123, 125, and 127.
b. [*AKM*]. Trans. Juan Rodriguez Chicago. *Decepción*. Buenos Aires: Ediciones Antonio Zamora, 1950. Bds. with dw., 495 pp.
c. [*BA*]. Trans. J. Martinez Alinari. *Coro de ángeles*. Buenos Aires: Guillermo Kraft Limitada, 1957. Paper with dw., 375 pp.
d. [*Cave*]. Trans. J. Martinez Alinari. *La caverna*. Buenos Aires: Guillermo Kraft Limitada, 1962. Paper with dw., 278 pp.
e. [*PTCT*]. Trans. Aníbal Leal. *Un lugar adonde llegar*. Buenos Aires: Javier Vergara, 1978. Paper, 531 pp.
J2 Belgium
a. [*WET*]. Trans. Jean H. P. Jacobs. *Het verleden laat niet los*. Antwerp: P. Vinck, 1957.
J3 Brazil
a. [*AKM*]. Trans. Hélio Pólvora. *Os capangas do chefe*. Rio de Janeiro: Edições Bloch, 1968. Introduction by Pólvora. Paper, 639 pp.
b. [*DP*]. Trans. Ronaldo Sérgio de Biasi. *Democracia & literatura*. Rio de Janeiro: Forense-Universitaria, [1977]. Paper, 112 pp.
J4 Bulgaria
a. [*AKM*]. Trans. Todor Viltchev. *Cjaloto kralsko vojnstvo*. Ed. Jenny Bozhilova. Sofia: Narodna Kultura, 1973. Introduction by Manon Dragostinova. Bds. with dw., 560 pp.
J5 Chile
a. ["When the Light Gets Green"]. "Cuando la luz palidece." *Antología de escritores contemporaneos de los estados unidos*. Ed. Ricardo A. Latcham. Santiago: Editorial Nascimento, 1944. I, 318–327. Paper, 2 vols.: 550, 563 pp.

b. [*WET*]. Trans. Lilian Lorca. *La vida es difícil (una novela romántica)*. Santiago: Zig-Zag, 1952. Paper, 698 pp.

J6 China

a. [*AKM*]. Washington, D.C.: United States Intelligence Agency, 1974. 2 vols.

J7 Czechoslovakia

a. [*AKM*]. Trans. A. J. Štàstný. *Všichni jsou zbrojnoši královi*.
1. Prague: Odeon, 1970. Afterword by Zdeněk Vančura. Bds. with dw., 527 pp.
2. Prague: Odeon, 1977. Afterword by Martin Hilský. Cloth with dw., 588 pp.

b. [*F*]. Trans. Eva Kondrysová. *Potopa*. Prague: Svoboda Jiskry, 1974. Bds. with dw., 462 pp.

c. [*AKM*]. Trans. Jana Ruppeldtová. *Guvernér*. Bratislava: Slovensky Spisovatel, 1976. Afterword by Juraj Vojtek.

d. [*AHG*]. Trans. Eva Kondrysová. *U nebeskych bran*. Prague: Svoboda Jiskry, 1979. Bds. with dw., 472 pp.

J8 Denmark

a. [*AKM*]. Trans. Annabeth Kruuse. *Alle kongens maend*.
1. Copenhagen: Grafisk Forlag, 1948. Paper, 414 pp.
2. Copenhagen: Fremad, 1969. Paper, 2 vols.: 254, 219 pp.

b. [*NR*]. Trans. Karina Windfeld-Hansen. *Hovslag l natten*. Copenhagen: Grafisk Forlag, 1949. Paper, 294 pp.

c. [*BA*]. Trans. Karina Windfeld-Hansen. *Om jeg blot kunne blive fri*. Copenhagen: Grafisk Forlag, 1957. Introduction by Henrik Hansen. Paper, 454 pp.

J9 Finland

a. [*AKM*]. Trans. Juhani Koskinen. *Kaikki kuninkaan miehet*. Jyväskylä. Gummerus, 1976. Bds. with dw., 573 pp.

b. [*PTCT*]. Trans. Juhani Koskinen. *Jokin tässä elämässä*. Jyväskylä: Gummerus, 1979. Bds. with dw., 452 pp.

J10 France

a. [*AKM*]. Trans. Pierre Singer. *Les Fous du roi*.
1. Paris: Librairie Stock, 1950. Introduction by Michel Mohrt. Paper, 559 pp.
2. Paris: Le Club Français du Livre, 1951.
3. Paris: Stock, 1968. Introduction by Michel Mohrt. Paper.
4. Paris: Stock, 1979. Introduction by Michel Mohrt. Paper, 734 pp.

Note: in "Foreign News: France," *Time*, 18 Dec. 1950, p. 32: a notice that *AKM* was awarded the international prize of the French Book Club for the French translation.

b. [*NR*]. Trans. Michel Mohrt. *Le Cavalier de la nuit*. Paris: Librairie Stock, 1951. Paper, 453 pp.

c. [*AHG*]. Trans. J[ean]-G[érard] Chauffeteau. *Aux portes du ciel*. Paris: Librairie Stock, 1952. Preface by Chauffeteau. Paper, 369 pp.

d. [*WET*]. Trans. Jean-Gérard Chauffeteau and Gilbert Vivier. *Le Grand Souffle*. Paris: Librairie Stock, 1955. Paper, 540 pp.

e. [Poems]. Trans. Alain Bosquet. *Profils*, 13 (Autumn 1955), 44–55.

Includes: "End of Season," "The Mango on the Mango Tree," and "History."

f. [*BA*]. Trans. Jean-Gérard Chauffeteau and Gilbert Vivier. *L'Esclave libre*.

    1. Paris: Librairie Stock, 1957. Paper, 382 pp.

    2. Paris: Club des éditeurs, 1957. Cloth, 428 pp.

g. ["Ernest Hemingway"]. Trans. Michel Minard et al. "Introduction to *A Farewell to Arms*." Ernest Hemingway issue. *La Revue des Lettres Modernes: Histoire des Idées et des Littératures*, 4, nos. 31–34 (4th Qtr 1957), 473–520.

Note: critical outline no. 2, pp. 9–56 in collaboration with RPW.

h. [*Seg*]. Trans. Jean-Luc Salvador. *Ségrégatión: Essai sur le problème noir en Amérique*. Paris: Librairie Stock, 1957. Paper, 94 pp.

i. ["William Faulkner"]. Trans. Michel J. Minard et al. "William Faulkner." *La Revue des Lettres Modernes: Histoire des Idées et des Littératures*, 5 (Winter 1958–59), 429–434.

j. [*Cave*]. Trans. Connie Fennell. *Le Caverne*. Paris: Librairie Stock, 1960. Paper, 379 pp.

k. [Poems]. Trans. Alain Bosquet. *Trente-cinq jeunes poètes américains*. Paris: Gallimard, 1960. Pp. 83–89.

Includes: "The Mango on the Mango Tree" and "Letter to a Friend."

l. [*W*]. Trans. Jean-Gérard Chauffeteau and Gilbert Vivier. *La Grande Forêt*. Paris: Librairie Stock, 1962. Preface by Chauffeteau. Paper, 268 pp.

m. [*LCW*]. Trans. Pierre Singer. *L'Héritage de la guerre civile*. Paris: Librairie Stock, 1962. Paper, 115 pp.

Note: excerpt, also translated by Singer: "La Guerre de Sécession continent les clefs de l'Amérique," *Le Figaro Littéraire*, 16 June 1962, p. 17.

n. [*F*]. Trans. Antoine Gentien. *Les Eaux montent: Un Roman de notre temps*. Paris: Librairie Stock, 1965. Paper, 322 pp.

o. [*WSN?*]. Trans. as "'Moi, je suis content d'être un noir!' un entretien avec Ralph Ellison," *Mensuel: Journal de Genève*, no. 30 (July 1970), pp. 2–3.

p. [*PTCT*]. Trans. Anne-Marie Soulac. *Un Endroit où aller*. Paris: Stock, 1979. Preface by Raymond Las Vergnas. Paper with dw., 460 pp.

J11 Germany

a. [*AKM*]. Trans. Ilse Krämer. *Der Gouverneur*.
    1. Hamburg: Krüger, 1951.
    2. Munich: Goldman, 1956.

b. [Poems]. Trans. Kurt Erich Meurer. *Perspektiren*, 13 (Autumn 1955), 42–53.
Includes: "Pursuit," "End of Season," "Monologue at Midnight," "Late Subterfuge," and "Letter to a Friend."

c. [*BA*]. Trans. Helmut Degner. *Amantha*. Gütersloh: C. Bertelsmann, 1957. Bds. with dw., 512 pp.

d. [*AKM*(p)]. Trans. Erwin Piscator and Hellmut Schlien. *Blut auf dem Mond: Ein Schauspiel in 3 Akten*. Emsdetten (Westf.): Lechte, 1957.

e. [Essay]. "Von der positiven Kraft der Kritik." *Neue deutsche Hefte*, 32 (March 1957), 664–667.

f. [*AHG*]. Trans. Helmut Degner. *Alle Wünsche dieser Welt*. Gütersloh: C. Bertelsmann, 1959. Bds. with dw., 526 pp.

g. [*Cave*]. Trans. Helmut Degner. *Die Höhle von Johntown: Roman*. Gütersloh: Sigbert Mohn Verlag, 1961. Bds. with dw., 380 pp.

h. [*SE*]. Trans. Hans Hennecke and Hans Walz. *Ausgewählte Essays*. Gütersloh: Sigbert Mohn Verlag, 1961. Cloth with dw., 366 pp.

i. [Poems]. Trans. Franz Link. *Amerikanische Lyrik*. Vol. 17. Stuttgart: Philipp Reclam, 1974. Pp. 360–365.
Includes: "The Garden" and "Bearded Oaks."

J12 Hungary

a. [*AKM*]. Trans. Valkay Sarolta. *Repül a nehéz kő*. Budapest: Magvető, 1970. Bds. with dw., 663 pp.

b. [*F*]. Trans. Bartos Tibor. *Vízözön*. Budapest: Európa Könyvkiadó, 1975. Bds. with dw., 483 pp.

J13 India

a. [Poems]. Washington, D.C.: United States Intelligence Agency, 1962.

J14 Israel

a. [*AKM*]. Trans. A. Ben-Dan. *Kol anshey ha-melekh.* Tel-Aviv: Idit, 1954.

b. [*BA*]. Trans. Moshe Ben-Rafael. *Havurat maleakhim.*
1. Tel-Aviv: Idit, 1959.
2. As *Havurat mal'akim.* Tel Aviv: Idit, 1964.

J15 Italy
a. ["Her Own People"]. *Inventario*, 1 (1946), 189–198.
b. [*AHG*]. Trans. Luisa Panella Coggi. *Alle porte del cielo.* Milan: Baldini & Castoldi, 1948. Bds. with dw., 405 pp.
c. [*AKM*]. Trans. Luigi Berti. *Tutti gli uomini del re.*
1. Milan: Bompiani, 1949. Paper with dw., 595 pp.
2. Milan: Garzanti, 1968. Paper, 577 pp.
d. [*WET*]. Trans. Glauco Cambon. *Nel vortice del tempo.* Milan-Verona: Arnoldo Mondadori, 1954. Bds. with dw., 631 pp.
e. [*NR*]. Trans. Maria Stella Ferrari. *Il cavaliere della notte.* Milan: Bompiani, 1954. Bds. with dw., 544 pp.
f. [*BD*]. Trans. Glauco Cambon. "Stirpe di draghi." *Inventario*, 7 (Jan.–June 1955), [95]–116.
g. [Poem]. "Fine di stagione." *Prospetti*, 13 (Autumn 1955), 50–53.
h. [*Seg*]. "La coscienza divisa Inchiesta sulla segregazione razziale— negli Stati del Sud." *Tempo presente*, 1 (Nov. 1956), [611]–629.
Note: excerpt from *Life*.
i. [*BA*]. Trans. Bruno Oddera. *La banda degli angeli.* Milan: Bompiani, 1957. Paper with dw., 452 pp.
j. [*CA*]. Trans. Bruno Oddera. *Il circo in soffitta.* Milan: Bompiani, 1959. Bds. with dw., 336 pp.
k. [Poems]. Trans. Izzo Carlo. "Tre poesie." *Tempo presente*, 5 (Aug. 1960), [555]–558.
Includes: "Debate: Question, Quarry, Dream," "Nursery Rhymes: Knockety-Knockety-Knock," and "Mother Makes the Biscuits."
l. [*Cave*]. Trans. Elsa Pelitti. *La caverna.* Milan: Bompiani, 1960. Bds. with plastic dw., 374 pp.
m. [*AKM*(p)]. Trans. Gerardo Guerrieri. "Tutti gli uomini del re: Un prologo e tre atti di RPW." *Sipario*, no. 176 (Dec. 1960), pp. 53–71. Illus. pp. 73–74. Introduction by RPW.
n. [Poems]. Trans. Luigi Berti. "'Elijah on Mount Carmel' e poesie da 'Promises.'" *Inventario*, 17 (May–Dec. 1962), [1]–16.
Includes: "To a Little Girl . . . ," "Promises / To Gabriel," and "Boschi Scuri."
o. [*WSN?*]. Trans. Ettore Capriolo. *Chi parla per i negri?* Milan: Valentino Bompiani, 1967. Paper, 334 pp.

p. [*W*]. Trans. Adriana Dell'orto. *Adam o della guerra civile*. Milan: Bompiani, 1970. Paper with dw., 309 pp.

q. [Poems]. Trans. Sergio Perosa. *Racconto del tempo e altre poesie, 1923–71*. Turin: Einaudi, 1971. Bds. with dw., 176 pp.

r. [Essay]. "Un saggio: La poesia in un'epoca di sfacelo." Trans. Giuseppe Pontiggia. *Almanacco della specchio*, no. 1 (1972), 153–162.

Note: RPW's acceptance speech for the 1970 National Medal for Literature.

J16 Japan

a. [Stories]. Trans. Katsugi Takamura, Kenji Kabayashi, and Tamo Hashiguchi. In an anthology whose title approximates *Mud Stream*. Tokyo: Naundo, n.d. Pp. 133–202.

Includes: "The Patented Gate," "Christian Education," "Her Own People," and "Christmas Gift."

b. [Stories]. Ed. Sōichi Minagawa. *Blackberry Winter and Other Stories*. Tokyo: Nan'un-do, 1956. Paper, 119 pp.

c. [*BA*]. Trans. Akira Namikawa. *Band of Angels*. Tokyo: Irachi Shuppan-sha, 1957. Bds. with wax paper dw., 432 pp.

d. [*CA*]. Trans. Tamotsu Hashiguchi. *Shûkyô kyôiku, etc*. Tokyo: Nan'un-dô, 1960.

e. [*AKM*]. Ed. Jūkichi Suzuki, Senichi Itō, and Tokizō Sanada. *All the King's Men* (abridged). Tokyo: Bunri Shoin, 1969. Paper with dw., 172 pp.

f. [Essay]. Ed. Naozo Uenc. *Why Do We Read Fiction?* Tokyo: Nan'un-do, 1971. Pp. 1–21. Paper, 82 pp.

g. [*LCW*]. Ed. Teruhiko Mukai and Nobuhiko Motoyama. *The Legacy of the Civil War*. Tokyo: Bunri, 1976.

J17 Korea

a. [*SSM*]. Trans. Byeong-taeg Yang and Gahyeong Lee. *Hyeondae yeongmi danpyeonseon*. Seoul: Euryumunhwasa, 1961.

b. [*BA*]. Washington, D.C.: United States Intelligence Agency, 1971.

J18 Latvia

a. [*AKM*]. Trans. Rute Runce. *Visā ķeniņe zemē neviens*. Rīgā: Liesma, 1972. Afterword by M. Tuguševa.

J19 Lithuania

a. [*AKM*]. Trans. Juozas Butenas. *Karaliaus visa kariauna*. Vilnius: Vaga, 1970. 595 pp.

J20 Netherlands

a. [*AKM*]. Trans. J. G. Alburg and M. Mok. *Zij gaven hem macht*. Amsterdam: Uitgeverij De Bezige Bij, 1950. Bds. with dw., 423pp.

b. [*BA*]. Trans. C. J. Kelk. *Slavin van de vrijheid*. Amsterdam:

Elsevier, 1956. Bds. with dw., 410 pp.

J21 Norway

a. [*AKM*]. Trans. Fredrik Wulfsberg. *All kongens menn.* Oslo: Norsk Forlag, 1948. Paper, 544 pp.

b. [*WET*]. Trans. Erling Sundve. *Det store bedrag.* Oslo: Gyldendal Norsk Forlag, 1952. Paper, 525 pp.

J22 Poland

a. [*AKM*]. Trans. Bronisław Zieliński. *Gubernator.*

  1. Warsaw: Państwowy Instytut Wydawniczy, 1960. Paper with dw., 736 pp.

  2. Warsaw: Państwowy Instytut Wydawniczy, 1962. Bds. with dw., 736 pp.

  3. Warsaw: Państwowy Instytut Wydawniczy, 1964. 2 vols. Paper.

b. [*W*]. Trans. Bronisław Zieliński. *Puszcza: Opowieść z czasów wojny domowej.* Warsaw: Państwowy Instytut Wydawniczy, 1964. Postscript by W. Sadkowski. Paper with dw., 239 pp.

c. [Story]. "Cirkus v podkroví." *Světová Literatura,* 13 (1968), 109–137.

d. [BW]. Trans. Krystyna Tarnowska. "Jagodowa Zima." *Współczesne opowiadania amerykańskie, 32.* Warsaw: Iskry, 1973. I, 64–91.

e. [*WSN?*]. Trans. Adam Kaska. *W imieniu murzynów?* Warsaw: Państwowy Instytut Wydawniczy, 1974. Paper with dw., 540 pp.

f. [*MMGG*]. Trans. Bronisław Zieliński. *Spotkajmy się w zielonej dolinie.* Warsaw: Państwowy Instytut Wydawniczy, 1975. Paper, 354 pp.

g. [*NR*]. Trans. Kazimierz Piotrowski. *Nocny jeździec.* Warsaw: Państwowy Instytut Wydawniczy, 1976. Paper, 466 pp.

J23 Portugal

a. [*NR*]. Trans. João B. Viegas. *O cavaleiro da noite.* Lisbon: Estúdiós Cor, 1959. Introduction by RPW. Paper, 468 pp.

J24 Russia

a. [*AKM*]. Trans. M. Tugushev. *Vsia korolevskaia rat, roman.*

  1. Serialized in *Novyi mir,* 44 (July 1968), 80–151; (Aug. 1968), 76–130; (Sept. 1968), 66–120; (Oct. 1968), 120–175; and (Nov. 1968), 119–176.

  2. Moscow: Izd-vo Tshk Vlksm, 1968. Bds. with dw., 544 pp.

J25 Spain

a. [*NR*]. Trans. E. Piñas. *El caballero de la noche.*

  1. Barcelona: Plaza & Janés, S.A., 1960. Bds. with dw., 446 pp.

  2. Barcelona: Ediciones G. P., 1963. Paper with dw., 448 pp.

b. [*AKM*]. Trans. Juan Rodriguez Chicago. *Todos los hombres del rey.*

In *Los premios Pulitzer de novela*. Vol. 8. Barcelona: Plaza & Janés, S.A., 1967. Pp. 1271–1802.

c. [*MMGG*]. Trans. Manuel Bartolomé. *Te espero en la verde espesura*. Barcelona: Noguer, 1973. Bds. with dw., 320 pp.

d. [*PTCT*]. Trans. Aníbal Leal. *Un lugar adonde llegar*. Barcelona: Javier Vergara, 1978. Paper, 531 pp.

J26 Sweden
a. [*AKM*]. Trans. Nils Holmberg. *Alla kungens män*. Stockholm: Bonnier, 1947.

b. [*WET*]. Trans. Nils Holmberg. *Nog av tid och rum: (En romantisk berättelse)*. Stockholm: Albert Bonniers Forlag, 1951. Paper with dw., 464 pp.

c. [*RA*]. Trans. Margareta Schlyter-Stiernstedt. *Slaget om fort alamo*. Stockholm: B. Wahlströms Bokförlag, 1965. Bds., 156 pp.

J27 Switzerland
a. [*AKM*]. Trans. Ilse Krämer. *Des Königs Tross*. Zürich: Büchergilde Gutenberg, 1949. Bds., 539 pp.

b. [Essay]. Trans. Maria von Scheinitz. "Ironie, die aus einer Mitte kommt: Katherine Anne Porter." In *Fahles Pferd und fahler Reiter: Drei Novellen aus dem amerikanischen übertragen Katherine Anne Porter*. Zürich: Diogenes Verlag, 1963.

J28 Turkey
a. [*AKM*]. Trans. Nermin Turkmen. *İktidar hirsi*. İstanbul: Türkiye Yayinevi, 1958.

b. [*WET*]. Trans. Sevinç Deger. *Intikam hirsi*. İstanbul: Türkiye Yayinevi, 1958.

J29 Venezuela
a. [Poem]. Trans. Hildamar Escalante. "Pro sua vita." In *Breve informe de peosia norteamericana*. Caracas: Tipografia la nacion, 1947. Pp. 123–126. Paper, 131 pp.

J30 Vietnam
a. [*CA*]. Trans. Hoa-Kỳ Tuyêt-tác Khác. "Mùa đông nở hoa dàu." In *Giâc mo mùa đông*. Saigon: Ziên Hồng, 1967. Pp. 153–182. Paper, 386 pp.

J31 Yugoslavia
a. [*BA*]. Trans. Boris Gerechtshammer. *Četa andjela*. Rijeka: Otokar Keršovani, 1958.

b. [*AKM*]. Trans. Stjepan Preveo Krešić. *Svi kraljevi ljudi*. Zagreb: Naprijed, 1960.

c. [*Cave*]. Trans. Omer Lakomica. *Pečina*. Rijeka: Otokar Keršovani, 1963.

Works about
Robert Penn Warren and
His Writing

K

Complete Books

K1 Hart, John A., chm. *All the King's Men: A Symposium.* Carnegie
Series in English, no. 3.
a. Pittsburgh: Carnegie Institute of Technology, 1957.
b. Rpt. Ann Arbor: University Microfilms, 1971.
  Contents: A. Fred Sochatoff, "Some Treatments of the Huey
Long Theme," pp. 3–15; Erwin R. Steinberg, "The Enigma of
Willie Stark," pp. 17–28; Robert C. Slack, "The Telemachus
Theme," pp. 29–38; Beekman W. Cottrell, "Cass Mastern and the
Awful Responsibility of Time," pp. 39–49; Neal Woodruff, Jr.,
"The Technique of *AKM*," pp. 51–62; John A. Hart, "Some Major
Images in *AKM*," pp. 63–74; and William M. Schutte, "The Dra-
matic Versions of the Willie Stark Story," pp. 75–90.

K2 Poenicke, Klaus. *Robert Penn Warren: Kunstwerk und krittische The-
orie.* Heidelberg: Carl Winter, 1959.
  Contents: chapters: "Die Agrarbewegung," "Die Konturen des
Mythos: RPW wider den Zeitgeist," "Die 'Neue Kritik' und War-
ren's Leitthema," "*NR*: Seine Struktur und die literarisch-geistige
Matrix," "*NR*: Fabel und Mythos," "*AHG*," "*AKM*: Studie einer
Metamorphose," "*CA*," "*WET*," and "*BA*"; plus "Bibliographischer
Anhang."

K3 Beebe, Maurice, ed. "Robert Penn Warren Special Number."
a. *Modern Fiction Studies*, 6 (Spring 1960).
b. Rpt. New York: Kraus Reprint, 1965.
  Contents: Everett Carter, "The 'Little Myth' of RPW," pp. 3–12;
John Lewis Longley, Jr., "'AHG': The Major Themes," pp. 13–
24; Elizabeth M. Kerr, "Polarity of Themes in 'AKM,'" pp. 25–
46; John W. Rathbun, "Philosophy, 'WET,' and the Art of the
Novel," pp. 47–54; Robert Berner, "The Required Past: 'WET,'"
pp. 55–64; Leonard Casper, "Journey to the Interior: 'Cave,'"
pp. 65–72; and Maurice Beebe and Erin Marcus, "Criticism of
RPW: A Selected Checklist," pp. 83–88.

K4 Casper, Leonard. *Robert Penn Warren: The Dark and Bloody Ground*.

a. Seattle: University of Washington Press, 1960.

b. Woodthorpe, England: W. S. Hall & Company, 1960.

c. Rpt. New York: Greenwood Press, 1971.

Contents: chapters: 1. "A Symposium of Voices," 2. "The New Criticism," 3. "The New Agrarianism," 4. "Approach to Literature," 5. "Poetry: The Golden Eye," 6. "Fiction and Biography: The Ornate Web," and 7. "The Running Gamble"; plus notes, selected bibliography, and index.

K5 Bohner, Charles H. *Robert Penn Warren*. Twayne's United States Authors Series, no. 69. New York: Twayne Publishers, 1964.

Contents: chapters: 1. "Southern Man of Letters," 2. "The Texture of the World," 3. "The Past Recaptured," 4. "The Past and Its Burden," 5. "The Detritus of History," and 6. "Interim Report"; plus chronology, selected bibliography, and index.

K6 Lynn, Robert H. *All the King's Men: Notes*. Lincoln, NE: Cliff's Notes, 1964.

K7 West, Paul. *Robert Penn Warren*. Pamphlets on American Writers, no. 44.

a. Minneapolis: University of Minnesota Press, 1964.

b. London: Oxford University Press, 1965.

K8 Gerhard, George B. *Robert Penn Warren's* All the King's Men. New York: Monarch Press, 1965.

K9 Longley, John Lewis, Jr., ed. *Robert Penn Warren: A Collection of Critical Essays*.

a. New York University Press, 1965.

b. Rpt. Westport, CT: Greenwood Press, 1979.

Contents: John M. Bradbury, "RPW's Novels: The Symbolic and Textual Patterns," pp. 3–17; Ralph Ellison and Eugene Walter, "The Art of Fiction XVIII: RPW," pp. 18–45; Alvan S. Ryan, "RPW's *NR*: The Nihilism of the Isolated Temperament," pp. 49–59; John Lewis Longley, Jr., "Self-Knowledge, the Pearl of Pus, and the Seventh Circle: The Major Themes in *AHG*," pp. 60–74; RPW, "*AKM*: The Matrix of Experience," pp. 75–81; Robert B. Heilman, "Melpomene as Wallflower; or, The Reading of Tragedy," pp. 82–95; Robert B. Heilman, "Tangled Web," pp. 96–109; Frederick P. W. McDowell, "The Romantic Tragedy of Self in *WET*," pp. 110–124; F. Cudworth Flint, "Mr. Warren and the Reviewers," pp. 125–139; Leonard Casper, "Miscegenation as Symbol: *BA*," pp. 140–148; Leonard Casper, "Journey to the Interior," pp. 149–158; Leonard Casper, "Trial by Wilderness: Warren's Exemplum," pp. 159–168; John Lewis Longley, Jr., "When All Is Said and Done: Warren's *F*," pp. 169–177; William C. Havard, "The Burden of the Literary Mind: Some Meditations on RPW as Historian," pp. 178–194; Frederick P. W. McDowell, "Psychology and Theme in *BD*," pp. 197–222; George P. Garrett, "The Recent Poetry of RPW," pp. 223–236; and RPW, "Knowledge and the Image of Man," pp. 237–246; plus introduction and selected bibliography.

K10 Strandberg, Victor H. *A Colder Fire: The Poetry of Robert Penn Warren*. [Lexington]: University of Kentucky Press, 1965.

   Contents: chapters: 1. "The Emerging of Vision and Voice: *SP* and Its Sources," 2. "*BD*: Warren's Best Book," 3. "*P*: A Legacy," and 4. "*YEO*: A Culmination"; plus introduction, "The Themes of RPW," and index.

K11 Beebe, Maurice, and Leslie A. Field, eds. *Robert Penn Warren's All the King's Men: A Critical Handbook*. Belmont, CA: Wadsworth Publishing Company, 1966.

   Contents: Hodding Carter, "Huey Long's Louisiana Hayride," pp. 1–14; T. Harry Williams, "The Achievements of Huey Long," pp. 14–21; Carl P. Leubsdorf, "The Legacy of Huey Long (an Associated Press release), pp. 21–23; RPW, "Louisiana Politics and *AKM*," pp. 23–28; Louis D. Rubin, Jr., "Huey Long in Fiction," pp. 28–39; Dante Alighiere, "Purgatorio: Canto Three," pp. 40–43; Niccolò Machiavelli, "On Political Expediency," pp. 43–45; William James, "On Pragmatism," pp. 46–48; RPW, "Selected Literary Criticism," pp. 48–54; RPW, "Knowledge and the Image of Man," pp. 55–62; Ralph Ellison and Eugene Walter, "An Interview with Warren," pp. 63–65; William M. Schutte, "The Dramatic Versions of the Willie Stark Story," pp. 65–77; Robert B. Heilman, "*AKM* as Tragedy," pp. 79–89; Joseph Baker, "Irony in *AKM*," pp. 90–100; Norton R. Girault, "The Narrator's Mind as Symbol," pp. 101–117; Malcolm O. Sillars, "A Study in Populism," pp. 117–125; Newton P. Stallknecht, "A Study in Nihilism," pp. 125–128; Norman Kelvin, "Warren as Puritan," pp. 129–132; Seymour L. Gross, "Warren as Moralist," pp. 133–139; James Ruoff, "Warren's Teleology," pp. 139–147; Joseph Frank, "Romanticism and Reality," pp. 147–149; Chester E. Eisinger, "The Conservative Quest," pp. 149–157; John Edward Hardy, "The Dialectic of

Self," pp. 157–167; Roger Sale, "Having It Both Ways," pp. 168–175; and Elizabeth M. Kerr, "Polarity of Themes," pp. 175–195; plus chronology and selected bibliography.

K12 Longley, John Lewis, Jr. *Robert Penn Warren*. Southern Writers Series, no. 2. Austin, TX: Steck-Vaughn Co., 1969.

K13 Moore, L. Hugh, Jr. *Robert Penn Warren and History: "The Big Myth We Live."* The Hague: Mouton, 1970.

Contents: chapters: "Introduction," "The Facts of the Past," "RPW's Philosophy of History: 'History is Blind, but Man is Not,'" "Man in History: Tradition and Myth," and "*W*: The 'Little Myth'"; plus selected bibliography.

K14 Light, James F., comp. *The Merrill Studies in* All the King's Men. Columbus, OH: Charles E. Merrill Publishing Company, 1971.

Contents: RPW, "*AKM*: The Matrix of Experience," pp. 2–7; Arthur M. Schlesinger, Jr., "The Messiah of the Rednecks," pp. 7–20; RPW, "Knowledge and the Image of Man," pp. 20–28; Rod W. Horton and Herbert W. Edwards, "From Evolution and Pragmatism," pp. 28–32; John Milton, "From *Paradise Lost*," pp. 32–34; Charles Kaplan, "Jack Burden: Modern Ishmael," pp. 34–42; Ted N. Weissbuch, "Jack Burden: Call Me Carraway," pp. 42–44; L. Hugh Moore, Jr., "RPW and The Terror of Answered Prayer," pp. 44–51; Robert Gorham Davis, "Dr. Adam Stanton's Dilemma," pp. 53–56; Charles R. Anderson, "Violence and Order in the Novels of RPW," pp. 56–73; James F. Light, "Structure, Meaning, and Technique in *AKM*," pp. 73–87; Malcolm O. Sillars, "A Study in Populism," pp. 87–96; Robert White, "RPW and the Myth of the Garden," pp. 96–104; James Ruoff, "Humpty Dumpty and *AKM*," pp. 104–113.

K15 Keenan, John J., ed. "Robert Penn Warren Issue." *Four Quarters* (La Salle College), 21 (May 1972).

Contents: Ruth Fisher, "A Conversation with RPW," pp. 3–17; John Hollander, "Rotation of Crops: For RPW" (poem), p. 18; Cleanth Brooks, "Brooks on Warren," pp. 19–22; Arthur H. Scouten, "Warren, Huey Long, and *AKM*," pp. 23–26; Victor Strandberg, "RPW: The Poetry of the Sixties," pp. 27–44; Robert Frank Cayton, "The Fictional Voices of RPW," pp. 45–52; H. D. Herring, "Madness in *AHG*," pp. 56–66; Earl Wilcox, "Right On! *AKM* in the Classroom," pp. 69–78; Curtis Whittington, Jr., "The Earned Vision: RPW's 'The Ballad of Billie Potts' and Albert Camus' *Le Malentendu*," pp. 79–90; James H. Justus, "Warren and the Doctrine of Complicity," pp. 93–99; Allen Shepherd, "Carrying Manty Home: RPW's *BA*," pp. 101–109; Leonard Casper, "Ark, *F*, and Negotiated Covenant," pp. 110–115; D. G. Kehl, "Love's Definition: Dream as Reality in RPW's *MMGG*," pp. 116–122.

K16 Guttenberg, Barnett. *Web of Being: The Novels of Robert Penn Warren*. Nashville: Vanderbilt University Press, 1975.

Contents: Each chapter is devoted to a single novel; includes a selected bibliography.

K17 Chambers, Robert H., ed. All the King's Men: *A Collection of Critical Essays*. TCI. Englewood Cliffs, NJ: Prentice-Hall, 1977.

Contents: Robert B. Heilman, "Melpomene as Wallflower; or, the Reading of Tragedy," pp. 17–28; Norton R. Girault, "The Narrator's Mind as Symbol: An Analysis of *AKM*," pp. 29–47; Robert C. Slack, "The Telemachus Theme in *AKM*," pp. 48–56; Jerome Meckier, "Burden's Complaint: The Disintegrated Personality as Theme and Style in RPW's *AKM*," pp. 57–72; James C. Simmons, "Adam's Lobectomy Operation and the Meaning of *AKM*," pp. 73–83; James Ruoff, "Humpty-Dumpty and *AKM*: A Note on RPW's Teleology," pp. 84–92; RPW, "Introduction to the Modern Library Edition of *AKM*," pp. 93–97; Ladell Payne, "Willie Stark and Huey Long: Atmosphere, Myth, or Suggestion?" pp. 98–115; Beekman W. Cottrell, "Cass Mastern and the Awful Responsibility of Time," pp. 116–125; Jonathan Baumbach, "The Metaphysics of Demagoguery: *AKM* by RPW," pp. 126–142; and Earl Wilcox, "Right On! *AKM* in the Classroom," pp. 143–153; plus introduction, chronology, and selected bibliography.

K18 Strandberg, Victor H. *The Poetic Vision of Robert Penn Warren*. [Lexington]: University Press of Kentucky, 1977.

Contents: chapters: 1. "The Themes of RPW," 2. "Poems of Passage," 3. "The Undiscovered Self," 4. "Mysticism," and 5. "Postscript: An Appreciation"; plus introduction, notes, and index.

K19 Newton, Thomas A. "A Character Index of Robert Penn Warren's Long Works of Fiction." *Emporia State Research Studies*, 26 (Winter 1978), 6–104.

K20 Styron, William. *Admiral Robert Penn Warren and The Snows of Winter*. Winston-Salem, NC: Palaemon Press Limited, 1978.

Note: a 20-pp. pamphlet in tribute 10 April 1975 at Lotos Club in New York City; other tributes by Lionel Trilling and John Palmer; 276 copies total (RPW, no. B).

K21 Tschöpl, Günter. *Zur Identitätsthematik bei Robert Penn Warren:*

Die Ermittlung des Ich in All the King's Men. SLRAAA, no. 12. Frankfort: Peter Lang, 1978. 195 pp.

K22   Walker, Marshall. *Robert Penn Warren: A Vision Earned.* Edinburgh: Paul Harris Publishing, 1979.

Contents: chapters: 1. "Regionalism, Agrarianism, and Literature," 2. "Early Poetry," 3. "Short Stories," 4. "Dreams and Identities," 5. "Uses of History," 6. "The Human Bond and a New Sense of Poetry," 7. "The Flesh and the Imagination," 8. "Uses of Pastoral," 9. "Country Hick"; plus introduction, conclusion, interview, selected bibliography, and index.

L

Partial Books

Note: Selections included in this section represent material dealing with RPW as part of a larger whole, that is, as part of a movement, part of a regional heritage, etc. Page numbers are provided when an author has devoted a substantial portion of the book to RPW; otherwise, readers should consult the indexes.

L1   Mims, Edwin. *The Advancing South: Stories of Progress and Reaction.* Garden City, NY: Doubleday, Page, 1926.

L2   Kreymborg, Alfred. *Our Singing Strength: An Outline of American Poetry (1620–1930).* New York: McCann, 1929.

L3   Williamson, George. "Donne and the Poetry of Today." *A Garland for John Donne, 1631–1931.* Ed. Theodore Spencer. Cambridge, MA: Harvard University Press, 1931.

L4   Couch, W. T., ed. *Culture in the South.* Chapel Hill: University of North Carolina Press, 1935.

L5   Deutsch, Babette. *This Modern Poetry.* New York: W. W. Norton & Co., 1935.

L6   Parks, Edd Winfield. *Segments of Southern Thought.* Athens: University of Georgia Press, 1938.

L7   Brooks, Cleanth. *Modern Poetry and the Tradition.* Chapel Hill: University of North Carolina Press, 1939.

L8   Moore, Merrill. *The Fugitive: Clippings and Comment.* Boston: Privately printed, 1939.

L9   Burke, Kenneth. *The Philosophy of Literary Form: Studies in Symbolic Action.*
   a. Baton Rouge: Louisiana State University Press, 1941.
   b. Rev. ed. New York: Vintage Books, 1957.
   c. 2d rev. ed. Baton Rouge: Louisiana State University Press, 1967.

L10   Mathiessen, F. O. *American Renaissance.* New York: Oxford University Press, 1941.

L11   Ransom, John Crowe. *The New Criticism.* Norfolk, CT: New Directions, 1941.

L12 Stallman, Robert Wooster. "The New Criticism and the Southern Critics." *A Southern Vanguard.* Ed. Allen Tate. New York: Prentice-Hall, 1947.

L13 Hyman, Stanley Edgar. *The Armed Vision: A Study in the Methods of Modern Literary Criticism.* New York: Alfred A. Knopf, 1948.

L14 O'Connor, William Van. *Sense and Sensibility in Modern Poetry.* Chicago: University of Chicago Press, 1948.

L15 Spiller, Robert E., et al. *Literary History of the United States.* New York: Macmillan, 1948; rev. ed., 1953; 3d ed., 1963; 4th ed., 1975.

L16 Stallman, Robert Wooster, ed. *The Critic's Notebook.* Minneapolis: University of Minnesota Press, 1950.

L17 Hoffman, Frederick J. *The Modern Novel in America, 1900–1950.* Chicago: Henry Regnery Co., 1951.

L18 Straumann, Heinrich. *American Literature in the Twentieth Century.*
  a. London: Hutchinson's University Library, 1951.
  b. Rev. ed. Harper Torchbook. New York: Harper & Row, 1965.

L19 Deutsch, Babette. *Poetry in Our Time.*
  a. New York: Henry Holt, 1952.
  b. New York: Columbia University Press, 1956.
  c. New York: Doubleday, 1963.

L20 O'Connor, William Van. *An Age of Criticism, 1900–1950.* Chicago: Henry Regnery Co., 1952.

L21 Prescott, Orville. "Political Novel: Warren, Orwell, Koestler." *In My Opinion: An Inquiry into the Contemporary Novel.* Indianapolis: Bobbs-Merrill, 1952. Pp. 22–39.

L22 Raiziss, Sona. *The Metaphysical Passion: Seven Modern American Poets and the Seventeenth-Century Tradition.* Philadelphia: University of Pennsylvania Press, 1952.

L23 Wagenknecht, Edward. *Cavalcade of the American Novel.* New York: Holt, Rinehart, and Winston, 1952.

L24 Rubin, Louis D., Jr., and Robert D. Jacobs, eds. *Southern Renascence: The Literature of the Modern South.* Baltimore: Johns Hopkins University Press, 1953. Pp. 207–235.

L25 Humphrey, Robert. *Stream of Consciousness in the Modern Novel.* Berkeley: University of California Press, 1954.

L26 Southworth, James G. *More Modern American Poets.*
  a. New York: Oxford University Press, 1954.
  b. Oxford: Basil Blackwell, 1954.

L27 Blotner, Joseph L. *The Political Novel.* Garden City, NY: Doubleday, 1955.

L28 Bogan, Louise. *Selected Criticism: Prose, Poetry.* New York: Noonday Press, 1955.

L29 Rossiter, Clinton. *Conservatism in America: The Thankless Persuasion.*
a. New York: Alfred A. Knopf, 1955.
b. 2d rev. ed. New York: Vintage Books, 1962.

L30 Beardsley, Monroe, Robert Daniel, and Glenn Leggett. *Theme and Form: An Introduction to Literature.* Englewood Cliffs, NJ: Prentice-Hall, 1956.

L31 Daiches, David. *Critical Approaches to Literature.* Englewood Cliffs, NJ: Prentice-Hall, 1956.

L32 Pritchard, John Paul. *Criticism in America: An Account of the Development of Critical Techniques from the Early Period of the Republic to the Middle Years of the Twentieth Century.* Norman, OK: University of Oklahoma Press, 1956.

L33 Angoff, Allan, ed. *American Writing Today: Its Independence and Vigor.* New York: New York University Press, 1957.

L34 McCormick, John. *Catastrophe and Imagination: An Interpretation of the Recent English and American Novel.* London: Longmans, Green, 1957.

L35 R[ice], J[ohn] A. "Introduction to *AKM.*" *American Panorama: Essays by Fifteen American Critics on 350 Books Past and Present Which Portray the U.S.A. in Its Many Aspects.* New York: New York University Press, 1957.

L36 Bradbury, John M. *The Fugitives: A Critical Account.* Chapel Hill: University of North Carolina Press, 1958. Pp. 172–255.

L37 Davidson, Donald. *Southern Writers in the Modern World.* Athens: University of Georgia Press, 1958.

L38 Heiney, Donald. *Recent American Literature.* Great Neck, NY: Barron's Educational Series, 1958.

L39 Stewart, Randall. *American Literature and Christian Doctrine.* Baton Rouge: Louisiana State University Press, 1958.

L40 Wilder, Amos N. *Theology and Modern Literature.* Cambridge, MA: Harvard University Press, 1958.

L41 Cowan, Louise. *The Fugitive Group: A Literary History.* Baton Rouge: Louisiana State University Press, 1959.

L42 Purdy, Rob Roy, ed. *Fugitives' Reunion: Conversations at Vanderbilt, May 3–5, 1956.* Nashville, TN: Vanderbilt University Press, 1959.

L43 Wasserstrom, William. *The Heiress of All the Ages: Sex and Sentiment in the Genteel Tradition.* Minneapolis: University of Minnesota

Press, 1959.

L44 Fiedler, Leslie A. *Love and Death in the American Novel.* New York: Criterion Books, 1960.

L45 Schlesinger, Arthur M., Jr. *The Age of Roosevelt: The Politics of Upheaval.* Boston: Houghton Mifflin, 1960. III, 42–68.

L46 Gold, Herbert, and David L. Stevenson, eds. *Stories of Modern America.* New York: St. Martin's Press, 1961.

L47 White, Ellington. "RPW." *South: Modern Southern Literature in Its Cultural Setting.* Ed. Louis D. Rubin, Jr., and Robert D. Jacobs. Garden City, NY: Doubleday, 1961. Pp. 198–209.

L48 Douglas, Wallace W. "Deliberate Exiles: The Social Sources of Agrarian Poetics." *Aspects of American Poetry.* Ed. Richard M. Ludwig. Columbus, OH: Ohio State University Press, 1962. Pp. 273–300.

L49 Foster, Richard. *The New Romanticism: A Reappraisal of the New Criticism.* Bloomington, IN: University of Indiana Press, 1962.

L50 Hagopian, John V. "The Blackberry Winter." *Insight I: Analyses of American Literature.* Ed. John V. Hagopian and Martin Dolch. Frankfurt: Hirschgraben, 1962.

L51 Scott, Wilbur S. *Five Approaches of Literary Criticism: An Arrangement of Contemporary Critical Essays.* New York: Macmillan, 1962.

L52 Spiller, Robert E. *A Time of Harvest: American Literature, 1910–1960.* American Century Series. New York: Hill and Wang, 1962.

L53 Weales, Gerald. *American Drama Since World War II.* New York: Harcourt, Brace and World, 1962.

L54 Bradbury, John M. *Renaissance in the South: A Critical History of the Literature, 1920–1960.* Chapel Hill: University of North Carolina Press, 1963.

L55 Brooks, Cleanth. *The Hidden God: Studies in Hemingway, Faulkner, Yeats, Eliot, and Warren.* New Haven: Yale University Press, 1963. Pp. 98–127.

L56 Eisinger, Chester E. *Fiction of the Forties.* Chicago: University of Chicago Press, 1963. Pp. 198–229.

L57 Fain, John Tyree, ed. *The Spyglass: Views and Reviews 1924–1930, by Donald Davidson.* Nashville: Vanderbilt University Press, 1963.

L58 Frank, Joseph. *The Widening Gyre: Crisis and Mastery in Modern Literature.* New Brunswick, NJ: Rutgers University Press, 1963. Pp. 179–202.

L59 Kallsen, Loren J., ed. *The Kentucky Tragedy: A Problem in Ro-*

mantic Attitudes. Indianapolis, IN: Bobbs-Merrill, 1963.

L60 Nemerov, Howard. *Poetry and Fiction: Essays*. New Brunswick, NJ: Rutgers University Press, 1963.

L61 Rubin, Louis D., Jr. *The Faraway Country: Writers in the Modern South*. Seattle: University of Washington Press, 1963. Pp. 105–130.

L62 Allen, Walter. *Tradition and Dream: The English and American Novel from the Twenties to Our Time*.

a. London: Phoenix House, 1964.

b. As *The Modern Novel in Britain and the United States*. New York: E. P. Dutton, 1964.

L63 Hardy, John Edward. *Man in the Modern Novel*. Seattle: University of Washington Press, 1964.

L64 Simonini, R. C., Jr. *Southern Writers*. Charlottesville: University Press of Virginia, 1964.

L65 Baumbach, Jonathan. *The Landscape of Nightmare: Studies in the Contemporary Novel*. New York: New York University Press, 1965. Pp. 16–34.

L66 Gossett, Louise Young. *Violence in Recent Southern Fiction*. Durham, NC: Duke University Press, 1965. Pp. 52–75.

L67 Stewart, John Lincoln. *The Burden of Time: The Fugitives and Agrarians, The Nashville Group of the 1920's and 1930's, and the Writing of John Crowe Ransom, Allen Tate, and Robert Penn Warren*. Princeton, NJ: Princeton University Press, 1965. Pp. 427–542.

L68 Straumann, Heinrich. *American Literature in the Twentieth Century*. Rev. ed. Harper Torchbook. New York: Harper & Row, 1965.

L69 French, Warren. *The Social Novel at the End of an Era*. Carbondale: Southern Illinois University Press, 1966.

L70 Karanikas, Alexander. *Tillers of a Myth: Southern Agrarians as Social and Literary Critics*. Madison: University of Wisconsin Press, 1966.

L71 Milne, Gordon. *The American Political Novel*. Norman: University of Oklahoma Press, 1966. Pp. 153–179.

L72 Scholes, Robert, and Robert Kellogg. *The Nature of Narrative*. New York: Oxford University Press, 1966.

L73 Stone, Edward. *Voices of Despair*. Athens: Ohio University Press, 1966.

L74 Stuckey, W. J. *The Pulitzer Prize Novels: A Critical Backward Look*. Norman: University of Oklahoma Press, 1966.

L75 Symons, Julian. *Critical Observations*. London: Hamish Hamilton, 1966.

L76 Davis, Richard Beale. "Mrs. Stowe's Characters——in Situations and a Southern Literary Tradition." *Essays on American Literature in Honor of Jay B. Hubbell.* Ed. Clarence Gohdes. Durham, NC: Duke University Press, 1967.

L77 Hoffman, Frederick J. *The Art of Southern Fiction.* Carbondale: Southern Illinois University Press, 1967.

L78 Ruland, Richard. *The Rediscovery of American Literature: Premises of Critical Taste, 1900–1940.* Cambridge, MA: Harvard University Press, 1967.

L79 Buchloh, Paul G., ed. *Amerikanische Erzählungen von Hawthorne bis Salinger: Interpretationen.* Neumünster: Karl Wachholtz, 1968.

L80 Coyle, William, ed. *The Young Man in American Literature.* New York: Odyssey Press, 1968.

L81 Hall, James. *The Lunatic Giant in the Drawing Room: The British and American Novel Since 1930.* Bloomington: Indiana University Press, 1968. Pp. 81–110.

L82 Inge, M. Thomas, ed. *Agrarianism in American Literature.* New York: Odyssey Press, 1968.

L83 Magill, Frank N., ed. *Masterplots.* 15 vols. New York: Salem Press, 1968. Annual supplements.

L84 Noble, David W. *The Eternal Adam and the New World Garden: The Central Myth in the American Novel Since 1830.* New York: George Braziller, 1968.

L85 Core, George, ed. *Southern Fiction Today: Renascence and Beyond.* Athens: University of Georgia Press, 1969.

L86 Gérard, Albert. *Les Tambours du néant: Essai sur le problème existential dans le roman américain.* [Paris]: La Renaissance du Livre, 1969.

L87 Jarrell, Randall. *The Third Book of Criticism.* New York: Farrar, Straus & Giroux, 1969.

L88 Tischler, Nancy M. *Black Masks: Negro Characters in Modern Southern Fiction.* University Park: Pennsylvania State University Press, 1969.

L89 Williams, T. Harry. *Huey Long.* New York: Alfred A. Knopf, 1969.

L90 Berry, Thomas Elliott. *The Newspaper in the American Novel, 1900–1969.* Metuchen, NJ: Scarecrow Press, 1970.

L91 Davenport, F. Garvin, Jr. *The Myth of Southern History: Historical Consciousness in Twentieth-Century Southern Literature.* Nashville: Vanderbilt University Press, 1970. Pp. 131–170.

L92 French, Warren, ed. *The Fifties: Fiction, Poetry, Drama*. Deland, FL: Everett/Edwards, 1970.

L93 Woodward, C. Vann. *The Burden of Southern History*. Rev. ed. Baton Rouge: Louisiana State University Press, 1970.

L94 Brooks, Cleanth. *The Poetry of Tension*. St. John's, Newfoundland: Memorial University, 1971.

L95 ———. *A Shaping Joy: Studies in the Writer's Craft*. New York: Harcourt Brace Jovanovich, 1971.

L96 Cady, Edwin H. *The Light of Common Day: Realism in American Fiction*. Bloomington: Indiana University Press, 1971.

L97 Cowan, Louise. *The Southern Critics: An Introduction to the Criticism of John Crowe Ransom, Allen Tate, Donald Davidson, Robert Penn Warren, Cleanth Brooks, and Andrew Lytle*. University of Dallas Studies in Literature. Dallas, TX: University of Dallas Press, 1971.

L98 Gross, Harvey. *The Contrived Corridor: History and Fatality in Modern Literature*. Ann Arbor: University of Michigan Press, 1971.

L99 Krieger, Murray. *The Classic Vision: The Retreat from Extremity in Modern Literature*. Baltimore: Johns Hopkins University Press, 1971.

L100 Stanzel, Franz. *Narrative Situations in the Novel*. Trans. from the German, James P. Pusack. Bloomington: Indiana University Press, 1971.

L101 Aldridge, John W. *The Devil in the Fire: Retrospective Essays on American Literature and Culture, 1951–1971*. New York: Harper's Magazine Press, 1972.

L102 Bungert, Hans, ed. *Die amerikanische Short Story: Theorie und Entwicklung*. Darmstadt: Wissenschaftliche, 1972.

L103 Holman, C. Hugh. *The Roots of Southern Writing: Essays on the Literature of the American South*. Athens: University of Georgia Press, 1972.

L104 Hubbell, Jay B. *Who Are the Major American Writers?* Durham, NC: Duke University Press, 1972.

L105 Kopcewicz, Andrzej. *Poezja amerykanskiego południa*. Poznan: [Wydawn. Naukowe Universytetu im Adama Mickiewicza], 1972.

L106 Murray, Edward. *The Cinematic Imagination: Writers and the Motion Picture*. New York: Frederick Ungar, 1972.

L107 Rubin, Louis D., Jr. *The Writer in the South: Studies in a Literary Community*. Mercer University Lamar Memorial Lectures, no. 15. Athens: University of Georgia Press, 1972.

L108 Skaggs, Merrill Maguire. *The Folk of Southern Fiction*. Athens: University of Georgia Press, 1972.

L109 Baym, Max I. *A History of Literary Aesthetics in America*. New York: Frederick Ungar, 1973.

L110 Hassan, Ihab. *Contemporary American Literature, 1945–1972: An Introduction*. New York: Frederick Ungar, 1973.

L111 Hayashi, Tetsumaro, ed. *Steinbeck's Literary Dimension: A Guide to Comparative Studies*. Metuchen, NJ: Scarecrow Press, 1973.

L112 Rougé, Robert. *L'Inquiétude religieuse dans le roman américain moderne*. Publications de l'université de Haute Bretagne, no. 4. Paris: Librairie C. Klincksieck, 1973.

L113 Wright, George T., ed. *Seven American Literary Stylists*. Minneapolis: University of Minnesota Press, 1973.

L114 Fain, John Tyree, and Thomas Daniel Young, eds. *The Literary Correspondence of Donald Davidson and Allen Tate*. Athens: University of Georgia Press, 1974.

L115 Rubin, Louis D., Jr., and C. Hugh Holman. *Southern Literary Study: Problems and Possibilities*. Chapel Hill: University of North Carolina Press, 1975.

L116 Simpson, Lewis P. *The Dispossessed Garden: Pastoral and History in Southern Literature*. Mercer University Lamar Memorial Lectures, no. 16. Athens: University of Georgia Press, 1975.

L117 Simpson, Lewis P., ed. *The Possibilities of Order: Cleanth Brooks and His Work*. Baton Rouge: Louisiana State University Press, 1976.

L118 Cerf, Bennett. *At Random: The Reminiscences of Bennett Cerf*. New York: Random House, 1977.

L119 Gray, Richard. *The Literature of Memory: Modern Writers of the American South*. Baltimore: Johns Hopkins University Press, 1977.

L120 Holman, C. Hugh. *The Immoderate Past: The Southern Writer and History*. Wesleyan College Lamar Memorial Lecture. Athens: University of Georgia Press, 1977.

L121 Watkins, Floyd C. *In Time and Place: Some Origins of American Fiction*. Athens: University of Georgia Press, 1977.

L122 Rubin, Louis D., Jr. *The Wary Fugitives: Four Poets and the South*. Baton Rouge: Louisiana State University Press, 1978. Pp. 327–361.

L123 Trilling, Diana. *Reviewing the Forties*. New York: Harcourt Brace Jovanovich, 1978.

L124 Hoffman, Daniel, ed. *Harvard Guide to Contemporary American Writing*. Cambridge, MA: Harvard University Press, 1979.
  Note: esp., A. Walton Litz, "Literary Criticism," pp. 56–58; Lewis P. Simpson, "Southern Fiction," pp. 167–173; and Daniel Hoffman, "Poetry: After Modernism," pp. 461–464.

M

Essays

Note: These essays are listed in chronological order and include primarily those items first appearing in journals and periodical publications. Essays reprinted in collections are cross-referenced with editor's last name, reference symbol, and page numbers. I have also listed inclusive page numbers of complete articles that pertain only in part to RPW.

M1 Knickerbocker, William S. "The Fugitives of Nashville." *SR*, 36 (April 1928), 211–224.

M2 Hartstock, Ernest. "Roses in the Desert: A View of Contemporary Southern Verse." *SR*, 37 (July 1929), 328–335.

M3 Ransom, John Crowe. "Hearts and Heads." *AmRev*, 2 (March 1934), 554–571.

M4 Starke, Aubrey. "The Agrarians Deny a Leader." *AmRev*, 2 (March 1934), 534–553.

M5 Brooks, Cleanth, Jr. "The Modern Southern Poet and Tradition." *VQR*, 11 (April 1935), 305–320.

M6 Davidson, Donald. "*I'll Take My Stand*: A History." *AmRev*, 5 (Summer 1935), 301–321.

M7 Fletcher, John Gould. "The Modern Southern Poets." *Westminster Magazine*, 23 (Winter 1935), 229–251.

M8 Parkes, H. B. "The American Cultural Scene (IV): The Novel." *Scrutiny*, 9 (June 1940), 2–8.

M9 Forgotson, E. S. "The Poetic Method of RPW." *AmPf*, 6 (Winter 1941), 130–146.

M10 Irish, Marion D. "Proposed Roads to the New South, 1941: Chapel Hill Planners vs. Nashville Agrarians." *SR*, 49 (Jan.–March 1941), 1–27.

M11 Pressly, Thomas J. "Agrarianism: An Autopsy." *SR*, 49 (April–June 1941), 145–163.

M12 Tate, Allen. "*The Fugitive*, 1922–1925: A Personal Recollection Twenty Years After." *PULC*, 3 (April 1942), 75–84.

M13 Cater, Catherine. "Four Voices Out of the South." *MAQR* (Winter 1944), pp. 166–173.
M14 Beatty, Richmond Croom. "Fugitive and Agrarian Writers at Vanderbilt."
  a. *THQ*, 3 (March 1944), 3–23.
  b. As "By Way of Background." *A Vanderbilt Miscellany, 1919–1944.* Ed. Richmond Croom Beatty. Nashville: Vanderbilt University Press, 1944. Pp. 11–27.
M15 Allen, Charles. "The Fugitive." *SAQ*, 43 (Oct. 1944), 382–389.
M16 Hendry, Irene. "The Regional Novel: The Example of RPW." *SR*, 53 (Jan.–March 1945), 84–102.
M17 Hardwick, Elizabeth. "Poor Little Rich Girls." *PR*, 12 (Summer 1945), 420–422.
M18 Walcutt, Charles C. "The Regional Novel and Its Future." *ArQ*, 1 (Summer 1945), 17–27.
M19 Southard, W. P. "Speculation I: The Religious Poetry of RPW." *KR*, 7 (Autumn 1945), 653–676.
M20 Basso, Hamilton. "The Huey Long Legend." *Life*, 9 Dec. 1946, pp. 106–108, 110, 112, 115–116, 118–121.
M21 O'Connor, William Van. "RPW: 'Provincial Poet.'" *A Southern Vanguard*. Ed. Allen Tate. New York: Prentice-Hall, 1947. Pp. 92–99.
M22 Heilman, Robert B. "Melpomene as Wallflower; or, The Reading of Tragedy."
  a. *SR*, 55 (Jan.–March 1947), 154–166.
  b. Longley, **K9**, pp. 82–95.
  c. Beebe and Field, **K11**, pp. 79–89.
  d. Chambers, **K17**, pp. 17–28.
M23 Matthiessen, F. O. "American Poetry, 1920–1940." *SR*, 55 (Jan.–March 1947), 24–55.
M24 West, Ray B., Jr. "Truth, Beauty, and American Criticism." *UKCR*, 14 (Winter 1947), 137–148.
M25 Flint, F. Cudworth. "RPW." *AmOx*, 34 (April 1947), 65–79.
M26 Girault, Norton R. "The Narrator's Mind as Symbol: An Analysis of *AKM*."
  a. *Accent*, 7 (Summer 1947), 220–234.
  b. *Critiques and Essays on Modern Fiction, 1920–1951.* Ed. John W. Aldridge. New York: Ronald Press, 1952. Pp. 200–216.
  c. Beebe and Field, **K11**, pp. 101–117.
  d. Chambers, **K17**, pp. 29–47.

M27 Ransom, John Crowe. "Poetry: I. The Formal Analysis." *KR*, 9 (Summer 1947), 436–456; "Poetry: II. The Final Cause." *KR*, 9 (Autumn 1947), 640–658.

M28 Cargill, Oscar. "Anatomist of Monsters."
a. *CE*, 9 (Oct. 1947), 1–8.
b. As "Afterword." *Toward a Pluralistic Criticism*. Carbondale: Southern Illinois University Press, 1965. Pp. 141–153.

M29 Bentley, Eric. "*AKM*." *Theater Arts*, 31 (Nov. 1947), 72–73.

M30 Runnquist, Ake. "Pärlan i ostronet: Några dragi RPW's romaner." *Bonniers litterära magasin* (Stockholm), 16 (Nov. 1947), 725–732.

M31 Baker, Joseph E. "Irony in Fiction: *AKM*."
a. *CE*, 9 (Dec. 1947), 122–130.
b. As "Irony in *AKM*." Beebe and Field, **K11**, pp. 90–100.

M32 O'Connor, William Van. "The Influence of the Metaphysicals on Modern Poetry." *CE*, 9 (Jan. 1948), 180–187.

M33 Fogle, Richard Harter. "A Recent Attack upon Romanticism." *CE*, 9 (April 1948), 356–361.

M34 Nemerov, Howard. "The Phoenix in the World." *Furioso*, 3 (Spring 1948), 36–46.

M35 Humbolt, Charles. "The Lost Cause of RPW." *Masses and Mainstream*, 1 (July 1948), 8–20.

M36 Bentley, Eric. "The Meaning of RPW's Novels."
a. *KR*, 10 (Summer 1948), 407–424.
b. As "Suche nach Selbsterkenntnis: Das Werk Robert Penn Warrens." *Die Amerikanische Rundschau*, 4 (Oct. 1948), 73–86.
c. In *Forms of Modern Fiction: Essays Collected in Honor of Joseph Warren Beach*. Ed. William Van O'Connor. Minneapolis: University of Minnesota Press, 1948. Pp. 269–286.
d. In *On Contemporary Literature: An Anthology of Critical Essays on the Major Movements and Writers of Contemporary Literature*. Ed. Richard Kostelanetz. New York: Avon Books, 1964. Pp. 616–633.

M37 Stewart, John L. "The Achievement of RPW." *SAQ*, 47 (Oct. 1948), 562–579.

M38 Brantley, Frederick. "The Achievement of RPW." *Modern American Poetry*. Ed. B. Rajan. *Focus* Five. London: Dennis Dobson, 1950. Pp. 66–80.

M39 Tyler, Parker. "Novel into Film: *AKM*."
a. *KR*, 12 (Spring 1950), 369–376.
b. *The Kenyon Critics: Studies in Modern Literature*. Ed. John Crowe Ransom. Cleveland: World Publishing Co., 1951. Pp. 225–232.

M40 Amacher, Richard E. "Warren's 'Original Sin: A Short Story.'"
a. *Expl*, 8 (May 1950), item 52.
b. Rpt. New York: Kraus, 1965.
c. *The Explicator Cyclopedia*. Ed. Charles Child Walcutt and J. Edwin Whitesell. Chicago: Quadrangle Books, 1966. I, 336–337.

M41 Gerhard, George. "*AKM*: A Symposium." *Folio* (Indiana University), 15 (May 1950), 4–11.

M42 Hudson, Richard B. "*AKM*: A Symposium." *Folio*, 15 (May 1950), 11–13.

M43 Raben, Joseph. "*AKM*: A Symposium." *Folio*, 15 (May 1950), 14–18.

M44 Ransom, John Crowe. "*AKM*: A Symposium." *Folio*, 15 (May 1950), 2–3.

M45 Stallknecht, Newton P. "*AKM*: A Symposium."
a. *Folio*, 15 (May 1950), 18–22.
b. As "A Study in Nihilism." Beebe and Field, **K11**, pp. 125–128.

M46 Fiedler, Leslie A. "Toward Time's Cold Womb."
a. *New Leader*, 22 July 1950, p. 24.
b. *PR*, 17 (Sept.–Oct. 1950), 739–743.
c. In *No! In Thunder*. Boston: Beacon Press, 1960. Pp. 119–126.

M47 Davidson, Donald. "Faulkner e Warren: A contribuição do sul dos Estados Unidos para a contemporánea." *Anhembi*, 1 (Dec. 1950), 34–43.
Note: published in Brazil.

M48 Gordon, Clifford M. "Warren's 'Original Sin: A Short Story.'"
a. *Expl*, 9 (Dec. 1950), item 21.
b. Rpt. New York: Kraus, 1965.
c. *The Explicator Cyclopedia*, **M40c**, I, 337–338.

M49 Beatty, Richmond Croom. "The Poetry and Novels of RPW." Vanderbilt Studies in the Humanities, no. 1. Nashville: Vanderbilt University Press, 1951. Pp. 142–160.

M50 Joost, N. "'Was All for Naught?': RPW and New Directions in the Novel." *Fifty Years of the American Novel: A Christian Appraisal*. Ed. Harold Charles Gardiner. New York: Charles Scribner's Sons, 1951. Pp. 273–291.

M51 Frohock, W. M. "Mr. Warren's Albatross."
a. *SWR*, 36 (Winter 1951), 48–59.
b. *The Novel of Violence in America*. 2d ed. Dallas, TX: Southern Methodist University Press, 1957. Pp. 86–105.
c. Rpt. Boston: Beacon Press, 1964.

M52 Gabrieli, Vittorio. "Romanticismo e visione tragica nel romanzo di RPW." *Lo spettatore italiane*, 4 (Jan. 1951), 12–14; 4 (Feb. 1951), 38–41.

M53 Heilman, Robert B. "Tangled Web."
a. *SR*, 59 (Jan.–March 1951), 107–119.
b. Longley, **K9**, pp. 96–109.

M54 Fitzell, Lincoln. "The Sword and the Dragon." *SAQ*, 50 (April 1951), 230–231.

M55 Frank, Joseph. "Romanticism and Reality in RPW."
a. *HudR*, 4 (Summer 1951), 248–258.
b. *The Widening Gyre: Crisis and Mastery in Modern Literature*. New Brunswick, NJ: Rutgers University Press, 1963. Pp. 179–202.
c. Beebe and Field, **K11**, pp. 147–149.

M56 Hynes, Sam. "RPW: The Symbolic Journey." *UKCR*, 17 (Summer 1951), 279–285.

M57 Prescott, Orville. "Political Novel: Warren, Orwell, Koestler." *In My Opinion: An Inquiry into the Contemporary Novel*. Ed. Orville Prescott. Indianapolis, IN: Bobbs-Merrill, 1952. Pp. 22–39.

M58 Jacobs, Robert D. "Poe and the Agrarian Critics." *Hopkins Review*, 5 (Spring 1952), 43–54.

M59 Beatty, Richmond Croom. "A Personal Memoir of the Agrarians." *Shenandoah*, 3 (Summer 1952), 11–13.

M60 "A Symposium: The Agrarians Today." *Shenandoah*, 3 (Summer 1952), 14–33.

M61 Heilman, Robert B. "The Southern Temper." *Hopkins Review*, 6 (Fall 1952), 5–15.

M62 Rouse, H. Blair. "Time and Place in Southern Fiction." *Hopkins Review*, 6 (Fall 1952), 37–61.

M63 Mohrt, Michel. "RPW and the Myth of the Outlaw."
a. Trans. Beth Brombert. *YFS*, no. 10 [1953], 70–84.
b. As "RPW ou le mythe du hors-la-loi." *Le Nouveau Roman américain*. Paris: Gallimard, 1955. Pp. 207–223.

M64 Anderson, Charles. "Violence and Order in the Novels of RPW."
a. *Hopkins Review*, 6 (Winter 1953), 88–105.
b. *Southern Renascence: The Literature of the Modern South*. Ed. Louis D. Rubin, Jr., and Robert D. Jacobs. Baltimore: Johns Hopkins University Press, 1953. Pp. 207–224.
c. *Modern American Fiction: Essays in Criticism*. Ed. A. Walton Litz. A Galaxy Book. New York: Oxford University Press, 1963. Pp. 278–295.

d. Light, **K14**, pp. 56–73.

M65 Campbell, Harry Modean. "Warren as Philosopher in *WET*."
a. *Hopkins Review*, 6 (Winter 1953), 106–116.
b. *Southern Renascence*, **M64b**, pp. 225–235.

M66 Sullivan, Walter. "Southern Novelists and the Civil War." *Hopkins Review*, 6 (Winter 1953), 133–146.

M67 Watkins, Floyd C. "Thomas Wolfe and the Nashville Agrarians." *GaR*, 7 (Winter 1953), 410–423.

M68 Frost, William. "Warren's 'Pursuit.'"
a. *Expl*, 11 (Feb. 1953), item 22.
b. Rpt. New York: Kraus, 1965.
c. *The Explicator Cyclopedia*, **M40c**, I, 338–339.

M69 Bradbury, John M. "RPW's Novels: The Symbolic and Textual Patterns."
a. *Accent*, 13 (Spring 1953), 77–89.
b. As "Warren's Fiction." *The Fugitives: A Critical Account*. Chapel Hill: University of North Carolina Press, 1958. Pp. 195–230.
c. Longley, **K9**, pp. 3–17.

M70 Jacobs, Robert D. "Faulkner's Tragedy of Isolation." *Hopkins Review*, 6 (Spring–Summer 1953), 162–183.

M71 Marion, Denis. "RPW." *NNRF*, 1 (April 1953), 725–728.

M72 Fergusson, Francis. "Three Novels." *Perspectives USA*, no. 6 (Winter 1954), pp. 30–44.

M73 Rubin, Louis D., Jr. "All the King's Meanings."
a. *GaR*, 8 (Winter 1954), 422–434.
b. As "Huey Long in Fiction." Beebe and Field, **K11**, pp. 28–29.
c. *The Curious Death of the Novel*. Baton Rouge: Louisiana State University Press, 1967. Pp. 222–238.

M74 White, Robert. "RPW and the Myth of the Garden."
a. *Faulkner Studies*, 3 (Winter 1954), 59–67.
b. Rpt. New York: Kraus, 1966.
c. Light, **K14**, pp. 96–104.

M75 Douglas, Wallace W. "Drug Store Gothic: The Style of RPW." *CE*, 15 (Feb. 1954), 265–272.

M76 Sherbo, Arthur. "Sherwood Anderson's *I Want to Know Why* and Messrs. Brooks and Warren." *CE*, 15 (March 1954), 350–351.

M77 Casper, Leonard. "The New Criticism and Southern Agrarianism." *Diliman Review* (Philippines), 2 (April 1954), 136–149.

M78 Ford, Newell F. "Kenneth Burke and RPW: Criticism by Obsessive Metaphor." *JEGP*, 53 (April 1954), 172–177.

M79 Casper, Leonard. "RPW: Method and Canon." *Diliman Review* (Philippines), 2 (July 1954), 263–292.

M80 ——. "RPW: An Assessment." *Diliman Review*, 2 (Oct. 1954), 400–424.

M81 Antonini, Giacomo. "Penn Warren e il primato dello stile." *La fiera letteraria*, 12 Jan. 1955, pp. 5–6.

M82 Stewart, James T. "Two Uses of Maupassant by RPW." *MLN*, 70 (April 1955), 279–280.

M83 Campbell, Harry Modean. "Notes on Religion in the Southern Renascence." *Shenandoah*, 6 (Summer 1955), 10–18.

M84 Cowan, Louise. "The Fugitive Poets in Relation to the South." *Shenandoah*, 6 (Summer 1955), 3–10.

M85 Lytle, Andrew Nelson. "A Summing Up." *Shenandoah*, 6 (Summer 1955), 28–36.

M86 McDowell, Frederick P. W. "RPW's Criticism." *Accent*, 15 (Summer 1955), 173–196.

M87 Rubin, Louis D., Jr. "The Eye of Time: Religious Themes in RPW's Poetry." *Diliman Review* (Philippines), 3 (July 1955), 215–237.

M88 Stewart, Randall, chm. "A Symposium: The Southern Renascence." *Shenandoah*, 6 (Summer 1955), 3–36.

M89 McDowell, Frederick P. W. "Psychology and Theme in *BD*."
a. *PMLA*, 70 (Sept. 1955), 565–586.
b. Longley, **K9**, pp. 197–222.

M90 Martin, Terence. "*BA*: The Definition of Self-Definition." *Folio* (Indiana University), 21 (Winter 1955–56), 31–37.

M91 Daniel, Robert. "The Critics of Nashville." *TSL*, no. 1 (1956), pp. 19–26.

M92 Savelli, Giovanni. "America meta di secolo." *Letteratura americana: Panorama critico introduttivo*. Rome: Del Centro Internaz, di Comparazione e Sintesi, 1956. Pp. 234–236.

M93 Antonini Giacomo. "Penn Warren: Nostalgia per il vecchio Sud: Il mito della dignità umana." *La fiera letteraria*, 22 Jan. 1956, pp. 1–2.

M94 Bloński, Jon. "RPW." *Twórczość* (Warsaw), 12 (March 1956), 164–167.

M95 Satterwhite, Joseph N. "RPW and Emily Dickinson." *MLN*, 71 (May 1956), 347–349.

M96 Magmer, James. "RPW's Quest for an Angel." *CathW*, 183 (June 1956), 178–183.

M97 Flint, F. Cudworth. "Mr. Warren and the Reviewers."

a. *SR*, 64 (Autumn 1956), 632–645.

b. Longley, **K9**, pp. 125–139.

M98 Létargez, J. "RPW's Views of History." *RLV*, 22 (Nov.–Dec. 1956), 533–543.

M99 Cottrell, Beekman W. "Cass Mastern and the Awful Responsibility of Time."

a. Hart, **K1**, pp. 39–49.

b. Chambers, **K17**, pp. 116–125.

M100 Hart, John A. "Some Major Images in *AKM*." **K1**, pp. 63–74.

M101 Schutte, William M. "The Dramatic Versions of the Willie Stark Story."

a. Hart, **K1**, pp. 75–90.

b. Beebe and Field, **K11**, pp. 65–77.

M102 Slack, Robert C. "The Telemachus Theme."

a. Hart, **K1**, pp. 29–38.

b. Chambers, **K17**, pp. 48–56.

M103 Sochatoff, A. Fred. "Some Treatments of the Huey Long Theme." Hart, **K1**, pp. 3–15.

M104 Steinberg, Erwin R. "The Enigma of Willie Stark." Hart, **K1**, pp. 17–28.

M105 Woodruff, Neal, Jr. "The Technique of *AKM*." Hart, **K1**, pp. 51–62.

M106 Byrne, Clifford M. "The Philosophical Development in Four of RPW's Novels." *McNR*, 9 (Winter 1957), 56–68.

M107 Gross, Seymour L. "Conrad and *AKM*." *TCL*, 3 (April 1957), 27–32.

M108 Holland, Robert B. "The Agrarian Manifesto: A Generation Later." *MissQ*, 10 (Spring 1957), 73–78.

M109 Kelvin, Norman. "The Failure of RPW."

a. *CE*, 18 (April 1957), 355–364.

b. As "Warren as Puritan." Beebe and Field, **K11**, pp. 129–132.

M110 Rubin, Louis D., Jr. "The Concept of Nature in Modern Southern Poetry." *AQ*, 9 (Spring 1957), 63–71.

M111 McDowell, Frederick P. W. "The Romantic Tragedy of Self in *WET*."

a. *Crit*, 1 (Summer 1957), 34–49.

b. Longley, **K9**, pp. 110–124.

M112 Mizener, Arthur. "The Pulitzer Prizes." *Atlantic*, July 1957, pp. 42–45.

M113 Thale, Jerome. "The Narrator as Hero." *TCL*, 3 (July 1957), 69–73.

M114 Kerr, Dell. "An Exercise on RPW's *AKM*." *Exercise Exchange*, 5 (Oct. 1957), 8–9.

M115 King, Roma A., Jr. "Time and Structure in the Early Novels of RPW." *SAQ*, 56 (Autumn 1957), 486–493.

M116 Ruoff, James. "Humpty Dumpty and *AKM*: A Note on RPW's Teleology."

a. *TCL*, 3 (Oct. 1957), 128–134.

b. Beebe and Field, **K11**, pp. 139–147.

c. *The Modern American Novel: Essays in Criticism*. Ed. Max Roger Westbrook. New York: Random House, 1967. Pp. 196–208.

d. Light, **K14**, pp. 104–113.

e. Chambers, **K17**, pp. 84–92.

M117 Sillars, Malcolm O. "Warren's *AKM*: A Study in Populism."

a. *AQ*, 9 (Fall 1957), 345–353.

b. Beebe and Field, **K11**, pp. 117–125.

c. Light, **K14**, pp. 87–96.

M118 Gross, Seymour L. "Laurence Sterne and Eliot's 'Prufrock': An Object Lesson in Explication." *CE*, 19 (Nov. 1957), 72–73.

M119 Wasserstrom, William. "RPW: From Paleface to Redskin." *PrS*, 31 (Winter 1957–58), 323–333.

M120 Whittemore, Reed. "A Few Ways of Pulling Apart a Poem." *NRep*, 9 Dec. 1957, pp. 15–19.

M121 Lombardo, Agostino. "Poesia di RPW." *Criterio*, 2 (1958), 33–41.

M122 Stewart, Randall. "Dreiser and the Naturalistic Heresy." *VQR*, 34 (Winter 1958), 100–116.

M123 Watkins, Floyd C. "Billie Potts at the Fall of Time." *MissQ*, 11 (Winter 1958), 19–28.

M124 Tindall, William York. "The Criticism of Fiction." *TQ*, 1 (Feb. 1958), 101–111.

M125 Allen, Charles. "RPW: The Psychology of Self-Knowledge." *L&P*, 8 (Spring 1958), 21–25.

M126 Davidson, Donald. "The Thankless Muse and Her Fugitive Poets."

a. *SR*, 66 (Spring 1958), 201–228.

b. *Southern Writers in the Modern World*. Athens: University of Georgia Press, 1958. Pp. 1–30.

M127 Rubin, Louis D., Jr. "The Image of an Army: Southern Novelists and the Civil War." *TQ*, 1 (Spring 1958), 17–34.

M128 Frank, William. "Warren's Achievement." *CE*, 19 (May 1958), 365–366.

M129 Gross, Seymour L. "The Achievement of RPW."
a. *CE*, 19 (May 1958), 361–365.
b. Beebe and Field, **K11**, pp. 133–139.

M130 Hashiguchi, Yasuo. "RPW as a Short Story Writer." *KAL* (Fukuoka, Japan), no. 1 (June 1958), pp. 19–25.

M131 Virtanen, Reino. "Camus' *Le Malentendu* and Some Analogues." *Comparative Literature*, 10 (Summer 1958), 232–240.

M132 Holman, C. Hugh. "Literature and Culture: The Fugitive-Agrarians." *Social Forces*, 37 (Oct. 1958), 15–19.

M133 Sutherland, Ronald. "Structural Linguistics and English Prosody." *CE*, 20 (Oct. 1958), 12–17.

M134 Wasiolek, Edward. "A Classic Maimed: A Translation of Bunin's 'The Gentleman from San Francisco' Examined." *CE*, 20 (Oct. 1958), 25–28.

M135 Wright, James. "The Stiff Smile of Mr. Warren." *KR*, 20 (Autumn 1958), 645–655.

M136 Link, Franz H. "Über das Geschichtsbewusstsein einiger amerikanischer Dichter des 20. Jahrhunderts: Hart Crane's 'The Bridge,' Stephen Vincent Benét's 'Western Star,' and RPW's *BD*." *JA*, 4 (1959), 143–160.

M137 Casper, Leonard. "Golden Eye, Unwinking."
a. *Perspective*, 10 (Winter 1959), 201–208.
b. *RPW: The Dark and Bloody Ground*. Seattle: University of Washington Press, 1960. Pp. 56–87.

M138 Ruoff, James E. "RPW's Pursuit of Justice: From Briar Patch to Cosmos." *Research Studies of the State College of Washington*, 27 (March 1959), 19–38.

M139 Stewart, John L. "RPW and the Knot of History." *ELH*, 26 (March 1959), 102–136.

M140 Casper, Leonard. "The Fallacy of Heresy." *Western Review*, 23 (Spring 1959), 283–287.

M141 Garrett, George P. "The Function of the Pasiphae Myth in *BD*." *MLN*, 74 (April 1959), 311–313.

M142 Hashiguchi, Yasuo. "A Critical Analysis of RPW's 'BW.'" *KAL* (Fukuoka, Japan), no. 2 (May 1959), pp. 23–27.

M143 Montague, John. "American Pegasus." *Studies* (Dublin), 48 (Summer 1959), 183–191.

M144 Casper, Leonard. "Miscegenation as Symbol: *BA*."

a. *Audience*, 1 (Autumn 1959), 66–74.

b. Longley, **K9**, pp. 140–148.

M145 Gross, Seymour L. "RPW." *Critic*, 18 (Oct.–Nov. 1959), 11–13, 80–82.

M146 Casper, Leonard. "Mirror for Mobs: The Willie Stark Stories." *Drama Critique*, 2 (Nov. 1959), 120–124.

M147 Dwyer, William F. "Light Religiously Dim: The Poetry of RPW." *Fresco*, NS 1 (1960), 43–55.

M148 Glazier, Lyle. "Reconstructed Platonism: RPW's *Cave*." *Litera*, 7 (1960), 16–26.

M149 Renguette, Dale T. "The Gray Pessimism of RPW." *Fresco*, NS 1 (1960), 34–42.

M150 Brooks, Cleanth. "Regionalism in American Literature." *JSH*, 26 (Feb. 1960), 35–43.

M151 Berner, Robert. "The Required Past: *WET*." *MFS*, 6 (Spring 1960), 55–64.

M152 Carter, Everett. "The 'Little Myth' of RPW." *MFS*, 6 (Spring 1960), 3–12.

M153 Casper, Leonard. "Journey to the Interior."

a. *MFS*, 6 (Spring 1960), 65–72.

b. Longley, **K9**, pp. 149–158.

M154 Current-Garcia, Eugene. "The Fugitive-Agrarian Movement: A Symposium Introduction." *MissQ*, 13 (Spring 1960), 53–54.

M155 Davis, Joe. "RPW and the Journey to the West." *MFS*, 6 (Spring 1960), 73–82.

M156 England, Kenneth. "They Came Home Again: Fugitives' Return." *GaR*, 14 (Spring 1960), 80–89.

M157 Kerr, Elizabeth. "Polarity of Themes in *AKM*."

a. *MFS*, 6 (Spring 1960), 25–46.

b. Beebe and Field, **K11**, pp. 175–195.

M158 Longley, John Lewis, Jr. "*AHG*: The Major Themes."

a. *MFS*, 6 (Spring 1960), 13–24.

b. As "Self-Knowledge, the Pearl of Pus, and the Seventh Circle: The Major Themes in *AHG*." Longley, **K9**, pp. 60–74.

M159 Rathbun, John W. "Philosophy, 'WET,' and the Art of the Novel." *MFS*, 6 (Spring 1960), 47–54.

M160 Sadaya, Shigenobu. [RPW: An Introduction]. *Works and Styles of Contemporary American Authors*. Research English Library. Tokyo: Tokyo Research Company, [May 1960]. Pp. 203–227.

M161 Engleborghs, M. "Drie Romans van RPW." *Kultuurleven*, 27 (July 1960), 446–454.

M162 Cowan, Louise. "The Communal World of Southern Literature." *GaR*, 14 (Fall 1960), 248–257.

M163 Gérard, Albert. "RPW, romancier de la responsabilité." *RGB*, 96 (Oct. 1960), 27–39.

M164 Hardy, John Edward. "RPW's Double-Hero." *VQR*, 36 (Fall 1960), 583–597.

M165 Kaplan, Charles. "Jack Burden: Modern Ishmael."
  a. *CE*, 22 (Oct. 1960), 19–24.
  b. Light, **K14**, pp. 34–42.

M166 Link, Franz H. "Das Verhaltnis der Dichtung zur Wirklichkeit bei Allen Tate und anderen *new Critics*." *DVLG*, 34 (Dec. 1960), 554–580.

M167 Cowan, Louise. "The *Pietas* of Southern Poetry." *South: Modern Southern Literature in Its Cultural Setting*. Ed. Louis D. Rubin, Jr., and Robert D. Jacobs. Garden City, NY: Doubleday, 1961. Pp. 95–114.

M168 Lemaire, Marcel. "Fiction in U.S.A. From the South . . . ." *RLV*, 27 (1961), 244–253.

M169 Yanazi, Küchirō. "*NR* and RPW's Ideas." *Bulletin of the University of Osaka Prefecture*, Series C, 9 (1961), 57–72.

M170 Weissbuch, Ted N. "Jack Burden: Call Me Carraway."
  a. *CE*, 22 (Feb. 1961), 361.
  b. *Light*, **K14**, pp. 42–44.

M171 Breyer, Bernard R. "A Diagnosis of Violence in Recent Southern Fiction." *MissQ*, 14 (Spring 1961), 59–67.

M172 Casper, Leonard. "Warren and the Unsuspecting Ancestor." *WSCL*, 2 (Spring–Summer 1961), 43–49.

M173 Nolde, M. Simon. "*The Violent Bear It Away*: A Study in Imagery." *Xavier University Studies*, 1 (Spring 1961), 180–194.

M174 Sale, Roger. "Having It Both Ways in *AKM*."
  a. *HudR*, 14 (Spring 1961), 68–76.
  b. Beebe and Field, **K11**, pp. 168–175.

M175 Barucca, Primo. "La caverna di Warren." *La fiera letteraria*, 16 (June 1961), 4.

M176 Clark, Marden J. "Religious Implications in the Novels of RPW." *BYUS*, 4 (Autumn 1961), 67–79.

M177 Rubin, Louis D., Jr. "The Southern Muse: Two Poetry Societies." *AQ*, 13 (Fall 1961), 365–375.

M178 Ryan, Alvan S. "RPW's *NR*: The Nihilism of the Isolated Temperament."
  a. *MFS*, 7 (Winter 1961–62), 338–346.

b. Longley, **K9**, pp. 49–59.

M179 Godfrey, Larry. "RPW's Vision of Time." *Osmania Journal of English Studies* (Osmania University, Hyderabad, India), no. 2 (1962), pp. 29–36.

M180 Heseltine, H. P. "The Deep, Twisting Strain of Life: The Novels of RPW." *Melbourne Critical Review*, no. 5 (1962), 76–89.

M181 O'Connor, William Van. *The Grotesque: An American Genre and Other Essays.* Carbondale: Southern Illinois University Press, 1962. Pp. 14–16.

M182 Justus, James H. "Warren's *WET* and Beauchamp's Confession." *AL*, 33 (Jan. 1962), 500–511.

M183 Hayashi, Nobunyuki. "On the Novels of RPW." *Jinbun Gakuko* (Tokyo Metropolitan University), no. 28 (March 1962), 3–24.

M184 Beebe, Keith. "Biblical Motifs in *AKM.*" *JBR*, 30 (April 1962), 123–130.

M185 Bostetter, Edward E. "The Nightmare World of *The Ancient Mariner.*" *Studies in Romanticism*, 1 (Summer 1962), 241–254.

M186 Rubin, Louis D., Jr. "The South and the Faraway Country."
a. *VQR*, 38 (Summer 1962), 444–459.
b. *The Faraway Country.* Seattle: University of Washington Press, 1963. Chapter 1.

M187 Antonini, Giacomo. "Il Sud di RPW." *La fiera letteraria*, 17 (Oct. 1962), 1 and 3.

M188 Casper, Leonard. "Trial by Wilderness: Warren's Exemplum."
a. *WSCL*, 3 (Fall 1962), 45–53.
b. Longley, **K9**, pp. 159–168.

M189 Samuels, Charles Thomas. "In the Wilderness." *Crit*, 5 (Fall 1962), 46–57.

M190 McElderry, B. R., Jr. "RPW and Whitman." *WWR*, 8 (Dec. 1962), 91.

M191 Fortin, Marilyn B. "Jack Burden's Search for Identity in *AKM.*" *Lit*, no. 4 (1963), 33–37.

M192 Clements, A. L. "Theme and Reality in *AHG* and *AKM.*" *Criticism*, 5 (Winter 1963), 27–44.

M193 Connelly, Thomas Lawrence. "The Vanderbilt Agrarians: Time and Place in Southern Tradition." *THQ*, 22 (March 1963), 22–37.

M194 Munro, David A. "A Case?—for 'Semi-Fiction.'" *Trace*, no. 48 (Spring 1963), 17–19.

M195 Tyler, Parker. "An American Theater Motif: The Psychodrama." *AQ*, 15 (Summer 1963), 140–151.

M196 Havard, W. C. "The Burden of the Literary Mind: Some Meditations on RPW as Historian."
a. *SAQ*, 62 (Autumn 1963), 516–531.
b. Longley, **K9**, pp. 178–194.

M197 Hicks, John. "Exploration of Values: Warren's Criticism." *SAQ*, 62 (Autumn 1963), 508–515.

M198 Jones, Madison. "The Novels of RPW." *SAQ*, 62 (Autumn 1963), 488–498.

M199 Ray, Robert J., and Ann Ray. "Time in *AKM*: A Stylistic Analysis." *TSLL*, 5 (Autumn 1963), 452–457.

M200 Rosenthal, M. L. "RPW's Poetry." *SAQ*, 62 (Autumn 1963), 499–507.

M201 Strugnell, John R. "RPW and the Uses of the Past." *REL*, 4 (Oct. 1963), 93–102.

M202 Weathers, Winston. "'BW' and the Use of Archetypes."
a. *SSF*, 1 (Fall 1963), 45–51.
b. *The Archetype and the Psyche: Essays in World Literature*. University of Tulsa, Department of English Monograph Series, no. 4 (1968), pp. 103–110.

M203 Williams, T. Harry. "The Achievement of Huey Long."
a. As "Introduction." *Every Man a King: The Autobiography of Huey P. Long*. Chicago: Quadrangle Books, 1964. Pp. vii–xxvi.
b. Beebe and Field, **K11**, pp. 14–21.

M204 Beardsley, Monroe C. "The New Criticism Revisited: An Affirmative View." *Four Quarters*, 13 (Jan. 1964), 11–19.

M205 Fuchs, Carolyn. "Words, Action, and the Modern Novel." *Kerygma*, 4 (Winter 1964), 3–11.

M206 Scott, James B. "The Theme of Betrayal in RPW's Stories." *Thoth* (Syracuse University), 5 (Spring 1964), 74–84.

M207 Schwartz, Elias. "Ransom's 'Bells for John Whiteside's Daughter.'" *ELN*, 1 (June 1964), 284–285.

M208 Samuels, Charles Thomas. "Mr. Trilling, Mr. Warren, and *An American Tragedy*." *YR*, 53 (Summer 1964), 629–640.

M209 Strandberg, Victor. "Theme and Metaphor in *BD*."
a. *PMLA*, 79 (Sept. 1964), 498–508.
b. *A Colder Fire*. [Lexington]: University of Kentucky Press, 1965. Pp. 139–168.
c. *The Poetic Vision of RPW*. [Lexington]: University of Kentucky Press, 1977. Pp. 170–189.

M210 Grantham, Dewey W., Jr. "Interpreters of the Modern South." *SAQ*, 63 (Autumn 1964), 521–529.

M211 Makita, Tokumoto. "The Study of the Cave." In Cultural Science, Sociology, and Education Series, no. 14 (Kanazawa University, Japan) (Dec. 1964), n.p.

M212 Garrett, George P. "The Recent Poetry of RPW." Longley, **K9**, pp. 223–236.

M213 Hagopian, John V. "In Defense of the Affective Fallacy." *SoR* (Adelaide, Australia), 1 (1965), 72–77.

M214 Longley, John Lewis, Jr. "When All Is Said and Done: Warren's *F.*" Longley, **K9**, pp. 169–177.

M215 Spilka, Mark. "The Affective Fallacy Revisited." *SoR* (Adelaide, Australia), 1 (1965), 57–70.

M216 Widmer, Kingsley. "The Father Killers of RPW." *Paunch*, no. 22 (Jan. 1965), 57–64.

M217 Longley, John Lewis, Jr. "RPW: American Man of Letters." *Arts and Sciences* (New York University), Spring 1965, pp. 16–22.

M218 Justus, James H. "The Uses of Gesture in Warren's *Cave*." *MLQ*, 26 (Sept. 1965), 448–461.

M219 Montgomery, Marion. "The Sense of Violation: Notes Toward a Definition of Southern Fiction." *GaR*, 19 (Fall 1965), 278–287.

M220 Moore, L. H. "RPW, William Styron, and the Use of Greek Myth." *Crit*, 8 (Winter 1965–66), 75–87.

M221 Fiedler, Leslie A. "The Blackness of Darkness: The Negro and the Development of American Gothic." *Images of the Negro in American Literature*. Ed. Seymour L. Gross and John Edward Hardy. Chicago: University of Chicago Press, 1966. Pp. 84–105.

M222 Davis, Richard Beale. "Spadework, American Literature, and the Southern Mind: Opportunities." *SAB*, 31 (March 1966), 1–4.

M223 Inge, M. Thomas. "The Educative Experience in *AKM*."
a. *Stylus* (The Magazine of the Washington Literary Society of Randolph-Macon College), 4 (Spring 1966), 21–26.
b. Rev. as "An American Novel of Ideas." *University College Quarterly*, 12 (May 1967), 35–40.

M224 Justus, James H. "The Mariner and RPW." *TSLL*, 8 (Spring 1966), 117–128.

M225 Montgomery, Marion. "Bells for John Stewart's Burden: A Sermon upon the Desirable Death of the 'New Provincialism' Here Typified." *GaR*, 20 (Summer 1966), 145–181.

M226 Gross, Harvey. "History as Metaphysical Pathos: Modern Literature and the Idea of History." *UDQ*, 1 (Autumn 1966), 1–22.

M227 Davis, Richard Beale. "Mrs. Stowe's Characters—in Situations and a Southern Literary Tradition." *Essays on American Literature in Honor of Jay B. Hubbell*. Ed. Clarence Gohdes. Durham, NC: Duke University Press, 1967. Pp. 109–125.

M228 Shepherd, Allen. "Character and Theme in RPW's *F*." *Crit*, 9, no. 3 [1967], 95–102.

M229 Davison, Richard Allan. "RPW's 'Dialectical Configuration' and *The Cave*." *CLAJ*, 10 (June 1967), 349–357.

M230 Mizener, Arthur. "RPW: *AKM*." *SoR*, NS 3 (Summer 1967), 874–894.

M231 Rock, Virginia. "The Fugitive-Agrarians in Response to Social Change." *SHR*, 1 (Summer 1967), 170–181.

M232 Scott, Nathan A., Jr. "Judgment Marked by a Cellar: The American Negro Writer and the Dialectic of Despair." *UDQ*, 2 (Summer 1967), 5–35.

M233 Moore, L. Hugh, Jr. "RPW and the Terror of Answered Prayer." *MissQ*, 21 (Winter 1967–68), 29–36.

M234 Wilcox, Earl. "*AKM*: Epigraph." *Expl*, 26 (Dec. 1967), item 29.

M235 Davison, Richard Allan. "Physical Imagery in RPW's 'BW.'" *GaR*, 22 (Winter 1968), 482–488.

M236 Strandberg, Victor H. "Warren's Osmosis." *Criticism*, 10 (Winter 1968), 23–40.

M237 Moore, John Rees. "RPW: You Must Go Home Again." *SoR*, NS 4 (Spring 1968), 320–332.

M238 Whittington, Curtis, Jr. "The 'Burden' of Narration: Democratic Perspective and First-Person Point of View in the American Novel." *SHR*, 2 (Spring 1968), 236–245.

M239 Durham, Frank. "The Southern Literary Tradition: Shadow or Substance." *SAQ*, 67 (Summer 1968), 455–468.

M240 Tate, Allen. "Faulkner's *Sanctuary* and the Southern Myth." *VQR*, 44 (Summer 1968), 418–427.

M241 Ward, Robert Stafford. "Still 'Christians,' Still Infidels." *SHR*, 2 (Summer 1968), 365–375.

M242 Payne, Ladell. "Willie Stark and Huey Long: Atmosphere, Myth, or Suggestion?"
a. *AQ*, 20 (Fall 1968), 580–595.
b. Chambers, **K17**, pp. 98–115.

M243 Burt, D. J. "A Folk Reference in Warren's *F.*" *MissQ*, 22 (Winter 1968–69), 74–76.

M244 Glick, Nathan. "Fifty Years of the American Novel." *Dialogue*, 2, no. 3 (1969), 34–43.

M245 Justus, James H. "All the Burdens of Warren's *AKM.*" *The Forties: Fiction, Poetry, Drama*. Ed. Warren French. Deland, FL: Everett/Edwards, 1969. Pp. 191–201.

M246 Nakadate, Neil. "RPW and the Confessional Novel." *Genre*, 2 (1969), 326–340.

M247 McCarthy, Paul. "Sports and Recreation in *AKM.*" *MissQ*, 22 (Spring 1969), 113–130.

M248 Brooks, Peter. "Nouvelle Critique et critique nouvelle aux Etats-unis." *Nouvelle Revue Française*, Sept. 1969, pp. 416–426.

M249 Burt, D. J., and A. C. Burt. "RPW's Debt to Ibsen in *NR.*" *MissQ*, 22 (Fall 1969), 359–361.

M250 Core, George. "In the Heart's Ambiguity: RPW as Poet." *MissQ*, 22 (Fall 1969), 313–326.

M251 Witt, R. W. "RPW and the 'Black Patch War.'" *RKHS*, 67 (Oct. 1969), 301–316.

M252 Justus, James H. "A Note on John Crowe Ransom and RPW." *AL*, 41 (Nov. 1969), 425–430.

M253 Martin, R. G. "Diction in Warren's *AKM.*" *EJ*, 58 (Nov. 1969), 1169–1174.

M254 Rubin, Louis D., Jr. "Southern Literature: A Piedmont Art." *MissQ*, 23 (Winter 1969–70), 1–16.

M255 Arnavon, Cyrille. "RPW: Interprète de l'histoire américaine." *Europe*, 48 (1970), 205–226.

M256 Core, George. "Southern Letters and the New Criticism." *GaR*, 24 (Winter 1970), 413–431.

M257 Shapiro, Edward. "The Southern Agrarians and the Tennessee Valley Authority." *AQ*, 22 (Winter 1970), 791–806.

M258 Simpson, Lewis P. "The Southern Writer and the Great Literary Secession." *GaR*, 24 (Winter 1970), 393–412.

M259 Kazin, Alfred. "Whatever Happened to Criticism?" *Commentary*, 49 (Feb. 1970), 58–63.

M260 Goldfarb, Russell M. "RPW's Tollivers and George Eliot's Tullivers." *UKCR*, 36 (March 1970), 209–213; 36 (Summer 1970), 275–279.

M261 Irvine, Peter L. "The 'Witness' Point of View in Fiction." *SAQ*, 69 (Spring 1970), 217–225.

M262 Meckier, Jerome. "Burden's Complaint: The Disintegrated Personality as Theme and Style in Warren's *AKM*."
a. *SNNTS*, 2 (Spring 1970), 7–21.
b. Chambers, **K17**, pp. 57–72.

M263 Shepherd, Allen. "RPW as a Philosophical Novelist." *WHR*, 24 (Spring 1970), 157–168.

M264 Spears, Monroe K. "The Latest Poetry of RPW." *SR*, 78 (Spring 1970), 348–358.

M265 Sullivan, Walter. "The Historical Novelist and the Existential Peril: RPW's *BA*."
a. *SLJ*, 2 (Spring 1970), 104–116.
b. *Death by Melancholy: Essays on Modern Southern Fiction*. Baton Rouge: Louisiana State University Press, 1972.

M266 Shepherd, Allen. "RPW's 'Prime Leaf' as Prototype of *NR*." *SSF*, 7 (Summer 1970), 469–471.

M267 Katope, Christopher G. "RPW's *AKM*: A Novel of 'Pure Imagination.'" *TSLL*, 12 (Fall 1970), 493–510.

M268 Strout, Cushing. "*AKM* and the Shadow of William James." *SoR*, NS 6 (Autumn 1970), 920–934.

M269 Berke, Jacqueline. "Further Observations on 'A Shaw Story and Brooks and Warren.'" *CEA Critic*, 33 (Nov. 1970), 28–29.

M270 Shepherd, Allen. "Warren's *A*: 'Issues in Purer Form' and 'The Ground Rules of Fact.'" *MissQ*, 24 (Winter 1970–71), 47–56.

M271 Herring, Henry D. "Politics in the Novels of RPW." *Recherches Anglaises et Américaines* (Université des Sciences Humaines, Strasbourg, France), no. 4 (1971), 48–60.

M272 Kopcewicz, A. "Assertion of Loneliness: RPW's 'The Ballad of Billie Potts.'" *Studia anglica posnaniensia*, 3 (1971), 107–113.

M273 Langman, F. H. "The Compelled Imagination: RPW's Conception of the Philosophical Novelist." *SoR* (Adelaide, Australia), 4 (1971), 192–202.

M274 Light, James F. "Structure, Meaning, and Technique in *AKM*." Light, **K14**, pp. 73–87.

M275 Miles, Josephine. "Twentieth-Century Donne." *Twentieth-Century Literature in Retrospect*, Harvard English Studies, no. 2 (1971), 205–224.

M276 Wilson, James D. "The Role of Slavery in the Agrarian Myth." *Recherches Anglaises et Américaines*, 4 (1971), 12–22.

M277 Bruffee, Kenneth A. "Elegiac Romance." *CE*, 32 (Jan. 1971), 465–476.

M278 Shepherd, Allen. "The Poles of Fiction: Warren's *AHG*." *TSLL*, 12 (Winter 1971), 709–718.

M279 Simmons, James C. "Adam's Lobectomy Operation and the Meaning of *AKM*."
a. *PMLA*, 86 (Jan. 1971), 84–89.
b. Chambers, **K17**, pp. 73–83.

M280 Shepherd, Allen. "Sugar-Boy as Foil in *AKM*." *Notes on Contemporary Literature*, 1 (March 1971), 15.

M281 Buffington, Robert. "The Poetry of the Master's Old Age." *GaR*, 25 (Spring 1971), 5–16.

M282 Shepherd, Allen. "Percy's *The Moviegoer* and Warren's *AKM*." *Notes on Mississippi Writers*, 4 (Spring 1971), 2–14.

M283 ——. "RPW as Allegorist: The Example of *W*." *Rendezvous*, 6 (Spring 1971), 13–21.

M284 Spies, George Henry, III. "John Steinbeck's *In Dubious Battle* and RPW's *NR*: A Comparative Study." *Steinbeck Quarterly*, 4 (Spring 1971), 48–55.

M285 Köhring, Klaus H. "The American Epic." *SHR*, 5 (Summer 1971), 265–280.

M286 Garrett, George P., and John Graham. "Talking with Shelby Foote—June 1970." *MissQ*, 24 (Fall 1971), 405–427.

M287 Tjader, Margurite. "Airmail Interview: Margurite Tjader." *Dreiser Newsletter*, 2 (Fall 1971), 11–17.

M288 Marsimova, V. "Etot 'svobodnyi mir'" [This Free World; on Ya. Gubenko's dramatization of *AKM*]. Moscow *Pravda*, 3 Dec. 1971.

M289 Dooley, D. M. "The Persona RPW in Warren's *BD*." *MissQ*, 25 (Winter 1971–72), 19–30.

M290 Shepherd, Allen. "Character and Theme in Warren's *MMGG*." *Greyfriar*, 13 (1972), 34–41.

M291 Slack, Robert C. "Willie Stark and William James." *Carnegie Studies in English*, no. 12 (1972), pp. 71–79.

M292 Sumner, D. Nathan. "The Function of Historical Sources in Hawthorne, Melville, and RPW." *Research Studies of Washington State University*, no. 40 (1972), pp. 103–114.

M293 Tatarinova, P. N. "Dva romana Roberta Penna Uorrena" [Two Novels of RPW]. *Krasnodar*, Nauchnye trudy Kubanskogo Universiteta, no. 155 (1972), pp. 145–161.

M294 Namba, Tatsuo. "Regionalism in RPW's *AKM*." *Studies in American Literature*, no. 8 (March 1972), pp. 63–79.

M295 Quinn, Sister M. Bernetta, O.S.F. "RPW's Promised Land." *SoR*, NS 8 (Spring 1972), 329–358.

M296 Brooks, Cleanth. "Brooks on Warren." *Hollins Critic*, 21 (May 1972), 19–22.

M297 Casper, Leonard. "Ark, *F*, and Negotiated Covenant." *Four Quarters*, 21 (May 1972), 110–115.

M298 Cayton, Robert Frank. "The Fictional Voices of RPW." *Four Quarters*, 21 (May 1972), 45–52.

M299 Herring, H. D. "Madness in *AHG*: A Metaphor of the Self in Warren's Fiction." *Four Quarters*, 21 (May 1972), 56–66.

M300 Justus, James H. "Warren and the Doctrine of Complicity." *Four Quarters*, 21 (May 1972), 93–99.

M301 Kehl, D. G. "Love's Definition: Dream as Reality in RPW's *MMGG*." *Four Quarters*, 21 (May 1972), 116–122.

M302 O'Brien, Joseph M. "Cultural History in *AKM*." *Notes on Contemporary Literature*, 2 (May 1972), 14–15.

M303 Scouten, Arthur H. "Warren, Huey Long, and *AKM*." *Hollins Critic*, 21 (May 1972), 23–26.

M304 Shepherd, Allen. "Carrying Manty Home: RPW's *BA*." *Four Quarters*, 21 (May 1972), 101–109.

M305 Strandberg, Victor. "RPW: The Poetry of the Sixties." *Hollins Critic*, 21 (May 1972), 27–44.

M306 Whittington, Curtis, Jr. "The Earned Vision: RPW's 'The Ballad of Billie Potts' and Albert Camus' *Le Malentendu*." *Four Quarters*, 21 (May 1972), 79–90.

M307 Wilcox, Earl. "Right On! *AKM* in the Classroom."
a. *Four Quarters*, 21 (May 1972), 69–78.
b. Chambers, **K17**, pp. 143–153.

M308 Bauerle, Richard F. "The Emblematic Opening of Warren's *AKM*." *Papers on Language and Literature*, 8 (Summer 1972), 312–314.

M309 Hahn, Paul D. "A Reformulation of New Criticism: 'Burnt Norton' Revisited." *Emporia State Research Studies*, 21 (Summer 1972), 5–64.

M310 Keith, Philip. "Whittier and Warren." *Shenandoah*, 23 (Summer 1972), 90–95.

M311 Shepherd, Allen. "The Case for RPW's Second Best Novel." *Cimarron Review* (July 1972), pp. 44–51.

M312 Gray, R. "The American Novelist and American History: A Revaluation of *AKM*." *Journal of American Studies*, 6 (Dec. 1972), 297–307.

M313 Bisanz, Adam J. "RPW: 'The Ballad of Billie Potts': Ein amerikanisches 'Memorabile' auf dem Hintergrund europäischer Überlieferung." *Fabula*, 14 (1973), 71–90.

M314 Dragostinova, Manon. "Za avtora" [About the Author]. *Cjaloto kralsko vojnstvo* [*AKM*]. Sofia: Narodna Kultura, 1973. Pp. 5–8. Introduces the novel.

M315 Justus, James H. "Fiction: The 1930's to the Present." *American Literary Scholarship* (Duke), no. 9 (1973), 209–244.

M316 Konikkara, Sister Cleopatra. "RPW's *AKM*." *Literary Studies: Homage to Dr. A. Sivaramasubramonia Aiyer*. Ed. K. P. K. Menon, M. Manuel, and K. Ayyappa Paniker. Trivandrum: St. Joseph's Press for the Dr. A. S. Aiyer Memorial Committee, 1973. Pp. 201–210.

M317 Prasad, Thakur. "The Author as Victim: A Study of RPW's *WET*." *Journal of Shivaji University* (Kolhapur), 6 (1973), 9–13.

M318 Stafford, William. "An Interval in a Northwest Life, 1950–1973." *Northwest Review*, 13 (1973), 6–9.

M319 Tatarinova, P. N. "Stanovlenie Uorrena-khudozhnika" [The coming into being of Warren the artist]. *Krasnodar*, Nauchnye trudy Kubanskogo Universiteta, no. 176 (1973), 100–113.

M320 Burt, David J. "RPW's Debt to Homer in *F*." *Notes on Contemporary Literature*, 3 (Jan. 1973), 12–14.

M321 Goldstein, Laurence. "Audubon and RPW: To See and Record All Life." *Contemporary Poetry: A Journal of Poetry Criticism* (Fairleigh Dickinson University), 1 (Winter 1973), 47–68.

M322 Shepherd, Allen. "RPW's *A*: The Epigraph." *Notes on Contemporary Literature*, 3 (Jan. 1973), 8–11.

M323 Montesi, Albert J. "Huey Long and *The Southern Review*." *Journal of Modern Literature*, 3 (Feb. 1973), 63–74.

M324 Olson, D. B. "Jack Burden and the Ending of *AKM*." *MissQ*, 26 (Spring 1973), 165–176.

M325 Mellon, Joan. "Film and Style: The Fictional Documentary." *Antioch Review*, 32 (June 1973), 403–425.

M326 Shepherd, Allen. "Warren's *AKM*: Using the Author's Guide to the Novel." *EJ*, 62 (July 1973), 704–708.

M327 ——. "Toward An Analysis of the Prose Style of RPW." *Studies in American Fiction*, 1 (Autumn 1973), 188–202.

M328 Cowley, Malcolm. "What Books Survive from the 1930's?" *Journal of American Studies*, 7 (Dec. 1973), 293–300.

M329 Bataille, Robert. "The Aesthetics and Ethics of Farming: The Southern Agrarian View." *Iowa State Journal of Research*, 49, no. 2, pt. 2 (1974), 189–193.

M330 Bisanz, Adam John. "Entfremdung und Heimkehr in RPWs 'Ballade von Billie Potts': Versuch einer Deutung des parenthetischen Kommentärs." *Sprachkunst*, 5 (1974), 76–95.

M331 Tzavela, Hristofor Trajkov. "Tvorčeski portret na R. P. Uorăn" [Portrait of RPW as a Writer]. *Cjaloto kralsko vojnstvo*. Sofia: Narodna Kultura, 1974. Pp. 5–8.

M332 Westendorp, Tj. A. "RPW: The Development of a Critic." *Handelingen van het tweeëndertigste Nederlands Filologencongres: Geheuden te Utrecht op woensdag 5, donderdag 6 en vrijdag 7 april 1972*. Amsterdam: Holland University Press, 1974. Pp. 221–222.

M333 Wilson, Mary Ann. "Search for an Eternal Present: *Absalom, Absalom!* and *AKM*." *ConnR*, 8, no. 1 (1974), 95–100.

M334 Simpson, Lewis P. "The Southern Recovery of Memory and History." *SR*, 82 (Winter 1974), 1–32.

M335 Cohen, Keith. "El 'New Criticism' en los Estados Unidos." *Revista de Occidente*, 12 (March 1974), 274–307.

M336 Justus, James H. "The Politics of the Self-Created: *AHG*." *SR*, 82 (Spring 1974), 284–299.

M337 Sullivan, Jeremiah J. "Conflict in the Modern American Novel." *Ball State University Forum*, 15 (Spring 1974), 28–36.

M338 Vauthier, Simone. "The Case of the Vanishing Narratee: An Inquiry into *AKM*." *Southern Literary Journal*, 6 (Spring, 1974), 42–69.

M339 Witte, Flo. "Adam's Rebirth in RPW's *W*." *Southern Quarterly*, 12 (July 1974), 365–377.

M340 Webb, Max. "Ford Madox Ford and the Baton Rouge Writers' Conference." *SoR*, NS 10 (Autumn 1974), 892–903.

M341 Bałazy, Teresa. "Warren's *MMGG*: An Interpretation." *Studia anglica posaniensia: An International Review of English Studies*, 6, nos. 1–2 (1975), 147–155.

M342 Mariani, Paul. "Vespers: RPW at Seventy." *Parnassus: Poetry in Review*, 4, no. 1 (1975), 176–188.

M343 Pumpyansky, A. "Kazhclyy chelovek-korol?" [Is each man a king?]. *Novyi mir* (Moscow), 6 [1975], 157–183.

M344 Justus, James H. "On the Restlessness of Southerners." *SoR*, NS 11 (Winter 1975), 65–83.

M345 Kay, Hunter. "The South, the Tradition, and the Traditionalist." *Versus* (Vanderbilt Student Communications, Inc.), Feb. 1975, pp. 19–20.

M346 McCarron, William E. "Warren's *AKM* and Arnold's 'To Marguerite—Continued.'" *AL*, 47 (March 1975), 115–116.

M347 Hiers, John T. "Buried Graveyards: Warren's *F* and Jones' *A Buried Land*." *Essays in Literature*, 2 (Spring 1975), 97–104.

M348 Howard, Richard. "Dreadful Alternatives: A Note on RPW." *GaR*, 29 (Spring 1975), 37–41.

M349 Walker, Marshall. "Making Dreams Work: The Achievement of RPW." *London Magazine*, 15 (Dec. 1975–Jan. 1976), 33–46.

M350 Ilacqua, Alma A. "Amanda Starr: Victim of Her Own False Assumption." *Hartford Studies in Literature*, 8, no. 3 (1976), 178–189.

M351 Nakadate, Neil. "Voices of Community: The Function of Colloquy in RPW's *BD*." *TSL*, no. 21 (1976), 114–124.

M352 Popp, Klaus-Jürgen. "RPW: 'BW' (1946)." *Die amerikanische Short Story der Gegenwart: Interpretationen*. Ed. Peter Frecse. Berlin: Schmidt, 1976. Pp. 77–83.

M353 Shaw, Patrick W. "A Key to RPW's 'When the Light Gets Green.'" *CEA Critic*, 38, no. 2 (1976), 16–18.

M354 Snyder, Robert E. "The Concept of Demagoguery: Huey Long and His Literary Critics." *Louisiana Studies*, 15 (1976), 61–83.

M355 Welch, Dennis M. "Image Making: Politics and Character Development in *AKM*." *Hartford Studies in Literature*, 8, no. 3 (1976), 155–177.

M356 Sullivan, Walter. "The Decline of Myth in Southern Fiction." *SoR*, NS 12 (Winter 1976), 16–31.

M357 Law, Richard. "Warren's *NR* and the Issue of Naturalism: The 'Nightmare' of Our Age." *Southern Literary Journal*, 8 (Spring 1976), 41–61.

M358 Quinn, Sister Bernetta, O.S.F. "Warren and Jarrell: The Remembered Child." *Southern Literary Journal*, 8 (Spring 1976), 24–40.

M359 Stitt, Peter. "RPW, the Poet." *SoR*, NS 12 (Spring 1976), 261–276.

M360 Hannaford, Richard. "Sugar-Boy and Violence in *AKM*." *Notes on Contemporary Literature*, 6 (May 1976), 10–13.

M361 Tjenos, William. "The Poetry of RPW: The Art to Transfigure." *Southern Literary Journal*, 9 (Fall 1976), 3–12.

M362 Chambers, Robert H. "Introduction." **K17**, pp. 1–15.

M363 *Notes from the Editors: RPW's* AKM. Franklin Center, PA: Franklin Library, 1977. 22 pp. *See* **A7.j1**.

M364 Rotella, Guy. "RPW's *YEO*." *Descant*, 21, no. 4 (1977), 36–48.

M365 Spiegelman, Willard. "The Poetic Achievement of RPW." *SWR*, 62 (1977), 411–415.

M366 Westendorp, Tj. A. "RPW as Critic and Novelist: The Early Phase." *Dutch Quarterly Review of Anglo-American Letters*, 7 (1977), 274–285.

M367 Plumly, Stanley. "Warren Selected: An American Poetry, 1923–1975." *Ohio Review*, 18 (Winter 1977), 37–48.

M368 Thomas, William. "The Fugitives, Recaptured." *Commercial Appeal* (Memphis, TN), *Mid-South*, 13 Feb. 1977, pp. 6–9, 14, 16.

M369 Wyatt, David M. "RPW: The Critic as Artist." *VQR*, 53 (Summer 1977), 475–487.

M370 Glassman, Peter. "American Romances: Fiction Chronicle." *HudR*, 30 (Autumn 1977), 437–450.

M371 Clausen, Christopher. "Grecian Thoughts in the Home Fields: Reflections on Southern Poetry." *GaR*, 32 (1978), 283–305.

M372 Clements, A. L. "Sacramental Vision: The Poetry of RPW." *SAB*, 43, no. 4 (1978), 47–65.

M373 Mansfield, Luther Stearns. "History and the Historical Process in *AKM*." *The Centennial Review* (E. Lansing, MI), 22 (1978), 214–230.

M374 Walling, William. "In Which Humpty Dumpty Becomes King." *The Modern American Novel and the Movies*. Ed. Gerald Peary and Roger Shatzkin. Ungar Film Library. New York: Ungar, 1978. Pp. 168–177.

M375 Wilkie, Everette C., Jr. "RPW's 1973 Literary Award." *AN&Q*, 16 (1978), 140.

M376 Clark, William Bedford. "A Meditation on Folk-History: The Dramatic Structure of RPW's 'The Ballad of Billie Potts.'" *AL*, 49 (Jan. 1978), 635–645.

M377 Law, Richard G. "*BD*: The Fact of Violence vs. the Possibility of Love." *AL*, 49 (Jan. 1978), 560–579.

M378 ——. "'The Case of the Upright Judge': The Nature of Truth in *AKM*." *Studies in American Fiction*, 6 (Spring 1978), 1–19.

M379 Rotella, Guy. "A Note on Warren's 'BW.'" *Notes on Contemporary Literature*, 8 (May 1978), 3–5.

M380 Wellek, René. "The New Criticism: Pro and Contra." *Critical Inquiry*, 4 (Summer 1978), 611–624.

M381 Rotella, Guy. "Evil, Goodness, and Grace in Warren's *A*." *Notre Dame English Journal*, 11 (Oct. 1978), 15–32.

M382 ———. "'One Flesh': RPW's *I*." *Renascence*, 31 (Autumn 1978), 25–42.

M383 Winchell, Mark R. "O Happy Sin! *Felix Culpa* in *AKM*." *MissQ*, 31 (Fall 1978), 570–585.

M384 Shaw, Robert B. In *Grolier's Masterplots, 1979 Annual*. Danbury, CT: Grolier, 1979. Pp. 235–238. On *NT*.

M385 Smith, Dave. "'He Prayeth Best Who Loveth Best': on RPW's Poetry." *American Poetry Review*, 8 (Jan.–Feb. 1979), 4–8.

M386 Rotella, Guy. "RPW's *Tale of Time*." *Essays in Arts and Sciences* (University of New Haven), 8 (May 1979), 45–61.

M387 McCarron, William E. "Tennyson, Donne, and *AKM*." *AN&Q*, 17 (May 1979), 140–141.

M388 Kington, Don M. "Pulitzer Prize Winner RPW and His Fort Knox 'Nugget.'" Louisville *Courier-Journal Magazine*, 3 June 1979, pp. 20–21.

N

Reviews

Note: The listing of books included in this section is chronological by publication date; reviews for each book are also in chronological order. For a few books I have been unable to locate a single review; nonetheless, those titles are listed in their proper places in the firm belief that their reviews will emerge, sooner or later.

The Warren deposit at the Beinecke Rare Book and Manuscript Library contains boxes and scrapbooks of reviews that publishers and clipping services have mailed to RPW. Many of these clippings are without page numbers but warrant inclusion because they represent a cross section of opinions about RPW's works. Some of the more substantial reviews, on the order of review-essays, are in the section on essays.

N1 *John Brown: The Making of a Martyr* (1929)
  a. Robbins, Frances Lamont. "The Week's Reading." *Outlook and Independent*, 13 Nov. 1929, p. 427.
  b. Ehrlich, Leonard. "John Brown's Body Is Dug Up by a Southerner." New York *Evening Post*, 16 Nov. 1929, p. 13m:4.
  c. Sifton, Paul. New York *World*, 1 Dec. 1929, p. 11m.
  d. Anon. Springfield [MA] *Sunday Union and Republican*, 12 Jan. 1930, p. 7e.
  e. Craven, Avery. *NYHTBR*, 12 Jan. 1930, p. 17.
  f. Kelly, F. F. *NYTBR*, 12 Jan. 1930, p. 7.
  g. Anon. Cleveland *News Open Shelf*, Feb. 1930, p. 7.
  h. Snow, Francis. *Current History*, 31 (Feb. 1930), 836.
  i. Munson, G. B. *Bookman*, 71 (March 1930), 114.
  j. Nevins, Allan. "Martyr and Fanatic." *NRep*, 19 March 1930, pp. 134–135.
  k. Anon. *Historical Outlook*, 21 (April 1930), 186.
  l. Gabriel, R. H. "Seven American Leaders." *YR*, 19 (Spring 1930), 590–596.

m. Harper, L. A. *University of California Chronicle*, 32 (July 1930), 387–390.

n. MacDonald, William. "John Brown." *Nation*, 2 July 1930, pp. 22–23.

o. Perkins, Dexter. "Figures in Perspective." *VQR*, 6 (Oct. 1930), 615–620.

N2 *I'll Take My Stand* (1930)

a. Hansen, Harry. New York *World*, 12 Nov. 1930, p. 12.

b. Moore, Virginia. *Books*, 30 Nov. 1930, p. 21.

c. Knickerbocker, W. S. "Back to the Land." *SatR*, 20 Dec. 1930, pp. 467–468.

d. James, F. C. *Annals of the American Academy of Political and Social Sciences*, 153 (Jan. 1931), 268.

e. Krock, Arthur. *NYT*, 4 Jan. 1931, p. 3.

f. Hazlitt, Henry. "So Did King Canute." *Nation*, 14 Jan. 1931, pp. 204–205.

g. Anon. Boston *Transcript*, 4 Feb. 1931, p. 2.

h. Anon. *Pittsburgh Monthly Bulletin*, 36 (March 1931), 27.

i. Anon. *Booklist*, April 1931, p. 359.

j. Phillips, Ulrich B. "Fifteen Vocal Southerners." *YR*, 20 (Spring 1931), 611–613.

k. Anon. *Management Review*, 20 (May 1931), 158.

l. Pennington, E. L. *Living Church*, 29 Aug. 1931, p. 594.

m. Young, Thomas Daniel. "To Preserve So Fine a Country." *SR*, 86 (Fall 1978), 595–604.

N3 *Thirty-Six Poems* (1935)

a. Flint, F. Cudworth. "Five Poets." *SoR*, 1 (Winter 1936), 650–674.

b. Lechlitner, Ruth. "Nostalgic, Fugitive Verse." *NYHTBR*, 16 Feb. 1936, p. 10.

c. Anon. "Shorter Notices." *Nation*, 25 March 1936, p. 391.

d. Holmes, John. "Five American Poets." *VQR*, 12 (April 1936), 288–295.

e. Z[abel], M[orton] D[auwen]. "Problems of Knowledge." *Poetry*, 48 (April 1936), 37–41.

f. Lann, Robert. "Some Poetry in Review." *NRep*, 15 July 1936, p. 304.

g. Leach, H. G. *Forum*, 96 (Aug. 1936), 96.

h. Walton, Eda Lou. "Poems by Robert Warren." *NYTBR*, 31 Jan. 1937, p. 19.

N4 *An Approach to Literature* (1936)
Note: I have been unable to locate any reviews for this title.

N5 *A Southern Harvest* (1937)
a. W., M. *NYTBR*, 21 Nov. 1937, p. 28.
b. Armfield, Eugene. "Moonshine and Honeysuckle." *SatR*, 18 Dec. 1937, pp. 10–11.
c. Anon. "Reprints, New Editions." *NYHTBR*, 9 Jan. 1938, p. 17.
d. Clark, Eleanor. *PR*, 4 (March 1938), 56–58.

N6 *Understanding Poetry* (1938)
a. Holmes, John. "Poetry Now." Boston *Evening Transcript*, 6 Aug. 1938, p. 3–2.
b. Walton, Eda Lou. "Schoolroom Anthology." *NYHTBR*, 28 Aug. 1938, p. 17.
c. Koch, V. C. *Quarterly Journal of Speech*, 25 (Oct. 1939), 499–500.
d. Kenner, Hugh. "Subways to Parnassus." *Poetry*, 84 (April 1954), 43–53.

N7 *Night Rider* (1939)
a. Routon, Lenora. "Warren Novel Tells Story of Kentucky Tobacco War." *Daily Reveille* (LSU), 4 March 1939, p. 8.
b. Gueymard, Claire L. "Author of Stirring Novel Based on Tobacco War in Kentucky Sees Analogy in Louisiana Berry Fight." Baton Rouge *State Times*, 16 March 1939, p. 11.
c. Davenport, Basil. *SatR*, 18 March 1939, p. 6.
d. Fadiman, Clifton. "Books." *NY*, 18 March 1939, pp. 68–69.
e. Davis, Hassoldt. *NYTBR*, 19 March 1939, p. 6.
f. Pruette, Lorine. "A Tobacco War in Kentucky." *NYHTBR*, 19 March 1939, p. 2.
g. B., R. W. "Mr. Warren Offers His Prize Novel." New Orleans *Times-Picayune*, 26 March 1939, p. 2–11.
h. Anon. "Tobacco War." *Time*, 27 March 1939, p. 73.
i. Brown, Harry. *Harvard Advocate*, April 1939, pp. 43–44.
j. Rahv, Philip. "A Variety of Fiction." *PR*, 6 (Spring 1939), 106–113.
k. T., F. H. *Vanderbilt Alumnus*, 24 (April 1939), 10–11.
l. Woodward, Frances. "Three First Novels." *AtMo*, April 1939, n.p.
m. Anon. Springfield [MA] *Sunday Union and Republican*, 9 April 1939, p. 7e.
n. Burns, John McDougal. "Laurels Richly Earned." Nashville *Tennessean*, 9 April 1939, p. 6D.
o. Jackson, Joseph Henry. "A Significant Novel Written Under Fel-

lowship Auspices." San Francisco *Chronicle*, 14 April 1939, p. 17.

p. Anon. *Booklist*, 15 April 1939, p. 271.

q. Curtiss, Mina. "Tragedy of a Liberal." *Nation*, 29 April 1939, pp. 507–508.

r. Isherwood, Christopher. "Tragic Liberal." *NRep*, 31 May 1939, p. 108.

s. Thompson, Ralph. "Outstanding Novels." *YR*, 28 (June 1939), vi.

t. Long, Louise. "Night Rider." *SWR*, 24 (July 1939), 498–500.

u. Muller, Herbert J. "Violence upon the Roads." *KR*, 1 (Summer 1939), 323–324.

v. Stegner, Wallace. "Conductivity in Fiction." *VQR*, 15 (Summer 1939), 443–447.

w. Baily, J. O. *Southern Literary Messenger*, 1 (Sept. 1939), 639–640.

x. Anon. "Drama in Tobacco." *TLS*, 20 Jan. 1940, p. 29.

y. West, Anthony. *New Statesman*, 20 Jan. 1940, p. 77.

z. Baker, Howard. "In Praise of the Novel: The Fiction of Huxley, Steinbeck, and [48] Others." *SoR*, 5 (Spring 1940), 778–800.

a². Wilson, Angus. "The Fires of Violence." *Encounter*, 4 (May 1955), 75–78.

b². Anon. *Books & Bookmen*, 18 (Sept. 1973), p. 135.

c². Anon. "Paperbacks: New and Noteworthy." *NYTBR*, 29 April 1979, p. 67.

N8 *Eleven Poems on the Same Theme* (1942)

a. Jack, Peter Monro. *NYTBR*, 26 April 1942, p. 4.

b. Beatty, Richmond Croom. "Rich, Fresh Imagery." Nashville *Banner*, 29 April 1942, p. 4x.

c. Anon. *NY*, 9 May 1942, p. 80.

d. Rushton, Peters. "The Unrationed Muse." *VQR*, 18 (Summer 1942), 478–480.

e. Williams, Oscar. "More Poets of the Month." *NRep*, 6 July 1942, p. 28.

f. Lechlitner, Ruth. "Selected New Poetry." *NYHTBR*, 19 July 1942, p. 13.

g. Jones, Frank. *Nation*, 26 Sept. 1942, p. 277.

h. Nims, John Frederick. "Two Intellectual Poets." *Poetry*, 61 (Dec. 1942), 505–508.

i. Tate, Allen. *Recent American Poetry and Poetic Criticism*. Washington, D.C.: Library of Congress, 1943. P. 9.

j. Untermeyer, Louis. "Cream of the Verse." *YR*, 32 (Winter 1943), 366–371.

k. Deutsch, Babette. "Poets—Timely and Timeless." *NRep*, 29 March 1943, pp. 420–421.

N9 *Understanding Fiction* (1943)

    a. Anon. *Dominicana*, 28 (June 1943), 144.

    b. Hintz, H. W. *CE*, 5 (Oct. 1943), 48.

N10 *At Heaven's Gate* (1943)

    a. Kelly, H. G. *Library Journal*, 68 (Aug. 1943), 625.

    b. Laughlin, James. *Accent*, 4 (Aug. 1943), 62–63.

    c. Varley, Lee. Springfield [MA] *Sunday Union and Republican*, 1 Aug. 1943, p. 7e.

    d. Skillin, Edward J. "Mighty Like Despair." *Commonweal*, 6 Aug. 1943, p. 398.

    e. Chamberlain, John. *NYT*, 19 Aug. 1943, p. 17.

    f. Anon. "Briefly Noted." *NY*, 21 Aug. 1943, p. 67.

    g. Daniels, Jonathan. "Scraping the Bottom of Southern Life." *SatR*, 21 Aug. 1943, p. 6.

    h. Engle, Paul. "Paul Engle Hails a New Novel as Outstanding Work of 1943." Chicago *Tribune*, 22 Aug. 1943, pt. 6, pp. 11 and 12.

    i. Geismar, Maxwell. "The Pattern of Dry Rot in Dixie." *NYTBR*, 22 Aug. 1943, p. 4.

    j. Gordon, Caroline. "Passionate Southern Eloquence." *NYHTBR*, 22 Aug. 1943, p. 5.

    k. Howell, Isabel. "Mr. Warren's Second Novel, 'AHG.'" Nashville *Tennessean*, 22 Aug. 1943, p. C-7.

    l. Leisure, Harold. "Life in a Southern City." San Francisco *Chronicle*, 22 Aug. 1943.

    m. North, Sterling. Chicago *Sun Book Week*, 22 Aug. 1943, p. 3.

    n. Cowley, Malcolm. "Luke Lea's Empire." *NRep*, 23 Aug. 1943, p. 258.

    o. Phillips, William. "Coils of the Past." *Nation*, 28 Aug. 1943, pp. 243–244.

    p. Anon. *AtMo*, Sept. 1943, p. 131.

    q. Anon. "Books Received." *Christian Century*, 1 Sept. 1943, p. 991.

    r. Lytle, Andrew. "AHG." *SR*, 51 (Oct.–Dec. 1943), 599–602.

    s. Prescott, Orville. "Outstanding Novel." *YR*, 33 (Autumn 1943), xii.

    t. Garrigue, Jean. "Many Ways of Evil." *KR*, 6 (Winter 1944), 135–138.

    u. Stevenson, Lionel. "The Threshold of War." *VQR*, 20 (Winter 1944), 144–145.

v. Fergusson, Francis. *American Oxonian*, 31 (April 1944), 125–126.
w. Reed, Henry. *The Listener* [London], 24 Oct. 1946, p. 570.
x. McIntire, Lucy B. "Notorious District in Tammany Era." Savannah *Morning News*, 25 Jan. 1959, p. 12.
y. Perkin, Robert L. "One Man's Pegasus: Reissue of an Excellent Novel." *Rocky Mountain News*, 1 Feb. 1959, p. 64.
z. Kohler, Dayton. "Reissued *AHG*." Louisville *Courier-Journal*, 1 Feb. 1959, p. 4–7.
a². Anon. *TLS*, 15 Jan. 1960, p. 29.
b². Jacobson, Dan. "Rednecks and Patricians." *Spectator*, 15 Jan. 1960, p. 83.
c². Waterhouse, Keith. "New Novels." *New Statesman*, 16 Jan. 1960, p. 79.
d². Price, R. G. G. "New Novels." *Punch*, 20 Jan. 1960, p. 139.

N11　*Selected Poems, 1923–1943* (1944)
　　a. Anon. *Bulletin from Virginia Kirkus' Bookshop Service*, 15 March 1944, p. 129.
　　b. Beatty, Richmond Croom. "Rich and Exciting Poetry." Nashville *Banner*, 5 April 1944, p. 12.
　　c. Kennedy, Leo. "Recent Books of Verse." Chicago *Sun Book Week*, 16 April 1944, p. 6.
　　d. Bogan, Louise. "Verse." *NY*, 22 April 1944, pp. 76–78.
　　e. Thorp, Willard. *NYTBR*, 7 May 1944, p. 4.
　　f. Ransom, John Crowe. "The Inklings of 'Original Sin.'" *SatR*, 20 May 1944, pp. 10–11.
　　g. Drew, Elizabeth. "Alert and Subtle Verse." *NYHTBR*, 25 June 1944, p. 11.
　　h. Arrowsmith, William. *Chimera*, 2 (Summer 1944), 44–45.
　　i. Flint, F. Cudworth. "Without a Common Denominator." *VQR*, 20 (Summer 1944), 464–473.
　　j. Van Ghent, Dorothy. *Rocky Mountain Review*, 8 (Summer 1944), 164–165.
　　k. Herschberger, Ruth. "Poised Between the Two Alarms . . . ."
　　　　1. *Accent*, 4 (Summer 1944), 240–246.
　　　　2. *Accent Anthology: Selections from* Accent, a Quarterly Journal of New Literature, *1940–1945*. Ed. Kerker Quinn and Charles Shattuck. New York: Harcourt, Brace, 1946. Pp. 610–618.
　　l. Mizener, Arthur. "Four Poets." *PR*, 11 (Summer 1944), 357–360.
　　m. Gregory, Horace. "Of Vitality, Regionalism, and Satire in Recent American Poetry."
　　　　1. *SR*, 52 (Autumn 1944), 572–593.

2. As "John Crowe Ransom, Allen Tate, RPW, and a Note on Laura Riding." *History of American Poetry, 1900–1940*. Ed. Horace Gregory and Zaturenska Marya Alexandroona. New York: Harcourt, Brace, 1944. Pp. 360–386.

n. Matthiessen, F. O. "American Poetry Now."

    1. *KR*, 6 (Autumn 1944), 683–696.

    2. As "Four American Poets, 1944." *Responsibilities of the Critic: Essays and Reviews*. Ed. John Rackliffe. New York: Oxford University Press, 1952. Pp. 121–124.

o. Fitts, Dudley. "Of Tragic Stature." *Poetry*, 65 (Nov. 1944), 94–101.

p. Dupee, F. W. "RPW and Others." *Nation*, 25 Nov. 1944, pp. 660 and 662.

q. Untermeyer, Louis. "Among the Poets." *YR*, 34 (Winter 1945), 341–346.

r. Anon. "Poems of Maturity." *TLS*, 21 Sept. 1951, p. 595.

N12 *All the King's Men* (1946)

a. Anon. *Bulletin from Virginia Kirkus' Bookshop Service*, 1 July 1946, p. 301.

b. Walbridge, Earle F. *Library Journal*, 71 (Aug. 1946), 1051.

c. Wood, James P. "Mr. Warren's 'Modern Realism.'" *SatR*, 17 Aug. 1946, p. 11.

d. Barry, Josephine. "Minnesota Faculty Man Does Impressive Novel." St. Paul *Pioneer Press* [MN], 18 Aug. 1946, p. 10.

e. Brookhouser, Frank. "Rise and Fall of a Southern Dictator in Tradition of Long." Philadelphia *Inquirer*, 18 Aug. 1946, p. SO-17.

f. Davis, Robert Gorham. "Dr. Adam Stanton's Dilemma."

    1. *NYTBR*, 18 Aug. 1946, pp. 3 and 24.

    2. Light, **K14**, pp. 53–56.

g. Engle, Paul. "Willie Stark—He Hits You Between the Eyes!" Chicago *Sunday Tribune Magazine of Books*, 18 Aug. 1946, pt. 4, pp. 1, 3, and 8.

h. Ethridge, William M., Jr. "'AKM' Novel Wins Enthusiastic Reception: Former Memphian's Book Called Exciting and Good Writing." Memphis *Commercial Appeal*, 18 Aug. 1946, p. IV–12.

i. Hamm, Victor M. "Demagog, Huey Long Style; an Ambitious, Ruthless Southern Politico Is the Hero of RPW's Intricately Plotted Novel." Milwaukee *Journal*, 18 Aug. 1946, p. V–5.

j. Harrison, Jane. "Pulitzer Prize Candidate." Nashville *Tennessean*, 18 Aug. 1946, p. 29-A.

k. Heritage, Donald. "'AKM' Is Analysis of Another American Dictator." Philadelphia *Record*, 18 Aug. 1946, p. M-9.

l. Jackson, Joseph Henry. "Powerful New Novel on the Life and Times of a U.S. Politician." San Francisco *Chronicle*, 18 Aug. 1946, p. 12.

m. Marsh, Fred. "Demagogue's Progress: A Novel of American Politics Following the Huey Long Story and Legend." *NYHTBR*, 18 Aug. 1946, p. 2.

n. S[cott], W[infield] T. "Two Top Novels of Summer: Warren's State Boss, Laxness's Farmer in Iceland." Providence *Journal*, 18 Aug. 1946, p. VI-8.

o. St. John, Wylby Folk. "Southern Demagogue." Atlanta *Journal*, 18 Aug. 1946, p. 10e.

p. Smith, Laban C. "A Wily Political Boss: From Lincolnesque to Huey Long-Like Role." Chicago *Sun Book Week*, 18 Aug. 1946, p. 3.

q. S[mith], P[aul] J[ordan]. "Story of Southern Boss Ably Told for First Time: RPW Produces His Best Novel in Dramatizing Dictator's Career." Los Angeles *Times*, 18 Aug. 1946, p. III-4.

r. Cournos, John. New York *Sun*, 19 Aug. 1946, p. 2–18.

s. Gannett, Lewis. "Books and Things." *NYHT*, 19 Aug. 1946, p. 17.

t. Hansen, Harry. "Southern Demagogue: RPW's New Novel Is Excellent Portrait of a Huey Long Type." New York *World-Telegram*, 19 Aug. 1946, p. 18.

u. Rogers, W. G. "RPW's Novel Draws Praise from AP Critic, Calls It Pulitzer Prize Work." Baton Rouge *Morning Advocate*, 20 Aug. 1946, p. 3.

v. Bond, Alice Dixon. "Picture of a Cracker Dictator; The War of Tedium and Inertia." Boston *Herald*, 21 Aug. 1946, p. 19.

w. Cheney, Brainard. "Powerful, Profound, Important Novel." Nashville *Banner*, 21 Aug. 1946, p. 22.

x. Gray, James. "Novelist Strips U.S. Conscience." Chicago *Daily News*, 21 Aug. 1946, p. 24.

y. Anon. "Briefly Noted: Fiction." *NY*, 24 Aug. 1946, p. 70.

z. Gardiner, Harold C. "Why Put Him Together?" *America*, 24 Aug. 1946, p. 503.

a². Trilling, Diana. "Fiction in Review." *Nation*, 24 Aug. 1946, p. 220.

b². Engle, Paul. "Willie Stark—He Hits You Between the Eyes!" *Chicago Sunday Tribune Magazine of Books*, 25 Aug. 1946, p. 7.

c². R., M. C. "Has Professor Warren's Book Brought to Us the Real Dictator Huey P. Long?" Washington *Star*, 25 Aug. 1946, p. C5.

d². Anon. *Time*, 26 Aug. 1946, p. 98.

e². D[aniel], T[homas] H. "Novel Based on Huey Long Wins Praise." Columbia [SC] *Record*, 29 Aug. 1946.

f². Meador, Frank. "More than Just the Kingfish." Boston *Globe*, 29 Aug. 1946, p. 19.

g². Anon. *Booklist*, 43 (Sept. 1946), 18.

h². Canby, Henry Seidel. *Book-of-the-Month Club News*, Sept. 1946, p. 13.

i². Dexter, Ethel Hathaway. "RPW's 'AKM': Southern Poet's Novel a Dramatic Story Based on the Real Life of a Famous Demagogue—Many Characters Add to Interest." Springfield [MA] *Sunday Union and Republican*, 1 Sept. 1946, p. 4d.

j². N[emerov], H[oward]. *Furioso*, 2 (Fall 1946), 69–71.

k². Ragan, Sam. "Chronicle of Southern Politics." Raleigh *News and Observer*, 1 Sept. 1946, p. II-8.

l². Mayberry, George. "On the Nature of Things." *NRep*, 2 Sept. 1946, pp. 265–266.

m². R., W. K. "Humpty Dumpty Had a Great Fall." *Christian Science Monitor*, 4 Sept. 1946, p. 14.

n². Commins, Saxe. "Some Powerful Variations on a Huey Long Theme." Cleveland *News Weekend Book Review*, 7 Sept. 1946, p. 3.

o². Lord, Ruth K. "Story of a Southern 'Boss' Has Pulitzer Prize Quality." Louisville *Courier-Journal*, 8 Sept. 1946, p. 3–15.

p². Spearman, Walter. "Literary Lantern." Charlotte [NC] *Observer*, 8 Sept. 1946, p. IV-4.

q². Anon. "Backwoods Humpty Dumpty." *Newsweek*, 9 Sept. 1946, pp. 114 and 116.

r². Fairall, Helen K. "RPW's Novel about a Benevolent Despot." Des Moines *Register*, 15 Sept. 1946, p. L–11.

s². Anon. "Native of Guthrie Wins High Praise for Book." Todd County *Standard* [Elkton, KY], 20 Sept. 1946, p. 8.

t². Draper, Arthur. "Warren Writes Political Boss Saga." Houston *Post*, 29 Sept. 1946, p. IV–18.

u². Anon. "Books: In Brief Review." *CE*, 8 (Oct. 1946), 49.

v². Hicks, Granville. "Some American Novelists." *American Mercury*, 63 (Oct. 1946), 494–500.

w². Kirschbaum, Leo. "Leading Pulitzer Contender." *Commentary*, 2 (Oct. 1946), 392–394.

x^2. Prescott, Orville. "Outstanding Novels." *YR*, 36 (Autumn 1946), 192.

y^2. West, Ray B., Jr. "A Note on American Fiction: 1946." *Western Review*, 11 (Autumn 1946), 45–48.

z^2. Rago, Henry. "Books of the Week." *Commonweal*, 4 Oct. 1946, pp. 599–600.

a^3. Anon. "Shorter Notices." *Catholic World*, 164 (Nov. 1946), 189.

b^3. Chamberlain, John. "The New Books." *Harper's Magazine*, Nov. 1946, n.p.

c^3. Hardwick, Elizabeth. *PR*, 13 (Nov.–Dec. 1946), 583–584.

d^3. [Swallow, Alan]. *United States Quarterly Book List*, 2 (Dec. 1946), 283–284.

e^3. Anon. "Books: Fiction." *Time*, 16 Dec. 1946, p. 112.

f^3. Wade, John D. "A Handsome Gift Indeed." *VQR*, 23 (Winter 1947), 138–141.

g^3. P[atterson], I[sabel] M. *NYHT*, 12 Jan. 1947, p. VII–19.

h^3. D., M. "Books and Authors." Baton Rouge *Morning Advocate*, 18 Jan. 1947, p. 6–A.

i^3. Weeks, Edward. *AtMo*, July 1947, p. 118.

j^3. Hale, Lionel. "Down South." [London] *Observer*, 2 May 1948, p. 3.

k^3. Symons, Julian. "The Boss on the Band Wagon." Manchester *Evening News*, 5 May 1948, p. 2.

l^3. Anon. "Southern Dictator." *TLS*, 8 May 1948, p. 257.

m^3. Quennell, Peter. "Life and Death of a Rabble-Raiser." [London] *Daily Mail*, 17 May 1948.

n^3. O'Connor, Frank. "Lay Off Hamlet!" [London] *Evening News*, 19 May 1948.

o^3. Allen, Walter. *New Statesman and Nation*, 5 June 1948, pp. 164–165.

p^3. Nathan, Monique. "Les Fous du Roi de RPW." *Critique* [Paris], 7 (May 1951), 467–470.

q^3. Anon. "Fables of Our Time." *TLS*, 27 Nov. 1959, p. 692.

r^3. Anon. *TLS*, 15 Jan. 1960, p. 29.

s^3. Duchene, Anne. "Suburbanised Faulkner." Manchester *Guardian*, 15 Jan. 1960, p. 83.

t^3. Jacobson, Dan. "Rednecks and Patricians." *Spectator*, 15 Jan. 1960, p. 83.

u^3. Miller, Karl. "Requiem for a Demagogue." [London] *Observer*, 17 Jan. 1960, p. 21.

v^3. Price, R. G. G. "New Novels." *Punch*, 20 Jan. 1960, p. 139.

w[3]. Anon. "In Brief . . . ." London *Tribune*, 22 Jan. 1960, p. 10.

x[3]. Anon. "New Editions of Two of RPW's Novels." *Eastern Daily Press*, 12 Feb. 1960, p. 8.

y[3]. S., G. D. "Pulitzer Winner Warren—A Novelist of the Top Rank." Bulawayo *Chronicle*, 13 March 1960, p. 8.

z[3]. M., W. "A Saga of American Guilt." Rhodesia *Herald*, 23 March 1960, p. 18.

a[4]. Anon. "Book Reviews." Calcutta *Statesman*, 3 April 1960, Magazine sec., p. 4.

b[4]. Anon. East African *Standard*, 29 April 1960, p. 14.

c[4]. Wolfman, Joe. "Thoughts on Re-Reading *AKM*." *Twin North Tribune* [Dallas, TX], 24 Nov. 1966, p. 5.

d[4]. Maloff, Saul. "Reconsideration: *AKM*." *NRep*, 3 March 1973, pp. 28–30.

e[4]. Anon. *New Statesman*, 11 Jan. 1974, p. 55.

f[4]. Symons, Julian. "At the Court of the Kingfisher." [London] *Sunday Times*, 20 Jan. 1974, p. 31.

g[4]. Anon. *Spectator*, 26 Jan. 1974, p. 106.

h[4]. Anon. *Books & Bookmen*, 19 (March 1974), 87.

N13   *Blackberry Winter* (1946)
Note: I have been unable to locate any reviews of this title.

N14   *The Rime of the Ancient Mariner* (1946)

a. Breit, Harvey. *NYHTBR*, 5 Jan. 1947, p. 5.

b. Blackmur, R. P. "Uncle! Uncle!" *Nation*, 15 March 1947, pp. 307–309.

c. Burke, Kenneth. "Towards Objective Criticism." *Poetry*, 70 (April 1947), 42–47.

d. Griggs, Earl Leslie. "Date Shells and the Eye of the Critic." *VQR*, 23 (April 1947), 297–301.

e. Olson, Elder.

1. *MP*, 45 (May 1948), 275–279.

2. As "A Symbolic Reading of *The Ancient Mariner*." *Critics and Criticism: Ancient and Modern*. Ed. R. S. Crane. Chicago: University of Chicago Press, 1952. Pp. 138–144.

N15   *The Circus in the Attic and Other Stories* (1947)

a. Anon. *Bulletin from Virginia Kirkus' Bookshop Service*, 15 Jan. 1948, p. 34.

b. Poore, Charles. *NYT*, 22 Jan. 1948, p. 25.

c. Anon. "Briefly Noted." *NY*, 24 Jan. 1948, pp. 80 and 82.

d. Dedmon, Emmett. "Southern Communities Brought to Life in

Warren Anthology." Chicago *Sunday Sun and Times Book Week*, 25 Jan. 1948, p. 5x.

e. Hicks, Granville. "Warren's Short Stories." *NYTBR*, 25 Jan. 1948, pp. 5 and 28.

f. Match, Richard. "Evidences of Artistic Growth." *NYHTBR*, 25 Jan. 1948, p. 4.

g. Anon. "On the Soft Side." *Time*, 26 Jan. 1948, p. 101.

h. Farrelly, John. "Fiction Parade: Delayed Action." *NRep*, 26 Jan. 1948, p. 32.

i. R., W. K. *Christian Science Monitor*, 30 Jan. 1948, p. 14.

j. Smith, Henry Nash. "Proustian Exploration." *SatR*, 31 Jan. 1948, pp. 14–15.

k. Jackson, Joseph Henry. "This World." San Francisco *Chronicle*, 3 Feb. 1948, p. 14.

l. Anon. *Booklist*, 15 Feb. 1948, p. 217.

m. Marshall, Margaret. "Notes by the Way." *Nation*, 21 Feb. 1948, pp. 216–217.

n. Eckman, Frederick. "Warren: A Southern Paragon." *Cronos*, 2 (March 1948), 75–76.

o. Anon. "Short Tales by Robert Warren." New Orleans *Times-Picayune*, 7 March 1948, p. 2–17.

p. Fremantle, Anne. "Books." *Commonweal*, 12 March 1948, p. 547.

q. Elledge, Scott. "Low Thought." *Furioso*, 3 (Spring 1948), 81–82.

r. Prescott, Orville. "Outstanding Novels." *YR*, 37 (Spring 1948), 575–576.

s. Anon. "Beneath the Surface." *TLS*, 18 April 1952, p. 261.

t. Anon. *United States Quarterly Book List*, 4 (June 1948), 140.

u. Glick, Nathan. "The Southern Temper." *Commentary*, 5 (June 1948), 577–578.

v. Daniel, Robert. "No Place to Go." *SR*, 56 (Summer 1948), 524–526.

w. Fiedler, Leslie A. "The Fate of the Novel." *KR*, 10 (Summer 1948), 519–527.

x. Frank, Joseph. "Recent Fiction." *HudR*, 1 (Summer 1948), 276–284, 286, and 288.

y. O'Connor, William Van. "RPW's Short Fiction." *Western Review*, 12 (Summer 1948), 251–253.

z. Anon. *VQR*, 24 (Autumn 1948), cxviii.

N16 *Modern Rhetoric* (1949)

a. Dykema, K. W. *CE*, 12 (Oct. 1950), 55–56.

b. Samuels, E. *CE*, 12 (Oct. 1950), 54–55.

c. Anon. *Choice*, 9 (July–Aug. 1972), 639.

N17 *Fundamentals of Good Writing* (1950)

a. Anon. *Bookmark*, June 1950, p. 207.

b. Barker, Shirley. *Library Journal*, 1 June 1950, p. 975.

c. Roverc, Richard H. "Salute to RPW." *Harper's*, July 1950, p. 105.

d. B., V. A. "New Critical Volumes for Reader and Writer." Chicago *Daily News*, 5 July 1950, p. 27.

e. Stauffer, Donald A. *NRep*, 10 July 1950, p. 21.

f. Stegner, Wallace. "The Art of the Right Word." *NYTBR*, 16 July 1950, pp. 5 and 20.

g. Anon. Springfield [MA] *Republican*, 6 Aug. 1950, p. 7B.

h. Anon. "The Art of Writing." *TLS*, 26 Sept. 1952, p. 630.

N18 *World Enough and Time* (1950)

a. Anon. *Bulletin from Virginia Kirkus' Bookshop Service*, 15 April 1950, p. 242.

b. McDonald, G. D. *Library Journal*, 1 May 1950, p. 775.

c. Anon. *Bookmark* (New York State Library), 9 (June 1950), 213.

d. Beauchamp, Elise. "People Live in Pages of This Novel." New Orleans *Times-Picayune*, 18 June 1950, p. 2–6.

e. O'Neill, Lois, and Ed O'Neill. "Kentucky in Fiction Again." Louisville *Courier-Journal*, 18 June 1950, Magazine sec., pp. 23–26.

f. Gill, Brendan. "One Bourbon on the Rocks, One Gin-and-Tonic." *NY*, 24 June 1950, pp. 89–90, 93.

g. Guthrie, A. B., Jr. "Virtue Plundered in Kentucky." *SatR*, 24 June 1950, pp. 11–12.

h. Cowley, Malcolm. "Mr. Warren's New Novel Is His Longest and Richest." *NYHTBR*, 25 June 1950, p. 1.

i. Dedmon, Emmett. "Truth Seems Strange in an Unusual Novel." Chicago *Sunday Sun-Times*, 25 June 1950, p. 2–5.

j. Engle, Paul. "Rich, Violent New Novel by RPW." Chicago *Sunday Tribune Magazine of Books*, 25 June 1950, p. 3.

k. Janeway, Elizabeth. "Man in Conflict, Mind in Torment." *NYTBR*, 25 June 1950, pp. 1 and 22.

l. Anon. "Kentucky Murder." *Newsweek*, 26 June 1950, pp. 88–90.

m. Anon. "The Web of Politics." *Time*, 26 June 1950, p. 98.

n. Jackson, Joseph Henry. "This World." San Francisco *Chronicle*, 26 June 1950, p. 18.

o. Anon. *Booklist*, 1 July 1950, p. 336.

p. Pickrel, Paul. "Outstanding Novel." *YR*, 39 (Summer 1950), 765–768.

q. Rolo, C. J. *AtMo*, July 1950, pp. 86–87.

r. Rovere, Richard H. "Salute to RPW." *Harper's*, July 1950, pp. 103–104.

s. Stoer, M. W. *Christian Science Monitor*, 1 July 1950, p. 6.

t. Jones, Ernest. "Through a Glass, Darkly." *Nation*, 8 July 1950, p. 42.

u. Anon. "Recent and Readable." *Time*, 10 July 1950, p. 83; 24 July 1950, p. 87.

v. Trese, L. J. *Commonweal*, 21 July 1950, p. 373.

w. Fiedler, Leslie A. "Toward Time's Cold Womb."

  1. *New Leader*, 22 July 1950, p. 24.

  2. *PR*, 17 (Sept.–Oct. 1950), 739–743.

  3. *No! In Thunder*. Boston: Beacon Press, 1960. Pp. 119–126.

x. Hatch, Robert. "The Hero and the Angel: A Kentucky Tragedy." *NRep*, 31 July 1950, pp. 18–19.

y. Sandrock, Mary. "New Novels." *CathW*, 171 (Aug. 1950), 394.

z. Baker, Carlos. *VQR*, 26 (Autumn 1950), 603–605.

a². Mizener, Arthur. "Amphibium in Old Kentucky." *KR*, 12 (Autumn 1950), 697–701.

b². Ridgely, Joseph V. "Tragedy in Kentucky." *Hopkins Review*, 4 (Fall 1950), 61–63.

c². Fowke, Edith. *Canadian Forum*, 30 (Dec. 1950), 214–215.

d². Schiller, Andrew. "The World Out of Square." *Western Review*, 15 (Spring 1951), 234–237.

e². Raymond, John. *New Statesman and Nation*, 22 Sept. 1951, pp. 318–319.

f². Anon. "The Path of Honour." *TLS*, 28 Sept. 1951, p. 617.

g². Symons, Julian. "At the Court of the Kingfisher." [London] *Sunday Times*, 20 Jan. 1974, p. 31.

  Note: combined review of *AKM* and *WET* reissues from Secker & Warburg.

h². Anon. "Paperbacks: New and Noteworthy." *NYTBR*, 29 April 1979, p. 67.

N19 *Brother to Dragons* (1953)

a. W[ilder], A[mos] N. "Revising the American Dream." *Christianity and Crisis*, 20 July 1953, pp. 97–98.

b. Anon. *Bulletin from Virginia Kirkus' Bookshop Service*, 1 Aug. 1953, p. 510.

c. Prescott, Orville. "Books of the Times." *NYT*, 21 Aug. 1953, p. 15.

d. Webster, Harvey Curtiss. "Virginia Cauldron." *SatR*, 22 Aug. 1953, pp. 11–12.

e. Ames, Alfred C. Chicago *Sunday Tribune of Books*, 23 Aug. 1953, p. 3.

f. Deutsch, Babette. "RPW's Savage Poem: Old Murder, Modern Overtones." *NYHTBR*, 23 Aug. 1953, p. 3.

g. Jarrell, Randall. "On the Underside of the Stone." *NYTBR*, 23 Aug. 1953, p. 6.

h. Anon. "Dark and Bloody Ground." *Time*, 24 Aug. 1953, p. 82.

i. Edwards, John. "This World." San Francisco *Chronicle*, 6 Sept. 1953, p. 18.

j. Schwartz, Delmore. "The Dragon of Guilt." *NRep*, 14 Sept. 1953, pp. 17–18.

k. Anon. *Booklist*, 15 Sept. 1953, p. 31.

l. Anon. *Bookmark* (New York State Library), 13 (Oct. 1953), 9.

m. Lowell, Robert. "Prose Genius in Verse." *KR*, 15 (Autumn 1953), 619–625.

n. Bogan, Louise. "Verse." *NY*, 24 Oct. 1953, pp. 157–159.

o. Anon. "Parable of Sin." *Nation*, 7 Nov. 1953, p. 376.

p. McDonald, G. D. *Library Journal*, 78 (Dec. 1953), 2221.

q. Swallow, Alan. *Talisman*, no. 4 (Winter 1953), pp. 38–42.

r. Tyler, Parker. "Ambiguous Axe." *Poetry*, 83 (Dec. 1953), 167–171.

s. Joost, Nicholas. "The Movement Toward Fulfillment." *Commonweal*, 4 Dec. 1953, pp. 231–232.

t. Deutsch, Babette. "Poetry Chronicle." *YR*, 43 (Winter 1954), 277–281.

u. Flint, F. Cudworth. "Search for a Meaning." *VQR*, 30 (Winter 1954), 143–148.

v. Kenner, Hugh. "Something Nasty in the Meat-House." *HudR*, 6 (Winter 1954), 605–610.

w. McCormick, John. "White Does and Dragons." *Western Review*, 18 (Winter 1954), 163–167.

x. O'Connor, William Van. "The Burden of Innocence." *SR*, 62 (Winter 1954), 143–150.

y. Fiedler, Leslie A. "Seneca in the Meat House."
    1. *PR*, 21 (March–April 1954), 208–212.
    2. *No! In Thunder*. Boston: Beacon Press, 1960. Pp. 127–131.

z. Honig, Edwin. "A Tale in Verse and Voices." *Voices*, no. 154 (May–Aug. 1954), pp. 41–44.

a². Anon. "American Tragedy." *TLS*, 11 June 1954, p. 378.

b². Kristol, Irving. "American Ghosts." *Encounter*, 3 (July 1954), 73–75.

Brother to Dragons: A New Version (1979)

c². Anon. *Kirkus Review*, 15 July 1979, p. 850.

d². Anon. *Booklist*, 1 Sept. 1979, p. 20.

e². Bloom, Harold. *NRep*, 1 and 8 Sept. 1979, p. 30.

f². Vest, Quentin. *Library Journal*, 1 Sept. 1979, p. 1703.

g². Henigan, Robert. "Warren Rewrites, 'Tightens' Verse." Springfield [MO] *Leader & Press*, 8 Sept. 1979, p. 6-A.

h². Holladay, Robert. "Warren at His Best with Novel in Verse." Nashville *Banner*, 15 Sept. 1979, p. 5.

i². Dickerson, James. "Poem Revisited." *Clarion-Ledger* [Jackson, MS], 16 Sept. 1979, p. 4.

j². White, Victor. "New Version of a Warren Classic." Dallas *Morning News*, 16 Sept. 1979.

k². Marten, Harry. "Warren and Kuntz: Poets in the American Grain." Washington *Post*, 30 Sept. 1979, p. 10.

l². Hall, Wade. "A Poet's Epic Visit to Man's Darkness." Louisville *Courier-Journal*, 28 Oct. 1979, p. D-5.

N20 *Anthology of Stories from* The Southern Review (1953)

Note: I have been unable to locate any reviews of this title.

N21 *Short Story Masterpieces* (1954)

a. Breit, Harvey. "Repeat Performances." *NYTBR*, 16 May 1954, p. 18.

N22 *Band of Angels* (1955)

a. Anon. *Bulletin from Virginia Kirkus' Bookshop Service*, 1 June 1955, p. 367.

b. Anon. "'Le Grand Souffle'—'Le complexe de Broadway': Le Nouveau Roman américain . . . et l'autre." *Le Journal des Lettres*, 27 June 1955, p. 2C.

c. Lalou, René. "Le Livre de la semaine." *Les Nouvelles Littéraires*, 30 June 1955, p. 3.

d. Bradshaw, L. M. *Library Journal*, 80 (Aug. 1955), 1699.

e. Benet, James. San Francisco *Chronicle*, 3 Aug. 1955, p. 17.

f. Faure, Maurice. "RPW romancier de la justice." *Observateur*, 18 Aug. 1955, pp. 17–19.

g. Cheney, Brainard. "A Strange and Fearful Tale." Nashville *Ban-*

ner, 19 Aug. 1955, p. 23.

h. Baker, Carlos. "Souls Lost in a Blind Lobby." *SatR*, 20 Aug. 1955, pp. 9–10.

i. Engle, Paul. Chicago *Sunday Tribune of Books*, 21 Aug. 1955, p. 1.

j. Groblewski, H. J. "Warren Novel Reflects Search for Self." Houston *Post*, 21 Aug. 1955, NOW sec., p. 34.

k. McManis, John. "Warren Misses in New Novel." Detroit *News*, 21 Aug. 1955, p. E-15.

l. Mizener, Arthur. "A Nature Divided Against Itself." *NYTBR*, 21 Aug. 1955, pp. 1 and 18.

m. Rosenberger, Coleman. "Romantic, Dramatic, Symbolic: A Major New Novel." *NYHTBR*, 21 Aug. 1955, p. 6.

n. Anon. *Time*, 22 Aug. 1955, p. 86.

o. Anon. "Year's Best—to Date." *Newsweek*, 22 Aug. 1955, p. 92.

p. Prescott, Orville. "Books of the Times." *NYT*, 22 Aug. 1955, p. 19.

q. O'Leary, Theodore M. "One of Year's Big Novels." Kansas City *Star*, 27 Aug. 1955, p. 10.

r. Melton, Amos. "Warren Handles Hackneyed Plot with His Usual Skill." Fort Worth *Star-Telegram*, 28 Aug. 1955, p. II-7.

s. Adams, Phoebe. *AtMo*, Sept. 1955, pp. 84–85.

t. Anon. *Booklist*, 1 Sept. 1955, p. 15.

u. Pickrel, Paul. "Which Way to Freedom?" *Harper's*, Sept. 1955, pp. 93–94.

v. Pippett, Roger. *Book-of-the-Month Club News*, Sept. 1955, p. 9.

w. R., C. F. Springfield [MA] *Union and Republican*, 4 Sept. 1955, p. 7c.

x. Derleth, August. "Minority Report." *Capitol Times* [Madison, WI], 22 Sept. 1955, pp. 25 and 29.

y. Paulding, Gouverneur. "New Orleans and New York: I. When Freedom Comes." *Reporter*, 22 Sept. 1955, pp. 46–47.

z. Craib, Roderick. "A Novel on Freedom." *New Leader*, 26 Sept. 1955, pp. 24–25.

a². Fiedler, Leslie A. "Romance in the Operatic Manner."

    1. *NRep*, 26 Sept. 1955, pp. 28–30.

    2. As "Fiction as Opera." *No! In Thunder*. Boston: Beacon Press, 1960. Pp. 131–133.

b². Brown, Ashley. *Shenandoah*, 7 (Autumn 1955), 87–91.

c². Coxe, L. O. "Recent Fiction." *YR*, 45 (Autumn 1955), 154–160.

d². Evans, M. Stanton. "Warren Agonistes." *Freeman*, 5 (Oct. 1955), 707.

e². Geismar, Maxwell. "Agile Pen and Dry Mind." *Nation*, 1 Oct. 1955, p. 287.

f². West, Anthony. *NY*, 15 Oct. 1955, pp. 170–173.

g². Clement, Sarah V. "RPW Blends Slavery, War, Love, and Hate in Thought-Provoking Novel." Jackson *Sun*, 30 Oct. 1955, p. 3.

h². Anon. *Bookmark* (New York State Library), 15 (Nov. 1955), 37.

i². Anon. *Voice of St. Jude*, Nov. 1955.

j². Hughes, Riley. *CathW*, 182 (Nov. 1955), 147.

k². Sullivan, J. F. "Gothic: Southern Style." *Commonweal*, 11 Nov. 1955, pp. 147–148.

l². Lombardo, Agostino. *Lo spettatore italiano*, 8 (Dec. 1955), 528–530.

m². McDowell, Frederick P. W. "And the Greatest of These Is Charity." *Western Review*, 20 (Winter 1956), 167–171.

n². Scott, Nathan A., Jr. "Warren: The Man to Watch." *Christian Century*, 29 Feb. 1956, pp. 272–273.

o². Lohner, Edgar. "Menschliche Irrfahrt." *Kritische Blätter*, 6 (March 1956), 9–11.

p². Vidal, Gore. "Book Report." *Zero*, 2 (Spring 1956), 95–98.

q². Anon. "New Fiction." London *Times*, 31 May 1956, p. 13.

r². Scott-James, Marie. "New Novels." London *Sunday Times*, 3 June 1956, p. 5.

s². Wain, John. "Timeless and Temporal." [London] *Observer*, 3 June 1956, p. 11.

t². Kane, Harnett T. *Civil War History*, Dec. 1956, p. 122.

u². Knab-Grzimek, Fränze. *Bücherei und Bildung*, 9 (1957), 547–548.

v². Röder, Rudolf. *Welt und Wort*, 12 (Aug. 1957), 248.

w². Musulin, Janko. "Onkel Toms Boudoir." *Wort und Wahrheit: Monatschrift für Religion und Kultur*, 13 (1958), 216–217.

x². Edmonds, Irene. "RPW and the 'Tragic Mulatto.'" *NYR*, 1 (Spring 1958), 19–22.

y². Anon. *Books & Bookmen*, 18 (Sept. 1973), 135.

N23 *Six Centuries of Great Poetry* (1955)

   Note: I have been unable to locate any reviews of this title.

N24 *Segregation* (1956)

   a. Anon. *Virginia Kirkus' Service Bulletin*, 1 July 1956, pp. 462–463.

   b. Brunn, Robert R. *Christian Science Monitor*, 30 Aug. 1956, p. 7.

   c. Hogan, William. "This World." San Francisco *Chronicle*, 31 Aug. 1956, p. 17.

   d. Adams, Phoebe. *AtMo*, Sept. 1956, pp. 83–84.

   e. Anon. *Wisconsin Library Bulletin*, 52 (Sept.–Oct. 1956), 209.

f. Ethridge, M., Jr. "Turmoil in the South." *SatR*, 1 Sept. 1956, p. 14.

g. Heimanson, R. H. *Library Journal*, 81 (Sept. 1956), 1998.

h. Pickrel, Paul. "We Are on a Journey . . . ." *Harper's*, Sept. 1956, pp. 83–84.

i. Furnas, J. C. "RPW Reports on Segregation in His Native South." *NYHTBR*, 2 Sept. 1956, p. 1.

j. McGill, Ralph. "A Southerner Talks with the South." *NYTBR*, 2 Sept. 1956, pp. 1 and 13.

Note: responses by David Antman, Max L. Jacobson, and Edward J. Sorock, *NYTBR*, 7 Oct. 1956, p. 44.

k. Norris, Hoke. "Author Probes Race Dilemma." Chicago *Sun-Times*, 2 Sept. 1956, p. II-4.

l. Ottley, Roi. "Reports on His Native South." Chicago *Sunday Tribune*, 9 Sept. 1956, p. 4–3.

m. Prothro, James W. "A Southerner's View of a Southerner's Book." *Reporter*, 20 Sept. 1956, pp. 46–47.

n. Reddick, L. D. "Whose Ordeal?" *NRep*, 24 Sept. 1956, pp. 9–10.

o. Anon. *Booklist*, 1 Oct. 1956, p. 62.

p. Anon. *Bookmark* (New York State Library), 16 (Oct. 1956), 8.

q. Anon. *NY*, 13 Oct. 1956, p. 200.

r. Clarke, M. M. *CathW*, 184 (Nov. 1956), 154–155.

s. Pfaff, William. "Segregation." *Commonweal*, 7 Dec. 1956, pp. 268–271.

t. Potter, D. M. "A Minority Within a Minority." *YR*, 46 (Winter 1957), 260–267.

u. Anon. "Uncle Tom's Legacy." *TLS*, 29 March 1957, p. 195.

v. Goodman, Paul. "A Southern Conceit."

1. *Dissent*, 4 (Spring 1957), 204–208.

2. *Voices of Dissent: A Collection of Articles from* Dissent Magazine. New York: Grove Press, 1958. Pp. 181–185.

w. Singer, Marie B. "The Black Mind." *Twentieth Century*, 161 (April 1957), 395–399.

x. MacKenzie, Norman. *New Statesman*, 3 Aug. 1957, p. 154.

y. Nichols, Charles H. "Negroes and Whites." *Commentary*, 24 (Oct. 1957), 370–373.

N25 *A New Southern Harvest* (1957)

a. Burnette, Frances. *Library Journal*, 1 Dec. 1956, p. 2847.

b. S., M. C. "Writing, South." New Orleans *Times-Picayune*, 13 Jan. 1957, p. 3–12.

N26 *Promises: Poems, 1954–1956* (1957)

a. Anon. *Virginia Kirkus' Service Bulletin*, 1 July 1957, p. 461.

b. Fitts, Dudley. "A Power Reaffirmed." *NYTBR*, 18 Aug. 1957, pp. 6 and 20.

c. Deutsch, Babette. "New Warren Poems, Tradition-Haunted, Forward-Gazing." *NYHTBR*, 25 Aug. 1957, p. 4.

d. Engle, Paul. "An Ornament of Our Literature." Chicago *Sun Tribune*, 8 Sept. 1957, p. 4–2.

e. Anon. *Booklist*, 1 Oct. 1957, p. 71.

f. Casper, Leonard. "The Founding Fathers." *Western Review*, 22 (Autumn 1957), 69–71.

g. McDonald, G. D. *Library Journal*, 82 (Oct. 1957), 2460.

h. Smith, W. J. "Words from a Ruined Fortress." *NRep*, 14 Oct. 1957, pp. 18–19.

i. Rodman, Selden. "The New Warren." *SatR*, 9 Nov. 1957, pp. 15 and 42.

j. Hecht, Anthony. "Poets and Peasants." *HudR*, 10 (Winter 1957–58), 606–613.

k. Flint, F. Cudworth. "Poetic Accomplishment and Expectation." *VQR*, 34 (Winter 1958), 118–119.

l. Whittemore, Reed. "Five Old Masters and Their Sensibilities." *YR*, 47 (Winter 1958), 281–288.

m. Rosenthal, M. L. "Out There in the Dark." *Nation*, 18 Jan. 1958, pp. 56–57.

n. Frumkin, Gene. "Going Somewhere." *Mainstream*, March 1958, pp. 52–53.

o. Dickey, James. "In the Presence of Anthologies." *SR*, 66 (Spring 1958), 294–314.

p. Fielde, Rolf. "The Ruined Stone and the Sea-Reaches." *Poetry*, 92 (April 1958), 49–52.

q. Garrett, George Palmer. *GaR*, 12 (Spring 1958), 106–108.

r. Wasserstrom, William. "Warren's New Poems." *PrS*, 32 (Spring 1958), 67–69.

s. M., J. *Voices*, no. 166 (May–Aug. 1958), pp. 48–51.

t. Wright, James. "The Stiff Smile of Mr. Warren." *KR*, 20 (Autumn 1958), 645–648, 650–652, 654–655.

u. Abbott, M. "Lyric Poems Rich in Mood, Insight." *Michigan Daily* [Ann Arbor], 23 Nov. 1958, p. 14.

v. Blum, Morgan. "Promises as Fulfillment." *KR*, 21 (Winter 1959), 97–120.

w. Skelton, Robin. *New Statesman*, 23 May 1959, p. 732.

x. Fuller, Roy. "Book Reviews." *London Magazine*, 6 (Aug. 1959), 68–69, 71, 73.

N27 *Selected Essays* (1958)

a. Nichols, Luther. "Literary Heart Explored." San Francisco *Examiner*, 27 June 1958, p. 2–3.

b. Anon. "The Good and the Evil." *Newsweek*, 30 June 1958, p. 86.

c. Whittington, Curtis, Jr. "Major Commentary on Writers' Significance." Nashville *Banner*, 4 July 1958, p. 18.

d. Engle, Paul. "Insight into Modern Literature." Chicago *Sunday Tribune*, 13 July 1958, p. 4–6.

e. Redman, Ben Ray. "Scholar-Gentleman." *SatR*, 19 July 1958, p. 28.

f. Nolan, James W. "One Southern Writer Looks at Some Others." New Orleans *Times-Picayune*, 20 July 1958, p. 3–6.

g. Evans, Joseph E. "In Quest of Meaning." *Wall Street Journal*, 28 Aug. 1958, p. 8.

h. Anon. "Books in Brief." *NYHTBR*, 31 Aug. 1958, p. 10.

i. Wermuth, P. C. *Library Journal*, 83 (Sept. 1958), 2318.

j. Hynes, Sam. "Outstanding Critic." *Commonweal*, 3 Oct. 1958, pp. 27–29.

k. Anon. *Booklist*, 1 Nov. 1958, p. 121.

l. Weales, Gerald. "Warren as Critic." *New Leader*, 8 Dec. 1958, pp. 17–18.

m. Anon. "Reader's Guide." *YR*, 48 (Winter 1959), vi–vii.

n. Casper, Leonard. "The Fallacy of Heresy." *Western Review*, 23 (Spring 1959), 283–287.

o. Kazin, Alfred. "The Seriousness of RPW." *PR*, 26 (Spring 1959), 312, 314–316.

p. Pulos, C. E. "Warren as Critic." *PrS*, 33 (Spring 1959), 1–2.

q. Anderson, Charles. *MLN*, 76 (Jan. 1961), 72–75.

r. Anon. "Well Judged." London *Times*, 13 Feb. 1964, p. 15.

s. Cohen, Peter. "Book Reviews." *The Listener*, 27 Feb. 1964, p. 364.

t. Davie, Donald. "Multi-Storey Structure." *New Statesman*, 13 March 1964, p. 406.

u. Anon. "Old New Criticism." *TLS*, 9 April 1964, p. 292.

v. Tanner, Tony. "The Great Symbol Hunt." *Spectator*, 10 April 1964, p. 492.

w. Igoe, W.J. *The Tablet*, 13 June 1964, p. 666.

N28 *Remember the Alamo!* (1958)

a. Anon. *Bulletin from Virginia Kirkus' Bookshop Service*, 15 July 1958, p. 511.

b. B., M. W. *Horn Book Magazine*, 34 (Oct. 1958), 392.

c. Graff, H. F. *NYTBR*, 2 Nov. 1958, p. 2–3.

d. Forsythe, Roberta. Chicago *Sunday Tribune*, 8 Nov. 1958, p. 2–36.

e. Maxwell, Emily. "Books: Christmas for Ages One and Upward." *NY*, 22 Nov. 1958, p. 214.

f. Taylor, Millicent. *Christian Science Monitor*, 26 Nov. 1958, p. 19.

g. Anon. *Booklist*, 1 Jan. 1959, p. 245.

N29 *How Texas Won Her Freedom* (1959)
Note: I have been unable to locate any reviews of this title.

N30 *The Cave* (1959)

a. Anon. *Bulletin from Virginia Kirkus' Bookshop Service*, 15 June 1959, p. 409.

b. Joysmith, Toby. "'Shadows which the Fire Throws on the Opposite Walls of the Cave . . . .'" Mexico City *News*, 16 Aug. 1959, sec. 1.

c. Cheney, Brainard. "Lusty Melodrama of Tennessee Hills." Nashville *Banner*, 21 Aug. 1959, p. 21.

d. Hicks, Granville. "Melodrama with Meaning." *SatR*, 22 Aug. 1959, p. 13.

e. Schott, Webster. "Fine Novel and Likely Popular." Kansas City *Star*, 22 Aug. 1959, p. 18.

f. Engle, Paul. Chicago *Sunday Tribune of Books*, 23 Aug. 1959, p. 1.

g. Mizener, Arthur. "In the Darkness They Found Light." *NYTBR*, 23 Aug. 1959, p. 1.

h. Norris, Hoke. "RPW's Descent into a Cave." Chicago *Sun-Times*, 23 Aug. 1959, p. III-4.

i. Rosenberger, Coleman. "Many Sided Tale of a Man Trapped, a Town Revealed." *NYHTBR*, 23 Aug. 1959, p. 1.

j. Sherman, John K. "Melodrama by Warren Poses Moral Dilemma." Minneapolis *Sunday Tribune*, 23 Aug. 1959, p. 6.

k. Sullivan, Walter. "Tennessee Is Setting for New Warren Novel." Nashville *Tennessean*, 23 Aug. 1959, p. 8-C.

l. Tunstall, Caroline. "Man's Rescue Bares Town Secrets." *Virginian-Pilot and Portsmouth Star*, 23 Aug. 1959, p. 6-F.

m. Anon. "A Distinguished Novel." *Newsweek*, 24 Aug. 1959, p. 84.

n. Anon. "Shadow and Substance." *Time*, 24 Aug. 1959, pp. 78–79.

o. Dorn, Norman K. "This World." San Francisco *Chronicle*, 24 Aug. 1959, p. 33.

p. Hanscom, Leslie. "Out of the Cave a Glimpse of Reality." New York *World-Telegram and Sun*, 24 Aug. 1959.

q. Hogan, William. "Floyd Collins' Story Retold in 'The Cave.'" San Francisco *Chronicle*, 24 Aug. 1959, p. 33.

r. Hutchens, John K. "The Cave." *NYHT*, 24 Aug. 1959, p. 15.

s. Prescott, Orville. "Books of the Times." *NYT*, 24 Aug. 1959, p. 19.

t. Smith, Harrison. "Tragedy in a Cave." *Sunday Herald-Leader*, 30 Aug. 1959, p. 57.

u. Simmons, George E. "Gloom, Symbolic, Real, Dominates." New Orleans *Times-Picayune*, 30 Aug. 1959, p. 2–10.

v. Wermuth, P. C. *Library Journal*, 84 (Sept. 1959), 2523–2524.

w. Hynes, Sam. "A Tale of Men Trapped in Their Own Darkness." *Commonweal*, 4 Sept. 1959, pp. 476–477.

x. Gardiner, Harold C. "Morality Tale in Hillbilly Terminology." *America*, 5 Sept. 1959, p. 676.

y. Martin, Terence. "Buried Alive." *NRep*, 7 Sept. 1959, pp. 20–21.

z. Drake, Robert Y., Jr. "The Myth of the Cave." *National Review*, 12 Sept. 1959, pp. 334–335.

a². Hatch, Robert. "Down to the Self." *Nation*, 12 Sept. 1959, pp. 138–139.

b². Anon. *Booklist*, 15 Sept. 1959, p. 52.

c². Maddocks, Melvin. *Christian Science Monitor*, 24 Sept. 1959, p. 9.

d². Price, Martin. "Six Recent Novels." *YR*, 49 (Autumn 1959), 124–132.

e². Rolo, Charles. *AtMo*, Oct. 1959, pp. 115–116.

f². Sandeen, Ernest. *Critic*, 18 (Oct.–Nov. 1959), 13 and 63.

g². Schickel, Richard. "Two Realities." *Progressive*, Oct. 1959, pp. 48–50.

h². Slatoff, Walter. "Notes, Reviews, and Speculations." *Epoch*, 10 (Fall 1959), 62–63.

i². Malcolm, Donald. "Books: Cavities." *NY*, 31 Oct. 1959, pp. 198, 201–202.

j². Hughes, Riley. *CathW*, 190 (Nov. 1959), 127.

k². McGrath, Thomas. "Carnival at a Death." *Mainstream*, Nov. 1959, pp. 60–63.

l². Anon. *Christian Century*, 11 Nov. 1959, p. 1315.

m². Anon. "Fables for Our Time." *TLS*, 27 Nov. 1959, p. 692.

n². Abel, Lionel. "Refinement and Vulgarity." *Commentary*, 28 (Dec. 1959), 541–544.

o². "Aswin." "The Literary Scene Abroad." *Indian P.E.N.*, 25 (Dec. 1959), 380–381.

p². DeMott, Benjamin. *HudR*, 12 (Winter 1959–60), 618–626.

q². Lister, Richard. "Man in a Cave Puts a Town on the Spot." [London] *Evening Standard*, 1 Dec. 1959, p. 15.

r². Coleman, John. "Property Values." *Spectator*, 4 Dec. 1959, p. 836.

s². Shrapnel, Norman. [Manchester] *Guardian*, 4 Dec. 1959, p. 13.

t². Waterhouse, Keith. *New Statesman*, 5 Dec. 1959, pp. 816–817.

u². Price, R. G. G. "New Novels." *Punch*, 9 Dec. 1959, p. 577.

v². Anon. "Once Over Lightly." *KR*, 22 (Winter 1960), 166–167.

w². Arimond, Carroll. *Extension*, 54 (Jan. 1960), 6.

x². Nemerov, Howard. "Four Novels." *PR*, 27 (Winter 1960), 174–176, 178–181, 183–185.

y². Pugh, Griffith T. "Recent Books." *EJ*, 49 (Feb. 1960), 140.

z². Gransden, K. W. "New Novels." *Encounter*, 14 (May 1960), 78–79.

a³. Allen, Charles A. *ArQ*, 16 (Summer 1960), 182–184.

b³. Davies, A. M. "Three New Novels and Some Short Stories." Cambridge [England] *Review*, 29 Oct. 1960, p. 97.

c³. Tick, Stanley. "America Writes." *Meanjin Quarterly*, 20, no. 1 (1961), 112–115.

d³. Kiley, Frederick S. *Clearing House*, 35 (March 1961), 444.

e³. Thompson, Frank H., Jr. "Not So Very, Very Good." *PrS*, 35 (Summer 1961), 173–175.

f³. Holmes, Theodore. "The Literary Mode." *Carleton Miscellany*, 4 (Winter 1963), 124–128.

N31 *The Gods of Mount Olympus* (1959)

   a. Anon. "Legacy Books: A New Series." *NYHTBR*, 1 Nov. 1959, p. 12.

   b. Fitts, Dudley. "Everyman's Heritage." *NYTBR*, 1 Nov. 1959, p. II-6.

   c. Mathes, Miriam S. *Library Journal*, 15 Nov. 1959, p. 3637.

   d. Anon. *SatR*, 19 Dec. 1959, p. 43.

N32 *The Scope of Fiction* (1960)

   Note: I have been unable to locate any reviews of this title.

N33 *All the King's Men: A Play* (1960)

   a. Gibbs, Wolcott. "The Theater." *NY*, 24 Jan. 1948, p. 43.

b. Crisler, B. R. "Again the Troublous Saga of Willie Stark." *Christian Science Monitor*, 22 July 1950, p. 7.

c. Atkinson, Brooks. "Theatre: Stage Politics." *NYT*, 17 Oct. 1959, p. 27; 25 Oct. 1959, p. 1.

d. Lipsett, Richard. *Theatre*, 2 (May 1960), 46.

e. Anon. *Booklist*, 1 June 1960, pp. 596–597.

f. Freedley, George. *Library Journal*, 85 (July 1960), 2615.

N34 *You, Emperors, and Others: Poems, 1957–1960* (1960)

a. Anon. *Virginia Kirkus' Service Bulletin*, 15 June 1960, p. 485.

b. Anon. *Booklist*, 1 Sept. 1960, p. 17.

c. Engle, Paul. "Poetry from a Charged, Nimble Mind." Chicago *Sunday Tribune Magazine of Books*, 4 Sept. 1960, p. 7.

d. Robie, Burton A. *Library Journal*, 85 (Oct. 1960), 3664.

e. Holmes, John. "The Lonely Fact of Humanness We Share." *NYHTBR*, 16 Oct. 1960, p. 12.

f. Fitts, Dudley. "Exercise in Metrical High Jinks." *NYTBR*, 23 Oct. 1960, p. 32.

g. Thompson, John. "A Catalogue of Poets." *HudR*, 13 (Winter 1960–61), 618–625.

h. Hartman, Geoffrey H. "Philosopher, Satyr, and Two Ghosts." *KR*, 23 (Spring 1961), 345–361.

i. Hayo, Samuel. *Poetry Dial*, 1 (Spring 1961), 45–46.

j. Martz, Louis L. "The Virtues of Collection." *YR*, 50 (Spring 1961), 441–447.

k. Morse, Samuel French. "Seven Poets, Present Time." *VQR*, 37 (Spring 1961), 291–296.

l. Hardy, John Edward. "You, RPW." *Poetry*, 99 (Oct. 1961), 56–62.

m. Zinnes, Harriet. "A New World Needed." *PrS*, 36 (Spring 1962), 85–87.

N35 *The Legacy of the Civil War* (1961)

a. Anon. *A Monthly Review of American Books* [Japan], 1961, p. 14.

b. Hogan, William. "This World." San Francisco *Chronicle*, 14 April 1961, p. 31.

c. McNaspy, C. J. "Historians Reassess Our 'Tragic Years.'" *America*, 15 April 1961, pp. 155–156.

d. Chamberlain, John. "Virtue and the Alibi." *Wall Street Journal*, 19 April 1961, p. 16.

e. Harwell, Richard. "1861–65: Perspective and Participation." Chicago *Sunday Tribune of Books*, 23 April 1961, p. 6.

f. Poore, Charles. *NYT*, 27 April 1961, p. 19.

g. Anon. "Briefly Noted." *NY*, 29 April 1961, p. 150.

h. Beatty, Richmond Croom. "RPW Discusses Our Rich Southern Heritage." Nashville *Tennessean*, 30 April 1961, p. 7-E.

i. Stedman, Alex. "Study Stresses War's Impact." Fort Worth *Star-Telegram*, 30 April 1961, p. III-20.

j. Brunn, Robert R. *Christian Science Monitor*, 1 May 1961, p. 13.

k. H., V. P. "Civil War's Meaning in a Brilliant Book." Omaha *World-Herald*, 7 May 1961, Magazine of the Midlands sec., p. 25.

l. Donald, David. "When the Smoke of Battle Cleared, an Ideal Had Been Born." *NYTBR*, 14 May 1961, p. 1–3.

m. Anon. *Booklist*, 15 May 1961, p. 567.

n. Heaps, Willard A. *Library Journal*, 15 May 1961, pp. 1884–1885.

o. Jones, Peter d'A. "The Struggle for the Union Continues." *NRep*, 15 May 1961, pp. 16–17.

p. Kazin, Alfred. "City of the Soul."

    1. *Reporter*, 9 June 1961, pp. 40, 42–44.

    2. As "The Southern 'City of the Soul.'" *Contemporaries*. Boston: Little Brown, 1962. Pp. 178–183.

q. Weaver, Richard M. "An Altered Stand." *National Review*, 17 June 1961, pp. 389–390.

r. Rubin, Louis D., Jr. "'Theories of Human Nature': Kazin or Warren?" *SR*, 69 (Summer 1961), 500–506.

s. Tobin, Richard L. "U.S. History's Great Single Event." *SatR*, 8 July 1961, pp. 23–24.

t. Anon. *THQ*, 20 (Sept. 1961), 285–286.

u. Wight, Willard E. *Civil War History*, 8 (Sept. 1961), 337.

v. Anon. "The Best of the Best." *Vogue*, 7 Sept. 1961, pp. 244 and 279.

w. Williams, T. Harry. "Warren's Book on Civil War Among the More Meaningful." Baton Rouge *Sunday Advocate*, 17 Sept. 1961, p. 2-E.

x. Hutchens, John K. "'Warren.'" *NYHT*, 17 Nov. 1961, p. 23.

y. Burger, Nash K. "Paperbacks in Review: The House Divided." *NYTBR*, 31 Jan. 1965, p. 42–43.

z. Chrismer, Wayde. "The Civil War Centennial—An Appraisal of Its Literature." *American Book Collector* 16 (May 1966), 9–11.

N36 *Wilderness* (1961)

    a. Gardiner, Harold C. "The Search of a Lamed Adam." *America*, 11 Nov. 1961, p. 206.

    b. Maslin, Marsh. "RPW Writes Modern Morality Play." San Francisco *Calendar Bulletin*, 11 Nov. 1961.

c. Hyman, Stanley E. "Coming Out of the Wilderness." *New Leader*, 13 Nov. 1961, pp. 24–25.

d. Anon. *Bulletin from Virginia Kirkus' Bookshop Service*, 15 Nov. 1961, p. 853.

e. Prescott, Orville. "Books of the Times." *NYT*, 15 Nov. 1961, p. 41.

f. Anon. "Author in a Box." *Time*, 17 Nov. 1961, p. 93.

g. Hicks, Granville. "Crusader in a World of Chance." *SatR*, 18 Nov. 1961, p. 19.

h. Anderson, Charles R. "Irony Pervades Warren Novel." Baltimore *Sun*, 19 Nov. 1961, p. A-7.

i. Butcher, Fanny. *Chicago Sunday Tribune of Books*, 19 Nov. 1961, pp. 1–2.

j. Haddican, James. "A 'Holy Crusade' That Disillusioned." New Orleans *Times-Picayune*, 19 Nov. 1961, p. 3–7.

k. Hynes, Samuel. "Quest of the Meaning of Freedom." *NYTBR*, 19 Nov. 1961, p. 58.

l. Tyler, Betty. "Strange Trio in Civil War Adventure." Bridgeport [CT] *Sunday Post*, 19 Nov. 1961, p. C-5.

m. Anon. "The Agony of Adam." *Newsweek*, 20 Nov. 1961, p. 109.

n. Adams, Phoebe. *AtMo*, Dec. 1961, p. 126.

o. Anon. *Booklist*, 1 Dec. 1961, pp. 226–227.

p. Nyren, Dorothy. *Library Journal*, 86 (Dec. 1961), 4309.

q. Bowen, Robert O. "The View from Beneath." *National Review*, 2 Dec. 1961, pp. 383–384.

r. Rosenberger, Coleman. "A Bavarian Jew in America's Civil War." *NYHTBR*, 3 Dec. 1961, p. 4.

s. Hertz, Robert N. "Spiritual Journey, Philosophical Detours." *NRep*, 18 Dec. 1961, p. 23.

t. Lacy, Bernard. *Christian Century*, 20 Dec. 1961, p. 1531.

u. Anon. "Notes on Current Books." *VQR*, 38 (Winter 1962), viii.

v. Hartt, J. J. "The Return of Moral Passion." *YR*, 51 (Winter 1962), 300–308.

w. Jackson, Katherine G. "Books in Brief." *Harper's*, Jan. 1962, p. 96.

x. Kleine, Don W. "RPW." *Epoch*, 11 (Winter 1962), 263–268.

y. Magmer, James. *CathW*, 194 (Jan. 1962), 244–245.

z. Wilson, James R. *Books Abroad*, 36 (Winter 1962), 81–82.

a[2]. McMichael, George. "This World." San Francisco *Chronicle*, 7 Jan. 1962, pp. 17–18.

b[2]. Gerard, David. *Civil War Times*, 3 (Feb. 1962), 20.

c². Sale, Roger. "Novels and Being a Novelist." *HudR*, 15 (Spring 1962), 134–142.

d². Anon. *Bookmark* (New York State Library), 21 (May 1962), 224.

e². Pugh, Griffith T. "From the Recent Books." *EJ*, 51 (May 1962), 374.

f². Adams, Jennifer. *Time and Tide—John O'London's*, 31 May 1962, p. 32.

g². Anon. "Loss of Illusion." *TLS*, 1 June 1962, p. 385.

h². Richardson, Maurice. "Dragooned." *New Statesman*, 1 June 1962, pp. 804–805.

i². Shrapnel, Norman. [Manchester] *Guardian*, 1 June 1962, p. 7.

j². Anon. "New Fiction." London *Times*, 7 June 1962, p. 10.

k². Price, R. G. G. "New Novels." *Punch*, 20 June 1962, pp. 953–954.

l². Daniel, John. "Cold Facts." *Spectator*, 22 June 1962, p. 834.

m². Bellasis, M. *The Tablet*, 18 Aug. 1962, p. 768.

n². Samuels, Charles Thomas. "In the Wilderness." *Critique*, 5 (Fall 1962), 46–57.

N37 *Selected Poems by Denis Devlin* (1963)

a. Smith, Ray. *Library Journal*, 15 Jan. 1963, p. 225.

b. Stepánchey, Stephen. *NYHTBR*, 11 Aug. 1963, p. 7.

c. Carruth, Hayden. *Poetry*, 103 (Dec. 1963), 191–192.

N38 *Flood* (1964)

a. Anon. *Publisher's Weekly*, 27 Jan. 1964, p. 212.

b. Anon. *Bulletin from Virginia Kirkus' Bookshop Service*, 15 March 1964, p. 321.

c. Thomas, Lucy. "RPW's Story of Dying Town Is Moving." *Southwest-Times Record* [Fort Smith, AK], 5 April 1964, p. 13-B.

d. Brady, Charles A. "New Face of South Shown in Romance of Changing Times." Buffalo *Evening News*, 18 April 1964, p. B-12.

e. LaFleche, Duane. "Penn Warren's 'F': The South's Loneliness." *Knickerbocker News* [Albany, NY], 18 April 1964, p. B-2.

f. Wharton, Will. "Last Days of Fiddlersburg." St. Louis *Globe Democrat*, 19 April 1964, p. 4-F.

g. Walker, Larry. "Moral Theme." *Sunday Oklahoman*, 19 April 1964, p. D-17.

h. Poore, Charles. *NYT*, 23 April 1964, p. 37.

i. Anon. "From an Aeolian Cave." *Time*, 24 April 1964, p. 106.

j. Dolbier, Maurice. *NYHT*, 24 April 1964, p. 23.

k. Hogan, William. "A Symbolical Story by RPW." San Francisco *Chronicle*, 24 April 1964, p. 37.

l. Hicks, Granville. "Fiddlers Before the Flood." *SatR*, 25 April 1964, pp. 29–30.

m. Moore, Harry T. "Warren Animates New Pompeii." Chicago *Daily News*, 25 April 1964, Panorama sec., p. 9.

n. Alderman, Nancy. "Man's Quest Universal—Unique." Nashville *Tennessean*, 26 April 1964, p. 7-B.

o. Baker, Carlos. "Visibly Receding from his High-Water Marks." Chicago *Sunday Tribune of Books*, 26 April 1964, pp. 6 and 10.

p. Bates, Dan. "Warren Novel Drowned in Flood of Digression." Fort Worth *Star-Telegram*, 26 April 1964, p. III-20.

q. Bergamo, Ralph. "Warren's 'F' Traces Erosion." Atlanta *Journal*, 26 April 1964, p. 6-D.

r. Crews, Frederick C. "A Search for Identity in Fiddlersburg." *NYTBR*, 26 April 1964, p. 6.

s. Ellison, Virginia P. "Artist-Come-Home New Warren Theme." New Orleans *Times-Picayune*, 26 April 1964.

t. Gilliam, Stanley. "Warren's New Novel of South Is Satisfying Study of Loneliness." Sacramento *Bee*, 26 April 1964, p. L-16.

u. Holmesly, Sterlin. "Another Good Novel by Warren." San Antonio *Express/News*, 26 April 1964.

v. Matthew, Christopher. "High Water in Tennessee: RPW Writes of a Doomed Town, Old Passions." Milwaukee *Journal*, 26 April 1964, p. V-4.

w. Moran, John G. "Destruction and Rebirth of Town and Its People." Houston *Chronicle*, 26 April 1964, p. N-40.

x. Popkin, George. "Warren's 'F' and Basso's 'Dragon.'" Providence *Journal*, 26 April 1964.

y. Powers, Dennis. "RPW's 'F.'" Oakland *Tribune*, 26 April 1964, p. 2-EL.

z. Torgersen, Margaret. "It Wrings the Reader Dry." Worchester *Sunday Telegram*, 26 April 1964.

a^2. Culligan, Glendy. "Old Pro'll Keep You Awake But Doesn't Penetrate Heart." Washington *Post*, 1 May 1964, p. A-4.

b^2. Fadiman, Clifton. *Book-of-the-Month Club News*, May 1964, pp. 12–13.

c^2. Gaines, E. J. *Library Journal*, 89 (May 1964), 2117.

d^2. Garrett, James. "Penn Warren's 'F' Washes Out as Novel." Cleveland *Press*, 1 May 1964, Showtime Magazine sec., p. 15.

e^2. Pfeiffer, Ted. "'F': A Washout of Sick Characters." Louisville *Times*, 1 May 1964, p. 1–9.

f². Moody, Minnie Hite. "Clarity and Passion in a Torrential Novel." Columbus *Dispatch*, 3 May 1964, p. 44.

g². Shaffer, Thomas L. "Warren: A Bit of Blue Sky." South Bend *Tribune*, 3 May 1964, p. 1–16.

h². Sullivan, Richard. Chicago *Sunday Tribune of Books*, 3 May 1964, pp. 6–7.

i². Anon. "Bourbon and Baccy." *Newsweek*, 4 May 1964, p. 93.

j². Anon. "Tale of Fiddlers Before the Flood." Sioux City *Journal*, 10 May 1964.

k². Cross, Leslie. "A Visit with RPW: A Busy Writer Looks Back, Ahead." Milwaukee *Journal*, 10 May 1964, p. 5–4.

l². Anon. *Booklist*, 15 May 1964, p. 868.

m². Wain, John. " After the Deluge, What?" *NRep*, 16 May 1964, pp. 23–25.

n². Reid, Margaret W. "A Search for Identity." Wichita Falls *Times*, 17 May 1964, p. 4.

o². Williams, Ernest E. "Predictability Mars 'F.'" Fort Wayne *News-Sentinel*, 23 May 1964, p. 4-A.

p². Thompson, Lawrence. "New Dam Menaces Mountain Town." Richmond *News Leader*, 27 May 1964, p. 13.

q². Chafee, Norman. "A Romance of Our Time." Tulsa *World*, 31 May 1964, Your World sec., p. 4.

r². Lewis, R. W. B. "*F.*" *NYTBR*, 31 May 1964, p. 18.

s². Barrett, William. *AtMo*, June 1964, p. 134.

t². Oppenheim, Jane. *Best Sellers*, 1 June 1964, p. 104.

u². Fass, Martin. "Melodrama Mars RPW Story." Los Angeles *Times-Calendar*, 7 June 1964, Magazine sec., p. 18.

v². Heath, Gary E. "Sunday News Book Review." Vermont *Sunday News*, 7 June 1964, p. 17.

w². Gardiner, Helen C. "Tales of Torment." *America*, 13 June 1964, p. 826.

x². French, Marion. Bangor *Daily News*, 20 June 1964, p. 16.

y². Hardy, John Edward. "RPW's 'F.'" *VQR*, 40 (Summer 1964), 485–489.

z². DeMott, Benjamin. "'One Hell of a Professor.'" *Reporter*, 2 July 1964, pp. 34, 36–37.

ε³. Hoyt, Charles Alva. "A Noble Failure." Louisville *Courier-Journal*, 12 July 1964, p. 4–5.

b³. Davenport, Guy. "Caution: Falling Prose." *National Review*, 14 July 1964, pp. 609–610.

c³. Halman, Talat. "*F*: A Romance of Our Time." *Village Voice*, 23 July 1964, pp. 5 and 12.

d³. West, Anthony. "Books: Playing the Games." *NY*, 21 Sept. 1964, pp. 204–205.

e³. Mizener, Arthur. "The Uncorrupted Consciousness." *SR*, 72 (Autumn 1964), 690–698.

f³. Hugh-Jones, Stephen. "Floods." *New Statesman*, 30 Oct. 1964, p. 666.

g³. Richler, Mordecai. "The Big Southern Novel Show." *Spectator*, 30 Oct. 1964, p. 581.

h³. Anon. "Après quoi le déluge?" *TLS*, 5 Nov. 1964, p. 993.

i³. Price, R. G. G. "New Novels." *Punch*, 18 Nov. 1964, p. 784.

j³. Berman, Ronald. *Masterplots*. Ed. Frank N. Magill. New York: Salem Press, 1965. Pp. 99–101.

k³. Longley, John Lewis, Jr. "RPW: The Deeper Rub." *SoR*, NS 1 (Autumn 1965), 968–980.

l³. Raleigh, J. "An End to Bravery." *Ramparts*, 3 (Jan.–Feb. 1965), 52–54.

m³. Stewart, J. L. "The Country of the Heart." *YR*, 54 (Winter 1965), 252–258.

N39 *Who Speaks for the Negro?* (1965)

a. Anon. *Bulletin from Virginia Kirkus' Bookshop Service*, 1 March 1965, pp. 280–281.

b. Smith, Frank. "Famed Novelist's Attempt to Define Negro Revolt." Washington *Post*, 19 May 1965, p. A-10.

c. Smith, Ted. "Southern Writers Support Negroes." San Francisco *News Call Bulletin*, 22 May 1965, p. 7.

d. Woodward, C. Vann. "Warren's Challenge to Race Dogma." *NRep*, 22 May 1965, pp. 21–23.

e. Dolbier, Maurice. *NYHT*, 28 May 1965, p. 19.

f. Anon. "Writers Look Southward in the New Spring Books." New Orleans *Times-Picayune*, 30 May 1965, p. 2–18.

g. Tolson, M. B. "Will the Real Moses Please Stand Up?" *NYHTBR*, 30 May 1965, pp. 5 and 8.

h. Poore, Charles. "Who Speaks for the Negro Speaks for Mankind." *NYT*, 1 June 1965, p. 37; 8 June 1965, p. 39.

i. Galphin, Bruce. "The Inward and the Outward Ear." *SatR*, 5 June 1965, p. 22.

j. Anon. "Faces of Change." *Newsweek*, 7 June 1965, pp. 84–86.
    Note: see RPW's reply, 5 July 1965, p. 2.

k. Hogan, William. "Too Many Books on Civil Rights?" San Francisco *Chronicle*, 11 June 1965, p. 43.
l. Kirsch, Robert R. "Negro Americans' Assessment of the Negro Revolution." Los Angeles *Times*, 13 June 1965, p. 13.
m. Lynch, Donna. "View of Negro Leaders Presented in Lengthy Book." Baton Rouge *Morning Advocate*, 13 June 1965, p. 2-E.
n. Nicholson, Joseph. "Wide Field of Negro Movement Studied Calmly." Fort Worth *Star-Telegram*, 13 June 1965, p. VI-6.
o. Casper, Leonard. "A Documented Account of Human Rights Fight." Boston *Traveler*, 15 June 1965.
p. Thompson, Thomas. Amarillo *Globe-Times*, 17 June 1965, p. 2.
q. Anon. "Books: Briefly Noted." *NY*, 19 June 1965, pp. 84–86.
r. Coughlin, Francis. "A Welter of Voices from a Shifting Scene." Chicago *Tribune*, 20 June 1965, Books Today sec., p. 1.
s. Murray, A. *New Leader*, 21 June 1965, pp. 25–27.
t. Hoffman, Nicholas von. "More on Civil Rights Themes." Chicago *Daily News*, 26 June 1965, Panorama sec., p. 9.
u. Bowden, Earle. "Story of South Being Rewritten." Pensacola *News-Journal*, 27 June 1965, pp. 1-B and 4-B.
v. Whitcraft, Carol. "Those Who Lead Them." Austin [TX] *American Statesman*, 27 June 1965, p. 19.
w. Brooks, Bob. "Diversity of Views by Negroes." Washington *Post*, 28 June 1965.
x. M[addocks], M[elvin]. *Christian Science Monitor*, 1 July 1965, p. 9.
y. Weeks, Edward. "Casing the Rebels." *AtMo*, July 1965, p. 137.
z. Highet, Gilbert. *Book-of-the-Month Club News*, July 1965, p. 8.
a². Handlin, Oscar. "A Conflict as Fateful as the Civil War." *NYTBR*, 4 July 1965, p. 3.
b². Woolsey, Bill. "The Negro Speaks Out with Voice of History." Louisville *Times*, 6 July 1965, p. 1-7.
c². Gallagher, J. J. "Books Reviews." *America*, 10 July 1965, pp. 60 and 62.
d². Anon. *Booklist*, 15 July 1965, p. 1044.
e². Footlick, Jerrold K. *National Observer*, 19 July 1965, p. 19.
f². Anon. *Playboy*, Aug. 1965, p. 30.
g². Peeples, William. "RPW on Civil Rights." Louisville *Courier-Journal*, 8 Aug. 1965, p. D-5.
h². Rubin, Louis D., Jr. "A Southern Novelist on Negro Leaders." Baltimore *Evening Sun*, 24 Aug. 1965, p. A-16.
i². Raines, C. A. *Library Journal*, 90 (Sept. 1965), 3469–3470.

j². Anon. *Choice*, 2 (Oct. 1965), 538.

k². Epstein, Joseph. "Down the Line." *Commentary*, 40 (Oct. 1965), 101–105.

l². Gaston, Paul M. "Speaking for the Negro." *VQR*, 41 (Autumn 1965), 612–618.

m². Hays, Forbes. *Carleton College Miscellany* [MN], 6 (Fall 1965), 69–77.

n². Meier, August. "The Question Is Not Answered." *Dissent*, 12 (Autumn 1965), 509–511.

o². Rabinowitz, V. *Science and Society*, 29 (Fall 1965), 458–459.

p². Haselden, Kyle. *Christian Century*, 6 Oct. 1965, pp. 1235–1236.

q². F[uller], H[oyt] W. *Negro Digest*, 15 (Dec. 1965), 93.

r². Kaledin, Arthur. *Commonweal*, 24 Dec. 1965, pp. 377–379.

s². Anon. *Publisher's Weekly*, 10 Jan. 1966, p. 90.

t². Karpathin, Marvin M. "How It Was." *Nation*, 31 Jan. 1966, pp. 134–136.

u². Cheney, Brainard. "Is There a Voice Unheard in Warren's Book Who Is Speaking for the Negro?" *SR*, 74 (Spring 1966), 545–550.

v². Anon. *SatR*, 23 April 1966, p. 51.

N40 *Selected Poems: New and Old, 1923–1966* (1966)

a. Anon. *Bulletin from Virginia Kirkus' Bookshop Service*, 1 Aug. 1966, p. 807.

b. Burke, H. C. *Library Journal*, 91 (Sept. 1966), 3962.

c. Rubin, Louis D., Jr. "Meditative and Lyrical." *NYTBR*, 9 Oct. 1966, p. 4.

d. Stafford, William. "Beyond Life's Awful Illogic." Chicago *Tribune Books Today*, 9 Oct. 1966, p. 10.

e. Gold, Arthur R. "Mr. Warren's Unspecific Gravity." *Book Week*, 23 Oct. 1966, p. 15.

f. Davison, Peter. *AtMo*, Nov. 1966, p. 137.

g. Wain, John. "RPW: The Drama of the Past." *NRep*, 26 Nov. 1966, pp. 16–18.

h. Anon. *Booklist*, 1 Dec. 1966, p. 401.

i. Carruth, H. "In Spite of Artifice." *HudR*, 19 (Winter 1966–67), 689–698.

j. Slater, Joseph. "Immortal Bard and Others." *SatR*, 31 Dec. 1966, pp. 24–25.

k. Anon. *Choice*, 3 (Jan. 1967), 1018.

l. Anon. *VQR*, 43 (Winter 1967), xvii.

m. Martz, Louis L. "Recent Poetry: Roethke, Warren, and Others." *YR*, 56 (Winter 1967), 275–284.

n. Stewart, Vincent. *Masterplots*. Ed. Frank N. Magill. New York: Salem Press, 1967. Pp. 298–302.

o. Gelpi, Albert J. *ChScM*, 19 Jan. 1967, p. 11.

p. Kennedy, William. "Saying the Unsayable: How a Poet Works." *National Observer*, 6 Feb. 1967, p. 31.

q. Spector, R. D. "The New Poetry of Protest." *SatR*, 11 Feb. 1967, pp. 38–40.

r. Anon. *Newsweek*, 20 Feb. 1967, p. 96.

s. Fuller, E. *Wall Street Journal*, 24 May 1967, p. 16.

t. Garrigue, Jean. "A Study of Continuity and Change." *New Leader*, 27 March 1967, pp. 23–25.

u. Vendler, Helen. "Recent American Poetry." *London Magazine*, 8 (Summer 1967), 641–660.

v. Simpson, Louis. "New Books of Poems." *Harper's*, Aug. 1967, p. 89.

w. Coleman, Elliott. "A Line of Light." *Poetry*, 110 (Sept. 1967), 416–419.

x. Bergonzi, Bernard. "Nature, Mostly American." *SoR*, NS 6 (Winter 1970), 205–215.

y. Spears, Monroe K. "The Latest Poetry of RPW." *SR*, 78 (Spring 1970), 348–358.

N41 *Faulkner: A Collection of Critical Essays* (1966)

a. Raines, C. A. *Library Journal*, 92 (Jan. 1967), 243.

b. Anon. *Booklist*, 1 April 1967, 831.

c. Merton, Thomas. "The Sounds Are Furious." *Critic*, 25 (April–May 1967), 76–80.

d. Anon. *AL*, 39 (May 1967), 263.

e. Hicks, Granville. "Faulkner Through Three Decades." *SatR*, 6 May 1967, pp. 27–28.

f. Anon. *Choice*, 4 (July 1967), 535.

g. Waggoner, Hyatt H. "Hemingway and Faulkner: The End of Something." *SoR*, NS 4 (Spring 1968), 458–466.

N42 *Randall Jarrell, 1914–1965* (1967)

a. Whittemore, Reed. *SatR*, 2 Sept. 1967, p. 26.

b. Moynahan, Julian. *NYTBR*, 3 Sept. 1967, p. 4.

c. Anon. *Time*, 15 Sept. 1967, p. 102.

d. Gaines, E. J. *Library Journal*, 1 Oct. 1967, p. 3423.

e. Spender, Stephen. *NYRB*, 23 Nov. 1967, p. 26.

f. Walsh, Chad. *Book World*, 3 March 1968, p. 4.

g. Levenson, J. C. "Lost World, Lost Poet." *VQR*, 44 (Spring 1968), 318–323.

h. Hoskins, Katherine. *Poetry*, 112 (May 1968), 118.

N43 *Incarnations: Poems, 1966–1968* (1968)

a. Anon. *Bulletin from Virginia Kirkus' Bookshop Service*, 15 Aug. 1968, p. 971.

b. Anon. *Publisher's Weekly*, 19 Aug. 1968, p. 71.

c. Katz, Bill. *Library Journal*, 93 (Sept. 1968), 3145.

d. Anon. "Notes on Current Books." *VQR*, 45 (Winter 1969), xv.

e. Anon. *Time*, 24 Jan. 1969, p. 74.

f. Anon. *Booklist*, 1 March 1969, p. 728.

g. Anon. "Warren: Impact Increases." Baltimore *Evening Sun*, 2 March 1969, p. D-5.

h. Spector, R. D. "Lyrics, Heroic and Otherwise." *SatR*, 15 March 1969, pp. 33–35.

i. D., D. M. "More on the Poetry Shelves." *National Observer*, 17 March 1969, p. 21.

j. Martz, Louis L. "Recent Poetry." *YR*, 58 (June 1969), 592–605.

k. Dickey, William. "A Place in the Country." *HudR*, 22 (Summer 1969), 347–364, 366, 368.

l. Maura, Sister, S.S.N.D. *Theology Today*, 26 (July 1969), 213–215.

m. Strandberg, Victor. "The Incarnations of RPW." *Shenandoah*, 20 (Summer 1969), 94–98.

n. Anon. *Choice*, 6 (Nov. 1969), 1226.

o. Fraser, G. S. "Public Voices." *PR*, 37, no. 2 (1970), 295–301.
   Note: erroneously listed as "*Incantations*" in the table of contents.

p. May, Derwent. "New Poetry." London *Observer*, 15 March 1970, p. 38.

q. Spears, Monroe K. "The Latest Poetry of RPW." *SR*, 78 (Spring 1970), 348–358.

r. Anon. "Fugitive from the Old South."
   1. *TLS*, 23 April 1970, p. 446.
   2. *T.L.S.: Essays and Reviews from* The Times Literary Supplement, *1970*. London: Oxford University Press, 1971. Pp. 90–94.

s. Plumly, Stanley. "RPW's Vision." *SoR*, NS 6 (Autumn 1970), 1201–1208.

N44 *Audubon: A Vision* (1969)

a. Anon. *Kirkus' Review*, 15 Aug. 1969, p. 920.

b. Cayton, Robert. *Library Journal*, 1 Nov. 1969, p. 4010.

c. Walsh, Chad. "Sing, Muse of Audubon and His Passion." Chicago *Tribune Book World*, 16 Nov. 1969, p. 3.

d. Anon. "Adam in the Wilderness." *Time*, 12 Dec. 1969, p. 107.

e. Lask, Thomas. "Books of the Times." *NYT*, 13 Dec. 1969, p. 37.

f. Kessler, Jascha. "The Last Word on Audubon." Los Angeles *Times*, 26 Dec. 1969, p. IV–11.

g. Nolan, James W. "One Name for Love Is Knowledge?" New Orleans *Times-Picayune*, 28 Dec. 1969, p. 4–14.

h. Workman, Charles. *Masterplots 1970*. Ed. Frank M. Magill. New York: Salem Press, 1970. P. 39.

i. Vendler, Helen. "A World of Beak and Claw and Fang." *NYTBR*, 11 Jan. 1970, p. 5.

j. Howes, Victor. "Poet's Vision of the Frontier." *Christian Science Monitor*, 15 Jan. 1970, p. 11.

k. Chappell, Fred. "A Curious 'Vision' of John J. Audobon [sic]." Greensboro [NC] *News*, 8 Feb. 1970, p. B-3.

l. [Quinn], Sister M. Bernetta. "'I continually dream of birds.'" *Sunday Herald Traveler*, 8 Feb. 1970, p. 10.

m. Anon. *Booklist*, 15 Feb. 1970, p. 710.

n. Pawlowski, R. *UDQ*, 5 (Spring 1970), 156–157.

o. Fuller, Edmund. "Audubon and Nature Honored." *Wall Street Journal*, 22 April 1970, p. 22.

p. Norman, Howard Allan. "An Adam in the Wilderness." Grand Rapids [MI] *Press*, 26 April 1970, p. 2-H.

q. Kessler, Jascha. "Keys to Ourselves." *SatR*, 2 May 1970, pp. 34–36.

r. Anon. *NYTBR*, 7 June 1970, p. 39.

s. Martz, Louis L. "Recent Poetry: Established Idiom." *YR*, 59 (Summer 1970), 551–569.

t. Anon. "Notes on Current Books." *VQR*, 46 (Autumn 1970), cxxxii.

u. Plumly, Stanley. "RPW's Vision." *SoR*, NS 6 (Autumn 1970), 1201–1208.

v. Martien, Norman. "I Hear America Singing." *PR*, 38, no. 1 (1971), 122–127.

w. Morris, Harry. "The Passions of Poets." *SR*, 79 (Spring 1971), 301–309.

N45 *Selected Poems of Herman Melville* (1970)

a. Grimshaw, James [A., Jr.]. "RPW's *Annus Mirabilis*." *SoR*, NS 10 (Spring 1974), 504–516.

N46 *John Greenleaf Whittier's Poetry* (1971)

a. Harding, Walter. *Library Journal*, 15 May 1971, p. 1715.

b. Anon. *Choice*, 8 (Oct. 1971), 1022–1023.

c. Anon. *AL*, 43 (Nov. 1971), 501.

d. Jolly, Ellen Roy. "Warren Appraises Whittier's Poetry." Baton Rouge *Morning Advocate*, 9 Jan. 1972, p. 2E.

e. Leary, Lewis. *SAQ*, 71 (Spring 1972), 273–274.

f. Ferguson, Suzanne. "Something Which the Past Has Hid." *SR*, 80 (Summer 1972), 493–498.

g. Keith, Philip. "Whittier and Warren." *Shenandoah*, 23 (Summer 1972), 90–95.

h. Grimshaw, James [A., Jr.]. "RPW's *Annus Mirabilis*." *SoR*, NS 10 (Spring 1974), 504–516.

N47 *Homage to Theodore Dreiser* (1971)

a. Anon. *Kirkus Review*, 1 July 1971, p. 733.

b. Anon. *Publisher's Weekly*, 26 July 1971, p. 46.

c. Duffy, Martha. *Time*, 30 Aug. 1971, p. 56.

d. Cayton, R. F. *Library Journal*, 96 (Sept. 1971), 2646.

e. Fadiman, Clifton. *SatR*, 4 Sept. 1971, p. 30.

f. Anon. *Playboy*, Oct. 1971, p. 28.

g. Anon. *NY*, 2 Oct. 1971, p. 131.

h. Anon. "Belles-Lettres." *SatR*, 27 Nov. 1971, p. 44.

i. Berthoff, Warner. "Dreiser Revisited." *Modern Occasions*, 2 (Winter 1972), 133–136.

j. Anon. *Choice*, 9 (March 1972), 64.

k. Rubin, Louis D., Jr. "Dreiser and *MMGG*: A Vintage Year for RPW." *Hollins Critic*, 9 (April 1972), 1–8, 10.

l. Light, Martin. *MFS*, 19 (1973), 611–612.

m. Grimshaw, James [A., Jr.]. "RPW's *Annus Mirabilis*." *SoR*, NS 10 (Spring 1974), 504–516.

N48 *Meet Me in the Green Glen* (1971)

a. Anon. *Kirkus Review*, 1 Aug. 1971, pp. 834–835.

b. Anon. *Publisher's Weekly*, 9 Aug. 1971, pp. 39–40.

c. Cayton, R. F. *Library Journal*, 96 (Sept. 1971), 2673.

d. Maddocks, Melvin. "Prince Charming Was on the Lam." *Life*, 8 Oct. 1971, p. 12.

e. Aldridge, John W. "The Enormous Spider Web of Warren's World." *SatR*, 9 Oct. 1971, pp. 31–32, 35–37.

f. Murray, J. J. *Best Sellers* (University of Scranton), 15 Oct. 1971, p. 318.

g. Stokely, Wilma D. "Penn Warren Novel about Tortured Relationship." Louisville *Courier-Journal*, 31 Oct. 1971, p. F-5.

h. Adams, Phoebe. *AtMo*, Nov. 1971, p. 152.

i. Anon. *Playboy*, Nov. 1971, p. 26.

j. Lask, Thomas. "All for the Love of a Woman." *NYT*, 6 Nov. 1971, p. 29.

k. Boatwright, James. "*MMGG*: Characters That Are, or Become, Moral Men." *NYTBR*, 7 Nov. 1971, p. 6.

l. Theroux, Paul. "Novels." *Book World*, 7 Nov. 1971, p. 2.

m. Hill, W. B. *America*, 20 Nov. 1971, p. 430.

n. Anon. *Booklist*, 1 Dec. 1971, p. 319.

o. Anon. *HudR*, 24 (Winter 1971–72), 716.

p. Donoghue, Denis. "Life Sentence." *NYRB*, 2 Dec. 1971, pp. 28–30.

q. Mano, D. K. *National Review*, 3 Dec. 1971, p. 1359.

r. Anon. *Antioch Review*, 31 (Winter 1972), 589.

s. Anon. "Notable Nominations." *American Libraries*, 3 (Jan. 1972), 87.

t. Warren, Bill. "Cassie's Cave." Austin [TX] *American Statesman*, 16 Jan. 1972, p. 31.

u. Hirsch, Foster. "That Not Yet Westering Moon." *Nation*, 24 Jan. 1972, pp. 124–125.

v. Pendelton, Elsa. *Progressive*, 36 (Feb. 1972), 49.

w. Atchity, Kenneth John. *Mediterranean Review*, 2 (Spring 1972), 63–66.

x. Rubin, Louis D., Jr. "Dreiser and *MMGG*: A Vintage Year for RPW." *Hollins Critic*, 9 (April 1972), 1–8, 10.

y. Anon. London *Observer*, 9 April 1972, p. 30.

z. Spurling, John. *New Statesman*, 14 April 1972, p. 496.

a[2]. Anon. *TLS*, 21 April 1972, p. 439.

b[2]. Anon. *Choice*, 9 (May 1972), 372.

c[2]. Anon. *Listener*, 11 May 1972, p. 628.

d[2]. Anon. *Books & Bookmen*, June 1972, p. 76.

e[2]. Lipsius, Frank. *Foylibra: Foyles Bookshop Magazine*, June 1972, p. 76.

f[2]. Cooke, Michael. "Recent Fiction." *YR*, 61 (Summer 1972), 599–609.

g[2]. Vergnas, Raymond Las. "L'Enchaînement au passé." *Les Nouvelles Littéraires*, 24–30 July 1972, p. 6.

h[2]. Grimshaw, James [A., Jr.]. "RPW's *Annus Mirabilis*." *SoR*, NS 10 (Spring 1974), 504–516.

N49 *American Literature: The Makers and the Making* (1973)
> *Note*: I have been unable to locate any reviews of this title.

N50 *Or Else—Poem/Poems, 1968–1974* (1974)

a. Anon. *Kirkus Review*, 15 Aug. 1974, p. 934.

b. Anon. *Booklist*, 15 Oct. 1974, p. 211.

c. Cayton, R. F. *Library Journal*, 15 Oct. 1974, p. 2607.

d. Broyard, Anatole. "How to Live. What to Do." *NYT*, 24 Oct. 1974, p. 39.

e. Etter, Dave. "Current Collections." *American Libraries*, 5 (Nov. 1974), 548–549.

f. Cheney, Frances N. "Collected Poems Span Six Years." Nashville *Tennessean*, 10 Nov. 1974, p. 10-F.

g. Girault, Norton. "With a Master Searcher." *Virginian-Pilot*, 17 Nov. 1974, p. C-6.

h. Meinke, Peter. *NRep*, 7 Dec. 1974, p. 29.

i. Anon. Washington *Post*, 8 Dec. 1974, Book World sec., p. 3.

j. Hall, Dan. "New Poetry Work Is a Career Milestone." Bridgeport [CT] *Sunday Post*, 8 Dec. 1974, p. F-4.

k. Kenny, Herbert A. "Poetry: 2 Men, 2 Styles—Reconciled and Wrangling." Boston *Sunday Globe*, 8 Dec. 1974, p. A-21.

l. Ricks, Christopher. "Two Poets on Poets and Other Writers." *NYTBR*, 23 Feb. 1975, pp. 6–7.

m. Anon. *Choice*, 12 (March 1975), 79.

n. Grimshaw, James [A., Jr.]. Colorado Springs *Sun, Sunday '75*, 2 March 1975, p. 9.

o. Chamberlain, J. E. "Poetry Chronicle." *HudR*, 28 (Spring 1975), 119–135.

p. Howard, Richard. "Dreadful Alternatives: A Note on RPW." *GaR*, 29 (Spring 1975), 37–41.

q. McClatchy, J. D. "Recent Poetry: Inventions and Obsessions." *YR*, 64 (Spring 1975), 422–432.

r. Moore, John Rees. "Redeeming Time." *SR*, 83 (Spring 1975), liv–lvii.

s. Mueller, Lisel. "Our Poets Deal with One Thing at a Time." *National Observer*, 21 June 1975, p. 21.

t. Walker, Cheryl. "Looking Backward, Looking Forward." *Nation*, 13 Sept. 1975, pp. 215–217.

u. Quinn, Sister Bernetta. *South Carolina Review*, 8 (Nov. 1975), 67–70.

v. Anon. *Poetry*, 128 (Sept. 1976), 349.

N51 *Democracy and Poetry* (1975)

a. Anon. *Publisher's Weekly*, 12 May 1975, p. 62.

b. Gollata, J. A. *Library Journal*, 15 May 1975, p. 989.

c. Broyard, Anatole. "The Poet as Ombudsman." *NYT*, 23 June 1975, p. 25.

d. Bedient, Calvin. *NYTBR*, 3 Aug. 1975, pp. 17–18.

e. Gray, Paul. *Time*, 18 Aug. 1975, p. 72.

f. Lauder, R. E. *America*, 13 Sept. 1975, p. 124.

g. Rosenthal, M. L. "Counteracting the Betrayal." *Nation*, 25 Oct. 1975, p. 408.

h. Miller, J. Hillis. "On Literary Criticism." *NRep*, 29 Nov. 1975, pp. 30–33.

i. Siff, David. *CE*, 37 (Dec. 1975), 431–435.

j. Smith, Henry Nash. "State of the Nation." *TLS*, 20 Feb. 1976, p. 199.

k. Anon. *American Poetry Review*, 5 (March 1976), 46.

l. Anon. *Choice*, 13 (April 1976), 217.

m. Howard, Richard. *GaR*, 30 (Spring 1976), 205–211.

n. Guttenberg, Barnett. "RPW and the Practice of Poetry." *SoR*, NS 14 (Winter 1978), 183–185.

N52 *Selected Poems, 1923–1975* (1976)

a. Anon. *Publisher's Weekly*, 24 May 1976, p. 56.

b. Stuart, Dabney. *Library Journal*, 1 Oct. 1976, p. 2069.

c. Anon. *Booklist*, 15 Oct. 1976, p. 300.

d. Bloom, Harold. *NRep*, 20 Nov. 1976, pp. 20, 22–23, 26.

e. Kramer, Hilton. *NYTBR*, 9 Jan. 1977, pp. 1 and 26.

f. Anon. *Kirkus Review*, 15 Jan. 1977, p. 85.

g. Anon. *Bookweek*, 23 Jan. 1977, p. E-8.

h. Hall, Wade. "A Warren Poetry Collection: The Search for Truth Past." Louisville *Courier-Journal & Times*, 30 Jan. 1977, p. D-5.

i. Bloom, Harold. "The Sunset Hawk." *New Leader*, 31 Jan. 1977, p. 19.

j. Howes, Victor. *Christian Science Monitor*, 10 Feb. 1977, p. 23.

k. Anon. *Kliatt Paperback Book Guide*, 11 (Spring 1977), 17.

l. Garrett, George. *Southern Booklore*, 1, no. 2 (Spring 1977).

m. Romano, John. *Commentary*, April 1977, p. 76.

n. Ryan, R. M. "Looming and Glimmering." *Subject to Change*, 3 (April 1977), 12.

o. Symons, Julian. "In the Southern Style." *TLS*, 29 April 1977, p. 506.

p. Anon. *Choice*, May 1977, p. 380.

q. Anon. London *Observer*, 1 May 1977, p. 24.

r. Cotter, J. F. *America*, 14 May 1977, p. 447.

s. Anon. *Books West*, June 1977, p. 40.

t. Anon. *HudR*, 30 (Summer 1977), 288.

u. Spiegelman, Willard. "The Poetic Achievement of RPW." *SWR*, 62 (Autumn 1977), vi–vii, 411–415.

v. Vendler, Helen. "Recent Poetry: Ten Poets." *YR*, 67 (Autumn 1977), 72–90.

w. McClatchy, J. D. *Poetry*, 131 (Dec. 1977), 169.

x. Anon. *Book World*, 11 Dec. 1977, p. E-6.

y. Spears, Monroe K. "Immersed in America." *NYRB*, 20 April 1978, pp. 38–41.

z. Schulman, Grace. *Nation*, 11 Nov. 1978, p. 519.

N53 *A Place to Come To* (1977)

a. Anon. *Kirkus Review*, 1 Jan. 1977, p. 19.

b. Anon. *Publisher's Weekly*, 17 Jan. 1977, p. 69.

c. Stuart, Dabney. "A Novel of Humor, Bitterness, Grace." *Library Journal*, 1 Feb. 1977, p. 406.

d. Anon. *Booklist*, 15 Feb. 1977, p. 880.

e. Broyard, Anatole. *NYT*, 2 March 1977, p. C-19.

f. Thomas, Phil. Colorado Springs *Gazette-Telegraph*, *Leisure Time*, 5 March 1977, p. 32-D.

g. Epstein, Seymour. "RPW's Latest Celebration of the Years." Chicago *Tribune Book World*, 6 March 1977, p. 7–1.

h. Fuller, Edmund. "Warren and the Metaphysics of Success." *Wall Street Journal*, 7 March 1977, p. 12.

i. Anon. *National Observer*, 12 March 1977, p. 20.

j. Lyons, Gene. "The Wandering Country Boy as Wandering Jew." *NYTBR*, 13 March 1977, pp. 4 and 24.

k. Sheppard, R. Z. "Sacred and Profane Gift." *Time*, 14 March 1977, p. 74.

l. Towers, Robert. *NYRB*, 17 March 1977, p. 4.

m. Howard, Richard. "A Technician's Romance." *SatR*, 19 March 1977, pp. 30 and 34.

n. Jefferson, Margo. *Newsweek*, 21 March 1977, p. 81.

o. Howes, Victor. *Christian Science Monitor*, 23 March 1977, p. 23.

p. Anon. *Playboy*, April 1977, p. 30.

q. Anon. *NY*, 11 April 1977, pp. 139–140.

r. Mathewson, Ruth. "A Placeless Southerner." *New Leader*, 11 April 1977, pp. 15–16.

s. Rosenbloom, Joseph. "RPW at 72: Is His Life the New Book's Plot?" Boston *Sunday Globe*, 17 April 1977, pp. 26–28.

t. Saussy, Marcelle. "Alabama Is Scene of Warren's New Novel." New Orleans *Times-Picayune*, 17 April 1977.

u. Anon. *Listener*, 28 April 1977, p. 555.

v. Symons, Julian. "In the Southern Style." *TLS*, 29 April 1977, p. 506.

w. Clapp, Susannah. *New Statesman*, 29 April 1977, p. 569.

x. Davison, Peter. *AtMo*, May 1977, p. 96.

y. Bergonzi, Bernard. "Tales from the South." London *Observer*, 1 May 1977, p. 24.

z. Wyatt, Robert. "No Place to Come To." Nashville *Tennessean*, 1 May 1977, p. 10-F.

a^2. Stahel, T. H. *America*, 14 May 1977, p. 448.

b^2. Anon. *Choice*, June 1977, p. 539.

c^2. Glassman, Peter. "American Romances: Fiction Chronicle." *HudR*, 30 (Autumn 1977), 437–450.

d^2. Anon. *Book World*, 11 Dec. 1977, p. E-2.

e^2. Clark, Lindley H., Jr. *Wall Street Journal*, 15 Dec. 1977, p. 20.

f^2. Anon. *Publisher's Weekly*, 6 Feb. 1978, p. 100.

g^2. Anon. *NYTBR*, 2 April 1978, p. 41.

h^2. Cooke, Michael G. "A Pure and Complex Writer." *YR*, 67 (Summer 1978), 605–608.

i^2. Halio, Jay L. "Persons Placed and Displaced." *SoR*, NS 15 (Winter 1979), 250–256.

N54 *Now and Then: Poems, 1976–1978* (1978)

a. Anon. *Kirkus Review*, 1 July 1978, p. 744.

b. Anon. *Publisher's Weekly*, 24 July 1978, p. 85.

c. Logan, William. *Library Journal*, Aug. 1978, p. 1516.

d. Anon. *Booklist*, 1 Sept. 1978, p. 20.

e. Nuckols, Carol. "Poet-Novelist Warren Offers Darker Musings." Fort Worth *Star-Telegram*, 3 Sept. 1978, p. 8e.

f. Bloom, Harold. *NRep*, 30 Sept. 1978, p. 34.

g. Anon. *Book World*, 22 Oct. 1978, p. E-4.

h. Piazza, Paul. "Intimations of Immortality." *Chronicle* [of Higher Education] *Review*, 30 Oct. 1978, p. R-11.

i. Pinsky, Robert. "Leaves from a Sturdy Tree." Los Angeles *Times*, 26 Nov. 1978, p. 34.

j. Anon. *Choice*, Dec. 1978, p. 1375.

k. Anon. *Book World*, 3 Dec. 1978, p. E-7.

l. Anon. *American Poetry Review*, Jan. 1979, p. 6.

m. Anon. *Kliatt Paperback Book Guide*, 13 (Winter 1979), 25.

n. Pettingele, Phoebe. *New Leader*, 12 Feb. 1979, p. 17.

o. Anon. *Best Sellers*, March 1979, p. 405.

p. Bedient, Calvin. "Poetry Comfortable and Uncomfortable." *SR*,

87 (Spring 1979), 296–304.

q. Stitt, Peter. *GaR*, 33 (Spring 1979), 214–217.

r. Anon. *HudR*, 32 (Spring 1979), 119.

s. Howes, Victor. "A Poet in His Own Time." *Christian Science Monitor*, 11 April 1979, p. 19.

N55 *Katherine Anne Porter: A Collection of Critical Essays* (1979)

   Note: I have been unable to locate any reviews on this title.

O

Biographical Sketches and Interviews

O1 DeVoto, Bernard. "Exiles from Reality." Rev. of *Exile's Return* by Malcolm Cowley. *SatR*, 2 June 1934, pp. 721–722.
  Note: Illus. on p. 722, "Malcolm Cowley and RPW Photographed near Nashville, home of the 'Fugitives.'"

O2 Anon. *LSU Alumni News*, 11 (Nov. 1934), 15. Photo.

O3 Moore, Merrill. *The Fugitive: Clippings and Comment about the Magazine and the Members of the Group That Published It*. Boston: n.p., 1939.

O4 "Second Southern Novel: RPW Plans Regional Story for Guggenheim Award." *LSU Alumni News*, 15 (March 1939), 3.

O5 Anon. "RPW." *Wilson Bulletin*, 13 (June 1939), 652. Autobiographical.

O6 Hart, James D., ed. *The Oxford Companion to American Literature*. New York: Oxford University Press, 1941. P. 806. 2d ed., 1948, p. 806; 3d ed., 1956, p. 806; 4th ed., 1965, pp. 896–897.

O7 Kunitz, Stanley J., and Howard Haycraft, eds. *Twentieth Century Authors*. New York: H. W. Wilson, 1942. Pp. 1476–1477.

O8 Allison, Margaret. "'Red' Warren." *Northwest Life*, July 1944, p. 18.

O9 Anon. "Who's Who in the Library of Congress: Mr. RPW." U.S. Library of Congress *Information Bulletin*, Sept. 1944, pp. 4 and 6.

O10 Anon. *Annual Report of the Librarian of Congress for the Fiscal Year Ended June 30, 1944*. Washington, D.C.: U.S. Government Printing Office, 1945. Pp. 36 and 60.

O11 Anon. *Annual Report of the Librarian of Congress for the Fiscal Year Ended June 30, 1945*. Washington, D.C.: U.S. Government Printing Office, 1946. Pp. 30, 90, and 147–148.

O12 Allison, Margaret. Minneapolis *Sunday Tribune*, 13 Oct. 1946, p. 1.

O13 Bonnefond, Laura. "Can Writing Be Taught?" *Mademoiselle*, Jan. 1947, pp. 202–203, 257, 259–260.

O14 Lerman, Leo. "Two-Facet Careers: Writers Who Teach." *Vogue*, 15 Aug. 1947, pp. 169, 208–211, 214.

O15 Anon. *The Americana Annual: 1948*. Ed. A. H. McDannald, John J. Smith, and Lavinia P. Dudley. New York: Americana, 1948. P. 729.

O16 G., R. "The Author." *SatR*, 24 June 1950, p. 11.

O17 Breit, Harvey. "Talk with Mr. Warren."
a. *NYTBR*, 25 June 1950, p. 20.
b. *The Writer Observed*. Cleveland: World Publishing, 1956. Pp. 131–133.

O18 Hutchens, John K. "On an Author." *NYHTBR*, 2 July 1950, p. 2.

O19 Berti, Luigi. "RPW: Con il vino dell 'elba scrirerà il suo capola-voro." *Omnibus*, 15 Oct. 1950, p. 26.

O20 Warfel, Harry R. *American Novelists of Today*. New York: American Book Company, 1951. Pp. 442–443.

O21 Anon. "Milestones." *Time*, 9 July 1951, p. 70.

O22 Anon. *The National Cyclopedia of American Biography*. New York: James T. White & Company, 1952. P. 332.

O23 "Some Important Fall Authors Speak for Themselves." *NYHTBR*, 11 Oct. 1953, p. 10.

O24 Richards, Robert F., ed. *Concise Dictionary of American Literature*. New York: Philosophical Library, 1955. P. 237.

O25 Kalb, Bernard. "The Author." *SatR*, 20 Aug. 1955, p. 9.

O26 Girson, Rochelle. "This Week's Personality." *SatR*, 27 Aug. 1955, p. 4.

O27 Ellison, Ralph, and Eugene Walter. "The Art of Fiction XVIII: RPW."
a. *Paris Review*, 4 (Spring–Summer 1957), 112–140.
b. *Writers at Work: The Paris Review Interviews*. Ed. Malcolm Cowley. New York: Viking Press, 1958. Pp. 183–207.
c. Longley, **K9**, pp. 18–45.
d. Beebe and Field, **K11**, pp. 63–65.

O28 Browning, D. C., and John W. Cousin, comps. *Everyman's Dictionary of Literary Biography, English and American*. New York: E. P. Dutton, 1958. P. 702.

O29 Magill, Frank N., ed. *Cyclopedia of World Authors*. New York: Harper & Brothers, 1958. Pp. 1126–1128.

O30 Anon. "Five Music Men of Words." *Newsweek*, 17 March 1958, p. 110.

O31 Anon. "Sketches of the Pultizer Prize Winners for 1958 in Letters, Music, and Journalism." *NYT*, 6 May 1958, p. 38.

O32 *American Annual 1959*. New York: Americana Corporation, 1959. P. 820.

O33 Hopy, Cyrus, moderator. "Interview [by students] with Flannery O'Connor and RPW." Nashville: Vanderbilt University, 23 April 1959. Sound recording.

O34 *NYTBR*, 14 June 1959, p. 5. Photo of RPW and family.

O35 Westbrook, John T. "The Fugitives Overhauled." *SWR*, 44 (Autumn 1959), 343.

O36 "An Interview with Flannery O'Connor and RPW."
a. *The Vagabond* [Vanderbilt], 4 (Feb. 1960), 9–16.
b. *Writer to Writer*. Ed. Floyd C. Watkins and Karl F. Knight. Boston: Houghton Mifflin, 1966. Pp. 71–90.

O37 Anon. "The Art of Fiction: An Interview with RPW." *Books & Bookmen*, Jan. 1960, pp. 11–12, 14–15, 34.

O38 Rock, Virginia J. "The Making and Meaning of *ITMS*: A Study of Utopian-Conservatism, 1925–1939." Ph.D., Minnesota, 1961.
Note: A shorter version of her biographical sketch of RPW appears in the Harper Torchbook edition of *ITMS*, pp. 381–383.

O39 Saporta, Marc. "Un entretien avec RPW." *Information & Documents*, 15 Oct. 1961, pp. 24–28.

O40 Anon. "Author in a Box." *Time*, 17 Nov. 1961, p. 93.

O41 Heryberg, Max J. *The Reader's Encyclopedia of American Literature*. New York: Thomas Y. Crowell Company, 1962. P. 1197.

O42 Griffin, Stuart. "Meeting the People: Dr. RPW." *Mainichi Daily News*, 27 Jan. 1962, p. 7.

O43 Anon. "RPW." *Study of Current English*, 17 (April 1962), 53–53.

O44 Wallace, Peter. "RPW: 'Just the Process.'" *Yale News*, 26 April 1962, pp. 1 and 8.

O45 "Works in Progress 1963." *Esquire*, July 1963, pp. 50–51, 55–56, 105.

O46 Saporta, Marc. "RPW." *Information & Documents*, no. 187, 15 Sept.–1 Oct. 1963, pp. 5–7, 19.

O47 Stewart, Randall. "RPW." *Encyclopedia Britannica* (1964), XXIII, 370.

O48 "Moths Against the Screen." *SatEP*, 4 April 1964, p. 41.
Note: in conjunction with an excerpt from *F*.

O49 Downs, Hugh. "The Today Show." New York: NBC Television, 17 May 1965.
Note: an interview regarding *WNS?*.

O50 Schöne, Annemarie. *Abriss der amerikanischen Literaturgeschichte in Tabellen*. Frankfurt: Athenäum, 1967. Pp. 211, 218, 229–230.

O51 McGill, Ralph. "Red Warren Soaked Up the South's Raw Agony." Nashville *Tennessean*, 28 Feb. 1967, p. 7.

O52 Braudy, Susan. "RPW: Voices in My Blood." *Yale Alumni Magazine*, March 1968, pp. 24–31.

O53 Schleuderer, Claude. "Interview with RPW." Hartford, CT: WWUH, 2 Feb. 1969. Rebroadcast 5 Feb. 1969, 7:00–8:00 p.m.

O54 Hoffman, Daniel. "RPW." *Contemporary Poets*. Ed. Rosalie Murphy. New York: St. Martin's Press, 1970. Pp. 1142–1146.

O55 Moritz, Charles, ed. *Current Biography Yearbook (1970)*. New York: H. W. Wilson, 1970. Pp. 432–435.

O56 Ward, A. C. *Longman Companion to Twentieth-Century Literature*. London: Longman, 1970. P. 558.

O57 Walker, Marshall. "RPW."
a. *Scottish International*, 9 (Feb. 1970), 3–9.
b. *RPW: A Vision Earned*. Edinburgh: Paul Harris, 1979. Pp. 241–263.

O58 Crawford, Jean. "A Conversation with RPW." *Vanderbilt Alumnus*, March–April 1970, pp. 20–21.

O59 Anon. "RPW." *Current Biography*, 31 (June 1970), 39–42.

O60 Sale, Richard B. "An Interview in New Haven with RPW." *SNNTS*, 2 (Fall 1970), 325–354.

O61 Casey, Phil. "RPW." Washington *Post*, 2 Dec. 1970, pp. C1–C2.

O62 Anon. "Incontri americani: RPW." *Studi americani*, 17 (1971), 379–389.

O63 Strandberg, Victor. "RPW." *Encyclopedia of World Literature in the 20th Century*. Ed. Wolfgang Bernard Fleischmann. New York: Frederick Ungar, 1971. III, 489–490.

O64 Downs, Hugh. "The Today Show." New York: NBC Television, 3 June 1971.
Note: an interview regarding *JGWP*.

O65 Kay, Ernest, ed. *International Who's Who in Poetry*. 3d ed. London: Melrose Press, 1972. P. 441. 4th ed., 1974, p. 490.

O66 Wegelin, Christof. "RPW." *Contemporary Novelists*. Ed. James Vinson. New York: St. Martin's Press, 1972. Pp. 1303–1307.

O67 B[rown], M[aria]. "RPW." *Hollins Critic*, 9 (April 1972), 9.

O68 Fisher, Ruth. "A Conversation with RPW." *Four Quarters*, 21 (May 1972), 3–17.

O69 Gado, Frank, ed. [An interview conducted with RPW 8 Feb. 1966].

  a. *The Idol*, 49 (Summer 1972), 1–23.

  b. *First Person: Conversations on Writers & Writing.* Schenectady, NY: Union College Press, 1973. Pp. 63–79.

O70 West, Paul. "RPW." *American Writers: A Collection of Literary Biographies.* Ed. Leonard Unger. New York: Charles Scribner's Sons, 1974. IV, 236–259.

O71 O'Sheel, Patrick. "Companion to Owls."

  a. *Humanities* [NEH], 4 (Feb. 1974), 1–2, 7–9.

  b. As "RPW: Creative Energy Spanning Generations." Washington *Post*, 28 April 1974, pp. F1–F3.

O72 Walker, Marshall. "RPW: An Interview." *Journal of American Studies*, 8 (Aug. 1974), 229–246. *See* **O57**.

O73 West, Richard S. "Ransom Honored by Prof. Daniel and Author Warren." *Kenyon Collegian*, 7 Nov. 1974, p. 2.

O74 Hofelich, Greg. "RPW." *Kentucky Kernel* [University of Kentucky], 14 March 1975, p. 7.

O75 McCullough, David. "Eye on Books." *Book-of-the-Month Club News*, June 1975, pp. 6–7.

  Note: mainly about Eleanor Clark but with insights to RPW.

O76 Anon. "What Kind of Future for America?" *U.S. News & World Report*, 7 July 1975, pp. 48–49.

O77 "A Conversation with Cleanth Brooks." *The Possibilities of Order: Cleanth Brooks and His Work.* Ed. Lewis P. Simpson. Baton Rouge: Louisiana State University Press, 1976. Pp. 1–124.

O78 Moyers, Bill. "Bill Moyers' Journal." New York: PBS Television, 4 April 1976.

O79 Baker, John. "RPW." *Conversations with Writers.* Eds. Matthew J. Bruccoli et al. Detroit: Gale Research, 1977. I, 279–302.

O80 *Notes from the Editors: RPW's AKM.* Franklin Center, PA: Franklin Library, 1977.

O81 *Who's Who 1977.* New York: H. W. Wilson, 1977. Pp. 2529–2530.

O82 DeMott, Benjamin. "Talk with RPW." *NYTBR*, 9 Jan. 1977, pp. 1, 22–25.

O83 Thomas, William. "The Fugitives, Recaptured." *Mid-South:* [Memphis] *Commercial Appeal Magazine*, 13 Feb. 1977, pp. 6–7; "RPW: Southerner," pp. 9, 14, 16.

O84 Hendrickson, Paul. "RPW." *National Observer*, 12 March 1977, p. 20.

O85 Cooper, Gerald. "A Talk with RPW." *Subject to Change*, 3 (April 1977), 10–13, 21.

O86 Rosenbloom, Joseph. "RPW at 72." Boston *Sunday Globe*, *New England* magazine sec., 17 April 1977, pp. 27–28, 30, 68.

O87 Anon. "Reviews, Good or Bad, Don't Impress RPW." Seattle *Post-Intelligencer*, 12 June 1977, p. H-10.

O88 Seymore, James. "RPW and Wife Eleanor Clark Battle a Writer's Nightmare: Her Loss of Sight." *People*, 27 June 1977, pp. 46–48.

    Note: Eleanor Clark's response, 25 July 1977, p. 5.

O89 Stitt, Peter. "An Interview with RPW." *SR*, 85 (Summer 1977), 467–477.

O90 Farrell, David. Oral history interview for the RPW Oral History Project, University of Kentucky, no. 01. Fairfield, CT, 6 Oct. 1977. Tape: 2 hr. 50 min.

O91 Harmer, Ruth. "A Celebration of Life.' *Modern Maturity*, Dec. 1977–Jan. 1978, p. 57.

O92 Anon. "Craft Interview with RPW." *New York Quarterly*, no. 23 (1978), pp. 13–25.

O93 Wilkie, Everett, and Josephine Helterman. "RPW." *Dictionary of Literary Biography*. Eds. Jeffrey Helterman and Richard Layman. Detroit: Gale Research, 1978. II, 513–524.

O94 Farrell, David. Oral history interview for the RPW Oral History Project, University of Kentucky, no. 10. New York, NY, 9 May 1978. Tape: 1 hr. 15 min.

O95 Anon. "An Interview with RPW and Eleanor Clark." *New England Review*, 1 (Autumn 1978), 49–70.

O96 Farrell, David. Oral history interview for the RPW Oral History Project, University of Kentucky, no. 15. Fairfield, CT, 7 Nov. 1978. Tape: 2 hr. 15 min.

O97 Anon. "Notes on HBJ Authors." *Shoptalk: The English Newsletter of the College Department of Harcourt Brace Jovanovich*, 2, no. 2 (1979), [6].

O98 Farrell, David. Oral history interview for the RPW Oral History Project, University of Kentucky, no. 17. Fairfield, CT, 25 Jan. 1979. Tape: 2 hr.

O99 Anon. NYT, 17 April 1979, p. B8.

O100 Farrell, David. Oral history interview for the RPW Oral History Project, University of Kentucky, no. 18. Fairfield, CT, 3 May 1979. Tape: 1 hr. 10 min.

O101 Cromwell, Sharon. "RPW: Working and Searching for Uncertain Truth." Hartford *Courant Magazine*, 9 Sept. 1979, pp. 10–12.

O102 Oney, Steve. "A Southern Voice." Atlanta *Journal & Constitution Magazine*, 16 Sept. 1979, pp. 12–15, 52, 54–55, 57–59.

O103 Williams, Shirley. "The Prolific RPW." Louisville *Courier-Journal*, 28 Oct. 1979, magazine sec., pp. 10, 12–15, 17, 48–50.

P

News Releases

Note: This section includes a selective sampling of those miscellaneous news items which cannot be conveniently catalogued elsewhere but which serve as documentation for particular events in RPW's literary career.

P1 Munson, Gorham B. Correspondence. *NRep*, 27 June 1928, p. 149.

P2 "Prominent Poets, Essayists, Novelists to Participate in Jubilee Conference." *Louisiana Leader*, April 1935, p. 2.

   Note: RPW was in charge of the conference.

P3 "The Recent Southern Novel." Rocky Mountain Writers' Conference, University of Colorado, July 1935.

   Reported in: Lawrance Thompson, *Robert Frost: The Years of Triumph, 1915–1938* (New York: Holt, Rinehart and Winston, 1970), pp. 423–424.

P4 "Publication of Southern Review Is Noteworthy Milestone in the Activities of the University." *Louisiana Leader*, July 1935, p. 8.

P5 "RPW Receives Poetry Magazine Prize." *Louisiana Leader*, Nov. 1936, p. 8.

P6 "RPW Wins Sinkler Prize." *Louisiana Leader*, June 1937, p. 1.

P7 Mitchiner, Nantelle. "Kentucky Tobacco War Is Theme of RPW's Novel." *DR* (LSU), 30 March 1938, p. 4.

P8 "RPW Is Winner of Guggenheim Award for 1939." *BRST*, 27 March 1939, p. 7.

P9 "Warren Receives Fellowship Award for Creative Work." *DR* (LSU), 28 March 1939, p. 2.

P10 "Warren Plans 2nd Novel with Southern Theme." *BRMA*, 2 April 1939, p. 8-B.

P11 "RPW Wins Guggenheim Award." *Louisiana Leader*, April 1939, p. 5.

P12 "Novelist Talks to Quota Club on Recent Book." *BRST*, 31 May 1939, p. 15.

P13 "RPW Plans Work in France and Italy." *DR* (LSU), 18 July 1939, p. 2.

P14 "RPW's 'Night Riders' [*sic*] Wins Honorable Mention." *BRST*, 27 Jan. 1940, p. 12.

P15 Walker, Norman. "LSU's Southern Review Ranks Tops' [*sic*] Among Literary Quarterlies." *BRST*, 20 May 1940, pp. 5 and 7.

P16 Wilson, Georgia L. "Warren Returns to L.S.U.; Author Discusses Play and Novel on Which He Has Been Working During the Past Year." *BRMA*, 15 Sept. 1940, p. 6-B.

P17 "On Campus After Year's Absence." *BRST*, 17 Sept. 1940, p. 2-A.

P18 "RPW Returns to University After Year's Leave to Work on Novel." *Louisiana Leader*, Oct. 1940, p. 5.

P19 *DR* (LSU), 17 Jan. 1941, p. 8.
Note: regarding RPW as a visiting lecturer in fiction, Iowa School of Letters.

P20 "War Reduces Poetry, Too, Says RPW." *DR* (LSU), 30 Oct. 1941, p. 3.

P21 "Southern Review Ends Publication on Spring Issue." *NOTP*, 6 Jan. 1942, p. 2.

P22 "Intellectualism Gets the Axe." *DR* (LSU), 8 Jan. 1942, p. 6.

P23 "Warren Gets Recognition for Poems." *DR* (LSU), 14 March 1942, p. 1.

P24 "Warren Reviews 'Fire in Summer.'" *DR* (LSU), 14 March 1942, p. 5.

P25 "Educators Protest LSU's Suspension of 'Southern Review.'" *BRST*, 17 March 1942, p. 13.

P26 "'Poet's Poet,' Reviewer Says of Warren." *BRST*, 29 April 1942, p. 2.

P27 "RPW Named 'Poet of the Month.'" *Louisiana Leader*, April 1942, p. 8.

P28 "Warren's Poetry Is Praised." *BRMA*, 3 May 1942, p. 8-C.

P29 "Warren to Lecture at Princeton Thursday." *DR* (LSU), 6 May 1942, p. 1.

P30 "RPW to Leave for Minnesota." *DR* (LSU), 9 May 1942, p. 1.

P31 Claitor, Jewel. "RPW—Minnesota's Gain, LSU's Loss." *DR* (LSU), 9 May 1942, p. 6.

P32 "Student Journal Blames LSU as Warren Resigns." *NOTP*, 10 May 1942, p. 11.

P33 "'At Heaven's Gate'—Warren Publishes Another." *DR* (LSU), 16 June 1943, p. 1.

P34 "RPW's Novel [*AKM*] Draws Praise from AP Critic, Calls It Pulitzer Prize Work." *BRMA*, 20 Aug. 1946, p. 3.

P35 Engle, Paul. "RPW Master of Great Poetry and Prose." Chicago *Sunday Tribune*, 25 Aug. 1946, p. 4–7.

P36 Hinternhoff, John F. "RPW Is No Apologist for the Evil-Doers About Whom He Writes." St. Louis *Globe-Democrat*, 15 Sept. 1946, p. 2E.

P37 Wallace, Frances J. "Notes and Quotes." *Wilson Library Bulletin*, 21 (Jan. 1947), 464.

P38 "Pulitzer Prize Won by Warren, Formerly of LSU." *BRST*, 5 May 1947, p. 1.

P39 "Warren's *AKM* Wins 1946 [*sic*] Pulitzer Novel Prize." *DR* (LSU), 6 May 1947, p. 1.
Note: no prize in fiction in 1946.

P40 "Pulitzer Award Winners Named." *NOTP*, 6 May 1947, p. 1.

P41 Hansen, Harry. "*AKM* Wins Pulitzer Award for Fiction." Chicago *Sunday Tribune Magazine of Books*, 11 May 1947, p. 4.

P42 Anon. *Publishers' Weekly*, 17 May 1947, p. 2502.

P43 "A Top Writer Is Assigned to *AKM*." *NOTP*, 20 July 1947, p. 2–12.

P44 Anon. *Time*, 4 Aug. 1947, pp. 80, 82–83.

P45 Rogers, W. G. "Warren Likes to Do His Writing on Foreign Soil." *NOTP*, 11 June 1950, p. 2–8.

P46 Hutchens, John K. "On an Author." *NYHTBR*, 2 July 1950, p. 2.

P47 Anon. "Foreign News: France." *Time*, 18 Dec. 1950, p. 32.

P48 "Some Important Fall Authors Speak for Themselves." *NYHTBR*, 11 Oct. 1953, p. 10.

P49 Washington *Post* and *Times Herald* Book and Author Luncheon, Washington, D.C., 5 Oct. 1955. With Morris Ernst and Louis Untermeyer. Program (Ctw).

P50 "Letters to the Editor." *NYTBR*, 15 Jan. 1956, p. 32.
Note: responses to RPW's essay, "A Lesson Read in American Books," **F30**.

P51 Morrissey, Ralph. "The Fugitives Return." *NYTBR*, 20 May 1956, p. 27.

P52 "Letters to the Editor." *NYTBR*, 7 Oct. 1956, p. 44.
Note: regarding *Seg*.

P53 Price, Ann. "Movie Based on Novel by RPW May Be Filmed in La." *BRMA*, 5 Oct. 1956, pp. 5–6.

P54 "Booksellers Cite 3 Writers' Works." *NYT*, 12 March 1958, p. 26.

P55 "Pulitzer, 1958." *NYT*, 6 May 1958, p. 34.

P56 "Sketches of the Pulitzer Prize Winners for 1958 in Letters, Music, and Journalism." *NYT*, 6 May 1958, p. 38.

P57 Miers, Virgil. "On the Scene." Dallas [TX] *Times Herald*, 20 Nov. 1958, p. 2.

P58 *Colloquium on Poetry.* Vanderbilt Literary Symposium, 22–23 April 1959. With Donald Davidson, Murray Krieger, Flannery O'Connor, and Jesse Stuart. Program (Ctw).

P59 Distinguished Lecture Series of the University of Louisville [KY], 27 April 1959. Notice in Louisville *Courier-Journal*, 29 April 1959.

P60 Atkinson, Brooks. "Theatre: Stage Politics." *NYT*, 17 Oct. 1959, p. 27; 25 Oct. 1959, p. 2–1.

P61 "[Three] Members Added by Arts Academy." *NYT*, 5 Dec. 1959, p. 8.

P62 "1959 Silver Anniversary All-America." *Sports Illustrated*, 21 Dec. 1959, p. 94.
 Note: names RPW as one of the judges.

P63 Rosenthal, A. M. "U.S. and Japanese Intellectuals Will Meet in Tokyo This Week." *NYT*, 22 Jan. 1962, p. 9.

P64 Kato, Takeyasu. "U.S. Novelist Lauds Japanese Culture." Mainichi *Daily News*, 29 Jan. 1962.

P65 Barr, John. "Writer Discusses Insides of Writing: That's Where It's Done, Novelist Warren Says." *Pacific Stars and Stripes*, 23 Feb. 1962, p. 16.

P66 Lask, Thomas. "Poets at Yale." *NYT*, 13 May 1962, p. 17X.

P67 *The Contemporary Novel.* Alumni Memorial Lecture, University of Massachusetts, 3 April 1963. Program (Ctw).

P68 Krasny, Janet R. "Warren Stresses Insight into Past." *Cornell Daily Sun*, 12 April 1963, p. 1.

P69 Paper on the history of the notion of alienated writers. Symposium at Princeton University, May 1963. With Ginsberg, Malamud, and Albee.
 Reported in: *Newsweek*, 6 May 1963, p. 96.

P70 *Readings.* The Poetry Center Calendar, YM–YWHA, New York, 12 May 1963. Program (Ctw).

P71 *The Contemporary Novel.* Eighth Annual Paideia Conference at Hill School, Pottstown, PA, 12 Oct. 1963. With Robert Gutwillig, novelist and trade book editor for McGraw-Hill. Program (Ctw).

P72 "RPW to Visit Hollins." *Hollins College Bulletin*, 14 (Dec. 1963), 1.

P73 "Famous Novelist to Give Lecture Here on Feb. 4." *DR* (LSU), 15 Jan. 1964, p. 1.

P74 "Pulitzer Prize Winner to Talk in LSU Series." *BRMA*, 16 Jan. 1964, p. 1.

P75 "RPW Lectures Here Tuesday." *DR* (LSU), 31 Jan. 1964, p. 1.

P76 "Warren Raps North's 'Self-Righteousness.'" *BRST*, 4 Feb. 1964, p. 8-A.

P77 Alston, Vernon. "Robert Warren Talks on Poetry of 1930's." *BRST*, 5 Feb. 1964, p. 1-C.

P78 Silverberg, Jane. "Need to Change Cited by Warren." *DR* (LSU), 5 Feb. 1964, pp. 1 and 5.

P79 Perez, Ed. "Noted Critic Relates Changing Styles in Poetry in LSU Talk." *BRMA*, 5 Feb. 1964, p. 9-B.

P80 *BD* reading; discussion of origin, writing, and development of *AKM*. Glasgow Endowment Committee, Washington and Lee University, 5–6 Nov. 1964. Program (Ctw).

P81 Barker, George. "Red Warren, Rebel in the Ivy League." Nashville *Tennessean Magazine*, 27 Dec. 1964, pp. 6–7.

P82 "American Life as Seen by Contemporary Writers." A Tele-Lecture Course. Stephens College, Columbia, MO, 15 Feb. 1965. (Ctw).

P83 Stonehill, Judy. "Warren, Lowell, Berryman Highlight Festival." *Michigan Daily* [Ann Arbor], 10 March 1965, pp. 1 and 10.
  Note: Creative Arts Festival, University of Michigan, 18 March 1965.

P84 McAffee, Paul. "Prize-Winning Author Talks from Stool." Fort Worth *Star-Telegram*, 6 May 1965.
  Note: Creative Writing Day Convention, Texas Christian University.

P85 "Author Says Rights Battle Won." Honolulu *Star-Bulletin*, 13 Sept. 1965, p. C-1.

P86 Sakamoto, Ed. "Author Warren Sees Civil Rights Success." Honolulu *Advertiser*, 13 Sept. 1965, pp. A-1 and A-6.

P87 "The End of an Era." *Vassar Miscellany News*, 8 Dec. 1965, p. 1.

P88 Talbott, Strobe. "Warren Reads, Discusses Poems from New Books." *YDN*, 8 March 1966, p. 1.

P89 Montgomery, Paul L. "Dinner Salutes Pulitzer Prizes." *NYT*, 11 May 1966, p. 33.

P90 Borders, William. "RPW Is Winner of the Bollingen Prize in Poetry." *NYT*, 6 Feb. 1967, pp. 1 and 32.

P91 "Poet and Arguer: RPW." *NYT*, 6 Feb. 1967, p. 32.

P92 "Warren's Poems Win Yale Prize." *YDN*, 6 Feb. 1967, p. 1.

P93 "Prized Poet." *Newsweek*, 20 Feb. 1967, p. 96.

P94 Gilroy, Harry. "Some New Poetry Is Read by Warren at Goldberg Home." *NYT*, 13 Dec. 1967, p. 41.

P95 "On the Twelfth Night . . . Parties." Washington *Post*, 7 Jan. 1968.

P96 *Readings: International Poetry Forum, Pittsburgh, PA, 3 Oct. 1968.* Program (Ctw).

P97 Lane, Calvin W. "RPW: The Writer as Historian." *UH News Liberated Press*, 5 Feb. 1969, pp. 6 and 14.

P98 Samplier, Louie. [Keller Lecture]. University of Hartford *News Liberated Press*, 5 Feb. 1969, p. 6.

P99 Raymont, Henry. "Writers Appeal for Soviet Jew." *NYT*, 3 Aug. 1969, p. 6.

P100 Whitman, Alden. "RPW: The Poet Prevails (Just Now)." *NYT*, 16 Dec. 1969, p. 54.
   Note: uses a working title, "A Definition of Love," for *MMGG*.

P101 *Founder's Day Address.* University of Virginia, 13 April 1970. Program (Ctw).

P102 "National Medal for Literature Awarded Warren." *BRST*, 22 July 1970, p. 14-A.

P103 Raymont, Henry. "RPW Gets Book Award." *NYT*, 22 July 1970, p. 33.

P104 "Former Professor at LSU Wins Literary Prize." *BRMA*, 3 Dec. 1970, p. 1-C.

P105 "Warren Receives '70 National Medal for Literature." *NYT*, 3 Dec. 1970, p. 60.

P106 Meehan, Thomas. "The Yale Faculty Makes the Scene." *NYT*, 7 Feb. 1971, sec. 6, pp. 12–13, 48–52. *See* **P108**.

P107 *Readings and Comments: The Humanities Series, Boston College, 18 Feb. 1971.* Program (Ctw).

P108 "Letters." *NYT*, 28 Feb. 1971, p. 6–4.
   Note: response to Meehan's article, **P106**.

P109 Gent, George. "2 More U.S. Novelists Come to Aid of Solzhenitsyn." *NYT*, 21 Dec. 1972, p. 28.

P110 "RPW Offers Solzhenitsyn Royalties from Latest Book." London *Times*, 22 Dec. 1972, p. 5h.

P111 "Warren Tapped for Distinguished Lecture." Bridgeport [CT] *Sunday Post*, 3 Feb. 1974, p. E-4.

P112 "Jefferson Lecture." *Antiquarian-Bookman's Weekly*, 18 Feb. 1974, p. 649.

P113 "RPW Delivers 1974 Jefferson Lecture." *Library of Congress Information Bulletin*, 17 May 1974, pp. 163–164.

P114 "Warren to Pay Tribute to Ransom." *Kenyon Collegian*, 31 Oct. 1974, p. 1.

P115 "Book of Poems Personal RPW Says." *Rocky Mountain News*, 6 Dec. 1974, p. 29.

P116 *Democracy and Poetry.* The Cecil B. Williams Memorial Lecture, Texas Christian University, 26 Feb. 1975; "Readings from His Poetry," 27 Feb. 1975 (a.m.). Program (Ctw).

P117 "Readings from His Poetry." University of Texas at Austin *Daily Texan*, 28 Feb. 1975, p. 2.

P118 "Warren Receives Copernicus Prize for Life's Poetry." *NYT*, 10 May 1976, p. 29.

P119 Russell, John. "Leonid Is Eulogized by Virgil Thomson / RPW Also Speaks . . . ." *NYT*, 6 Oct. 1976, p. 46.

P120 Gallagher, Jim. "RPW Flips Through the Chapters of His Illustrious Literary Life." Chicago *Tribune*, 7 March 1977, p. 1.

P121 "'Toward Sunset at a Great Height.'" *Vanderbilt Hustler*, 8 April 1977, p. 6.

P122 "People, etc." Colorado Springs *Gazette-Telegraph*, 10 April 1977, p. 3-D.

P123 "MacLeish Receives '78 National Medal for Literature." *NYT*, 7 April 1978, p. C-22.
   Note: RPW presented the medal.

P124 "Pulitzers Announced." Colorado Springs *Gazette-Telegraph*, 17 April 1979, p. 1-A.

P125 Lask, Thomas. "Brooks, 40 Years Later, Says New Criticism Was Misunderstood." *NYT*, 28 May 1979, p. C-11.

P126 "Random House Is Reissuing 3 Contemporary Classics . . . ." *NYT*, 30 Sept. 1979, p. G-47.
   Note: *BD*(nv) is included.

Q

Unpublished Works

Note: The scope of this section is only representative of the attention graduate students have paid RPW's works, for it is impossible to encompass all schools that grant advanced degrees.

Q1 Blum, Morgan. "The Traditionist Post-War Poetry." M.A., Louisiana State University, 1936.

Q2 Almand, Claude M. "'Pondy Woods': A Symphonic Episode Based on the Poem of RPW." M.M., Louisiana State University, 1938.

Q3 Pockwinse, Florence B. "A History of *The Fugitive* and the Fugitives." M.A., Boston University, 1938.

Q4 Bonds, Georgia A. "Basic Themes in the Poetry of Ransom, Warren, and Tate: A Study of the Problem of Abstraction in the Poetry of Mr. John Crowe Ransom, Mr. RPW, and Mr. Allen Tate." M.A., Louisiana State University, 1940.

Q5 Meyer, Sr. M. Carmel, C.S.A. "New Poetry of the American South: A Study of Its Art, Its Tradition, and Its Critical Ideas." M.A., Loyola University (Chicago), 1943.

Q6 Rowlison, Mariena. "Kentucky Schools in Fiction." M.Ed., Western Kentucky College, 1944.

Q7 Duncan, Joseph E. "The Relationship of Seventeenth-Century and Twentieth-Century Metaphysical Poetry." M.A., University of Louisville, 1946.

Q8 Woodward, Barbara C. "Theories of Meaning in Poetry, 1915–1940: A Critical History." Ph.D., University of Michigan, 1946.

Q9 Harrison, Jane. "The Fiction of RPW: A Study in Technique." M.A., Vanderbilt University, 1947.

Q10 Stewart, John L. "The Fugitive-Agrarian Writers: A History and a Criticism." Ph.D., Ohio State University, 1947. Cf. **L67.**
    Abstract appears in *Abstracts of Dissertations, Ohio State University*, no. 55 (1949), pp. 295–302.

Q11 Bennett, John B. "The Iron Beach: A Study of the Poetry of RPW." M.A., Vanderbilt University, 1948.

Q12 Bradbury, John M. "The Fugitive Critics: A Critical History." Ph.D., State University of Iowa, 1948. Cf. **L36**.

Q13 Hynes, Sam L. "The Poet as Dramatist: RPW and Some Predecessors." M.A., Columbia University, 1948.

Q14 O'Connor, John W. "Sense and Sensibility in Modern Poetry." Ph.D., Columbia University, 1948.

Q15 Casey, James R. "The Short Stories in the *Southern Review* (1935–1942)." M.A., Vanderbilt University, 1949.

Q16 Kinnaird, John W. "Prometheus, Evil and Humpty Dumpty: The Poetry and Fiction of RPW." M.A., Columbia University, 1949.

Q17 Ransom, John B. "Integration of the Individual in the Fiction of RPW." M.A., Stanford University, 1949.

Q18 Coleman, Thomas E. "Form as Function in the Novels of RPW." M.A., University of Louisville, 1950.

Q19 Burke, Lawrence M. "The Conditions for the 'Good Man' in the Novels of RPW." M.A., University of Washington, 1951.

Q20 Church, Ralph B. "A Synthesis of the Novels of RPW." M.A., Columbia University, 1951.

Q21 Santmyer, Sue P. "The 'Nashville Agrarians' as Critics of American Society." M.A., Vanderbilt University, 1951.

Q22 Simmons, James Elden. "The Philosophical Content of RPW's Novels." M.A., University of Oklahoma, 1951.

Q23 Tritschler, Charles A. "'Circus in the Attic': A Study of the Fiction of RPW." B.A., Amherst College, 1951.

Q24 Hochman, Stanley. "RPW: Four in Pursuit of Definition." M.A., Columbia University, 1952.

Q25 Justus, James H. "The Kentucky Tragedy in Simms and Warren: A Study in Changing Milieux." M.A., University of Tennessee, 1952.

Q26 Welker, Robert L. "The Underlying Philosophy of RPW: A Study in the Poetic Attitude." M.A., Vanderbilt University, 1952.

Q27 Abrams, Richard J. "RPW: A Southern Paradox." B.A., Williams College (Williamstown, MA), 1953.

Q28 Casper, Leonard R. "The Lost Sense of Community and the Role of the Artist in RPW." Ph.D., University of Wisconsin, 1953. Cf. **K4**.

    Abstract appears in *Summaries of Doctoral Dissertations: University of Wisconsin*, 14 (1954), 426–428.

Q29 Cowan, Louise. "*The Fugitive*: A Critical History." Ph.D., Vanderbilt University, 1953. Cf. **L41.**

Q30 Khairallah, George A. "A Study of the Ethical Content of RPW's *AKM*." M.A., Columbia University, 1953.

Q31 Spicehandler, Daniel. "Self-Knowledge in the Novels of RPW." M.A., Columbia University, 1953.

Q32 Altgelt, Frederick. "RPW: A Study of Symbolism in *NR* and *WET*." M.A., Vanderbilt University, 1954.

Q33 Bankowsky, Richard J. "A Natural History of Supernaturalism: A Study of Three Poems by RPW." M.A., Columbia University, 1954.

Q34 Bowen, Frances J. "The New Orleans *Double Dealer*: 1921– May, 1926, A Critical History." Ph.D., Vanderbilt University, 1954.
   DA, 14, no. 11 (1954), 2063.

Q35 Brown, Jane E. "The 'New Criticism' and the Study of Poetry." M.A., University of Montana, 1954.

Q36 Godsey, Edwin S. "The Development of Tragedy in Four Novels by RPW." M.A., Vanderbilt University, 1954.

Q37 Montesi, Albert J. "*The Southern Review*: A History and Evaluation (1935–1942)." Ph.D., Pennsylvania State University, 1955.

Q38 White, Frank H. "RPW: His Critical Work as It Relates to the Form and Content of His Novels." B.A., Harvard University, 1955.

Q39 Whittington, Curtis C., Jr. "Dialectic Humanism and the Theme of RPW." M.A., Vanderbilt University, 1955.

Q40 Davis, Ellen A. "The Nature of Reality: A Study of the Poetry of RPW." M.A., Mississippi Southern College, 1956.

Q41 Girod, John G. "The Rednecks: A Study of the Use of the Huey Long Story in Five American Novels." B.A., Southwestern Louisiana Institute, 1956.

Q42 Klammer, Enno E. "The Philosophy of Man in the Novels of RPW." M.A., University of Nebraska, 1956.

Q43 Lane, Calvin W. "Narrative Art and History in RPW's *WET*." Ph.D., University of Michigan, 1956.
   DA, 17, no. 6 (1957), 1340.

Q44 Aden, William C. "RPW's Novels: The Major Theme." M.A., Cornell University, 1957.

Q45 Clark, Marden J. "Symbolic Structure in the Novels of RPW." Ph.D., University of Washington, 1957.
   DA, 18, no. 1 (1958), 229–230.

Q46 Eickhoff, Michael E. "*WET*, and RPW's Dialectic of Freedom and Necessity." M.A., University of Notre Dame, 1957.

Q47 England, Kenneth. "The Decline of the Southern Gentleman Character as He Is Illustrated in Certain Novels by Present-Day Southern Novelists." Ph.D., Vanderbilt University, 1957.

DA, 17, no. 11 (1957), 2594.

Q48 Geske, Anna D. "Conflict and Synthesis in RPW's Concept of Human Nature." M.A., University of Iowa, 1957.

Q49 Linenthal, Mark, Jr. "RPW and the Southern Agrarians." Ph.D., Stanford University, 1957.

DA, 17, no. 11 (1957), 2611–2612.

Q50 New, Ina C. "The Kentucky Tragedy as a Literary Source." M.A., Louisiana State University, 1957.

Q51 Poenicke, Klaus. "Schopferische Dialektik: Kunstwerk und kritische Theorie bei RPW." Ph.D., Freie Univeritat (Berlin), 1957. Cf. **K2.**

Q52 Strauss, Gerald H. "The *Double Dealer* (1921–1926): A Little Magazine from the South." M.A., Columbia University, 1957.

Q53 Borchers, Nancy N. "RPW's Novels: The Differences within the Framework of the Similarities." M.A., Vanderbilt University, 1958.

Q54 DiLorenzo, Ronald E. "The Literary Criticism of RPW." M.A., University of Iowa, 1958.

Q55 Samuels, Charles T. "As Brutus Killed Caesar: Tragedy in the Novels of RPW." M.A., Ohio State University, 1958.

Q56 Welker, Robert L. "Evelyn Scott: A Literary Biography." Ph.D., Vanderbilt University, 1958.

DA, 19, no. 5 (1958), 1080.

Q57 White, Paula S. "RPW's Image of the South." M.A., University of Hawaii, 1958.

Q58 Engelbrecht, Donald H. "*BD*: The Many Voices of RPW." M.A., Arizona State University, 1959.

Q59 Prater, Neal Byron. "Point of View in the Novels of R.P.W." M.A., Vanderbilt University, 1959.

Q60 Pryor, William L. "An Examination of the Southern Milieu in Representative Plays by Southern Dramatists, 1923–1956." Ph.D., Florida State University, 1959.

DA, 20, no. 2 (1959), 674–675.

Q61 Stuckey, William J. "A Critical History of the Pulitzer Prize Novels." Ph.D., Washington University, 1959.

DA, 20, no. 9 (1960), 3755.

Q62 Ward, Frank W., III. "The Problem of Focus of Narration in *AKM*." M.A., Texas Christian University, 1959.

Q63 Brubaker, DeLacy P. "The Theme of the Father in the Novels of RPW." M.A., Columbia University, 1960.

Q64 Estes, Phoebe B. "RPW's Philosophy of Existence: A Study of *AKM*." M.A., Duke University, 1960.

Q65 Helbling, Sister Mary Raphael. "Responsibility and the Self in RPW's *AKM*." M.A., University of Notre Dame, 1960.

Q66 Maguire, Merrill A. "The Role of the Negro in RPW's Work." M.A., Duke University, 1960.

Q67 Peck, Robert A. "RPW and the Philosophical Novel." B.A., Dartmouth College, 1960.

Q68 Stone, Edith O. "Democratic Values in Modern Narrative Poems." Ph.D., University of Michigan, 1960.

DA, 21, no. 2 (1960), 345.

Q69 Whyte, Samuel W. "Agrarianism and Father Rejection in Three RPW Novels." M.A., Bowling Green State University, 1960.

Q70 Williamson, Jerry M. "The Patterned Protagonist in RPW's Novels." M.A., Florida State University, 1960.

Q71 Bamberg, Robert D. "Plantation and Frontier: A View of Southern Fiction." Ph.D., Cornell University, 1961.

DA, 22, no. 6 (1961), 1973–1974.

Q72 Baumback, Jonathan. "The Theme of Guilt and Redemption in the Post-Second-World-War American Novel." Ph.D., Stanford University, 1961.

DA, 22, no. 5 (1961), 1620–1621.

Q73 Conwell, Ina C. "Justice in RPW's *WET*." M.A., Emory University, 1961.

Q74 Gossett, Louise Y. "Violence in Recent Southern Fiction." Ph.D., Duke University, 1961. Cf. **L66**.

DA, 23, no. 1 (1962), 233–234.

Q75 Hudnall, Clayton E. "Nathaniel Hawthorne and RPW: Studies in the Uses of Evil." M.A., University of Iowa, 1961.

Q76 Justus, James H. "The Concept of Gesture in the Novels of RPW." Ph.D., University of Washington, 1961.

DA, 22, no. 9 (1962), 3201.

Q77 Reedy, Jerry E. "RPW and the Criticism of Warren's Novels." M.A., University of South Dakota, 1961.

Q78 Rock, Virginia J. "The Making and Meaning of *ITMS*: A Study in Utopian-Conservatism, 1925–1939." Ph.D., University of Minnesota, 1961.
DA, 23, no. 10 (1964), 4197–4198.

Q79 Samuels, Charles T. "RPW: The End and the Beginning." Ph.D., University of California at Berkeley, 1961.
DA, 22, no. 13 (1962), 143, without abstract.

Q80 Shaw, Ann B. "Conradian Elements in the Novels of RPW." M.A., University of Tennessee, 1961.
In Kentucky Microcards, Series A; Modern Language Series, no. 112 (SAMLA).

Q81 Buchsbaum, Betty S. "RPW: Philosophical Novelist and the Psychological Novel." M.A., Brown University, 1962.

Q82 Elliott, Mary A. "The Southern Fugitives: Their Opposition to the Mid-Western School of Whitmanesque Poetry." M.A., University of Maryland, 1962.

Q83 Hebert, Laurel A. "Self-Knowledge in the Novels of RPW." M.A., University of Oregon, 1962.

Q84 Kauth, Priscilla J. "Hemingway, Steinbeck, Warren, and Faulkner: The Sense of the Past." M.A., Stetson University, 1962.
Noted in Nakadate, p. 345.

Q85 McDonald, Alma J. "Pure and Impure Poetry: RPW's *SP*." M.A., University of South Carolina, 1962.

Q86 McPherson, David C. "RPW and the South." M.A., University of Texas at Austin, 1962.

Q87 Nicholson, Paul J., Jr. "RPW's Philosophy: The Theme of Knowledge in *AKM*." M.A., Oklahoma State University, 1962.

Q88 Roden, Jerry. "Technique and Tragedy in the Novels of RPW." Ph.D., Auburn University, 1962.

Q89 Strandberg, Victor H. "RPW as Poet: A Close Analysis of *SP*, *BD*, *P*, and *YEO*." Ph.D., Brown University, 1962. Cf. **K10**.
DA, 23, no. 6 (1962), 2141–2142.

Q90 Blum, Ida S. "Webs and Wilderness: The Development of RPW as a Novelist." B.A., University of Pennsylvania, 1963.

Q91 Dunn, Sharon K. E. "Isolation and Definition of the Individual: Related Themes in the Novels of RPW." M.A., Stanford University, 1963.

Q92 Harrington, Catherine S. "Southern Fiction and the Quest for Identity." Ph.D., University of Washington, 1963.
DA, 25, no. 2 (1964), 1210–1211.

Q93 Reaves, Gary R. "The Significance of Time in the Novels of RPW." M.A., Sam Houston State Teachers College, 1963.

Q94 Waggoner, William H. "Politics and the Image of Man in RPW's Early Novels." M.A., Brown University, 1963.

Q95 Whittington, Joseph R. "The Regional Novel of the South: The Definition of Innocence." Ph.D., University of Oklahoma, 1963.
 DA, 24, no. 10 (1964), 4202–4203.

Q96 Hohl, Edward D. "RPW and Pragmatism." M.A., Stanford University, 1964.

Q97 Moore, Littleton Hugh, Jr., "RPW and History: 'The Big Myth We Live.'" Ph.D., Emory University, 1964. Cf. **K13**.
 DA, 25, no. 9 (1965), 5283–5284.

Q98 Poe, John W. "An Emerging Consciousness in Southern Literature in Twain, Faulkner, Warren, and McCullers." M.A., Kansas State Teachers College, 1964.

Q99 Scott, Willye B. "RPW: A Modern Novelist's Image of American Experience." M.A., North Carolina Central University, 1964.

Q100 West, Mary A. B. "The Image of Man: The Problem of Self-Definition in the Novels of RPW." M.A., Washington State University, 1964.

Q101 Attinello, Eleanor V. "Romanticism as a Literary Theme: RPW and Some Predecessors." M.A., Columbia University, 1965.

Q102 Freeman, Mary G. "The Betrayal Theme in RPW's Novels." M.A., University of Tennessee, 1965.

Q103 Hornsby, Samuel G. "The Problem of Evil in the Early Novels of RPW." M.A., University of Georgia, 1965.

Q104 Lewis, Ann H. "The Logic of Experience: RPW's Use of History in *W*." M.A., Emory University, 1965.

Q105 McWalters, Mary E. "Archetypal Patterns in RPW's *AKM*." M.A., University of Virginia, 1965.

Q106 Milliner, Gladys W. "The Sense of Guilt and Isolation in Faulkner and Warren." M.A., Tulane University, 1965.

Q107 Shepherd, Allen G., III. "A Critical Study of the Fiction of RPW." Ph.D., University of Pennsylvania, 1965.
 DA, 26, no. 12 (1966), 7325–7326.

Q108 Steadmon, Jerry D. "Search for Identity in the Novels of RPW." M.A., Eastern New Mexico University, 1965.

Q109 Webber, Winona L. "Old Court and New Court: Justice in RPW's Fiction." M.A., Duke University, 1965.

Q110 Bishoff, Robert E. "Pragmatic Man in Search of Himself: A Study of the Novels of RPW." M.A., New Mexico Highlands University, 1966.

Q111 Byrd, John C. "The Troubled Southerner: RPW as a Social Critic." M.A., University of Arizona, 1966.

Q112 Cheney, Thomas P. "An Analysis of the Poetry of RPW for Oral Interpretation." M.A., Baylor University, 1966.

Q113 Crane, John K. "The Psychological Experience of Time in the Novels of Thomas Hardy." Ph.D., Pennsylvania State University, 1966.

    Note: discusses *AKM*, pp. 11–13.

Q114 Crick, J. Brian. "RPW and 'A Poem of Pure Imagination.'" M.A., University of Western Ontario, 1966.

Q115 Dooley, Dennis M. "'The Awful Responsibility of Time': A Study of Warren's Concept of the Hero in Early Novels." M.A., Kent State University, 1966.

Q116 Halverstadt, Barbara H. "The Culmination of Images in RPW's *Cave*." M.A., University of North Carolina at Chapel Hill, 1966.

Q117 Hill, Michael F. "Primitivism in the Novels of RPW." M.A., McNeese State University, 1966.

Q118 Lankford, Willard P. "A Consideration of the Concept of 'The Speaking Voice': How It Is Used as a Technique for Character Development in *AKM*." M.A., Indiana University of Pennsylvania, 1966.

    Noted in Nakadate, p. 347.

Q119 Platzker, Doris A. "Public Vistas, Private Visions: Aspects of the Modern American Political Imagination." Ph.D., Yale University, 1966.

    DA, 28, no. 1 (1967), 241A.

Q120 Cioffari, Philip E. "Major Themes in Southern Fiction Since World War II." Ph.D., New York University, 1967.

    DA, 30, no. 10 (1970), 4402A.

Q121 Cook, Martha E. "From Fact to Fiction: A Study of RPW's *WET*." M.A., Vanderbilt University, 1967.

Q122 Cramer, James M. "Moral Structure in the Novels of RPW." B.A., Rutgers University, 1967.

Q123 Davenport, F. Garvin, Jr. "The Myth of Southern History— Twentieth-Century Variations." Ph.D., University of Minnesota, 1967. Cf. **L91**.

DA, 28, no. 9 (1968), 3666A.

Q124 Kehl, Delmar G. "The Dialectics of Reality in the Fiction of RPW." Ph.D., University of Southern California, 1967.

DA, 28, no. 11 (1968), 4633A.

Q125 Leahy, Paula A. "Time in Selected Novels of RPW and William Faulkner." B.A., Arizona State University, 1967.

Q126 Pfeiffer, Andrew H. "The Historical Dimension and the Modern Southern Novel: Studies in the Use of History and the Philosophy of History in the Novels of Mary Johnston, Ellen Glasgow, and RPW." M.A., Vanderbilt University, 1967.

Q127 Ross, Joe C. "RPW and the Negro." Ph.D., Vanderbilt University, 1967.

DA, 29, no. 12 (1969), 4501–4502A.

Q128 Wenstrand, Thomas E. "An Analysis of Style: The Application of Sector Analysis to Examples of American Prose Fiction." Ph.D., Columbia University, 1967.

DA, 28, no. 5 (1967), 1799A.

Q129 Wilson, G. Ronald. "Comparing and Contrasting Characters as a Device in the Development of RPW's Novel *W*." M.A., Indiana University of Pennsylvania, 1967.

Q130 Cayton, Robert F. "Point of View in the Novels of RPW." Ph.D., Ohio University, 1968.

DA, 30, no. 1 (1969), 313–314A.

Q131 Fridy, Wilford E. "RPW's Use of Kentucky Materials in His Fiction as a Basis for His New Mythos." Ph.D., University of Kentucky, 1968.

DA, 30, no. 4 (1969), 1523A.

Q132 Grimshaw, James A., Jr. "*AKM*: Tragedy or Melodrama?" M.A., Texas Technological College, 1968.

Q133 Herring, Henry Dunham. "The Environment in RPW's Fictional South." Ph.D., Duke University, 1968.

DA, 29, no. 9 (1969), 3141A.

Q134 Huff, Mary Nance. "RPW: A Bibliography." M.A., Vanderbilt University, 1968. Cf. **R16**.

Q135 Moses, Henry Clay, III. "History as Voice and Metaphor: A Study of Tate, Warren, and Faulkner." Ph.D., Cornell University, 1968.

DA, 29, no. 11 (1969), 4014A.

Q136 Rosenkrantz, Josi D. "RPW and the Fragmentation of the Twentieth-Century Mind: Putting Humpty-Dumpty Together

Again." M.A., University of Wisconsin, 1968.

Q137 Schmidt, Mary P. "Betrayal and Identity in RPW: A Study of *BW*, *CA*, and *WET*." M.A., Wichita State University, 1968.

Q138 Chambers, Robert H., III. "RPW: His Growth as a Writer." Ph.D., Brown University, 1969.

  DA, 31, no. 1 (1970), 381–382A.

Q139 Colbert, William J. "RPW: The Enduring Search for Self-Knowledge." M.A., University of Mississippi, 1969.

Q140 Elkins, Dean R. "A Bibliographical and Critical Essay upon the RPW Collection at the University of Kentucky with a Sample Catalogue." M.A., University of Louisville, 1969.

Q141 McNutt, Anne S. "A Critical Analysis of the Women in RPW's Novels." M.A., East Tennessee State University, 1969.

Q142 Michaelson, Edith L. "Self-Knowledge and History in Three Novels by RPW." M.A., Hunter College, 1969.

Q143 Norris, Carolyn B. "The Image of the Physician in Modern American Literature." Ph.D., University of Maryland, 1969.

  DA, 31, no. 2 (1970), 765A.

Q144 Orta, Marjorie P. H. "'Identity,' the 'Unconscious Self,' and the 'Journey to the West' as Themes in RPW's *BD*." M.A., University of Georgia, 1969.

Q145 Summers, Marcia P. "The Use of Subordinate Characters as Dramatized Narrators in Twentieth-Century Novels." Ph.D., University of Illinois, 1969.

  DA, 30, no. 9 (1969), 3024A.

Q146 Tretter, Irene S. "RPW's Southern Experience." M.A., University of Iowa, 1969.

Q147 Wallace, Margaret. "RPW's Dialectic Argument for Knowledge." M.A., Murray State University (Kentucky), 1969.

Q148 Woods, Linda L. "The Language of RPW's Poetry." Ph.D., Emory University, 1969.

  DA, 30, no. 5 (1969), 2049A.

Q149 Alexander, Jeanette. "RPW: Prejudice and the Southern Intellect." M.A., Emory University, 1970.

Q150 Benton, Paul F., Jr. "The Doubleness of Life: A Study of the First Four Novels of RPW." Ph.D., Princeton University, 1970.

  DA, 31, no. 2 (1971), 6590A.

Q151 Clark, Mary Scott. "Religious Currents in the Work of RPW." M.A., University of Maine, 1970.

Q152 Dooley, Dennis M. "This Collocation of Memories: The Poetic Strategy of RPW." Ph.D., Vanderbilt University, 1970.

DA, 31, no. 3 (1970), 1268–1269A.

Q153 Hillard, Jane O. "The Burden of Incomplete Knowledge: RPW's *AKM*." M.A., University of Louisville, 1970.

Q154 Kemmerle, Mark F. "The Philosophy and World View of RPW in *BD*." B.A., Brown University, 1970.

Q155 Lentz, Perry C. "Our Missing Epic: A Study in Novels about the American Civil War." Ph.D., Vanderbilt University, 1970.

DA, 31, no. 10 (1971), 5412A.

Q156 Love, Patrick J. "The Significance of the Parallels Between T. S. Eliot's *The Waste Land* and RPW's *AKM*." M.A., Texas A&M University, 1970.

Q157 Olson, H. Lynette. "The American Negro in Selected Writings of RPW." M.A., South Dakota State University, 1970.

Q158 Patton, Jon W. "Huey Long in American Fiction." M.A., University of Tennessee, 1970.

Q159 Stitt, Peter Allison. "The Poetry of Agrarianism: A Study of Donald Davidson, John Crowe Ransom, Allen Tate, and RPW." Ph.D., University of North Carolina at Chapel Hill, 1970.

DA, 31, no. 8 (1971), 4181A.

Q160 Sullivan, James P. "A Study of the Critical Theory and Pedagogical Works of Cleanth Brooks and RPW." Ph.D., New York University, 1970.

DA, 31, no. 5 (1970), 2403–2404A.

Q161 Brown, Harry N. "Warren's Continuing Quests: A Trinity." Ph.D., Ohio University, 1971.

DA, 32, no. 5 (1971), 2676A.

Q162 Burke, Lawrence M. "The Lonely Choice: A Study of the Early Fiction of RPW." Ph.D., Columbia University, 1971.

DA, 35, no. 7 (1975), 4501–4502A.

Q163 Chushman, Mortimer A. "Continuing Tradition in America: The Fugitive / Southern Agrarian Resurrection of New Humanist Values." Ph.D., University of Maryland, 1971.

DA, 32, no. 7 (1972), 3914A.

Q164 Hoskins, Robert V. "The Symbol of the Severed Head in Twentieth-Century British and American Fiction." Ph.D., University of Kentucky, 1971.

DA, 33, no. 2 (1972), 756A.

Q165 Phillips, Billie R. S. "RPW's Archetypal Triptych: A Study of the Myths of the Garden, the Journey, and Rebirth in *Cave*, *W*, and *F*." Ph.D., North Texas State University, 1971.

DA, 32, no. 12 (1972), 6998A.

Q166 Thomas, Leroy. "An Analysis of the Theme of Alienation in the Fictional Works of Five Contemporary Southern Writers." Ph.D., Oklahoma State University, 1971.
DA, 33, no. 2 (1972), 768A.

Q167 Allmon, Charmaine. "The Agrarian Myth as Metaphor in Novels of the Nineteenth-Century South." Ph.D., University of North Carolina at Chapel Hill, 1972.
DA, 33, no. 4 (1972), 1711A.

Q168 Golden, Daniel. "Shapes and Strategies: Forms of Modern American Fiction in the Novels of RPW, Saul Bellow, and John Barth." Ph.D., Indiana University, 1972.
DA, 33, no. 6 (1972), 2933–2934A.

Q169 Grimshaw, James A., Jr. "RPW: A Bibliographical Catalogue, Being a Description of His First American Editions Printed Through 31 December 1971, along with Individual Titles, an Annotated Checklist of Secondary Sources, and an Index." Ph.D., Louisiana State University, 1972.
DA, 33, no. 5 (1972), 2375A.

Q170 Guttenberg, Barnett. "The Novels of RPW." Ph.D., Cornell University, 1972. Cf. **K16**.
DA, 33, no. 3 (1972), 1169A.

Q171 Nakadate, Neil E. "The Narrative Stances of RPW." Ph.D., Indiana University, 1972.
DA, 33, no. 5 (1972), 2386A.

Q172 Thompson, David, J. S. "Societal Definitions of Individualism and the Critique of Egotism as a Major Theme in American Fiction." Ph.D., Brown University, 1972.
DA, 33, no. 8 (1973), 4435A.

Q173 Tipton, Juanita E. "RPW's South from *JB* to *F*." M.A., University of Georgia, 1972.

Q174 Yeatman, John R. "Narrators and Commentators in Four Novels by RPW." Ph.D., University of Oregon, 1972.
DA, 33, no. 5 (1972), 2399A.

Q175 Ahlport, Daniel B. "Time and the Search for Self in Warren's *AHG*." M.A., University of North Carolina at Chapel Hill, 1973.

Q176 Appleyard, Diane P. "RPW and the Spirit of History: A Study of *AHG*." M.A., Vanderbilt University, 1973.

Q177 Clark, William B. "The Serpent of Lust in the Southern Garden: The Theme of Miscegenation in Cable, Twain, Faulkner, and Warren." Ph.D., Louisiana State University, 1973.
DA, 34, no. 9 (1974), 5958–5959A.

Q178 Ellis, Helen E. "Sunday School and Satire—the Tension in RPW's Novels." Ph.D., University of Massachusetts, 1973.
 DA, 34, no. 7 (1974), 4257–4258A.

Q179 Law, Richard G. "'The Mastering Vision': The Early Fiction of RPW." Ph.D., University of Washington, 1973.
 DA, 34, no. 12 (1974), 7762–7763A.

Q180 Stevens, Gary W. "The Novels of RPW: The Theme of Community." Ph.D., University of Illinois, 1973.
 DA, 34, no. 9 (1974), 5996–5997A.

Q181 Vliet, Rodney M. "The Concept of Evil in the Novels of RPW." Ph.D., Michigan State University, 1973.
 DA, 35, no. 3 (1974), 1677A.

Q182 Williams, Mina G. "The Sense of Place in Southern Fiction." Ph.D., Louisiana State University, 1974.
 DA, 34, no. 6 (1973), 3440–3441A.

Q183 Betz, Norman J. "RPW and Pragmatism." Ph.D., University of North Carolina at Chapel Hill, 1974.
 DA, 36, no. 1 (1975), 299A.

Q184 Williams, Wallace A. "Religious Ethics in the Writings of RPW." Ph.D., Southern Baptist Theological Seminary, 1974.
 DA, 35, no. 8 (1975), 5519–5520A.

Q185 Saine, James H. "Southern Agrarianism and the Civil War Biographies of Allen Tate, Andrew Nelson Lytle, and RPW." M.A., University of North Carolina at Chapel Hill, 1975.

Q186 Jabol, George J. "RPW: Philosopher-Novelist." Ph.D., University of Michigan, 1976.
 DA, 37, no. 10 (1977), 6485–6486A.

Q187 Lubarsky, Richard J. "The Instructive Fact of History: A Study of RPW's *BD*." Ph.D., University of Pennsylvania, 1976.
 DA, 37, no. 11 (1977), 7130–7131A.

Q188 Rotella, Guy L. "'Mediation of the Heart': The Tragic Theme in the Poetry of RPW." Ph.D., Boston College, 1976.
 DA, 37, no. 3 (1976), 1553–1554A.

Q189 Witteveld, Peter J. "A Light in the Dark Place: The Hawthorne-Warren Relationship." Ph.D., Brown University, 1976.
 DA, 38, no. 1 (1977), 270–271A.

Q190 Bartsch, Friedemann K. "The Redemptive Vision: RPW and Spiritual Autobiography." Ph.D., Indiana University, 1977.
 DA, 38, no. 4 (1977), 2117–2118A.

Q191 Carman, Phillip L. "A Bibliographical Study of the Major Fugitive Poets: Donald Davidson, John Crowe Ransom, Allen Tate and RPW." Ph.D., Tulsa University, 1977.

    DA, 38, no. 3 (1977), 1385A.

Q192 Ford, Thomas W. "Indian Summer and Blackberry Winter: Emily Dickinson and RPW." Paper read at the South Central Society for the Study of Southern Literature, 1977.

Q193 Haynes, Robert P. "Warren the Novelist." Ph.D., University of Illinois at Urbana-Champaign, 1977.

    DA, 38, no. 6 (1977), 3499A.

Q194 Lee, Young-Oak. "After the Fall: Tragic Themes in the Major Works of Nathaniel Hawthorne and RPW." Ph.D., University of Hawaii, 1977.

    DA, 38, no. 10 (1978), 6195–6196A.

Q195 Surrency, Jack E. "The Kentucky Tragedy in American Literature: From Thomas Holley Chivers to RPW." Ph.D., University of Tennessee, 1977.

    DA, 38, no. 2 (1977), 792–793A.

Q196 Ahlport, Daniel B. "The Redeeming Form: Tradition in Ransom, Davidson, Tate, Lytle, and Warren." Ph.D., University of North Carolina at Chapel Hill, 1978.

    DA, 40, no. 1 (1979), 255A.

Q197 Burnes, Ann P. "Mannerist Mythopoesis: A Reading of Warren's *BD*." Ph.D., St. Louis University, 1978.

    DA, 39, no. 3 (1978), 1560–1561A.

Q198 Hanson, Sandra S. "'In Separateness Only Does Love Learn Definition': The Idea of Love in the Novels of RPW." Ph.D., New York University, 1978.

    DA, 39, no. 6 (1978), 3558–3559A.

Q199 Bell, Marie O. K. "The Personified Author in Fiction: Hawthorne, Warren, and Fowles." Ph.D., University of North Carolina at Chapel Hill, 1979.

    DA, 40, no. 5 (1979), 2659–2660A.

Q200 Funk, Ruth C. "Order and Chaos: A Study of Cultural Dialectic in Adams, James, Cather, Glasgow, Warren, and Fitzgerald." Ph.D., Syracuse University, 1979.

    DA, 40, no. 5 (1979), 2679A.

Q201 Newlin, Louisa F. "RPW's Use of History in *AKM*." Ph.D., American University, 1979.

    DA, 40, no. 2 (1979), 857A.

R

Checklists

R1 Stallman, Robert Wooster. "RPW: A Checklist of His Critical Writings." *University of Kansas City Review*, 14 (Autumn 1947), 78–83.

R2 Arms, George, and Joseph M. Kuntz. *Poetry Explication*. Denver: Alan Swallow, 1950; rev. ed., 1962. Pp. 276–279.

R3 Leary, Lewis, ed. *Articles on American Literature, 1900–1950*. Durham: Duke University Press, 1951; *1950–1967*, 1970; and continuing.

R4 Elton, William. *A Guide to the New Criticism*. Chicago: University of Chicago Press, 1953.

R5 Cheney, Frances, comp. *Sixty American Poets, 1896–1944*. Rev. ed. Washington, D.C.: Library of Congress, 1954. Pp. 139–141.

R6 Leary, Lewis, ed. *Contemporary Literary Scholarship: A Critical Review*. New York: Appleton-Century-Crofts, 1958.

R7 Ludwig, Richard M., ed. *Literary History of the United States: Bibliographical Supplement*. New York: Macmillan Company, 1959. Pp. 234–236. *Bibliographical Supplement II, 1958–1970*, 1972.

R8 Beebe, Maurice, and Erin Marcus. "Criticism of RPW: A Selected Checklist." *MFS*, 6 (Spring 1960), 83–88.

R9 Casper, Leonard. *RPW: The Dark and Bloody Ground*. Seattle: University of Washington Press, 1960. Pp. 191–208. **K4**.

R10 Jones, Joseph, et al. *American Literary Manuscripts: A Checklist of Holdings in Academic, Historical, and Public Libraries in the United States*. Austin: University of Texas Press, 1960. P. 391.

R11 Millett, Fred B. *Contemporary American Authors: A Critical Survey and 219 Bio-Bibliographies*. New York: Harcourt, Brace and Company, 1960. Pp. 628–629.

R12 Nyren, Dorothy, ed. *A Library of Literary Criticism: Modern American Literature*. New York: Frederick Ungar, 1960. Pp. 503–508.

R13 Thurston, Jarvis, et al. *Short Fiction Criticism: A Checklist of In-

terpretation Since 1925 of Stories and Novelettes. Denver: Alan Swallow, 1960.

R14   Gerstenberger, Donna, and George Hendrick. *The American Novel, 1789–1959: A Checklist of Twentieth-Century Criticism on Novels Written Since 1789.* Denver: Alan Swallow, 1961. Pp. 252–254. Vol. II, *Criticism Written 1960–1968.* Chicago: Swallow Press, 1970.

R15   Meriwether, James B. "RPW." *South: Modern Southern Literature in Its Cultural Setting.* Ed. Louis D. Rubin, Jr., and Robert D. Jacobs. Garden City, NY: Doubleday, 1961. Pp. 425–428.

R16   Walker, Warren S. *Twentieth-Century Short Story Explication: Interpretations, 1900–1960 Inclusive, of Short Fiction Since 1800.* Hamden, CT: Shoe String Press, 1961. Pp. 347–348. Supplements issued.

R17   Gohdes, Clarence. *Bibliographical Guide to the Study of the Literature of the U.S.A.* Rev. ed. Durham: Duke University Press, 1963.

R18   Ethridge, James M., and Barbara Kopala, eds. *Contemporary Authors: A Bio-Bibliographical Guide to Current Authors and Their Works.* Detroit: Gale Research, 1965. Pp. 462–463.

R19   Huff, Mary Nance, comp. *RPW: A Bibliography.* A Fugitive Bibliography. New York: David Lewis, 1968. *See* **Q134**.

R20   Rock, Virginia J. "Agrarianism: Agrarian Themes and Ideas in Southern Writing." *MissQ*, 21 (Spring 1968), 145–156.

R21   Elkins, Dean R. "A Bibliographical and Critical Essay upon the RPW Collection at the University of Kentucky with a Sample Catalogue." M.A., University of Louisville, 1969. *See* **Q140**.

R22   Phillips, Robert S. *The Achievement of William Van O'Connor: A Checklist of Publications and an Appreciation; with an Inventory of His Manuscripts in the George Arents Research Library at Syracuse University Compiled by Glenn B. Skillin.* [Syracuse]: George Arents Research Library, Syracuse University, 1969.

R23   Strandberg, Victor H. "RPW (1905–)." *A Bibliographical Guide to the Study of Southern Literature.* Ed. Louis D. Rubin, Jr. Baton Rouge: Louisiana State University Press, 1969. Pp. 316–320.

R24   Nevius, Blake. *The American Novel: Sinclair Lewis to the Present.* Goldentree Bibliographies. Northbrook, IL: AHM Publishing Corp., 1970. Pp. 93–96.

R25   Justus, James H. "Fiction: The 1930's to the Present." *American Literary Scholarship*, no. 9 (1971), pp. 245–276.

R26   Adelman, Irving, and Rita Dworkin. *The Contemporary Novel: A Checklist of Critical Literature on the British and American Novel Since 1945.* Metuchen, NJ: Scarecrow Press, 1972. Pp. 534–548.

R27 B[ethel], D[enise], and M[aria] B[rown]. "Books by RPW." *Hollins Critic*, 9 (April 1972), 6–7.

R28 Grimshaw, James A., Jr. "RPW: A Bibliographical Catalogue . . . ." Ph.D., Louisiana State University, 1972. *See* **Q169**.

R29 Woolmer, J. Howard. *A Catalogue of the Fugitive Poets*. With an essay by Louis D. Rubin, Jr. Focus Series, no. 3. Andes, NY: n.p., 1972.

R30 Grimshaw, James A., Jr. "RPW's *AKM*: An Annotated Checklist of Criticism." *RALS*, 6 (Spring 1976), 23–69.

R31 Carman, Phillip L. "A Bibliographical Study of the Major Fugitive Poets: Donald Davidson, John Crowe Ransom, Allen Tate, and RPW." Ph.D., Tulsa University, 1977. *See* **Q191**.

R32 Grimshaw, James A., Jr. "RPW [A Collector's Checklist]." *First Printings of American Authors*. Ed. Matthew J. Bruccoli and C. E. Frazer Clark, Jr. Detroit: Gale Research, 1977. I, 401–406.

R33 Nakadate, Neil. *RPW: A Reference Guide*. Boston: G. K. Hall, 1977.

R34 Williams, Jerry T., comp. *Southern Literature, 1968–1975: A Checklist of Scholarship*. SSSL. Boston: G. K. Hall, 1978. Pp. 197–202.

Appendixes

Appendix I

Manuscripts of Published Works

A TENTATIVE CATALOGUE

Note: Manuscripts of unpublished works are noted in section **I**. Arrangement of this appendix is by genre—fiction, poetry, drama, and nonfiction (all textbooks and anthologies are considered nonfiction, regardless of their subject matter); alphabetical by title within each genre; and alphabetical by location for each title. If a title is omitted, then I have been unable to locate the manuscript. Primary location designations are Ctw = the RPW deposit at the Beinecke Library at Yale; KyU = the Margaret I. King Library, Special Collections and Archives, University of Kentucky at Lexington; and SoR = *The Southern Review* files at Louisiana State University at Baton Rouge. One-item location abbreviations are listed in the front matter. The following abbreviations describe the manuscript holdings: OH = original holograph; CH = carbon holograph; OTS = original typescript; CTS = carbon typescript; O/CTS = mixed MS; MTS = multilith typescript; TTS = Thermofax typescript; XTS = Xerox typescript; GP = galley proofs; and PP = page proofs. An Arabic numeral in parentheses following the manuscript description indicates the number of copies unless specified otherwise. A Roman numeral indicates chapter, poem within a sequence, or act, as appropriate. Dates and other parenthetical data within quotation marks are found on the manuscripts, usually in RPW's own handwriting.

Occasionally I have noted the number of pages contained in the manuscripts, but I have not attempted to give page count for the longer entries. Readers might also note that the Ctw holdings are only on deposit and still belong to RPW. Understandably, that deposit has not yet been catalogued. The KyU holdings, on the other hand, have a preliminary catalogue prepared by Ms. Claire McCann.

A. FICTION

1. *AKM. Ctw*: OTS (with note, "For information concerning a passage omitted in printed book, see correspondence under Levensohn, Alan / dcg / March 1964"), CTS (canceled I, which begins, "The Boss was a son-of-a-bitch . . ."; for a reproduction of those first four pages, see Tschöpl, pp. 176–179); OTS (II, with note to see ltr., B. Cheney, 11/9/45), CTS; O/CTS (III, with extensive corrections); OTS, CTS (IV–X); OH (working notes); OTS, CTS (setting copy); GP (preliminary matter); PP.
2. *AHG. Ctw*: O/CTS, OTS (setting copy), CTS (summary of plot).
3. *BA, Ctw*: OTS (setting copy); OTS (with OH rev.); OH, OTS, and CTS (notes); TTS (V, frag.); GP (2, "14 April 1955" and "27 May 1955"); PP ("22 April 1955"); plate proofs. *KyU*: (CTS (background outline).
4. "Blackberry Winter." *Ctw*: OTS, CTS (frag., "first draft revised").
5. "Cass Mastern's Wedding Ring." *Ctw*: OTS (excerpt from *AKM*).
6. *Cave. Ctw*: OH (notes), OTS (I–XI, with title, "The Man Below"), CTS (complete), CTS (I–III), CTS (IV, frag.), OH ("notes for version C"), OTS ("canceled sheets, discarded in version C"), CTS (version C), C/TTS (with revisions), OTS (setting copy), GP ("29 April 1959"), PP. *KyU*: CTS (frag.), CTS (version C with notes by David Clay), GP.
7. "A Christian Education." *Ctw*: OTS.
8. "The Circus in the Attic." *Ctw*: OTS (early version, marked "deleted" and word count "19,750"), OTS (1st draft with comments by Paul Engle).
9. *CA. Ctb*: GP. *Ctw*: OTS (setting copy with CTS inserts), PP.
10. "The Confession of Brother Grimes." *Ctw*: OTS (2), CTS.
11. *F. Ctw*: OH (notes, frag. 1st draft), OTS (5, at various stages), CTS (4, some rejected leaves, *KR* excerpt), O/CTS (2), XTS (2, one excerpt for *SatEP* with title, "Playing Hell in Fiddlersburg"), GP (2, one dated "29 Oct. 1963"). *KyU*: OH and CTS (*SatEP* excerpt), CTS (2, one 1st draft, XVII wanting; the other, 2d draft), GP.
12. "Goodwood Comes Back." *Ctw*: OTS, CTS.
13. "Her Own People." *Ctw*: OTS (2).
14. "How Willie Proudfit Came Home." *Ctw*: OTS.
15. "The Life and Work of Professor Roy Millen." *Ctw*: OTS (2), CTS.

16. "The Love of Elsie Barton: . . . ." *Ctw*: OTS (3), CTS (3).
17. *MMGG*. *Ctw*: OH ("running work notes"), OH (I-VIII, with title, "Flight"), OTS (I–V, with title, "Love in a Valley"), CTS (I–IV, "2 Aug. 1963"; V–IX), XTS (7: one with comments on dialogue by P. M. Pasinetti; one with comments from Jordan Stokes, III; one with title, "But Not the Nightingale"; one, "draft—spring 1970"; one with comments by Eleanor Clark; one unmarked; one setting copy), GP (3: one "23 April 1971"; one "2 June 1971"; one undated), PP; plus assortment drafts of individual chapters at various stages of revision. *KyU*: CH and CTS (I–IV, with title, "Escape"), CH and CTS (V–XII, with title, "Love in the Valley").
18. *NR*. *KyU*: OTS (background material).
19. "The Patented Gate and the Mean Hamburger." *Ctw*: OTS, CTS. *KyU*: OH (1st draft), CTS (rev.).
20. *PTCT*. *Ctw*: OH (with I dated "23 Nov. 1971" and notes), OTS ("version 2 [Fall 1975]"), XTS (of chapters and worksheets), GP, PP, (3), blues (2); plus designer's layout of title page.
21. "Testament of Flood." *Ctw*: OTS (3).
22. "Unvexed Isles." *Ctw*: OTS.
23. "When the Light Gets Green." *Ctw*: OTS ("1st draft, 1933").
24. *W*. *KyU*: CTS (1st draft), OTS (2d draft), CTS (2d draft with corrections), OH (notes), OTS and CTS (summary of projected novel), OTS (with corrections of RPW's note for *Wings*), GP.

B. POETRY

1. "Acquaintance with Time in Autumn." *Ctw*: OH, OTS (3), CTS (6).
2. "Address of Soul to Body . . . ." *Ctw*: OTS (*NY* version), CTS (4).
3. "Adieu Sentimentale." *Ctw*: OTS.
4. "Admonition to the Dead." *Ctw*: OTS (3, one dated "1923").
5. "Admonition to Those Who Mourn." *Ctw*: OTS (with subtitle, "In Memoriam T.U.S.").
6. "After Teacups." *Ctw*: OTS.
7. "Aging Man in Woodland at Timeless Noon of Summer." *Ctw*: OH, OTS (3), CTS (3).
8. "Ah, Anima!" *Ctw*: OH ("10–11 Aug. 1976"), CTS.
9. "Amazing Grace in the Back Country." *Ctw*: OH, OTS.
10. "American Portrait: . . . ." *Ctw*: XTS (*NY* version).

11. "Apologia for Grief." *Ctw*: OTS.

12. "An Argument for Prayer." *Ctw*: OH ("23–25 Aug." [1977]), OTS (2), CTS (2), XTS. *SoR*: OTS.

13. "Arrogant Law." *Ctw*: OH, OTS, CTS. *KyU*: CTS ("15–18 Sept. 1958").

14. "Aspen Leaf in Windless World." *Ctw*: OH, OTS (3), CTS (4).

15. "Atheist at Hearthside." *Ctw*: OH (2), OTS, CTS (2).

16. "Athenian Death." *Ctw*: OTS.

17. *A. Ctw*: OH (prefatory note), OH (I–V, I "2 Feb." and V "10 Feb."), OH (IVc–e and Vc), OTS (1 p. with corrections), CTS (2 pp. with corrections), OTS (preliminary matter), OTS (I–III, V with corrections), OTS and XTS (with corrections marked "last revision"), O/CTS (setting copy), GP ("10 July 1969"), GP (*NY* version), PP. *KyU*: CTS (worksheets), CTS. *TNJ*: GP (uncorrected).

18. "August Moon." *Ctw*: OH ("29–31 July" [1978]), OTS, CTS (2).

19. "August Revival: Crosby Junction." *Ctw*: OTS (3), CTS.

20. "Auto-da-Fé." *Ctw*: OH, OTS (2), CTS (2).

21. "Bad Year, Bad War: . . . ." *Ctw*: OH, OTS, CTS. *KyU*: CH, CTS.

22. "Ballad: Between the Box Cars (1923)" seq. *Ctw*: OH, OTS, CTS. *KyU*: OH, CH, CTS (I); CH, CTS (II); CH, CTS (III, "6–7 Oct. 1958").

23. "Ballad of a Sweet Dream of Peace" subseq. *Ctw*: OH (2 versions), OTS, CTS (2).

24. "Ballad of Mr. Dutcher and the Last Lynching in Gupton." *Ctw*: OH ("3 March 1973"), OTS, CTS (2), MTS (with title, "Ballad of Mr. Crutcher and the Last Lynching in Guthrie").

25. "Better than Counting Sheep." *Ctw*: OH ("10–11 Feb." [1978]), CTS (2, one labeled "last version—Feb. 13").

26. "Bicentennial Ode." *Ctw*: OH, OTS (2), GP (*Esquire*).

27. "Birth of Love." *Ctw*: OH, OTS (2), CTS.

28. "Blow, West Wind." *Ctw*: OH, OTS (2 versions), CTS. *KyU*: CH, CTS.

29. "Boy Wandering . . . to Simm's Valley." *Ctw*: OH, OTS ("25 Aug." [1977]), CTS.

30. "Boy's Will . . ." seq. *Ctw*: OH, OTS (2), CTS (2).

31. *BD. Ctw*: OH, OTS, CTS (early version bearing title, "Ballad of the Brothers: A Murder Mystery"), CTS (with comments by A. Tate, S. Monk, and W. Van O'Connor), CTS (with rev.), OTS ("version IV" with corrections), CTS (2), OTS (pp. 21–24 and pp. 35–187), CTS (with "REPLACEMENT" typed at top of each

page), CTS (in folder marked "Rejected pages to version IV"), OH and OTS (assorted pages in two separate envelopes), OTS (setting copy), CTS (with note, "This is the last work version, from which final revisions were made. By accident a number of revisions on this copy were omitted from final printing / RPW" and labeled "version IV-3, copy 5"), *BD* (1st printing, labeled "work copy" with pp.97–98 torn out and penciled rev. throughout and dated on dw. "1960–1970"), GP (3: one with "4 June 1953"; another, "30 June 1953"), designer's corrections, PP.

32. "Caveat." *Ctw*: OH, OTS.
33. "Chain Saw in Vermont, in Time of Drouth." *Ctw*: OH, OTS (2 versions), CTS (2 versions, 3 copies of one, 1 copy of the other). *KyU*: CTS ("5 Aug. 1965").
34. "Code Book Lost." *Ctw*: OH (2, one dated "29–30 Aug." [1977]), OTS, CTS.
35. "Composition in Gold and Red-Gold." *Ctw*: OTS (2 versions), CTS (2 versions with title, "Autumn Composition . . .").
36. "Country Burying: 1919." *Ctw*: OH, OTS (2 versions).
37. "Courtmartial." *Ctw*: OH, OTS (2 versions).
38. "The Cross (A Theological Study)." *Ctw*: OH, OTS (2), CTS (3).
39. "Crusade." *Ctw*: OTS.
40. "Dark Night Of." *Ctw*: OH, OTS, CTS.
41. "Dark Woods" subseq. *Ctw*: OH, OTS (2).
42. "The Day Mr. Knox Did It" seq. *Ctw*: OH, OTS (3 versions), CTS (2 copies each of 2 versions). *KyU*: CTS (bears various dates between "8–20 Dec. 1965" with "Knott" instead of "Knox" in title).
43. "Debate: Question, Quarry, Dream." *Ctw*: OH ("8–15 March 1958"), OTS (2), CTS.
44. "Departure." *Ctw*: OH (2, one "17–19 Nov. 1976"), CTS.
45. "The Diver." *Ctw*: OH, OTS ("2–3 Oct." [1977]). *SoR*: OTS.
46. "Do You Agree with What I Say? . . . ." *Ctw*: OH, CTS. *KyU*: CH, CTS ("25–27 July 1959").
47. "Dragon Country: To Jacob Boehme." *Ctw*: OH, OTS.
48. "Dragon Tree." *Ctw*: OH, OTS, CTS. *KyU*: CH, CTS.
49. "Dream." *Ctw*: OH ("18–19 Sept." [1976]), OTS, CTS.
50. "Dream of a Dream." *Ctw*: OH ("20–25 July 1976"), CTS (2). *SoR*: OTS.
51. "Dream of a Dream the Small Boy Had." *Ctw*: OTS (2 versions), CTS (2 versions, with title, "If You Knew Everything You Would Be Smarter than God"). *KyU*: OH, CTS ("March 1965" and "22 July 1965").

52. "Dreaming in Daylight." *Ctw*: OH (2), CTS ("12–14 March" [1979]).
53. "Eagle Descending." *Ctw*: OH, OTS.
54. *EP*. *Ctw*: OH/OTS (poems in various versions).
55. "Elijah on Mt. Carmel." *Ctw*: OH, OTS (2).
56. "Empire." *Ctw*: OTS.
57. "Equinox on Mediterranean Beach." *Ctw*: OH, OTS, CTS. *KyU*: CH, CTS ("11–15 Sept. 1958").
58. "Evening Hawk." *Ctw*: OH, CTS ("9–12 Aug." [1975]).
59. "Evening Hour." *Ctw*: OH ("1–3 Aug. 1979"), CTS.
60. "Fairy Story." *Ctw*: OTS (*NY* version).
61. "Fall Comes in Back-Country Vermont" seq. *Ctw*: OH, OTS (2 versions), CTS (3). *KyU*: OH, CH, CTS (with title, "Life and Death in Back-Country Vermont").
62. "A Faring" seq. *Ctw*: OH. *KyU*: OH, CH (with heading, "The True Nature of Time").
63. "A Few Axioms for a Young Man." *Ctw*: OH, OTS, CTS (4), XTS.
64. "Filling Night with the Name." *Ctw*: OH, OTS (2, one "6–9 June 1978"; with subtitle, "Funeral as Local Color"), CTS (5).
65. "Finisterre." *Ctw*: CH, OTS. *KyU*: OH (with title, "Brittany Sunset").
66. "First Dawn Light." *Ctw*: OH ("9 July 1976"), CTS.
67. "Flaubert in Egypt." *Ctw*: OH, OTS, MTS (2), XTS.
68. "Folly on Royal Street . . . ." *KyU*: CH, CTS.
69. "Foreign Shore . . . ." *Ctw*: OH, OTS.
70. "Forever O'Clock." *Ctw*: OH ("9 April 1973"), OTS (2), CTS (2), MTS.
71. "Founding Fathers . . . ." *Ctw*: OH, OTS (2).
72. "From the Thicket Afar." *Ctw*: OH, CTS.
73. "Garland for You" seq. *Ctw*: OH (2), OTS (2), CTS, GP (*YR* version, "23 April 1958"). *KyU*: CH, CTS.
74. "Globe of Gneiss." *Ctw*: OH, CTS (2).
75. "Gold Glade." *Ctw*: OH, OTS.
76. "Goodbye." *Ctw*: OH, OTS (3), CTS (2).
77. "Grackles, Goodbye!" *Ctw*: OH, OTS, CTS (2).
78. "Heart of Autumn." *Ctw*: OH, OTS (2, rev. dated "12–14–16 Oct." [1976]), CTS.
79. "Heat Lightning." *Ctw*: OH ("10–18 Aug." [1977]), OTS (3), CTS (2).

80. "Heat Wave Brakes." *Ctw*: OH ("1–3 Sept. 1977"), CTS (with title, "Heat Wave").
81. "Holly and Hickory." *Ctw*: OH, OTS (2), CTS.
82. "Holy Writ" seq. *KyU*: CH, CTS ("begun 1960, finished 1965").
83. "Homage to Emerson . . ." seq. *Ctw*: OH (notes), OTS (3 versions), CTS (frag.); plus OTS (I, *NY* version). *KyU*: CH ("28 Dec. 1965"), CTS (2, one frag.).
84. "Homage to Theodore Dreiser" seq. *Ctw*: OH, CTS. *KyU*: CH, CTS.
85. "How To Tell a Love Story." *Ctw*: OH, OTS (with title, "How To Tell a Story").
86. "Hunting Season Opens . . . ." *Ctw*: OH, CTS.
87. "I knew not down what windy nights I fled." *Ctw*: OTS (with title, "Apocalypse").
88. "Ile de Port Cros . . ." seq. *Ctw*: OH, OTS, CTS.
89. "In Italian They Call the Bird *Civetta*." *Ctw*: OH, OTS (2, one "22 Sept. 1958"), CTS.
90. "In Moonlight, Somewhere, They Are Singing." *Ctw*: OH, OTS (4), CTS (2).
91. *I*. *Ctw*: OTS, CTS, GP (2, both dated "24 May 1968"); plus designer's layout of title page. *KyU*: GP (dup. set), PP.
92. "Inevitable Frontier." *Ctw*: OH, OTS (3, one "28 Nov. 1976"), CTS (2).
93. "Infant Boy at Midcentury" subseq. *Ctw*: OH, OTS (4).
94. "Internal Injuries" seq. *Ctw*: OH, CTS. *KyU*: CH, CTS (I–VIII).
95. "Into Broad Daylight." *Ctw*: OH, OTS, CTS, XTS. *KyU*: CH, CTS ("24 Oct. 1960").
96. "Images on the Tomb" seq. *Ctw*: OTS (IV, "1924").
97. "Iron Beach." *Ctw*: OTS.
98. "Island of Summer" seq. *Ctw*: CTS (I & V). *KyU*: CH, CTS (I–XV).
99. "It Is Not To Be Trusted." *Ctw*: OH, CH, OTS. *KyU*: CH, CTS ("3–21 June" with title, "Delight II").
100. "Language Problem." *Ctw*: OH, OTS (with title, "Language Barrier"), CTS (2, one "22 Nov. 1978").
101. "Last Laugh." *Ctw*: OH (2), OTS, CTS (2, one "12 Aug." [1977]).
102. "Lessons of History." *Ctw*: OH, OTS (with title, "Lessons in History"), CTS. *SoR*, CTS.

103. "The Limited." *Ctw*: OTS ("1931").

104. "Little Black Heart of the Telephone." *Ctw*: OH (2, one "summer 1975"), OTS.

105. "Little Boy and Lost Shoe." *Ctw*: OTS. *KyU*, OH.

106. "Lord Jesus, I Wonder." *Ctw*: OTS (2), CTS (5, one "10–12 May" [1979]).

107. "Loss, of Perhaps Love, ..." *Ctw*: OH, OTS (2, one is *NY* version), CTS ("15 Dec. 1974").

108. "Love at First Sight." *Ctw*: OH, CTS.

109. "Love: Two Vignettes" seq. *Ctw*: OH, CTS (5, four copies of one version, one copy of another). *KyU*: CH, CTS ("1 March 1965").

110. "Lullaby." *Ctw*: OH, OTS (2).

111. "Lullaby: A Motion Like Sleep." *Ctw*: OH, OTS, CTS.

112. "Mad Young Aristocrat on Beach." *Ctw*: OH, OTS.

113. "Man in Moonlight" seq. *Ctw*: OH, OTS (2), CTS (2).

114. "Man in the Street." *Ctw*: OH, OTS (2), CTS.

115. "Midnight." *Ctw*: OTS.

116. "Midnight Outcry." *Ctw*: OH ("19–21 Aug. 1975"), OTS.

117. "The Mirror." *Ctw*: CTS.

118. "The Mission." *Ctw*: OH, OTS, CTS (2).

119. "The Moon." *Ctw*: OTS.

120. "The Moonlight's Dream." *Ctw*: OH, OTS, CTS (5).

121. "Mortmain" seq. *Ctw*: OH (I–V), OTS (I & V), CTS (I & V). *KyU*: CH (II–V), CTS (V).

122. "Mountain Plateau." *Ctw*: OH, OTS (2), CTS (with comments by William Meredith).

123. "The Mouse." *Ctw*: OTS (2).

124. "Mr. Dodd's Son." *Ctw*: OTS.

125. "Myth on Mediterranean Beach: . . . ." *Ctw*: OH, CTS.

126. "The Natural History of a Vision." *Ctw*: OH, OTS (3), CTS, XTS ("8 March 1973").

127. "News Photo." *Ctw*: OH (2, with title, "News Photo of Man Coming Down Steps of Court House after Acquittal"), OTS (5), CTS (3). *KyU*: CH, CTS.

128. "Night Walking." *Ctw*: OH, OTS (2, one "2 Dec. 1978"), CTS (10). *SoR*: OTS.

129. "No Bird Does Call." *Ctw*: OH ("23 Oct." [1978]), CTS (3).

130. "Nocturne." *Ctw*: OTS.

131. "Nocturne: Traveling Salesman in Hotel Bedroom." *Ctw*: OH,

CTS. *KyU*: CH, CTS (dated as begun "Aug. 1949" and finished "1–2 March 1959").

132. "Not Quite Like a Top." *Ctw*: OH, CTS.

133. *NT*. *Ctw*: OTS (setting copy), CTS, GP (2), PP (2), blues; plus designer's layout of title page.

134. "Nursery Rhyme." *Ctw*: OH, OTS (2), CTS.

135. "October Picnic Long Ago." *Ctw*: OH ("1–4 Aug." [1978]), CTS (2).

136. "Old Flame." *Ctw*: OH, CTS.

137. "Old Nigger on One-Mule Cart . . . ." *Ctw*: OH, OTS (2, one is *NY* version), CTS ("4 April 1975").

138. "One Way to Love God." *Ctw*: OH, OTS, CTS ("2–8 Aug. 1975").

139. "The Only Poem." *Ctw*: OH, OTS, CTS (3).

140. *OEP*. *Ctb*: GP (uncorrected). *Ctw*: CTS, GP (2), XTS ("Master Copy—9 Nov. 1973"), XTS (with title, "Essay Toward the Human Understanding: Poem/Poems 1968–1973"), XTS (frag.), PP, blues.

141. "Or, Sometimes, Night." *Ctw*: OH, OTS, CTS ("23–26 March" [1973]).

142. "Ornithology in a World of Flux." *Ctw*: OH ("8 June 1958"), OTS (4), CTS.

143. "Orphanage Boy." *Ctw*: OH, CTS.

144. "Paradox." *Ctw*: OH, CTS.

145. "Patriotic Tour and Postulate of Joy." *Ctw*: OTS, CTS.

146. "Penological Study: . . ." seq. *Ctw*: OH, OTS, CTS. *KyU*: CH, CTS (I–VII).

147. "Penthesileas and Achilles . . . ." *Ctw*: OH, OTS (2), CTS (2, one "23 June 1958"). *KyU*: CH, CTS.

148. "Portraits of Three Ladies" seq. *Ctw*: OTS.

149. "Prairie Harvest." *Ctw*: OH, CTS (2, one "3–4 Dec." [1978]).

150. "Praise." *Ctw*: OH, CTS.

151. "Praises for Mrs. Dodd." *Ctw*: OTS (with title, "Praises for Mrs. Dodd Deceased").

152. "Preternaturally Early Snowfall in Mating Season." *Ctw*: OH, OTS ("29–31 Jan. 1979"), CTS (2), XTS (with title, "Big Early Snowfall").

153. "Pro Sua Vita." *Ctw*: OTS (2, "1926" and "1927").

154. "A Problem in Spatial Composition." *Ctw*: OH, OTS (2), CTS.

155. "Promises" seq. *Ctw*: OTS (3: one is setting copy; another is *YR*

version), CTS (sent to A. Tate for comment).

156. *P. Ctb*: GP ("uncorrected proof for advance readers"). *Ctw*: OTS (setting copy), GP (2, one "7 June"), PP. *KyU*: CTS (frag., with marginal notes by Denis Devlin), CTS (frag., with duplicate copies of several poems).

157. "Prognosis: . . ." seq. *Ctw*: OTS. *KyU*: OH, CTS (2).

158. "Rather Like a Dream." *Ctw*: OH, CTS (2). *SoR*: OTS.

159. "Rattlesnake Country." *Ctw*: OH, OTS, CTS, XTS (3, one is *Esquire* version), XP (2), PP.

160. "Reading Late at Night . . . ." *Ctw*: OH (with title, "Late Night Reading, Thermometer Falling"), OTS, CTS (2).

161. "Red Tail Hawk . . . ." *Ctw*: OH ("15 March 1977"), OTS (3), CTS (2).

162. "Remark for Historians." *Ctw*: OH, CTS (2, one "12 Aug. 1978").

163. "Saul." *Ctw*: OH, OTS, CTS (3).

164. "School Lesson Based on Word . . . ." *Ctw*: OH, OTS (2 versions, one with title, "School Lesson: A Short Story, But Not Too Short, For It Goes on Forever").

165. *SP*. *Ctw*: OTS (2, one setting copy); plus proofs of front matter.

166. *SPNO*. *Ctw*: OTS, CTS (setting copy), XTS (with rev. from previous vols.), XTS (cut and tape), GP (3, one "5 May 1966" and another "15 June 1966"), PP (2). *KyU*; GP (3).

167. *SP75*. *Ctw*: C/XTS ("author's working copy"), XTS (2, one stamped "setting copy"), GP (3), PP; also "master set repros" and OH (preface to Franklin Library ed.).

168. "Shoes in Rain Jungle." *Ctw*: CTS. *KyU*: OH, CTS.

169. "Short Thoughts for Long Nights" seq. *Ctw*: OH, OTS (2), CTS (2). *KyU*: CH, CTS ("8 June 1958").

170. "Sister Water." *Ctw*: OH, CTS (3).

171. "Small White House." *Ctw*: OH, OTS (with title, "Little White House").

172. "The Smile." *Ctw*: OH ("25–30 March" [1977]), CTS (with comments by William Meredith).

173. "Snowshoeing Back to Camp in Gloaming." *Ctw*: OH, OTS (4), CTS (5, one "5–6 March" [1978]).

174. "So many are the things that she has learned." *Ctw*: OTS (with title, "Mrs. Dodd's Daughter").

175. "Some Quiet, Plain Poems" seq. *Ctw*: entered by ind. poem. *KyU*: CH. CTS.

176. "Something Is Going to Happen." *Ctw*: OH, OTS (2 versions), CTS (3, one of one version, two of another). *KyU*: CH, CTS, XTS (with corrections).
177. "Somewhere." *Ctw*: OH ("28 Sept.–4 Oct." [1977]), CTS. *SoR*: OTS.
178. "Sonnet of a Rainy Summer." *Ctw*: OTS.
179. "Sonnet of August Drouth." *Ctw*: OTS.
180. "Speleology." *Ctw*: OH ("13–14 March 1978"), OTS, CTS (2).
181. "Star Fall." *Ctw*: OH, OTS, CTS.
182. "Stargazing." *Ctw*: OTS.
183. "Summer Storm (Circa 1916) and God's Grace." *Ctw*: OH, OTS (3), CTS.
184. "Sunset Walk in Thaw-Time in Vermont." *Ctw*: OH, OTS. *SoR*: OTS.
185. "Swimming in the Pacific." *Ctw*: OH, OTS (3), CTS (2).
186. "Switzerland." *Ctw*: OH, OTS (2), CTS (3).
187. "Synonyms" seq. *Ctw*: OH, OTS, CTS ("3–12 Feb." [1979]).
188. "Tale of Time" seq. *Ctw*: OH, OTS, CTS (I–VI). *KyU*: CTS (I–VI with title, "Toward Way of Solution").
189. "There's a Grandfather's Clock in the Hall." *Ctw*: OTS, CTS, MTS.
190. *TSP*. *Ctw*: OTS (some poems in several versions).
191. "[Three] Nursery Rhymes" seq. *Ctw*: OH, OTS (III), CTS (3, I & II; 2, III). *KyU*: CH, CTS ("from 16 March 1958 to 27 Sept. 1958").
192. "Time as Hypnosis." *Ctw*: OTS (3), XTS.
193. "Timeless, Twinned." *Ctw*: OH, OTS, CTS.
194. "Tires on Wet Asphalt at Night." *Ctw*: OH ("28–30 Sept." [1978]), OTS, CTS.
195. "To a Little Girl, One Year Old, ..." *Ctw*: OH, OTS, CTS (2, one is "final draft"), XTS.
196. "Trips to California." *Ctw*: OH ("1–2 Dec. 1978"), CTS (2).
197. "Truth." *Ctw*: OH, OTS, CTS (2).
198. "Trying To Tell You Something." *Ctw*: OH, CTS.
199. "Two Pieces after Suetonius" seq. *Ctw*: OTS (2), CTS (3). *KyU*: OH, OTS.
200. "Two Poems about Suddenly and a Rose" subseq. *Ctw*: OH, OTS (3 versions), CTS. *KyU*: CH, CTS ("17–18 Oct.").
201. "Two Studies in Idealism: . . ." seq. *Ctw*: OH (I & II), OTS (3, II), CTS (2, I; 3, II). *KyU*: CH, CTS ("Oct. 1958").

202. "Unless." *Ctw*: OH, OTS, CTS (3, one "16 Aug. 1976").
203. "Vision." *Ctw*: OH ("21–23 Oct. 1978"), OTS, CTS (2).
204. "Vision under the October Mountain: . . . ." *Ctw*: OH, OTS (2 versions), CTS (2 versions). *KyU*: CTS ("18–19 Sept. 1965").
205. "Waiting." *Ctw*: OH ("5 July 1976"), CTS.
206. "Waking to Tap of Hammer." *Ctw*: OH ("8–10 July 1977"), CTS (2).
207. "Ways of Day." *Ctw*: OH, OTS (3 versions). *KyU*: CH, CTS.
208. "Weather Report." *Ctw*: OH ("12 Aug." [1978]), OTS (with title, "Weather Report at Equinox"), CTS (2).
209. "The Well-House." *Ctw*: OH, OTS, CTS (2).
210. "What Is the Voice That Speaks." *Ctw*: OH, OTS (2), CTS (6, with one "final—8 Jan. 1979").
211. "What Was the Promise That Smiled . . . ?" *Ctw*: OH, OTS (2 versions).
212. "When Life Begins." *Ctw*: OH ("28 April–3 May" [1979]), CTS.
213. "When the Tooth Cracks—Zing!" *Ctw*: OH (2, "summer 1974" and "27–30 Oct. 1976"), CTS.
214. "Why?" *Ctw*: OH, CTS (2).
215. "The Wrestling Match." *Ctw*: OTS, CTS.
216. *YEO*. *Ctw*: OTS (setting copy), GP (2, "13 May 1960" and "10 June 1960"), PP. *KyU*: CTS (with extensive corrections), GP.
217. "Youth Stares at Minoan Sunset." *Ctw*: OH, OTS ("16 June 1976"), CTS.
218. "Youthful Truth-Seeker, Half Naked, ..." *Ctw*: OH, OTS (2), CTS (4, with title, "Truth Seeker . . .").

C. DRAMA

1. *AKM*. *Ctw*: CTS (3) and MTS (earlier version), O/CTS (mixed and marked: "revision," "A," "B," and "new version"), MTS (with comments by Aaron Frankel), OTS (with corrections and "1 Oct. 1959" marked "26"), OTS and CTS (prompt script), MTS (original prose version).
2. "Ballad of a Sweet Dream of Peace." *Ctw*: CTS and XTS (early versions), OTS and CTS (3, one with corrections of "Charade"), OH (notes and ltr. to Don Gallup, 23 Jan. 1971, regarding background of "Charade"), MTS (2), XTS ("Final: 1 Sept. 1971" and ref. to ltr. to Don Gallup, 4 Dec. 1970).

3. *BA* (screenplay). *KyU*: MTS (no. 162, "26 Dec. 1956" with subsequent changes dated on blue paper).

D. NONFICTION

1. "*AKM*: The Matrix of Experience." *Ctw*: OTS (with corrections). *KyU*: OH, CTS (with corrections).
2. *AL*. *Ctw*: OH and OTS ("Intro 1826–1861"); OH and OTS ("Intro 1865–1914"); OH and OTS ("Harlem Renaissance"); OH and OTS ("Henry Adams" with rev.); OH and OTS ("Sherwood Anderson"); OH and OTS ("James Fenimore Cooper" with corrections); OH and OTS ("Stephen Crane" with rev.); OH and OTS ("W. E. B. DuBois"); OH and OTS ("P. L. Dunbar"); OH and OTS ("Fitzgerald"); OH and OTS ("Bret Harte"); OTS and CTS ("Hawthorne" with extensive rev.); OH ("Ernest Hemingway"); OH and OTS ("Oliver Wendell Holmes" with rev.); OTS ("Julia Ward Howe" with rev.); OH (6 pp.), CTS (5 pp.), and OTS ("Langston Hughes"); OH ("Washington Irving"); OH ("James Weldon Johnson"); OH, OTS, and CTS ("Longfellow"); OH and OTS ("William James" with rev.); OH, CTS, and XTS ("Robert Lowell" with rev.); OH ("Henry Miller"); OTS ("Jean Toomer" with corrections); OH and OTS ("Booker T. Washington"); OH and OTS ("Whittier"); OH and OTS ("Richard Wright"); plus OTS (various headnotes to selected pieces); XPP (pp. 1–2970). *KyU*: CH and CTS ("Intro 1826–1861"); CH and CTS ("Intro 1865–1914"); OH and CTS ("Literature of the Non-Literary World"); CH and CTS ("Harlem Renaissance"); CH and CTS ("F. Scott Fitzgerald"); CTS and XTS ("Hawthorne"); OH ("*Scarlet Letter*" headnote); CH and CTS ("Hemingway"); CH ("*A Farewell to Arms*" headnote); CH and CTS ("Irving"); CH and O/CTS ("Longfellow"); CH and CTS ("James Russell Lowell"); CH and CTS ("Richard Wright").
3. "*An American Tragedy*." *Ctw*: OTS, CTS (with rev.). *KyU*: XTS (with ltr., Aaron Asher, World Pub. Co., 7 June 1962).
4. "Americanism." *KyU*: CTS (rev.).
5. "Andrew Lytle's *The Long Night*." *Ctw*: OH, OTS. *SoR*: OTS.
6. *ATL* (4th ed.). *KyU*: OH, CTS ("Preface"), publisher's MS (pp. 1–1833), GP, PP ("reader's set").
7. "Asides and Diversions" (rev.). *Ctw*: CTS.

8. "Basic Themes in Frost." *Ctw*: OTS (2, one "2d draft").

9. "The Blind Poet: Sidney Lanier" (rev.). *Ctw*: OTS.

10. "The Briar Patch." *Ctw*: OTS.

11. *Conversations on the Craft of Poetry*. *Ctw*: MTS (of the following transcripts: Lowell, Brooks, RPW; Ransom, Brooks, RPW—with rev.; Frost, Brooks, RPW—with rev.).

12. "Death of a Salesman—Southern Style" (rev.). *KyU*: OH, CTS.

13. "Democracy and Poetry." *SoR*: OTS ("8/10/74").

14. *DP*. *Ctw*: OH (notes, worksheets, and background material), OTS ("master, 5 Oct. 1974" with rev.), XTS (2); OTS (lecture I with rev.), XTS (lecture II with rev.), O/XTS (worksheets).

15. "Divided South Searches Its Soul." *Ctw*: GP.

16. "Edmund Wilson's Civil War" (rev.). *KyU*: OH (notes, worksheets, corrected drafts), OTS, CTS.

17. "Elizabeth Madox Roberts: . . . ." *Ctw*: CTS ("first draft"). *KyU*: OH (notes and worksheets), OH (1st draft), OTS (2), CTS, GP.

18. *FCCE*. *Ctw*: XTS, GP (2), PP. *KyU*: OH (worksheets and notes).

19. "Faulkner: The South, the Negro, and Time." *Ctw*: OH, OTS (with rev.), O/CTS (rev. version), CTS (5, one the uncut speech version), GP (*SoR* version). *KyU*: OH, OTS (pp. 1–11), CTS (pp. 1–25), CTS (rev.). *SoR*: OTS.

20. "A First Novel" (rev.). *KyU*: OTS (with notes).

21. "Five Tributes [to Eudora Welty]." *Ctw*: OH (with title, "Out of the Strong"), CTS. *KyU*: CH.

22. "Formula for a Poem." *Ctw*: OTS, CTS (with title, "How Poems Come About," with rev.).

23. "Function of Criticism." *Ctw*: OTS (frag.).

24. "The Gamecock" (rev.). *KyU*: CTS.

25. "Georgian Laureate" (rev.). *Ctw*: OTS (with corrections).

26. "Georgian Middle Life" (rev.). *KyU*: CTS.

27. *GMO*. *Ctw*: OTS (worksheets), OTS. *KyU*: CTS.

28. "Hawthorne, Anderson, and Frost" (rev.). *KyU*: CTS.

29. "Hemingway." *Ctw*: OTS (2d draft with rev.), OTS, CTS (1st draft), OTS (setting copy), GP—(all for "Intro. to *AFTA*").

30. "Homage to Oliver Allston" (rev.). *Ctw*: OTS.

31. "Homage to Theodore Dreiser." *SoR*: OTS.

32. *HTD*. *Ctw*: OH (worksheets), CH, CTS (2), CTS (1st draft), OTS (2d draft), OH (frag.), CTS (discarded leaves with rev.), O/CTS (canceled sheets and added material), XTS (4), GP (3 plus layout of front matter), PP (frag.).

33. *HTWHF*. *KyU*: OH (worksheets and notes), CTS (with titles, "Houston and San Jacinto" and "Sam Houston and San Jacinto"), GP ("11 Dec. 1957").
34. Introduction for program for Harvard production of Webster's *White Devil*. *Ctw*: OH (notes).
35. "Introduction [to *FCCE*]: Faulkner: Past and Future." *Ctw*: CTS. *KyU*: CH, CTS.
36. Introduction to *The Hero in America*. *Ctw*: OH.
37. *JB*. *Ctw*: OTS (setting copy), CTS (2, both frags. of 1st draft).
38. "John Crowe Random (1888–1974)." *SoR*: OTS.
39. "John Crowe Ransom: A Study in Irony." *Ctw*: OTS.
40. "John Crowe Ransom: Some Random Remarks." *Ctw*: OH, CTS ("1st draft—to appear in Ransom issue, *Shenandoah*"). *KyU*: CTS.
41. *JGWP*. *KyU*: OH (worksheets and notes), CH and CTS (1st draft).
42. "Knowledge and the Image of Man." *Ctw*: OH (notes), CTS, MTS (program).
43. "Lambert Davis: . . . ." *Ctw*: CTS (2 pp.).
44. "Lavender and Old Ladies" (rev.). *Ctw*: OTS, CTS (frag.).
45. *LCW*. *Ctw*: OH (notes with title, "Civil War and the American Imagination"), OTS (5 versions), CTS (6, of various versions), GP (4), PP (2, one with designer's sketches, front matter). *KyU*: OH and CTS (notes and worksheets), OH and CTS.
46. "A Lesson Read in American Books." *Ctw*: OH (notes), OTS (1st draft), MTS (4 pp.). *KyU*: CTS (2, headed "This material is not for publication").
47. "Literature as Symptom." *Ctw*: OTS.
48. "Love and Separateness in Eudora Welty." *Ctw*: OTS.
49. "Malcolm X: Mission and Meaning." *Ctw*: OH, CTS. *KyU*: CH (worksheets and rev. draft), CTS.
50. "Mark Twain." *Ctw*: OH, OTS (1st draft unrevised). *SoR*: OTS.
51. "Melville's Poems." *SoR*: OTS.
52. "Merrill Moore's Sonnets" (rev.). *KyU*: OTS.
53. *MR*. *KyU*: CTS (intro. and II), GP, PP.
54. *MR* (2d ed.). *KyU*: CTS (on argument, diction, metaphor, exposition, description, narration, paragraph, sentence, situation and tone, style and personality, handbook of grammar, and summary along with miscellaneous notes and rough drafts), GP.
55. "The Negro Movement in Upheaval" (rev.). *Ctw*: OTS (with extensive rev.). *KyU*: CTS.

56. "*Nostromo.*" *Ctw*: OH (notes), OTS (quotations from other sources), OTS (with rev.), OTS (title, "Joseph Conrad: Master of Illusion"), CTS.
57. "A Note on Three Southern Poets." *KyU*: CTS.
58. "Notes on the Poetry of John Crowe Ransom at His Eightieth Birthday." *Ctw*: OTS (frag.), CTS (with rev.). *KyU*: CH, CTS.
59. "Now and History." *Ctw*: OTS (2), MTS (with 1974 copyright by Regents of Univ. of Calif.).
60. "Old Words" (rev.). *KyU*: CTS.
61. "A Plea in Mitigation . . . ." *Ctw*: OH, OTS (3, two of 2d draft, one of "short version"), CTS (2, one of 1st draft, one of short version).
62. "A Poem of Pure Imagination: . . . ." *Ctw*: OH (notes), OTS (2 versions), OTS (setting copy), OTS (used for *SE* version), CTS (rev. 2d draft). *KyU*: CTS.
63. Porter, Katherine Anne, early intro. to her works. *Ctw*: OTS.
64. Prefatory note to Cass Mastern episode for *This Is My Best*. *Ctw*: OH, CTS. *KyU*: CH, CTS.
65. "Principle and Poet" (rev.). *Ctw*: OTS.
66. "Pure Poetry and the Structure of Poems" (speech). *KyU*: CTS.
67. "Race" (rev.). *Ctw*: OTS. *KyU*: CTS.
68. *RA. KyU*: CTS (3, one 1st draft, one rev. draft, one with corrections), GP (*Holiday*).
69. Review of *1×1*, by E. E. Cummings. *Ctw*: OTS.
70. Review of *No Bright Banner*, by DeCapite. *Ctw*: OTS.
71. Review of *The Zodiac*, by James Dickey. *Ctw*: OH, OTS, CTS (with rev.).
72. Review of *The Portable Steinbeck*, ed. by Lewis Gannett. *Ctw*: OTS.
73. Review of *Selected Poems of Herman Melville*, by F. O. Matthiessen. *Ctw*: OTS.
74. *SF. KyU*: PP (master set dated "11 March 1960").
75. "The Second American Revolution" (rev.). *KyU*: CTS.
76. *Seg. Ctw*: OH (notes and worksheets), OTS, CTS (setting copy), GP ("31 May" and "13 June"), PP. *KyU*: background material (newspaper clippings, pamphlets, handouts, news reports) on segregation issue.
77. *SE. Ctw*: OTS (setting copy), GP (2, "26 March 1958" and "3 May 1958"), PP. *KyU*: CTS ("Preface" with John E. Palmer's notes and with corrections).

78. *SPDD*. *Ctw*: OTS (material on DD and correspondence), CTS (poems), GP. *KyU*: OH ("preface").

79. *SPHM*. *Ctw*: OH (notes), OTS (8 of intro., notes, and headnotes), CTS (10), XTS (7), GP (4, one "29 Dec. 1969," one "14 Jan. 1970," and one "19 May 1970"), PP (2); plus various background material, copies of poems, etc. *KyU*: CH (intro. 1st draft), CTS (intro. rev.), CTS (intro. final).

80. *SSGP*, *KyU*: CTS (intro.).

81. "The Snopes World" (rev.). *Ctw*: OTS.

82. "T. S. Stribling: A Paragraph in the History of Critical Realism." *Ctw*: OTS.

83. "Uncorrupted Consciousness: The Stories of Katherine Anne Porter." *KyU*: CH, CTS.

84. *UF*. *Ctw*: OH, OTS (with rev. of explication of "I Want To Know Why"), OTS (frag. of "'The Killers'"). *KyU*: CTS (on plot, theme, glossary, notes, biographical sketches, miscellaneous notes [mainly in Brooks's handwriting]), publisher's MS.

85. *UF* (2d ed.). *KyU*: GP, PP.

86. *UP* (rev. ed.). *Ctw*: OTS (intro.). *KyU*: CTS (foreword), notes, on Eliot, ambiguity, metaphor, tone, Wordsworth, miscellaneous notes and parts of chapters), publisher's MS, GP, PP.

87, "Uses of the Past." *Ctw*: OH.

88. "Walker Evans" (tribute). *Ctw*: OH, XTS ("2 Feb. 1971").

89. "Whittier." *Ctw*: CTS ("Final for magazine version" with rev.).

90. *WSN?*. *KyU*: CH (preface), CH and CTS (I), O/CTS (II), CTS (III with corrections), CTS (VI), CTS (I–VI, "proof reader's copy"); plus miscellaneous notes, inserts, and tearsheets from the *Congressional Record*; GP (3, one dated "11 Feb. 1965"); and 34 interviews with civil rights leaders by RPW, some on tape, some transcribed (ltr., Susan E. Allen, Oral History Program, KyU, 3 Oct. 1979).

91. "Why Do We Read Fiction?" *Ctw*: OH (3, one marked version "B," another "C"), OTS (7, with various draft markings), CTS (6, with one titled, "Fiction: The Dancer and the Dance"), tearsheets (*Time and Tide*).

92. "William Carlos Williams, 1883–1963." *Ctw*: OH, OTS. *KyU*: OH (notes with inserts), CTS ("22 May 1963").

93. "William Faulkner." *Ctw*: OTS.

94. "William Styron." *Ctw*: OTS, CTS. *KyU*: OH, CTS.

95. "Working Toward Freedom" (rev.). *Ctw*: OTS.

96. "The World of Daniel Boone." *Ctw*: OH (1st draft). *KyU*: OH (with notes), GP (*Holiday*).
97. "The World of Huey Long." *Ctw*: CTS (intro. to *AKM* published by Secker & Warburg).
98. "Writer at Work: How a Story Was Born . . . ." *Ctw*: OTS. *KyU*: CTS.

Appendix II

Miscellaneous Items

Note: This section is arranged in four parts: items by RPW, his work set to music, audiovisual presentations about RPW and his work, and tributes not mentioned elsewhere.

A. BY RPW

1. ". . . RPW Reading from His *SP*." Cambridge, MA: Harvard Film Service (P-1086-1089), 1944. Two records (12 in., 78 rpm) in one album; Harvard University Vocarium Records.
   Includes: "Crime," "Terror," "Monologue at Midnight," "Bearded Oaks," and "Mexico Is a Foreign Country" (II & IV).
2. "John Gould Fletcher, John Malcolm Brinnin, William Carlos Williams, and RPW Read Their Own Poems." A Phonodisc. Washington, D.C.: Library of Congress Recording Laboratory, 1949. P17 (78 rpm); PL4, 1953 (33⅓ rpm).
   Includes: "Terror" and "Pursuit."
3. "On Ezra Pound." WYBC (Yale), New Haven, CT, 1955.
4. "On Writing." The Creative Mind and Method Series. WGBH-FM, Boston, for the National Association of Educational Broadcasts, 1959.
5. "RPW Reading His Own Poetry in the Yale Series of Recorded Poets" (YP 313). Phonodisc. Carillon Records, 1961.
   Includes: Side One: (1) "Mortmain": (a) "After Night Flight Son Reaches Bedside . . ."; (b) "A Dead Language: Circa 1885"; (c) "Fox-fire: 1956"; (d) "In the Turpitude of Time: N.D."; (e) "A Vision: Circa 1880." (2) "Clearly About You." (3) "The Letter About Money, Love, or Other Comfort, If Any." (4) "Arrogant Law." (5) "Tiberius on Capri." Side Two: (1) "The Garden." (2) "Founding Fathers, Nineteenth-Century Style, Southeast U.S.A." (3) "Country Burying (1919)." (4) "Debate: Question, Quarry, Dream." (5) "Original Sin: A Short Story." (6) "Dragon Country: To Jacob

Boehme." (7) "Two Studies in Idealism: Short Survey of American, and Human, History" (a) "Bear Track Plantation: Shortly after Shiloh"; (b) "Harvard '61: Battle Fatigue."

6. Williams, Oscar, ed. "A Little Treasury of 20th-Century American Poetry." Vol. II. Colpix Records, 1963. PS 1001.
   Includes: Warren reading "Terror."

7. "A Retrospective Reading Prepared by RPW." Washington, D.C.: Black Box, 1967. Tape, 55 mins. (C-823).

8. Newman, Edwin. "Speaking Freely." WNBC-TV. Taped 17 Dec. 1970; aired 3 Jan. 1971.
   Note: RPW has a transcript.

9. "RPW Reads from His Own Works." Yale Series of Recorded Poets. Decca, DL9148 (33⅓ rpm). [1975].
   Note: a reissue of **IIA5**.

10. Recipe. In *John Keats's Porridge: Favorite Recipes of American Poets*. Ed. Victoria McCabe. Iowa City: University of Iowa Press, 1975. P. 101. Rpt. *University Publishing*, 8 (Fall 1979), 13.

11. "Moments in History." Shell Oil Company's Bicentennial Program, 26 Dec. 1976.

B. WORK SET TO MUSIC

1. Buskirk, Carl Van. "The Land Between the Rivers." Libretto (English), n.d.
   Note: "The land between the rivers. A two-act libretto based upon characters and incidents in 'The Ballad of Billie Potts' . . . ."

2. Almand, Claude M. "Pondy Woods: A Symphonic Episode . . . ," 1938. See **Q2**.

3. Haieff, Alexei. "Ballad of a Sweet Dream of Peace," 1975. *See* **E9**.

C. AUDIOVISUAL PRESENTATIONS

1. Schneider, Robert L. "*AKM*." Twentieth-Century American Writers Series, no. 76. Ed. Warren French. Deland, FL: Everett/Edwards, 1973. Cassette tape.

2. Core, George. "RPW." Modern American Poetry Criticism Series, no. 813. Ed. Richard Calhoun. Deland, FL: Everett/Edwards, 1976. Cassette tape.

3. Grimshaw, James A., Jr. "The Works of RPW." Southern Ameri-

can Writers Series, no. 924. Ed. C. Hugh Holman. Deland, FL: Everett/Edwards, 1976. Cassette tape.

4. Denbo, Bruce. Oral history interview for the RPW Oral History Project, University of Kentucky, no. 02. Lexington, KY, 14 Dec. 1977. Tape: 50 min.

5. Howell, Sarah. Film on the Southern Agrarians. Middle Tennessee State University: Department of History, 1978.

6. Irvin, John. Oral history interview for the RPW Oral History Project, University of Kentucky, no. 03. Minneapolis, MN, 25 Jan. 1978. Tape: 1 hr.

7. Unger, Leonard. Oral history interview for the RPW Oral History Project, University of Kentucky, no. 04. Minneapolis, MN, 25 Jan. 1978. Tape: 1 hr. 10 min.

8. Lewis, R. W. B. Oral history interview for the RPW Oral History Project, University of Kentucky, no. 06. Chapel Hill, NC, 22 March 1978. Tape: 35 min. Transcript: 20 l.

9. Rubin, Louis D., Jr. Oral history interview for the RPW Oral History Project, University of Kentucky, no. 05. Chapel Hill, NC, 22 March 1978. Tape: 15 min.

10. Strandberg, Victor H. Oral history interview for the RPW Oral History Project, University of Kentucky, no. 07. Durham, NC, 23 March 1978. Tape: 1 hr. Transcript: 25 l.

11. Foster, Charles H. Oral history interview for the RPW Oral History Project, University of Kentucky, no. 08. Luray, VA, 27 March 1978. Tape: 1 hr. 45 min.

12. Monk, Samuel H. Oral history interview for the RPW Oral History Project, University of Kentucky, no. 09. Charlottesville, VA, 28 March 1978. Tape: 30 min.

13. Stein, Arnold S. Oral history interview for the RPW Oral History Project, University of Kentucky, no. 11. Baltimore, MD, 22 June 1978. Tape: 1 hr. 15 min.

14. O'Connor, Mary. Oral history interview for the RPW Oral History Project, University of Kentucky, no. 12. Davis, CA, 3 Aug. 1978. Tape: 1 hr. 45 min.

15. Heilman, Robert B. Oral history interview for the RPW Oral History Project, University of Kentucky, no. 13. Seattle, WA, 4 Aug. 1978. Tape: 1 hr. 35 min.

16. Wellek, René. Oral history interview for the RPW Oral History Project, University of Kentucky, no. 14. Woodbridge, CT, 21 Nov. 1978. Tape: 50 min.

17. Palmer, John E. Oral history interview for the RPW Oral History Project, University of Kentucky, no. 16. New Haven, CT, 24 Jan. 1979. Tape: 1 hr.

D. TRIBUTES

1. Hollander, John. "Rotation of Crops: For RPW" (poem). *Four Quarters*, 21 (May 1972), 18.
2. Styron, William. *Admiral RPW and the Snows of Winter*. Winston-Salem, NC: Palaemon Press, 1978. **K20**.
3. *Vanderbilt Poetry Review*, 2, nos. 3 & 4 (1977). Intro. by Allen Tate. Poems by contributors in tribute.
4. "A Portfolio of Portraits." *SatR*, Dec. 1978, p. 19. Photo by Hiro.
5. Lehman, David. "In Praise of RPW" (poem). *Poetry*, 135 (Nov. 1979), 85.

Appendix III

Chronology of Significant Events

1905	April 24. RPW born to Robert Franklin and Anna Ruth Penn Warren in Guthrie, Todd County, KY.
1922	Attends Citizens Military Training Camp, Fifth Corps Area, Camp Knox, KY, where he publishes his first poem, "Prophecy"; fall, enters Vanderbilt University.
1924	Feb. Elected to membership in the Fugitives.
1925	B.A. from Vanderbilt (*summa cum laude*).
1927	M.A. in English from the University of California at Berkeley; enters Yale Graduate School.
1928	Rhodes Scholar at Oxford.
1929	Nov. 2. Publishes first book, *JB*.
1930	B.Litt. from Oxford.
ca. 1930	Marries Emma Cinina Brescia.
1930–31	Assistant Professor of English at Southwestern College, Memphis, TN.
1931–34	Assistant Professor of English at Vanderbilt.
1934–42	Associate Professor of English at Louisiana State University at Baton Rouge.
1935	One of founders of *The Southern Review*.
1936	Helen Haire Levinson Prize for Poetry; Caroline Sinkler Prize of the Poetry Society of South Carolina; Houghton Mifflin Fellowship for Fiction.
1937	Caroline Sinkler Prize.
1938	Caroline Sinkler Prize; Phi Beta Kappa address, University of Oklahoma.
1939–40	Guggenheim Fellowship; Houghton Mifflin Literary Fellowship.
1942	Poet of the Month Award (*EP*).
1942–50	Professor of English at the University of Minnesota.
1943	Shelley Memorial Award.
1944–45	Second occupant of the Chair of Poetry at the Library of Congress.

1946   Aug. 17. *AKM* published.
1947   Pulitzer Prize for Fiction (*AKM*); Southern Author's Award
            (Southern Women's National Democratic Organization).
1947–48   Guggenheim Fellowship.
1949   Robert Meltzer Award of the Screen Writers' Guild
            (*AKM*); Honorary D.Litt. from the University of
            Louisville.
1950   Joins Yale faculty; membership in the National Institute
            of Arts and Letters; Chancellor, American Academy
            of Poets; Distinguished Alumnus Award, Vanderbilt
            University.
1951   Divorces Emma Cinina Brescia.
1951–56   Professor of Playwriting at Yale.
1952   Elected to the American Philosophical Society; Honorary
            D.Litt. from Kenyon College; marries Eleanor Clark,
            by whom he has two children—Rosanna Phelps Warren
            and Gabriel Penn Warren.
1955   *BA* is Literary Guild Selection for Sept.
1956   Honorary D.Litt. from Colby College.
1957   Aug. 15. Publishes *P*; Sidney Hillman Award for Journal-
            ism (*Seg.*); Edna St. Vincent Millay Prize of the Ameri-
            can Poetry Society (*P*); Honorary D.Litt. from Univer-
            sity of Kentucky.
1958   Pulitzer Prize for Poetry (*P*); National Book Award for Po-
            etry (*P*); membership in The Century Association.
1959   Selected for membership in the American Academy of
            Arts and Letters; Honorary D.Litt. from Swarthmore
            College.
1960   Honorary D.Litt. from Yale University.
1961–73   Rejoins Yale facuty as Professor of English.
1965   Irita Van Doren Award (*NYHT*); Honorary LLD from the
            University of Bridgeport (CT).
1967   Bollingen Prize in Poetry (*SPNO*).
1967–68   Member, English Committee of the Board of Overseers of
            Harvard College.
1968   National Arts Foundation Award.
1969   Honorary D.Litt. from Fairfield University (CT).
1970   National Medal of Literature; Van Wyck Brooks Award
            (*A*); Honorary D.Litt. from Wesleyan University.
1972   Fall. Ten Best Teachers Award, Yale; Chancellor, Ameri-
            can Academy of Poets.

1973   Professor Emeritus, Yale; University of South Caro-
         lina Award for Distinction in Literature; Honorary
         D.Litt. from Harvard University and from New Haven
         University.

1974   Delivers Third Annual Jefferson Lecture in the Human-
         ities (NEH); Honorary D.Litt. from the University of
         the South, from Southwestern College, and from Uni-
         versity of Meridian (TN); Honorary Fellow, MLA.

1975   Elected to the American Academy of Arts and Sciences;
         Emerson-Thoreau Award from AAAS.

1976   Copernicus Award (*OEP*) of the Academy of American
         Poets; Borestone Mountain Poetry Award.

1977   Harriet Monroe Prize for Poetry; Wilma and Roswell Mes-
         sing, Jr., Award from Associates of St. Louis Univer-
         sity Libraries; Honorary D.Litt. from Johns Hopkins
         University.

1978   Sept. *NT* published; Honorary D.Humane Letters from
         Berea College (KY).

1979   Pulitzer Prize for Poetry (*NT*).

Index

Index

Note: This index includes authors, titles, major literary figures, and selected subject headings referred to in this bibliography. Under "Warren, Robert Penn" is a list of selected subject references. To differentiate among the titles, I have used the following abbreviations: (a), anthology; (d), drama; (e), essay; (ex), excerpt; (j), news release; (ms), manuscript; (n), novel; n, note; (p), poem; (r), review; (s), short fiction; (tr), translation; and (u), unpublished material.

Brother to Dragons (p), A11; J15f; P80, 126; App. IB31; criticism of, F28, K9, 10, M89, 136, 141, 209, 289, 351, 377, Q58, 89, 144, 154, 197; (d),E6; (ex), C99, 100; reviews of, E6c, N19
"*BD*: A Play in Two Acts," E6d
"*BD*: The Fact of Violence vs. the Possibility of Love" (e), M377
"*BD*: The Many Voices of RPW" (u),Q58
"Brotherhood in Pain" (p), A35; C345
Brothers Three (r), G35
Brower, Reuben, C319a
Brown, Ashley, N22b²
Brown, Francis, H95
Brown, Harry, G50; N7i
Brown, Harry N., Q161
Brown, Jane E., Q35
Brown, Maria, O67; R27
Browning, D. C., O28
Broyard, Anatole, N50d, 51c, 53e
Brubaker, DeLacy P., Q63
Bruccoli, Matthew J., A3.c1(n2); O79; R32
Bruffee, Kenneth A., M277
Brunn, Robert R., N24b, 35J
Bücherei und Bildung, N22u²
Buchloh, Paul G., L79
Buchsbaum, Betty S., Q81
Buckler, William E., H74
Buffalo [NY] *Evening News*, N38d
Buffington, Robert, M281
Bulawayo *Chronicle*, N12y³
Bulletin from Virginia Kirkus' Bookshop Service, N11a, 12a, 15a, 18a, 19b, 19c², 22a, 24a, 26a, 28a, 30a, 34a, 36d, 38b, 39a, 40a, 43a, 44a, 47a, 48a, 50a, 52f, 53a, 54a
Bulletin of the University of Osaka Prefecture, M169
Bungert, Hans, L102
Burden, M. S., A32.c1
"The Burden of Incomplete Knowledge . . ." (u), Q153
"The Burden of Innocence" (r), N19x
"The 'Burden' of Narration . . ." (e), M238
The Burden of Southern History, L93
The Burden of Time, L67
"The Burden of the Literary Mind: Some Meditations on RPW as Historian" (e), K9; M196

"Burden's Complaint . . ." (e), K17; M262
"Burden's Landing: *AKM* and the Modern South" (e), L61
Burger, Nash K., N35y
"Buried Alive" (r), N30y
"Buried Graveyards: Warren's *F* and Jones's *A Buried Land*" (e), M347
A Buried Land, M347
A Buried Treasure, G20
Burke, H. C., N40b
Burke, Kenneth, L9; M78; N12c
Burke, Lawrence M., Q19, 162
Burkett, Eva M., H109
Burnes, Ann P., Q197
Burnett, Whit, H119
Burnette, Frances, N25a
Burns, John M., N7n
Burr, Michael R., F46b
Burt, A. C., M249
Burt, David J., M243, 249, 320
Buskirk, Carl Van, App. IIB1
"But no scream now, and under his hand" (p), A30, 35; C291
"But Not the Nightingale," see *Meet Me in the Green Glen*
"But the solution: You" (p), A28, 35; C215
Butcher, Fanny, N36i
Butenas, Juozas, J19a
"Butterflies over the Map" (p), A6, 28, 35; C92
"Button, Button" (r), G46
Buzzati, Dino, B14.a1(n3)
"By Way of Background" (e), M14
Byrd, John C., Q111
Byrne, Clifford M., M106

El caballero de la noche (n), J25a
Cable, G. W., Q177
Cady, Edwin H., L96
Calcutta *Statesman*, N12a⁴
Calder, Alexander, B16; F17a
"Calendar" (p), A2, 6; C76
A Calendar of Sin (r), G20
Calhoun, Richard, App. IIC2
"Call Me Early," *see* "So Clear, O Victory"
Cambon, Glauco, J15d, 15f
Cambridge Review, N30b³
Campbell, Charlotte, A27.a1(n1)
Campbell, H. M., M65, 83

dite as Logos" (p), A29, 35; C244;
App. IB125

Nakadate, Neil, M246, 351; Q171; R33
Namba, Tatsuo, M294
Namikawa, Akira, J16c
"Narrative Art and History in RPW's
   WET" (u), Q43
Narrative Situation in the Novel, L100
"The Narrative Stances of RPW" (u),
   Q171
"The Narrator as Hero" (e), M113
"Narrators and Commentators in Four
   Novels by RPW" (u), Q174
"The Narrator's Mind as Symbol" (e),
   K11, 17; M26
"The 'Nashville Agrarians' as Critics of
   American Society" (u), Q21
Nashville Banner, N7b, 11b, 12w, 19h[2],
   22g, 27c, 30c
Nashville Tennessean, C37b; G4–8; N7n,
   10k, 12j, 30k, 35h, 38n, 50f, 53z;
   O51; P81
Nashville: The Faces of Two Centuries, F90
Nathan, Monique, N12p[3]
Nathaniel Hawthorne: A Study in Solitude
   (r), G13
"Nathaniel Hawthorne and RPW . . ."
   (u), Q75
Nathaniel Hawthorne Journal, F69e; H135
Nation, C42a, 81, 84a, 90a; G39, 41–45,
   47, 51; N1n, 2f, 3c, 7q, 8g, 100, 11p,
   12a[2], 14b, 15m, 18t, 190, 22e[2], 26m,
   30a[2], 39t[2], 48u, 50t, 51g, 52z
National Book Award, F34(n); I76
The National Cyclopedia of American Biog-
   raphy, O22
National Medal for Literature, F69;
   J15r; P102, 123
"National Medal for Literature Awarded
   Warren" (j), P102
National Observer, N39e[2], 40p, 43i, 50s,
   53i; O84
National Review, N30z, 35q, 36q, 38b[3],
   48q
"Native of Guthrie Wins High Praise
   for Book" (r), N12s[2]
"Natural History" ["In the rain the
   naked old father . . ."] (p), A33, 35;
   C318
"Natural History" ["Many have died
   here . . ."] (p), A29, 35; C252
"The Natural History of a Vision" (p),

see "I Am Dreaming of a White
   Christmas . . ."
"Natural History of Ikey Sumpter . . ."
   (ex), A19.a1(n2)
"A Natural History of Supernatural-
   ism . . ." (u), Q33
"A Nature Divided Against Itself" (r),
   N22l
"The Nature of a Mirror" (p), A33, 35;
   C320
The Nature of Narrative, L72
"The Nature of Reality . . ." (u), Q40
"The Necessity for Belief" (p), A15;
   C115
"The Necklace" (s), M82
"The Need for Re-evaluation" (p), A33,
   35; C332
"Need to Change Cited by Warren" (j),
   P78
Negro Digest, N39q[2]
"The Negro Movement in Upheaval"
   (r), G61; App. ID55
"Negro Now" (e), F53
"The Negro Speaks Out with Voice of
   History" (r), N39b[2]
Neill-Hall, W. P., A36.e1(n)
Nel vortice del tempo (n), J15d
Nemerov, Howard, L60; M34; N12j[2],
   30x[2]
Neue deutsche Hefte, J11e
Nevins, Allan, N1j
Nevius, Blake, R24
New, Ina Claire, Q50
The New Criticism, L11
"The New Criticism and Southern
   Agrarianism" (e), M77
"The New Criticism and the Southern
   Critics" (e), L12
"The 'New Criticism' and the Study of
   Poetry" (u), Q35
"El 'New Criticism' en los Estados Uni-
   dos" (e), M335
"The New Criticism: Pro and Contra"
   (e), M380
"The New Criticism Revisited: An Af-
   firmative View" (e), M204
New England Review, C397–399; O95
New English Review, C32d, 79d; D10b,
   12a, 14b
New English Review Magazine, C54d
The New Equality (r), G57
New Leader, C190a; M46a; N18w(1),
   22z, 27l, 36c, 39s, 40t, 52i, 53r, 54n